SELF-CATERING

Houndapitt Farm Cottages

★ ★ ★
SELF CATERING

Set in a 100 acre estate overlooking Sandymouth Bay. We provide quality accommodation at very competitive prices. • cottages sleep from two to nine people • countryside setting • spectacular views • one mile from beach • 10 minutes from main town • coastal and country walks • large games room • coarse fishing lake • adventure playground

Terms include electricity and heating.
(Sorry, we do not allow pets.)

Detailed Colour Brochure from:
Mr & Mrs F. S. Heard, Houndapitt Farm,
Sandymouth, Bude, Cornwall EX23 9HW. **Tel: 01288 355455**
e-mail: info@houndapitt.co.uk • website: www.houndapitt.co.uk

BOARD

TREMAINE GREEN

Pelynt, Near Looe PL13 2LT

"A beautiful Hamlet" of 11 traditional cosy craftsmen's cottages, between Polperro and Looe. Clean, comfortable and well equipped, for two to eight people. Set in lovely grounds with country/coastal walks and Eden Project nearby. Cottages from only £89 per week. Pets welcome (£16 pw).

Tel: 01503 220333
e-mail: j7p@tremaine.sagehost.co.uk

BOARD

Colin and Rosemary Haskell

Borwick Lodge

Silver
SILVER AWARD

GUEST
ACCOMMODATION

Outgate, Hawkshead, Ambleside, Cumbria LA22 0PU
Tel & Fax: Hawkshead (015394) 36332
e-mail: borwicklodge@talk21.com • website: www.borwicklodge.com

Award-winning delightful 17th century house nestling in three acres of secluded gardens. Breathtaking panoramic lake and mountain views. Ideally situated. Close to Hawkshead village with good choice of restaurants and inns. Beautiful en suite rooms with colour televisions and tea-making facilities. King-size four-poster rooms. Somewhere special in this most beautiful corner of England. Ample parking. NON-SMOKING THROUGHOUT. Bed and Breakfast from £25 Residential licence.

See Board Section – Ambleside, Cumbria

Derwent Manor

Portinscale, KESWICK, Cumbria, England, CA12 5RE

E-mail: info@derwentwater-hotel.co.uk   Web: www.derwentwater-hotel.co.uk

Derwent Manor

Luxury Lakeland Holiday Cottages and Apartments

This former gentleman's country residence now provides some of Lakeland's finest self-catering accommodation amid tranquil surroundings on the fringe of a picturesque village. Wander down to the shores of Lake Derwentwater through 16 acres of private, unspoilt meadows – a recognised conservation area, or stroll along footpaths and over the River into the village of Keswick.

Our tastefully converted one or two bedroomed self-catering apartments and cottages are all superbly appointed and offer a uniquely high standard of facilities. Fully fitted feature kitchens (many with dishwashers), independent central heating, remote control teletext colour televisions with video player, CD player and direct dial telephone, whilst the bedrooms are complete with hairdryer, trouser press and radio alarms.

Your accommodation comes complete with welcoming tea tray, bouquet of fresh flowers, fruit basket, beds made and towels supplied. Even fresh milk in the fridge, and to be sure your holiday starts with a sparkle, a bottle of chilled Champagne.

But that's not all.

With our compliments, you may have Sunday lunch at the adjacent award winning and highly commended Derwentwater Hotel. Likewise, breakfast on your departure morning is also included, and there is more, ample free parking, takeaway meal and grocery delivery service, and a special welcome for pets.

For that really special occasion try our Glaramara Cottage, which is tucked away in the corner of the grounds and enjoys king size, half tester bed making an ideal romantic hideaway.

*Derwent Manor ...
an unrivalled location
with quality accommodation
and a range of
services and facilities
seldom matched.*

*Call us now for
our full colour brochure
on 01768 772211.*

E-mail: info@derwentwater-hotel.co.uk
Web: www.derwentwater-hotel.co.uk

BOWER HOUSE INN

Eskdale, Holmrook, Cumbria CA19 1TD
Tel: 019467 23244 Fax: 019467 23308
E-mail: info@bowerhouseinn.freeserve.co.uk
Website: www.bowerhouseinn.co.uk

A 17th century inn of considerable character, the Bower House is as popular with the locals as it is with tourists, always a good recommendation for any establishment. Tastefully furnished throughout and designed with an eye to comfort as well as style. All guest rooms have private facilities, colour television and telephone. Cuisine is of a consistently good standard, with fresh produce from nearby farms featuring extensively in skilfully prepared and well presented dishes, and the wine cellar should satisfy the most demanding palate.

ETC ★★　　AA ★★

Ashfield Farm, *Calwich*, *near Ashbourne DE6 2EB*

Five modern six-berth caravans, fully equipped, with mains electricity. Ashfield Farm overlooks the peaceful Dove Valley and is convenient for the Peak District, the old market town of Ashbourne only two miles away with golf courses, swimming pool, squash and bowling.
Within easy reach of stately homes like Haddon Hall and Chatsworth, with the Potteries and Lichfield 25 miles distant, Uttoxeter 10 miles away and Alton Towers Theme Park is under five miles away.
Prices and brochure on request.

English Tourist Board
COMMENDED
♣ ♣ ♣ ♣

Telephone 01335 324279 or 324443

SIDESMILL FARM

Mrs Catherine Brandrick

Snelston, Ashbourne, Derbyshire DE6 2GQ
Telephone: 01335 342710
Website: www.sidemill.demon.co.uk

Peaceful dairy farm located on the banks of the River Dove. A rippling mill stream flows quietly past the 18th century stone-built farmhouse. Traditional English breakfast, excellent local pubs and restaurants. One double room en suite, one twin-bedded room with private bathroom, tea/coffee making facilities. Ideal base for touring; within easy reach of Dovedale, Alton Towers, stately homes and many other places of interest.

Open February-November. Car necessary, parking available.
Bed and Breakfast from £20 per person. A non-smoking establishment. ETC ◆◆◆◆

PUBLISHER'S NOTE

While every effort is made to ensure accuracy, we regret that FHG Publications cannot accept responsibility for errors, omissions or misrepresentations in our entries or any consequences thereof. Prices in particular should be checked because we go to press early. We will follow up complaints but cannot act as arbiters or agents for either party.

SELF-CATERING

BONEHAYNE FARM
COLYTON, DEVON EX24 6SG

Enjoy a relaxing holiday, deep in the tranquil Devon countryside, on 250 acre working farm. Situated on the banks of the river Coly in a beautiful sheltered valley, ideal for trout fishing, or spot a kingfisher. Two miles from Colyton and four-and-a-half miles from coast, our self-catering, spacious cottage, part of farmhouse (south facing) has many olde worlde features and is fully equipped including four-poster. Two luxury caravans each on own site (south facing) in farmhouse's spacious garden. Well equipped, laundry room, barbecue, picnic tables and chairs. B&B also available.

Mrs S. Gould 01404 871416 or Mrs R. Gould 01404 871396.
website: www.members.netscapeonline.co.uk/thisfarm33 • e-mail: thisfarm33@netscapeonline.co.uk

Lower Ford Farm

A warm, friendly welcome awaits you at our 15th century farmhouse, set in a peaceful, unspoilt valley close to Tiverton, Cullompton and the M5 (J 28). Guests can enjoy a relaxed family holiday on our 300 acre working farm. Excellent farmhouse cooking, special diets welcome. Diningroom, lounge with colour TV, games room. All bedrooms are en suite with tea/coffee making facilities. Children welcome. Open all year, except Christmas. Bed, Breakfast and Evening Meal from £28.50 daily, £188 weekly.

For further details and brochure phone:
Mrs Diane Pring, Lower Ford Farm, Cullompton, Devon
01884 252354

DEVON
CONNECTION
Beautiful Barns, cottages and farmhouses in an Area of Outstanding Natural Beauty - Come and enjoy

• 87A Fore Street • Kingsbridge • Devon TQ7 1AB
• Tel: 01548 852572 • website: www.devonconnection.co.uk

IDYLLIC SETTING. Luxury cottage or apartment in a beautiful Georgian country house with breathtaking sea views and a virtually private beach. Nestling in four acres of grounds of outstanding natural beauty. Numerous facilities include heated **SHELL COVE HOUSE** *Country House Apartments and Cottages* pool, tennis court, badminton, croquet, bird hide gazebo and indoor play room. Central heating, dishwashers, videos, linen and all comforts. A unique holiday. Open all year with short breaks in the Spring and Autumn.

Shell Cove House, Old Teignmouth Road, Dawlish, Devon EX7 0NJ
Tel & Fax: 01626 862523

CARAVAN & CAMPING

SELF-CATERING

BOARD

LANCOMBES HOUSE HOLIDAY COTTAGES

Lancombes House, West Milton, Bridport DT6 3TN • Tel: 01308 485375

Lancombes House is a 200-year-old stone barn built 300 feet above sea level set in 10 acres; there are tame animals for children to play and help with including horses, ponies, goats and ducks. Panoramic views to the sea only four miles away. Four superbly converted cottages, each with its own sitting-out area, barbecue and garden furniture. Spacious open plan living areas, most with wood burning stoves. Modern fitted kitchens, double and twin-bedded rooms. Electric central heating, shared laundry. Deep in the heart of Hardy country, this is a delightful area to explore whether on foot or horseback. Many things to do and pets and children are very welcome

Prices start at £140 for mini-breaks
Open all the year round
Proprietors: Carol and Karl Mansfield

LULWORTH COUNTRY COTTAGES

Five family owned properties on historic 1200 acre estate. Coastguard Cottage, 400 yards from Lulworth Cove, sleeps 7; Home Farm, sleeps 7; St. Mary's sleeps 10, 48 East Lodge sleeps 4 and 49 east Lodge sleeps 3. All cottages are well equipped with washing machines, tumble driers, fridge/freezers, microwaves, dishwashers and colour TV. Central heating, duvets with linen, and electricity are inclusive. Secure gardens and parking. Situated in an area of exceptional natural beauty. Open throughout the year. Short breaks by arrangement.

For brochure contact:
Mrs E. S. Weld, Lulworth Castle House, East Lulworth, Wareham, Dorset BH20 5QS
Tel & Fax: 01929 400100

Cardsmill Farm Holidays

Whitchurch Canonicorum, Charmouth
Bridport, Dorset DT6 6RP
Tel & Fax: 01297 489375 • e-mail: cardsmill@aol.com
website: www.farmhousedorset.com

Stay on a real working family farm in the Marshland Vale, an Area of Outstanding Natural Beauty. Enjoy country walks to the village, coast and around farm and woods. Watch the daily milking, see baby calves and lambs, and seasonal activities here on this 590 acre farm. En suite family and double rooms available with CTV, tea/coffee trays.

Also available, two large, rural quiet farmhouses. Each has half acre gardens and parking spaces. Taphouse farmhouse has five bedrooms, two bathrooms, lounge, 22x15 ft kitchen/diner, games room, oil-fired Rayburn, log fire, central heating and payphone. Courthouse has four bedrooms, two bathrooms, lounge, kitchen/diner, small conservatory and full central heating. Both available all year for long or short stays. Phone for a brochure.

ETC ♦♦♦   🏠 *Approved*
B & B £18 - £24 per person

GREENWOOD GRANGE FARM COTTAGES

Higher Bockhampton, Dorchester, Dorset DT2 8QH
Tel & Fax: 01305 268874
e-mail: enquiries@greenwoodgrange.co.uk
website: www.greenwoodgrange.co.uk

Set in glorious rolling countryside Greenwood Grange Cottages, converted from barns built by Thomas Hardy's father in 1849. Superb leisure facilities: magnificent Roman-style indoor swimming pool, sauna, separate purpose-built fitness/games building with solarium, table tennis, table football, pool table and bar billiards; indoor and outdoor play area with swings for infants. Grounds for strolling and relaxing, two all weather tennis courts, lawns for croquet and badminton. Cottages accommodating between two and seven people. Family cottages sleeping two-six plus two luxury houses and a single storey cottage suitable for disabled. Country setting, two miles Dorchester, six miles coast.

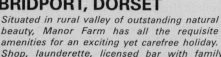

Superior Self Catering Holiday Accommodation

A working farm set in the heart of the beautiful and unspoilt Dorset countryside with stunning views and a peaceful, traffic free environment. Luccombe offers quality accommodation for 2-7 people in a variety of converted and historic farm buildings, with original timbers and panelling.

Well equipped kitchens. Large shower or bath. Cosy lounge/dining with colour TV. Bed linen, duvets, towels provided. Laundry room. Children and well behaved pets welcome. Ample parking. Disabled access. Riding, tennis, games room, Clay pigeon shooting and fishing nearby. Post office and village stores in local village. Open throughout the year Group/family enquiries welcome. Short breaks available

Luccombe Farm

★★★★
SELF CATERING

Murray and Amanda Kayll, Luccombe, Milton Abbas, Blandford Forum, Dorset DT11 0BE
Tel:(01258) 880558   Fax: (01258) 881384 E-mail: mkayll@aol.com

---

WOOLSBRIDGE MANOR

FARM CARAVAN PARK AA ▶▶▶ ETC ★★★

Situated approximately three-and-a-half-miles from the New Forest market town of Ringwood – easy access to the south coast. Seven acres level, semi-sheltered, well-drained spacious pitches. Quiet country location on a working farm, ideal and safe for families. Showers, mother/baby area, laundry room, washing up area, chemical disposal, payphone, electric hook-ups, battery charging. Children's play area on site. Site shop. Dogs welcome on leads. Fishing adjacent. Moors Valley Country Park golf course one mile. Pub and restaurant 10 minutes' walk.

Three Legged Cross, Wimborne Dorset BH21 6RA   Telephone: 01202 826369

ETC ♦♦♦♦ SILVER AWARD

WHITEWAYS FARMHOUSE

A warm welcome awaits you at this Hamstone and Flint Farmhouse. Situated at the head of the Blackmore Vale, the character rooms enjoy panoramic views over unspoilt countryside, ideal for walks along the Wessex Way and Hardy Trail. A working farm in the centre of Dorset but within a half hour drive of the sea, families are very welcome. All rooms are spacious with en suite bathroom/dressing room, tea/coffee making facilities, colour TV and central heating for all year round breaks. Breakfast is served in an attractive dining room with inglenook fireplace. Bed and Breakfast from £20.

Bookham, Buckland Newton, Dorchester, Dorset DT2 7RP
Tel & Fax: 01300 345511 • e-mail: bookhamfarm@netscapeonline.co.uk

---

Grafton Villa Farm Grafton, Hereford HR2 8ED

Tel & Fax: 01432 268689 • e-mail: jennielayton@ereal.com

A loved and cherished farmhouse, set in an acre of lawns and garden, overlooking ancient Roman fortifications and woodlands. Furnished with flair, using beautiful fabrics and antiques. Peaceful en suite bedrooms, delicious award-winning breakfasts - farmhouse portions. Ideal start to day visiting Hereford's secrets, market towns, Ledbury, Bromyard, Ross-on-Wye, Hay-on-Wye (book lover's haven), wonderful gardens and churches, Dore Abbey, Kilpeck and many more. Non-smoking. Bed & Breakfast from £21.00 pp.

AA ♦♦♦♦
Guest Accommodation

Silver SILVER AWARD

Mainoaks Farm Cottages
Goodrich, Ross-on-Wye

Six units sleeping two, four, six and seven. Mainoaks is a 15th century listed farm which has been converted to form six cottages of different size and individual character. It is set in 80 acres of pasture and woodland beside the River Wye in an area of outstanding natural beauty and an SSSI where there is an abundance of wildlife. All cottages have exposed beams, pine furniture, heating throughout, fully equipped kitchen with microwave, washer/dryer etc, colour TV. Private gardens, barbecue area and ample parking. Linen and towels provided. An ideal base for touring the local area with beautiful walks, fishing, canoeing, pony trekking, golf, bird-watching or just relaxing in this beautiful tranquil spot. Open throughout the year. Short breaks available. Pets by arrangement. Brochure on request.

Mrs P. Unwin, Hill House, Chase End, Bromsberrow, Ledbury, Herefordshire HR8 1SE
Telephone 01531 650448   ETC ★★★ to ★★★★ Highly Commended

Langstone Court Farmhouse

14th Century farmhouse. Lounge and dining room each measure 15 x 18 feet. Farmhouse wing sleeps 15 plus cots, Cidermill flat sleeps 5-7 plus cot or can be let as one unit sleeping up to 22 plus cots. Very popular for hen parties, birthdays and family get-togethers.

Two ground floor bedrooms, 1 double, 1 single. Central heating, log fires, laundry, payphone, bike storage, dishwashers. Set in beautiful Herefordshire Countryside. Large groups please book early. Short Breaks available all year except August.

Tel: 01989 770747

Colour brochure: Lesley Saunders, Dales Barn, Langstone, Llangarron, Ross-on-Wye HR9 6NR

Rakefoot Farm

ETC ◆◆◆◆ Bed and Breakfast
ETC ★★★/★★★★ Self Catering

Tel: Chipping 01995 61332 or 07889 279063 Chaigley near. Clitheroe BB7 3LY

Working family farm peacefully situated in the beautiful countryside of the Ribble Valley in the Forest of Bowland. Panoramic views. 3 miles Chipping village. 8 miles M6 J31a. Warm welcome whether on holiday or business, refreshments on arrival. **Bed and Breakfast or Self Catering** in renovated 17th century farmhouse and traditional stone barn conversion. Superbly furnished, wood-burning stoves, central heating, exposed beams and stonework. Most bedrooms en suite, some ground floor. Excellent home-cooked meals, laundry; pubs/restaurants nearby. Indoor/outdoor play areas, garden and patios. Dogs by arrangement.
"NWTB Silver Award for Self Catering holiday of the year 2000"

Self Catering properties sleeping 2 to 8, (3 interconnect sleepimg 16) From £75-£459 weekly. Short Breaks available. Bed and Breakfast £15-£20 pppn sharing.

WOODTHORPE HALL COUNTRY COTTAGES

Very well appointed luxury one and three bedroomed cottages, overlooking the golf course, all with central heating, colour TV, microwave, washer, dryer, dishwasher and fridge freezer. Woodthorpe is situated approximately six miles from the coastal resort of Mablethorpe and offers easy access to the picturesque Lincolnshire Wolds. Adjacent facilities include golf, fishing, garden centre, aquatic centre, snooker, pool and restaurant with bar and family room. ETC ★★★★. For further details contact:

Woodthorpe Hall, Woodthorpe, Near Alford, Lincs LN13 0DD - Telephone: 01507 450294

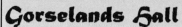
BOARD

SELF-CATERING

SELF-CATERING

Withy Grove Farm ETC★★

Come and enjoy a relaxing and friendly holiday "Down on the Farm" set in beautiful Somerset countryside. Peaceful rural setting adjoining River Huntspill, famed for its coarse fishing. The farm is ideally situated for visiting the many local attractions including Cheddar Gorge, Glastonbury, Weston-super-Mare and the lovely sandy beach of Burnham-on-Sea. Self-catering cottages are tastefully converted, sleeping four -five. Fully equipped with colour TV.

★ Heated Swimming Pool
★ Licensed Bar and Entertainment *(in high season)*
★ Games Room ★ Skittle Alley ★ Laundry

For more information please contact: **Mrs Wendy Baker, Withy Grove Farm, East Huntspill, Near Burnham-on-Sea, Somerset TA9 3NP. Telephone: 01278 784471.**

HALL FARM COUNTRY HOLIDAYS
Tel & Fax: 01386 881298 • e-mail: daphnestow@aol.com

Six cottages of character converted from 19th century barns in peaceful village setting in Vale of Evesham. Ranging from three bedrooms/two bathrooms to one and two bedrooms (all ensuite) they all have many original features and a wealth of old timbers. Furnished and equipped to a very high standard they have a welcoming atmosphere. Set amidst large lawned gardens. Ample parking, heated outdoor pool (summer months), grass tennis court. Only a short drive to many Cotswold beauty spots, interesting towns (Worcester, Cheltenham, Stratford-on-Avon), farm parks and pick-your-own. Brochure from:

Mrs Daphne Stow, Sedgeberrow, Evesham, Worcs WR11 6UB   ETC ★★★/★★★★

'Langber Country Guest House'

Ingleton, "Beauty Spot of the North" in the National Park area. Renowned for waterfalls, glens, underground caves, magnificent scenery and Ingleboro' Mountain (2,373 feet), an excellent centre for touring Dales, Lakes, coast and Three Peaks/National Park area. "Langber", a detached country house, is set amidst beautiful scenery with four-and-a-half acres of fields and gardens. There are three family, three double or twin and one single bedrooms, some en-suite. Central heating, comfortably furnished throughout. Fire precautions. Babysitting offered. Open all year except Christmas and New Year. Highly Recommended. Reductions for children under 10 sharing parents' room. Good food and a warm welcome. SAE please.

ETC ◆◆◆   Mrs Mollie Bell, Langber Country Guest House Ingleton, North Yorkshire LA6 3DT Telephone: 015242 41587.

Tel: 01348 837724
Fax: 01348 837622
E-mail: stay@lochmeyler.co.uk
Web: www.lochmeyler.co.uk

Mrs Morfydd Jones
Llandeloy,
Pen-y-Cwm,
Near Solva,
St. Davids, Pembrokeshire
SA62 6LL

A warm welcome awaits you at Lochmeyler, a 220 acre dairy farm in the centre of the St David's Peninsula. It is an ideal location for exploring the beauty of the coast and countryside.

There are 16 bedrooms, eight of them in the adjacent cottage suites. All are en-suite, non-smoking, luxury rooms with colour TV, video and refreshment facilities. Optional evening dinner with choice of menu including vegetarian. Children are welcome and there is a children's play area. Dogs free. Kennel facilities are free for owners wishing to leave their dogs during the day. Well behaved dogs can sleep in bedrooms providing they have their own bedding on the floor.

Open all year. Credit cards accepted. Colour brochure on request.

 AA/RAC ♦♦♦♦♦   WTB ★★★★ FARM   GOLD

Skerryback

Sandy Haven, Haverfordwest, Pembrokeshire SA62 3DN

Telephone: 01646 636598

Our 18c farmhouse is a working farm set in a sheltered garden adjoining the Pembokeshire coast footpath. It is an ideal situation for walkers and bird lovers to explore the secluded coves and beaches of the area, or take a boat trip to see the puffins on Skomer Island.

The two attractive double rooms, both en suite, look out across horses grazing in the meadow, the guests' lounge has colour TV and central heating backed up by log fires on chilly evenings. A welcoming cup of tea/coffee on arrival plus hospitality trays in the bedrooms.

Skerryback breakfasts are a real treat, the perfect way to start a day of strenuous walking or just relaxing on the nearest beach.

★★★
Farmhouse Award

Gwarmacwydd

Gwarmacwydd is a country estate of over 450 acres, including two miles of riverbank. See a real farm in action, the hustle and bustle of harvest, newborn calves and lambs. Children are welcomed. On the estate are five character stone cottages, Tourist Board Grade Four. Each cottage has been lovingly converted from traditional farm buildings, parts of which are over 200 years old. Each cottage is fully furnished and equipped with all modern conveniences. All electricity and linen included. All cottages are heated for year-round use. Colour brochure available.

Tel: 01437 563260 Fax: 01437 563839
e-mail: info@a-farm-holiday.org
website: www.a-farm-holiday.org

**Mrs Angela Colledge,
Llanfallteg, Whitland,
Pembrokeshire. SA34 0XH**

UPPER GENFFORD FARM
GUEST HOUSE • SELF-CATERING

Set amongst the most spectacular scenery of the Brecon Beacons National Park, Upper Genfford Farm is an ideal base for exploring the Black Mountains, Wye Valley and the Brecon Beacons, an area of outstanding beauty, rich in historical and archaeological interest, with Roman camps and Norman castles. Picturesque mountain roads will lead you to reservoirs, the Gower coast with its lovely sandy beaches and Llangorse Lake – well known for all kinds of water sports.

The charming Guest House accommodation includes one double and one twin-bedded rooms, both with en suite facilities. They are beautifully decorated and furnished, including tea/coffee making facilities, central heating, colour TV and hairdryer. The cosy lounge has a wealth of personal bric-a-brac, maps and paintings. Very much a home from home, with colour TV and books. Guests are made welcome with home-made cakes and tea on arrival. The local pub and restaurant is nearby and Hay-on-Wye, 'The Town of Books', is a short distance away.

Our self-catering cottage is fully-equipped with fridge-freezer, electric cooker, microwave, and oil-fired Rayburn for cooking. There is a cosy, comfortable lounge with colour TV, open log fire (logs provided), pretty bathroom and two attractive bedrooms (one with two single beds, the second with one double and one single). Ample parking in attractive patio adjacent to the cottage. Play area for Children, also a friendly pony.

Bed & Breakfast from £18 to £20 per person.

Terms from £150 to £180 weekly.

MRS PROSSER, UPPER GENFFORD FARM GUESTHOUSE, TALGARTH, BRECON LD3 0EN

TELEPHONE: 01874 711360

AA
Guest Accommodation
♦♦♦

Awarded Plaque of Recommendation from the Welsh Tourist Board
Nominated "Landlady of the Year" 1999   Winner of FHG Diploma

AA
QQQQ

The Highland Estate of

- **PEACE**
- **SECLUSION**
- **VARIETY OF INTERESTS**
- **FREEDOM**
- **HISTORY**
- **OUTSTANDING SCENERY**

Ellary

and Castle Sween

This 15,000 acre Highland Estate lies in one of the most beautiful and unspoilt areas of Scotland and has a wealth of ancient historical associations within its bounds. There is St. Columba's Cave, probably one of the first places of Christian Worship in Britain, also Castle Sween, the oldest ruined castle in Scotland, and Kilmory Chapel where there is a fascinating collection of Celtic slabs. There is a wide range of accommodation, from small groups of cottages, many of the traditional stone-built estate type to modern holiday chalets, super luxury and luxury caravans at Castle Sween.

Most of the cottages accommodate up to six, but one will take eight.

All units fully equipped except linen. Television reception is included.

Ellary is beautiful at all times of the year and is suitable for windsurfing, fishing, swimming, sailing and the observation of a wide variety of wildlife; there are paths and tracks throughout the estate for the visitor who prefers to explore on foot, and guests will find farmers and estate workers most helpful in their approach.

For further details, brochure and booking forms, please apply to:

ELLARY ESTATE OFFICE, by LOCHGILPHEAD, ARGYLL PA31 8PA

Tel: 01880 770232/770209 or 01546 850223

Fax: 01880 770386

e-mail: info@ellary.com • website: www.ellary.com

BRECHIN CASTLE CENTRE

Haughmuir,
by Brechin, Angus
Tel: 01356 626813

One of the largest tourist attractions in Angus
and a great day out for all the family.

~ HIGH QUALITY GARDEN CENTRE *and* COFFEE SHOP ~
~ COUNTRY PARK *with* ~ ORNAMENTAL LAKE ~ *picnic and enjoy the tranquillity;*
walk around the park to the FARM, *touch the animals* ~ SUMMER EVENTS ~
Brochure on request

SELF-CATERING

REELIG GLEN HOLIDAY COTTAGES & CHALETS

In the Scottish Highlands near Inverness

Holiday cottages with character and cedarwood chalets set individually among the trees or fields of a beautiful old Highland estate. They all have colour television, electric fires, four-ring cooker and microwave oven, night storage and electric water heating and adjoining car parking space. The cottages also have open fires. The countryside with all the untrammelled joys of nature is at the door – Butterflies find what butterflies need. Nearby is the Forestry Commission's Forest Walk with some of the tallest trees in Britain. Reelig is an excellent central base from which to see all parts of the Highlands. Fishing, pony trekking and dozens of interests are available locally. Rates are reduced in spring and autumn. STB ★ to ★★

Brochure available from Malcolm Fraser, Reelig Glen Estate, Kirkhill, Inverness-shire IV5 7PR
Telephone 01463 831208 (24 hours) Fax: 01463 831413 E-mail: Reelig@aol.com Website: www.reelig.com

---

SELF-CATERING

DALARABAN

STB ★★★

Dalaraban is a large comfortable centrally heated house built to accommodate eight people. High on top of the hill ¾ of a mile from Fort William, it has an unrivalled position with panoramic views of Loch Linnhe and the Morven mountains to the front and Ben Nevis to the rear. All power, bed linen and towels included. Electric blankets on all beds. Off road parking. One pet welcome. Open all year. Short breaks welcome in winter months. £250 - £660 per week. Brochure on request; ask for Malcolm or Eileen.

See also advert in Bed and Breakfast section.

**Strone Farm, Banavie, By Fort William
PH33 7PB Tel & Fax: 01397 712773**

BOARD

Newmill Farm

STB ★★★ B&B

Mrs Ann Guthrie, Newmill Farm, Stanley, Perthshire PH1 4QD
Telephone: (01738) 828281 E-mail:guthrienewmill@sol.co.uk
Website: www.newmillfarm.com

Newmill Farm is situated only six miles from Perth, in 330 acres of lovely farmland. Twin and double en suite rooms available and a family room with private bathroom; lounge, sittingroom, diningroom; bathroom, shower room and toilet. The many castles and historic ruins around Perth are testimony to Scotland's turbulent past. Situated at the "Gateway to the Highlands" the farm is ideally placed for those seeking some of the loveliest unspoilt scenery in Western Europe. Many golf courses and trout rivers nearby. Bed and breakfast from £18, Evening meal on request. Reductions and facilities for children. Pets welcome.

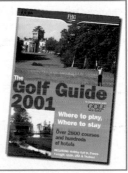
PUBLISHER'S NOTE

While every effort is made to ensure accuracy, we regret that FHG Publications cannot accept responsibility for errors, omissions or misrepresentations in our entries or any consequences thereof. Prices in particular should be checked because we go to press early. We will follow up complaints but cannot act as arbiters or agents for either party.

THE ASSOCIATION OF SCOTLAND'S SELF CATERERS

Selected Self-Catering Holidays in Scotland

Members of the ASSC are committed to high and consistant standards in self catering.
Contact your choice direct and be assured of an excellent holiday.

Brochures: 0990 168 571 • Web site: www.assc.co.uk

Owner-Operators ready to match our standards and interested in joining are requested to
contact our Secretary for information – 0990 168 571

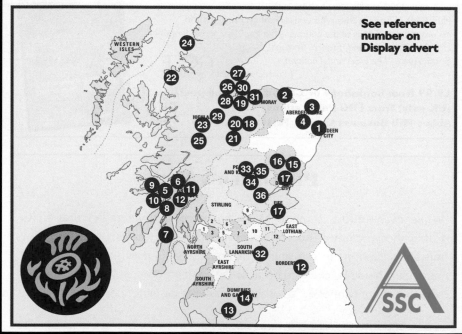

See reference
number on
Display advert

THE ROBERT GORDON UNIVERSITY TEL: 01224 262134 FAX: 01224 262144

The Robert Gordon University in the heart of Aberdeen offers a wide variety of accommodation to visitors from June through to August. Aberdeen is ideal for visiting Royal Deeside, Castles and historical buildings, playing golf or touring the Malt Whisky Trail. The city itself is a place to discover, and Aberdonians are friendly and welcoming people. We offer self-catering accommodation for individuals or for groups of people at superb rates. Each of our flats is self-contained, centrally heated, fully furnished and suitable for children and disabled guests. All flats have colour TV

Kepplestone   *King Street*

and some have microwave facilities. Bed linen and cooking utensils are all provided as is a complimentary 'welcome pack' of basic groceries. Towels available on request. Each residence has laundry and telephone facilities as well as ample car parking.

Contact: The Robert Gordon University, Business and Vacation Accommodation, Customer Services Dept, Schoolhill, Aberdeen. AB10 1FR
e-mail: accommodation@rgu.ac.uk • website: www.scotland2000.com/rgu

---

North East Farm Chalet *Near Elgin*

One 'A' frame chalet on working farm. 'Habitat' furnished, fully equipped for two – six people, colour TV, bed linen, duvets. Beautiful rural location in Moray – famous for flowers – district of lowlands, highlands, rivers, forests, lovely beaches, historic towns, welcoming people. Excellent local facilities. Moray golf tickets available. *From £170–£300 (January-December)*
Contact: Mrs. J. M. Shaw, Sheriffston, Elgin, Moray IV30 8LA
Tel & Fax: 01343 842695 • e-mail: jennifer.shaw@moray.gov.uk

DYKESIDE AND TANAREE COTTAGES (SLEEPS FOUR AND SIX)

STB ★★★★ SELF-CATERING. A warm welcome awaits you at Logie Newton Farm, eight miles east of Huntly. Two charming single-storey cottages are available, both extremely well equipped including colour TV, video, payphone, etc. The farm has its own walks, children's lead-rein pony rides, stone circles and Roman camp site. For further information and bookings please contact:
Mrs Rhona Cruickshank, LOGIE NEWTON FARM, by Huntly, Aberdeenshire AB54 6BB.
Tel: 01464 841229 • Fax: 01464 841277 • website: www.logienewton.co.uk

---

THE GREENKNOWE

A comfortable, detached, renovated cottage in a quiet location at the southern edge of the village of Kintore. Ideally situated for touring castles and pre-historic sites or for walking, fishing and golfing. The cottage is on one level with large sittingroom facing south and the garden. Sleeps four.   **WALKERS WELCOME SCHEME**

Terms £225–£350 per week including electricity and linen.
Mr & Mrs P. A. Lumsden, Kingsfield House, Kingsfield Road,
Kintore, Aberdeenshire AB51 OUD
Tel: 01467 632366 • Fax 01467 632399 • e-mail: kfield@clara.net

---

WEST COAST CHARACTER COTTAGES

Interesting selection of five individual privately owned holiday homes beautifully located (some with loch views) in rural areas within easy driving distance of Oban. All equipped/presented to a high standard and personally supervised by the local owners. Walking, fishing and many other pursuits to be enjoyed amongst wonderful scenery. Sleep 2 to 7. **Call for a Brochure**
Tigh Beag, Connel, By Oban, Argyll PA37 1PJ
Tel/Fax: 01631 710504 • Mobile: 07808 109005 • e-mail: Ejtricker@aol.com

---

LAGNAKEIL HIGHLAND LODGES

Our timber lodges are nestled in seven acres of scenic wooded glen overlooking Loch Feochan, only 3 miles from the picturesque harbour town of Oban: **"Gateway to the Isles"**. Fully equipped lodges to a high standard, including linen and towels, country pub a short walk. O.A.P. discount. Free loch fishing. Special Breaks from £38 per lodge per night, weekly from £170. Our colour brochure will tell lots more. **Colin and Jo Mossman,**
Lerags, Oban, Argyll, PA34 4SE • Tel: 01631 562746 • website: www.lagnakeil.co.uk

---

West Loch Tarbert, Argyll – Dunmore Court

Four cottages in architect design conversion of home farm on the estate of Dunmore House. Furnished to the highest standards all have stone fireplaces for log fires. Spacious accommodation for 5-7 persons. Bird-watching, sailing, sea fishing and walking. Easy access to island ferries. Pets welcome. Open all year. Colour brochure. From £165-£425

Contact: Mrs Amanda Minshall, Dunmore Court, Kilberry Road, Near Tarbert, Argyll PA29 6XZ **Telephone: 01880 820654**

STB ★★★ to ★★★★

HIGHLAND HIDEAWAYS   Argyllshire

This is one of several high quality self-catering properties of individual character we have to offer in outstanding coastal, town and country locations in Argyll including the Oban area and around Loch Awe. Sleeping 2 to 12 from £130 to £950 per week. Up to STB ★★★★ grade.

For further details contact:

Highland Hideaways,
5/7 Stafford Street, Oban, Argyll PA34 5NJ
Tel: 01631 562056 Fax: 01631 566778
e-mail: info@highlandhideaways.co.uk

Cologin Farm Holiday Chalets
Oban

All Scottish Glens have their secrets: let us share ours with you – and your pets !

Our cosy holiday chalets, set on an old farm in a peaceful private glen, can sleep from two to six people in comfort. They all have private parking, central heating, colour TV and bed linen.

✛ Tranquil country glen, just three miles from Oban
✛ Free fishing and dinghy use on our hill loch
✛ Excellent walks for you and your dogs
✛ Home-cooked food and licensed bar in our converted farm-house byre
✛ A safe haven for pets and children
✛ A friendly, family run complex with a good range of facilities

CALL NOW FOR OUR COLOUR BROCHURE AND FIND OUT MORE

Open all year round. Rates from £120 to £420 per week. Autumn Gold breaks and mid-week deals also available

MRS LINDA BATTISON, COLOGIN FARMHOUSE, LERAGS GLEN, BY OBAN, ARGYLL PA34 4SE
Tel: (01631) 564501   Fax: (01631) 566925
e-mail: cologin@oban.org.uk
STB ★★ to ★★★★ Self Catering

APPIN HOLIDAY HOMES

**Midway between Oban and Fort William
. . . in the Scottish Highlands**

Fine hill and shoreline walks amid natural beauty. Warm welcoming lodges and lochside caravan, set apart within landscaped park. Fishing (FREE), boating, cycling, pony trekking, Sealife Centre, Castle Stalker, licensed inn, all nearby. Lots to do and see. Price guide £155 - £375 per unit weekly. Sleeps two - five. Free colour brochure.

Mr & Mrs I. F. Weir, Appin Holiday Homes, Appin, Argyll PA38 4BQ

Tel: 01631 730287 – Web: www.appinholidayhomes.co.uk • E-mail: info@appinholidayhomes.co.uk

Mr & Mrs E. Crawford
Blarghour Farm

Loch Awe-side, by Dalmally, Argyll PA33 1BW
Tel: 01866 833246   Fax: 01866 833338
e-mail: blarghour@aol.com • web: www.blarghour.com

At Blarghour Farm one may choose from four centrally heated and double glazed holiday homes sleeping from two to eight people, all enjoying splendid views of lovely Loch Awe. Kitchens are well appointed, lounges tastefully decorated and furnished with payphone, TV and gas fire, beds are made up and towels supplied while the two larger houses have shower rooms in addition to bathrooms, all with shaver point. The two larger houses are suitable for children and have cots and high chairs. No pets are allowed.
Open all year. Centrally situated for touring. Illustrated brochure on request.

Mill House, Letterbox & Stockman's Cottages – Three recently renovated, quality Cottages, each sleeping four, on a working farm three miles from Jedburgh. All ideal centres for exploring, sporting holidays or getting away from it all. Each cottage has two public rooms (ground floor available). Minimum let two days. Terms £190–£310. Open all year. Bus three miles, airport 54 miles.
Green Tourism Business Award – SILVER.
Mrs A. Fraser, Overwells, Jedburgh, Roxburghshire TD8 6LT
Telephone: 01835 863020 • Fax: 01835 864334

BAREND HOLIDAY VILLAGE

SANDYHILLS, DALBEATTIE

Barend Holiday Village, near Sandyhills, on the beautiful south west coast of Scotland, with sixteen golf courses within a twenty mile drive; yet only one hour's drive from England.

Our Scandinavian style log chalets are centrally heated for all year round use, with TV and video. All chalets have docks or verandahs, some overlooking the loch, or the adjacent Colvend 18 hole golf course. On site launderette, bar, restaurant, sauna and indoor heated pool.

The two and three bedroomed chalets accommodate up to eight people, are £240-£640 p.w. including linen, heating and swimming. Short breaks all year round from £145 for four. STB ★★★ Self Catering

Tel: 01387 780663; Fax: 01387 780283
website: www.barendholidayvillage.co.uk

SHEPHERD AND STOCKMAN FLATS – DUMFRIES

Listed farm steading flats in peaceful pastoral valley surrounded by wooded hills and forest lanes. Two bedrooms each plus sofa bed and cot. TV, linen and central heating provided. Electricity metered. Outside facilities include drying room, bicycle shed, stable, dog run, barbecue and picnic area. Management is eco-sound and nature friendly. Lower flat and forest walks are wheelchair compatable. Village shop one-and-a-half miles, Thornhill nine miles, Dumfries 11 miles, Riding four miles, fishing two miles, Mountain bike course is two miles and Queensberry is five miles.

Contact: David and Gill Stewart,
Gubhill Farm, Ae, Dumfries DG1 1RL
Telephone: 01387 860648
E-mail: stewart@creaturefeature.freeserve.co.uk

STB ★★★ UPSTAIRS / CATEGORY 1
DISABILITY DOWNSTAIRS

GLENPROSEN COTTAGES – Glenprosen is one of the lovely, secret, Glens of Angus, foothills of the Cairngorms, and one of the most accessible, yet least spoilt parts of the Scottish Highlands. Only 40 minutes from Dundee, and 1½ hours from Edinburgh, the hills reach to over 3000 ft and the glen is exceptionally rich in wildlife. Peter Pan was conceived in these hills, James Barrie, spent his best holidays here.
A wide range of completely individual self-catering cottages, and houses. All traditionally stone built, but fully modernised and comfortable. Wide range of size (two-eight) from shepherd's cottage, to Georgian mansion.
Visit our website or ring for brochure 01575 540302. website: www.glenprosen.co.uk

SUMMER WATERSPORTS AND WINTER SKIING

Just six miles south of Aviemore these superb log chalets are set in 14 acres of woodland in the magnificent Spey Valley, surrounded on three sides by forest and rolling fields with the fourth side being half a mile of beach frontage. Free watersports hire for guests, 8.30-10am/4-5.30pm daily. Watersports, salmon fishing, archery, dry ski slope skiing. Hire/instruction available by the hour, day or week mid April to end October. Boathouse Restaurant on the shore of Loch Insh offers coffees, bar meals, children's meals and evening à la carte. Large gift shop and bar. Children's adventure area, interpretation trail, ski slope, mountain bike hire and stocked trout lochan are open all year round. Ski hire and instruction available December-April.

**Loch Insh Chalets, Kincraig,
Inverness-shire PH21 1NU
Tel: 01540 651272 Fax: 01540 651208
e-mail: office@lochinsh.com
website: www.lochinsh.com**

21

Innes Maree Bungalows, Poolewe IV22 2JU

Only a few minutes walk from the world-famous Inverewe Gardens in magnificent Wester Ross. A purpose built complex of six superb modern bungalows, all equipped to the highest standards of luxury and comfort. Each bungalow sleeps six with main bedroom en suite. Children and pets welcome. Terms from £175 to £425 inclusive of bed linen and electricity. Brochure available. **Tel & Fax 01445 781454**
STB ★★★★
E-mail: innes-maree@lineone.net • Website: www.assc.co.uk/innesmaree

22

HIGH GARRY LODGES
INVERGARRY

Four Scandinavian lodges set in an elevated position with superb views. Double glazed, electric central heating. One twin, two double bedrooms, large lounge with breakfast bar and well-equipped kitchen and bathroom. £160 - £440.

One newly converted cottage nestling at a lower level within the confines of this small working farm. One double, one twin bedroom. Tastefully renovated to a high standard. £190 - £470.

Visitors may participate at feeding times
Ideal for touring West Highlands. Fishing,
Golf and Bird-watching.

Brochure available.

**Mr & Mrs Wilson, High Garry Lodges,
Ardgarry Farm, Faichem, Invergarry,
Inverness-shire. PH35 4HG**

Tel: 01809 501226
Fax: 01809 501307

23

Clashmore Holiday Cottages Our three croft cottages at Clashmore, are the ideal base for a holiday in the Highlands. They are cosy and fully equipped, with linen provided. Nearby there are sandy beaches, mountains and lochs for wild brown trout fishing. Children welcome but sorry no pets. Open all year, sleeping two-five £160-£330 per week.
**Contact Mr and Mrs Mackenzie, Lochview,
216 Clashmore, Stoer, Lochinver, Sutherland IV27 4JQ
Tel & Fax: 01571 855226 e-mail: clashcotts@aol.com**

24

Pets Welcome! Free Fishing!

RIVERSIDE LODGES

INVERGLOY, SPEAN BRIDGE, INVERNESS-SHIRE PH34 4DY
TEL/FAX 01397 712684
e-mail: riverside.lodges@dial.pipex.com
web: www.ykm09.dial.pipex.com

Peace and quiet are synonymous with Riverside, where our three identical lodges each sleep up to six people. Accessible from the A82 but totally hidden from it, our 12 acres of woodland garden front on Loch Lochy. Cots, linen, boat, fishing tackle, barbecue, all for hire. Pets welcome. There is a nominal charge for fishing on our stocked lochan or you can fish free from our shingle beach on Loch Lochy.
Brochure gladly provided.

25

26

TOMICH HOLIDAYS, Guisachan Farm, Tomich. Inverness-shire   **Sleep 4 to 6**
Working farm housing 3 courtyard cottages and indoor pool. Also 2 storey wooden chalets, amid woodlands and Victorian Dairy. All include central heating, hot water and electricity, so your comfort is assured. Set in the highlands, Tomich is near Glen Affric and close to Loch Ness. An ideal base for walking, touring or relaxing. Open all year. Pets welcome. Terms from £165 to £505. STB ★★★/★★★★ SELF-CATERING   **Bookings/Colour Brochure:**
Donald and Sue Fraser, Tomich Holidays, Guisachan Farm, Tomich, Inverness-shire IV4 7LY • Tel: 01456 415332
• Fax 01456 415499 • e-mail: admin@tomich-holidays.co.uk • website: www.tomich-holidays.co.uk

27

SUTHERLAND
HIGHLAND GLEN LODGES

Superb ★★★★ luxury lodges set high on a hillside in the northern Highlands. Panoramic mountain views from your armchair or private balcony. Centrally located for touring the north. Glorious walks from the lodges. Each lodge is beautifully furnished and cosy at any time of the year. Dogs welcome. Open all year. Sleeps 4, bed linen and towels included, free electricity, digital satellite TV, video, fully fitted kitchen, bathroom with power shower. Ground floor accommodation with parking by the door. Credit card and secure online bookings available. Short and weekend breaks possible.

Southlins, High Street
Dornoch, Sutherland IV25 3SH
Telephone: 01862 811579

www.highlandlodges.co.uk

28

EASTER DALZIEL FARM HOLIDAY COTTAGES
DALCROSS, INVERNESS-SHIRE IV1 2 JL — TEL/FAX: 01667 462213

Three cosy, traditional stone-built cottages in a superb central location, ideal for touring, sporting activities and observing wildlife. Woodland and coastal walks. The cottages are fully equipped including linen and towels. Pets by arrangement. Terms from £130 low season to £415 high season per cottage per week.
Recommended in the Good Holiday Cottage Guide. Open all year for long or short breaks.
Brochure on request. STB ★★★ and ★★★★ SELF CATERING.

29

South Loch Ness. 'Giusaichean', Ault-na-Goire, Errogie

Sleeps 4/6 plus cot. Secluded but not isolated. Giusaichean is a converted croft at Loch Ness, centrally placed for touring the Highlands. Two double bedrooms upstairs, also bathroom with bidet, shower and bath. Downstairs second WC and kitchen with electric hob and oven, microwave, washing machine, tumble dryer, dishwasher, fridge and freezer. Spacious lounge with wood-burning stove, colour TV. Oil central heating and electricity free. Payphone. Fenced garden, safe for pets and children. Open all year. Other self catering also in Loch Ness area.

Brochure, contact Rosemary and Andy Holt,
Wilderness Cottages, Island Cottage,
Inverfarigaig, Inverness IV2 6XR.

Tel/Fax: 01456 486631 • E-mail: andy@wildernesscottages.com • Website: www.wildernesscottages.com

30

LOCHLETTER LODGES

BALNAIN, GLENURQUHART, INVERNESS. IV63 6TJ
Tel: 01456 476313 Fax: 01456 476301
e-mail: mary@lochletter.freeserve.co.uk
website: www.lochletter.freeserve.co.uk

Lochletter Lodges are situated in beautiful Glenurquhart.
Plodda, Divach and Guisachan lodges all have double bed, one twin bedded room and two adult sized bunk bedded rooms. Bathrooms have shower toilet etc. Glomach is a two bedded lodge with one double and one twin bedded room with extra stowaway beds. Full bathroom facilities.

★ *Access for disabled.* ★ *Electricity inclusive.* ★ *Badminton and games room on site*
★ *Washing machine and tumble dryer.* ★ *Car Parking - room for two cars* ★ *Linen provided.*
★ *Delicious home made bread available.* ★ *Walking and Cycling.* ★ *Golf* ★ *Fishing*

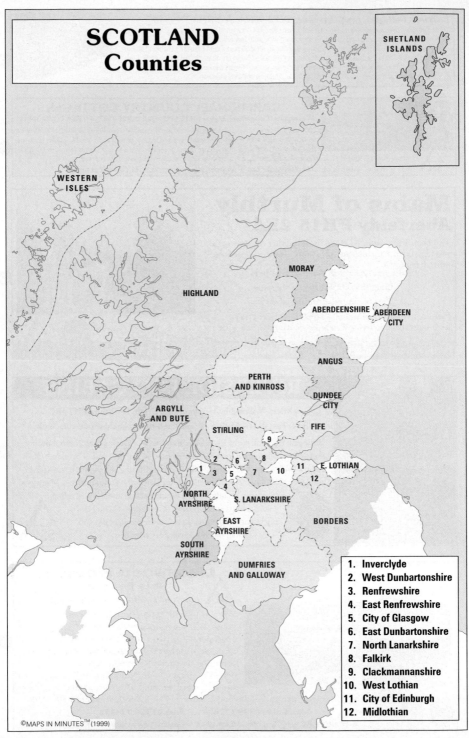

SCOTLAND
Counties

SHETLAND ISLANDS

WESTERN ISLES

MORAY

HIGHLAND

ABERDEENSHIRE   ABERDEEN CITY

ANGUS

PERTH AND KINROSS

ARGYLL AND BUTE

DUNDEE CITY

STIRLING   FIFE

9

2 6 8
1 3 5 7 10 11 E. LOTHIAN
4 12

NORTH AYRSHIRE

S. LANARKSHIRE

EAST AYRSHIRE   BORDERS

SOUTH AYRSHIRE

DUMFRIES AND GALLOWAY

1. Inverclyde
2. West Dunbartonshire
3. Renfrewshire
4. East Renfrewshire
5. City of Glasgow
6. East Dunbartonshire
7. North Lanarkshire
8. Falkirk
9. Clackmannanshire
10. West Lothian
11. City of Edinburgh
12. Midlothian

©MAPS IN MINUTES™ (1999)

The Farm Holiday Guide to

Holidays in

England, Scotland, Wales, Ireland
& The Isle of Man

Farms, guest houses and country hotels;
cottages, flats and chalets; caravans and camping;
activity holidays; country inns.

CONTENTS

ENGLAND

BOARD

CONTENTS

SCOTLAND

WALES

NORTHERN IRELAND

REPUBLIC OF IRELAND

FARM HOLIDAY GUIDE
ENGLAND, SCOTLAND, WALES, IRELAND
& THE CHANNEL ISLANDS

This 54th edition of FARM HOLIDAY GUIDE offers a comprehensive choice of all types of accommodation, in all parts of the country, for direct booking. All the entries are well described and generally give an indication of rates. We advise if children or pets are welcome, and whether the premises are suitable for disabled guests. So why not phone and have a talk with one or two different proprietors, and remember to ask about any special facilities or other points not mentioned in the description which are important to you. While on holiday, you may like to visit some of the places of interest in the area and our entries usually give some information about the local attractions to help you plan these outings. Our selection of Country Inns, starting on page 193, may also give you some idea of where to stop for refreshments.

Anne Cuthbertson
Editor

ISBN 185055 317 3
© IPC Media Ltd 2001
Cover photographs: Main picture – Photo Bank; smaller picture – Graham Bell
Cover design: Oliver Dunster, Focus Network

Maps: ©MAPS IN MINUTES™ (1999)

Typeset by FHG Publications Ltd. Paisley.
Printed and bound in Great Britain by William Clowes, Beccles, Suffolk.

Distribution. Book Trade: WLM, Unit 11, Newmarket Court, Newmarket Drive, Derby DE24 8NW
(Tel: 01332 573737. Fax: 01332 573399).
News Trade: Market Force (UK) Ltd, 247 Tottenham Court Road, London WIP 0AU
(Tel: 020 7261 6809; Fax: 020 7261 7227).

Published by FHG Publications Ltd., Abbey Mill Business Centre,
Seedhill, Paisley PA1 ITJ (Tel: 0141-887 0428 Fax: 0141-889 7204).
e-mail: fhg@ipcmedia.com

US ISBN 1-55650 917 0
Distributed in the United States by
Hunter Publishing Inc., 130 Campus Drive, Edison, N.J. 08818, USA

The Farm Holiday Guide is an FHG publication, published by
IPC Country & Leisure Media Ltd, part of IPC Media Group of Companies.

Ratings You Can Trust

ENGLAND

The **English Tourism Council** (formerly the English Tourist Board) has joined with the **AA** and **RAC** to create a new, easily understood quality rating for serviced accommodation, giving a clear guide of what to expect.

HOTELS are given a rating from One to Five **Stars** – the more Stars, the higher the quality and the greater the range of facilities and level of services provided.

GUEST ACCOMMODATION, which includes guest houses, bed and breakfasts, inns and farmhouses, is rated from One to Five **Diamonds**. Progressively higher levels of quality and customer care must be provided for each one of the One to Five Diamond ratings.

HOLIDAY PARKS, TOURING PARKS and CAMPING PARKS are now also assessed using **Stars**. Standards of quality range from a One Star (acceptable) to a Five Star (exceptional) park.

Look out also for the new *SELF-CATERING* Star ratings. The more *Stars* (from One to Five) awarded to an establishment, the higher the levels of quality you can expect. Establishments at higher rating levels also have to meet some additional requirements for facilities.

NB Some self-catering properties had not been assessed at the time of going to press and in these cases the old-style KEY symbols will still be shown.

SCOTLAND

Star Quality Grades will reflect the most important aspects of a visit, such as the warmth of welcome, efficiency and friendliness of service, the quality of the food and the cleanliness and condition of the furnishings, fittings and decor.

THE MORE STARS, THE HIGHER THE STANDARDS.

The description, such as Hotel, Guest House, Bed and Breakfast, Lodge, Holiday Park, Self-catering etc tells you the type of property and style of operation.

In England, Scotland and Wales, all graded properties are inspected annually by Tourist Authority trained Assessors.

WALES

Places which score highly will have an especially welcoming atmosphere and pleasing ambience, high levels of comfort and guest care, and attractive surroundings enhanced by thoughtful design and attention to detail

STAR QUALITY GUIDE FOR SERVICED ACCOMMODATION AND HOLIDAY PARKS

★★★★★ *Exceptional quality*
★★★★ *Excellent quality*
★★★ *Very good quality*
★★ *Good quality*
★ *Fair to good quality*

SELF-CATERING ACCOMMODATION

The **DRAGON GRADES** spell out the quality. They range from Grade 1 (simple and reasonable) to Grade 5 (excellent quality). The grades reflect the overall quality, not the range of facilities.

FHG Diploma Winners 2000

Each year we award a small number of diplomas to holiday proprietors whose services have been specially commended by our readers. The following were our FHG Diploma Winners for 2000.

England

CUMBRIA

- Mr & Mrs Haskell, Borwick Lodge, Outgate, Hawkshead, Cumbria LA22 0PU (015394 36332).

- Mrs Val Sunter, Higher House Farm, Oxenholme Lane, Natland, Kendal, Cumbria LA9 7QH (015395 61177).

DEVON

- Jenny Fox, Highstead Farm, Bucks Cross, Bideford, Devon EX39 5DX (01237 431201).

DORSET

- Mr & Mrs Reynolds, The Vine Hotel, 22 Southern Rd, Southbourne, Bournemouth, Dorset BH6 3SR (01202 428309).

HAMPSHIRE

- Mrs Ellis, Efford Cottage Guest House, Milford Road, Everton, Lymington, Hampshire SO41 0JD (015906 42315).

KENT

- Pam & Arthur Mills, Cloverlea, Bethersden, Ashford, Kent TN26 3DU (01233 820353)

Wales

ANGLESEY & GWYNEDD

- Jim & Marion Billingham, Preswylfa, Aberdovey, Gwynedd LL35 0LE (01654 767239)

NORTH WALES

- Bob & Nesta Wivell, Pen-Y-Bont Fawr, Cynwyd, Near Corwen, North Wales LL21 0ET (01490 412663)

Scotland

ABERDEENSHIRE, BANFF & MORAY

- Garth Hotel, Grantown on Spey, Morayshire PH26 3HN (01479 872836)

PERTH & KINROSS

- The Windlestrae Hotel, The Muirs, Kinross, Tayside KY13 7AS (01577 863217)

HELP IMPROVE BRITISH TOURIST STANDARDS

Why not write and tell us about the holiday accommodation you have chosen from one of our popular publications?

Complete a nomination form giving details of why you think YOUR host or hostess should win one of our attractive framed diplomas.

*Be a giant in a magical miniature world of make-believe depicting rural England in the 1930's.
"A little piece of history that is forever England."*

Open: 10am to 5pm daily 17th February to 28th October.

Directions: Junction 16 M25, Junction 2 M40.

The world's leading collection of lighthouse equipment. AV theatre and reconstructed living quarters.

DOGS ON LEADS

Open: Sunday to Friday 10.30am to 4.30pm Easter to 31st October 2001

Directions: A30 into Penzance

World's finest steamboat collection and premier all-weather attraction. Swallows and Amazons exhibition, model boat pond, tea shop, souvenir shop. Free guided tours "Dolly": 1850-2000 Exhibition.

Open: 10am to 5pm 3rd weekend in March to last weekend October

Directions: on A592 between Windermere and Bowness-on-Windermere

---

A collection of cars from film and TV, including Chitty Chitty Bang Bang, James Bond cars, Del Boy's van, Fab1 and many more.

PETS MUST BE KEPT ON LEAD

Open: Daily 10am-5pm. Closed February half term. Weekends only in December.

Directions: In centre of Keswick close to car park

An underground wonderland of stalactites, stalagmites, rocks, minerals and fossils. Home of the unique Blue John stone – see the largest single piece ever found. Suitable for all ages.

Open: March to October opens 9.30am, November to February opens 10am. Enquire for last tour of day and closed days.

Directions: ½ mile west of Castleton on A6187 (old A625)

Visit 1000+ gnomes and pixies in two acre beech wood. Gnome hats are loaned free of charge - so the gnomes think you are one of them - don't forget your camera! Also 2-acre wild flower garden with 250 labelled species.

Open: daily 10am to 6pm 21st March to 31st October

Directions: Between Bideford and Bude; follow brown tourist signs from A39/A388/A386

Award-winning centre sited on Plymouth's famous Hoe telling the story of the city, from the epic voyages of Drake, Cook and the Mayflower Pilgrims to the devastation of the Blitz. A must for all the family

Open: Summer daily 9am - 6pm; Winter Tuesday- Sunday 9am - 5pm. For current information Tel: 01752 600608

Directions: follow signs from Plymouth City Centre to the Hoe and seafront

"England for Excellence" award-winning rural attraction combining traditional rural crafts with hilarious novelties such as sheep racing and duck trialling, Indoor adventure zone for adults and children.

Open: daily, 10am to 6pm April - Oct Phone for Winter opening times and details

Directions: on A39 North Devon link road, two miles west of Bideford Bridge

An exciting working wool museum with machinery that spins yarn and weaves cloth, including the Devon tartan. Mill machinery, restaurant, gardens in a waterside setting. Home of the giant New World tapestry.

Open: April to November daily 10.30am to 5pm; November to April Monday to Friday 10.30am to 5pm

Directions: Two miles from Junction 27 M5; follow signs to Willand (B3181) then brown tourist signs to Museum

Britain's best preserved lead mining site – and a great day out for all the family, with lots to see and do. Underground Experience – Park Level Mine now open.

Open: April 1st to October 31st 10.30am to 5pm daily

Directions: alongside A689, midway between Stanhope and Alston in the heart of the North Pennines.

On three floors of a Listed Victorian warehouse telling 200 years of inland waterway history. • Historic boats • Painted boat gallery • Blacksmith • Archive film • Hands-on displays
"A great day out"

Open: Summer 10am to 5pm
Closed Christmas Day

Directions: Junction 11A or 12 off M5 – follow brown signs for Historic Docks. Railway and bus station 10 minute walk. Free coach parking.

The museum of everyday life in Roman Britain. An award-winning museum with re-created Roman rooms, hands-on discovery areas, and some of the best mosaics outside the Mediterranean

Open: Monday to Saturday
10am-5.30pm
Sunday 2pm-5.30pm

Directions: St Alban's

Open-air museum with historic buildings housing exhibitions on Kent life over past 100 years. Sample Kentish fare in the tearoom. Medway boat trip, adventure playground, free parking.

DOGS MUST BE KEPT ON LEAD

Open: daily March to November 4th
10am to 5.30pm

Directions: just off Junction 6 M20, A229 to Maidstone

The world's largest collection of Grand Prix racing cars – over 130 exhibits within five halls, including McLaren Formula One cars.

Open: daily 10am to 5pm (last admission 4pm). Closed Christmas/New Year.

Directions: 2 miles from M1 (J23a/24) and M42/A42; to north-west via A50.

Large wildlife park with Reptile Land, Tropical House, Insectarium, Birds of Prey Centre, farm animals, wallaby enclosure, llamas; adventure playground, tea room and gift shop.

Open: daily from 10am
April to end October

Directions: off A17 at Long Sutton

Visit the Discovery Centre and you'll become a time traveller, experiencing extinct creatures, submerged forests, Viking raids and the Victorian seaside along your voyage of discovery. TIME is an exciting interactive exhibition.

Open: Open daily 10am to 5pm (Please check for seasonal variations), except Christmas/Boxing/New Year's Days

Directions: Follow Lakeside signs from Cleethorpes seafront, A180 or A15 through Grimsby

Lions, snow leopards, chimpanzees, penguins, reptiles, aquarium and lots more, set amidst landscaped gardens. Gift shop, cafe and picnic areas.

Open: all year round from 10am

Directions: on the coast 16 miles north of Liverpool; follow the brown and white tourist signs

Come to the world's greatest medieval adventure and enter our world of mystery and merriment. Jump on the magical 'Travel Back in Time' and ride in search of Robin.

Open: daily 10am to 6pm (last admission 4.30pm)

Directions: near Nottingham Castle in city centre – follow brown tourist signs

750-year old man-made cave system beneath a modern day shopping centre. Discover how the caves were used with a unique 40-minute audio tour.

Open: daily Mon-Sat 10am to 4.15pm, Sundays 11am to 4pm

Directions: In Nottingham city centre, within Broadmarsh Shopping Centre

* Britain's most spectacular caves
* Traditional paper-making
* Penny Arcade
* Magical Mirror Maze *

Open: Summer 10am to 5pm; Winter 10.30am to 4.30pm. Closed 17-25 Dec.

Directions: from M5 J22 follow brown-and-white signs via A38 and A371. Two miles from Wells.

Falconry centre with animals - flying displays, animal handling, feeding and bottle feeding - in 15th century NT farmyard setting on Exmoor. Also falconry and outdoor activities, hawk walks and riding

Open: 10.30am to 4.30pm

Directions: A39 west of Minehead, turn right at Allerford, half-mile along lane on left

---

The world's largest display of Royal Doulton figures past and present. Video theatre, demonstration room, museum, restaurant and shop. Factory Tours by prior booking weekdays only.

Open: Monday to Saturday 9.30am to 5pm; Sundays 10.30am to 4.30pm Closed Christmas week

Directions: from M6 Junction 15/16; follow A500 to junction with A527. Signposted.

Discover one of Britain's best indoor Botanic Gardens and Paradise Water Gardens, an inspiration for garden lovers. Other attractions include the Planet Earth Exhibition with amazing fossils and moving dinosaurs, the Sussex History Trail and Pleasure Gardens.

Open: Open daily, except Christmas Day and Boxing Day.

Directions: signposted off A26 and A259

Experience history and nostalgia at its very best at one of the South of England's favourite attractions. Over 30 room and shop displays bring the park to life

PETS NOT ALLOWED IN CHILDRENS PLAY AREA

Open: 10am to 6pm (last admission 4.45pm, one hour earlier in winter)

Directions: Just off A21 in Battle High Street opposite the Abbey

---

100 acres of parkland, home to hundreds of duck, geese, swans and flamingos. Discovery centre, cafe, gift shop; play area.

Open: every day except Christmas Day

Directions: signposted from A19, A195, A1231 and A182

Wander through a lush landscape of exotic foliage where a myriad of multi-coloured butterflies sip nectar from tropical blossoms. Stroll past bubbling streams and splashing waterfalls; view insects and spiders all safely behind glass.

Open: 10am to 6pm summer, 10am to dusk winter

FHG PUBLICATIONS, ABBEY MILL BUSINESS CENTRE, PAISLEY PA1 1TJ

Around 100 vintage and classic cars, motorbikes and commercials, with over 30 taxed. Superb view of Wiltshire Downs; children's play and picnic area

Open: Sunday to Thursday 11am to 5pm (1st April to 31st Oct); 11am to 4pm (1st Nov to 31st March)

Directions: A4 from Calne to Marlborough, follow brown tourist signs

FHG PUBLICATIONS, ABBEY MILL BUSINESS CENTRE, PAISLEY PA1 1TJ

Award-winning bird of prey centre featuring free-flying demonstrations daily. 30 species on permanent display including the largest bird of prey in the world – the Andean Condor. Children's adventure playground. Tea-room and gift shop.

Open: daily 10am to 5pm

Directions: just outside Settle on the A65 Skipton to Kendal road.

FHG PUBLICATIONS, ABBEY MILL BUSINESS CENTRE, PAISLEY PA1 1TJ

Steam train operate over a 4½ mile line from Bolton Abbey Station to Embsay Station. Many family events including Thomas the Tank Engine take place during major Bank Holidays.

Open: steam trains run every Sunday throughout the year and up to 7 days a week in summer. 11am to 4.15pm

Directions: Embsay Station signposted from the A59 Skipton by-pass; Bolton Abbey Station signposted from the A59 at Bolton Abbey.

FHG PUBLICATIONS, ABBEY MILL BUSINESS CENTRE, PAISLEY PA1 1TJ

A fascinating display of railway carriages and a wide range of railway items telling the story of rail travel over the years.

ALL PETS MUST BE KEPT ON LEADS

Open: daily 11am to 4.30pm

Directions: Approximately one mile from Keighley on A629 Halifax road. Follow brown tourist signs

FHG PUBLICATIONS, ABBEY MILL BUSINESS CENTRE, PAISLEY PA1 1TJ

FHG

READERS' OFFER 2001

The Grassic Gibbon Centre

Arbuthnott, Laurencekirk, Aberdeenshire AB30 1PB

Tel: 01561 361668   e-mail: lgginfo@grassicgibbon.com

website: www.grassicgibbon.com

Two for the price of one entry to exhibition

Valid during 2001 (not groups)

NOT TO BE USED IN CONJUNCTION WITH ANY OTHER OFFER

FHG

READERS' OFFER 2001

STORYBOOK GLEN

Maryculter, Aberdeen, Aberdeenshire AB12 5FT

Tel: 01224 732941

10% discount on all entries

valid until end 2001

NOT TO BE USED IN CONJUNCTION WITH ANY OTHER OFFER

FHG

READERS' OFFER 2001

Kelburn Castle & Country Centre

Fairlie, Near Largs, Ayrshire KA29 0BE

Tel: 01475 568685 e-mail: info@kelburncountrycentre.com

website: www.kelburncountrycentre.com

One child free for each full paying adult

Valid until October 2001

NOT TO BE USED IN CONJUNCTION WITH ANY OTHER OFFER

FHG

READERS' OFFER 2001

CREETOWN GEM ROCK MUSEUM

Chain Road, Creetown, Near Newton Stewart, Kirkcudbrightshire DG8 7HJ

Tel: 01671 820357 • E-mail: gem.rock@btinternet.com

Website: www.gemrock.net

10% off admission prices

valid during 2001

NOT TO BE USED IN CONJUNCTION WITH ANY OTHER OFFER

FHG

READERS' OFFER 2001

MYRETON MOTOR MUSEUM

Aberlady, East Lothian EH32 0PZ

Tel: 01875 870288

One child FREE with each paying adult

valid during 2001

NOT TO BE USED IN CONJUNCTION WITH ANY OTHER OFFER

Visitor centre dedicated to the much-loved Scottish writer Lewis Grassic Gibbon. Exhibition, cafe, gift shop. Outdoor children's play area. Disabled access throughout.

Open: daily April to October 10am to 4.30pm. Groups by appointment including evenings.

Directions: On the B967, accessible and signposted from both A90 and A92.

28-acre theme park with over 100 nursery rhyme characters, set in beautifully landscaped gardens. Shop and restaurant on site.

Open: 1st March to 31st Oct: daily 10am-6pm; 1st Nov to end Feb: Sat/Sun only 11am- 4pm

Directions: 6 miles west of Aberdeen off B9077

The historic home of the Earls of Glasgow. Waterfalls, gardens, famous Glen, unusual trees. Riding school, stockade, play areas, exhibitions, shop, cafe and The Secret Forest.

PETS MUST BE KEPT ON LEAD

Open: daily 10am to 6pm Easter to October

Directions: On A78 between Largs and Fairlie, 45 mins drive from Glasgow

---

Worldwide collection of gems, minerals, crystals and fossils
•Erupting Volcano•Audio Visual•
•Crystal Cave•Unique Giftshop•
•Relax in our themed tea room•
•Internet Cafe •

Open: Open daily Easter to 30th November; Dec/Feb – weekends only.

Directions: 7 miles from Newton Stewart, 11 miles from Gatehouse of Fleet; just off A75 Carlisle to Stranraer road.

Motor cars from 1896, motorcycles from 1902, commercial vehicles from 1919, cycles from 1880, British WWII military vehicles, ephemera, period advertising etc

Open: daily October to Easter 10am to 5pm; Easter to October 10am to 6pm. Closed Christmas Day and New Year's Day

Directions: off A198 near Aberlady. two miles from A1

FHG

READERS' OFFER 2001

Almond Valley Heritage Centre

Millfield, Livingston, West Lothian EH54 7AR

Tel: 01506 414957 e-mail: almondheritage@cableinet.co.uk

Free child with adult paying full admission

Valid during 2001

NOT TO BE USED IN CONJUNCTION WITH ANY OTHER OFFER

FHG

READERS' OFFER 2001

EDINBURGH CRYSTAL VISITOR CENTRE

Eastfield, Penicuik, Midlothian EH26 8HB

Tel: 01968 675128

Two for the price of one (higher ticket price applies)

valid April 2001 until April 2002

NOT TO BE USED IN CONJUNCTION WITH ANY OTHER OFFER

FHG

READERS' OFFER 2001

Deep Sea World

North Queensferry, Fife KY11 1JR

Tel: 01383 411880/0906 941 0077 (24hr info line, calls cost 10p per minute)

One child FREE with a full-paying adult

valid until end 2001

NOT TO BE USED IN CONJUNCTION WITH ANY OTHER OFFER

FHG

READERS' OFFER 2001

Highland and Rare Breeds Farm

Elphin, Near Ullapool, Sutherland IV27 4HH

Tel: 01854 666204

One FREE adult or child with adult paying full entrance price

valid May to September 2001

NOT TO BE USED IN CONJUNCTION WITH ANY OTHER OFFER

FHG

READERS' OFFER 2001

New Lanark Visitor Centre

New Lanark Mills, Lanark, Lanarkshire ML11 9DB

Tel: 01555 661345

One child FREE with each full paying adult

valid during 2001

NOT TO BE USED IN CONJUNCTION WITH ANY OTHER OFFER

An innovative museum exploring the history and environment of West Lothian on a 200-acre site packed full of things to see and do, indoors and out.

Open: daily (except Christmas and New Year) 10am to 5pm

Directions: 15 miles from Edinburgh, follow "Heritage Centre" signs from A899

FHG PUBLICATIONS, ABBEY MILL BUSINESS CENTRE, PAISLEY PA1 1TJ

Visitor Centre with Exhibition Room, factory tours (children must be able to wear safety glasses provided), Crystal Bargains, gift shop, licensed tea room. Facilities for disabled visitors.

Open: Visitor Centre open daily; Factory Tours weekdays (9am-3.30pm) all year, plus weekends (11am-2.30pm) April to September.

Directions: 10 miles south of Edinburgh on the A701 Peebles road; signposted a few miles from the city centre

FHG PUBLICATIONS, ABBEY MILL BUSINESS CENTRE, PAISLEY PA1 1TJ

Scotland's award-winning aquarium where you can enjoy a spectacular diver's eye view of our marine environment through the world's longest underwater safari. New 'Amazing Amphibians' display, behind the scenes tours. Aquamazing entertainment for all the family

Open: daily except Christmas Day and New Year's Day

Directions: from Edinburgh follow signs for Forth Road Bridge, then signs through North Queensferry. From North, follow signs through Inverkeithing and North Queensferry.

FHG PUBLICATIONS, ABBEY MILL BUSINESS CENTRE, PAISLEY PA1 1TJ

Highland croft open to visitors for "hands-on" experience with over 35 different breeds of farm animals – "stroke the goats and scratch the pigs". Farm information centre and old farm implements. For all ages, cloud or shine!

Open: daily mid-May to third week in September 10am to 5pm

Directions: on A835 15 miles north of Ullapool

FHG PUBLICATIONS, ABBEY MILL BUSINESS CENTRE, PAISLEY PA1 1TJ

200-year old conservation village with award-winning Visitor Centre, set in beautiful countryside

Open: daily all year round 11am to 5pm

Directions: one mile south of Lanark; well signposted from all major routes

FHG PUBLICATIONS, ABBEY MILL BUSINESS CENTRE, PAISLEY PA1 1TJ

A delightful ride by narrow gauge steam train along the shore of Wales largest natural lake through the beautiful scenery of Snowdonia National Park

Open: Easter to end September; daily except some Mondays and Fridays early/late season

Directions: Easily accessible via A55 and A494

FHG PUBLICATIONS, ABBEY MILL BUSINESS CENTRE, PAISLEY PA1 1TJ

Nine rooms in a Georgian house filled with items illustrating the happier times of family life over the past 150 years. Joyful nostalgia unlimited.

Open: March to end October

Directions: opposite Beaumaris Castle

FHG PUBLICATIONS, ABBEY MILL BUSINESS CENTRE, PAISLEY PA1 1TJ

Walk through the Rabbit Hole to the colourful scenes of Lewis Carroll's classic story set in beautiful life-size displays. Recorded commentaries and transcripts available in several languages

Open: 10am to 5pm daily (closed Sundays Easter to November); closed Christmas/Boxing/New Year's Days.

Directions: situated just off the main street, 250 yards from coach and rail stations

FHG PUBLICATIONS, ABBEY MILL BUSINESS CENTRE, PAISLEY PA1 1TJ

A unique theme attraction presenting the history and culture of the Celts. Audio-visual exhibition, displays of Welsh and Celtic history, soft play area, tea room and gift shop. Events throughout the year.

Open: 10am to 6pm daily (last admission to exhibitions 4.40pm)

Directions: in restored mansion just south of clock tower in town centre; car park just off Aberystwyth road

FHG PUBLICATIONS, ABBEY MILL BUSINESS CENTRE, PAISLEY PA1 1TJ

Make a pit stop whatever the weather! Join an ex-miner on a tour of discovery, ride the cage to pit bottom and take a thrilling ride back to the surface. AV presentations, period village street, children's adventure play area, restaurant and gift shop. Full disabled access.

Open: Open daily 10am to 6pm (last tour 4.30pm). Closed Mondays October to Easter, also Christmas/Boxing days

Directions: Exit Juntion 32 M4, signposted from A470 Pontypridd. Trehafod is located between Pontypridd and Porth

FHG PUBLICATIONS, ABBEY MILL BUSINESS CENTRE, PAISLEY PA1 1TJ

ENGLAND

Board Accommodation

LONDON

FREE or REDUCED RATE entry to Holiday Visits and Attractions — see our READERS' OFFER VOUCHERS on pages 43-60

BEDFORDSHIRE

SANDY. Mrs M. Codd, Highfield Farm, Great North Road, Sandy SG19 2AQ (01767 682332; Fax: 01767 692503).

Tranquil welcoming atmosphere on attractive arable farm. Set well back off A1 giving quiet, peaceful seclusion yet within easy reach of the RSPB, the Shuttleworth Collection, the Greensand Ridge Walk, Grafham Water and Woburn Abbey. Cambridge 22 miles, London 50 miles. All rooms have tea/coffee making facilities, most have bathroom en suite and two are on the ground floor. There is a separate guests' sittingroom with TV. Family room. Dogs welcome by arrangement. No smoking. Guestaccom "Good Room" Award. Most guests return! Prices from £25 per person per night. ETC ◆◆◆◆◆

SANDY. Mrs Anne Franklin, Village Farm, Thorncote Green, Sandy SG19 1PU (01767 627345)

Village Farm is a family run working farm, mixed arable with a flock of 1000 free range laying hens, plus turkeys and geese for Christmas trade. Accommodation comprises one double bedroom, two twin/family rooms, both en suite. Full farmhouse breakfast plus beverages in room. Thorncote Green is a picturesque hamlet within easy reach of many interesting places:- Shuttleworth Collection, Swiss Gardens, R.S.P.B headquarters, Greensand Ridge walk, Woburn Abbey, Wimpole Hall and Cambridge. Bed and Breakfast from £20 per person per night. ETC ◆◆

BUCKINGHAMSHIRE

AYLESBURY. Anita and John Cooper, Poletrees Farm, Ludgershall Road, Brill, Near Aylesbury HP18 9TZ (Tel: 01844 238276; Fax: 01844 238462).

We would like to welcome you to our home and working farm. We rear British beef and sheep. Our three grandchildren can be hilarious; we understand your needs when travelling with children. We have one family room so please bring them; you will be made very comfortable. We provide spacious, comfortable accommodation in our historic house with oak-beamed ceilings, wattle and daub walls. Guests have their own diningroom and TV lounge where we can sit and chat to you. Perhaps you would like a cup of tea in our lovely garden. We can cater for dietary requirements if you let us know. Evening Meals or cold suppers can be booked. Winners of Roy Castle Award for a smoke-free house. Bed and Breakfast from £23 - £28. ETC ◆◆◆.

MILTON KEYNES. Mrs Christina Payne, Spinney Lodge Farm, Hanslope, Milton Keynes MK19 7DE (01908 510267).

Spinney Lodge is an arable, beef and sheep farm. The lovely Victorian farmhouse with its large garden and rose pergola has en suite bedrooms with colour TV and tea-making facilities. Close to Woburn Abbey, Stowe Gardens and Silverstone; M1 Junction 15 eight minutes, 12 minutes to Northampton, 15 minutes Milton Keynes. Bed and Breakfast from £20 to £25; Evening Meal by arrangement. Open all year except Christmas.

CAMBRIDGESHIRE

CAMBRIDGE. Cristina's Guest House, 47 St. Andrews Road, Cambridge CB4 1DH (01223 365855/327700; Fax: 01223 365855). Guests are assured of a warm welcome here, quietly located in the beautiful city of Cambridge, only 15 minutes' walk from the city centre and colleges. All rooms have colour TV, hairdryer, alarm/clock radio and tea/coffee making equipment. Most rooms have private shower and toilet. Centrally heated with comfortable TV lounge. Private car park, locked at night. No smoking house. **ETC/AA** ◆◆◆

CAMBRIDGE. Mrs Jean Wright, White Horse Cottage, 28 West Street, Comberton, Cambridge CB3 7DS (01223 262914). A 17th century cottage with all modern conveniences situated in a charming village four miles south-west of Cambridge. Junction 12 off M11 - A603 from Cambridge, or A428 turn-off at Hardwick turning. Accommodation includes one double room, twin and family rooms. Own sitting room with colour TV; tea/coffee making facilities. Full central heating; parking. Golfing facilities nearby. Excellent touring centre for many interesting places including Cambridge colleges, Wimpole Hall, Anglesey Abbey, Ely Cathedral, Imperial War Museum at Duxford, and many more. Bed and Breakfast from £20 per person. Children welcome.

CAMBRIDGE near. Mrs J.L. Bygraves, Elms Farm, 52 Main Road, Little Gransden SG19 3DL (01767 677459). Situated south west of Cambridge on B1046 from Junction 12 on the M11 or from A1 at St. Neots. Excellent touring centre for Cambridge, Duxford War Museum, Wimpole Hall, Woburn Abbey, Audley End House, Ely Cathedral, etc. Working arable farm with rural views and country walks around picturesque village. Farmhouse offers a warm and friendly atmosphere. Accommodation comprises one double, one twin with en suite facilities and one single bedroom, all with colour TV, tea/coffee making facilities and central heating. Four pubs nearby for evening meals. Bed and Breakfast from £20 per person. No smoking.

CAMBRIDGE near. Vicki Hatley, Manor Farm, Landbeach, Cambridge CB4 4ED (01223 860165). Five miles from Cambridge and 10 miles from Ely. Vicki welcomes you to her carefully modernised Grade II Listed farmhouse, which is located next to the church in this attractive village. All rooms are either en suite or have private bathroom and are individually decorated. TV, clock radios and tea/coffee making facilities are provided in double, twin or family rooms. There is ample parking and guests are welcome to enjoy the walled gardens. Bed and Breakfast from £20 per person double, and £30 single.

Please mention The Farm Holiday Guide when writing to enquire about accommodation

ELY. Mrs Linda Peck, Sharps Farm, Twenty Pence Road, Wilburton, Ely CB6 3PX (01353 740360).

Between Ely (six miles) and Cambridge (12 miles) our modern farmhouse offers guests a warm welcome and a relaxed atmosphere. All rooms have en suite or private bathroom, central heating, colour TV, radio alarm, tea/coffee making facilities, hair dryer and views over surrounding countryside. Breakfast is served in the Conservatory, with home-made preserves and free range eggs. Special diets catered for. Disabled facilities. Ample parking. No smoking. Bed and Breakfast from £19.00. Short Breaks available.

WELNEY. Mrs C.H. Bennett, Stockyard Farm, Wisbech Road, Welney, Wisbech PE14 9RQ (01354

610433). A warm welcome awaits you at this cosy former farmhouse in the heart of the Fens. Equidistant from Ely and Wisbech it makes an ideal base from which to explore the numerous historic sites, watch wildlife at the nearby nature reserves or fish the famous Fenland waters. Whatever your interests Cindy and Tim can offer advice and information. Both the double bedroom and the twin have washbasins and hot drinks facilities. Breakfast is served in the conservatory adjoining the guests' TV lounge. Free range produce. Full central heating. Private parking. Non-smokers only. Pets by arrangement. Prices range from £15 to £21 per person depending on length of stay and choice of breakfast (full English or Continental).

WICKEN. Mrs Valerie Fuller, Spinney Abbey, Wicken, Ely CB7 5XQ (01353 720971).

Working farm. Spinney Abbey is an attractive Grade II Listed Georgian stone farmhouse with views across pasture fields. It stands in a large garden with tennis court next to our dairy farm which borders the National Trust Nature Reserve Wicken Fen. One double and one family room, both en suite, and twin-bedded room with private bathroom, all with TV, hospitality tray, etc. Full central heating, guests sittingroom. Regret no pets and no smoking upstairs. Situated just off A1123, half-a-mile west of Wicken. Open all year. Bed and Breakfast from £22 per person. ETC ◆◆◆◆
e-mail: spinney.abbey@tesco.net

CHESHIRE

CHESTER. Mr and Mrs Aplas, Aplas Guest House, 106 Brook Street, Chester CH1 3DU (01244 312401). Patricia and Michael Aplas welcome you to the Aplas Guest House. We are a small family run guest house and have been established for 15 years. We are ideally located, some five minutes walk to the city centre and about the same to the railway station. For those coming by car - parking is available. Most of our rooms are en suite and can be booked on a 'room only' or 'Bed & Breakfast' basis. Our prices range from £13 per person to £17.50 per person and discounts are available for long stays and children.

CHESTER. Mrs Arden, Ivy Farm, Coddington,Tattenhall, Chester CH3 9EN (01829 782295). Friendly working farm eight miles from Chester. Close to Welsh Border, Beeston and Peckforton Castles and Carden Park Golf and pursuits park. Large gardens and car park. One double and one family room, both en suite and with coloured TV. From £19 per person.

CHURCH MINSHULL. Brian and Mary Charlesworth, Higher Elms Farm, Minshull Vernon, Crewe CW1 4RG (01270 522252). A 400-year-old farmhouse on working farm. Oak-beamed comfort in dining and sittingrooms, overlooking Shropshire Union Canal. No dinners served but four pubs within two miles. Interesting wildlife around. Convenient for M6 but tucked away in the countryside; from M6 Junction 18, off A530 towards Nantwich. Family room, double, twin and single rooms are all en suite, with colour TV and tea/coffee facilities. Well behaved pets welcome. Within 15 miles of Jodrell Bank, Oulton Park, Bridgemere Garden World, Stapeley Water Gardens, Nantwich and Chester. Bed and Breakfast from £23. Half price for children under 12 years

CONGLETON. Mrs Sheila Kidd, Yew Tree Farm, North Rode, Congleton CW12 2PF (01260 223569; Fax: 01260 223328). Discover freedom, relaxation, wooded walks and beautiful views. Meet a whole variety of pets and farm animals on this friendly working farm. Your comfort is our priority and good food is a speciality. Generous scrummy breakfasts and traditional evening meals. A true taste of the countryside — just for you! Bed and Breakfast from £19; optional Evening Meal £10. Brochure on request. **ETC ◆◆◆◆**.
e-mail: kidyewtreefarm@netscapeonline.co.uk

When making enquiries please mention FHG Publications

HYDE, (Near Manchester). Mrs Charlotte R. Walsh, Needhams Farm, Uplands Road, Werneth Low, Gee Cross, near Hyde SK14 3AQ (0161 368 4610; Fax: 0161-367 9106). Working farm. A cosy 16th century farmhouse set in peaceful, picturesque surroundings by Werneth Low Country Park and the Etherow Valley, which lie between Glossop and Manchester. The farm is ideally situated for holidaymakers and businessmen, especially those who enjoy peace and quiet, walking and rambling, golfing and riding, as these activities are all close by. At Needhams Farm everyone, including children and pets, receives a warm welcome. Good wholesome meals available in the evenings. Residential licence and Fire Certificate held. Open all year. Bed and Breakfast from £20 single minimum to £34 double maximum; Evening Meal £7. RAC Acclaimed. **ETC/AA ◆◆◆**

e-mail: charlotte@needhamsfarm.demon.co.uk
website: www.needhamsfarm.demon.co.uk

MACCLESFIELD. Susan Brocklehurst, Hill Top Farm, Wincle, Macclesfield SK11 0QH (01260 227257). Working farm. Overlooking the beautiful Dane Valley in this unspoilt region of the East Cheshire countryside, Hill Top is a working dairy and sheep farm situated in the tiny village of Wincle. Pretty bedrooms, a cosy television lounge and separate diningroom, together with good food and a friendly service make this the ideal base from which to explore the Peak District National Park, either by car or as a walker. Bed and Breakfast from £20 per person. Evening meal also available.

MACCLESFIELD. Mrs P.O. Worth, Rough Hey Farm, Leek Road, Gawsworth, Macclesfield SK11 0JQ (01260 252296). Featured in "Which?" B&B Guide. Delightfully situated overlooking the Cheshire Plain and on the edge of the Peak National Park in an area of outstanding natural beauty, Rough Hey is an historic former hunting lodge dating from before the 16th century, tastefully modernised yet retaining its old world character. This 300 acre sheep farm, with long horn cattle, consists of wooded valleys and hills with plenty of wildlife and lovely walks. In the locality there are numerous old halls and villages to visit. Double room en suite, twin room en suite and two single rooms, all with washbasin, TV and tea/coffee making facilities. Large comfortable lounge with TV. No smoking. A warm and friendly welcome is assured. Terms from £20. **ETC ◆◆◆◆**

NANTWICH. Mrs West, Stoke Grange Mews, Stoke Grange Farm, Chester Road, Nantwich CW5 6BT (01270 625525). Comfortable canal side farmhouse B&B with en suite rooms, colour TV, tea/coffee facilities plus a four-poster bed. Balcony giving panoramic views of canal and countryside. Log burning fire in diningroom and wonderful antique tapestry in the lounge. We also have a two-bedroomed self-catering cottage with all mod cons in a converted barn across from the farmhouse. Shared garden. Pets corner. Meals can be obtained from two pubs in the village of Barbridge only a ten minute walk away along the canal or road. B&B from £30 single, £50 - £60 double. Self-catering from £225 - £375 per week. **ETC ◆◆◆**

Please mention *The Farm Holiday Guide* when making enquiries about accommodation featured in these pages.

LEA FARM

Charming farmhouse set in landscaped gardens, where peacocks roam, on 150 acre dairy farm. Working farm, join in. Spacious bedrooms with washbasins, colour TV, electric blankets, radio alarm and tea/coffee making facilities. Family, double and twin bedrooms, en suite facilities. Luxury lounge, diningroom overlooking gardens. Pool/snooker; fishing in well stocked pool in beautiful surroundings. Bird watching. Children welcome, also dogs if kept under control. Help feed the birds and animals and see the cows being milked. Near to Stapeley Water Gardens, Bridgemere Garden World. Also Nantwich, Crewe, Chester, the Potteries and Alton Towers. Bed and Breakfast from £18 per person; Evening Meal from £11. Children half price. Weekly terms available.

Mrs Jean E. Callwood, Lea Farm, Wrinehill Road,

AA◆◆◆   **Wybunbury, Nantwich CW5 7NS • Tel & Fax: 01270 841429**

NORTHWICH. Mrs T.H. Campbell, Manor Farm, Cliff Road, Acton Bridge, Northwich CW8 3QP (Tel & Fax: 01606 853181). *WELCOME HOST.* Peaceful, rural, elegantly furnished traditional country house with open views from all rooms. Situated away from roads down a long private drive, above the wooded banks of the River Weaver. Absorb the tranquillity of our garden providing access to a private path through our woodland into the picturesque valley. In the heart of Cheshire, we are an ideal location for business or pleasure. Within easy reach of Chester, Merseyside, Manchester/Liverpool Airports and the motorway network (M56 Junction 10). All rooms have en suite/private bathroom and beverage tray and TV. Ample safe parking. Bed and Breakfast from £20. **ETC ◆◆◆◆**

FOR THE MUTUAL GUIDANCE OF GUEST AND HOST

Every year literally thousands of holidays, short breaks and overnight stops are arranged through our guides, the vast majority without any problems at all. In a handful of cases, however, difficulties do arise about bookings, which often could have been prevented from the outset.

It is important to remember that when accommodation has been booked, both parties – guests and hosts – have entered into a form of contract. We hope that the following points will provide helpful guidance.

GUESTS: When enquiring about accommodation, be as precise as possible. Give exact dates, numbers in your party and the ages of any children. State the number and type of rooms wanted and also what catering you require – bed and breakfast, full board etc. Make sure that the position about evening meals is clear – and about pets, reductions for children or any other special points.

Read our reviews carefully to ensure that the proprietors you are going to contact can supply what you want. Ask for a letter confirming all arrangements, if possible.

If you have to cancel, do so as soon as possible. Proprietors do have the right to retain deposits and under certain circumstances to charge for cancelled holidays if adequate notice is not given and they cannot re-let the accommodation.

HOSTS: Give details about your facilities and about any special conditions. Explain your deposit system clearly and arrangements for cancellations, charges etc. and whether or not your terms include VAT.

If for any reason you are unable to fulfil an agreed booking without adequate notice, you may be under an obligation to arrange suitable alternative accommodation or to make some form of compensation.

While every effort is made to ensure accuracy, we regret that FHG Publications cannot accept responsibility for errors, omissions or misrepresentations in our entries or any consequences thereof.

Prices in particular should be checked because we go to press early. We will follow up complaints but cannot act as arbiters or agents for either party.

CORNWALL

©MAPS IN MINUTES™ (1999)

Isles of Scilly

A39

A388

Bude
Bude
Bay
Holsworthy
A30

A388

A30

A30

Tintagel
A39
Launceston
A395

Trevose Head
A388

Dartmoor

Padstow
Wadebridge
Bodmin Moor
Tavistock
Ashburton
A38

CORNWALL
Bodmin
A390
A39
Liskeard
Buckfastleigh

Newquay
A30
Saltash
PLYMOUTH
Totnes

A392
St Austell
Fowey
Looe
Plympton
Torpoint
A391
A390
A30
Truro
A379
St Ives
Redruth
Dodman Point
Kingsbr
Camborne
St Mawes
Salcombe
St Just
Penzance
A394
St Mawes
Falmouth
Sennen
Helston
Land's End

Mount's Bay

Lizard
Lizard Point

BODMIN. Mrs Gill Hugo, Bokiddick Farm, Lanivet, Bodmin PL30 5HP (Tel & Fax: 01208 831481).

Lovely Georgian farmhouse with oak beams and wood panelling, tucked away in beautiful countryside , yet only two miles from the main A30. Peaceful location, magnificent views. Our dairy farm situated in Central Cornwall is an ideal touring base for all of Cornwall from moor to shore. We are very close to magnificent National Trust Lanhydrock House and Gardens. The exciting Eden Project and Saints Way Walk are on our doorstep. The house is furnished to a high standard including three pretty en suite bedrooms. All have tea/coffee facilities, colour TV and hairdryers. Enjoy delicious breakfasts cooked on the Aga. A warm welcome awaits you. Bed and Breakfast from £21. **ETC** ◆◆◆◆◆ *GOLD AWARD.*
e-mail: gillhugo@bokiddickfarm.co.uk
website: www.bokiddickfarm.co.uk

BODMIN. Mrs Joy Rackham, High Cross Farm, Lanivet, Near Bodmin PL30 5JR (01208 831341).

Working farm. Traditional granite farmhouse circa 1890 on a 91 acre working farm. The village of Lanivet is the geographical centre of Cornwall and is therefore ideal for the north and south coastal beaches ad the moor. Riding, fishing and cycle tracks are close by also new Eden Project. The bedrooms have washing facilities and shaver points. There is a separate lounge and dining room for guests with tea and coffee making facilities. Bed and Breakfast £15 daily. Evening Meal optional.

BODMIN. Mrs Margaret Oliver, Tremeere Manor, Lanivet, Near Bodmin PL30 5BG (01208 831513).

Tremeere is a 17th Century Manor House set in a 240 acre dairy farm in mid-Cornwall on the halfway mark for the Saints Way, 15 minutes' drive from the Eden Project. There are spacious comfortable rooms comprising two double en suite bedrooms and one twin-bedded room, with lovely views of the surrounding countryside. Central heating, tea/coffee making facilities and a comfortable guests' lounge with TV. Prices are from £18 per person. No smoking. Nearby is Bodmin town with its ancient Gaol and Steam Railway. Lanhydrock House (N.T.), The Lost Gardens of Heligan or walking on Bodmin Moor and visiting the famous Jamaica Inn. Coastal walks and beaches are within easy reach as well as walking the Camel Trail.

BOSCASTLE. Mrs Jackie Haddy, Home Farm, Minster, Boscastle PL35 0BN (Tel & Fax: 01840 250195).

Home Farm is a beautifully situated working farm overlooking picturesque Boscastle and its heritage coastline. The farm is surrounded by National Trust countryside and footpaths through unspoilt wooded valleys to Boscastle village, restaurants and harbour. Traditional farmhouse with beautiful furnishings has three charming en suite rooms with colour TV with satellite link, tea-making facilities; cosy guest lounge with log fire. Good home cooking; walled garden; plenty of friendly farm animals. Beaches, golf courses, riding stables, coastal paths and many other activities for you to enjoy. A warm welcome awaits you. ETC ◆◆◆
e-mail: jackie.haddy@btclick.com

BOSCASTLE. Mrs P. E. Perfili, Trefoil Farm, Camelford Road, Boscastle PL35 0AD (01840 250606).
Trefoil is non-smoking accommodation, only a short walk to the picturesque village of Boscastle. En suite rooms, tea/coffee making facilities, colour TV's. Comfortable accommodation, good home cooking, vegetarians catered for. Sandy beaches, a haven for walkers and a photographer's dream. The ideal base for North and South coasts. Reductions for weekly bookings and children. A warm welcome awaits you. Bed & Breakfast from £19.

BOSCASTLE. Mrs Cheryl Nicholls, Trerosewill Farm, Paradise, Boscastle PL35 0DL (01840 250545).

Working farm. Luxurious Bed and Breakfast accommodation in modern farmhouse on working farm, only a short walk from the picturesque village of Boscastle. Rooms have spectacular coastal and rural views, all en suite with tea making facilities. Colour TVs and telephone available if required. Mineral water and bath-robes provided. Licensed. Centrally heated. Seasonal log fires. Large gardens. Traditional farmhouse fayre. Feed the calves. Superb coastal and countryside walks. One-way walks arranged. Packed Lunches available. Spring and Autumn breaks. Bed and Breakfast from £19. Strictly no smoking. FHG Diploma Award. Good Food Award Winner of Farmhouse Bed and Breakfast for Cornwall 2000. ETC ◆◆◆ *SILVER AWARD*

BOSCASTLE. Mrs V.M. Seldon, Tregatherall Farm, Boscastle PL35 0EQ (01840 250277).

Working sheep farm of 120 acres, set in an area of outstanding natural beauty. Two miles from the picturesque harbour and village of Boscastle, and three miles from Tintagel and King Arthur's Castle. The magnificent surfing beaches of North Cornwall are close by and the location is ideal for walking or touring. Tregatherall is a refurbished farmhouse, all bedrooms with tea/coffee making facilities. Separate lounge with satellite TV. Ample parking and large garden with swings. Open April to October. Reductions for children. Cot available. Bed and Breakfast from £17 per night. Cornish Tourist Board registered. Self-catering accommodation also available.

Please mention The Farm Holiday Guide when writing to enquire about accommodation

BUDE. Mrs J. Crocker, Cann Orchard, Howard Lane, Stratton, Bude EX23 9TD (01288 352098). Cann Orchard is an ancient farmstead, dating from the Domesday Book, situated down a quiet country lane in a sheltered little valley, minutes from the stunning beaches and coastline of Bude and North Cornwall. The farmhouse is beautifully furnished, centrally heated and very comfortable. All windows have wonderful views of the ten acres of gardens orchards and ponds surrounding the house, bursting with wildlife. Bedrooms, two of which are en suite, have colour TV, tea/coffee making facilities, and old oak-beamed ceilings. The guests' lounge, with colour TV/video, has a magnificent fireplace with log burning stove for cool nights. Ample parking. No pets. No smoking. B & B from £16 to £22.50. Open all year. Self-catering also available. **ETC ◆◆◆◆**.

BUDE. Mrs Christine Nancekivell, Dolsdon Farm, Boyton, Launceston PL15 8NT (01288 341264).

Dolsdon was once a 17th century coaching inn, now modernised, situated on the Launceston to Bude road within easy reach of sandy beaches, surfing, Tamar Otter Park, leisure centre with heated swimming pool, golf courses, fishing, tennis and horse riding and is ideal for touring Cornwall and Devon. Guests are welcome to wander around the 260 acre working farm. All bedrooms have washbasins and tea making facilities (en suite family room available). Comfortably furnished lounge has colour TV. Plenty of good home cooking assured - full English breakfast. Parking. Bed and Breakfast from £15; reductions for children. Brochure available.

BUDE. Mrs Sylvia Lucas, Elm Park, Bridgerule, Holsworthy EX22 7EL (01288 381231). Elm Park is a

205 acre dairy, beef and sheep farm. Six miles from surfing beaches at Bude and ideal for touring Devon/Cornwall. Children are especially welcomed with pony rides. Games room available with snooker, table skittles, darts, etc, and golf putting. There are spacious family rooms (two en-suite) and a twin-bedded room, all with colour TV and tea/coffee making facilities. Ample four-course dinners with freshly produced fare and delicious sweets. Bed, Breakfast and Evening Meal, reasonable terms. Reductions for children and everyone is made welcome and comfortable. Brochure available.

BUDE. Jan and Paul Hudson, Little Bryaton, Morwenstow, Near Bude EX23 9SU (01288 331755).

OS Grid Reference 221156. Lovely old farmhouse in tranquil, peaceful setting, close to Heritage coastal footpath, surfing beaches, rocky coves, impressive cliffs and the seaside resort of Bude. Luxurious accommodation comprises two double bedrooms and one family suite, all with en suite bathroom; central heating; colour TV and tea/coffee-making facilities. Guests have own private conservatory and diningroom. Bed and Breakfast from £19.50. Three-course Candlelit Dinner from £10.50. Reductions for mini-breaks, weekly bookings and children. Cots and high chairs available. Open all year. ALSO highly recommended self-contained annexe beautifully equipped, oak-beamed. Sleeps two to four. Available all year. Telephone or e-mail us soon to book your holiday.
e-mail:little.Bryaton@dial.pipex.com
website: www.little.bryaton.dial.pipex.com

BUDE. Mrs Pearl Hopper, West Nethercott Farm, Whitstone, Holsworthy (Devon) EX22 6LD (01288 341394). Working farm, join in. Personal attention and a warm welcome await you on this dairy and sheep farm. Watch the cows being milked, help with the animals. Free pony rides, scenic farm walks. Short distance from sandy beaches, surfing and the rugged North Cornwall coast. Ideal base for visiting any part of Devon or Cornwall. We are located in Cornwall though our postal address is Devon. The traditional farmhouse has washbasins and TV in bedrooms; diningroom and separate lounge with colour TV. Plenty of excellent home cooking. Access to the house at anytime. Bed and Full English Breakfast from £15, Evening Meal and pack lunches available. Children under 12 years reduced rates. Weekly terms available.

BUDE. Mrs J. Dauncey, East Woolley Farm, Morwenstow, Bude EX23 9PP (01288 331525). East Woolley is a small dairy farm just half-a-mile off the A39, with magnificent cliff walks and beaches nearby. Tintagel, Boscastle, Hartland and the quaint fishing village of Clovelly with its cobbled street are all within easy reach. Accommodation consists of self-contained en suite rooms in a converted barn. Breakfast is served in the farmhouse diningroom. All rooms have tea and coffee making facilities, TV and clock radios. Guests are welcome to sit and relax in the conservatory or laze in the garden. Bed and Breakfast from £19 - £22. Non-smoking. **ETC** ◆◆◆◆.

COLAN. Mrs Anna Machin-Weaver, Colan Barton, Colan, Near Newquay TR8 4NB (01637 874395; Fax: 01637 881388). Colan Barton is a 17th century farmhouse set in its own 11 acres, surrounded by stunning Cornish countryside. Relax in this peaceful atmosphere and know that you will be well looked after. Coastal walks, fishing lakes, golf courses, lovely beaches, riding stables and cycle routes are all nearby. We are not a working farm but we do have a menagerie of animals for you to meet! You can visit the Norman Church up the lane or stroll in the woods. All our bedrooms have country views, central heating, colour TV and tea/coffee making facilities. Prices from £16 to £24. Children welcome. Sorry, no pets. AA ◆◆◆◆. e-mail: colanbarton.hotmail.com@barclays.net

FOWEY. Mrs S.C. Dunn, Menabilly Barton, Par PL24 2TN (01726 812844). Working farm. Menabilly Barton is a secluded farmhouse set in a wooded valley leading to a quiet sandy beach. Spacious diningroom, lounge with TV, peaceful garden open during the day. Good traditional farmhouse food. Three large bedrooms, en suite available. Bathroom with shower, two toilets. Facilities for making drinks and microwave if required. Coastal walks, National Trust properties, Heligan Gardens and The Eden Project all nearby. Local village pub serves good food. Historic port of Fowey three miles, North Coast only 40 minutes' drive. Bed and full English Breakfast. Reductions for children. Colour brochure on request.

HELSTON. Mrs P. Roberts, Hendra Farm, Wendron, Helston TR13 0NR (01326 340470). Hendra Farm, just off the main Helston/Falmouth road, is an ideal centre for touring Cornwall; three miles to Helston, eight to both Redruth and Falmouth. Safe sandy beaches within easy reach – five miles to the sea. Beautiful views from the farmhouse of the 60-acre beef farm. Two double, one single, and one family bedrooms; bathroom and toilets; sittingroom and two diningrooms. Cot, babysitting and reduced rates offered for children. No objection to pets. Car necessary, parking space. Enjoy good cooking with roast beef, pork, lamb, chicken, genuine Cornish pasties, fish and delicious sweets and cream. Open all year except Christmas. Evening Dinner, Bed and Breakfast from £125 per week which includes cooked breakfast, three course evening dinner, tea and home-made cake before bed. Bed and Breakfast only from £14 per night also available.

LAUNCESTON. Hurdon Farm, Launceston PL15 9LS (01566 772955). Elegant Listed 18th century

farmhouse, idyllically tucked away amidst our 500 acre mixed working farm. Centrally positioned on Devon/Cornwall border, it is ideally located for exploring the many attractions in both counties. Six luxurious and spacious en suite bedrooms, all with colour TV, radio, tea/coffee facilities and central heating. Comfortable guests' lounge. Superb English breakfasts and delicious four-course dinners, freshly prepared and cooked, are served at separate tables in the dining room. Open May till November. Bed and Breakfast from £20. **AA/RAC/ETC** ◆◆◆◆

LAUNCESTON. Mary Rich, "Nathania", Altarnun, Launceston PL15 7SL (01566 86426). A warm

welcome awaits you, for accommodation on a small farm on Bodmin Moor within easy reach of coast, moors, towns, lakes and fishing. Visit King Arthur country – Tintagel, Dozmary Pool, the famous Jamaica Inn, Wesley Cottage and cathedral of the moors. One mile from A30, very quiet, ideal for overnight stop for West Cornwall. Double room en suite, twin rooms with bathroom adjoining. Tea making facilities and TV. Payphone. Conservatory and lounge for quiet relaxation. We look forward to meeting you for one night, or why not book your holiday with us and tour Cornwall. You will enjoy the quiet, happy, relaxing atmosphere. Prices from £10.50 per person per night. Please telephone, or write, for details – SAE, thank you.

LISKEARD. Mrs Stephanie Rowe, Tregondale Farm, Menheniot, Liskeard PL14 3RG (Tel & Fax: 01579

342407). Working farm, join in. Feeling like a break near the coast? Come and relax, join our family with the peace of the countryside — breathtaking in Spring — on a 200 acre mixed farm, situated near Looe between A38 and A390. See pedigree South Devon cattle and sheep naturally reared, explore the new woodland farm trail amidst wildlife and flowers. This stylish, characteristic farmhouse, which dates back to the Domesday Book, has featured in the Daily Telegraph, and is a Cream of Cornwall member, provides exceptional comfort with en suite suite bedrooms all with colour TV, tea/coffee making facilities, lounge diningroom with log fires. A conservatory to enjoy each day's warmth capturing a beautiful view over the farm, set in an original walled garden including picnic table, tennis court and play area. Special activities can be arranged — golf, fishing, cycling and walking. Home and local produce a speciality, full English Breakfast; try our delicious optional Evening Meal from £11. Bed and Breakfast from £21. Open all year. Self-catering character cottage also available (★★★★). A warm welcome awaits you to discover the beauty of Cornwall. Please phone for a brochure and discuss your requirements. **ETC/AA** ◆◆◆◆ *SILVER AWARD*

LISKEARD. Mrs Lindsay M. Pendray, Caduscott, East Taphouse, Liskeard PL14 4NG (Tel & Fax:

01579 320262). Working farm Sweet dreams and restful nights broken only by the owl's hooting in the clear night sky. From Stargazers to Shellseekers, all the ingredients are here to match your mood. Attractive 17th century Listed farmhouse. Central heating log fires. Traditional Bed and Breakfast (from £17 to £21 non-smoking) served in large lounge/diningroom; double room (en suite, toilet/shower), adjoining twin-bedded room, ideal for families. The Pendrays have farmed Caduscott for over 70 years and will make every effort to ensure that you discover Cornwall. ETC ◆◆◆
e-mail: caduscott@farmline.com

FREE or REDUCED RATE entry to Holiday Visits and Attractions — see our READERS' OFFER VOUCHERS on pages 43-60

LOOE. Mrs J.M. Gill, Cleese Farm, Nomansland, Looe PL13 1PB (01503 240224). Stay in a traditional

farmhouse, in peaceful countryside a half-a-mile off the Plymouth Road, two miles from Looe, and get a behind-the-scenes taste of the real Cornwall. By the house, which overlooks rolling fields and the distant sea, is a working farm with dairy cattle, horses, dogs, cats, ducks, chickens and a rooster for your early morning call! Cleese is within a short distance of picturesque fishing villages, beautiful beaches, dramatic moorland and seacoasts, historical houses and gardens, a wide variety of attractions, and sport and activity centres. There is ample space for six guests; three tasteful and charming bedrooms with TV, beverage facilities and modern facilities, a fully equipped bathroom and a large sitting/dining room, plus your own front door. Full English breakfast served each morning. Heaven in a farmhouse! Well behaved dogs welcome. Smoking accepted downstairs. £17 to £18 B&B per person per night; reductions for children.

LOOE. Mrs Lynda Wills, Polgover Farm, Widegates, Looe PL13 1PY (01503 240248). Working farm.

Polgover Farm is situated in picturesque countryside, four miles from Looe on the B3252 and ideally situated to explore Cornwall and South Devon. Local attractions include horse riding, golf, fishing, water sports, Monkey Sanctuary and many beaches. There is always a warm welcome at Polgover's spacious 16th century Listed farmhouse, where you can have a peaceful and relaxing holiday. There are three tastefully decorated bedrooms, all with washbasin, colour TV and tea/coffee making facilities. Guests' bathroom. Lounge with colour TV incorporating breakfast room with separate tables. Sorry, no pets. Open Easter to October. Ample parking. Bed and Breakfast from £16. Weekly and child reductions. Brochure available. Also luxury six-berth fully equipped self-catering caravan in its own garden available at the farm.
website: www.polgoverfarm_homestead.com

LOOE. Mrs D. Eastley, Bake Farm, Pelynt, Looe PL13 2QQ (01503 220244). Working farm.

This is an old farmhouse, bearing the Trelawney Coat of Arms (1610), situated midway between Looe and Fowey. There are three double bedrooms all with washbasin, (one with en suite), tea/coffee making facilities and night storage heater; shower room/toilet; sittingroom/diningroom. Children welcome at reduced rates. Sorry, no pets. Open from April to October. A car is essential for touring the area, ample parking. There is much to see and do here - horse riding, coastal walks, golf and National Trust Properties within easy reach. The sea is only five miles away and there is shark fishing at Looe. Bed and Breakfast from £17. Cleanliness guaranteed. Brochure available on request. **ETC ◆◆◆.**

LOOE. Mrs Keilthy, Cardwen Farm, Pelynt, Looe PL13 2LU (01503 220213). Cardwen is a 17th century

Grade 11 Listed Farmhouse set in three acres of notable gardens with a stream and pond. The village of Pelynt is half-a-mile, Looe and Polperro, two beautiful fishing villages, are both four miles away and the Eden Project is under 10 miles away. The Coastal Path nearby is judged to be one of the most beautiful stretches of coast in the world. We have two en suite double bedrooms and one twin room, all overlooking the garden and surrounding fields. Two well-equipped cottages sleeping four to six also available all year.

FHG PUBLICATIONS LIMITED
publish a large range of well-known accommodation guides.
We will be happy to send you details or you can use the order form
at the back of this book.

LOOE. Mrs Angela Eastley, Little Larnick Farm, Pelynt, Looe PL13 2NB (01503 262837). Little Larnick

is situated in a sheltered part of the West Looe river valley. Walk to Looe from our working dairy farm and along the coastal path to picturesque Polperro. The character farmhouse and barn offers twin, double and family en suite rooms. The bedrooms are superbly equipped and decorated to a high standard. The family room is in a downstairs annexe overlooking the garden. Our newly renovated barn offers three self-contained bedrooms with their own lounge areas. Cycling shed, drying room and ample parking. No pets. No smoking. Bed and Breakfast from £20 to £23. Open all year. **ETC** ◆◆◆◆

MARAZION. Jenny Birchall, Mount View House, Varfell, Ludgvan, Penzance TR20 8AH (01736 710179). Mount View House is a Victorian former farmhouse

standing in half-an-acre of gardens overlooking St. Michael's Mount. The house is furnished in traditional style and offers one room with sea views and another with rural views. Rooms have washbasins, central heating and tea/coffee making facilities. Guests' WC and shower room; sitting/diningroom with open fire. Children welcome, cot available. Situated approximately three miles from Penzance and five miles from St. Ives. We are the ideal touring stopover. Our close proximity to the heliport (one mile) makes an ideal break en route to the Scilly Isles. Bed and Breakfast from £16 per person per night. Four night low season breaks £100 for two people sharing. Self-catering accommodation also available.

MEVAGISSEY. Mrs Dawn Rundle, Lancallan Farm, Mevagissey, St. Austell PL26 6EW (Tel/Fax: 01726 842284). Lancallan is a large 17th century farmhouse on a

working 700 acre dairy and beef farm in a beautiful rural setting, one mile from Mevagissey. We are close to Heligan Gardens, lovely coastal walks and sandy beaches, and are well situated for day trips throughout Cornwall. Also six to eight miles from the Eden Project. Enjoy a traditional farmhouse breakfast in a warm and friendly atmosphere. Accommodation comprises one twin room and two double en suite rooms (all with colour TV and tea/coffee facilities); bathroom, lounge and diningroom.Terms and brochure available on request. SAE please.
e-mail: dawn/rundle@lancallan.freeserve.co.uk

MEVAGISSEY. Mrs Anne Hennah, Treleaven Farm, Mevagissey PL26 6RZ (01726 842413). Working farm. Treleaven Farm is situated in quiet, pleasant surroundings

overlooking the village and the sea. The 200-acre mixed farm is well placed for visitors to enjoy the many attractions of Mevagissey with its quaint narrow streets and lovely shops. Fishing and boat trips are available and very popular. Also, visit the Lost Gardens of Heligan. The house offers a warm and friendly welcome with the emphasis on comfort, cleanliness and good food using local produce. A licensed bar and solar heated swimming pool add to your holiday enjoyment, together with a games room and putting green. Tastefully furnished throughout, with central heating, there are five double bedrooms and one family bedroom, all en suite with tea/coffee making facilities and TV; bathroom, two toilets. Sittingroom and diningroom. Open February to November for Bed and Breakfast from £22. Dinner £12. Sorry, no pets. SAE, please, for particulars or telephone.

MULLION. Mrs Joan Hyde, Campden House, The Commons, Mullion TR12 7HZ (01326 240365). Campden House offers comfortable accommodation in a peaceful setting with large gardens and a beautiful sea view. It is within easy reach of Mullion, Polurian and Poldhu Coves, and is ideally situated for exploring the beautiful coast and countryside of the Lizard. Mullion golf course is less than one mile away. All eight bedrooms have handbasin with hot and cold water and comfortable beds; some rooms have en suite shower. There is a large sun lounge, TV lounge with colour TV and a large dining room and bar. Guests have access to the lounges, bedrooms and gardens at all times. Children and pets welcome. Bed and Breakfast from £15.50.

NEWQUAY. Mrs B. L. Harvey, Shepherds Farm, Fiddlers Green, St. Newlyn East, Newquay TR8 5NW

(01872 540502). Working farm. A warm welcome awaits you on our family-run 600 acre mixed working farm. Come and share our warm and friendly atmosphere with first class service in affordable quality accommodation. Cleanliness guaranteed. All rooms en suite and have colour TV and tea making facilities. Large garden. Central location, ideal for touring. The farm is set in rural, small hamlet of Fiddlers Green three miles from beautiful Cornish coastline, five miles from Newquay; 20 minutes from south coast. Glorious sandy beaches, ideal for surfing, little rivers for the very young. Beautiful breathtaking views and walks along scenic clifftops. One-and-a-half miles from National Trust property of Trerice. Good pub food close by. Come and join us! Bed and Breakfast from £16 to £19. Free horse riding seasonal. Also self-catering available. ETC ◆◆◆◆

PADSTOW. Andrew and Sue Hamilton, Trevone Bay Hotel, Trevone, Near Padstow PL28 8QS (01841

520243; Fax: 01841 521195). On arrival relax with a pot of tea, then stroll through the tranquil village to the beautiful sandy bay. Follow the coast path along the rocky bay, then back across the fields to your comfortable hotel. Does this tempt you? How about an excellent home-cooked meal, coffee watching the sunset and an evening socialising in the bar. Our hotel is non-smoking throughout. All bedrooms en suite. Ideal for walking, touring, bird watching or relaxing on the beach. From £35.00 for Dinner, Bed and Breakfast. Open April to October. If this sounds like your sort of holiday, write or phone for brochure. ETC ◆◆◆◆

PADSTOW. Mrs Sandra May, Trewithen Farm, St Merryn, Near Padstow PL28 8JZ (01841 520420).

Trewithen farmhouse is a newly renovated Cornish Roundhouse, set in a large garden and situated on a working farm enjoying country and coastal views. The picturesque town of Padstow with its pretty harbour and narrow streets with famous fish restaurants is only three miles away. St Merryn Parish boasts seven beautiful sandy beaches and bays. Also coastal walks, golf, fishing and horse riding on neighbouring farm. Hire a bike or walk along the Camel Trail cycle and footpath - winding for 18 miles along the River Camel. The accommodation has been tastefully decorated to complement the exposed beams and original features. All bedrooms are en suite or have vanity units, with hot drink facilities. Parking. Full English breakfast. Evening Meal optional. TV lounge. Bed and Breakfast from £22 per person per night. Weekly rates and Winter weekend breaks available. ETC ◆◆◆

PAR Mr and Mrs Rowe, Tregaminion Farm House, Menabilly, Par PL24 2TL. En suite and self contained

family B&B throughout the year. Our farm nestles in the hollows of the South Cornish Coast set deep within the Du Maurier countryside. We can offer you a peaceful, relaxed and friendly holiday in our family-run farmhouse. We are within easy walking distance of Polkerris and Polridmouth Bays, both beautiful, small, safe beaches for you and your children to enjoy. The ancient port of Fowey is also within walking distance, approximately two to three miles. Stay with us for as little or as long as you like. For more information and prices please contact **Jill Rowe (01726 812442).**

PENZANCE. Mrs M.D. Olds, Mulfra Farm, Newmill, Penzance TR20 8XP (01736 363940). This hill farm

with cows and calves, high on the edge of the Penwith Moors, offers superb accommodation which attracts many of our guests to return year after year. The 17th century stone-built, beamed farmhouse has far reaching views, is attractively decorated and furnished, and offers two double en suite bedrooms with tea and coffee making facilities, TV, shaver socket; comfortable lounge with inglenook fireplace, diningroom with separate tables and conservatory. Car essential, ample parking. Warm friendly atmosphere, good food, beautiful walking country, ideal centre for exploring west Cornwall. Bed and Breakfast £130 per person per week. Evening Meal by arrangement. Further details with pleasure.

PENZANCE. Mrs Rosalind Wyatt, South Colenso Farm, Goldsithney, Penzance TR20 9JB (01736

762290). Working farm. South Colenso Farm is a 76 acre working arable farm. The spacious Georgian style farmhouse is set in beautiful unspoilt countryside, peaceful and secluded, yet not isolated. Ideally situated between Marazion and Praa Sands, a perfect location for touring both coasts of Cornwall, with sandy beaches and pretty coves nearby. The large en suite bedrooms (two double and one family rooms) have tea/coffee making facilities and a lovely country view. Relax in our comfortable lounge with colour television and log fire. Full English Breakfast is served in our sunny diningroom with separate tables. Ample private parking. Non-smoking. Children over six years welcome. Please write or call for terms.

PENZANCE. Mrs Penny Lally, Rose Farm, Chyanhal, Buryas Bridge, Penzance TR19 6AN (01736

731808). Rose Farm is a small working farm in a little hamlet close to the picturesque fishing villages of Mousehole and Newlyn and seven miles from Land's End. The 200-year-old granite farmhouse is cosy with pretty, en suite rooms. One double, one family suite and a romantic 15th century four-poster room in barn annexe. We have all manner of animals, from pedigree cattle to pot-bellied pigs! Open all year (closed Christmas). ETC/AA ◆◆◆◆

website: www.rosefarmcornwall.co.uk

PENZANCE (near Porthcurno). Mrs P. M. Hall, Treen Farmhouse, Treen, St. Levan, Penzance TR19 6LF (01736 810253). Situated just off the south-west coastal footpath, Treen Farm is a family-run dairy farm in the village of Treen, set in 80 acres of pastureland by the sea near Land's End (four miles). Visitors are welcome to use the gardens, walk around the farm and watch the milking. Pub, shop, cafe, campsite and beaches nearby. Ideal for walking and sightseeing. Comfortable farmhouse Bed and Breakfast accommodation, single, twin and double (en suite) rooms with tea/coffee making facilities, some with TV, views of gardens, pastureland and sea. Traditional English Breakfast served. Guests' lounge with open fire and television. Private parking. Pets welcome. Reductions for children. Sorry, no smoking. Bed and Breakfast from £15.00. Self-catering also available for two people (plus cot) from £150.

PORT ISAAC. Chris and Liz Bolton, Trewetha Farm, Port Isaac PL29 3RU (01208 880256). 18th

century traditional farmhouse in Betjeman country in an area designated as outstanding natural beauty. Spectacular views over the sea and surrounding countryside. Pet the miniature Shetland ponies, help feed the hens or watch the sheep graze. Ideal location for sandy beaches, walking, cycling and all water sports. The double and twin en suite rooms are tastefully decorated and centrally heated. Each has colour TV and tea/coffee making facilities. ENQUIRE ABOUT OUR COASTAL WALKING BREAKS: full English breakfast, packed lunch, three-course dinner and transport to the start of the walk. Self-catering cottages also available.

ROSELAND PENINSULA. Mrs Shirley E. Pascoe, Court Farm, Philleigh, Truro TR2 5NB (01872 580313). Working farm. Situated in the heart of the Roseland Peninsula at Philleigh, with its lovely Norman church and 17th century Roseland Inn, this spacious and attractive old farmhouse, set in over an acre of garden, offers Bed and Breakfast accommodation. There are double, single and family bedrooms with washbasins and tea making facilities; bathroom, separate toilet; large comfortable lounge with colour TV. Enjoy a full English breakfast in the traditional farmhouse kitchen. Children welcome, cot, high chair, babysitting available. Sorry, no pets indoors. Car essential – ample parking. The family livestock and arable farm includes 50 acres of woodlands which border the beautiful Fal Estuary providing superb walking, picnic areas and bird-watching opportunities, while the nearest beaches are just over two miles away. Please write or telephone for brochure and terms.

ST. AUSTELL. Mrs Liz Berryman, Polgreen Farm, London Apprentice, St. Austell PL26 7AP (Tel & Fax: 01726 75151). Polgreen is a family-run dairy farm nestling in the Pentewan Valley in an area of outstanding natural beauty. One mile from the coast and four miles from the picturesque fishing village of Mevagissey. A perfect location for a relaxing holiday in the glorious Cornish countryside. Centrally situated, Polgreen is ideally placed for touring all of Cornwall's many attractions. Cornish Way Leisure Trail adjoining farm. Within a few minutes drive of the spectacular Eden Project and Heligan Gardens. All rooms with private facilities, colour TV, tea/coffee making facilities, guest lounge, children welcome. Terms from £18 per person per night. **ETC ◆◆◆◆** e mail: polgreen.farm@btclick.com

ST. IVES. Mrs N.I. Mann, Trewey Farm, Zennor, St. Ives TR26 3DA (01736 796936). Working farm. On the main St Ives to Land's End road, this attractive granite-built farmhouse stands among gorse and heather-clad hills, half a mile from the sea and five miles from St Ives. The mixed farm covers 400 acres, with Guernsey cattle and fine views of the sea; lovely cliff and hill walks. Guests will be warmly welcomed and find a friendly atmosphere. Five double, one single and three family bedrooms (all with washbasins; bathroom, toilets; sittingroom, diningroom. Cot, high chair and babysitting available. Pets allowed. Car essential – parking. Open all year. Electric heating. Bed and Breakfast only. SAE for terms, please.

ST IVES. Mrs S. Britnell, Little Pengelly Farmhouse, Trenwheal, Leedstown, Hayle TR27 6BP (01736 850452). 17th century picturesque farmhouse in central location midway between St. Ives and Helston off the B3302. Spacious accommodation, washbasins all rooms plus excellent shower and bathroom facilities. Early morning tea and generous breakfast with home-baked bread. Guest TV lounge and conservatory. Considerate pet owners welcome. Sorry no smoking and not suitable for young children. Open Easter to end October. Terms £17 per person per night. Central for touring West Cornwall. Hot and cold savouries served 1pm to 7pm daily. Large two-person SELF CATERING barn conversion available. Patio and garden. Pets welcome. No smoking. Open all year. Three day off-peak breaks. Please write or phone for full details.
e-mail: britnell@littlepengelly.co.uk
website: www.littlepengelly.co.uk

ST MAWES/TRURO. Mrs A. Palmer, Trenestrall Farm, Ruan High Lanes, Truro TR2 5LX (01872 501259). Working farm, join in. A tastefully restored 200 year old barn, now a farmhouse offering comfortable accommodation on a 300 acre mixed farm. Situated on beautiful Roseland Peninsula, within easy reach of St. Mawes and Truro. Close to safe beaches and beautiful Fal estuary for sailing, bird watching etc. Accommodation consists of double or twin room with en suite and tea/coffee facilities, own sittingroom with TV, bathroom and shower room. Amenities include private fishing lake and snooker room, table tennis and pony riding. Pride taken with presentation of food using home produce whenever possible. Children welcome, babysitting service. Pets accepted. Phone or write for details of Bed and Breakfast from £17 per person per night.

TORPOINT. Mrs Sarah Blake, Stone Farm, Whitsand Bay, Millbrook, Torpoint PL10 1JJ (Tel & Fax: 01752 822267). Dairy farm 400 yards from the cliff path leading to miles of sandy beaches in an Area of Outstanding Natural Beauty with panoramic views from Rame to Looe. Large garden with croquet lawn. Everyone can help feed the animals or watch the milking. Children's pony rides and games room. Open all year except Christmas. Bed and Breakfast from £17. **ETC** ◆◆◆◆

TRURO. Mrs M.A. Hutchings, Lands Vue, Three Burrows, Truro TR4 8JA (01872 560242). You will find a warm welcome at our peaceful country house, set in two acres of garden where you may relax or enjoy a game of croquet. There are three lovely bedrooms all with en suite facilities, TV and tea making facilities. There is a cosy lounge with open fire and large diningroom with superb views over the Cornish countryside, where we serve a delicious farmhouse breakfast. Being very central for all of Cornwall's famous gardens and coastline, Lands Vue is an ideal base highly recommended by many of our guests who return year after year. Write or phone Molly Hutchings for brochure. **AA** ◆◆◆◆

TRURO. Mrs Pamela Carbis, Trenona Farm, Ruan High Lanes, Truro TR2 5JS (01872 501339). Trenona Farm is a working mixed farm of 210 acres situated on the unspoilt Roseland Peninsula. Safe, sandy beaches and coastal footpath nearby. Central for touring and close to Gardens at Heligan, Trelissick and Trewithen. The 19th century farmhouse has four guest bedrooms. All can accommodate two to four persons and have their own washbasin and tea making facilities. Two have en suite shower and toilet and TV. Guest lounge with colour TV. Separate diningroom. Children and pets welcome. Terms from £14 to £20 per night, £98 per week. Brochure available. Open April to October

TRURO. Mrs S. Hicks, Pengelly Farmhouse, Trispen, Truro TR4 9BG (Tel & Fax: 01872 510245). Working farm, join in. Situated in the centre of the county, Pengelly Farm is the ideal base for seeing all of Cornwall. The north coast beaches, with magnificent cliffs and surf are only a 10 minute drive away, the more peaceful south coast beaches are an easy 20 minute drive and Lands End and other attractions are easily accessible within an hour. The farmhouse is centrally heated throughout and has four bedrooms to let, two en suite and two sharing a main bathroom. All have washbasin, colour TV, tea/coffee making facilities and hairdryer. A friendly personal service is assured. Bed and Breakfast from £16 to £25. Also available is our self-catering unit, sleeping six - terms from £125 per week. Please write or call for our brochure.

FREE or REDUCED RATE entry to Holiday Visits and Attractions — see our READERS' OFFER VOUCHERS on pages 43-60

WADEBRIDGE. Mrs E. Hodge, Pengelly Farm, Burlawn, Wadebridge PL27 7LA (01208 814217).

A Listed Georgian farmhouse situated in a quiet location on a 150 acre farm overlooking wooded valleys, approximately one-and-a-half miles from Wadebridge. Ideal location for touring or walking and cycling close to the Camel Trail. There are a number of beaches plus sailing, golf, horse riding and much more within 20 minutes' drive. Large garden for relaxing or for children to play. Three prettily decorated bedrooms all with own vanity units, tea/coffee making facilities, colour TV, and hair dryers. Traditional English breakfast or special requests by prior arrangement. Lounge with colour TV. Children welcome - cot and highchair available, babysitting on request. Bed and Breakfast £18. **ETC ◆◆◆**, *CORNWALL TOURIST BOARD REGISTERED.*

WADEBRIDGE. Carol Fielding Brown, Treglown House, Haywood Farm, St. Mabyn, Bodmin PL30 3B

(Tel & Fax: 01208 841896). There is a special welcome at our peaceful, friendly farmhouse amidst lovely countryside, yet only a short stroll from the delightful village of St Mabyn. Lord Falmouth built this sturdy house with granite lintels and Delabole slate roof at the end of the 19th century. On arrival guests are treated to a cream tea served in the garden or, on chilly days, in the sittingroom by a cosy log fire. Our en suite rooms have TV, radio and beverage tray. Children and pets are especially welcome. There are lots of interesting animals to enjoy and space to roam in. Treglown House lies four miles from Wadebridge, 11 miles Padstow, 17 miles Eden Project. Terms £18- £25. **ETC ◆◆◆**

e-mail: treglownhouse@stmabyn.fsnet.co.uk

ZENNOR. Sue & John Wilson, Tregeraint House, Zennor, St. Ives TR26 3DB (Tel & Fax: 01736

797061). Traditional cottage in an acre of gardens overlooking the Atlantic coastline in one of the most beautiful parts of Cornwall. The house has been lovingly restored, providing a base from which to explore this fascinating area. Each bedroom (one twin, one double, one family) is comfortably furnished with a plumbed in traditional pine washstand and central heating. Tea and coffee making facilities. Vegetarian and other diets can be catered for and there are nearby pubs where reasonable meals can be had, while St. Ives and Penzance offer excellent eating, artistic and other facilities. Open all year except at Christmas. £20 per person (£2 single supplement).
e-mail: suewilson@yahoo.co.uk

When making enquiries or bookings, a stamped addressed envelope is always appreciated

CUMBRIA

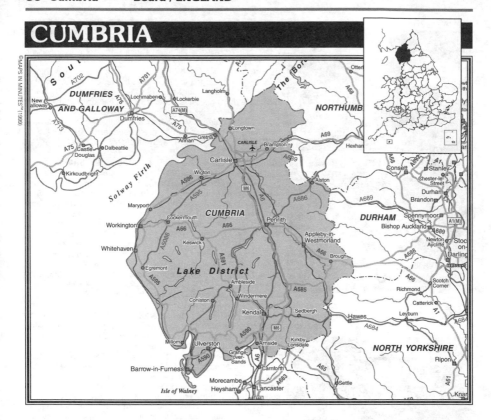

©MAPS IN MINUTES™ (1999)

AMBLESIDE. Peter and Anne Hart, Bracken Fell, Outgate, Ambleside LA22 0NH (015394 36289).. A delightful country residence with 2 acres of gardens, situated in beautiful open countryside between Ambleside and Hawkshead in the picturesque hamlet of Outgate. This comfortable home with its lovely accommodation and friendly service is ideally located for exploring the Lake District. Each bedroom has its own private facilities, colour TV, hairdryer, complimentary tea and coffee and a super view. There is a comfortable lounge, dining room and ample private parking. Two country inns are within walking distance where evening meals are available. Bed and Breakfast from £23. No pets or children under 12 years. Non smoking. Self-catering accommodation also available. Write or phone for brochure. **ETC** ◆◆◆
e-mail: hart.brackenfell@virgin.net.
website: www.brackenfell.com

Bracken Fell

AMBLESIDE. Mrs S. Briggs, High Wray Farm, High Wray, Near Ambleside LA22 0JE (015394 32280).
Working farm. Charming 17th century olde worlde farmhouse with Beatrix Potter connections. Original oak beams, cosy lounge with log burning fire, pretty colour co-ordinated bedrooms, all with en suite facilities. Heating and tea/coffee trays are in all rooms. Situated in a quiet unspoilt location, panoramic views and lake shore walks close by. A warm welcome awaits all who visit us, where comfort, cleanliness and personal attention are assured. Follow the B5286 from Ambleside towards Hawkshead turn left for Wray. Follow road to High Wray, the farm is on the right. Families welcome. Terms from £20. FHG Diploma Winner.
ETC ◆◆◆◆

BORWICK LODGE
Outgate, Hawkshead, Ambleside
LA22 0PU Telephone: Hawkshead 015394 36332.

Colin and Rosemary Haskell

A leafy driveway entices you to the most enchantingly situated house in the Lake District, a very special 17th century country lodge with magnificent panoramic lake and mountain views, quietly secluded in beautiful gardens. Ideally placed in the heart of the Lakes and close to Hawkshead village with its good choice of restaurants and inns. Beautiful en suite bedrooms with colour television and tea/coffee facilities, including "Special Occasions" and "Romantic Breaks", two king-size four-poster rooms. Tourist Board ◆◆◆◆ and SILVER AWARD. Four times winner of FHG Diploma for Accommodation and Service. Colin and Rosemary welcome you to their "haven of peace and tranquillity" in this most beautiful corner of England. Ample parking. NON-SMOKING. Bed and Breakfast from £25. May we send our brochure?

See also Colour Advertisement on page 4

AMBLESIDE. Rothay House, Rothay Road, Ambleside LA22 0EE (015394 32434). Rothay House is an

attractive modern detached guest house set in pleasant gardens with views of the surrounding fells. All bedrooms are comfortable and well furnished with en suite facilities, colour TV, tea and coffee tray. Our visitors are assured of warm and friendly service in attractive surroundings. The house is within easy walking distance of the village centre. Ambleside has a variety of interesting shops and restaurants and makes an ideal base for walking, touring or enjoying sailing, watersports and angling on Lake Windermere. Car not essential, but ample parking. Open all year. Children welcome; sorry, no pets. Bed and Breakfast from £20 to £25; Winter Weekend Breaks available.

AMBLESIDE. Mr D. Woodhouse, Glenside, Old Lake Road, Ambleside LA22 0DP (015394 32635).

Janice and David welcome you to their non-smoking three-bedroomed old farm cottage dating back to the 18th century and offering a high standard of accommodation. All bedrooms have the original beamed ceilings, cottage-style furnishings, washbasin and tea and coffee making facilities. They all share two well-appointed shower/bathrooms, cosy TV lounge and quaint diningroom serving a traditional English breakfast. The house is situated midway between the village and Lake Windermere and lovely walks start from the door. Private parking. Bed and Breakfast from £17 to £18 per person. **ETC** ◆◆◆◆

AMBLESIDE. Mrs C. Irvine, Tock How Farm, High Wray, Ambleside (015394 36106). A beautiful

Lakeland farm giving the visitor an opportunity to sample the peaceful life of a Lake District farmer. It is set in idyllic surroundings overlooking Blelham Tarn with magnificent panoramic views of the Langdale Pikes, Coniston Old Man, the Troutbeck Fells and Lake Windermere. High Wray is a quiet unspoilt hamlet set between Ambleside and Hawkshead making this an ideal base for walking or touring. Visitors can expect to taste at breakfast the culinary delights of a working farmhouse kitchen. Sky TV and tea/coffee making facilities are provided in all en suite rooms. Please telephone for further details.

Please mention *The Farm Holiday Guide* when making enquiries about accommodation featured in these pages.

AMBLESIDE. Liz, Mary and Craig, Wanslea Guest House, Lake Road, Ambleside LA22 0DB (01539

433884). Wanslea is a spacious family-run Victorian non-smoking guest house with fine views, situated just a stroll from the village and Lake shore with walks beginning at the door. We offer a friendly welcome and comfortable rooms, all of which have colour TV and tea/coffee tray; most rooms are en suite. A good breakfast will start your day before enjoying a fell walk or maybe a more leisurely stroll by the lake. Relax in our licensed residents' lounge with a real fire on winter evenings. Children are welcome and pets accepted by arrangement. Bed and Breakfast from £17.50 per person, Evening Meal also available to party bookings. Autumn, Winter, Spring Breaks at reduced rates. Brochure on request. **ETC** ◆◆◆.
e-mail: wanslea.guesthouse@virgin.net

AMBLESIDE. Judith and Edward Ireton, Holmeshead Farm, Skelwith Fold, Ambleside LA22 0HU

(015394 33048; Fax: 015394 31337). Working farm. Nestling between Ambleside and Hawkshead, Holmeshead is situated in the hamlet of Skelwith Fold, at the gateway to the Langdale Valley. Holmeshead is a spacious 17th century farmhouse which has been updated while still retaining its intrinsic character. Part of its charm is that Holmeshead is a working Lakeland farm. All three guest rooms have a peaceful, southerly outlook across the lawn to the farm fields beyond. Each room is cosily furnished and contains a three-piece shower room, TV, and tea/coffee making facilities.

| See also Colour Display Advertisement | **APPLEBY. The Gate Hotel, Bongate, Appleby CA16 6LH (017683 52688; Fax: 017683 53858).** An attractive family-run business on the outskirts of Appleby in easy reach of the town centre with its shops, castle and swimming pool and approximately one mile from the golf course. It is tastefully decorated with panelling from the steam ship 'Berengaria'. A traditional log fire enhances the warm and friendly service offered all year round. Our rooms are en suite and well furnished with colour TV and tea/coffee trays. There is ample parking, a pleasant enclosed garden and play area. Pets welcome by arrangement. Specialising in Thai food we also offer conventional English food. Licensed. Bed and Breakfast from £25 to £30 per person; Evening Meal from £4.95 to £12.50
Website: www.appleby/web.co.uk/gate

APPLEBY. Mrs C. Jackson, Wickerslack Farm, Crosby Ravensworth, Penrith CA10 3LN (01931 715236) A very warm welcome awaits you on our family run working farm. Peaceful rural setting with superb views, ideal base for walking and touring holidays or just to relax. Beautifully decorated, spacious accommodation with three rooms, two en suite. Guests' lounge with TV and log fire which is accessible all day. Light suppers available. For bookings or further details contact: Christine Jackson. **ETC** ◆◆◆

BRAMPTON. Mrs Margaret Mounsey, Walton High Rigg, Walton, Brampton CA8 2AZ (016977 2117).

A friendly welcome to our attractive Georgian Listed farmhouse with very comfortable spacious rooms. A washbasin, TV and tea/coffee facilities in the bedroom, a separate diningroom, a pool/snooker table is available, also a private bathroom if requested. This is a working dairy/sheep farm where the children can help to feed the hens and baby calves. We have spectacular views of the Pennines and Lake District from the bedrooms. It is an excellent site to explore Hadrian's Wall country, the Lakes or Scotland. The farm is three quarters of a mile from the village of Walton, ten miles from Carlisle and M6. Fishing, golf and horse riding available locally. **ETC** ◆◆◆, *WELCOME HOST*

BRAMPTON. Mrs Elizabeth Woodmass, Howard House Farm, Gilsland, Brampton CA8 7AJ (016977

47285). Working farm, join in. A 250 acre mixed farm with a 19th century stone-built farmhouse situated in a rural area overlooking the Irthing Valley on the Cumbria/Northumbria border. Half-a-mile from Gilsland village and Roman Wall; Haltwhistle five miles and the M6 at Carlisle, 18 miles. Good base for touring – Roman Wall, Lakes and Scottish Borders. Trout fishing on farm. Guests' lounge with colour TV where you can relax anytime in comfort. Diningroom. One double room en suite, one twin and one family room with washbasins, bath or shower. All bedrooms have tea/coffee making facilities. Bathroom with shower, toilet. Children welcome at reduced rates. Sorry, no pets. Car essential - parking. Open January to December for Bed and Breakfast from £20 to £23; Evening Meal optional. Weekly terms available. SAE or telephone for brochure. **ETC ◆◆◆◆**

CALDBECK. Mr and Mrs A. Savage, Swaledale Watch, Whelpo, Caldbeck CA7 8HQ (Tel & Fax:

016974 78409). Ours is a mixed farm of 300 acres situated in beautiful countryside within the Lake District National Park. Central for Scottish Borders, Roman Wall, Eden Valley and Lakes. Primarily a sheep farm (everyone loves lambing time). Visitors are welcome to see farm animals and activities. Many interesting walks nearby or roam the peaceful northern fells. Enjoyed by many Cumbrian Way walkers. Very comfortable accommodation with excellent home cooking. All rooms have private facilities. Central heating. Tea making facilities. We are a friendly Cumbrian farming family and make you very welcome. Bed and Breakfast from £18 to £24; Evening Meal from £12, Tuesday, Wednesday, Thursday and Saturday only. **ETC/AA ◆◆◆◆.**
e-mail: nan.savage@talk21.com

CARLISLE. Mrs Dorothy Nicholson, Gill Farm, Blackford, Carlisle CA6 4EL (01228 675326; mobile:

07808 571586). In a delightful setting on a beef and sheep farm, this Georgian style farmhouse dated 1740 offers a friendly welcome to all guests breaking journeys to or from Scotland or having a holiday in our beautiful countryside. Near Hadrian's Wall, Gretna Green and Lake District. Golf, fishing, swimming and large agricultural auction markets all nearby; also cycle path passes our entrance. Accommodation is in one double room en suite, one family and one twin/single bedrooms. All rooms have washbasins, shaver points and tea/coffee making facilities. Two bathrooms, shower; lounge with colour TV; separate diningroom. Open all year. Reductions for children; cot provided. Central heating. Car essential, good parking. Pets permitted. Bed and Breakfast from £18. Telephone for further details or directions.

CARLISLE. Mrs L. Lawson, Craigburn Farm, Catlowdy, Longtown CA6 5QP (01228 577214). A

warm welcome awaits you at our family-run guest house. Delicious homemade meals, sweets our speciality. Residential licence. Stopover to and from Scotland and Northern Irleland. We look forward to meeting you.

Readers are requested to mention this guidebook
when seeking accommodation (and please enclose
a stamped addressed envelope).

COCKERMOUTH. Mrs B. Woodward, Toddell Farm, Brandlingill, Cockermouth CA13 0RB (01900

828423). Beautifully restored 17th century barn with open beams, self-contained lounge with TV and tea/coffee making facilities. One double bed and a slumber loft above with two singles, also a bed setttee for extras! Private entrance leads to this very spacious suite with its own private bathroom. Situated three miles from Cockermouth, yet within the National Park, Toddell Farm is set in seven acres. With splendid views from the house, the fells provide some very good walks from the property. Dogs welcome. Bed and Breakfast from £25.

COCKERMOUTH. Mrs Chester, Birk Bank Farm, Brandlingill, Cockermouth CA13 0RB (01900 822326). Birk

Bank is a traditional Lakeland farm situated up a short drive from the public road, four miles from Cockermouth. Within easy reach of Lakes and coast. Enjoy home cooking using local produce and free range eggs served in guests' diningroom with separate tables. Lounge with TV and log fire on chilly evenings; tea/coffee in lounge with home-made biscuits. Morning tea if requested. One double and one triple room; electric blankets. Bathroom and shower room. Bed and Breakfast from £16 - £18. Evening Meal if booked in advance £9. Children over five welcome. Sorry no pets. Open March - October.

COCKERMOUTH near. Mrs Nicholson, Swinside End Farm, Scales, High Lorton, Near Cockermouth

CA13 9VA (01900 85134). Working farm situated in a peaceful part of Lorton Valley, the perfect base for your Lakeland holiday. Ideal for hill walking and touring around the Lake District. All rooms have central heating, washbasins, tea/coffee making facilities and hairdryer. TV lounge with open fire. Magnificent views. Packed lunches available. A warm welcome awaits you. Open all year. Pets by arrangement. Bed and Breakfast from £15 per person per night.

CONISTON. Mr Richard Nelson, Townson Ground, East of the Lake, Coniston LA21 8AA (01539

441272). Nestling amidst breathtaking scenery on the tranquil eastern side of Coniston Water, our fascinating 16th century farmhouse provides the perfect country retreat, a home from home with emphasis on quality, comfort, peace and quiet. Delightful bedrooms offer en suite facilities, tea trays and televisions; a couple overlook the lake and surrounding fells. Relax by roaring log fires in our lounge, enjoy a hearty breakfast and unwind in the lovely garden. An ideal base for touring, walking, cycling and watersports (we have private lake access and jetty). One dog permitted. Bed & Breakfast from £20 per person. **ETC ◆◆◆◆**
e-mail: info@townsonground.co.uk
website: www.townsonground.co.uk

DALTON-IN-FURNESS. Mrs Nicholson, Park Cottage, Dalton-in-Furness LA15 8JZ (01229 462850). Over 300 years old, Park Cottage overlooks Burlington Lake and has four acres of grounds mainly woodland and garden with 31 types of wild bird feeding and nesting. Surrounded by public footpaths in open countryside and farmland we enjoy a very peaceful location. Two lounges cater for smokers and non-smokers, with a separate diningroom. All bedrooms have splendid views, are en suite and have co-ordinated furnishings, TV/video, tea/coffee making facilities and central heating. Wide choice for Breakfast, Evening Meals available. Packed lunches, suggested itineraries and maps. Ideally situated for walking, fishing (trout and coarse) and bird-watching. Excellent standards and value at £18 per person Bed and Breakfast. Phone for brochure.

HAWKSHEAD. Colin and Rosemary Haskell, Borwick Lodge, Outgate, Hawkshead, Ambleside LA22 0PU (015394 36332). A leafy driveway entices you to the most enchantingly situated house in the Lake District, a very special 17th century country lodge with magnificent panoramic lake and mountain views, quietly secluded in beautiful gardens. Ideally placed in the heart of the Lakes and close to Hawkshead village with its good choice of restaurants and inns. Beautiful en suite bedrooms with colour TV and tea/coffee facilities including "Special Occasions" and "Romantic Breaks" two king-size four-poster rooms. Colin and Rosemary welcome you to their "haven of peace and tranquillity" in this most beautiful corner of England. Ample parking. NON-SMOKING. Bed and Breakfast from £25. May we send our brochure? **ETC** ◆◆◆◆ *SILVER AWARD.*
e-mail: borwicklodge@talk21.com
website: www.borwicklodge.com

KENDAL. Glynis Byrne, Marwin House, Duke Street, Holme, Near Carnforth LA6 1PY (01524 781144). Marwin House is a delightful country cottage situated in the small unspoilt village of Holme, gateway to the Lake District and Yorkshire Dales, yet only five minutes from M6 Junction 36. We are an ideal base for walking. Bedrooms are comfortable and tastefully decorated with colour TV, tea/coffee making facilities and central heating. Private lounge with colour TV/video. Children are most welcome. Off road parking. Breakfast a speciality served in a warm friendly atmosphere. Bed and Breakfast from £16 to £18. Open all year. **ETC** ◆◆.

KENDAL near. Mrs Betty Fishwick, Stock Bridge Farm, Staveley, Kendal LA8 9LP (01539 821580). A comfortable, well appointed 17th century farmhouse on edge of by-passed village, just off A591 Kendal-Windermere Road. Situated at the foot of the Kentmere Valley. Ideal for walking. All bedrooms have fitted washbasins with shaver points. Bathroom with shower and toilet, plus separate toilet. Cosy lounge/diningroom with open fire, colour TV. Fire Certificate held. Full central heating. Full English Breakfast served at separate tables; friendly personal service. Good off-road parking facilities. Three good village pubs within walking distance of the farm. Excellent stop-off for England-Scotland routed through beautiful English Lakeland.

KESWICK. Mrs M. M. Beaty, Birkrigg Farm, Newlands, Keswick CA12 5TS (017687 78278). **Working farm.** Birkrigg is a working beef and sheep farm, very pleasantly and peacefully situated, with an excellent outlook in the lovely Newlands Valley. Five miles from Keswick between Braithwaite and Buttermere. Being in a beautiful mountainous area makes this an ideal place to stay especially for those wishing to walk or climb. Centrally located for touring the many beauty spots in the Lake District. Clean, comfortable accommodation awaits you. A good Breakfast is offered at 8.30am, Evening Tea at 9.30pm. Packed Lunches available. Sorry, no Evening Meals. Local inns all provide good food, two to four miles away. Open March to November. **ETC** ◆◆

KESWICK. Mrs E. M. Richardson, Fold Head Farm, Watendlath, Borrowdale, Keswick CA12 5UW (017687 77255). Working farm. Fold Head Farmhouse is a white Lakeland farmhouse situated on the banks of Watendlath Tarn in this picturesque hamlet. It is a 3000 acre sheep farm and an ideal centre for touring, climbing, fell-walking and fishing. Fly-fishing for rainbow trout at Watendlath Tarn; permits available. Guests are accommodated in two double bedrooms and one twin bedroom, with washbasins; bathroom, two toilets; sittingroom; diningroom. Full central heating; separate TV lounge. Pets are allowed free. Open from February to December. Car essential; parking. Sir Hugh Walpole used this farmhouse in his book "Judith Paris" as the home of Judith Paris. Evening Dinner/ Bed and Breakfast. Terms on request.

KESWICK. Mr & Mrs Bradley, Rickerby Grange Country House Hotel, Portinscale, Keswick, Cumbria CA12 5RH (017687 72344). Set within its own garden with private car parking, in the picturesque village of Portinscale near the shores of Lake Derwentwater within walking distance of the market town of Keswick, ideally situated for exploring all parts of the Lakes. Offering comfort, friendly service, these being the essential qualities provided by the resident proprietor. A well stocked bar, comfortable lounge and elegant diningroom where a five-course dinner can be enjoyed, with a varied selection of fine wines. Three ground floor bedrooms, all rooms en suite with tea and coffee making facilities, colour TV, direct dial telephone. Bed and Breakfast from £28, Double Bed and Breakfast from £41, Winter Rates Available (Special Breaks) Open all Year, including Christmas and New Year. Brochure sent on request. **ETC/AA/RAC** ◆◆◆◆ *SPARKLING AWARD.*
e-mail: val@ricor.demon.co.uk
website: www.ricor.demon.co.uk

KESWICK. Mrs Deborah Mawson, Dalton Cottage, Bassenthwaite CA12 4QG (017687 76952). Dalton Cottage is a traditional Lakeland farm cottage nestling at the foot of Skiddaw. Its situation is idyllic, with spectacular views over Bassenthwaite Lake to the front, Ullock Pike and Skiddaw to the rear, making it an ideal base for walking and touring the Lakes. Both bedrooms are tastefully decorated and are en suite with tea/coffee making facilities. We serve hearty English breakfasts and local inns provide good food nearby in the evenings. Dalton Cottage is typical of the period, with beams, open log fires and antiques. It is the perfect place to relax and unwind and is ideal for families – cot and high chair available. Open all year. Bed and Breakfast from £22, £145 weekly. Friday/Saturday/Sunday Special Breaks £63. Deborah and Martyn look forward to meeting you.
E-mail: deborah.dalt.cottage@talk21.com
Website: www.daltoncottage.co.uk

Readers are requested to mention this guidebook
when seeking accommodation (and please enclose
a stamped addressed envelope).

KESWICK. Colin and Lesley Smith, Mosedale House, Mosedale, Mungrisdale, Cumbria CA11 0XQ

(017687 79371). Traditional 1862 built, lakeland farmhouse. A smallholding with donkeys, hens and pet pig. It enjoys a magnificent position, nestling at the foot of Carrock Fell, overlooking the river Caldew, three-and-a-half miles from the A66 Keswick to Penrith road. Four-course dinners, licensed, vegetarians welcome. Home-baked bread, our own free-range eggs. Packed Lunches. No smoking. En suite rooms. Attractive lounge. Bed and Breakfast £25.50. Dinner £13.75. Delightful two bedroomed self-catering cottage. Peaceful location, fell-walking from the door. Abundant wildlife. Visit us on our website below. Grade One facilities for disabled guests. **ETC** ◆◆◆◆
e-mail: colin.smith2@ukonline.co.uk
website: www.keswick.org

KESWICK. Val and Alan Heiver, The Paddock Guest House, Wordsworth Street, Penrith Road, Keswick-on-Derwentwater CA12 4HU (017687 72510).

Personally run by Val and Alan this delightful residence of charm and character dates from the mid 1800's. With six guest bedrooms (all en suite) including family room. All rooms have tea/coffee, colour TV, hairdryers, clock radios and central heating. Enjoy our guest lounge with an open log fire. Built from Lakeland slate stone and minerals. A hearty English, vegetarian or Continental breakfast is served between 8.15 and 8.45. In a quiet residential area only five minutes' walk back to the centre and ten minutes to the lake, close by the beautiful and tranquil Fitz Park. No smoking. Off street parking available.

KESWICK. Lyndhurst Guest House, 22 Southerby Street, Keswick CA12 4EF (017687 72303). Well established Bed and Breakfast for non-smokers, two minutes' walk from town centre and ideally situated for local walks. All rooms are fully en suite and have colour TV, central heating and tea/coffee making facilities. Family, twin and double rooms available. Children and groups welcome; child discount applies. Cyclists welcome and cycle storage available. Packed lunches available. Bed and full English Breakfast £19.50 per person, two or more nights £18.50.

NEAR SAWREY. Miss Gillian Fletcher, High Green Gate Guest House, Near Sawrey, Ambleside LA22 0LF (015394 36296). The Guest House is a converted 18th century farmhouse in the quiet hamlet where Beatrix Potter lived and wrote. Her house, owned by the National Trust, is close by and open to the public. The area abounds with pleasant easy walks and is a good centre for the Southern Lakes. Open from March to October. Good food and service under the personal attention of the owner. Spacious diningroom, lounge and separate TV lounge. All bedrooms have hot and cold water and individual heating in addition to central heating. Rooms with private facilities available. Reduced rates for children sharing with parents. Cot and highchair are available and babysitting can be arranged. Dogs welcome. A car is desirable and there is parking for seven cars. Bed and Breakfast from £23 per night; Bed, Breakfast and Evening Meal from £33 per night (£209 weekly). **ETC/AA/RAC** ◆◆◆

NEAR SAWREY. Mrs Elizabeth Mallett, Esthwaite How Farmhouse, Near Sawrey, Ambleside LA22 0LB (015394 36450). A warm and friendly welcome awaits you at Esthwaite How Farmhouse, situated in this lovely village where Beatrix Potter wrote her books. Beautiful views of the countryside and the lake (where part of the television film about her life was made) can be seen from bedrooms and the diningroom. Ideal for walking, fishing and touring. Accommodation comprises one double and one family bedrooms with washbasins; bathroom with shower; dining/sitting room with open log fire, central heating. Children welcome; babysitting can be arranged. Open all year. Car essential, parking for two cars. Bed and Breakfast from £15; Bed, Breakfast and Evening Meal from £23. Half rates for children sharing room.

Please mention The Farm Holiday Guide when writing to enquire about accommodation

NEWBIGGIN ON LUNE. Mrs Brenda Boustead, Tranna Hill, Newbiggin on Lune, Kirkby Stephen CA17 4NY (015396 23227 or 07989 892368). Tranna Hill offers a relaxing and friendly atmosphere in a non-smoking environment.

Five miles from M6 Junction 38, ideal base for walkers, fishermen and golfers with Howgill Fells Nature Reserve, fish farm and golf course only minutes away. Well placed for breaking your journey or touring the Lakes and Dales. Private parking and large gardens. En suite rooms with TV, refreshment trays, central heating and beautiful views. Delicious breakfasts. All for £18pppn. **ETC** ◆◆◆

PENRITH. Mrs Yvonne Dent, Bridge End Farm, Kirkby Thore, Penrith CA10 1UZ (01768 361362).

Relax in our 18th century farmhouse on a dairy farm in the Eden Valley. Lovely spacious en suite bedrooms, tastefully furnished with antiques, featuring beautiful handmade patchwork quilts and craft work. All rooms have coffee/tea making facilities, hair dryer, clock radio and TV. Enjoy delicious home made breakfast and dinner served in the dining room. All the food is freshly prepared and you will never forget Yvonne's sticky toffee pudding. Finish the evening in front of the fire in the delightfully furnished guest lounge or take a stroll along the banks of the River Eden. Private fishing available. **ETC** ◆◆◆◆◆

PENRITH. Mr and Mrs D. L. and M. Brunskill, Brookfield, Shap, Penrith CA10 3PZ (01931 716 397).

Situated one mile from M6 motorway (turn off at Shap interchange No. 39), first accommodation off motorway. Excellent position for touring Lakeland, or overnight accommodation for travelling north or south. Central heating throughout, renowned for good food, comfort and personal attention. All bedrooms are well-appointed and have en suite facilities remote-control colour TV, hospitality tray and hairdryer; Diningroom where delicious home cooking is a speciality. Well-stocked bar. Residents' lounge. Sorry, no pets. Open from January to December. Terms sent on request. Ample parking. Full Fire Certificate. **AA** ◆◆◆◆.

PENRITH. Mrs Brenda Preston, Pallet Hill Farm, Penrith CA11 0BY (017684 83247). Pallet Hill Farm is

pleasantly situated two miles from Penrith on the Penrith-Greystoke-Keswick road (B5288). It is four miles from Ullswater and has easy access to the Lake District, Scottish Borders and Yorkshire Dales. There are several sports facilities in the area - golf club, swimming pool, pony trekking; places to visit such as Lowther Leisure Park and the Miniature Railway at Ravenglass. Good farmhouse food and hospitality with personal attention. Double, single, family rooms; diningroom and sittingroom. Children welcome - cot, high chair available. Sorry, no pets. Car essential, parking. Open Easter to November. Bed and Breakfast from £10.50 (reduced rates for children and weekly stays).

PENRITH. Mrs Mary Milburn, Park House Farm, Dalemain, Penrith CA11 0HB (Tel & Fax: 017684 86212). Wordsworth often visited here. A working sheep farm

with 18th Century farmhouse. Peace and tranquillity with glorious views over to Barton Fell. Situated in the Lake District National Park, three miles from Ullswater or M6 (J40) or A592 entering via Dalesmain Mansion (Historic House) ignoring the 'no cars sign.' Genuine country hospitality at its best – home made biscuits are a typical gesture. Attractive en suite rooms. TV lounge with open fire. Hospitality tray. Evening meals available locally. Sorry no pets in house. Bed and Breakfast from £19 to £22. Farm Holiday Bureau member and featured in "Special Places to Stay". **ETC** ◆◆◆.
website: www.eden-in-cumbria.co-uk/parkhouse

PENRITH. Mrs C Bousfield, Trainlands, Maulds Meaburn, Penrith CA10 3HX (017683 51249). This

17th/18th century farmhouse and working farm is situated away from busy roads between the Eden and Lyvennet Valleys, but within easy reach of the M6 and A66. Five miles west of Appleby and 13 miles south of Penrith. Guest TV lounge/dining room with a real fire await those who need to get away from it all, but with plenty of walking for those with the energy. Evening meal by arrangement. For bookings or further information contact Carol Bousfield on the above number or by e-mail: bousfield@trainlands.u-net.com

PENRITH. Mrs Margaret Taylor, Tymparon Hall, Newbiggin, Stainton, Penrith CA11 0HS (Tel and Fax: 017684 83236). Working farm. Enjoy a relaxing break in the

beautiful North Lakes and explore the Eden Valley. A delightful 18th century Manor House and colourful summer garden situated on a 150 acre sheep farm in a peaceful rural area close to Lake Ullswater. Enjoy old-fashioned hospitality, home cooked farmhouse breakfasts and three-course dinners. Guests' bedrooms, en suite or standard, offer space and tranquillity with every facility for a memorable time. Evening Dinner, Bed and Breakfast. Brochure on request with SAE. **ETC** ◆◆◆◆

PENRITH. Mrs P Bonnick, Scalehouse Farm, Scalehouses, Renwick, Penrith CA10 1JY (Tel & Fax: 01768 896493). A traditional Cumbrian farmhouse in a tiny

hamlet overlooking the unspoilt Eden Valley. The North Pennines is an area of outstanding natural beauty, known as 'England's Last Wilderness'. Wildlife, rare elsewhere, is common here with hares, skylarks, lapwings, curlews, snipe, etc. There are lots of interesting places to visit - Carlisle Castle, Hadrian's Wall and Ullswater are just 25 minutes drive away, and so much more. All rooms have period furniture, books, paintings and central heating. The cosy drawingroom has a log fire, TV and games. Home made evening meals are available, with produce from our garden in season. Two double bedrooms and one twin room available. Children welcome. Bed & Breakfast from £14 per person. We are a non-smoking house.

POOLEY BRIDGE. Mrs Coulston, Hole House Farm, Pooley Bridge, Penrith CA10 2NG (017684

86325). 17th Century character Farmhouse, tastefully furnished and decorated, in a quiet location next to River Eamont yet only a ten minute walk into Pooley Bridge for shops, pubs, steamer trips and fell walks. Two double bedrooms, one with extra bed, both with wash hand basin, one with shower; separate bathroom with W.C. Both with colour TV and tea/coffee making facilities. On the B5320, half a mile out of Pooley Bridge.

TROUTBECK. Gwen and Peter Parfitt, Hill Crest, Troutbeck, Penrith CA11 0SH (017684 83935). Gwen

and Peter assure you of a warm and friendly welcome at Hill Crest, their unique Lakeland home which offers two en suite double/family rooms, one twin room. Home cooking, choice of menu including vegetarian; lounge/dining room, early morning tea, bedtime drinks; packed lunches. Panoramic mountain views. Aira Force waterfalls, Ullswater 10 minutes, Keswick 15 minutes, a good base for walking, boating, touring, Lakes, Hadrian's Wall and the Borders. Books, maps and hints from Gwen on what to see. Walkers, children and dogs welcome. Bed and Breakfast £14 per person twin room, £16 per person en suite rooms. Children half price sharing. Dinner from £5 (optional). Weekly rates. 10 minutes Junction 40 M6. At Hill Crest we aim to create a relaxed and informal atmosphere where guests are treated as part of the family. Highly recommended by previous guests. Non smoking establishment.

See also Colour Display Advertisement

WINDERMERE. Irene and George Eastwood, Sandown, Lake Road, Windermere LA23 2JF (015394 45275). Superb Bed and Breakfast accommodation. All rooms en suite with colour TV and tea/coffee making facilities. Situated two minutes from Lake Windermere, shops and cafes. Many lovely walks. Open all year. Special out of season rates, also two-day Saturday/Sunday Breaks. Well-behaved dogs welcome. Each room has own safe private car parking. SAE or telephone for further details.

DERBYSHIRE

AMBERGATE. Mrs Carol Oulton, Lawn Farm, Whitewells Lane (off Holly Lane), Ambergate DE56 2DN

(01773 852352). Working farm, join in. Enjoy comfortable Bed and Breakfast accommodation on a working beef and sheep farm, one mile from the A6 at Ambergate. Ambergate has many woodland walks and a picturesque canal which leads to nearby Cromford, home of the Arkwright Mill. Matlock Bath is 10 miles away and offers many attractions including cable cars. Within easy travelling distance of Haddon Hall, Chatsworth House and Gardens, The Peak District National Park and The National Tramway Museum at Crich. Accommodation comprises double en suite room and family room with handbasin. Children welcome at reduced rates. Pets welcome by arrangement. Terms on request from £17.50 per night. Non-smokers preferred.
e-mail: caroloulton@farming.co.uk

ASHBOURNE. Mrs E.M. Smail, New House Farm, Kniveton, Ashbourne DE6 1JL (01335 342429).

Working farm. Organically managed, this traditional family farm is in the South Peak District. Carsington Water is two miles, Ashbourne three miles and Dovedale a lovely five mile walk; Alton Towers 10 miles. There are pets, free-range livestock, archaeological features and farm shop. Guided farm walks. We serve organic, free-range and fair-traded foods. Vegetarians and other diets welcome. Children's teas, light suppers, babysitting and play area available. Pets welcome. Tea/coffee facilities, central heating, TV and radio in rooms. We also arrange FREE WORKING HOLIDAYS, individual/group camping and a venue for courses. Bed and Breakfast from £8 to £15.50.

See also Colour Display Advertisement

ASHBOURNE. Mrs Catherine Brandrick, Sidesmill Farm, Snelston, Ashbourne DE6 2GQ (01335 342710). Peaceful dairy farm located on the banks of the River Dove. A rippling mill stream flows quietly past the 18th century stone-built farmhouse. Traditional English Breakfast, excellent local pubs and restaurants. One double room en suite, one twin-bedded room with private bathroom, tea/coffee making facilities. Ideal base for touring, within easy reach of Dovedale, Alton Towers, stately homes and many other places of interest. Open February - November. Car necessary, parking available. Bed and Breakfast from £20 per person. A non-smoking establishment. ETC ◆◆◆◆
website: http://www.sidemill-demon.co.uk

Located between the towns of Buxton and Bakewell, this is an ideal hideaway for your break – whatever the time of year. As part of a traditional working dairy farm, this striking 18th century farmhouse is an ideal base to enjoy peace and quiet whilst experiencing the joys of green meadows roped in woodland. Shallow Grange is set away from the main road and a stone's throw from your door there are a variety of unspoilt walks where you can venture out on nature trails. Take your choice of cycling by heather-covered moors, walking through rocky valleys or picturesque villages nearby. Your comfort is our business and we have made sure that you will be well looked after at Shallow Grange, which is centrally heated, double-glazed and all bedrooms are oak-beamed and have en suite bathroom, colour television and tea and coffee making facilities. Down on the farm you can experience the atmosphere of the countryside. Throughout the year there is plenty of farm activity with calving, lambing and haymaking.

Shallow Grange

PROPRIETOR: CHRISTINE HOLLAND

Shallow Grange, Chelmorton, Near Buxton, Derbyshire SK17 9SG
Telephone: (01298) 23578 Fax: (01298) 78242 Mobile: 07836 535353

BAKEWELL. Mrs Alison Yates, Smerrill Grange, Middleton By Youlgrave, Bakewell DE45 1LQ (01629 636232). Working farm. Traditional bed and breakfast on beef cattle and sheep farm. Beautiful setting in heart of Peak District. Very old farmhouse. Many tourist attractions within short driving distance, eg Chatsworth House and Haddon Hall. Bakewell and Matlock six miles. Glorious walks in Derbyshire Dales. Double en suite, double and twin bedrooms with private bathroom. Tea/coffee making facilities. Private guests' sitting and dining rooms. Bed and Breakfast from £17. Reductions for children. Dogs by arrangement.

BASLOW. Mrs S. Mills, Bubnell Cliff Farm, Wheatlands Lane, Baslow, Bakewell DE45 1RH (01246 582454). Working farm. A 300 acre working farm situated half-a-mile from the village of Baslow in the beautiful Derbyshire Peak District. Guests can enjoy, from their bedroom window, breathtaking views of Chatsworth Park and surrounding area. Chatsworth House, the majestic home of the Duke of Devonshire, medieval Haddon Hall and the traditional market town of Bakewell (famous for its puddings), are all close by. Accommodation comprises one double and one family room, guests' lounge/diningroom with TV and log fires in the winter. NON-SMOKERS ONLY. Bed and Breakfast from £17 per person. Reductions for children. Varied breakfast menu.

CHINLEY, Near Buxton. Mrs Barbara Goddard, Mossley House Farm, Maynestone Road, Chinley, High Peak SK23 6AH (Tel & Fax: 01663 750240). Working farm.

Enjoy a stay at our 150 acre hill farm situated in a Special Landscaped Area in the lovely Peak District. A traditional spacious farmhouse offering a high standard of comfort and hospitality. One family room en suite, one double room with private bathroom. Colour TV. Central heating. Children welcome. Village half a mile away. Ideal spot for a holiday. Open all year. Bed and Breakfast from £19. ETC ◆◆◆

DOVEDALE, Near Ashbourne. Margaret & Frank, St. Leonard's Cottage, Thorpe, Ashbourne DE6 2AW (01335 350224).

One of the oldest cottages in the village, St. Leonard's stands in its own grounds of one third of an acre, overlooking the village green, near to the entrance to Dovedale. Thorpe Cloud rises in the background. The village of Thorpe is ideally situated for touring in the Peak District with many historic houses easily reached. For walkers the Manifold Valley and Tissington Trail are close by, along with Carsington Water for fishing and sailing. The cottage is fully modernised but retains the original oak beams. Three bedrooms all en suite with tea/coffee facilities. Centrally heated throughout. Dining room and sitting room with colour TV. The cottage is open all day for guests. Sorry no pets and no smoking. Ample parking. Full Fire Certificate held. Bed & Breakfast from £20.00 per person.

FREE or REDUCED RATE entry to Holiday Visits and Attractions — see our READERS' OFFER VOUCHERS on pages 43-60

DOVEDALE, Mrs Joan Wain, Air Cottage Farm, Ilam, Ashbourne DE6 2DB (01335 350475). Working Farm, Join in. Holidaymakers to the Peak District will enjoy staying at Air Cottage Farm situated at the edge of Dovedale with picturesque views of Thorpe Cloud and Dovedale Valley. The famous Stepping Stones are just 10 minutes away and it is an ideal base for touring the Peak District National Park, stately homes and many other places of local historic interest. Unlimited walks in the Manifold Valley and the Tissington Nature Trail and scenic routes for motorists. Within easy reach of Alton Towers and Carsington Reservoir for water sports. Activities available include swimming, squash and horse riding, all within easy reach. Two double bedrooms and one single (sleeping two); bathroom, two toilets; sittingroom; diningroom. Cot and high chair provided for children. Open March to November. A car essential – parking. Terms and further details on request.

GLOSSOP. Graham and Julie Caesar, Windy Harbour Farm Hotel, Woodhead Road, Glossop SK13 7QE

(01457 853107). Situated in the heart of the Peak District on the B6105, approximately one mile from Glossop town centre and adjacent to the Pennine Way. Our 10-bedroom hotel with outstanding views of Woodhead and Snake Passes and the Longdendale Valley is an ideal location for all outdoor activities. A warm welcome awaits you in our licensed bar and restaurant serving a wide range of excellent home-made food. Bed and Breakfast from £18 per night singles to £40 per night family.

HARTINGTON. Mrs Jane Gibbs, Wolfscote Grange Farm, Hartington, Near Buxton SK17 0AX (01298

84342). A more beautiful setting would be hard to find – Wolfescote Grange nestling beside the Dove Valley with stunning scenery. The farmhouse, steeped in history, dates back to the Domesday Book and is full of fine oak. The lounge and well-appointed bedrooms have views of the hills enveloping the valley. Separate diningroom with antique fireplace and oak-mullioned window seat; pretty en suite bedrooms (one double, one twin/family and one single) with tea/coffee facilities. Fresh linen and towels welcome travellers; wake to the birds singing, the smell of fresh bread, and the beauty of the Peak District on the doorstep. Bed and Breakfast from £22 to £26. **ETC** ◆◆◆ e-mail: wolfscote@btinternet.com

KIRK LANGLEY. Mrs. Diane Buxton, New Park Farm, Lodge Lane, Kirk Langley DE6 4NX (01332

824262). Working farm. An early 19th century farmhouse situated seven miles from Ashbourne and four miles from Derby, within easy reach of Alton Towers and The American Adventure Park, Dovedale, Carsington Water, two miles from Kedleston Hall. Hotels and pubs are only a few miles away where good food is served. Accommodation consists of one double bedroom, one family bedroom and one twin bedroom, all with TV and tea/coffee making facilities. Parking is off road, close by the house. Situated in peaceful surroundings overlooking Kirk Langley Village and countryside. Bed and Breakfast from £14 per person. Reductions for children. Self-catering flat also available. Open all year. Write or telephone for details.

MATLOCK. Mrs D. Wootton, Old School Farm, Uppertown Lane, Uppertown, Ashover, Near Chesterfield S45 0JF (01246 590813). Working farm, join in. This working farm in a small hamlet on the edge of the Peak District enjoys unspoilt views. Ashover is three miles away and mentioned in the Domesday Book; Chatsworth House, Haddon Hall, Hardwick Hall, Matlock Bath and Bakewell all within seven miles. Accommodation comprises two family rooms with en suite facilities, one double, one single rooms. Washbasin in two of the rooms; shared bathroom for guests' use only. Plenty of hot water; fitted carpets; large livingroom/diningroom with colour TV. Car essential. No smoking in bedrooms. NO PETS. Disabled guests welcome. Children welcome. Open from April to October. Bed and Breakfast from £22 per person per night; Bed, Breakfast and Evening Meal £30 per person per night. Evening meal minimum two persons. Reductions for children. Take the B5057 Darley Dale Road off the A632 Chesterfield to Matlock main road. Take second left. Keep on this road for approximately one mile. Old School Farm is on left opposite the stone water trough. **ETC/RAC** ◆◆◆ *SPARKLING DIAMOND AWARD.*

MATLOCK. Mrs Linda Lomas, Middlehills Farm Bed and Breakfast, Grange Mill, Matlock DE4 4HY (01629 650368). We know the secret of contentment - we live in the most picturesque part of England. Share our good fortune, breathe the fresh air, absorb the peace, feast your eyes on the beautiful scenery that surrounds our small working farm, with our pot bellied pig who just loves to have her ears scratched, and Bess and Ruby who are ideal playmates for children of all ages. Retire with the scent of honeysuckle and waken to the aroma of freshly baked bread and sizzling bacon then sample the delights of the Peak District and Derbyshire Dales such as Dovedale, Chatsworth and Haddon Hall.

MELBOURNE near. Mrs Mary Kidd, Ivy House Farm, Stanton-by-Bridge, Near Melbourne DE73 1HT (Tel & Fax: 01332 863152). Working farm, join in. Ivy House Farm is a 400 acre arable farm with horses at livery. The farmhouse was built in the 17th century and has been 'open house' for bed and breakfast guests since 1992. We have now converted some cowsheds into chalets, all of which are en suite with tea/coffee making facilities and TV. Each chalet has a theme – Cowshed, Sheep Pen, Stable and Pigsty. The area has lots to do and see, such as Calke Abbey, ski slopes, Alton Towers, motor racing at Donington Park. There are also lots of places to eat. Children and pets are welcome, but we are strictly non- smoking. Ample off-road parking. Bed and Breakfast from £20.

DEVON

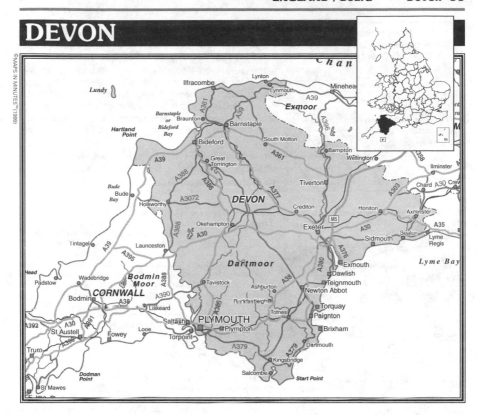

©MAPS IN MINUTES™ (1999)

ASHBURTON. Mrs Mary Lloyd-Williams, Hooks Cottage, Bickington, Near Ashburton TQ12 6JS (01626 821312). Situated in 12 acres of woods and fields in a very quiet and picturesque setting at the end of a long farm lane with lovely walks on the doorstep. Relax by the swimming pool or enjoy the river that runs through the property. Central for the areas many attractions, and the beaches and moors. Family suite for guests comprising double room and twin-bedded room with connecting bathroom, dining room, lounge, colour TV, tea making facilities. Excellent meals with fresh produce a speciality. Bed and Breakfast with optional Evening Meal. Children very welcome. Please ring for brochure.
e-mail: hookscottage@yahoo.com

ASHBURTON. Margaret Phipps, New Cott Farm, Poundsgate, Ashburton, Newton Abbot TQ13 7PD (Tel & Fax: 01364 631421). A friendly welcome, beautiful views, pleasing accommodation await you at New Cott in the Dartmoor National Park. Enjoy the freedom, peace and quiet of open moorland and the Dart Valley. Farm trail, birds and animals on the farm. Riding, golf, leisure centre locally. Bedrooms en suite, tea/coffee/chocolate, central heating. Ideal for less able guests, special diets catered for - lots of lovely homemade food. Bed and Breakfast from £18.50 Evening Dinner £11. Weekly reductions, short breaks welcome. Open all year. **AA QQQQ. ETC ◆◆◆◆**
e-mail: newcott@ruralink.co.uk
website: www.newcott-farm.co.uk

BAMPTON. Mrs Lindy Head, Harton Farm, Oakford, Tiverton EX16 9HH (01398 351209). Working farm, join in. Real farm holidays for country lovers. A unique rural experience for children and the chance to meet the animals on our traditional non-intensive farm near Exmoor. Tranquil 17th century stone farmhouse, secluded but accessible, ideal touring centre. Comfortable accommodation in three double bedrooms with washbasin and tea making facilities; luxury bathroom with a view; dining room serving real country cooking with farm-produced additive-free meat and organic vegetables; home baking a speciality; guests' lounge with colour TV. Home spun wool. Garden. Children over four welcome. Pets accepted. Car essential - parking. Open for Evening Meal, Bed and Breakfast from £24; Bed and Breakfast from £16. Reductions for children. Farm walks. Fishing, shooting, riding can be arranged. Vegetarian meals available on request.

BAMPTON. Mrs Anne Boldry, Newhouse Farm, Oakford, Tiverton EX16 9JE (01398 351347). Enjoy a real taste of country living at our 400 year old farmhouse on the edge of Exmoor. Choose between twin or double bedded rooms, thoughtfully furnished with all those extras - en suite bathrooms, tea and coffee trays, remote-control colour TV. Spend the day exploring this beautiful part of Devon; National Trust houses, thatched villages, country pubs, market towns, moors and coasts are all nearby. Come home to tea in the garden, and our award winning dinner if you wish. Featured in Good B & B Guide and Guide to Good Food in the West Country. B & B from £21, dinner £13, weekly reductions. Send for brochure. **AA ◆◆◆◆.**

BARNSTAPLE. Mrs Sheelagh Darling, Lee House, Marwood, Barnstaple EX31 4DZ (01271 374345). Stone-built Elizabethan Manor House dating back to 1256, standing in its own secluded gardens and grounds with magnificent views over rolling Devon countryside. James II ceilings, an Adam fireplace, antiques and the work of resident artist add interest. Easy access to coast and moor. Marwood Gardens one mile. Family-run, friendly and relaxing atmosphere. Walking distance to local pub with excellent food. Open April to October. One double, one twin room and one four-poster room, all en suite with colour TV and tea/coffee making facilities. Bed and Breakfast from £20. No children under 12 years. Well-behaved pets welcome.

Please mention The Farm Holiday Guide when writing to enquire about accommodation

BARNSTAPLE. Mr and Mrs D. Woodman, The Old Rectory, Challacombe, Barnstaple EX31 4TS (01598 763342).

Within the Exmoor National Park, easily accessible on a good road, The Old Rectory is tucked away peacefully on the edge of Challacombe. A glance at the map of North Devon will show how excellently the house is placed, either for touring the spectacular coastline or for walking on Exmoor. Superbly furnished bedrooms, with tea/coffee making equipment, washbasins and heating. Ample bathroom, toilet, shower facilities. Comfortable dining room, lounge with colour TV. Bed and Breakfast from £18 per night, from £120 per week. No VAT charge. Further particulars on request.

BARNSTAPLE near. Mrs J. Ley, West Barton, Alverdiscott, Near Barnstaple EX31 3PT (01271 858230).

Working farm. Our family run working farm of 250 acres is situated in a small rural village between Barnstaple and Torrington on the B3232. Ideal base for your holiday within easy reach of Exmoor or visiting our rugged coastline of many sandy beaches. Also Dartington Glass, RHS Rosemoor Gardens, Clovelly and many other beauty spots. West Barton farmhouse is situated beside the B3232 with panoramic views of the beautiful North Devon countryside. Children welcome with reductions. Comfortable accommodation family room, twin beds, single and double rooms available. Visitors' own lounge with colour TV. Dining room. Good farmhouse cooking including a variety of our own produce when available. Basic Food Hygiene Certificate. Regret no pets. Bed and Breakfast from £16; Evening Meal optional. Weekly terms on request.

BIDEFORD. Mrs S. Wade, Collaberie Farm, Welcombe, Bideford EX39 6HF (01288 331391).

Situated on Devon/Cornwall border. Modern farmhouse on 90 acre beef farm overlooking wooded valley to Atlantic Ocean. Just one-and-a-half miles from Welcombe Mouth, voted cleanest beach in Britain in 1993. Clovelly, Hartland Quay, Bideford, Westward Ho! and Bude all within easy reach. Two bedrooms (one family, one double) both with washbasin and tea/coffee making facilities; bathroom, toilet; lounge with colour TV, video; diningroom. Children welcome - high chair, cot; babysitting usually available. Open all year except Christmas. Fire Certificate held. Bed and Breakfast from £17. Evening meal optional. Reductions for children.

BIDEFORD near. Mrs Yvonne Heard, West Titchberry Farm, Hartland, Near Bideford EX39 6AU (01237 441 287). Working farm, join in.

Spacious, completely renovated 17th century farmhouse, carpeted and well appointed throughout. One family room with washbasin, one double room with washbasin and one twin room; all with tea/coffee facilities and radio. Bathroom and toilet, separate shower room. Downstairs lounge with colour TV; diningroom where excellent home cooking is served using fresh produce whenever possible. A games room and sheltered walled garden are available for guests' use. The easily accessible coastal footpath winds its way around this 150 acre mixed farm situated between Hartland Lighthouse and the National Trust beauty spot of Shipload Bay. Hartland three miles, Clovelly six miles, Bideford and Westward Ho! 15 miles, Bude 18 miles. Children welcome at reduced rates; cot, high chair and babysitting available. Open all year except Christmas. Sorry no pets. Bed and Breakfast from £16.00 per person per night; Evening Meal (optional) £8.00. Reduced weekly terms available. Also self-catering cottage available (3 Keys COMMENDED).

PLEASE SEND A STAMPED ADDRESSED ENVELOPE WITH ENQUIRIES

BRAUNTON. Mrs Roselyn Bradford, "St. Merryn", Higher Park Road, Braunton EX33 2LG (01271

813805). Set in beautiful, sheltered garden of approximately one acre, with many peaceful sun traps. Ros extends a warm welcome to her guests. Rooms (£20 per person) include single, double and family rooms, with washbasin, central heating, colour TV and tea/coffee making facilities. All rooms either en suite or with private bathrooms. Evening meal (£12) may be served indoors or out. Guests may bring own wine. Guest lounge with colour TV, patio door access to garden. Swimming pool, fish ponds, hens and thatched summerhouse plus excellent parking. Self-catering flat also available. Please send for brochure.

CHERITON BISHOP. Mrs N.M. Stephens, Horselake Farm, Cheriton Bishop, Exeter EX6 6HD (Tel & Fax:

01647 24220). Horselake Farm offers unique accommodation in a lovely 16th century Grade II Listed Tudor farmhouse. Set in beautiful gardens with outside heated swimming pool. Owner runs an Arabian horse stud and fruit farm. The accommodation comprises three rooms – one four-poster, one en suite and a twin room; all have washbasin, TV and tea/coffee making facilities. Central heating, log fires in winter. Children welcome. Bed and Breakfast from £18 to £22 per person.

CHULMLEIGH. Mrs S. Weeks, Great Burridge Farm, Chawleigh, Chulmleigh EX18 7HY (01363 83818).

A warm welcome awaits you in this picturesque, thatched farmhouse set in the stunning, wooded valley of the Little Dart River, on the beautiful Ridge and Valley walk. Pretty, centrally heated, en suite bedrooms, cosy sittingroom and secluded garden. Bed and Breakfast from £20; Bed and Breakfast and Evening Meal from £30.

COLYTON. Mrs Norma Rich, Sunnyacre, Northleigh, Colyton EX24 6DA (01404 871422). Working

farm, join in. A warm and friendly welcome awaits you. Come and enjoy a relaxing holiday on our working farm, which is set in an area of outstanding natural beauty amongst the rolling hills of East Devon. Children may help with animal feeding, includes calves, chickens, ducks, lambs etc., and collect the free range eggs for their breakfast (adults are welcome to help as well!). There is a Full English Breakfast. Fresh and mainly homegrown produce is used to make excellent and varied Evening Meals. Sweets are all homemade and served with clotted cream. Early Morning Tea. Evening drinks. Three bedrooms with washbasin, seperate w.c. TV in lounge, games room, sun room, Wendy house, sandpit. Cot and high chair available. Please enquire for reasonable rates.

COLYTON. Mrs Maggie Todd, Smallicombe Farm, Northleigh, Colyton, EX24 6BU (01404 831310).

Featured in 1998 'Guide to Good Food in the West Country'. Come and escape the stress to an idyllic rural setting, little changed since chronicled in the Domesday Book. Meet our friendly farm animals. Taste real pork from rare breed pigs. Explore this unspoilt corner of Devon with an abundance of wildlife, yet be close to the coast. Watch the buzzards soar overhead and try to spot the shy roe deer and badgers emerging from the wood. All rooms en suite, one ground floor. From £18.50 per night Bed and Breakfast. Reductions for children and weekly. Evening meals available. Open all year. **ETC ◆◆◆.**
website: www.smoothhound.co.uk/hotels/smallico.html

COLYTON. Bonehayne Farm, Colyton EX24 6SG. Working farm. Enjoy a relaxing holiday, deep in the tranquil Devon countryside, on a 250-acre working farm. Situated on the banks of the River Coly, ideal for trout fishing, or spot a kingfisher in a beautiful sheltered valley. Two miles from Colyton and four-and-a-half miles from coast, is situated our spacious self-catering cottage. It is part of the farmhouse (south-facing), with many olde worlde features, and is fully equipped, including a four-poster. There are also two luxury caravans, each on its own site (south-facing), situated in the farmhouse's spacious garden. They are well-equipped; laundry room, barbecue, picnic tables and chairs. Bed and Breakfast also available. Details from **Mrs S. Gould (01404 871416) or Mrs R. Gould (01404 871396).**
e-mail: thisfarm33@netscapeonline.co.uk
website: www.members.netscapeonline.co.uk/thisfarm33

CREDITON. Mrs M Reed, Hayne Farm, Cheriton Fitzpaine, Crediton EX17 4HR (01363 866392). Guests are welcome to our 17th century working beef and sheep farm, situated between Cadeleigh and Cheriton Fitzpaine. Exeter nine miles, Tiverton eight miles. South and North coast, Exmoor and Dartmoor within easy reach. Three local pubs nearby. Good farm fayre. Fishing lake; summer house overlooking duck pond. Bed and Breakfast from £18, reduction for children. **ETC ◆**.

CREDITON. Mrs Janet Bradford, Oaklands, Black Dog, Crediton EX17 4QJ (01884 860645). Janet and Ivor warmly welcome you to enjoy a relaxing stay, long or short, in peaceful surroundings with lovely views and countryside walks. Large comfortable bedrooms with en suite, tea/coffee facilities, colour TV and central heating. Large guest lounge with Sky TV and open fire in winter. Large garden with surrounding 20 acres of farmland where guests are free to wander. Walking distance of the 17th century Black Dog Inn pub/restaurant. Oaklands is situated between Dartmoor and Exmoor, ideal for touring all parts of Devon. Bed and Breakfast from £18. Reductions for children. Open all year.

CREDITON. Mrs S. Pugsley, Great Park Farm, Crediton EX17 3PR (01363 772050). A warm welcome awaits at this Listed farmhouse. Outstanding views and country walks within a peaceful location. Easy walking distance of town and leisure facilities. Delightfully furnished rooms, all with colour TV and tea/coffee making facilities. One en suite. Beautifully decorated TV lounge for you to relax. Over all, property has a peaceful ambience of the highest standard. Bed and Breakfast: single room from £17, double room from £32. **ETC ◆◆**
e-mail: susan@pugsley40freeserve.co.uk

CULLOMPTON. Mrs Diane Pring, Lower Ford Farm, Cullompton EX15 1LX (01884 252354).Working farm, join in. A warm and friendly welcome awaits you at our 15th century farmhouse, set in a peaceful unspoilt valley, three miles from Tiverton, Cullompton, M5/J28. Guests can enjoy a relaxed family holiday in our 300 acre working farm. Excellent farmhouse cooking and special diets welcome. Diningroom, lounge with colour TV, games room and all bedrooms have washbasin and en suite, tea/coffee facilities. Children welcome. Open all year except Christmas. Bed, Breakfast and Evening Meal from £28.50 daily. From £188 weekly.

CULLOMPTON. Mrs Margaret Chumbley, Oburnford Farm, Cullompton EX15 1LZ (01884 32292).

Working farm, join in. Treat yourself to a "special break" and enjoy our welcoming friendly family atmosphere. Mentioned in the Domesday Book, Oburnford is a dairy farm where guests may watch the milking and the making of clotted cream. The Listed Georgian farmhouse is set in large gardens, and is ideally situated for the coasts, Exmoor, Dartmoor, coarse fishing and several National Trust properties. Cullompton (M5 J28) two-and-a-half miles. The spacious en suite bedrooms all have tea/coffee facilities; the guest lounge has a colour television; separate dining room. Generous farmhouse hospitality, licensed, full menu, four-course evening meals and fresh clotted cream all make for a perfect relaxing break at anytime of the year. Special diets welcome. Bed and Breakfast £19. Bed, Breakfast and Evening Meal £190 per week. Phone now "free wine", "free child". Open all year.

DARTMOUTH. Mrs Jane Reeves, New Barn Farm, Dartmouth TQ6 0NH (01803 832410). New Barn is

a 200-year-old working sheep farm, we also keep rare breed poultry. Set in a quiet valley yet only five minutes drive from the ancient port of Dartmouth, and close to Blackpool and Slapton Sands. Within easy reach of Dartmoor National Park, National Trust Properties and specialist plant nurseries. We offer hearty farmhouse breakfasts and comfortable bedrooms. Twin, double and family with tea and coffee makiing facilities. Guests are welcome to spend time in our lovely garden, full of birds, where badgers feed at night and can be watched from the house. Ample safe parking. Bed and Breakfast from £18 per person.

DARTMOUTH. Mrs Stella Buckpitt, Middle Wadstray, Blackawton, Totnes TQ9 7DD (01803

712346). Cosy Devon Longhouse on working farm. About one mile from Woodlands Leisure Park and Dartmouth Golf Club, four miles from Dartmouth or beaches, and easy reach of Torbay, Salcombe and Dartmoor. Farm walks and large garden with stream and lake with small boat for guest use. Children spend hours paddling and fishing in the stream for tadpoles, pond skaters etc. Bring your wellies and have fun anytime of the year Enjoy some evenings playing scrabble, puzzles or board games. Regret no pets or smoking indoors. Family and single rooms with private shower room and toilet, double and twin room with private bathroom. Bed and full English Breakfast daily from £17.50. Reductions for children and longer stays. See also details of cottage in Self-Catering section. Grid Ref. SX824 513.

DARTMOUTH. John and Chris Drew, Blackdown Farm, Washbourne, Dartmouth TQ9 7DN (01803

712396). Our recently extended and renovated Devon farmhouse is in a peaceful area near Dartmouth, Toynes and beaches. We have three spacious, light, letting rooms with good quality en suite. Tea/coffee tray and television in all rooms. The large sittingroom is for your use with log fires when the evenings draw in. Traditional breakfast is served in the livingroom which opens onto the lawns and pond. We like you to relax and enjoy a flexible stay. Walk over our fields and enjoy "patchwork Devon" scenery. Bed and Breakfast from £20 per person, discount for longer stays. Please telephone for a brochure. No smoking in Farmhouse please.

Please mention *The Farm Holiday Guide* when making enquiries about accommodation featured in these pages.

EAST PRAWLE. Mrs Linda Tucker, Welle House, East Prawle, Kingsbridge, Devon TQ7 2BU (01548 511531). Working farm. Welle House is part of a working mixed farm situated in the most southerly point of Devon's beautiful, unspoilt coastline. The house is in a quiet location with ample safe parking, a large garden with plenty of grass for games and views towards the village of East Prawle and the sea. All rooms (two double, one twin and one family) have en suite facilities and central heating. Access at all times and guests' lounge with colour TV and log fire. Help yourself to tea and coffee at any time. Flexible meal times. Children most welcome. Regret no pets. Good pubs within easy walking distance. Bed and Breakfast from £15.

EXETER. Mrs Dudley, Culm Vale Guest House, Stoke Canon, Exeter EX5 4EG (Tel & Fax: 01392 841615; Mobile: 07974 707296). A fine old country house of great charm and character, giving the best of both worlds as we are only three miles to the north of the Cathedral city of Exeter, with its antique shops, yet situated in the heart of Devon's beautiful countryside on the edge of the pretty village of Stoke Canon. An ideal touring centre. Our spacious comfortable Bed and Breakfast accommodation includes full English breakfast, colour TV, tea/coffee facilities, washbasin and razor point in all rooms, some with bathrooms en suite. Full central heating. Our lovely gardens boast a beautiful swimming pool and there is ample free parking. Bed and Breakfast £15 to £25 per person per night according to room and season. Credit cards accepted.

EXETER. Mrs Heather Glanvill, Holbrook Farm, Clyst Honiton, Exeter EX5 2HR (Tel & Fax: 01392 367000). Our dairy farm is pleasantly situated in a quiet location one mile between the Sidmouth A3052 and A30. The spacious en suite rooms are furnished to a high standard with TV and hot drinks facilities, enjoying beautiful views. Guests have their own key and entrance, access unrestricted. Treat yourself to our freshly prepared breakfast using local produce, separate tables. The historic city of Exeter, spectacular East Devon coastline and Dartmoor are close at hand. At the end of your day relax and enjoy one of our tasty suppers or visit one of the excellent pubs nearby. Bed and Breakfast £19 to £21. **ETC/AA** ◆◆◆◆.
e-mail: heatherglanvill@holbrookfarm.co.uk
website: www.holbrookfarm.co.uk

FREE or REDUCED RATE entry to
Holiday Visits and Attractions — see our
READERS' OFFER VOUCHERS on pages 43-60

EXETER. Joyce Dicker, Moor Farm, Dunsford, Exeter EX6 7DP (01647 24292). Working farm.

The farmhouse is quietly situated on the edge of Dartmoor, in the area where "Down To Earth" was filmed. The guests have their own wing of the farmhouse, ideal for all ages. Good quality food is served. One double room, one family room, each with tea/coffee facilities. Open March-October. **ETC** ◆

EXETER. Karen Williams, Stile Farm, Starcross, Exeter EX6 8PD (Tel & Fax: 01626 890268). Enjoy a peaceful break in beautiful countryside. Close to the Exe Estuary and only two miles to the nearest sandy beach. Take a stroll to the village (only-half-a-mile) to discover many eating places, or a little further to some specially recommended ones. Birdwatching, golf, fishing, racing, etc. all nearby, and centrally situated for exploring all the lovely countryside and coastline in the area. Good shopping in Exeter. Comfortable rooms, guests' lounge, English breakfast. Nice garden. Plenty of parking. NON-SMOKING. Personal service and a 'home from home' atmosphere guaranteed. Bed and Breakfast from £16 per person per night, £105 weekly.

EXETER. Mrs Sally Glanvill, Rydon Farm, Woodbury, Exeter EX5 1LB (01395 232341). Working farm. Come, relax and enjoy yourself in our lovely 16th century Devon longhouse. We offer a warm and friendly family welcome at this peaceful dairy farm. Three miles from M5 Junction 30 on B3179. Ideally situated for exploring the coast, moors and the historic city of Exeter. Only 10 minutes' drive from the coast. Inglenook fireplace and oak beams. All bedrooms have central heating, private or en suite bathrooms, hair dryers and tea/coffee making facilities. One room with romantic four-poster. A traditional farmhouse breakfast is served with free range eggs and there are several excellent pubs and restaurants close by. Pets by arrangement. Farm Holiday Bureau member. Open all year. Colour brochure available. Bed and Breakfast from £24 to £27. **ETC/AA** ◆◆◆◆

GITTISHAM. Christine and Alan Broom, Catshayes Farm, Gittisham, Honiton EX14 3EA (Tel & Fax: 01404 850302). Countryside lovers will enjoy peace and tranquillity in our 15th century thatched Devon Longhouse. Working dairy farm surrounded by unspoilt rural landscape, amid quiet country lanes. Near charming thatched village, ancient church, woodland walks, abundance of wildlife. Three miles Honiton, established centre for antiques, Honiton lace, golf course and markets stalls lining the streets Tuesdays and Saturdays. Seven miles Sidmouth beach, 10 miles Exeter Airport, 15 miles Cathedral City of Exeter. Farmhouse cooking, spacious bedrooms, log fires, oak beams; shooting and riding by arrangement. Studio nearby offering creative and personal development workshops. Evening meals available. Children welcome. Open all year. **ETC** ◆◆

HOLSWORTHY. Mrs C. A. Chant, The Barton, Pancrasweek, Holsworthy EX22 7JT (01288 381315). A peaceful holiday awaits you on our 200 acre working cattle farm situated on the Devon/Cornwall border. Six miles from Cornish coast with quaint fishing villages, beautiful beaches and famous Clovelly. Fishing, sailing, sailboarding at Tamar Lakes, also close to leisure pool and sports centre. Historic Dartmoor and Bodmin Moor within easy reach. The 16th century farmhouse has three bedrooms for guests - two double and one twin, all en suite with tea making facilities. Lounge with TV, separate diningroom. Traditional farmhouse cooking with home grown produce when available. Open Easter to end September. Bed and Breakfast from £19; Evening Meal £8.50.

HONITON. Pamela Boyland, Barn Park Farm, Stockland Hill, Near Stockland, Honiton EX14 9JA

(Tel & Fax: 01404 861297; Freephone: 0800 328 2605). Barn Park Farm is a working dairy farm situated one-and-a-half miles off A30/A303 junction, road sign marked Axminster/ Stockland. Within reach of many beauty spots. Coast nine miles. Traditional farmhouse breakfasts using eggs from our free-range hens. Barn Park farm has en suite/private bathrooms. All bedrooms having beverage tray (TV on request). The farmhouse is brimming with character with a homely atmosphere. We are open all year except Christmas Day. TV Lounge, quiet sittingroom. Ground floor bedroom by arrangement. Bed and Breakfast from £16. Evening meal if required, £9. No smoking in the house please. website: www.stockland.cx

HONITON. Mrs Elizabeth Tucker, Lower Luxton Farm, Upottery, Honiton EX14 9PB (01823 601269).

Working farm. If you are looking for a quiet, peaceful and relaxing holiday, come to Lower Luxton Farm, where a warm and friendly welcome awaits you. Situated in an area of outstanding natural beauty in the centre of the Blackdown Hills, overlooking the Otter Valley. Ideal centre for touring. Carp and tench fishing in our farm pond. Olde worlde farmhouse with inglenook and beams, fully modernised and offering family, double or twin rooms with tea/coffee making facilities, TV, en suite/private bathroom. Good home cooking assured and plenty of it! Bed and Breakfast from £16 per night. Weekly Bed and Breakfast with six Evening Dinners from £130 per week. Children and pets welcome. Open all year. SAE, or telephone, for our brochure.

HONITON near. Mrs M Bennett, Lane End Farm, Broadhembury Honiton EX14 0LU (Tel & Fax: 01404

841563). A warm welcome awaits you at Lane End, a working family farm, set in a beautiful river valley with an abundance of colourful wild flowers and varied wildlife, in an area designated as "Outstanding Natural Beauty".A bridle path meanders through the farm and takes you to the village centre with thatched cob cottages. There are many footpaths and walks giving a unique opportunity to see the Devon countryside at its best. The accommodation consists of two en suite family or double rooms and a twin room. All bedrooms have tea and coffee making facilities, clock radio; colour TV and video in lounge and full central heating. Delicious home cooking consisting of traditional full English breakfast, with an optional evening meal. **ETC ◆◆◆**.

IVYBRIDGE near. Mrs Susan Winzer, "The Bungalow", Higher Coarsewell Farm, Ugborough, Near

Ivybridge PL21 0HP (01548 821560). Working farm. Higher Coarsewell Farm is part of a traditional family-run dairy farm situated in the heart of the peaceful South Hams countryside, near Dartmoor and local unspoilt sandy beaches. It is a very spacious bungalow with beautiful garden and meadow views. One double room with bathroom en suite and one en suite family room. Guest lounge/dining room. Good home cooked food, full English breakfast served. Children welcome - cot, high chair and babysitting available. Bed and Breakfast from £16 daily; optional Evening Meal extra. Open all year. A3121 turn-off from the main A38 Exeter to Plymouth road.

KINGSBRIDGE. Mrs M. Darke, Coleridge Farm, Chillington, Kingsbridge TQ7 2JG (01548 580274).

Coleridge Farm is a 600 acre working farm situated half-a-mile from Chillington village, midway between Kingsbridge and Dartmouth. Many safe and beautiful beaches are within easy reach, the nearest being Slapton Sands and Slapton Ley just two miles away. Plymouth, Torquay and the Dartmoor National Park are only an hour's drive. Visitors are assured of comfortable accommodation in a choice of one double and one twin-bedded rooms; private shower; toilet; shaver points and tea/coffee making facilities. Spacious lounge with TV. A variety of eating establishments in the locality will ensure a good value evening meal. Children welcome. Small dogs by arrangement. Terms on request.

KINGSBRIDGE. Mrs Angela Foale, Higher Kellaton Farm, Kellaton, Kingsbridge TQ7 2ES (Tel & Fax 01548 511514). Working farm. Smell the fresh sea air, delicious Aga-cooked breakfast in the comfort of this lovely old farmhouse. Nestled in a valley, our farm with friendly animals welcomes you. Spacious, well-furnished rooms, en suite, colour TVs, tea/coffee making facilities, own lounge, central heating and log fires. Flexible meal times. Attractive walled garden. Safe car parking. Situated between Kingsbridge and Dartmouth. Visit Salcombe by ferry. One-and-a-half miles to the lost village of Hallsands and Lanacombe Beach. Beautiful, peaceful, unspoilt coastline with many sandy beaches, paths, wild flowers and wildlife. Ramblers' haven. Good pubs and wet-weather family attractions. Open Easter to October. Non-smoking. B & B from £16.50 .**ETC** ◆◆◆.

e-mail: higherkellatonfarm@agriplus.net
website: www.welcometo/higherkellaton

KINGSBRIDGE. Mrs J. Robinson, Coombe Farm, Kingsbridge TQ7 2JG (01548 852038). Come and enjoy the peace and beauty of Devon in our lovely 16th century farmhouse. Coombe Farm occupies a quiet valley position just one mile from Kingsbridge. It is a family-run farm offering Bed and Breakfast accommodation. Wonderful breakfast, large elegant rooms all en suite and having colour TV, hot drinks facilities. Artists have use of an art studio and fishermen can enjoy the well known Coombe Water fishery (coarse). Open April to October. Bed & Breakfast from £22.50. **ETC** ◆◆◆◆.

KINGSBRIDGE (Near). Mrs M. Newsham, Marsh Mills, Aveton Gifford, Kingsbridge TQ7 4JW (Tel & Fax: 01548 550549). Georgian Mill House, overlooking the River Avon, with mill pond, mill leat and duck pond. Small farm with friendly animals. Peaceful and secluded, just off A379, Kingsbridge four miles, Plymouth 17 miles. Bigbury and Bantham with their beautiful sandy beaches nearby, or enjoy a walk along our unspoilt river estuary, or the miles of beautiful South Devon coastal paths. We are only eight miles from Dartmoor. One double and one double/twin room, both en suite with colour TV; other rooms have washbasin, and there is a guest bathroom with additional separate WC. All bedrooms have tea/coffee making facilities and room heaters. Guests have their own lounge/dining room with colour TV. Beautiful gardens, ample car parking. Bed and Breakfast from £18 per night. Phone, fax or SAE for brochure or enquiries.

e-mail: Newsham@Marshmills.co.uk
website: www.Marshmills.co.uk

MORETONHAMPSTEAD. Mrs T.M. Merchant, Great Sloncombe Farm, Moretonhampstead TQ13 8QF (01647 440595). Working farm. Share the magic of Dartmoor all year round while staying in our lovely 13th century farmhouse full of interesting historical features. A working dairy farm set amongst peaceful meadows and woodland abundant in wild flowers and animals, including badgers, foxes, deer and buzzards. A welcoming and informal place to relax and explore the moors and Devon countryside. Comfortable double and twin rooms with en suite facilities, TV, central heating and coffee/tea making facilities. Delicious Devonshire suppers and breakfasts with new baked bread. Open all year. No smoking. Farm Holiday Bureau member. **ETC** ◆◆◆◆ *SILVER AWARD*. **AA** ◆◆◆◆.

NEWTON ABBOT near. Mrs Angela Dallyn, Bulleigh Park, Ipplepen, Near Newton Abbot TQ12 5UA

(Tel and Fax: 01803 872254). A warm welcome awaits you at this family farm, with prize-winning pedigree Aberdeen Angus cattle and ponies. In a delightful rural setting with superb panoramic views of the tranquil Devon countryside, but centrally located for Torbay, Totnes, Dartmoor, the coast, also sporting facilities: golf (one-and -a-half miles), tennis, bowling, Newton Abbot races plus many local attractions. The beautiful, spacious farmhouse accommodation consists of a double/twin/family en suite and a pretty double room with a balcony and guest bathroom with separate toilet. Both rooms have beverage facilities, colour TV, clock radio alarms and basins with shaver points. Lounge with colour Ceefax TV, Baby Grand piano and open fire. Lovely Edwardian Conservatory. Excellent farmhouse breakfast, with local home-made produce whenever possible and preserves. Special diets a speciality. Good restaurant, pubs nearby, one within walking distance. Ample parking. Large secluded garden. Central heating. Open all year. Self-catering available. Tea/coffee with home-made cakes on arrival. AA AND GUESTACCOM RECOMMENDED.

NORTH TAWTON. Mrs J. Pyle, Lower Nichols Nymet Farm, Lower Nichols Nymet, North Tawton,

Devon EX20 2BW (Tel & Fax: 01363 82510). Jane and David Pyle welcome you to their home. We offer a haven of comfort and rest on our 180 acre farm. It is set in rolling countryside in the centre of Devon, just north of Dartmoor. On holiday, food becomes important, we serve hearty and healthy breakfasts and candle-lit dinners using local produce. Our elegantly furnished en suite bedrooms have glorious views. There are many National Trust properties and other attractions to visit. This is a perfect base for exploring the beauties of the south west. A non-smoking establishment. Brochure available. Bed and Breakfast from £20. Open Easter to October inclusive. .

OKEHAMPTON. Mrs Jenny King, Higher Cadham Farm, Jacobstowe, Okehampton EX20 3RB (01837

851647). Working farm. 139 acre beef and sheep farm just off the A3072, five miles from Dartmoor. 16th century farmhouse with barn conversions offering a total of nine rooms, five en suite, the rest have washbasin, shaver point, etc., with bathroom and toilets close by. Two of the four lounges are non-smoking as is the diningroom. The accommodation is of the highest standard with plenty of hearty Devonshire food, a residential licence and a warm welcome. Babies and dogs are accepted by arrangement only but older children are very welcome. We have farm walks, ducks on the ponds and other animals to amuse all the family. Walkers on the Tarka Trail are fully catered for with drying room, packed lunches, etc. AA QQQQ Selected and DATI Warmest Welcome Award 1992 has helped make Higher Cadham Farm the "place to stay" when in West Devon. Bed and Breakfast from £18.50; Dinner £12. Weekly from £190; supplement for en suite rooms. Member of Farm Holiday Bureau. AA Landlady of the Year Top 20 Finalist, 1998. **ETC** ◆◆◆◆.
e-mail: jenny@highercadham.freeserve.co.uk
website: www.internetsouthwest.co.uk/highercadham

OKEHAMPTON. Mrs Rosemary Ward, Parsonage Farm, Iddesleigh EX19 8SN (01837 810318).

A warm welcome awaits you in our period farmhouse, home of the famous Parson Jack Russell, situated approximately one mile from the picturesque village of Iddesleigh and three miles from the market town of Hatherleigh. The Tarka Trail passes through our farmyard, with fishing available on the farm boundary. An ideal base from which to explore Dartmoor, Exmoor and coastlines. Accommodation consists of one family room and one double room, both en suite with tea/coffee making facilities and colour TV. Bed and Breakfast from £20 per person per night. Open Easter to October. No smoking or pets. Reductions for children. **ETC** ◆◆◆◆ SILVER AWARD

PLYMOUTH. Mrs Margaret MacBean, Gabber Farm, Down Thomas, Plymouth PL9 0AW (01752 862269). Working farm, join in. Come and join us on this 120 acre working farm in an area of outstanding natural beauty with lovely walks on the farm and coastline. It is ideally situated for touring and near the historic city of Plymouth. Good food and a warm welcome are assured with Bed and Breakfast or Bed, Breakfast and Evening Meal available. One double and one family room en suite, two twin and a family room with washbasins. All have tea/coffee making facilities and clock radio. Iron, ironing board, hairdryer available. TV lounge, diningroom. Fire Certificate. Bed and Breakfast from £16.50. Special rates for Senior Citizens and children. Brochure available on request.

SIDMOUTH. Mrs Betty S. Sage, Pinn Barton, Peak Hill, Sidmouth EX10 0NN (Tel & Fax: 01395 514004). A warm welcome awaits you at Pinn Barton a 330 acre working farm set peacefully just off the coastal road, only two miles from the sea front at Sidmouth. Safe, clean beaches and lovely cliff walks. All bedrooms have bathroom en suite; colour TV; central heating; free hot drinks facilities; electric blankets. Children very welcome. Ample parking. Reductions for children sharing parents' room. Open all year. Guests have their own keys. Bed and breakfast from £20 to £22. Please contact Mrs Betty Sage for more details. **ETC** ◆◆◆◆

SIDMOUTH. Mrs Elizabeth Tancock, Lower Pinn Farm, Peak Hill, Sidmouth EX10 0NN (01395 513733). Working farm. Lower Pinn is in an area of outstanding natural beauty, two miles west off the unspoilt coastal resort of Sidmouth and one mile to the east of the pretty village of Otterton. Comfortable, spacious en suite rooms with colour TV, hot drink facilities, electric blankets and central heating. Guests have their own keys and may return at all times throughout the day. Ample parking. Substantial breakfast served in dining room. Local inns and restaurants nearby provide excellent evening meals. Children and pets welcome. Open all year. Bed and Breakfast from £20 to £23. Full details on request. **ETC** ◆◆◆◆

SIDMOUTH. Kerstin Farmer, Higher Coombe Farm, Tipton St John, Sidmouth EX10 0AX (Tel & Fax: 01404 813385). Find a warm, friendly welcome and comfortable, fully equipped rooms in our Victorian farmhouse, family owned since 1913. We offer total relaxation and a superb breakfast, using local produce. After exploring East Devon's towns and villages, rolling countryside and beaches, take tea on the patio overlooking mature garden. Ideal for families. Easily reached, four miles inland from Sidmouth seafront. One family, one single and two double rooms (one with en suite shower). Bed & Breakfast £18 - £22 per person per day, half price for children in family room. Open March to December. **ETC** ◆◆◆
e-mail: KerstinFarmer@farming.co.uk
website:www.SmoothHound.co.uk/hotels/higherco

SIDMOUTH. Mrs B.I. Tucker, Goosemoor Farm, Newton Poppleford, Sidmouth EX10 0BL (01395 568279). Goosemoor Farmhouse is an old Devon Long House with a bread oven in the dining room. The 25-acre mixed farm is on the Exeter - Lyme Regis bus route, about four miles from the sea, and has streams running through its meadows. There are many delightful walks in country lanes, or over Woodberry and Alsbeare Commons. Guests may wander freely on the farmland. Coarse fishing available also. There are two double and one family rooms, all with washbasins; two bathrooms, three toilets; sitting room; dining room. Open all year with log fires. Central heating throughout. Car not essential, but there is parking. Also self-catering available- two bedrooms, sleeps five. Own entrance. Bed and Breakfast from £15. Cream teas also available.

SOUTH MOLTON near. Messrs H.J. Milton, Partridge Arms Farm, Yeo Mill, West Anstey, Near South Molton EX36 3NU (01398 341217; Fax: 01398 341569).

Now a working farm of over 200 acres, four miles west of Dulverton, "Partridge Arms Farm" was once a coaching inn and has been in the same family since 1906. Genuine hospitality and traditional farmhouse fare await you. Comfortable accommodation in double, twin and single rooms, some of which have en suite facilities. There is also an original four-poster bedroom. Children welcome. Animals by arrangement. Residential licence. Open all year. Fishing and riding available nearby. Bed and Breakfast from £21.00 to £26.50; Evening Meal from £10.00. Farm Holiday Guide Diploma Winner.

STOKEINTEIGNHEAD (Near Torquay). Mrs R. Wilkinson, Deane Thatch Accommodation, Stokeinteignhead, Near Torquay TQ12 4QU (Tel & Fax: 01626 873724).

A charming thatched Devonshire cob cottage, and thatched cob Linhay. Situated in a secluded rural spot enjoying uninterrupted views of farmland with an atmosphere of total tranquillity. Half-a-mile from the village of Stokeinteignhead and just one mile from the sea. Ideally situated for Torquay (the English Riviera) and Dartmoor National Park. All rooms have colour TV, private bathroom, shower or bidet and tea/coffee making facilities; king-size bed in Linhay. Children welcome, reduced rates and babysitting available. Open all year. Bed and Breakfast from £20, discounts for weekly rate. Brittany Ferries recommended. ETC ◆◆◆
e-mail:deanethatch@hotmail.com
websites: http://come.to/deanethatch
www.ukchoice.net/17/deanethatch.htm

TAVISTOCK. Hilary Tucker, Beera Farm, Milton Abbot, Tavistock PL19 8PL (Tel & Fax: 01822 870216).

Beera is a working farm on the river Tamar, providing an ideal base for touring Devon and Cornwall. Visit the north and south coasts with rugged cliffs, sandy beaches and quaint fishing villages, Saltram House where 'Sense and Sensibility' was filmed and many other National Trust properties nearby. Play golf, walk the Tamar Trail and the farm and admire the beautiful scenery; off-road driving, archery, clay pigeon shooting can be arranged. Enjoy excellent evening meals using local and home grown produce. Packed lunches available. Two doubles, one twin all en suite with tea/coffee, central heating, clock/radios, hair dryers. Brochure available. Children welcome. Open all year. Bed and Breakfast from £20, Evening Meal from £10.50. ETC ◆◆◆◆
email: robert.tucker@farming.co.uk

TEIGN VALLEY. S. and G. Harrison-Crawford, Silver Birches, Teign Valley, Trusham, Newton Abbot TQ13 0NJ (01626 852172).

A warm welcome awaits you at Silver Birches, a comfortable bungalow at the edge of Dartmoor. A secluded, relaxing spot with two acre garden running down to river. Only two miles from A38 on B3193. Exeter 14 miles, sea 12 miles. Car advisable. Ample parking. Excellent pubs and restaurants nearby. Good centre for fishing, bird watching, forest walks, golf, riding; 70 yards salmon/trout fishing free to residents. Centrally heated guest accommodation with separate entrance. Two double bedded rooms, one twin bedded room, all with own bath/shower, toilet. Guest lounge with colour TV. Diningroom, sun lounge overlooking river. Sorry, no children under eight. Terms including tea on arrival - Bed and full English Breakfast from £25 per person per night, £168 weekly. Evening Meal optional. Open all year. Self catering caravans also available from £135.

TIVERTON. Mr & Mrs B. Reader, Lodgehill Farm Hotel, Tiverton EX16 5PA (01884 251200; Fax: 01884

242090). In a peaceful setting off the A396, just one mile south of Tiverton, overlooking the beautiful Exe valley. Each en suite bedroom is individually furnished with TV, radio and telephone, and is non-smoking. The bar is well stocked and equipped with ash trays! For evening meals, we have a modest wine list and a comfortable diningroom. Dinner is informal and local produce is the main ingredient. Easy access from Tiverton–Bickleigh road, 400 metres up a private drive. Lodge Hill Farm is no longer a working farm but is still shown on OS maps. It enjoys the solitude of an old farmhouse with the convenience of a hotel. Why not relax with the Readers!
e-mail: lodgehill@dial.pipex.com
website: www.lodgehill.co.uk

TIVERTON. Mrs L Arnold, The Mill, Lower Washfield, Tiverton EX16 9PD (01884 255297). A warm

welcome awaits you at our newly converted mill, beautifully situated on the banks of the picturesque River Exe. Wonderful views to the National Trust's Knightshayes Court and on the route of the Exe Valley Way. Easy access to both the north and south coasts, Exmoor and Dartmoor. Only two-and-a-half miles from the market town of Tiverton. Relaxing and friendly atmosphere with delicious farmhouse fare. En suite bedrooms with tea/coffee making facilities. Bed and Breakfast from £17.

TORQUAY. Peter and Carol White, Braddon Hall Hotel, Braddons Hill Road East, Torquay TQ1 1HF

(01803 293908). This delightful personally-run hotel is situated in a peaceful yet convenient position, only a few minutes from the harbour, shopping centre and entertainments. All en suite rooms are individual in character and tastefully decorated and have remote control colour TV and tea/coffee making facilities. Romantic four-poster bed available for that special occasion. Full central heating for those early and late breaks. Discounts for the over 55's on weekly bookings out of season. Parking. Bed and Breakfast from £16 to £20 per person per night. **ETC** ◆◆◆

TOTNES. Mrs J. Allnutt, The Old Forge at Totnes, Seymour Place, Totnes TQ9 5AY (01803

**As seen on BBC TV's
Holiday Programme**

862174). A charming 600-year-old stone building, delightfully converted from blacksmith and wheelwright workshops and coach houses. Traditional forge, complete with blacksmith's prison cell. We have our own bit of "rural England" close to the town centre. Very close to the River Dart steamer quay, shops and station (also steam train rides). Ideally situated for touring most of Devon - including Dartmoor and Torbay coasts. A day trip from Exeter, Plymouth and Cornwall. Elizabethan costume markets on Tuesdays in Summer (May to September). Double, twin and family rooms, all en suite. Ground floor rooms suitable for most disabled guests. All rooms have colour TV, telephone, beverage tray (fresh milk), colour co-ordinated continental bedding, central heating. Licensed lounge and patio.
Conservatory-style leisure lounge with whirlpool spa. No smoking indoors. Parking, walled gardens. Excellent choice of breakfast menu including vegetarian and special diets. Children welcome but sorry, no pets. Bed and Breakfast from £27 to £37 per person. (en suite). Cottage suite for two to six persons, suitable for disabled visitors. AA Selected QQQQ Award and ETB Highly Commended since 1987. **ETC** ◆◆◆◆

WOOLACOMBE. Dave and Chris Ellis, Crossways Hotel, The Seafront, Woolacombe EX34 7DJ (Tel & Fax: 01271 870395). Cosy, family-run, licensed hotel, situated in one of the finest sea front positions in Woolacombe, overlooking the pretty Combesgate beach and Lundy Island and being surrounded by National Trust land. Bathing and surfing from hotel and ideally situated for golf, horse riding and beautiful walks. Menu choice for breakfast and evening dinner, and children's menu. Varied bar snacks available at lunchtime. All bedrooms individually refurbished to a high standard, many en suite and with fabulous sea views. Colour TV and tea/coffee making facilities in all rooms. Children half-price or Free. Pets welcome. Free on-site parking. Why not find out why many of our guests return year after year? **ETC** ★ *SILVER AWARD,.* **AA, RAC** *DINING AWARD*

YELVERTON. Mrs E. Wills, Callisham Farm, Meavy, Yelverton PL20 6PS (Tel & Fax: 01822 853901) A warm Devonshire welcome and a homely atmosphere awaits you in our traditional Dartmoor Farmhouse. Nestling in the wooded and very pretty valley of Meavy, Callisham is easily accessible from the A386. A perfect centre for walking, cycling and lake or river fishing. Golf, riding and shopping nearby. Guests can enjoy charming en suite bedrooms offering comfortable beds, colour TV and tea making facilities. After a good night's rest you can savor a huge breakfast of your choice with special diets and requests catered for. Cosy in winter with log fires and full central heating **ETC** ◆◆◆.

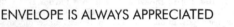
See also Colour Display Advertisement

YELVERTON. Mrs Linda Landick, Eggworthy Farm, Sampford Spiney, Yelverton PL20 6LJ (01822 852142) Holiday on Dartmoor! In the beautiful Walkham Valley. Moorland and valley walking within yards of the accommodation or just relax in the garden and adjoining woodland. Many local attractions. Comfortable rooms, one double en suite, one family suite with private bathroom. Both rooms have colour TV, tea/coffee facilities. Full English breakfast. Non-smoking. Pets welcome. Open all year except Christmas. Brochure available. Terms from £18-£22. We look forward to seeing you. **ETC** ◆◆◆.

DORSET

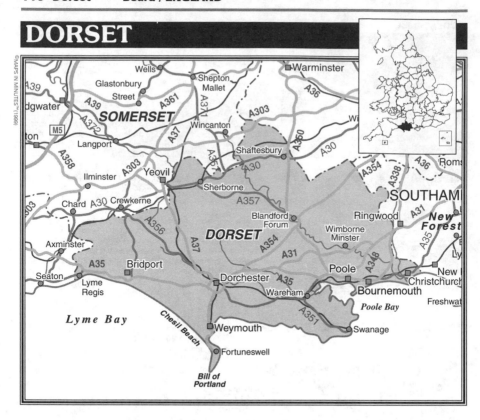

BEAMINSTER. Mrs Hasell, Kitwhistle Farm, Beaminster Down, Beaminster DT8 3SG (Tel & Fax: 01308 862458). Kitwhistle Farm is a working dairy farm situated on the peaceful Beaminster Down. We are two miles away from the small town of Beaminster with its many eating houses. The town is featured in many of Thomas Hardy's tales. The accommodation available is a family en suite, consisting of two bedrooms - one double room and one twin room. Bed and Breakfast from £17.00 per adult per night with full English Breakfast. Directions:- from Beaminster Square take North Street to the top of the hill, turn right (signposted Maiden Newton); Kitwhistle Farm is half a mile on the right. **ETC ◆◆◆.**

BLANDFORD FORUM. Mrs C.M. Old, Manor House Farm, Ibberton, Blandford Forum DT11 0EN (01258 817349). Working farm, dairy and sheep. Situated nine miles west of Blandford Forum. Small 16th century manor house, now a farmhouse, surrounded by large colourful garden in a quiet unspoilt village which at one time was given to Katherine Howard by Henry VIII. The oak beams and nail studded doors confirm its centuries-old past. One double bedroom, one double or twin (both en suite), and one twin bedroom (separate bathroom); all with tea making facilities. Bathroom and toilet; lounge with TV, diningroom with separate tables. Children welcome, cot and high chair provided. Bed and Breakfast from £14 to £18. Open all year. No evening meal. Good food at Crown Inn nearby. Self catering accommodation also available.

BRIDPORT. Jane Greening, New House Farm, Mangerton Lane, Bradpole, Bridport DT6 3SF (Tel & Fax:

01308 422884). Stay in a modern, comfortable farmhouse on a small working farm set in the rural Dorset hills and become one of the family. A large wild garden where you are welcome to sit or stroll round. Two large rooms available, both en suite, both with lovely views over the surrounding countryside, both with television and tea/coffee making facilities. There is also a large sittingroom where you can relax. We are near to Bridport and the seaside, golf courses, fossil hunting, beautiful gardens, wonderful walking, coarse fishing lake - lots to do. Simple traditional farmhouse evening meals can be provided, subject to booking. Bed and Breakfast from £20. **ETC** ◆◆◆.

BRIDPORT. Mrs D.P. Read, The Old Station, Powerstock, Bridport DT6 3ST (01308 485301). Peacefully

situated deep in the glorious Dorset countryside, one mile south east of Powerstock, in two-and-a-half acres of garden, this former railway station enjoys beautiful views. Conveniently situated for drives into neighbouring counties; many rural walks; can be reached by public transport. Two double bedrooms, one single, all with washbasins and tea-making facilities; bathroom, three toilets; central heating. Daytime access. Off road parking; tennis, fun golf. Hearty English breakfast prettily served (vegetarian breakfast by previous arrangement). Open March through October, from £16. Badger watching possible most evenings from house. SAE, please, for details. Sorry no children or pets. No smoking.

BRIDPORT. Britmead House Hotel, West Bay Road, Bridport DT6 4EG (Tel: 01308 422941; Fax:

01308 422516). Personal service and putting guests' comfort first means visitors return time after time. Situated between Bridport and West Bay Harbour with its Beaches, Golf Course, Chesil Beach and the Dorset Coastal Path. Full en suite rooms (one ground floor), all with colour TV, tea-making facilities, hairdryer and mini-bar. South-facing lounge and diningroom overlooking the garden. Licensed. Private parking. B&B from £48 to £58 for two nights; £72 to £78 for three nights. Rates for longer stays on request. **ETC/AA** ◆◆◆◆ *GUESTACCOM GOOD ROOM AWARD 1998/9.*
website: www.britmeadhouse.co.uk

BRIDPORT near. Mrs Sue Norman, Frogmore Farm, Chideock, Bridport DT6 6HT (01308 456159).

Working farm. Set in the rolling hills of West Dorset, enjoying splendid sea views, our delightful 17th century farmhouse offers comfortable, friendly and relaxing accommodation. An ideal base from which to ramble the many coastal and country footpaths of the area (nearest beach Seatown one-and-a-half miles) or tour by car the interesting places of Dorset and Devon. Bedrooms with en suite shower rooms, TV and tea making facilities. Guests' dining room and cosy lounge with woodburner. Well behaved dogs welcome. Open all year; car essential. Bed and Breakfast from £17 (evening meal optional). Brochure and terms free on request.

CERNE ABBAS. Mrs T. Barraclough, Magiston Farm, Sydling St. Nicholas, Dorchester DT2 9NR

(01300 320295). Working farm. Magiston is a 400 acre working farm with a comfortable 17th century cob and brick farmhouse set deep in the heart of Dorset. Large garden with river. Half-an-hour's drive from coast and five miles north of Dorchester. The farmhouse comprises double, twin and single bedrooms including a twin on the ground floor. Delicious evening meals served. Children over 10 years and pets welcome. Central heating. Open January to December. Bed and Breakfast from £18.50 per person per night. Please write or telephone for further details. **ETC** ◆◆◆.

CHARMOUTH. Mrs S. M. Johnson, Cardsmill Farm, Whitchurch, Canonicorum, Charmouth, Bridport DT6 6RP (Tel & Fax: 01297 489375). Working farm, join in. A Grade II Listed comfortable quiet farmhouse in the picturesque Marshwood Vale, three miles from Charmouth. Ideal location for touring, safe beaches, fossil hunting, golf and walking the coastal path. See the farm animals, pets and crops. Family and double en suite rooms available, each with CTV, shaver points, tea/coffee trays. Cot available. Full central heating and double glazed windows throughout. Lounge with Inglenook fireplace, woodburning stove, oak beams, colour TV, games and books. Dining area with separate tables. English and varied breakfasts. Access at all times. Children and well behaved pets welcome. Large garden with patio, picnic table and seats. Bed and Breakfast from £18 - £24 per person per night. Open Febuary till end of November. Please phone or write for a brochure. Also two self-catering farmhouses each to sleep 11-12 plus cot, for long or short stays all year. **ETC** ◆◆◆
e-mail: cardsmill@aol.com
website: www.farmhousedorset.com

CHARMOUTH. Marshwood Manor, Bettiscombe Near Bridport, Near Charmouth DT6 5NS (01308 868442). Five tastefully furnished en suite rooms. Close to Charmouth and Lyme Regis. Bed and Breakfast with Evening Meal on request. Speciality home cooking. Outdoor heated swimming pool. Weekly or Short Breaks available. Brochure on request. AA Listed. **ETC** ◆◆◆◆.
website: www.marshwoodmanor.co.uk

DORCHESTER. Mrs Jane Rootham, The Old Post Office, Martinstown, Dorchester DT2 9LF (01305 889254). Situated in the Winterbourne Valley, The Old Post Office is a stone and slate Georgian cottage used as the village post office until 1950. It is part of a row of cottages that are all listed buildings. Winterbourne St Martin (Martinstown) is in the heart of Hardy country, two miles from the Neolithic Hill Fort of Maiden Castle, Hardy's monument and the town of Dorchester. The coast and beach are five miles away and it is an ideal walking and touring base. The bedrooms all have washbasins, tea/coffee making facilities and some have TV. Pets and children welcome. Bed and Breakfast from £15 to £25.

DORCHESTER. Michael and Jane Deller, Churchview Guest House, Winterbourne Abbas, Near Dorchester DT2 9LS (Tel/fax: 01305 889296). Our 17th century guest house, noted for warm hospitality and delicious Breakfasts and Evening Meals, makes an ideal base for touring beautiful West Dorset. Our character bedrooms are all comfortable and well appointed. Meals, served in our beautiful diningroom, feature local produce, with relaxation provided by two attractive lounges and licensed bar. Your hosts Jane and Michael Deller are pleased to give every assistance with local information to ensure a memorable stay. NON-SMOKING. Terms: Dinner, Bed and Breakfast £36 to £44; Bed and Breakfast £22 to £32. **ETC/AA** ◆◆◆.
e-mail: stay@churchview.co.uk
website: www.churchview.co.uk

Please mention The Farm Holiday Guide when writing to enquire about accommodation

DORCHESTER. Mrs Lisa Bowden, Higher Came Farmhouse Bed and Breakfast, Higher Came, Dorchester DT2 8NR (Tel & Fax: 01305 268908). Working farm. Come and relax in our beautiful 17th century Listed farmhouse peacefully nestling in the heart of Dorset's Thomas Hardy country. Located just two miles from the historic market town of Dorchester this traditional farmhouse has spacious and attractively furnished bedrooms. Family room with large en suite bathroom plus two further rooms with both a double and a single bed and private facilities. Each room has TV, tea/coffee making facilities and hairdryer. Delicious home-cooked farmhouse breakfast using local produce. Relax in our comfortable resident's lounge or take a stroll and enjoy the gardens. Central heating and log fire. Open all year. Children and pets welcome. Bed and Breakfast from £21 to £34.

DORCHESTER. Mrs N. Foot, Whiteways Farmhouse, Bookham, Buckland Newton, Dorchester DT2 7RP (Tel & Fax: 01300 345511). A warm welcome awaits you at this Hamstone and Flint Farmhouse. Situated at the head of the Blackmore Vale, the character rooms enjoy panoramic views over unspoilt countryside; ideal for walks along the Wessex Way and Hardy Trail. A working farm in the centre of Dorset but within a half hour drive of the sea. Families are very welcome. All rooms are spacious with en suite bathroom/dressing room, tea/coffee making facilities, colour TV and central heating for all year round breaks. Breakfast is served in an attractive dining room with inglenook fireplace. Bed and Breakfast from £20. ETC ◆◆◆◆
SILVER AWARD
e-mail: bookhamfarm@netscapeonline.co.uk

FURZEHILL. Mrs King, Stocks Farm, Furzehill, Wimborne BH21 4HT (Tel & Fax: 01202 888697). Stocks Farm is a family-run farm and nursery situated in peaceful countryside just one-and-half miles from the lovely country town of Wimborne Minster, off the B3078. Surrounded by lovely Dorset countryside and pretty villages; coastline, beaches and New Forest within easy reach. Bed and Breakfast accommodation consists of one double en suite bedroom and one twin bedroom with private bathroom, both on ground level. Disabled guests are very welcome. Tea and coffee making facilities in both rooms. All accommodation is non-smoking. Situated in secluded garden with patio for guests to enjoy breakfast outside. Local pubs and restaurants offer varied menus. Bed and Breakfast from £19 to £20 per person per night.

Buckland Farm

Situated in quiet and unspoilt surroundings with gardens and grounds of five acres which are ideal for guests to relax or stroll in; about three miles from the lovely coastal resorts of Lyme Regis and Charmouth. A warm welcome awaits you. Accommodation mainly on the ground floor. Two family bedrooms, one double en suite shower and one twin bedded room, all with TV, washbasin, tea/coffee making facilites. Bathroom, shower in bath, separate WC. Lounge with colour TV, video and log fire. Dining area with separate tables. A good English Farmhouse breakfast served, a real home from home plus our very friendly dog. Friendly pub within two minutes' walk for evening meals. Payphone. No smoking. Bed and Breakfast from £15. Send SAE for further details. Self-catering caravan and chalet Bungalow available. Sheila and David Taylor.

Raymonds Hill, Near Axminster EX13 5SZ
Tel/Fax: 01297 33222 or e-mail: sheilataylor@bucklandfarm@fsnet.co.uk

---

POOLE. Mrs Stephenson, Holly Hedge Farm, Bulbury Lane, Lytchett Matravers, Poole BH16 6EP

(01929 459688). Built in 1892, Holly Hedge Farm is situated next to Bulbury Woods Golf Course, set in 11 acres of wood and grassland adjacent to lake. We are just 15 minutes away from the Purbecks, the beach and the forest. The area is ideal for walking or cycling and Poole Quay and Harbour are also nearby. Accommodation comprises two double/family rooms, one twin and one single, all with en suite showers, colour TV, tea/coffee making facilities, radio alarms and central heating. Prices for a single room £25 to £30, double £42, per night. Open all year round for summer or winter breaks. Full English or Continental breakfast served.

SHERBORNE. Mrs J. Mayo, Almshouse Farm, Hermitage, Holnest, Sherborne DT9 6HA (Tel and Fax:

01963 210296). This charming old farmhouse was a monastery during the 16th century, restored in 1849 and is now a listed building. A family-run working dairy farm, it is surrounded by 140 acres overlooking the Blackmoor Vale, just one mile off the A352. Accommodation is in three comfortable en suite rooms with colour TV and tea/coffee making facilities. Diningroom with inglenook fireplace, lounge with colour TV, for guests' use at all times. Also garden and lawn. Plenty of reading material and local information provided for this ideal touring area. Bed and Breakfast from £20. Excellent evening meals in all local inns nearby. Situated six miles from Sherborne with its beautiful Abbey and Castle. SAE for further details. **ETC/AA ◆◆◆◆, ETC** *SILVER AWARD.*

SHERBORNE. Mrs E. Kingman, Stowell Farm, Stowell, Near Sherborne DT9 4PE (01963 370200). A

15th century former Manor House that has retained some lovely historical features. Now a farmhouse on a family-run dairy and beef farm. It is in a beautiful rural location yet only five miles from the A303, two miles from A30 and two hours by train from London. An ideal place to relax and unwind, enjoy traditional home baking and a warm friendly atmosphere. Close to the abbey town of Sherborne, National Trust properties and many other places of interest to suit all people. Accommodation – one double room, one twin room, guest bathroom, and lounge with colour TV and log fires. From £18 per person per night, reductions for children under 10 years and weekly stays. Evening Meal by arrangement.

Terms quoted in this publication may be subject to increase if rises in costs necessitate

SHERBORNE. Mrs Penny Luxmoore, Caphays House, Caundle Marsh, Near Sherborne DT9 5LX (Tel & Fax: 01963 23325). Set in idyllic unspoilt countryside, only four miles from Sherborne, half-a-mile up its own 'no through lane', Caphays House is a 400-year-old former dairyhouse offering very friendly and comfortable accommodation. Lovely beamed sittingroom with inglenook and log fire for the sole use of guests. A perfect place to stay for a relaxing break in this unspoilt and beautiful part of Dorset. Bed and Breakfast from £22 per person per night. **ETC ★★★**

SHERBORNE. David, Hazel, Mary and Gerry Wilding, White Horse Farm, Middlemarsh, Sherborne DT9 5QN (01963 210222). Set in beautiful Hardy countryside, we offer a warm welcome in comfortable surroundings, with a hearty farmhouse breakfast. The property is surrounded by three acres of paddock and garden with a duck pond. We lie between the historic towns of Sherborne, Dorchester and Cerne Abbas and are situated next door to an inn serving good food and local ales. Delightful coastal attractions are some 30-40 minutes' drive away. All rooms have en suite showers, colour TV, central heating and tea/coffee making facilities. There is also a private conservatory/lounge and dining room. Ample parking. B&B from £20. Self-catering cottages also available. **ETC Listed**
e-mail: enquiries@whitehorsefarm.co.uk
website: www.whitehorsefarm.co.uk

SHILLINGSTONE. Mrs Rosie Watts, Pennhills Farm, Sandy Lane, off Lanchards Lane, Shillingstone, Blandford DT11 0TF (01258 860491). Pennhills Farmhouse set in 100 acres of unspoiled countryside, is situated one mile from the village of Shillingstone in the heart of the Blackmore Vale, an ideal peaceful retreat, short break or holiday. It offers spacious comfortable accommodation for all ages; children welcome, pets by arrangement. One downstairs bedroom. All bedrooms en suite with TV and tea/coffee making facilities, complemented by traditional English breakfast with home produced bacon and sausages. Vegetarians catered for. Good meals available locally. Brochure sent on request. A warm and friendly welcome is assured from your host Rosie Watts. From £18 per person

SWANAGE. Mrs Rosemary Dean, Quarr Farm, Valley Road, Swanage BH19 3DY (01929 480865). Quarr is a working family farm steeped in history dating back to the Domesday Book. Animals kept naturally - cows, calves, horses, poultry. Bring your children to feed ducks, chickens, peacocks and watch steam trains passing through our meadows. Accommodation in family room with en suite bathroom, own sittingroom with colour TV, real log fire, tea making facilities. Bed and Breakfast. Cot available. Easy reach high class restaurants, pubs; sea three miles. Studland, sandy beach just five miles away. Ideal for walking, cycling, coastal path, RSPB Reserves, golf courses, riding. Please telephone for further details and terms.

SWANAGE. Mrs Justine Pike, Downshay Farm, Haycrafts Lane, Harmans Cross, Swanage BH19 3EB (01929 480316). Working dairy farm in the heart of beautiful Isle of Purbeck, midway between Corfe Castle and Swanage. This Victorian Purbeck stone farmhouse has family room en suite and one double with private shower room close by. Both rooms have colour TV and tea/coffee making facilities. Steam railway within walking distance, coastal path and sandy beaches three miles away. Excellent pubs and restaurnats to be found locally. Open Easter to October for Bed and Breakfast from £18 per person.

WIMBOURNE. Mrs A. C. Tory, Hemsworth Manor Farm, Witchampton, Wimbourne BH21 5BN (01258 840216; Fax: 01258 841278). Our lovely old Manor Farmhouse which is mentioned in the Domesday Book, is situated in an exceptionally peaceful location, yet is only half-an-hour's drive from Salisbury, Dorchester, Poole, Bournemouth and the New Forest. Hemsworth is a working family farm of nearly 800 acres, providing some lovely walks. The farm is mainly arable, but is also home to cattle, sheep, pigs, horses, ponies and various domestic pets. We have three fully equipped en suite bedrooms, and one double room with private bathroom. All have colour TV. Separate lounge for guests use. There are excellent pubs locally. Brochure available. **ETC** ◆◆◆◆

WINTERBORNE ZELSTON. Mrs Irene Kerley, Brook Farm, Winterborne Zelston, Blandford DT11 9EU (Tel & Fax: 01929 459267). A warm welcome awaits you at Brook Farm, a friendly working farm situated in a pretty, peaceful hamlet overlooking the River Winterborne, between Wimborne and Dorchester. Central for visiting the many attractions of Dorset. Two large double/twin en suite rooms and one twin room with private facilities. Colour TV, beverage making facilities, hairdryer etc. in all rooms. Guests have own keys, plenty of parking space. Hearty English breakfasts are served with our free-range eggs and home-made marmalade. Excellent food at the local country inns. Open all year except Christmas. Children over 10 years welcome, regret no pets or smoking. Terms from £20 to £22 per person per night, (extra for single occupancy) with reductions for three or more nights and favourable weekly terms. **ETC** ◆◆◆

DURHAM

CHESTER LE STREET. Mrs H. Johnson, Low Urpeth Farm, Ouston, Chester Le Street DH2 1BD (0191 4102901; Fax: 0191 4100081). Superb farmhouse accommodation, spacious rooms, well furnished in a very traditional style. Beverage facilities, TV and comfortable chairs. Our large square stone farmhouse is within easy distance of county cricket at Chester-le-Street, Beamish Museum, Durham Cathedral (a World Heritage site), Durham Dales and Castles and coastline of Northumberland. Directions: leave A1M at Junction 63, follow A693, one-and-a-half miles turn right to Ouston, continue a further one-and-a-half miles, down hill, over roundabout, turning left at "Trees Please", sign into Low Urpeth. Bed and Breakfast from £20 to £25. Closed Christmas and New Year .**ETC** ◆◆◆◆.

CORNFORTH. Mrs D. Slack, Ash House, 24 The Green, Cornforth DL17 9JH (01740 654654). Built mid 19th Century, Ash House is a beautifully appointed period home combining a delicate mixture of homeliness and Victorian flair. Elegant rooms, individually and tastefully decorated, combining antique furnishings, beautiful fabrics, carved four posters and modern fittings. Spacious and graceful, filled with character, Ash House offers a warm welcome to both the road-weary traveller and those wishing merely to unwind in the quiet elegance of this charming home on quiet village green. Private parking. 10 minutes Historic Durham City, and adjacent A1 (M) motorway. Well placed between York and Edinburgh. Excellent value.

MIDDLETON-IN-TEESDALE. Mrs Eileen Dent, Wythes Hill Farm, Lunedale, Middleton-in-Teesdale DL12 0NX (01833 640349). Wythes Hill is a working hill farm on the Pennine Way, three miles from Middleton-in-Teesdale. Accommodation is available in an en suite double/family room and a single room; both have panoramic views of the Dales. New full central heating. Bed and Breakfast £18; Evening Meal by arrangement. Open March to October. Children welcome. Pets not permitted.

STANLEY. Mrs P. Gibson, Bushblades Farm, Harperley, Stanley DH9 9UA (01207 232722). Ideal stopover when travelling north or south. Only 10 minutes from A1(M) Chester-le-Street. Durham City 20 minutes, Beamish Museum two miles, Metro Centre 15 minutes, Hadrian's Wall and Northumberland coast under an hour. Comfortable Georgian farmhouse set in large garden. Twin ground floor en suite room plus two double first-floor bedrooms. All rooms have tea/coffee making facilities, colour TV and easy chairs. Ample parking. Children welcome over 12 years. Sorry, no pets. Bed and Breakfast from £17 to £19.50 per person per night, single £20 to £25. Self-catering accommodation also available. Leave A1(M) at Chester-le-Street for Stanley on the A693, then Consett half-a-mile after Stanley. Follow signs for Harperley Farm on right, half a mile from Crossroads. **ETC** ◆◆◆

ESSEX

BRAINTREE. Mrs A. Butler, Brook Farm, Wethersfield, Braintree CM7 4BX (01371 850284). Beautiful Listed farmhouse, parts dating back to 13th century, on a 100-acre mixed farm set on the edge of a picturesque village. Essex can offer many picturesque places to visit and the Suffolk villages of Long Melford, Lavenham and Dedham, as well as Constable Country, are all within easy reach. Warm, spacious and comfortable rooms, guests' lounge, safe parking. Thirty minutes from Stansted Airport. Camping also available. Open all year. Prices from £20 per person in double, twin or family rooms; from £25 single. **ETC** ◆◆◆.

GLOUCESTERSHIRE

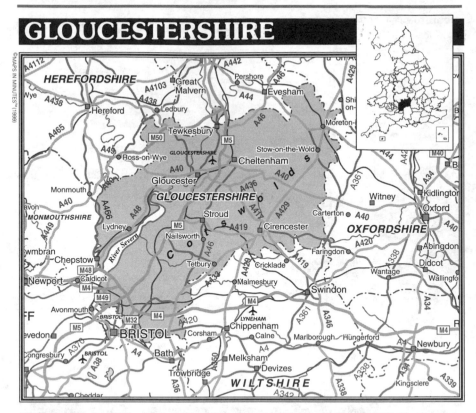

BATH near. Mrs Pam Wilmott, Pool Farm, Wick, Bristol BS30 5RL (0117 937 2284). Working farm, join in. Welcome to our 350 year old Grade II Listed farmhouse on a working dairy farm. On A420 between Bath and Bristol and a few miles from Exit 18 of M4, we are on the edge of the village, overlooking fields, but within easy reach of pub, shops and golf club. We offer traditional Bed and Breakast in one family and one twin room with tea/coffee facilities; TV lounge. Central heating. Ample parking. Open all year except Christmas. Terms £18 to £22.

BLAISDON. Ms N. Klaiber, Tan House Farm, Blaisdon, Longhope GL17 0AH (01452 830202) Converted 18th century Listed timber framed barn offering ground floor double and family rooms with en suite shower rooms. Separate lounge, dining room and playroom. Working farm on the edge of the Forest of Dean. Ideal centre for touring. Bed and Breakfast: Double room £20 per person per night. Family room £25 per person per night, Children reduced rates.

BRISTOL. Mrs Marilyn Collins, Box Hedge Farm, Coalpit Heath, Bristol BS36 2UW (01454 250786).

Box Hedge Farm is set in 200 acres of beautiful rural countryside on the edge of the Cotswolds. Local to M4/M5, central for Bristol and Bath and the many tourist attractions in this area. An ideal stopping point for the South West and Wales. We offer a warm, friendly atmosphere with traditional farmhouse cooking. All bedrooms have colour TV and tea/coffee making facilities. Bed and Breakfast £20 single standard, £29 single en suite, £35 double standard, £46 double en suite. Family rooms - prices on application. Dinner £8.50. All prices include VAT. Self-catering accommodation also available.

BROADWAY. Mrs P Hutcheon, Burhill Farm, Buckland, Broadway WR12 7LY (Tel & Fax: 01386

858171). A warm welcome awaits our guests at our mainly grass farm lying in the folds of the Cotswolds just two miles south of Broadway. Both guest rooms are en suite and have tea/coffee making facilities, colour TV and hairdryers. The farm lies near the top of a no- through road so is very peaceful with many lovely walks including the Cotswold Way which runs through the farm. Stratford-upon-Avon and Cheltenham are a half-hour's drive away, and there are many lovely villages to visit. Come and enjoy the peace and quiet. Bed and Breakfast from £20. **ETC** ◆◆◆◆◆ *GOLD AWARD.*

CHELTENHAM. Mrs Carole M. Rand, "Cleevely", Wadfield Farm, Corndean lane, Winchcombe,

Cheltenham GL54 5AL (01242 602059). A family run arable/sheep farm with the Cotswold Way running through. Half-timbered Cotswold stone house overlooking Sudeley and Winchcombe Valley. Splendid views. Excellent base for exploring the Cotswolds. Winter breaks, log fires, TV lounge. Traditional farmhouse cusine. Twin en suite, double/family room with private bathroom, both with tea/coffee making facilities. Ample parking. Twin en suite from £20 per person per night, Double/family room (maximum four people) with private bathroom from £55. Three course Evening Meal from £8.50 to £10.00 per person. Vegetarian and special diets catered for. Packed lunches by arrangement. **ETC** ◆◆◆

CHELTENHAM. Mr John Sparrey, Parkview, 4 Pittville Crescent, Cheltenham GL52 2QZ (01242

575567). We offer accommodation in Cheltenham's nicest area but only ten minutes' walk from the centre. The bedrooms are large and airy and have TV, tea, coffee and provide views onto Pittville Park. This fine Regency house is inspected annually by the Tourist Authority; the RAC and "Which?" Bed and Breakfast Guide also inspect. Cheltenham is famous for horse racing and festivals of music and literature while nearby Prestbury is the most haunted village in England. The Cotswold villages stand in the surrounding hills while Stratford is one hour's drive. Tours can be arranged.Bed and Breakfast terms from £20 per person. **ETC** ◆◆◆

CHIPPING CAMPDEN. Mrs Sue Harrison, Greystone Farm, Blockley, Moreton-in-Marsh GL56 9LN

(01386 700482). The farmhouse has been sympathetically renovated to a high standard, offering a comfortable en suite twin bedroom, central heating, colour TV and tea/coffee making facilities. It stands in the middle of our family run 200 acre dairy farm, and has outstanding panoramic views to be seen from the bedroom windows. Home-made jams, marmalade and free-range eggs from our own hens are offered for your breakfast. Ideally situated for walking and touring the Cotswolds, with Stratford-upon-Avon, Warwick, Oxford, Stoneleigh and Cheltenham all within easy reach. Plenty of local pubs and restaurants within a three mile radius. Non-smoking. Ample private parking. Bed and Breakfast from £22 to £28 per person per night.
e-mail: susanharrison@farmersweekly.net

CHIPPING CAMPDEN. Lucy King, Manor Farm, Weston Sub-Edge, Chipping Campden GL55 6QH (01386 840390; mobile: 07889 108812; Fax: 0870 1640638; Int. Fax: 4487 01640638). Working farm, join in.

A warm friendly welcome and a hearty, full English breakfast is assured for all guests at Manor Farm, a traditional 17th century Cotswold stone, oak-beamed farmhouse. An excellent base for exploring the Cotswolds and Shakespeare Country from our 800 acre working farm with sheep, cattle and horses. Lots of excellent walks around beautiful countryside. Only one-and-a-half miles from Chipping Campden which is not only a lovely old market town, but also has a good selection of pubs, restaurants and shops. Open all year round. All rooms en suite with TV, tea/coffee making facilities, etc. Bed and Breakfast from only £22.50 per person per night.
e-mail: lucy@manorfarmbnb.demon.co.uk

CHIPPING CAMPDEN. Mrs Gené Jeffrey, Brymbo, Honeybourne Lane, Mickleton, Chipping Campden GL55 6PU (01386 438890; Fax: 01386 438113). A warm and welcoming farm building conversion with large garden in beautiful Cotswold countryside, ideal for walking and touring.

COTSWOLD COUNTRY
BED AND BREAKFAST

Close to Stratford-upon-Avon, Broadway, Chipping Campden and with easy access to Oxford and Cheltenham. All rooms are on the ground floor, with full central heating. The comfortable bedrooms all have colour television and tea/coffee making facilities. Sitting room with open log fire. Breakfast room. Children and dogs welcome. Parking. Maps and guides to borrow. Sample menus from local hostelries for your information. Home-made preserves a speciality. FREE countryside tour of area offered to three-night guests. Rooms: two double, two twin, one family. Bathrooms - three en suite, two shared. Bed and Breakfast from £18.00 per person, en suite £21.00. Brochure available. **ETC** ◆◆◆◆
e-mail: enquiries@brymbo.com
website: www.brymbo.com

CIRENCESTER. Ann and Martin Shewry-Fitzgerald, Manby's Farm, Oaksey, Malmesbury SN16 9SA (01666 577399; Fax: 01666 577241). Our new farmhouse, situated within stunning countryside on the Wiltshire/Gloucestershire border is close to the Cotswold Water Park. We offer luxury accommodation from where you can enjoy the peace and quiet or plan a visit to one of the many places of interest, such as Malmesbury, Castle Combe, Oxford, Stratford-upon-Avon, Stonehenge, Longleat and many more. Our farmhouse has full central heating and snooker room with indoor swimming pool adjacent. Three double/twin en suite bedrooms with tea/coffee making facilities, radio and colour TV; family room also available. A log fire in the inglenook will ensure our winter guests are kept warm. A hearty English breakfast is served, with three-course dinner and packed lunches available by

arrangement. Bed and Breakfast from £20 per person, discount for more than three nights. Visa and Access accepted. **AA/ETC** ◆◆◆◆
e- mail: DJHackle@compuserve.com

DURSLEY. Burrows Court, Nibley Green, North Nibley, Dursley GL11 6AZ (Tel & Fax: 01453 546230). This 18th century mill is idyllically set in an acre of garden surrounded by open country with beautiful views of the Cotswolds. Decorated and furnished in the country style. The house has six bedrooms, all with private bathroom, colour TV, beverage facilities and radio. Other facilities include two lounges, one with residents' bar; central heating. There is a good choice of restaurants and pubs nearby. Children over five years welcome. Bed and breakfast from £20 to £25 per person. Close to M5 motorway between Junctions 13 and 14. RAC Highly Acclaimed. **ETC** ◆◆◆

DURSLEY near. Gerald and Norma Kent, Hill House, Crawley Hill, Uley, Near Dursley GL11 5BH (01453

860267). Cotswold stone house situated on top of a hill with beautiful views of the surrounding countryside, near the very pretty village of Uley. Ideal spot for exploring the various walks in the area including the Cotswold Way and there are many places of interest within reasonable driving distance of Uley. Choice of bedrooms with or without en-suite facilities, all with washbasins, central heating, shaver points, tea/coffee making facilities and TV. Your hosts' aim is to make your stay in the Cotswolds an enjoyable and memorable one, with comfort and hospitality of prime importance. Bed and Breakfast from £18 per person; Evening Meals are normally available if required. Non Smoking Please phone or write for brochure.

DURSLEY near. Mrs Catherine Bevan, Hodgecombe Farm, Uley, Near Dursley GL11 5AN (01453

860365). Situated in the lower Cotswolds, Hodgecombe Farm lies in a quiet valley between Uley and Coaley, tucked under the Uley Bury Roman Fort with spectacular views across open countryside to the River Severn and beyond. The Cotswold Way winds lazily past Hodgecombe Farm and visitors find this the perfect place to relax in unspoilt surroundings. Three double rooms, one en suite, are comfortably furnished with armchairs, tea/coffee, clock radios and central heating. Bed and Breakfast from £18 to £23 per person; Evening Meal £10. Sorry no smokers, animals or under five-year-olds. Open March to October. **AA** ◆◆◆◆

GLOUCESTER. Mrs Jackie Guilding, Oaktree Farm, Little Haresfield, Standish GL10 3DS (01452

883323). Working farm, join in. Enjoy that well-earned break in the friendly atmosphere of our mixed dairy farm, situated on the western edge of the Cotswolds in an Area of Outstanding Natural Beauty, with open views of the Malvern Hills, Forest of Dean and the Cotswolds. Guests are welcome to watch the daily running of the farm or just relax in the garden. Choice of breakfast is served in the conservatory overlooking the surrounding countryside. All rooms are en suite with colour TV, tea/coffee making facilities and are equipped with the little extras to make your stay enjoyable. Children welcome, sorry no pets. Bed and Breakfast from £20 to £25. **ETC** ◆◆◆◆.
e-mail: jackie@oaktree.fsnet.co.uk

GLOUCESTER near. S.J. Barnfield, "Kilmorie Smallholding", Gloucester Road, Corse, Staunton,

Gloucester GL19 3RQ (Tel & Fax: 01452 840224) Quality all ground floor accommodation. "Kilmorie" is Grade II Listed (c1848) within conservation area in a lovely part of Gloucestershire, deceptively spacious yet cosy, tastefully furnished. Double, twin, family or single bedrooms, all having tea tray, colour TV, radio, mostly en suite. Very comfortable guests lounge, traditional home cooking is served in the separate dining room overlooking lage garden where there are seats to relax, watch our free range hens (who provide excellent eggs for breakfast!) or the wild birds and butterflies we encourage to visit. Perhaps walk waymarked farmland footpaths which start here. Children may "help" with our child's pony, Pygmy goats, whose tiny pretty kids arrive in Spring, and hens. Rural yet ideally situated to visit Cotswolds, Royal Forest of Dean, Wye Valley and Malvern Hills. Children over five years. Bed, full English Breakfast and Evening Dinner from £23.50; Bed and Breakfast from £16. Ample parking. **ETC** ◆◆◆
e-mail: kilmorie.bb@freeuk.com

Please mention *The Farm Holiday Guide* when making enquiries about accommodation featured in these pages.

GOTHERINGTON. Mrs Janet Newman, Pardon Hill Farm, Prescott, Gotherington, Cheltenham GL52 9RD (Tel & Fax: 01242 672468). Working farm, join in.

Pardon Hill Farm is a working farm and family home set in 300 acres of peaceful grassland, cornfields and woodland. We have a friendly domestic menagerie of cats, dogs, horses and ponies, and our rolling hillsides are home to cattle and sheep that our family has been raising here for the past 100 years. The house is made of Cotswold stone with all modern internal comforts. All three bedrooms are en suite with hospitality tray, television and views from every window. A choice of breakfast is served in the conservatory. A warm welcome awaits you at Pardon Hill Farm. Children and pets welcome. **ETC ◆◆◆.**
e-mail: janet@pardonhillfarm.freeserve.co.uk
website: www.margintrip.co.uk/pardonhill.shtml

LECHLADE (Near). Mrs Elizabeth Reay, Apple Tree House, Buscot, Near Faringdon, Oxfordshire SN7 8DA (01367 252592). 17th century listed house situated in

small interesting National Trust village, two miles Lechlade, four miles Faringdon on A417. River Thames five minutes' walk through village to Buscot lock and weirs. Ideal touring centre for Cotswolds, Upper Thames, Oxford, etc. Good fishing, walking and cycling area. Access at all times to the three guest bedrooms all of which have washbasin, razor point, tea/coffee making facilities and central heating when necessary. En suite room available. Private facilities to all rooms if required. Residents' TV lounge with log fire in winter. Prices from £38 for double or £26 single when sharing bathroom; choice of many restaurants, etc within five mile radius of Buscot. I look forward to welcoming you to Apple Tree House. **ETC ◆◆◆.**
e-mail: emreay@aol.com

MINCHINHAMPTON, (Near Stroud). Mrs Margaret Helm, Hunters Lodge, Dr Brown's Road, Minchinhampton Common, Near Stroud GL6 9BT (01453 883588; Fax: 01453 731449). Hunters Lodge is a beautiful

stone-built Cotswold country house set in a large secluded garden adjoining 600 acres of National Trust common land at Minchinhampton. Accommodation available - one double room en suite; two twin/double-bedded rooms both with private bathrooms. All have tea/coffee making facilities, central heating and colour TV and are furnished and decorated to a high standard. Private lounge with TV and a delightful conservatory. Car essential, ample parking space. Ideal centre for touring the Cotswolds, Bath, Cheltenham, Cirencester, with many delightful pubs and hotels in the area for meals. You are sure of a warm welcome, comfort, and help in planning excursions to local places of interest. Bed and Breakfast from £22 per person. Non-smokers. Children over 10. No dogs. SAE please, or telephone. **AA ◆◆◆◆◆**

NEWENT. Mrs Katrina Cracknell, Withyland Heights, Beavan's Hill, Kilcot, Newent GL18 1PG (01989 720582; Fax: 01989 720238). Situated on the

Herefordshire/Gloucestershire border, Withyland Heights has two bedrooms which are spacious and attractively furnished with tea and coffee making facilities. The double/family room has en suite facilities and panoramic views of surrounding countryside. The twin/triple room has original beams and private bathroom, sleeps six. Non-smoking. Children welcome. Open all year. Bed and Breakfast from £16 to £23. **ETC ◆◆◆.**

STOW-ON-THE-WOLD. Robert and Dawn Smith, Corsham Field Farmhouse, Bledington Road, Stow-on-the-Wold GL54 1JH (01451 831750). Homely farmhouse with traditional features and breathtaking views, one mile from Stow-on-the-Wold. Ideally situated for exploring all the picturesque Cotswold villages such as Broadway, Bourton-on-the-Water, Upper and Lower Slaughter, Chipping Campden, Snowshill, etc. Also central point for places of interest such as Blenheim Palace, Cotswold Wildlife Park, Stratford and many stately homes and castles in the area. Twin, double and family rooms, most with en suite facilities, others with washbasins, TV and tea/coffee making facilities. Pets and children welcome. Good pub food five minutes' walk away. Bed and Breakfast from £17 to £23 per person. **AA/ETC ◆◆◆.**

ASTON HOUSE

Aston House is a chalet bungalow overlooking fields in the peaceful village of Broadwell, 1¹/2 miles from Stow-on-the-Wold. It is centrally situated for all the Cotswold villages, while Blenheim Palace, Warwick Castle, Oxford, Stratford-upon-Avon, Cheltenham, Cirencester and Gloucester are within easy reach. Accommodation comprises of a twin-bedded and double/twin room, both en-suite on the first floor, and a double room with private bathroom on the ground floor. All rooms have tea/coffee making facilities, radio, colour TV, hair dryer and electric blankets for the colder nights. Bedtime drinks and biscuits are provided. Guests, and children over ten years, are welcomed to our home February to November. No smoking. Car essential, parking. Pub within walking distance. Bed & good English breakfast from £22 - £24 pp daily; weekly from £155 per person. ETC ◆◆◆

Mrs F.J. Adams, Aston House, Broadwell, Moreton-in-Marsh GL56 0TJ
Telephone: 01451 830475 • E-mail: fja@netcomuk.co.uk
Website: www.netcomuk.co.uk/~nmfa/aston_house.html

STOW-ON-THE-WOLD. Mrs S. Davis, Fairview Farmhouse, Bledington Road, Stow-on-the-Wold, Cheltenham GL54 1JH (Tel and Fax: 01451 830279). You are assured of a warm welcome at Fairview Farmhouse situated one mile from Stow-on-the-Wold on a quiet B road with outstanding panoramic views of the surrounding Cotswold Hills. Ideal base for touring the pretty villages of Bourton-on-the-Water, The Slaughters, Broadway, Chipping Campden, also famous Stratford etc. The cosy bedrooms are furnished to a high standard with a king-size four-poster de luxe for that special occasion; all are en suite with colour TV and tea/coffee making equipment. Lounge and additional lounge area with books, maps, etc. Central heating. Ample parking. Open all year. Prices from £45 to £55 (two people sharing). ETC ◆◆◆◆ SILVER AWARD.

STOW-ON-THE-WOLD. Graham and Helen Keyte, The Limes, Evesham Road, Stow-on-the-Wold GL54 1EN (01451 830034/831056; Fax: 01451 830034). Over the last 29 years this RAC Listed and AA QQQ guesthouse has established a reputation for its homely and friendly atmosphere. It is just four minutes' walk from the town centre; central for visiting Stratford-upon-Avon, Burford, Bourton-on-the-Water, Cirencester, Cheltenham, etc. The Limes overlooks fields and has an attractive large garden with ornamental pool and waterfall. Double, twin and family rooms with washbasins. Four rooms en suite, one four-poster and family room; other doubles. All rooms have tea/coffee making facilities and colour TV; hairdryers available. Central heating. TV lounge. Diningroom. Children welcome, cot. Pets welcome. Car park. Fire Certificate held. Bed and full English Breakfast from £20 to £25 per person per night. Reductions for children. Vegetarians catered for. Open all year except Christmas. AA ◆◆◆, RAC Listed

---

TEWKESBURY. Mrs Bernadette Williams, Abbots Court, Church End, Twyning, Tewkesbury GL20 6DA (Tel & Fax: 01684 292515). Working farm. A large, quiet farmhouse set in 350 acres, built on the site of monastery between the Malverns and Cotswolds, half a mile M5-M50 junction. Six en suite bedrooms with colour TV and tea making facilities. Centrally heated. Open all year except Christmas. Large lounge with open fire and colour TV. Spacious diningroom. Licensed bar. Good home cooked food in large quantities, home produced where possible. Children's own TV room, games room and playroom. Tennis lawn. Play area and lawn. Cot and high chair available. Laundry facilities. Ideally situated for touring with numerous places to visit. Swimming, tennis, sauna, golf within three miles. Coarse fishing available on the farm. Bed and Breakfast from £17.50 to £19.50. Reduced rates for children and Senior Citizens. ETC ◆◆◆

Please mention The Farm Holiday Guide when
writing to enquire about accommodation

HAMPSHIRE

BROCKENHURST (NEW FOREST). Mrs Pauline Harris, Little Heathers, Whitemoor Road, Brockenhurst SO42 7QG (01590 623512; Fax: 01590 624255; Mobile: 07775 715584). A friendly welcome awaits you at our spacious bungalow situated on the outskirts of Brockenhurst, in the heart of the New Forest, where ponies roam free. Wonderful countryside for walking, cycling, riding, touring etc. Golf courses nearby. Four miles from Lymington with its Yacht Haven and Isle of Wight ferry. Colour TV, hairdryer and beverage facilities in double and twin bedded ground-floor bedrooms with en suite facilities; guest lounge, large garden in quiet location. Full English or Vegetarian Breakfast, special diets or smaller appetites catered for. NO SMOKING. Children welcome. Brochure available. From £22 per person per night (special short breaks reduced rates). **ETC ◆◆◆◆** *SILVER AWARD*
e-mail: little_heathers@hotmail.com
website: www.newforest.demon.co.uk/littleheathers.htm

LYNDHURST. Penny Farthing Hotel, Romsey Road, Lyndhurst SO43 7AA (023 8028 4422; Fax: 023 8028 4488). The Penny Farthing is a cheerful small Hotel ideally situated in Lyndhurst village centre, the capital of "The New Forest". The Hotel offers en suite single, double, twin and family rooms with direct dial telephones, tea/coffee tray, colour TV and clock radios. We also have some neighbouring cottages available as Hotel annexe rooms or on a self-catering basis. These have been totally refitted, much with "Laura Ashley" decor, and offer quieter, more exclusive accommodation. The hotel has a licensed bar, private car park and bicycle store. Lyndhurst has a charming variety of shops, resturants, pubs ,and bistros and "The New Forest Information Centre and Museum". All major credit cards accepted. **AA/RAC/ETC ◆◆◆◆.**
website: www.pennyfarthinghotel.co.uk.

NEW FOREST. Mrs Sandra Hocking, Southernwood, Plaitford Common, Salisbury Road, Near Romsey SO51 6EE (01794 323255 or 322577). Modern country family home, surrounded by farmland, on the edge of the New Forest. Two double, one family and one twin bedrooms; lounge. Full English Breakfast. Cots and high chairs available for babies. Four miles from M27 off A36. Salisbury, Southampton 11 miles, Stonehenge 17 miles, Portsmouth half-an-hour, Winchester 14 miles, Romsey five miles and within easy reach of continental ferries. Large garden. Ample parking. TV. Tea/coffee always available. Horse riding, golf, fishing, swimming, walking in New Forest (10 minutes). Local inns for good food. Terms from £15. Open all year.

NEW FOREST (Fritham). John and Penny Hankinson, Fritham Farm, Fritham, Lyndhurst SO43 7HH (Tel & Fax: 023 8081 2333). Lovely farmhouse on working farm in the heart of the New Forest. Dating from the 18th century, all three double/twin bedrooms have en suite facilities and provision for tea/coffee making. There is a large comfortable lounge with TV and log fire. Fritham is in a particularly beautiful part of the New Forest, still largely undiscovered and with a wealth of wildlife. It is a wonderful base for walking, riding, cycling and touring. Non-smoking. Children 10 years and over welcome. Come and enjoy peace and quiet in this lovely corner of England. Bed and Breakfast from £20 to £22. **ETC/AA ◆◆◆◆**

RINGWOOD, NEW FOREST. Mrs M. E. Burt, Fraser House, Salisbury Road, Blashford, Ringwood BH24 3PB (01425 473958).

Fraser House is situated one mile from the market town of Ringwood, overlooking the Avon Valley. This comfortable family house is on the edge of the New Forest, famous for its ponies, deer and pleasant walks. It is ten miles from Bournemouth and the South Coast, and is convenient for visiting Southampton, Stonehenge and the cathedral city of Salisbury. All rooms have en suite bath or shower facilities, central heating, comfortable beds, colour TV, tea/coffee making facilities. Guest lounge with TV. Fishing and water sports available nearby. Non-smokers preferred. Ample parking space. Open all year. Most major credit cards accepted. Bed and Breakfast from £22 per night. **ETC ◆◆◆**

ROMSEY. Mrs Christina Pybus, Pyesmead Farm, Plaitford, Romsey SO51 6EE (01794 323386).

A warm welcome awaits you on the northern edge of the New Forest, at our family-run stock farm with its own coarse fishing lakes and heated indoor swimming pool and sauna. Many activities locally including horse riding, trout fishing, golf and forest walks. Within easy reach of Salisbury, Winchester, Southampton and the coast. Excellent pubs providing good food within quarter-of-a-mile. Children welcome. Open all year except Christmas. Bed and Breakfast from £17. **ETC ◆◆◆.**

WINCHESTER near. Mays Farm, Longwood Dean, Near Winchester SO21 1JS (01962 777486; Fax 01962 777747).

Twelve minutes' drive from Winchester, (the eleventh century capital city of England), Mays Farm is set in rolling countryside on a lane which leads from nowhere to nowhere. The house is timber framed, originally built in the sixteenth century and has been thoroughly renovated and extended by its present owners, James and Rosalie Ashby. There are three guest bedrooms, (one double, one twin and one either), each with a private bathroom or shower room. A sitting room with log fire is usually available for guests' use. Ducks, geese, chickens and goats make up the two acre "farm". Prices from £23 per person per night for bed and breakfast. Booking is essential. Please telephone or fax for details.

FREE or REDUCED RATE entry to Holiday Visits and Attractions — see our READERS' OFFER VOUCHERS on pages 43-60

HEREFORDSHIRE

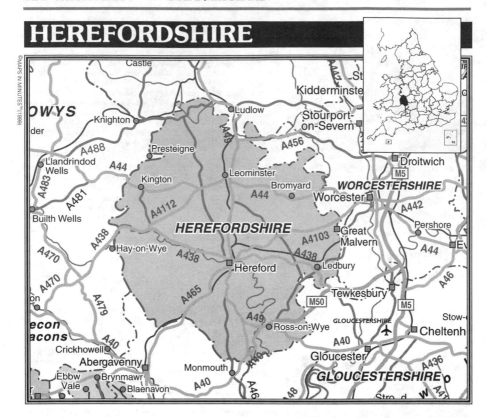

BREDENBURY. Mrs G. Evans, Red Hill Farm, Bredenbury, Bromyard HR7 4SY (01885 483255 or 01885 483535). 17th century farmhouse situated in the beautiful peaceful countryside, within easy driving distance of Worcester, Hereford, Malvern, Ledbury and Ludlow. Guest accommodation includes one family room, two double bedrooms, one twin-bedded room all with washbasin and TV; bathroom and shower; lounge with colour TV; central heating throughout. Good food at local pub (one mile) at reasonable prices. Home from home. Children and pets welcome. Equestrian horse centre (all-weather gallop, half-a-mile). Bed and Breakfast from £16 to £17 per person. Situated on A44. From Worcester take A44 to Bromyard, proceed towards Leominster for two miles; farm on right with Tourist Board sign at farm entrance. You will receive a very warm welcome on arrival. ETC ◆◆

BROADWAY. Mrs Helen Perry, Mount Pleasant Farm, Childswickham, Broadway WR12 7HZ (01386 853424). Working farm.

Large Victorian farmhouse set in 850 acres of mixed farm with cattle and horses. Excellent views. Open all year round, guests are offered a warm welcome and a good, traditional farmhouse breakfast. An ideal centre for touring the Cotswolds - three miles from Broadway, 15 miles from Stratford-upon-Avon, within easy reach of Warwick, Oxford, Cheltenham, Buxford and many other attractions. All the bedrooms are en suite with TV, tea/coffee facilities and central heating. Bed and Breakfast from £24 per person. ◆◆◆◆. Superior self-catering accommodation also available in converted barns sleeping two to eight persons. Graded 4 KEYS by Tourist Board.

FELTON HOUSE

Felton, Near Hereford HR1 3PH Tel/Fax: (01432) 820366
E-mail: bandb@ereal.net
Website: www.SmoothHound.co.uk/hotels/felton.html
www.herefordshirebandb.co.uk

Marjorie and Brian Roby offer guests, children and pets a very warm welcome to their home, a country house of immense character set in beautiful tranquil gardens in the heart of unspoilt rural England. Relax with refreshments in the library, drawing room or garden room. Taste excellent evening meals at local inns. Sleep in an antique four poster or brass bed and awake refreshed to enjoy, in a superb Victorian dining room, the breakfast you have selected from a wide choice of traditional and vegetarian dishes. Felton House is 20 minutes by car from Hereford, Leominster, Bromyard and Ledbury, off A417 between A49 and A465. Non Smoking, Children and pets welcome. Tourist Board Highly Commended.

B&B £23 per person with en suite or private bathroom. AA & ETC ◆◆◆ *Silver Award*

HEREFORD. David Jones, Sink Green Farm, Rotherwas, Hereford HR2 6LE (01432 870223). Working farm. Warm and friendly atmosphere awaits your arrival at this 16th century farmhouse, on the banks of the River Wye. Three miles south of the cathedral city of Hereford, with Ross-on-Wye, Leominster, Ledbury, Malvern and the Black Mountains within easy reach. All rooms en suite, tea/coffee making facilities and colour TV. One room with four-poster, family room by arrangement. Guests' own lounge. Pets by arrangement. Bed and Breakfast from £20 per person. AA QQQQ.

HEREFORD. Mrs Diana Sinclair, Holly House Farm, Allensmore, Hereford HR2 9BH (01432 277294; Fax: 01432 261285; mobile 07885 830223). Spacious luxury farmhouse and over 10 acres of land with horses, situated in beautiful and peaceful open countryside. Bedrooms en suite or with private bathroom, central heating, TV and tea/coffee making facilities. We are only five miles south-west of Hereford city centre. Ideal base for Welsh Borders, market towns, Black Mountains, Brecon and Malvern Hills and the Wye Valley. We have a happy family atmosphere and pets are welcome. Brochure on request. From £20 per person per night and with our delicious English Breakfast you will be fit for the whole day! e-mail: hollyhousefarm@aol.com

See also Colour Display Advertisement HEREFORD. Jennie Layton, Grafton Villa, Grafton, Hereford HR2 8ED (Tel & Fax: 01432 268689). A loved and cherished farmhouse, set in an acre of lawns and garden, overlooking ancient Roman fortifications and woodlands. Furnished with flair, using beautiful fabrics and antiques. Peaceful en suite bedrooms, delicious award winning breakfasts, farmhouse portions. An ideal way to start the day visiting Hereford's secrets, market towns, Ledbury. Bromyard, Ross-on-Wye, Hay-on-Wye (book lovers' haven) and wonderful garden and churches, Dore Abbey, Kilpeck and many more. Self-catering cottage available, suitable for wheelchair guests. Sleeps 4/5. **ETC** ◆◆◆◆ *SILVER AWARD*, **AA** ◆◆◆◆. e-mail: jennielayton@creal.com

FHG PUBLICATIONS LIMITED

publish a large range of well-known accommodation guides. We will be happy to send you details or you can use the order form at the back of this book.

LEDBURY. Mrs Jane West, Church Farm, Coddington, Ledbury HR8 1JJ (01531 640271). Church Farm

is a Black and White Listed farmhouse on a working farm in quiet hamlet. Oak beamed accommodation in two double and one twin bedroom. Close to Malvern Hills. Ideal touring base being equidistant between Ross-on-Wye, Hereford, Worcester and Gloucester. Plenty of space and fields for walking dogs. Warm hospitality assured in a quiet, relaxed atmosphere. Plenty of good English fare. Evening meals if required. Log fires, TV. Bed and Breakfast from £22. Excellent self-catering unit also available.

LEDBURY. Mrs C. Gladwin, Hill Farm, Eastnor, Ledbury HR8 1EF (01531 632827). HILL FARM is a 300-

year-old stone and brick farmhouse surrounded by woodland at the foot of the Malvern Hills, one mile from Ledbury and one mile from Eastnor Castle. Accommodation comprises one twin room and two family rooms also used as twin/double rooms all with washbasin, TV and tea/coffee making facilities. Guests own sittingroom with log fire and the diningroom look out onto a large garden and rural views. Bed and Breakfast from £17.50. Evening Meal by arrangement from £10.00.

LEOMINSTER. Mrs J. Williams, Lowe Farm, Pembridge, Leominster HR6 9JD (01544 388395). Standing

on its own in two hundred acres of beautiful rolling countryside a Grade 11 Listed 14th century farmhouse on working farm. A warm welcome awaits you from Juliet and Clive, with high standards and service, but with that home-from-home feeling. Guests have exclusive use of beautifully furnished dining, sittingroom areas. Fully centrally heated. Spacious car parking. Open all year round, we offer a non-smoking environment and late breakfasts. Bedrooms with TV, tea/coffee making facilities with private en suite. In house chilled cabinet for indoors and the garden, which is half an acre of trees/shrubs and has well designed gazebo, seating areas, with use of gas barbecue. **ETC ♦♦♦♦** *SILVER AWARD*
e-mail: williams_family@lineone.net

LONGTOWN. Mrs I. Pritchard, Olchon Cottage Farm, Longtown, Hereford HR2 0NS (Tel & Fax: 01873 860233). Working farm. Small working farm. An ideal

location for a peaceful holiday in lovely walking country close to Offa's Dyke Path and Welsh Border. The farmhouse is noted for its good, wholesome, home produced food and many guests return to enjoy the homely, relaxing atmosphere. Magnificent views and many places of interest to visit. Accommodation comprises two family bedrooms (also used as singles/doubles) both en suite with colour TV, radio, hairdryer and tea/coffee facilitiies. Guests' sittingroom and diningroom with separate tables. Towels provided. Reductions for children under 10 years; cot, high chair and babysitting offered. Open all year except Christmas. Bed, Breakfast and Evening Meal or Bed and Breakfast from £20. Car essential, parking. Terms on application, with stamp for brochure please. Welcome Host Award. **ETC ♦♦♦**
website: www.golden-valley.co.uk/olchon

NEWTON ST MARGARETS. Mrs Dido Windham, Shobdon Farm, St Margarets HR2 0QW (01981 510310). Set in its own grounds on a small working sheep farm between Hay-on-Wye and Hereford, but off the beaten track. We are ideally placed for outdoor activities in the area and walking and sightseeing in the Black Mountains, Border towns and the Golden Valley. This is a family house with a large farmhouse kitchen where breakfast is served. The bedrooms are spacious with tea/coffee facilities. One double en suite and one twin/family room with separate shower etc and lots of hot water. Dogs by arrangement – outdoor kennel and stabling if required. B & B from £20 per person per night.

ROSS-ON-WYE. Mrs M. E. Drzymalska, Thatch Close, Llangrove, Ross-on-Wye HR9 6EL (01989 770300). Working farm, join in. Secluded peaceful Georgian farmhouse set in large colourful gardens in 13 acres of pasture situated in the beautiful Wye Valley between Ross and Monmouth. Thatch Close offers a comfortable, homely atmosphere where guests are welcome to help feed the pigs, cows, calves, or just relax and enjoy this traditionally run farm. Places of scenic beauty and historic attractions nearby include Forest of Dean, Black Mountains, Cathedral Cities, old castles and buildings. Guests have their own lounge and diningroom with colour TV. Twin bedroom and one double room, both with bathrooms en suite, one double room with private bathroom; all bathrooms have shower and bath. Central heating. Non-smokers please. Breakfast and optional Evening Meal are prepared using mainly home grown produce. Vegetarian and diabetic meals arranged. Bed and Breakfast from £18 with reductions for longer stays. Reduced rates for children. SAE for further details. ETC ◆◆◆

ISLE OF WIGHT

COWES. Judith Shanks, Youngwoods Farm, Whitehouse Road, Porchfield, Newport PO30 4LJ (Tel & Fax: 01983 522170). Enjoy a friendly welcome at our grassland farm set in open countryside, among the ancient oak trees with magnificent views of the West Wight. The 18th century stone farmhouse is peacefully situated well off the road and retains its original character, with two spacious twin/double bedrooms and one single bedroom. Tea/coffee making facilities and central heating throughout. Close to Newtown Nature Reserve with red squirrels and good bird watching hides. Cowes sailing centre four miles, historic Carisbrooke Castle three miles and beaches all round. Children from eight years and non-smokers welcome. Open all year. Terms from £18 to £25 per person per night. ETC ◆◆◆.

KENT

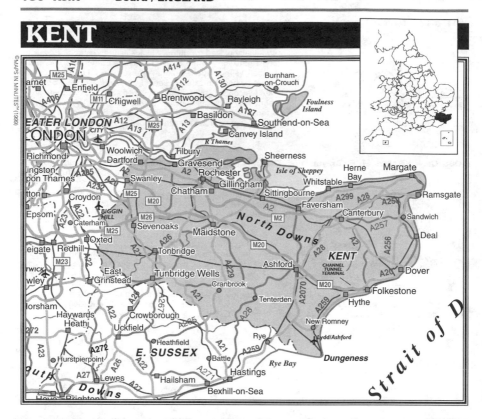

©MAPS IN MINUTES™ (1999)

BIDDENDEN Mrs Susan Twort, Heron Cottage, Biddenden, Ashford TN27 8HH (01580 291358).

Peacefully situated in own grounds amidst six acres of arable farmland, boasting many wild animals and birds, a stream and pond for coarse fishing. Within easy reach of Leeds Castle and many National Trust. properties including Sissinghurst Castle. You can choose between three tastefully furnished rooms with en suite facilities and TV or two rooms with separate bathrooms. All rooms are centrally heated and have tea/coffee making facilities. There is a residents' lounge with log fire. Evening meals by arrangement. Bed and Breakfast from £17.50 to £25.00 per person per night.

CANTERBURY. Mrs Lewana Castle, Great Field Farm, Misling Lane, Stelling Minnis, Canterbury CT4 6DE (01227 709223).

Situated in beautiful countryside, our spacious farmhouse is about eight miles from Canterbury and Folkestone, 12 miles from Dover and Ashford. We are a working farm with some livestock including friendly ponies and chickens. We provide a friendly and high standard of accommodation with full central heating and double glazing, traditional breakfasts cooked on the Aga, courtesy tray and colour TV in each of our suites/bedrooms. Our annexe suite has a private staircase, lounge, kitchen, double bedroom and bathroom and is also available for self-catering holidays. Our cottage suite has its own entrance, stairs, lounge, bathroom and twin-bedded room. Our large double/family bedroom has en suite bathroom and air-bath. There is ample off-road parking and good pub food nearby. Bed and Breakfast from £18per person; reductions for children. Non-smoking establishment.

BLERIOT'S

47 Park Avenue, Dover, Kent CT16 1HE   Telephone (01304) 211394

A Victorian Residence set in a tree lined avenue, in the lee of Dover Castle. Within easy
reach of trains, bus station, town centre, Hoverport and docks. Channel Tunnel approximately
10 minutes' drive. Off-road parking. We specialise in one night 'stop-overs' and Mini Breaks.
Single, Double, Twin and Family rooms with full en suite. All rooms have colour TV, tea
and coffee making facilities, and are fully centrally heated. Full English Breakfast served
from 7am. Reduced rates for room only. Open all year.

Rates: Bed & Breakfast: £18 to £23 per person per night.

Mini-Breaks: January-April and October-December £18 per person per night.

MASTERCARD AND VISA ACCEPTED   *AA* INSPECTED

CANTERBURY. Mrs A. Hunt, Bower Farmhouse, Stelling Minnis, Near Canterbury CT4 6BB (01227

709430). Anne and Nick Hunt welcome you to Bower Farm
House, a traditional 17th century Kentish farmhouse situated in the
midst of Stelling Minnis, a medieval common of 125 acres of
unspoilt trees, shrubs and open grassland; seven miles south of
the cathedral city of Canterbury and nine miles from the coast; the
countryside abounds in beauty spots and nature reserves. The
house is heavily beamed and maintains its original charm. The
accommodation comprises a double room and a twin bedded
room, both with private facilities. Full traditional English breakfast
is served with home-made bread, marmalade and fresh free-
range eggs. Children welcome; pets by prior arrangement. Open
all year (except Christmas). Car essential. Excellent pub food five
minutes away. Bed and Breakfast from £21.00 per person. **ETC**
◆◆◆◆ *SILVER AWARD.*

CANTERBURY. Mr and Mrs R. Linch, Upper Ansdore, Duckpit Lane, Petham, Canterbury CT4 5QB (Tel:

01227 700672; Fax: 01227 700840). Beautiful secluded
Listed Tudor farmhouse with various livestock, situated in an
elevated position with far-reaching views of the wooded
countryside of the North Downs. The property overlooks a Kent
Trust Nature Reserve, it is five miles south of the cathedral city of
Canterbury and only 30 minutes' drive to the ports of Dover and
Folkestone. The accommodation comprises three double and
one twin bedded room, and a family room. All have shower, WC
en suite and tea making facilities. Dining/sittingroom, heavily
beamed with large inglenook. Car essential, bed and Full English
Breakfast from £21 per person. AA QQQ.

PLEASE NOTE

All the information in this book is given in good faith in the
belief that it is correct. However, the publishers cannot
guarantee the facts given in these pages, neither are they
responsible for changes in policy, ownership or terms that may
take place after the date of going to press. Readers should
always satisfy themselves that the facilities they require are
available and that the terms, if quoted, still apply.

FAVERSHAM. N.J. and C.I. Scutt, Leaveland Court, Leaveland, Faversham ME13 0NP (01233 740596).

Guests are warmly welcomed to our enchanting timbered 15th century farmhouse which nestles between Leaveland Church and woodlands in rural tranquillity. Offering high standards of accommodation whilst retaining their original character, all bedrooms are en suite with colour TV and hot drinks trays. Traditional breakfasts, cooked on the Aga, are available with a choice of alternatives. There is a large attractive garden with heated outdoor swimming pool for guests' use and ample car parking. Ideally situated for visiting Kent's historic cities, castles, houses and gardens with Canterbury only 20 minutes by car and also easy access to Channel ports, 30 minutes. Good walking country, being close to both the Pilgrim's Way and the coast. Open February to November. Terms from £24 for Bed and Breakfast. **ETC** ◆◆◆◆.

MAIDSTONE. Mrs Diane Leat, Bramley Knowle Farm, Eastwood Road, Ulcombe, Maidstone ME17 1ET (01622 858878; Fax: 01622 851121).

A warm welcome awaits you at our modern farmhouse built in the style of a Kentish Barn. Set in 45 acres of peaceful Kentish countryside, yet only ten minutes' drive from M20 Junction 8. Evening meals within walking distance. Ideal location for visiting Leeds Castle, Sissinghurst Gardens, Canterbury and Rye. Three-quarters of an hour's drive from Channel Ports. London one hour by train. Accommodation consists of one double en suite, one double and one single sharing guests-only bathroom. TV and tea/coffee making facilities in all bedrooms. Dining/sitting room with TV and video. Non smoking. Children over three welcome. Bed and Breakfast from £20.00 per person. **ETC** ◆◆◆.

FOR THE MUTUAL GUIDANCE
OF GUEST AND HOST

Every year literally thousands of holidays, short breaks and overnight stops are arranged through our guides, the vast majority without any problems at all. In a handful of cases, however, difficulties do arise about bookings, which often could have been prevented from the outset.

It is important to remember that when accommodation has been booked, both parties – guests and hosts – have entered into a form of contract. We hope that the following points will provide helpful guidance.

GUESTS: When enquiring about accommodation, be as precise as possible. Give exact dates, numbers in your party and the ages of any children. State the number and type of rooms wanted and also what catering you require – bed and breakfast, full board etc. Make sure that the position about evening meals is clear – and about pets, reductions for children or any other special points.

Read our reviews carefully to ensure that the proprietors you are going to contact can supply what you want. Ask for a letter confirming all arrangements, if possible.

If you have to cancel, do so as soon as possible. Proprietors do have the right to retain deposits and under certain circumstances to charge for cancelled holidays if adequate notice is not given and they cannot re-let the accommodation.

HOSTS: Give details about your facilities and about any special conditions. Explain your deposit system clearly and arrangements for cancellations, charges etc. and whether or not your terms include VAT.

If for any reason you are unable to fulfil an agreed booking without adequate notice, you may be under an obligation to arrange suitable alternative accommodation or to make some form of compensation.

While every effort is made to ensure accuracy, we regret that FHG Publications cannot accept responsibility for errors, omissions or misrepresentations in our entries or any consequences thereof.
Prices in particular should be checked because we go to press early. We will follow up complaints but cannot act as arbiters or agents for either party.

LANCASHIRE

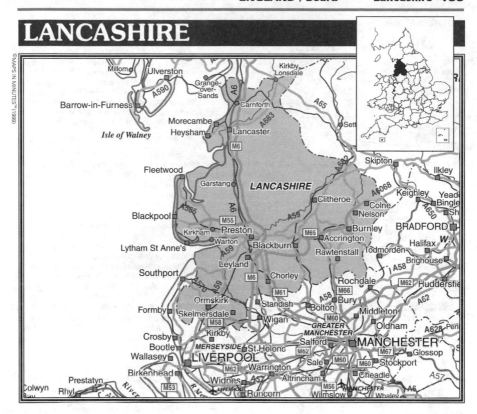

©MAPS IN MINUTES™ (1999)

BACUP. Ann Isherwood, Pasture Bottom Farm, Bacup OL13 9UZ (Tel & Fax: 01706 873790).

Pasture Bottom Farm is situated at the head of the Rossendale Valley on the Lancashire–Yorkshire border. It is set in an elevated position with panoramic views. It is a working beef farm. We are within a short distance from the main road on a private lane with no passing traffic. All rooms are centrally heated. Two twin rooms, one en suite, one with private bathroom, and one double room en suite. TV in each room and tea/coffee facilities. Tariff from £16 per person per night. **ETC ◆◆◆.**
e-mail: ha.isherwood@zen.co.uk

CARNFORTH. Mrs Vera Casson, Galley Hall Farm, Shore Road, Carnforth LA5 9HZ (01524 732544).

A 17th century farmhouse on a stock rearing farm on the North Lancashire coast, near Junction 35 M6, close to Leighton Moss RSPB, historic Lancaster; ideal base for touring the Lake District or the coastal resorts. Double, twin and single rooms; tea/coffee, washbasin and radio in all rooms; TV available. Sorry, no pets or smoking. Central heating, log fires. Lounge with TV. Evening meals on request. Good golf courses and fishing in the area. We offer a homely and friendly atmosphere. Open all year except Christmas. Bed and Breakfast from £18 per person. **ETC ◆◆◆◆**

CLITHEROE. Mrs Frances Oliver, Wytha Farm, Rimington, Clitheroe BB7 4EQ (01200 445295).

Working farm, join in. Farmhouse accommodation on stockrearing farm in Ribble Valley with extensive views. Within walking distance of Pendle Hill. Ideal touring centre for Lake District, Yorkshire Dales, Bronte Country, interesting and historic Clitheroe. Children welcome. Babysitting service. Beautiful picnic area. Packed lunches available. Farm produce when possible, and home cooking. Accommodation comprises en suite double and family rooms; TV lounge; central heating. Ample car parking. Pets by prior arrangement (£1 per day). Bed and Breakfast from £15; Evening Meal £8. Reduced rates for children under 11 years. Open all year.

CLITHEROE near. Miss J.M. Simpson and Mr N.E. Quayle, Middle Flass Lodge, Settle Road, Bolton-by-Bowland, Clitheroe BB7 4NY (01200 447259; Fax: 01200 447300). A warm and friendly welcome awaits in this family-run tastefully converted barn. Unrivalled views across the countryside. Situated in the Forest of Bowland at the heart of the Ribble Valley, ideal base for the Dales and Lakes. We are a small guest house with four en suite bedrooms, all with tea/coffee making facilities, colour teletext TV and room controlled central heating. Residents' lounge. Full English breakfast and four-course table d'hôte dinner served in our dining room using fresh local produce whenever possible, all chef prepared. Licensed. Gardens. Ample private parking. Bed and Breakfast from £20 per person. Please telephone for further details. **AA/ETC ◆◆◆◆.**

See also Colour Display Advertisement **CLITHEROE. Mrs P. M. Gifford, Rakefoot Farm, Chaigley, Near Clitheroe BB7 3LY (01995 61332/07889 279063).** Working family farm offering accommodation in standard and en suite rooms, some with private lounge. Panoramic views of Longridge Fell and Pendle Hill, ideally situated for walking or touring the Dales, Lakes and coast. Excellent cooked breakfasts; other meals by arrangement. Also self-catering. Bed and Breakfast from £15 to £20 per person per night depending on room and length of stay. Children welcome, reductions for sharing. **ETC ◆◆◆◆**

LUNE VALLEY. Mrs Shirley Harvey, Low House Farm, Claughton, Lancaster LA2 9LA (015242 21260).

Working farm, join in. Low House is a mixed dairy working farm set in the heart of the beautiful Lune Valley, yet easily accessible from M6 Motorway. Within easy reach of Lake District, North West coast and Yorkshire Dales. Convenient for fishing, golf, waymarked walks and country cycle track. Accommodation in large comfortable farmhouse with guests' own sittingroom. Colour TV and tea/coffee making facilites in bedrooms, two of which have own bath shower room. Visitors are welcome to relax in large beautiful garden which also has some play facilities for children. Country pub serving meals approximately 150 yards. Bed and Breakfast from £20. **ETC ◆◆◆**

ORMSKIRK. Mrs A. Mercer, The Meadows, New Sutch Farm, Sutch Lane, Ormskirk L40 4BU (01704 894048). Lovely 17th century farmhouse situated down a private country lane. Relaxed and friendly atmosphere. Three pretty en suite ground floor bedrooms with all home comforts. Both lounge and diningroom overlook beautiful gardens. Enjoy a hearty breakfast whilst listening to the birdsong. Welcome pot of tea. M6, 15 minutes, A59 five minutes. Bed and Breakfast from £19.50. Open all year.

ORMSKIRK near. Mrs Wilson, Brandreth Barn, Tarlscough Lane, Burscough, Near Omskirk L40 0RJ

(Tel & Fax: 01704 893510). Situated alongside the Martin Mere Wildfowl Trust, an 18th century brick-built barn conversion dated 1774. Five minutes from A59, 15 minutes from M6. Ideal for touring the Lake District and the Yorkshire Dales. Three double and five twin rooms, all en suite with colour TV, full central heating, and tea/coffee making facilities. Licensed restaurant using fresh homegrown produce. Evening meal by arrangement. Also disabled facilities. Single room £25, double room £40. Open all year except Christmas.

PILLING. Beryl and Peter Richardson, Bell Farm, Bradshaw Lane, Scronkey, Pilling, Preston PR3 6SN

(01253 790324). Beryl and Peter welcome you to their 18th century farmhouse situated in the quiet village of Pilling, which lies between the Ribble and Lune Estuaries. The area has many public footpaths and is ideal for cycling. From the farm there is easy access to Blackpool, Lancaster, the Forest of Bowland and the Lake District. Accommodation consists of one family room with en suite facilities, one double and one twin with private bathroom. Tea and coffee making facilities. Lounge and dining room. All rooms en suite. All centrally heated. Children and pets welcome. Full English Breakfast is served. Open all year, except Christmas and New Year. Bed and Breakfast from £20.00.

SOUTHPORT. Mrs Wendy E. Core, Sandy Brook Farm, 52 Wyke Cop Road, Scarisbrick, Southport PR8

5LR (01704 880337). Bill and Wendy Core offer a homely, friendly atmosphere at Sandy Brook, a small working farm situated three-and-a-half miles from the seaside resort of Southport and five miles from the historic town of Ormskirk. Motorways are easily accessible, and the Lake District, Trough of Bowland, Blackpool and North Wales are within easy reach. Six en suite bedrooms with colour TV and tea/coffee making facilities. Central heating throughout. Sittingroom with colour TV; diningroom. High chair, cots, and babysitting available. Room available for wheelchair/disabled guests. Open all year round. Bed and Breakfast from £17. Reductions for children. Weekly terms on request. NWTB Silver Award Winner "Place to Stay" Farmhouse Category. **ETC ◆◆◆**

LEICESTERSHIRE including Rutland

BELTON-IN-RUTLAND, Near Uppingham.

The Old Rectory, Belton-in-Rutland, Oakham LE15 9LE (01572 717279; Fax: 01572 717343). Guest accommodation. Victorian country house and guest annexe in charming village overlooking Eyebrook valley and rolling Rutland countryside. Comfortable and varied selection of rooms, mostly en suite, with direct outside access. Prices from £16 to £30 per person per night including breakfast. Small farm environment (horses and sheep) with excellent farmhouse breakfast. Public House 100 yards. Lots to see and do: Rutland Water, castles, stately homes, country parks, forestry and Barnsdale Gardens. Non-smoking. Self catering also available. RAC ◆◆◆
e-mail: bb@stablemate.demon.co.uk

MELTON MOWBRAY. Mrs D. N. Mellows,

Somerby House Farm, Somerby, Near Melton Mowbray LE14 2PZ (01664 454225). Bed and Breakfast in 18th century farmhouse. Single and double rooms and bath. Family room with bath, WC. TV. Central heating. Children and dogs welcome. Open all year. Stabling for horses May to August. Inns and riding school in village. Nearby places of interest include Rutland Water for boating and water sports, Oakham Castle, Belvoir Castle, Rockingham Castle and Burghley House. The Nene Valley Railway is also close by.

MELTON MOWBRAY. Mrs Margaret Spencer,

White Lodge Farm, Nottingham Road, Ab Kettleby, Melton Mowbray LE14 3JB (01664 822286). A warm welcome and comfortable accommodation await you on our working farm at the edge of the Vale of Belvoir, three miles north of Melton Mowbray, home of the pork pie and Stilton cheese. Ground floor, self-contained rooms overlook the garden, all en suite with central heating, colour TV, tea coffee-making facilities and electric blankets. Open all year. Non-smoking. Bed and Breakfast from £19 per person per night. ETC ◆◆◆◆

LINCOLNSHIRE

BENNIWORTH. Kay Olivant, Skirbeck Farm, Panton Road, Benniworth LN3 6JN (01507 313682; Fax: 01507 313692). Enjoy a stay on a working farm whilst visiting the beautiful Lincolnshire Wolds. The peaceful location is surrounded by good walking country including the Viking Way. It is 16 miles east of the cathedral City of Lincoln and only a few miles from the interesting market towns of Louth, Norcastle and Market Rasen. The east coast and South Yorkshire (via the Humber Bridge), all within easy touring distance. The farm has its own coarse and fly fishing lakes and over four miles of natural lakes. Local atractions include Benniworth Springs off-road driving track, Hemswell antiques, Market Rasen Races and Cadwell racing circuit. The farmhouse is comfortably furnished, has central heating and log fires. All bedrooms have colour TV, Teasmaid and own bathroom. Sun lounge overlooking secluded garden. Children welcome. Non-smokers please. Self-catering cottages also available.

HORNCASTLE. Mrs C.E. Harrison, Baumber Park, Baumber, Near Horncastle LN9 5NE (01507 578235; Fax: 01507 578417). Spacious elegant farmhouse of character in quiet parkland setting on a mixed farm. Large gardens, wildlife pond and grass tennis court. Fine bedrooms with lovely views, period furniture and log fires. Central in the county and close to the Lincolnshire Wolds, this rolling countryside is little known and quite unspoilt. Bridleways and lanes ideal for walking, cycling or riding: stabling for horses available. Two championship golf courses at nearby Woodhall Spa. Well located for historic Lincoln, interesting market towns and many antique shops. Single, double en suite and twin with private bathroom. Bed and Breakfast from £20. A warm welcome awaits. **ETC** ◆◆◆◆

HORNCASTLE. Mrs Judy Bankes Price, Greenfield Farm, Minting, Near Horncastle LN9 5PJ (Tel & Fax 01507 578457; mobile 07768 368829). Judy and Hugh welcome you to stay in their lovely, peaceful, spacious home, surrounded by extensive grounds and dominated by a wonderful wildlife pond. It is centrally placed and easy to find (A158 one mile); Lincoln Cathedral is 15 minutes' drive and the peaceful, rolling Wolds just five minutes away. The bedrooms have wonderful views, modern en suite shower rooms and heated towel rails. The bedrooms comprise one double and one twin with en suite facilities, and one double with a private bathroom. There is ample easy parking and a tennis court. Non-smoking household. Traditional pub one mile. Bed and Breakfast from £21.50. **AA** ◆◆◆◆.
e-mail: greenfieldfarm@farming.co.uk

MARTIN, By Timberland. Mr and Mrs N. Forman, Beechwood Barn, North Moor Lane, Linwood Road, Martin, By Timberland LN4 3RA (01526 378339). Beechwood Barn, built in 1853 and now managed as a smallholding, has been tastefully converted into a comfortable home retaining its original character. There are many exposed beams together with an imposing spiral staircase winding its way to a double en suite bedroom which was originally the old hay-loft. A further spiral staircase from this room leads to the grounds of Beechwood Barn giving guests their own private entrance. The pretty twin-bedded room has a washbasin and adjoining private bathroom. Both rooms have colour TV and tea/coffee making facilities. An ideal location for a peaceful and relaxing break. There are numerous places of interest to visit in this area with the Wolds and coast just a short drive away. The city of Lincoln with its famous cathedral is just 14 miles from the village. A full English breakfast is served using our own free-range eggs cooked to your liking. Unfortunately dogs are not allowed and Beechwood Barn is a non-smoking home. You are however always assured of a warm welcome. Open all year. **ETC** ◆◆◆◆.

SPALDING. Chris Cave, Sycamore Farm, 6 Station Road, Gedney Hill, Spalding PE12 0NP (Tel & Fax: 01406 330445; Mobile: 07889 147001). Exploring East Anglia? Why not spend a while in the "Land of the Big Sky"? A warm and comfortable welcome awaits you at this 150-year-old home, which is on the B1166, in the small Lincolnshire village of Gedney Hill. Your exclusive accommodation includes lounge with TV, diningroom, and shower/bathroom. Only a stone's throw away is a 'real' village shop, bakery, post office, and pubs with local 'flavour'. Flying, gliding, golf and fishing are also available. Bed and Breakfast £25 per adult per night. Sited within the grounds of the farmhouse is a fully serviced eight-berth static caravan. Hard or grass standings for caravans or tents are also available.

e-mail: sycamore.farm@virgin.net
website: http://homepage.ntlworld.com/christine.cave

THORPE FENDYKES. Mrs S. Evans, Willow Farm, Thorpe Fendykes, Wainfleet, Skegness PE24 4QH (01754 830316). In the heart of the Lincolnshire Fens, Willow Farm is a working smallholding with free range hens, goats, horses and ponies. Situated in a peaceful hamlet with abundant wildlife, ideal for a quiet retreat - yet only 15 minutes from the Skegness coast, shops, amusements and beaches. Bed and Breakfast is provided in comfortable en suite rooms at £15 per person per night, reductions for children (suppers and sandwiches can be provided in the evening on request). Rooms have tea and coffee making facilities and a colour TV and are accessible to disabled guests. Friendly hosts! Ring for brochure.

WRAGBY, near. Sarah Stamp, The Grange, Torrington Lane, East Barkwith, Near Wragby LN8 5RY (01673 858670). The Grange is perfectly positioned in a peaceful, rural location, amidst the wonderful Lincolnshire countryside, with views of the Cathedral to the west and the rolling Wolds to the east. Situated on the family farm, immaculate in every respect, a genuine warm welcome is offered, together with the peace and tranquillity for a relaxing and memorable break. The house is spacious, with two luxury en suite double rooms, tastefully furnished and equipped to provide every facility for comfort and care. Excellent home-produced food using fresh local produce ensures hearty appetites are met. Enjoy walks along the farm trail, as each season has something special to offer. Relax by the secluded trout lake and admire the sunsets. Children welcome. No pets. Non-smoking. Lawn tennis. Highly commended in the ETC 'England for Excellence' Awards. Bed and Breakfast from £22.50 per person. **ETC** ◆◆◆◆ *SILVER AWARD.*

NORFOLK

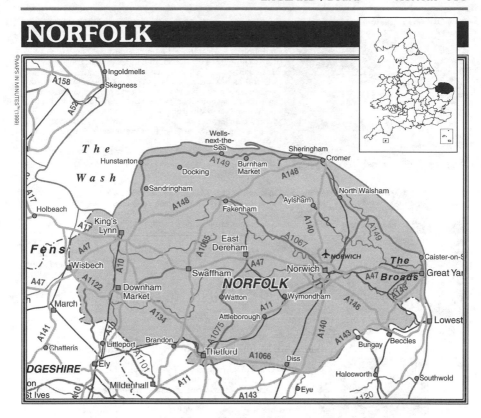

ATTLEBOROUGH. Hill House Farm, Deopham Road, Great Ellingham, Attleborough NR17 1AQ (01953 453113). A working farm in quiet rural setting situated within easy reach of all local attractions. We offer our guests a warm welcome, children welcome, pets by arrangement only. Attractions include Banham Zoo, world famous Butterfly Gardens, Snetterton Racing Circuit and fishing lakes are closeby; seaside resorts and Norfolk Broads are approximately 40 miles distant. Comfortable rooms with washbasins, tea/coffee facilities and colour TV. Ample parking. Open all year. Awarded Good Food Hygiene Certificate. Terms from £19 per person per night. Reduction for children up to 10 years.

BECCLES (Near). Mrs Rachel Clarke, Shrublands Farm, Burgh St. Peter, Near Beccles, Suffolk NR34 0BB (Tel & Fax: 01502 677241). This attractive homely farmhouse offers a warm and friendly welcome, is peacefully situated in the Waveney Valley on the Norfolk/Suffolk border, and is surrounded by one acre of garden and lawns. The River Waveney flows through the 550 acres of mixed working farmland; opportunities for bird-watching. Ideal base for touring Norfolk and Suffolk; Beccles, Lowestoft, Great Yarmouth and Norwich are all within easy reach. The house has two double rooms with en suite facilities and one twin-bedded room with private bathroom, shower room and toilet. All have satellite colour TV and tea/coffee making facilities; diningroom, lounge with colour satellite TV. Non-smoking rooms. No pets. Car essential, ample parking. Tennis court available. Swimming pool and food at River Centre nearby. Open all year except Christmas. Bed and Breakfast from £20 per person. Reductions for longer stays. SAE please. **ETC** ◆◆◆◆

BUNGAY. Mrs B. Watchorn, Earsham Park Farm, Harleston Road, Earsham, Bungay NR35 2AQ (01986 892180; Fax: 01986 894796).

Escape into the beautiful East Anglian countryside in this family-run quiet and friendly farmhouse surrounded by lovely gardens and farm walks. Superbly set on a hill overlooking the gorgeous Waveney Valley. The rooms are all spacious and beautifully furnished, but with comfort as a priority. Two large doubles (one with four-poster), and one twin room, all en suite. All rooms have extensive facilities, including easy chairs, colour TV, tea tray, radio, etc., whilst thick fluffy towels and embroidered linen add to your comfort. The farm's own produce is used in the excellent breakfasts. The famous Earsham Otter Trust is at the bottom of the drive. Your hosts have a wealth of local knowledge. A non-smoking house. B&B from £22 per person, based on two people sharing. **ETC** ◆◆◆◆ *SILVER AWARD*, **AA** ◆◆◆◆
e-mail: watchorn_s@freenet.co.uk

DEREHAM. Hill House, 26 Market Place, Dereham NR19 2AP (01362 699699).

Relax in the comfort of an elegant town centre location period residence with comfortable rooms and charming gardens. All bedrooms en suite, with colour TV, radio and tea/coffee making facilities; one four-poster. Full English breakfast; vegetarians and special diets welcomed. Ample off-road parking, secure cycle unit; laundry and drying facilities. Ideal touring base, situated in the heart of Norfolk with Norwich, the coast and Broads,Gressenhall, historic and other attractions a short drive away. Ground floor room for those with walking difficulty. More rooms planned for 2001. No smoking, no children under 16. Bed and Breakfast from £25.

FAKENHAM. Mrs Carol Pointer, Manor Farm, Sculthorpe, Fakenham NR21 9NJ (01328 862185; Fax: 01328 862033).

Manor Farm is a mixed working farm set in peaceful surroundings. This Georgian House has two en suite rooms and one with private bath and shower; all with central heating, colour TV and tea/coffee making facilities. Ideal base for exploring Norfolk's beaches, National Trust properties and unspoilt villages. Well behaved dogs allowed by arrangement and children over 10. Bed and full English breakfast from £20 per person per night. Open all year except Christmas. We look forward to welcoming you. **ETC** ◆◆◆◆ *SILVER AWARD, FARM HOLIDAY BUREAU MEMBER.*
e-mail: mddwo2@dial.pipex.com

HARLESTON. Mrs June E. Holden, Weston House Farm, Mendham, Harleston IP20 0PB (01986 782206; Fax: 01986 782414).

Peacefully located 17th century Grade II Listed farmhouse on a 300 acre mixed farm just outside village of Mendham in the heart of the Waveney Valley. Within easy reach of Suffolk heritage coast, Norfolk Broads, historic city of Norwich and nearby Otter Sanctuary. Comfortable, spacious accommodation comprises two double and one twin bedded rooms, all with en suite facilities, TV, hostess tray, clock radio and shaver points. Guest lounge with colour TV, games, books and piano. Attractive dining room overlooking large garden. Adequate parking space. Non-smoking. Bed and Breakfast £27 single, £45 double. Discounts for longer stays. **ETC/AA** ◆◆◆.

Holmdene Farm

Mrs G. Davidson, Holmdene Farm, Beeston,
King's Lynn, Norfolk, PE32 2NJ

Holmdene Farm is a small livestock farm situated in central Norfolk within easy reach of Coast and Broads. Sporting activities are available locally and the village pub is nearby. The 17th century beamed farmhouse is comfortable and welcoming with log fires for those chilly evenings. One double, one twin and two single rooms, all with beverage trays. Pets welcome. B & B from £18 per person. Evening meal for £12. Weekly terms and child reduction available. *Two self catering cottages, one sleeping five and the other up to eight persons. Terms on request. Please telephone for further details.*

ETC ★★★/♔♔♔

Working Farm • Cycles for hire
Telephone: 01328 701284

HOLT. Mrs Lynda-Lee Mack, Hempstead Hall, Holt NR25 6TN (01263 712224). Working farm. Enjoy

a relaxing holiday with a friendly atmosphere in our 18th century flint farmhouse, beautifully set on a 300 acre arable farm with ducks, donkeys and large gardens. Close to the north Norfolk coast and its many attractions. Take a ride on the steam train or a boat trip to Blakeney Point Seal Sanctuary. There is a five mile circular walk through our conservation award winning farm to Holt Country Park. Large en suite family room, double with private bathroom. Colour TV, tea/coffee facilites. Large lounge with log burning stove. Non-smoking. Sorry, no pets indoors. Bed and Breakfast from £20 per person. Children's reductions. Member of Farm Holiday Bureau. **ETC** ◆◆◆◆
website: www.broadland.com/hempsteadhall

KING'S LYNN. Roger and Helen Roberts, North Farmhouse, Station Road, Docking, King's Lynn PE31 8LS (01485 518493). North Farmhouse is a rambling old

farmhouse situated in Docking. The village is a central point for North-West Norfolk with its beautiful sandy beaches and historic houses, ideal for golf, bird watching, cycling and walking. We love this house and are sure you will too. The accommodation consists of one twin and one double with private bathrooms and a two room family suite. Breakfasts are delicious and the welcome very warm. No smoking, Children and dogs are welcome.
e-mail: northfarmhouse@aol.com

KNAPTON. Colin and Fiona Goodhead, White House Farm, Knapton NR28 0RX (Tel & Fax: 01263

721344). Enjoy a taste of country living at White House Farm, our Grade II Listed farmhouse. Whether walking along the nearby sandy beaches or just relaxing in our peaceful gardens, you can certainly get away from it all. The quiet village location combines the historic character of a tradtional flint and brick home with the modern touches you need to relax (en suite facilities, four-poster bed, log fires). Our full English breakfast includes homemade bread and jams and Fiona will be delighted to cook your evening meals, by arrangement. Bed and Breakfast £17 to £24. Self-catering cottages also available. We want you to enjoy and remember your visit; please telephone to discuss your booking or to obtain our brochure. **AA** ◆◆◆◆
e-mail: GOODHEAD@whfarm.swinternet.co.uk
website: www.broadland.com/whitehousefarm

When making enquiries or bookings,
a stamped addressed envelope is always appreciated

LONG STRATTON, near Norwich. Mrs Joanna Douglas, Greenacres Farmhouse, Woodgreen, Long

Stratton, Norwich NR15 2RR (01508 530261). Period 17th century farmhouse on 30 acre common with ponds and natural wildlife, 10 miles south of Norwich (A140). The beamed sitting room with inglenook fireplace invites you to relax. A large sunny dining room encourages you to enjoy a traditional leisurely breakfast. All en suite bedrooms (two double/twin) are tastefully furnished to complement the oak beams and period furniture, with tea/coffee facilities and TV. Full size snooker table and all-weather tennis court for guests' use. Jo is trained in therapeutic massage, aromatherapy and reflexology and is able to offer this to guests who feel it would be of benefit. Come and enjoy the peace and tranquillity of our home. When sunny, you can sit in the garden; when cold, warm yourself by the fire. Bed and Breakfast from £20. Reductions for two nights or more. Non-smoking. **ETC** ◆◆◆◆

NORFOLK BROADS (Neatishead). Alan and Sue Wrigley, Regency Guest House, The Street,

Neatishead, Near Norwich NR12 8AD (Tel & Fax: 01692 630233). An 18th century guest house in picturesque, unspoilt village in heart of Broadlands. Personal service top priority. Long established name for very generous English Breakfasts. 20 minutes from medieval city of Norwich and six miles from coast. Ideal base for touring East Anglia - a haven for wildlife, birdwatching, cycling and walking holidays. Number one centre for Broads sailing, fishing and boating. Guesthouse, holder of "Good Care" award for high quality services, has five bedrooms individually Laura Ashley style decorated and tastefully furnished. Rooms, including two king-size doubles, and family room have TV and tea/coffee making facilities and most have en suite bathrooms. Two main bathrooms. Separate tables in beamed ceiling breakfast room. Guests' sittingroom. Cot, babysitting, reduced rates children and all stays of more than one night. Pets welcome. Parking. Open all year. Fire Certificate held. There are two good eating places within walking distance from guest house. Bed and Breakfast from £22. **AA/ETC** ◆◆◆◆.

NORWICH. Mrs Marion Jones, Lower Farm, Horsford, Norwich NR10 3AW (01603 891291).

Enjoy the comfort and warm welcome at Lower Farm, a mixed farm with sheep and cattle. Beautiful old farmhouse ideal for Norwich, the coast and Broads. Attractive, spacious accommodation in two en suite rooms (one family, one double) with TV and beverage trays. Superb views and traditional farmhouse fayre. Cot, babysitting service. Non-smoking. Open all year. Bed and Breakfast from £19 per person per night. **ETC** ◆◆◆◆ *SILVER AWARD.*

THURSFORD. Mrs Sylvia Brangwyn, The Heathers, Hindringham Road, Thursford, Fakenham NR21

0BL (01328 878352). Very quiet country location ideal for touring, walking and visiting stately homes (i.e. Sandringham, Holkham Hall, Blickling and Felbrigg), bird watching at Cley, Titchwell and Blakeney Point; Walsingham Shrine four miles. There is one ground floor double room with one twin and one double on first floor; all rooms have private en suite with shaver point, colour TV and tea/coffee making facilities. Full central heating. Christmas and New Year breaks. Car is essential; ample parking facilities. Bed and Breakfast from £19 to £21 per person per night on two people sharing; optional Evening Meals by prior arrangement.

"The Heathers"

WYMONDHAM. Mrs Joy Morter, Home Farm, Morley, Wymondham NR18 9SU (01953 602581).

Comfortable accommodation set in four acres, quiet location, secluded garden. Conveniently situated off A11 between Attleborough and Wymondham, an excellent location for Snetterton and only 20 minutes from Norwich and 45 minutes from Norfolk Broads. Accommodation comprises two double room and one twin-bedded room, all with TV, tea/coffee facilities and central heating. Children over five years old welcome, but sorry no animals and no smoking. Bed and Breakfast from £18 per person per night.

WYMONDHAM. Mrs J. Durrant, Rose Farm, School Lane, Suton, Wymondham NR18 9JN (01953 603512).

17th Century farmhouse set in eight acres of pasture where our donkeys graze. Rose Farm is situated two-and-a-half miles from Attleborough and the charming market town of Wymondham, with its historic twin-towered abbey church and three-quarters-of-a-mile from A11 London to Norwich trunk road, giving easy access to coastal resorts. All bedrooms are ground floor and have colour TV and beverage making facilities. Central heating throughout. Convenient for Snetterton Race Course. Bed and Breakfast from £19. Reductions for children under 10 years.

FOR THE MUTUAL GUIDANCE OF GUEST AND HOST

Every year literally thousands of holidays, short breaks and overnight stops are arranged through our guides, the vast majority without any problems at all. In a handful of cases, however, difficulties do arise about bookings, which often could have been prevented from the outset.

It is important to remember that when accommodation has been booked, both parties – guests and hosts – have entered into a form of contract. We hope that the following points will provide helpful guidance.

GUESTS: When enquiring about accommodation, be as precise as possible. Give exact dates, numbers in your party and the ages of any children. State the number and type of rooms wanted and also what catering you require – bed and breakfast, full board etc. Make sure that the position about evening meals is clear – and about pets, reductions for children or any other special points.

Read our reviews carefully to ensure that the proprietors you are going to contact can supply what you want. Ask for a letter confirming all arrangements, if possible.

If you have to cancel, do so as soon as possible. Proprietors do have the right to retain deposits and under certain circumstances to charge for cancelled holidays if adequate notice is not given and they cannot re-let the accommodation.

HOSTS: Give details about your facilities and about any special conditions. Explain your deposit system clearly and arrangements for cancellations, charges etc. and whether or not your terms include VAT.

If for any reason you are unable to fulfil an agreed booking without adequate notice, you may be under an obligation to arrange suitable alternative accommodation or to make some form of compensation.

While every effort is made to ensure accuracy, we regret that FHG Publications cannot accept responsibility for errors, omissions or misrepresentations in our entries or any consequences thereof.
Prices in particular should be checked because we go to press early. We will follow up complaints but cannot act as arbiters or agents for either party.

NORTHAMPTONSHIRE

KETTERING. Mrs A. Clarke, Dairy Farm, Cranford St. Andrew, Kettering NN14 4AQ (01536 330273).

Enjoy a holiday in our comfortable 17th century farmhouse with oak beams and inglenook fireplaces. Four-poster bed now available. Peaceful surroundings, large garden containing ancient circular dovecote. Dairy Farm is a working farm situated in a beautiful Northamptonshire village just off the A14, within easy reach of many places of interest or ideal for a restful holiday. Good farmhouse food and friendly atmosphere. Open all year, except Christmas. Bed and Breakfast from £22 to £32 (children under 10 half price); Evening Meal £14. **ETC** ◆◆◆ *SILVER AWARD.*

OUNDLE. Trudy Dijksterhuis, Lilford Lodge Farm, Barnwell, Oundle, Peterborough PE8 5SA (Tel & Fax: 01832 272230).

Mixed farm set in the attractive Nene Valley, situated on the A605 three miles south of Oundle and five miles north of the A14. Peterborough and Stamford are within easy reach. Guests stay in the recently converted original 19th century farmhouse. All bedrooms have en suite bathrooms, central heating, TV, radio and tea/coffee making facilities. Comfortable lounge and separate dining room. Open all year except Christmas and New Year. Children welcome. Coarse fishing available. Bed and Breakfast from £21. Reductions for children and for longer stays. **ETC** ◆◆◆◆
e-mail: trudy@lilford-lodge.demon.co.uk
website: www.lilford-lodge.demon.co.uk

QUINTON. Mrs Margaret Turney, Quinton Green Farm, Quinton NN7 2EG (01604 863685; Fax: 01604 862230).

The Turney family look forward to welcoming you to their comfortable, rambling 17th century farmhouse only 10 minutes from Northampton, yet overlooking lovely rolling countryside. We are close to Salcey Forest with its wonderful facilities for walking. M1 Junction 15 is just five minutes away; central Milton Keynes 20 minutes. All rooms en suite. Children and pets welcome. Piano and billiards room. Open all year. Bed and Breakfast from £25 single, £45 double. **ETC/AA** ◆◆◆◆ *SILVER AWARD*

Visit the FHG website
www.holidayguides.com
for details of the wide choice of accommodation
featured in the full range of FHG titles

NORTHUMBERLAND

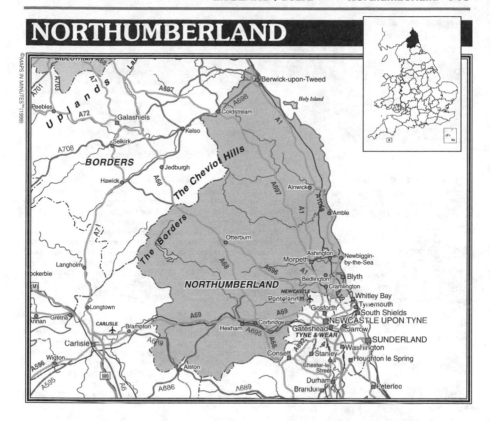

ALLENDALE. Mrs Carol Davison, Oakey Dene, Allendale, Hexham NE47 9EL (01434 683572; Mobile: 07989 047693). A warm welcome awaits you at Oakey Dene, a comfortable home with log fires if the weather is cold. Try our delicious full breakfast with home made bread and preserves. Visitors have their own sitting room and dining room with wonderful views of the surrounding countryside. Our double bedroom is en suite and the twin bedroom has a private bathroom. Single bedroom has washbasin and toilet. We are close to the golf course, pony trekking and wonderful walks. Spectacular scenery, many castles to visit and only 15 minutes from Hadrian's Wall. Children may like to see our herd of prize winning Toggenburg Goats. Packed lunches available.Bed and Breakfast from £19 to £25 per person per night. **ETC ◆◆◆◆,** *WELCOME HOST ESTABLISHMENT.*

ALNMOUTH. Mrs A. Stanton, Mount Pleasant Farm, Alnmouth, Alnwick NE66 3BY (01665 830215). Mount Pleasant is situated on top of a hill on the outskirts of the seaside village of Alnmouth, with spectacular views of the surrounding countryside. We offer fresh air, sea breezes, green fields, beautiful beaches, country roads and peace and quiet. There are two golf courses and a river meanders around the farm with all its bird life. There are castles, Holy Island, the Farnes and the Cheviots to explore. Farmhouse has large rooms, TV, tea making and en suite facilities. Ample parking. Prices from £20. Self-catering available.

ALNWICK. Mrs B. Sutherland, Rock Midstead Organic Farm, Rock Midstead, Alnwick NE66 2TH (01665 579225; Fax: 01665 579326). Enjoy a relaxing stay on our peaceful organic dairy farm. Comfortable farmhouse has guests own lounge and choice of two double/twin bedrooms with en suite or private bathrooms. Tea/coffee making facilities in every room, with colour TV and radio. Delicious breakfasts and evening meals using produce from the farm and fresh baked bread every day, located five miles from the market town of Alnwick, the farm is convienient for the A1 and within easy reach of the Northumbrian coast, Cheviot Hills, Northumberland National Park, and many castles, historical sites and golf courses. Children welcome, dogs by arrangement. Sorry, no smoking. Bed and Breakfast from £18. **ETC** ◆◆◆
e-mail: ian@rockmidstead.freeserve.co.uk

ALNWICK near. Mrs Celia Curry, Howick Scar Farm House, Craster, Alnwick NE66 3SU (Tel & Fax: 01665 576665). Comfortable farmhouse accommodation on working mixed farm situated on the Heritage Coast between the villages of Craster and Howick. Ideal base for walking, golfing, bird-watching or exploring the coast, moors and historic castles. The Farne Islands famous for their colonies of seals and seabirds, and Lindisfarne (Holy Island) are within easy driving distance. Accommodation is in two double rooms with washbasins. Guests have their own TV lounge/dining room with full central heating. Bed and Breakfast from £17.50. Open Easter to November. Also member of Farm Holiday Bureau. **ETC** ◆◆◆.

HEXHAM. Mrs Ruby Keenleyside, Struthers Farm, Catton, Allendale, Hexham NE47 9LP (01434 683580). Struthers Farm offers a warm welcome in the heart of England, with many splendid local walks from the farm itself. Panoramic views. Situated in an area of outstanding beauty. Double/twin rooms, en suite, central heating. Good farmhouse cooking. Ample safe parking. Come and share our home and enjoy beautiful countryside. Children welcome, pets by prior arrangement. Open all year. Bed and Breakfast from £20; Evening Meal from £10. Farm Holiday Bureau Member.

HEXHAM. Ros Johnson, West Wharmly, Hexham NE46 2PL (Tel & Fax: 01434 674227). Set on a 400 acre working farm. We offer a warm welcome to our well-appointed accommodation which has outstanding views over the South Tyne Valley. The 18th century farmhouse has a self-contained wing which is decorated to a high standard and has full central heating. A large private sittingroom, complete with open fire oak beams and colour TV, provides a homely retreat for the evenings. Two large bedrooms, both en suite, have colour TVs and tea/coffee making facilities. Ideal for families. Close to Hadrian's Wall and very accessible to Northumberland's many attractions. Bed and Breakfast from £20 to £22. **ETC** ◆◆◆◆

MORPETH. Mrs Lorna Thornton, Cornhills, Kirkwhelpington, Morpeth NE19 2RE (01830 540232; Fax: 01830 540388). Large Victorian farmhouse standing in an acre of garden, with spectacular views over open countryside, on an all grass working farm. Three beautifully decorated bedrooms (Two en suite) with tea/coffee, radio and hair dryers. Residents' lounge with TV open all day. Ideal for visiting Wallington, Cragside, Belsay Hall or fishing at Sweethope Lough. Enjoy the beautiful peaceful atmosphere offered at Cornhills. Bed and Breakfast from £20 per person per night. Children welcome, sorry no smokers or pets. Holiday cottage available. Sleeps 5. (NTB four stars) £220 to £330 per week. **ETC** ◆◆◆◆ *SILVER AWARD*.
e-mail: cornhills@farming.co.uk
website: www.northumberlandfarmhouse.co.uk

NINEBANKS. Mrs Mavis Ostler, Taylor Burn, Ninebanks, Hexham NE47 8DE (01434 345343). Warm welcome, good food on quiet working hill farm with spectacular views of Pennine Dales, three miles above Ninebanks. Large, comfortable, centrally heated farmhouse with spacious bedrooms, hospitality trays; guests' bathroom; guests' lounge with log fire and colour TV; you will be our only visitors. Excellent for walkers, ornithologists, country lovers - but no smoking. Pets welcome. Guests free to join in farm activities, observe cattle, sheep, free-range hens - even learn to work a sheepdog or build a stone wall. Bed and Breakfast £18 per adult; Evening Meal £10. Special diets catered for, home produce whenever available. 10% reductions for one week's stay. Write or ring for personal reply.

ROTHBURY. Mrs Helen Farr, Lorbottle West Steads, Thropton, Morpeth NE65 7JT (01665 574672).

Situated in the quite beautiful Whittingham Vale, five miles from Rothbury on a 320 acre farm. Stone-built spacious farmhouse with panoramic views of Thrunton Craggs, Simonside and Cheviot Hills, a perfect base for exploring Northumberland's natural beauty and heritage. Many facilities within four miles, e.g. golf, pony-trekking, mountain bikes, fishing and woodland walks. The farmhouse offers spacious TV lounge/diningroom with open fires in colder weather. Bedrooms have tea/coffee making facilities and TV. Guests' bathroom and use of garden. Bed and Breakfast from £18. Self-catering cottage, sleeps five, also available. Further details on request. **ETC ◆◆◆**

*Please mention The Farm Holiday Guide when writing
to enquire about accommodation*

NOTTINGHAMSHIRE

BLYTH. Mrs Vera Hambleton, Priory Farm Guesthouse, Hadsock Priory Estate, Blyth S81 0TY.

(01909 591515). The guest house is located on Hadsock Priory Country Estate with its beautiful five acre garden which is open to the public and famous for its display of snowdrops which carpet the garden in February/March. The guest house is located within one mile of the A1 and within 10 miles of the M1 giving easy access to the East Midlands and Northern England. Businessmen, tourists, children and dogs are all welcome. All rooms have tea/coffee making facilities and there are en suite facilities in two of the four bedrooms. The lounge with its log fire and TV is the ideal place to relax after a traditional home-cooked evening meal. Bed and Breakfast from £20 – £50..
e-mail: vera@guesthse.force9.co.uk
website: www.guesthse.force9.co.uk

EDWINSTOWE. (Near Mansfield). Robin Hood Farmhouse, Rufford Road, Edwinstowe NG21 9JA

(Tel & Fax: 01623 824367). Traditional olde English farmhouse in Robin Hood's village in the middle of Sherwood Forest. We are in close proximity of Clumber and Rufford Country Parks and adjacent to Center Parcs and South Forest Leisure Complex. Easy access to Nottingham and Lincoln. The farmhouse which is set in extensive gardens is open and centrally heated all year round. Accommodation comprises double/family and twin room, colour TV, tea/coffee making facilities in all rooms. Tariff from £17.50 per person per night. Reductions for children and extra nights. Pets and special requirements available on request. Ample secure parking.
e-mail: robinhoodfarm@aol.com

FARNSFIELD. Ken and Margaret Berry, Lockwell House, Lockwell Hill, Old Rufford Road, Farnsfield, Newark NG22 8JG (01623 883067). Set in 25 acres with 10 acres of woodland and situated on the edge of Sherwood Forest near Rufford Park on the A614, we are within easy reach of Nottingham, Newark, Mansfield, Worksop and all local country parks and tourist attractions. Small family-run Bed and Breakfast offering friendly service and comfort. All bedrooms are en suite and have tea/coffee making facilities. TV. Full English Breakfast. Ample car parking. Good pubs and restaurants nearby. Brochure available. Rates from £20.

STANTON-ON-THE-WOLDS. Mrs V. Moffat, Laurel Farm, Browns Lane, Stanton-on-the-Wolds,

Nottingham NG12 5BL (0115 9373488). Laurel Farm is an old farmhouse in paddocks with many pets and a National Garden Schemes standard garden. All rooms are spacious and newly refurbished, with en suite or private facilities. Teatrays, TV, hair dryer and bath robes for non en suite room. Laurel Farm is on a quiet lane with easy access from M1, A46 and A606. Convenient for tourist attractions. Breakfast is served in a spacious diningroom and only local produce and our own free-range eggs used. Strictly no smoking. Bed and Breakfast from £21.00 double/twin, £25.00 single per person per night. **ETC** ◆◆◆

OXFORDSHIRE

BANBURY near. Mrs E. J. Lee, The Mill Barn, Lower Tadmarton, Near Banbury OX15 5SU (01295 780349). Tadmarton is a small village, three miles south-west of Banbury. The Mill, no longer working, was originally water powered and the stream lies adjacent to the house. The Mill Barn has been tastefully converted, retaining many traditional features such as beams and exposed stone walls, yet it still has all the amenities a modern house offers. Two spacious en suite bedrooms, one downstairs, are available to guests in this comfortable family home. Base yourself here and visit Stratford, historic Oxford, Woodstock and the beautiful Cotswolds, knowing you are never farther than an hour's drive away. Open all year for Bed and Breakfast from £20, reductions for children. Weekly terms available.

BRAILES. Mrs M. Cripps, Agdon Farm, Brailes, Banbury OX15 5JJ (Tel & Fax: 01608 685226).

Working farm. A warm welcome awaits all our guests. Our comfortable Cotswold stone farmhouse is set in 500 acres of mixed farming, in an unspoilt part of the countryside. Two miles from B4035, five miles from A422. Within walking distance of Compton Wynyates, in close driving range of the Cotswolds, Warwick, 10 miles Stratford-upon-Avon and Banbury Cross. Many local village pubs. Accommodation with TV room, separate diningroom, guests' bathroom, pleasant bedrooms with tea/coffee making facilities. Central heating. Evening Meals available.

CHIPPING NORTON. Mrs Meyrick, Bould Farm, Bould, Near Idbury, Chipping Norton, OX7 6RT (Tel & Fax: 01608 658850).

Bould Farm is a 17th century Cotswold farmhouse on a 300 acre family farm set in beautiful countryside, 10 minutes' drive from Stow-on-the-Wold, Bourton-on-the-Water and Burford. Within easy reach of Blenheim Palace and the Cotswold Wildlife Park. Children welcome. Non-smoking. Spacious rooms with TV, tea/coffee making facilities. Large garden. Good local pubs. Open February to November. Bed and Breakfast from £22.50. **ETC** ◆◆◆

FARINGDON (Oxon). Mr D. Barnard, Bowling Green Farm, Stanford Road, Faringdon, Oxfordshire SN7 8EZ (01367 240229; Fax: 01367 242568).

Attractive 18th century period farmhouse offering 21st century comfort, situated in the Vale of White Horse, just one mile south of Faringdon on the A417. Easy access to the M4 Exit 13 for Heathrow Airport. An ideal place to stay for a day or longer. This is a working farm of cattle and horse breeding, poultry and ducks. Large twin-bedded/family room (en suite) on ground floor. All bedrooms have colour TV, tea/coffee making facilities and full central heating throughout. Ideal area for riding, golf, fishing and walking the Ridgeway. Interesting places to visit include Oxford, Bath, Windsor, Burford, Henley-on-Thames, Blenheim Palace and the Cotswolds. Open all year. Member of Farm Holiday Bureau. **ETC** ◆◆◆

HENLEY-ON-THAMES. Mrs Liz Roach, The Old Bakery, Skirmett, Near Henley-on-Thames RG9 6TD (01491 638309).

This welcoming family house is situated on the site of an old bakery, seven miles from Henley-on-Thames and Marlow; half-an-hour from Heathrow and Oxford; one hour from London. It is in the Hambleden Valley in the beautiful Chilterns with many excellent pubs selling good food. Excellent village pub in Skirmett within easy walking distance. Two double rooms with TV, one twin-bedded and two single rooms; two bathrooms. Open all year. Parking for five cars (car essential). Children and pets welcome. Bed and Breakfast from £25 to £30 single, £45 to £50 double.

LONG HANBOROUGH. Miss M. Warwick, The Close Guest House, Witney Road, Long Hanborough OX8 8HF (01993 882485).

We offer comfortable accommodation in house set in own grounds of one-and-a-half acres. Two family rooms, one double room; all are en suite and have colour TV and tea/coffee making facilities. Lounge. Full central heating. Use of garden and car parking for eight cars. Close to Woodstock, Oxford and the Cotswolds. Babysitting. Open all year except Christmas. Bed and Breakfast from £15.

MINSTER LOVELL. Mrs Katherine Brown, Hill Grove Farm, Crawley Road, Minster Lovell OX8 5NA (01993 703120; Fax: 01993 700528).

Hill Grove is a mixed family-run 300 acre working farm situated in an attractive rural setting overlooking the Windrush Valley. Ideally positioned for driving to Oxford, Blenheim Palace, Witney (Farm Museum) and Burford (renowned as the Gateway to the Cotswolds and for its splendid Wildlife Park). New golf course one mile. Hearty breakfasts. One double/private shower, one twin/double en suite bedrooms. Children welcome. Open all year except Christmas. Bed and Breakfast from £22 per person per night for double/private shower; £24 per person per night for double/twin en suite. Non-smoking. **ETC** ◆◆◆◆

POSTCOMBE. Jackie Graham, Beech Farm, Salt Lane, Postcombe, Oxon OX9 7EE (Tel & Fax: 01844 281240),

Our modern farm bungalow on a working farm has rural views towards the Chiltern Hills. It is in a quiet rural location yet close to Junction 6 M40. The two comfortable bedrooms are in a separate wing. Breakfast on local produce in conservatory and watch Red Kites circling over landscaped garden. Excellent local eateries. Ramblers have instant access to open countryside and Ridgeway. Golfers have several choices. Many excellent gardens to visit. Other places of interest Oxford, Blenheim Palace, Whipsnade Zoo, Beaconscott Model Village, Bicester Village outlet stores. "Oxford Tube" coach runs into London (40 miles) every 10 minutes. Outdoor kennel and run.
e-mail: jackie.beech.farm.bb@talk21.com
website: www.ukworld.net/beechfarm.htm

FREE or REDUCED RATE entry to Holiday Visits and Attractions — see our READERS' OFFER VOUCHERS on pages 43-60

WOODSTOCK. The Leather Bottel, East End, North Leigh, Near Witney OX8 6PY (01993 882174).

Joe and Nena Purcell invite you to The Leather Bottel guest house situated in the quiet hamlet of East End near North Leigh, convenient for Blenheim Palace, Woodstock, Roman Villa, Oxford and the Cotswolds. Breathtaking countryside walks. Two double en suite bedrooms, one family room with own bathroom, one single bedroom, all with colour TV and tea/coffee making facilities. Bed and Breakfast £30 per night for single room, from £40 for double. Children welcome. Open all year. Directions: follow signs to Roman Villa off A4095. **ETC** ◆◆◆.

See also Colour Display Advertisement

WOODSTOCK. Mr and Mrs N. Hamilton, Gorselands Hall, Boddington Lane, North Leigh, Witney OX8 6PU (01993 882292; Fax: 01993 883629). Lovely old Cotswold stone farmhouse with oak beams and flagstone floor in delightful rural setting. Large secluded garden, grass tennis court and croquet lawn. Ideal for Blenheim Palace, the Cotswolds and Oxford. Roman villa close by. Good walking country. Comfortable, attractively furnished bedrooms with views of the garden or the surrounding countryside. All rooms are en suite, with colour television and tea/coffee making facilities. Non-smoking. Lounge with snooker table for residents' use. A choice of excellent pubs within easy reach. Bed and Breakfast from £22.50. Winter discounts available. **ETC** ◆◆◆
e-mail: hamilton@gorselandshall.com
website: www.gorselandshall.com

Formal water gardens at Blenheim Palace, near Oxford

SHROPSHIRE

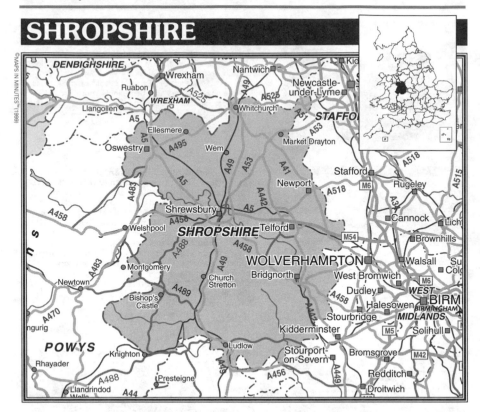

©MAPS IN MINUTES™ (1999)

BISHOP'S CASTLE. Mrs Ann Williams, Shuttocks Wood, Norbury, Bishop's Castle SY9 5EA (01588 650433; Fax: 01588 650492). Shuttocks Wood is a Scandinavian house in woodland setting situated within easy travelling distance of the Long Mynd and Stiperstone Hills. Accommodation consists of one double and two twin-bedded rooms, all en suite and with tea/coffee facilities and colour TV. Good walks and horse riding nearby and a badger set just 20 yards from the door! Ample parking. Non-smoking establishment. Children over 12 years welcome. Sorry, no pets. Open all year. Bed and Breakfast from £22 per person per night. Credit Cards accepted.

BUCKNELL. Mrs Christine E. Price, The Hall, Bucknell SY7 0AA (Tel & Fax 01547 530249). You are assured of a warm welcome at The Hall, which is a Georgian farmhouse with spacious accommodation. The house and gardens are set in a secluded part of a small South Shropshire village, an ideal area for touring the Welsh Borderland. Offa's Dyke is on the doorstep and the historic towns of Shrewsbury, Hereford, Ludlow and Ironbridge are within easy reach as are the Church Stretton Hills and Wenlock Edge. One triple bedroom with private bathroom, one twin en suite. Both have tea-making facilities and TV. Guest lounge. Ample parking. Bed and Breakfast from £20 to £22; Evening Meal £11. SAE, please, for details. **ETC** ◆◆◆.

e-mail: hall@ukworld.net
website: www.ukworld.net/hall

CHURCH STRETTON. Mrs Mary Jones, Acton Scott Farm, Acton Scott, Church Stretton SY6 6QN (01694 781260; Fax: 0870 129 4591). Working farm. Lovely 17th century farmhouse in peaceful village amidst the beautiful hills of South Shropshire, an area of outstanding natural beauty. The house is full of character; the rooms, which are all heated, are comfortable and spacious. Bedrooms have washbasin and tea/coffee making facilities; en suite or private bathroom. Colour TV lounge. Children welcome, pets accepted by arrangement. We are a working farm, centrally situated for visiting Ironbridge, Shrewsbury and Ludlow, each easily reached within half-an-hour. Visitors' touring and walking information available. Bed and full English Breakfast from £19 per person. Non-smoking. Farm Holiday Bureau member. Open all year excluding November, December and January. **ETC** ◆◆◆

CHURCH STRETTON. Mrs Josie Griffiths, Gilberries Farm Cottage, Wall-under-Heywood, Church Stretton SY6 7HZ (01694 771400; Fax: 01694 771663). Country cottage adjoining family farm. Quoted as 'an oasis – a haven of peace and tranquillity'. One double en suite bedroom, one twin bedded bedroom with private bathroom; both with tea making facilities, radios and hairdryer. Guests' lounge with colour TV and separate diningroom are available to guests at all times. Log fires, central heating, spacious parking. A warm welcome awaits. Bed and Breakfast from £18 per person. Excellent evening meals available within a five minutes' drive. **ETC** ◆◆◆◆

See also Colour Display Advertisement **CHURCH STRETTON. Mrs Lyn Bloor, Malt House Farm, Lower Wood, Church Stretton SY6 6LF (01694 751379).** Olde worlde beamed farmhouse situated amidst specacular scenery on the lower slopes of the Long Mynd hills. We are a working farm producing beef cattle and sheep. One double and one twin bedrooms, both with en suite bathrooms, colour TV, hair dryer and tea tray. Good farmhouse cooking is served in the dining room. Private guests' sitting room. Non-smoking. Regret no children or pets. Bed and Breakfast from £18.50 per person per night; Evening Meal from £15.00 per person. Now fully licensed. **AA** ◆◆◆

CLEOBURY MORTIMER (Near Kidderminster). Dinah M. Thompson, Cox's Barn, Bagginswood, Cleobury Mortimer, Near Kidderminster DY14 8LS (01746 718415; Fax 01746718277). A warm welcome awaits at our converted barn set in beautiful farmland overlooking the Wyre Forest. Within easy reach of Bridgnorth, Bewdley, Ludlow, the Wyre and Mortimer forests, the Long Mynd and Wenlock Edge, many English Heritage and National Trust properties to visit. The accommodation is maintained to a high standard; three double en suite bedrooms offering full central heating, tea and coffee making facilities, colour TV and clock radio alarms. Excellent home cooking, optional evening meals. Non-smoking. Bed and Breakfast £20 reduced rates after four nights. **ETC** ◆◆◆◆

CLUN. Mrs M. Jones, Llanhedric, Clun, Craven Arms SY7 8NG (01588 640203). Working farm. Put your feet up and relax in the recliners as the beauty of the garden, the trickle of the pond, and the views of Clun and its surrounding hills provide solace from the stress of modern day life. Receive a warm welcome at this traditional oak-beamed farmhouse set back from the working farm. Three bedrooms, double en suite, tea/coffee facilities and good home cooking. Visitors' lounge with inglenook fireplace; separate dining room. Walks, history and attractions all close by. Bed and Breakfast from £18, Bed, Breakfast and Evening Meal from £28.00. Reductions for children. Non-smoking household. Regret no dogs in house. Open April to October. **ETC** ◆◆◆

CRAVEN ARMS. Mrs S .J. Williams, Hurst Mill Farm, Clun, Craven Arms SY7 0JA (01588 640224).

Working farm. Winner "Great Farm Breakfast". Hurst Mill Farm is situated in the prettiest part of the Clun Valley, renowned as a completely unspoilt part of England. One mile from the small town of Clun, which has a Saxon church and a Norman castle. Legend says one is wiser after crossing Clun Bridge. Within easy reach are Ludlow, Newtown, Elan Valley, Ironbridge and Long-Mynd Hills. Through the fields runs the River Clun where one can bathe. Woods and hills provide wonderful walks, which can be organised. Fishing and pony trekking locally. The farm has cattle, sheep, one quiet riding pony. Three double bedrooms, twin en suite and tea/coffee making facilities; guests' lounge, diningroom. Parking. Children and pets welcome; cot and babysitting. Good food, pretty garden. Dinner, Bed and Breakfast from £28; Bed and Breakfast from £21. Lunches. Open all year. AA Recommended. Mrs Williams is the Winner of "Shropshire's Great Farm Breakfast Challenge". Also three holiday cottages available. ETC ◆◆◆.

CRAVEN ARMS. Mrs I. J. Evans, Springhill Farm, Clun, Craven Arms SY7 8PE (01588 640337). Working farm on Offa's Dyke footpath. Ideal for walkers, weekend breaks. Full English breakfast, evening meals on request. Pets by arrangement. Call for further details.

DORRINGTON. Ron and Jenny Repath, Meadowlands, Lodge Lane, Frodesley, Dorrington SY5 7HD

(01694 731350). Former farmhouse attractively decorated, set in eight acres of gardens, paddocks and woodland. Quiet location in a delightful hamlet seven miles south of Shrewsbury. The guest house lies on a no-through-road to a forested hill rising to 1000ft. Meadowlands features panoramic views over open countryside to the Stretton Hills. Guest accommodation includes en suite facilities and every bedroom has a colour TV, drink making facilities and a silent fridge. Guests lounge with maps and guides for loan. Drinks on arrival. Central heating. Plenty of parking space. Strictly no smoking. Bed and Breakfast from £18; Evening Meal from £10 by arrangement. Brochure available. ETC ◆◆◆

IRONBRIDGE. Virginia Evans, Church

Farm, Rowton, Wellington, Near Telford TR6 6QY (Tel & Fax: 01952 770381). Central for Ironbridge, Shrewsbury, Telford, Ludlow, Chester. Come and enjoy a large country breakfast in our 300 year old Listed farmhouse. Spacious en suite bedrooms, twins, singles all with washbasins, complimentary beverage trays and towels. From £20 per person. Short Breaks available. Also three beautifully converted barn cottages, equipped and furnished to a high standard, enclosed patio gardens, ground floor bedrooms, fishing, quiet location. Sleeps two-eight persons. From £160 – £400 per week.
e-mail: church.farm@bigfoot.com
website: www.virtual-shropshire.co.uk/churchfarm

LUDLOW Near. Mrs Rachel Edwards, Haynall Villa, Little Hereford, Near Ludlow SY8 4BG (Tel & Fax:

01584 711589). Relax in our early 19th century farmhouse, with many original features, oak stairs lead to comfortable rooms (one en suite), all with tea/coffee making facilities, with views over the beautiful, unspoilt countryside. We have a large attractive garden and private fishing (carp). We are ideally situated, approximately two miles from the A49, within easy reach of Ludlow, National Trust Properties, gardens and lovely villages. Walk by the river or experience panoramic views from the Shropshire hills. Sample the local foods. Combine your visit with the Ludlow Festival or one of it's many events. Bed and Breakfast from £17 per person per night. Evening meal - check price and availability. Non-smoking. Pets by arrangement. Children over six years welcome. **AA** ◆◆◆

LYDBURY NORTH. The Powis Arms, Lydbury North SY7 8PR (01588 680232). Bed and Breakfast available in country pub. Good food from snacks to full à la carte with friendly and professional service. Accommodation comprises four en suite bedrooms; sittingroom with TV, lounge bar and diningroom. Parking. Fishing and walking. Ideally situated for exploring Shropshire and the Welsh Borders and mediaeval towns of Ludlow and Shrewsbury. Nearby are the world famous Ironbridge and walking or bicycling country of Offa's Dyke, the Long Mynd, Stiperstones and Wenlock Edge. Prices from £25. Self-catering flats and caravan site accommodation also available.

LYDBURY NORTH. Mr and Mrs R. Evans, "Brunslow", Lydbury North SY7 8AD (01588 680244).

Working farm, join in. "Brunslow" is a beautiful Georgian style farmhouse, centrally heated throughout, ideal for walking and for those who enjoy the peace and quiet of unspoiled countryside. The house is set in large gardens with lovely views in all directions and the farm produces mainly milk; pigs, poultry and calves are reared and "feeding time" is very popular with younger guests. One double, one single and two family rooms, all having washbasin and tea/coffee making facilities. Central heating throughout. Bathroom, toilets; separate sittingroom and diningroom; colour TV, high chair and babysitting available. Open all year, except Christmas, for Bed and Breakfast from £18; Evening Dinner £8 if required. SAE please for terms. Packed lunches available. Car essential, parking.

NEWPORT. Mrs Green, Peartree Farmhouse, Farm Grove, Newport TF10 7PX (01952 811193).

Charming farmhouse set in picturesque gardens, enjoying the best of both worlds on the very edge of historic market town yet in country setting. Immaculate modern accommodation, non-smoking environment, TV lounge. All rooms satellite TV, tea/coffee making facilities, controllable central heating, mostly en suite. Ample private parking. Very convenient for Telford, Ironbridge etc. Bed and Breakfast from £20 per person.

OSWESTRY. Mrs Margaret Jones, Ashfield Farmhouse, Maesbury, Near Oswestry SY10 8JH (Tel & Fax: 01691 653589; Mobile: 07989 477414).

Scented roses, scarlet creepers and lacy Wisterias ramble over this delightful 16th century coach-house and Georgian farmhouse, one mile from Oswestry, A5 and A483 amidst an English/Welsh border mix. Very pretty, cosy, yet spacious en suite rooms (one has luxury private bath/shower room), all fully equipped. TV, payphone, hostess tray, etc., plus great Welsh mountain views. Olde worlde dining and sittingrooms, log fires, ample books, games. Many original features throughout. Five minutes walk to canalside inn, good food and boat hire. Beautiful area overflowing with castles, lakes, mountains, woodlands. Chester, Hangollen, Shrewsbury 20/30 minutes drive. North Wales, South Shropshire on doorstep. Bed and Breakfast from £19.75 per person per night. Short Breaks. Telephone for brochure. **ETC** ◆◆◆◆ *SILVER AWARD.*
website: www.ashfieldfarmhouse.co.uk

OSWESTRY near. Pam Morrissey, Top Farm House, Knockin, Near Oswestry SY10 8HN (01691 682582).

Full of charm and character, this beautiful 16th century Grade 1 Listed black and white house is set in the delightful village of knockin. Enjoy the relaxed atmosphere and elegant surroundings of this special house with its abundance of beams, open fires in winter, and fresh flowers all year round. Sit in the comfortable drawing room where you can read, play the piano, listen to music, or just sit and relax. Hearty breakfasts from our extensive menu are served in the lovely dining room which looks out over the flower-filled garden. The large bedrooms are all en suite, attractively decorated and furnished. All have tea /coffee making facilities, colour TV, etc. The main bathroom has a sauna cabinet and spa bath for guests' use. Convenient for the Welsh Border, Shrewsbury, Chester and Oswestry. Bed and Breakfast from £21 per person **ETC** ◆◆◆◆ *SILVER AWARD,* **AA** ◆◆◆◆.
e-mail: p.a.m@knockin.freeserve.co.uk

SHREWSBURY. Mrs Vanessa Bromley, North Farm, Eaton Mascot, Shrewsbury SY5 6HF (01743 761031; Fax: 01743 761854). Farmhouse Bed and Breakfast. Situated within peaceful countryside, yet within easy access to Shrewsbury, M54, Telford, Ironbridge and Church Stretton. We are a working farm of 270 acres, farming cereals and sheep. The accommodation consists of large twin en suite, one large double en suite and one double with private bathroom (family rooms can be made on request). All rooms have TV, hospitality tray and central heating. Easy car parking. Tariff £23 per person en suite, £18 per person with private bathroom. 'Stay on a Farm' Member. **ETC** ◆◆◆◆
e-mail: northfarm@talk21.com
website: www.virtualshropshire.co.uk/northfarm

TELFORD. Mrs Mary Jones, Red House Farm, Longdon-on-Tern, Wellington, Telford TF6 6LE (01952 770245). Red House Farm is a late Victorian farmhouse in the small village of Longdon-on-Tern, noted for its aqueduct, built by Thomas Telford in 1796. Two double bedrooms have private facilities, one family room has its own separate bathroom. All rooms are large and comfortable. Excellent Breakfast. Farm easily located, leave M54 Junction 6, follow A442, take B5063. Central for historic Shrewsbury, Ironbridge Gorge museums or modern Telford. Several local eating places. Open all year. Families most welcome, reductions for children. Pets also welcome. Bed and Breakfast from £18.
email: rhf@virtual-shropshire.co.uk
website: www.virtual-shropshire.co.uk/red-house-farm

TELFORD. John and Rosemarie Hawkins, Hill View Farm, Buildwas, Near Ironbridge, Telford TF8 7BP (01952 432228). Hill View Farm is set in open countryside with splendid views of the Severn Valley, situated on the A4169 road between the historic town of Much Wenlock and also convenient for Telford and Shrewsbury. Accommodation is non-smoking, peaceful, clean and friendly offering guests hearty breakfasts or lighter options if preferred. Bedrooms are traditional in decor with beverage tray, washbasin with bathrooms next door. Rates from £17.50 to £20.00 per person per night. Reductions for three nights or more.

WHITCHURCH. Miss J. Gregory, Ash Hall, Ash Magna, Whitchurch SY13 4DL (01948 663151). Working farm. An early 18th century house set in large garden with ample room for children to play, on a medium-sized farm with pedigree Friesians. Situated in the small North Shropshire village of Ash, approximately one-and-a-half miles from A41. Within easy reach of Chester and Shrewsbury (about 20 miles); Crewe 15 miles. Interesting features of this house are two oak-panelled reception rooms and an oak staircase; one of the two guest bedrooms is also panelled. One bedroom has en suite facilities. Bathroom, toilet; sittingroom; diningroom. Children welcome. Reduced rates available. Open all year for Bed and Breakfast. **ETC** ◆◆

SOMERSET

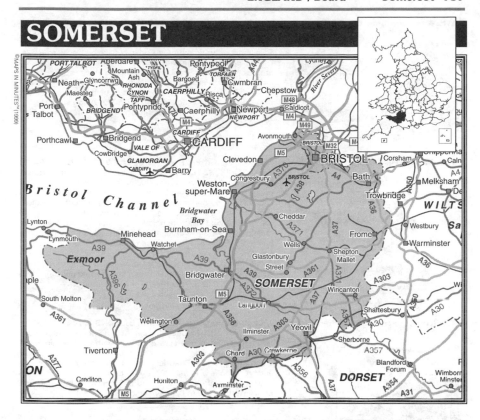

ASHBRITTLE. Mrs Ann Heard, Lower Westcott Farm, Ashbrittle, Wellington TA21 0HZ (01398 361296). On Devon/Somerset borders, 230 acre family-run farm with Friesian herd, sheep, poultry and horses. Ideal for walking, touring Exmoor, Quantocks, both coasts and many National Trust properties. Pleasant farmhouse, tastefully modernised but with olde worlde charm, inglenook fireplaces and antique furniture, set in large gardens with lawns and flower beds in peaceful, scenic countryside. Two family bedrooms with private facilities and tea/coffee making. Large lounge, separate diningroom offering guests every comfort. Noted for relaxed, friendly atmosphere and good home-cooking. Brochure by request. Bed and Breakfast from £18; Dinner £10 per person. Reductions for children. **ETC** ◆◆◆

AXBRIDGE. Mrs M. A. Counsell, Rooksbridge House, Rooksbridge, Axbridge BS26 2UL (01934 750630). Rooksbridge House is a charming Georgian farmhouse surrounded by a large garden on a working farm on the Somerset Levels. The accommodation, which has its own entrance, consists of a suite of rooms in a wing of the house. Upstairs a large family bedroom with four-poster bed has its own spacious bathroom. The sittingroom has a wonderful flagstone floor and oak beamed fireplace with log fires in winter. Rooksbridge is just a short distance from Junction 22 of the M5 and makes an ideal centre for touring Somerset. Well behaved pets welcome. Bed and Breakfast £30; childrens' discounts.**ETC** ◆◆◆◆. Self-catering cottage also available.

BATH. Mrs Colin Smart, Leigh Farm, Pensford, Near Bristol BS39 4BA (01761 490281; Fax: 01761 490270). Working farm. Close to Bath, Bristol, Cheddar, Mendip Hills. Spacious, comfy, stone-built farmhouse with lawns. Twin, family, double rooms, en suite; cot and high chair available. Guests' private lounge with night storage heating and open log fires in cold weather. Traditional farmhouse breakfasts. Tea/coffee facilities, hair dryer. Carp and tench fishing. Close to Blagdon and Chew Valley lakes, both renowned for trout fishing. No pets. Car park. Bed and Breakfast from £23. Also self-catering accommodation available (all units with night storage heating) from £150 to £400 weekly.

BATH. Mrs Chrissie Besley, The Old Red House, 37 Newbridge Road, Bath BA1 3HE (01225 330464; Fax: 01225 331661). Welcome to our romantic Victorian "Gingerbread" house which is colourful, comfortable and warm; full of unexpected touches and intriguing little curiosities. The leaded and stained glass windows are now double glazed to ensure a peaceful night's stay. Each bedroom is individually furnished with canopied or king size bed, colour TV, complimentary beverages, radio alarm clock, hair dryer and either en suite shower or private bathroom. Generous four course breakfasts are served. Waffles, pancakes or kippers are just a few alternatives to our famous hearty English grill. Dinner is available at the local riverside pub, just a short stroll away. We are non-smoking and have private parking. Prices range from £20 to £33 per person in double rooms.
e-mail: oldredhouse@amserve.net

BATH (Near). Betty Clothier, Franklyns Farm, Chewton Mendip, Near Bath BA3 4NB (01761 241372). Come and relax in peaceful setting, comfortable and cosy farmhouse, set in one acre of garden with hard tennis court. Delicious breakfasts with free range eggs. Ideal for visiting Bath, Glastonbury, Wells, Cheddar, Longleat and the coast is within easy reach. We are just off the A39 on the Emborough B3114 road. Half-a-mile along the road is Franklyns Farm. Bed and Breakfast from £19 to £20 per person. ETC ◆◆◆.

BATH Near. Mrs P Foster, Pennsylvania Farm, Newton-St-Loe, Bath BA2 9JD (01225 314912) Pennsylvania Farm is set in 280 acres of land close to Bath, Bristol, Cheddar and Wells. The farmhouse is a Listed 17th century building which is well appointed, warm and comfortable. It has three bedrooms, two with en suite bathrooms (power showers), one with private bathroom; a cosy dining room and a pleasant sunny sitting room with log fire. Wonderful farmhouse breakfasts; lunches and evenign meals available. Adjacent to the farmhouse is a lovely converted cottage with two bedrooms and its own kitchen and lounge (sleeps four). **ETC ◆◆◆◆**
website: www.pennsylvaniafarm.co.uk

BECKINGTON, Near Bath. Mrs Barbara Keevil, Eden Vale Farm, Mill Lane, Beckington, Near Bath BA3 6SN (01373 830371). Eden Vale Farm nestles down in a valley by the River Frome. Enjoying a picturesque location, this old watermill offers a selection of rooms including en suite facilities, complimented by an excellent choice of full English or continental breakfasts. Beckington is an ideal centre for visiting Bath, Longleat, Salisbury, Cheddar, Stourhead and many National Trust Houses including Lacock Village. Only a ten minute walk to the village pub, three-quarters of a mile of river fishing. Local golf courses and lovely walks. Very friendly animals. Dogs welcome. Please phone or write for more information. Open all year. ETC ◆◆◆

Brinsea Green Farm

**Mrs Delia Edwards,
Brinsea Green Farm
Brinsea Lane,
Congresbury, Near Bristol
BS19 5JN
Tel: (01934) 852278**

Brinsea Green is a Period farmhouse surrounded by open countryside. Set in 500 acres of farmland, it has easy access from the M5, (J21), A38 and Bristol Airport. Close to the Mendip Hills, the historic towns of Bath, Bristol and Wells, plus the wonders of Cheddar Gorge and Wookey Hole. Beautifully furnished en suite/shower bedrooms offer lovely views, comfortable beds, complimentary hot drinks and biscuits, radio, alarm, toiletries, sewing kit and hair dryer for your convenience. Both guest lounge (with TV) and dining room have inglenook fireplaces providing a warm, home from home atmosphere. Choose from our wide range of books and enjoy real peace and tranquillity. Early booking recommended

---

BRIDGWATER. Mrs Judith Denning, Apple View, Temple Farm, Chedzoy, Bridgwater TA7 8QR (Tel & Fax: 01278 423201). Relax and indulge yourself in our country retreat. Situated three miles from M5 J23 and on the Sustrans Western Way and CT Land End/John O' Groats cycle routes, central to all Somerset's attractions. On a working livestock farm, see lambs and calves born, chicks and ducklings hatch and watch the milking. Sleep between pure cotton sheets and soft woollen blankets and pamper yourself in our luxurious en suite bedrooms adorned with brass effect trimmings and heated towel rails. Breakfast on dry cure bacon, home-made preserves, free range eggs and freshly baked bread and croissants. Non-smoking. Category 2 disabled access. **ETC ◆◆◆◆**.

BRIDGWATER Near. Model Farm, Perry Green, Wembdon, Near Bridgwater TA5 2BA (01278 433999). Model Farm is a licensed country house situated in a peaceful rural setting, close to the North Somerset/Devon coast, Quantock Hills, and country towns. Ideally located for both leisure and business guests, the property is a 17th century farmhouse (non working) with an imposing Victorian frontage. Spacious, comfortable bedrooms with en suite shower facilities and a range of hot beverages provided. By arrangement a set three-course evening meal is available, guests being joined by the owners around a refectory table. A warm and friendly atmosphere awaits all who visit. No smoking throughout. Bed and Breakfast £25 to £35 per person per night. Visa/Mastercard accepted. **ETC/AA ◆◆◆◆**.
e-mail: Rmodelfarm@aol.com

See also Colour Display Advertisement

BUTCOMBE. Barry and Josephine Harvey, Butcombe Farm, Aldwick Lane, Butcombe BS40 7UW (01761 462380; Fax: 01761 462300). Sympathetically refurbished 14th Century manor house and farm buildings offering en suite B&B rooms and individual self-catering cottages. Set in several acres of field and woodland amid the tranquil Somerset countryside, excellent on-site facilities include heated outdoor pool and evening meals. Bath, Bristol, Cheddar, Glastonbury and Wells are all within easy drive. Special activities include fishing, cycling, horse riding, aromatherapy massage and wine-tasting. **ETC ◆◆◆◆** (Board), **ETC ★★★** (Self-Catering).
e-mail: info@butcombe-farm.demon.co.uk
website: www.butcombe-farm.demon.co.uk

CREWKERNE. Mrs Catherine Bacon, Honeydown Farm, Seaborough Hill, Crewkerne TA18 8PL (Tel & Fax: 01460 72665). We are a working dairy farm on the Somerset/Dorset border, one and a half miles from Crewkerne, with panoramic views. National Trust properties, private gardens and numerous other places of interest are within easy reach, and the coast is only 14 miles away. Golfing, fishing, riding, walking and cycling all available locally. Centrally heated accommodation comprises one twin and two double rooms, all with washbasins, tea/coffee trays and clock/radio. Enjoy the patio and garden or relax in the guest lounge with books, stereo or television. Non smoking. Bed and Breakfast from £18 per person per night. Brochure available.
e-mail: cb@honeydown.freeserve.co.uk
website: www.honeydown.freeserve.co.uk

CREWKERNE. Mr and Mrs A. Emery, Manor Farm, Dunsham Lane, Wayford TA18 8QL (01460 78865; mobile: 04676 20031). Beautiful Victorian country home (Portman style) in peaceful location with superb views within easy reach of the coast at Lyme Regis (12 miles), Forde Abbey and Cricket St. Thomas Wildlife Park (three miles). Approximately 20 acres of land with three small coarse fishing lakes, stabling. All bedrooms have en suite facilities, colour TV, tea/coffee tray and are centrally heated. Open all year. Excellent eating establishments close by. Bed and full English Breakfast £22 per person. Reduced rates for children. There is also a self-catering annexe, fully equipped for up to five persons from £150 per week. **AA ◆◆◆◆.**

DULVERTON. Mrs Carole Nurcombe, Marsh Bridge Cottage, Dulverton TA22 9QG (01398 323197). This superb accommodation has been made possible by the refurbishment of this Victorian former ex-gamekeeper's cottage on the banks of the River Barle. The friendly welcome, lovely rooms, delicious (optional) evening meals using local produce, and clotted cream sweets are hard to resist! Open all year, and in autumn the trees that line the river either side of Marsh Bridge turn to a beautiful golden backdrop. Just off the B3223 Dulverton to Exford road, it is easy to find and, once discovered, rarely forgotten. From outside the front door footpaths lead in both directions alongside the river. Fishing available. Terms from £16.50 per person Bed and Breakfast or £28.00 per person Dinner, Bed and Breakfast.

EXMOOR. Mrs Blackshaw, North Down Farm, Pyncombe Lane, Wiveliscombe, Taunton TA4 2BL (Tel & Fax: 01984 623730). In tranquil secluded surroundings on the Somerset/Devon Border. Traditional working farm set in 100 acres of natural beauty with panoramic views of over 30 miles. M5 motorway seven miles away and Taunton ten miles. All rooms tastefully furnished to high standard, include en suite facilities, TV and tea/coffee making. Family room, double or single available. Dining room and lounge with log fires for guests' comfort; central heating and double glazed. Drying facilities. Delicious home-produced food a speciality. Fishing, golf, horse riding and country sports nearby. Dogs welcome. Bed and Breakfast from £20 per person, generous discounts on stays of seven nights or more. North Down Break - three nights Bed, Breakfast and Evening Meal £80 per person. **ETC ◆◆◆.**

Cockhill Farm

Farmhouse accommodation on a working farm keeping a small beef suckler herd in the heart of the Mendips. A friendly atmosphere is assured in this Victorian farmhouse. Excellent home cooking using local produce. We also cater for vegetarians. Bed and Breakfast, optional Evening Meal. Spacious rooms with period furnishings, TV, tea/coffee making facilities. Ideally situated for the Cathedral City of Wells, Glastonbury, Cheddar, Georgian Bath and historic Bristol. Royal Bath and West Showground 10 minutes. Magnificent Chew Valley Lake for bird-watching, fly fishing and picnicking 20 minutes. Good local pubs and peaceful country walks. Children welcome, baby facilities available. One family, three double and one twin room. Open all year. Bed and Breakfast from £17.50.

Mrs Jacqueline Hawkins, Marchants Hill, Gurney Slade, Near Bath BA3 4TY (01749 840125)

GLASTONBURY. Mrs D. P. Atkinson, Court Lodge, Butleigh, Glastonbury BA6 8SA (01458 850575).

A warm welcome awaits at attractive, modernised 1850 Lodge with homely atmosphere. Set in picturesque garden on the edge of Butleigh, three miles from historic Glastonbury. Only a five minute walk to pub in village which serves lovely meals. Accommodation in one double, one twin and two single bedrooms; constant hot water, central heating. Bathroom adjacent to bedrooms. TV lounge, Tea/coffee served. Bed and Breakfast from £15.50; Evening Meal by arrangement. Children welcome at reduced rates. **AA/RAC Recommended**

GLASTONBURY (Near). Mrs M. White, Barrow Farm, North Wootton, near Glastonbury BA4 4HL (01749 890245). Working farm. Barrow is a dairy farm of 146

acres. The house is 15th century and of much character, situated between Wells, Glastonbury and Shepton Mallet. It makes an excellent touring centre for visiting Somerset's beauty spots and historic places, for example, Cheddar, Bath, Wookey Hole and Longleat. Guest accommodation consists of two double rooms, one family room, one single room and one twin-bedded room, each with washbasin, TV and tea/coffee making facilities. Bathroom, two toilets; two lounges, one with colour TV; diningroom with separate tables. Guests can enjoy farmhouse fare in generous variety, home baking a speciality. Bed and Breakfast, with optional four-course Dinner available. Car essential; ample parking. Children welcome; cot and babysitting available. Open all year except Christmas. Sorry, no pets. Bed and Breakfast from £14 to £17. Dinner £10. AA QQQ Listed.

LANGPORT. Mrs Ann Woodborne, Muchelney Ham Farm, Muchelney Ham, Langport TA10 0DJ (Tel & Fax: 01458 250737). Working farm. A warm welcome

awaits you at this 17th century farmhouse situated near the historic village of Muchelney with its abbey and priest's house. We are in an excellent centre for exploring Somerset and its wide variety of places of interest. Each room has its own unique character with oak and elm beams, period furniture and comfortable furnishings. All bedrooms are en suite, and guests may also enjoy our large, peaceful garden. A traditional English/Continental Breakfast is included. The combination of comfortable surroundings and modern conveniences will ensure that your stay is enjoyable and memorable. Please telephone or write for brochure. Self-catering wing sleeping four/five also available. ETC ◆◆◆◆◆ *GOLD AWARD*
website: www.muchelneyhamfarm.co.uk

Terms quoted in this publication may be subject to increase if rises in costs necessitate

MARTOCK. Mrs H. Turton, "Wychwood", 7 Bearley Road, Martock TA12 6PG (Tel & Fax: 01935

825601). Comfortable accommodation in our small, pleasant B&B located in a quiet position just off A303. Two double rooms en suite, one twin room with own private bathroom. Tea/coffee making facilities and remote control TV in bedrooms. Close to the ten "Classic" Gardens including: Montacute, Tintinhull, Barrington Court and Lytes Cary (National Trust). Visit Glastonbury Abbey, Wells Cathedral, the coast at Lyme Regis. Parking available. No smoking. Open March - November. Credit cards accepted. From £22 per person. Top 20 finalist for "AA Landlady of the Year". Also, national finalist – "England for Excellence" Awards 2000. Recommended by 'Which? Good B&B'. **ETC/AA** ◆◆◆◆.
e-mail: wychwoodmartock@yahoo.co.uk
website: www.theaa.co.uk/region8/76883.html

NORTH PETHERTON. Mrs Sue Milverton, Lower Clavelshay Farm, North Petherton, Near Bridgwater

TA6 6PJ (01278 662347). Working farm. 17th century farmhouse on a working dairy farm set in its own peaceful valley on the edge of the beautiful Quantock Hills. Off the beaten track but within easy reach of the many attractions in Somerset. Only 10 minutes from Junction 24 o f the M5 and 15 minutes from Taunton. Two en suite double bedrooms and one family room with private bathroom. Experience simple pleasures - beautiful countryside, long walks, fresh air, wildlife, wild flowers, log fires, starry nights, comfy beds, peace and tranquillity, good food, good books and good humour. Bring your family and your horse! Stables available - wonderful riding on the doorstep. Horse heaven! All meals with fresh local produce - our own where possible. Doubles £20 per person per night; family room £48 per night. Evening Meals on request (£9.50 adult, £4.75 child). **AA** ◆◆◆

SHERBORNE near. Mrs Sue Stretton, Beech Farm, Sigwells, Charlton Horethorne, Near Sherborne,

Dorset DT9 4LN (Tel & Fax: 01963 220524). Comfortable farmhouse with relaxed atmosphere on our 137 acre dairy farm carrying beef and horses in an area with wonderful views and excellent for walking, cycling and horse riding (guests' horses welcome). Located on the Somerset/Dorset border, six miles from Wincanton, four miles from Sherborne and just two miles off the A303. A comfortable, spacious, centrally heated farmhouse with a double room en suite, a twin room and family room with guest bathroom, all with tea/coffee trays. Pets welcome. Bed and Breakfast £16 per person. Less 10% for three or more nights. Evening meals at village inn or by prior arrangement. Open all year.

SUTTON MONTIS. Mrs E. Kerton, Parsonage Farm, Sutton Montis, Yeovil BA22 7HE (01963 220256).

17th Century farmhouse below King Arthur's Cadbury Castle, just off the A303 between Wincanton and Sparkford. This is a 160 acre beef and sheep farm; we have several home bred Shire horses. The area is unspoilt and an ideal centre for many interests. Close to Sherbourne, RNAS Yeovilton and several National Trust Properties. We also have lovely gardens, and are ideally situated for the Leland and MacMillan Trails. Two twin rooms and one double; two bathrooms; comfortable sitting room with TV. Good breakfasts, local produce, homemade bread, marmalade and free range eggs. Good local pubs for evening meals. Open April to October. £18 to £20 per person.

TAUNTON. Richard and Jill Gothard, Lower Marsh Farm, Kingston St Mary, Taunton TA2 8AB (Tel & Fax: 01823 451331).

Jill and Richard welcome you to their recently refurbished farmhouse on their family-run working farm half-a-mile from the quaint village of Kingston St Mary, which nestles at the foot of the Quantock Hills. Our accommodation comprises two en suite double/family rooms and one twin-bedded room, all with colour TV and tea/coffee making facilities. A delicious full English breakfast is served in the tastefully furnished dining room, which adjoins the drawing room with colour TV and log fire. All fully centrally heated. No pets and no smoking. Bed and Breakfast from £22.50 per night, reductions for children. Evening Meals by arrangement. **AA ◆◆◆.**
e-mail: mail@lowermarshfarm.co.uk

THEALE. Gill and Vern Clark, Yew Tree Farm, Theale, Near Wedmore BS28 4SN (01934 712475). A lovely large 17th Century farmhouse with a very friendly atmosphere - near to Wookey Hole, Cheddar, Wells and golf courses, with the cities of Bath and Bristol near by. Weston and Brean are also a short distance away. Idyllic walks are close at hand as well as the Somerset Levels and bird sanctuaries. There are three large super bedrooms, two double and one twin bedded. Own lounge with colour TV, as well as coffee and tea making facilities. Complimentary tea or coffee pot on arrival. Large car park. Tuesday to Friday; three course dinner on request. From £16 per person per night.

WASHFORD. Mrs Sarah Richmond, Hungerford Farm, Washford, Watchet TA23 0JZ (01984 640285).

Hungerford Farm is a comfortable 13th century farmhouse on a 350-acre mixed farm, three-quarters of a mile from the West Somerset Steam Railway. Situated in beautiful countryside on the edge of the Brendon Hills and Exmoor National Park. Within easy reach of the North Devon coast, two and a half miles from the Bristol Channel and Quantock Hills. Marvellous country for walking, riding, and fishing on the reservoirs. Family room and twin-bedded room, both with colour TV; own bathroom, shower, toilet. Own lounge with TV and open fire. Children welcome at reduced rates, cot and high chair. Sorry, no pets. Bed and Breakfast from £17. Evening drink included. Open February to November.
e-mail: sarah.richmond@virgin.net

WESTONZOYLAND. John and Liz. Knight, Staddlestones, 3 Standards Road, Westonzoyland TA7 0EL (01278 691179; Fax: 01278 691333).

Bed and Breakfast in the spacious comfort of our elegant Georgian home. Centrally located in the historic village of Westonzoyland and close to Junction 23 of the M5 motorway, Staddlestones provides an ideal base for exploring Somerset. Scenically beautiful and rich in history, natural life and country crafts, this lesser-known area of England offers a wealth of attractions to the visitor and will delight those who are not already familiar with its many treasures. Please contact us for full details of our quality facilities but do note that we have a no-smoking policy at Staddlestones and do not accept children. **ETC ◆◆◆** *SILVER AWARD.*
e-mail: staddlestones@euphony.net

WICK. Jackie Bishop, Toghill House Farm, Freezing Hill, Wick BS15 5RT (01225 891261; Fax: 01225 892128). Warm and cosy 17th century farmhouse on working farm with outstanding views, yet only three miles north of the historic city of Bath. All rooms en suite with tea making facilities and colour TV, or choose one of our luxury self-catering barn conversions which are equipped to a very high standard and include all linen. Children and pets welcome.

WRINGTON. Mr Hemmens, West Hay Farm, West Hay Road, Wrington BS40 7NR (01934 863549; Mobile: 0781 8625770).Situated within the beautiful Wrington Vale, nicely secluded at the end of a track yet close to all ammenities and overlooking breathtaking views of the Mendip Hills. Less than 10 minutes from Bristol Airport, with Bath, Bristol the seaside resort of Weston-super-Mare and Cheddar not far away. Double and twin rooms, all en suite with TV and hot drinks facilities. Enjoy breakfast of local produce including our own popular free-range eggs in a relaxed and friendly atmosphere. Excellent food served at the local pub just five minutes away. Please send for further information and terms.

STAFFORDSHIRE

ALBRIGHTON. Mrs Margaret Shanks, Parkside Farm, Holyhead Road, Albrighton, Near Wolverhampton WV7 3DA (01902 372310; Fax: 01902 375013). Whether on business or visiting tourist attractions, Parkside Farm offers comfortable accommodation in a friendly atmosphere, overlooking picturesque countryside. It is a working arable farm with three bedrooms all with private facilitites, TV and tea/coffee making. Family rooms are also available. It is located within easy distance of the A41, A5, M54 Junctions 3 and 4, Bridgnorth, Wolverhampton and Telford. There are plenty of pubs, bars and restaurants, the nearest within two minutes' walking distance. No dogs allowed in rooms, no smoking on premises; open parking available. Bed and Breakfast from £25 per person per night. ETC ◆◆◆◆
e-mail: jmshanks@farming.co.uk
website: www.parksidefarm.com

ECCLESHALL. M. Hiscoe-James, Offley Grove Farm, Adbaston, Eccleshall ST20 0QB (01785 280205). You'll consider this a good find! Quality accommodation and excellent breakfasts. Small traditional mixed farm surrounded by beautiful countryside. The house is tastefully furnished and provides all home comforts. En suite rooms available. Whether you are planning to book here for a break in your journey, stay for a weekend or take your holidays here, you will find something to suit all tastes among the many local attractions. Situated on the Staffordshire/Shropshire borders we are convenient for Alton Towers, Stoke-on-Trent, Ironbridge, etc. Just 15 minutes from M6 and M54; midway between Eccleshall and Newport, four miles from the A519. Reductions for children. Play area for small children. Open all year. Bed and Breakfast all en suite from £20. Many guests return. Self-catering cottages available. Brochure on request. AA/RAC ◆◆◆
e-mail: accomm@offleygrovefarm.freeserve.co.uk
website: www.offleygrovefarm.freeserve.co.uk

LEEK. Mrs Elizabeth Winterton, Brook House Farm,Cheddleton, Leek ST13 7DF (01538 360296).

Working farm. Brook House is a stockrearing farm in a picturesque and secluded valley, yet only half a mile from the A520. All our five rooms are en suite, have central heating, colour TV's, tea/coffe trays, hairdryer and comfortable beds. Relax in our lounge with log fires in winter and breakfast in our lovely conservatory with fine country views. Explore the Staffordshire Moorlands and the Peak District. Experience the thrills of Alton Towers, browse in the world famous pottery factory shops of Wedgwood, Royal Doulton etc, or visit the many stately homes in the area. Whatever you decide to do a warm welcome is assured. **ETC** ◆◆◆.

LEEK. Mrs P. Simpson, Summerhill Farm, Grindon, Leek ST13 7TT (01538 304264).

Traditional family farm set in the Peak District amid rolling countryside with panoramic views. Wonderful for walkers. All three rooms are en suite and have tea and coffee making facilities, colour TV, clock radios. Children welcome. Alton Towers only 15 minutes away, 35 minutes to Potteries. Open all year for Bed and Breakfast from £18.50 to £20; Dinner from £10. Directions – Leek to Ashbourne Road A523 through Onecote, first right for Grindon, three-quarters of a mile up no through road. **ETC/AA** ◆◆◆◆

LEEK. Gwen Sheldon, Middle Farm, Apesford, Bradnop, Leek ST13 7EX (01538 382839). Middle Farm is situated next to Coombes Valley off the A523 Leek to Ashbourne Road at Apesford, near Bradnop. Within easy reach of Alton Towers, Leek town centre, Peak District National Park and the Potteries where you will find the famous makes. i.e. Royal Doulton, Wedgwood and others. All rooms en suite, tea/coffee making facilities, TV, radio. Private parking. The dairy has recently been converted into a family room with the elderly and disabled in mind. Bed and Breakfast from £20. **ETC** ◆◆◆

SUFFOLK

BURY ST EDMUNDS. Mrs Kathy Parker, Grange Farm, Woolpit, Bury St. Edmunds IP30 9RG (01359 241143; Fax: 01359 244296).

Grange Farm is a Grade II Listed farmhouse, on a working arable farm in the heart of Suffolk, only one mile from the A14 corridor giving easy access to East Anglia. Woolpit is "Village of the Year" for Suffolk. Bury St. Edmunds and Stowmarket are 10 minutes away and historic Lavenham and Long Melford are close, via delightful country lanes and pretty villages. All rooms have tea/coffee making facilities, colour TV, alarm radio and hair dryer. One double/one twin en suite, one twin with private facilities. Breakfast is freshly prepared using local produce. Self catering, Caravan Club CL and fishing are situated on the farm. **ETC ◆◆◆◆**
e-mail: grangefarm@btinternet.com
website: www.farmstayanglia.co.uk/grangefarm

EYE. Janet and Gerald Edgecombe, Moat Farm, Thorndon, Eye IP23 7LX (01379 678437; Fax: 01379 678023).

Moat Farm is an old Suffolk farmhouse complete with horses, family of ducks and newly converted Granary. Situated in a quiet village, two miles off the A140, close to local pubs and restaurants. The en suite bedrooms are all beautifully furnished with a wealth of beams. A blazing log fire in the inglenook fireplace welcomes you to breakfast, chosen from our large and varied menu. The historic town of Eye, with its unique theatre and beauty parlour, Thornham, walks, golf, horse riding, antique shops all within a few miles. Two cycles for guests. Scenic coast about 25 miles.
e-mail: geralde@clara.co.uk
website: www.moatfarm.co.uk

FRAMLINGHAM. Mr and Mrs Kindred, High House Farm, Cransford, Framlingham, Woodbridge IP13 9PD (01728 663461; Fax: 01728 663409). Working farm.

Beautifully restored 15th Century Farmhouse on family-run arable farm, featuring exposed oak beams and inglenook fireplaces, with spacious and comfortable accommodation. One double room, en suite and one large family room with double and twin beds and private adjacent bathroom. A warm welcome awaits all, children's cots, high chairs, books, toys, and outside play equipment available. Attractive semi-moated gardens, farm and woodland walks. Explore the heart of rural Suffolk, local vineyards, Easton Farm Park, Framlingham and Orford Castles, Parham Air Museum, Saxtead Windmill, Minsmere, Snape Maltings, Woodland Trust and the Heritage Coast. Bed and Breakfast from £20. Reductions for children and stays of three nights or more. Self catering available in three-bed Gamekeeper's house set in woodland. **ETC ◆◆◆**.
e-mail: b&b@highhousefarm.co.uk
website: www.highhousefarm.co.uk

FRAMLINGHAM. Mrs Jennie Mann, Fiddlers Hall, Cransford, Near Framlingham, Woodbridge IP13 9PQ (01728 663729). Working farm, join in.

Signposted on B1119, Fiddlers Hall is a 14th century, moated, oak-beamed farmhouse set in a beautiful and secluded position. It is two miles from Framlingham Castle, 20 minutes' drive from Aldeburgh, Snape Maltings, Woodbridge and Southwold. A Grade II Listed building, it has lots of history and character. The bedrooms are spacious; one has en suite shower room, the other has a private bathroom. Use of lounge and colour TV. Plenty of parking space. Lots of farm animals kept. Traditional farmhouse cooking. Bed and Breakfast terms from £22.

FRAMLINGHAM. Mrs J. R. Graham, Woodlands Farm, Brundish, Near Framlingham, Woodbridge

IP13 8BP (01379 384444). Woodlands Farm has a cottage-type farmhouse set in quiet Suffolk countryside. Near historic town of Framlingham with its castle and within easy reach of coast, wildlife parks, Otter Trust, Easton Farm Park and Snape Maltings for music lovers. Open all year. Twin room wih private shower, washbasin and WC; two double bedrooms with bathroom en suite. Diningroom and sittingroom with inglenook fireplaces for guests' use. Good home cooked food assured. Full central heating. Car essential, good parking. Sorry, no pets. Bed and Breakfast from £20 to £22.50; Evening Meal by arrangement £14. SAE or telephone. FHB Member. ETC ◆◆◆◆

FRAMLINGHAM. Mrs C. Jones, Bantry, Chapel Road, Saxtead, Woodbridge IP13 9RB (01728 685578).

Bantry is set in half-an-acre of gardens overlooking open countryside in the picturesque village of Saxtead, which is close to the historic castle town of Framlingham. Best known for its working windmill beside the village green, Saxtead is a good central base from which to discover East Anglia. Accommodation is offered in self-contained apartments (one ground floor), each comprising its own private diningroom/TV lounge and bathroom for secluded comfort. Terms: Bed and Breakfast from £19.50 per night. Non-smoking.

FRAMLINGHAM. Mary and Anthony Wilkinson, Wayside, Glemham Road, Sweffling, Near

Saxmundham IP17 2BQ (01728 663256). We warmly welcome you to our family-run B & B home situated in the valley of the River Alde with its unspoilt water meadows rich in wildlife. The spacious en suite bedrooms, one double and one twin, have TV and tea/coffee facilities. Good walking country, and being on the Suffolk cycleway we have secure storage for cycles and ample parking for cars. Ideally placed for visiting the Heritage Coast, Minsmere Bird Reserve, Snape Maltings, Framlingham and Oxford Castles as well as Suffolk's many interesting churches. Folding beds for children accommodated with parents. No smoking. Bed and Breakfast from £40. Double. ETC ◆◆◆◆.

FRAMLINGHAM. Brian and Phyllis Collett, Shimmens Pightle, Dennington Road, Framlingham,

Woodbridge IP13 9JT (01728 724036). Shimmens Pightle is situated in an acre of landscaped garden, surrounded by farmland, within a mile of the centre of Framlingham, with its famous castle and church. Ideally situated for the Heritage Coast, Snape Maltings, local vineyards, riding, etc. Cycles can be hired locally. Many good local eating places. Double and twin bedded rooms, with washbasins, on ground floor. Comfortable lounge with TV overlooking garden. Morning tea and evening drinks offered. Sorry, no pets or smoking indoors. Bed and traditional English Breakfast, using local cured bacon and home made marmalade. Vegetarians also happily catered for. SAE please. Open mid March to November. Bed and Breakfast from £21 per person. Reduced weekly rates. ETC ◆◆◆

LOWESTOFT. Elisabeth Edwards, Church Farm, Corton, Near Lowestoft NR32 5HX (01502 730359;

Fax: 01502 733426). Britain's most easterly farm, near rural beach and cliff walks. Victorian farmhouse with attractive high standard en suite double bedrooms (one on ground level), all with colour TV and tea/coffee making facilities. Generous traditional breakfast. German spoken. Directions: A12 from Lowestoft to Yarmouth into Stirrups Lane opposite parish church. Ample parking. Bed and Breakfast from £22.50 to £25. Which? Good B&B, Time Out magazine. Welcome Host. ETC ◆◆◆◆◆
e-mail: medw149227@aol.com

STOKE-BY-NAYLAND. Mr and Mrs A. J. Geater, Ryegate House, Stoke-by-Nayland, Colchester CO6 4RA (01206 263679). Situated on the B1068 within the Dedham Vale, in a quiet Suffolk village, Ryegate House is a modern property built in the style of a Suffolk farmhouse. It is only a few minutes' walk from the local shops, post office, pubs, restaurants and church and an ideal base for exploring Constable country. A warm welcome, good food and comfortable accommodation in a peaceful setting with easy access to local historic market towns, golf courses and the East Coast. Comfortable en suite bedrooms with colour TV, radio alarm, tea/coffee making facilities, shaver point and central heating. Children welcome. Parking for six cars. Open all year except Christmas. Bed and Breakfast from £30 to £35 per night single, £42.50 to £50 double. **AA/ETC** ◆◆◆◆ *GOLD AWARD.* e-mail: ryegate@lineone.net

SURREY

KINGSTON-UPON-THAMES Chase Lodge, 10 Park Road, Hampton Wick, Kingston-upon-Thames KT1 4AS (020 8943 1862; Fax: 020 8943 9363). An award-winning hotel with style and elegance, set in tranquil surroundings at affordable prices. Easy access to Kingston town centre and all major transport links; 20 minutes from Heathrow Airport; Full English breakfast and à la carte menus; licensed bar. Ideal for wedding receptions. Various golf courses within easy reach. Major credit cards accepted. From £40 per person Bed and Breakfast; from £50 per person Dinner, Bed and Breakfast. Full details on request. **LTB/AA** ★★★, **RAC** *HIGHLY ACCLAIMED, LES ROUTIERS.* website: www.chaselodgehotel.com

LINGFIELD. Mrs Vivienne Bundy, Oaklands, Felcourt Road, Lingfield RH7 6NF (01342 834705). Oaklands is a spacious country house of considerable charm dating from the 17th century. It is set in its own grounds of one acre and is about one mile from the small town of Lingfield and three miles from East Grinstead, both with rail connections to London. It is convenient to Gatwick Airport and is ideal as a "stop-over" or as a base to visit many places of interest in south east England. Dover and the Channel Ports are two hours' drive away whilst the major towns of London and Brighton are about one hour distant. One family room en-suite, one double and one single bedrooms with washbasins; three bathrooms, two toilets; sittingroom; diningroom. Cot, high chair, babysitting and reduced rates for children. Gas central heating. Open all year. Parking. Bed and Breakfast from £22; Evening Meal by arrangement.

LINGFIELD. Mrs Vanessa Manwill, Stantons Hall Farm, Eastbourne Road, Blindley Heath, Lingfield RH7 6LG (01342 832401). Stantons Hall Farm is an 18th century farmhouse set amidst 18 acres of farmland and adjacent to Blindley Heath Common. Family, double and single rooms, most with toilet, shower and washbasin en suite. Separate bathroom. All rooms have colour TV, tea/coffee making facilities and are centrally heated. There are plenty of parking spaces. We are conveniently situated within easy reach of M25 (London Orbital), Gatwick Airport (car parking facilities for travellers) and Lingfield Park Racecourse. Enjoy a traditional English Breakfast in our large farmhouse kitchen. Bed and Breakfast from £23 per person, reductions for children sharing. Cot and high chair available. Well behaved dogs welcome by prior arrangement.

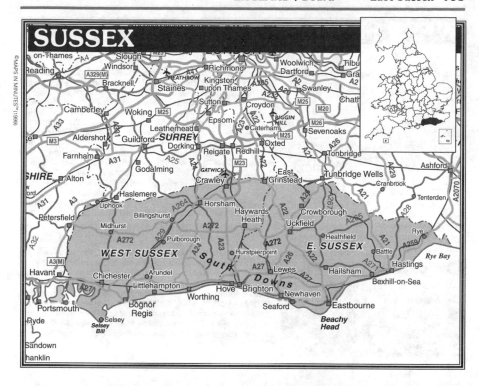

SUSSEX

EAST SUSSEX

BATTLE. Mrs June Ive, Moonshill Farm, The Green, Ninfield, Battle TN33 9LH (Tel & Fax: 01424 892645) Every comfort in quiet, peaceful farmhouse situated in 10 acres of garden, orchard and stables, in the centre of the village of Ninfield. Enjoy beautiful walks, golf and riding arranged. Comfortable rooms with hospitality tray and TV, three en suite, central heating, electric fires, lounge. Parking. Babysitting service. Bed and Breakfast from £17.50-£20.00. Open January to November. **ETC** ◆◆◆

BURWASH. Mrs E. Sirrell, Woodlands Farm, Burwash, Etchingham TN19 7LA (Tel & Fax: 01435 882794). Working farm, join in. Woodlands Farm stands one-third-of-a mile off the road, surrounded by fields and woods. This peaceful and beautifully modernised 16th century farmhouse offers comfortable and friendly accommodation. Sitting/dining room; two bathrooms, one en suite, double or twin-bedded rooms (one has four poster bed) together with excellent farm fresh food. This is a farm of 108 acres with mixed animals, and is situated within easy reach of 20 or more places of interest to visit and half-an-hour from the coast. Open all year. Central heating. Literature provided to help guests. Children welcome. Dogs allowed if sleeping in owner's car. Parking. Evening Meal optional. Bed and Breakfast from £20 to £23 per person per night. Telephone or SAE, please. AA QQ.
e-mail: liz_sir@lineone.net

WEST SUSSEX

HENFIELD. Mrs J. Forbes, Little Oreham Farm, off Horne Lane, Near Woodsmill, Henfield BN5 9SB

(01273 492931). Delightful old Sussex farmhouse situated in rural position down lane, adjacent to footpaths and nature reserve. One mile from Henfield village, eight miles from Brighton, convenient for Gatwick and Hickstead. Excellent base for visiting many gardens and places of interest in the area. The farmhouse is a listed building of great character; oak-beamed sittingroom with inglenook fireplace (log fires), and a pretty diningroom. Three comfortable attractive bedrooms with en suite shower/bath; WC; colour TV; tea making facilities. Central heating throughout. Lovely garden with views of the Downs. Situated off Horne Lane, one minute from Woodsmill Countryside Centre. Winner of Kellogg's award: "Best Bed and Breakfast" in the South East. You will enjoy a friendly welcome and pleasant holiday. Sorry, no children under 10. Bed and Breakfast from £20 per person. Evening Meals by arrangement. Non-smoking. Open all year.

PETWORTH. Phyl Folkes, "Drifters", Duncton, Petworth GU28 0JZ (01798 342706). Welcome to a quiet,

friendly, comfortable house overlooking countryside. One double en suite, two twin and one single rooms. Duncton is three miles from Petworth on the A285 Chichester Road, South Downs Way close by and many interesting places to visit. Petworth House and Gardens, Roman Villa, Chichester Cathedral and Theatre, Goodwood House and racecourse, Weald and Downland Museum and many more. TV and tea/coffee making facilities in all rooms. Sorry no young children and no smoking. Bed and Breakfast from £20.00 to £25.00 per person.

Reflections in the pond at Midhurst, West Sussex

WARWICKSHIRE

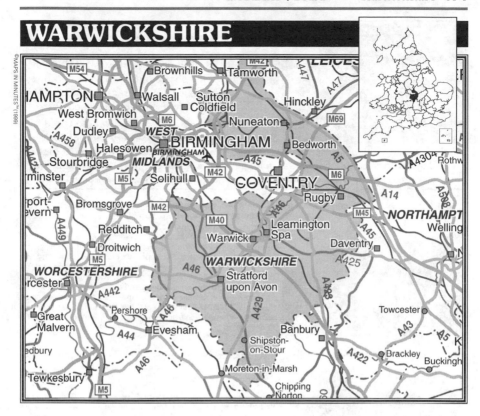

ALCESTER. John and Margaret Canning, Glebe Farm, Exhall, Alcester B49 6EA (Tel & Fax: 01789 772202). Shakespeare named our village "Dodging Exhall" and it has somehow "dodged" the passing of time, so if you want a true taste of rural England, come and relax in our quaint old farmhouse - parts of it dating from Tudor times - with its log fires, four-poster bed and country hospitality. One double, one twin and two single rooms, all with tea/coffee trays, electric blankets. Smoking in lounge. Payphone. Laundry. Children and pets welcome. Ample parking. Bed and Breakfast from £20 to £25. Open all year except Christmas and New Year.

COVENTRY Near. Mrs Sandra Evans, Camp Farm, Hob Lane, Balsall Common, Near Coventry CV7 7GX (01676 533804). Camp Farm is a farmhouse 150 to 200 years old. It is modernised but still retains its old world character. Nestling in the heart of England in Shakespeare country, within easy reach of Stratford-upon-Avon, Warwick, Kenilworth, Coventry with its famous Cathedral, and the National Exhibition Centre, also the National Agricultural Centre, Stoneleigh. Camp Farm offers a warm homely atmosphere and good English food, service and comfortable beds. The house is carpeted throughout. Diningroom and lounge with colour TV. Bedrooms – three double rooms or three single rooms, all with washbasin. The house is suitable for partially disabled guests. All terms by letter or telephone.

Cooperage Farm

Old Road, Meriden, Near Coventry CY7 7JP
Telephone 01676 523493
Website: www.cooperagefarm.co.uk
E-mail: info@cooperagefarm.co.uk

Cooperage Farm is a 300 year old Listed farmhouse situated in the very heart of England in the attractive village of Meriden. A friendly, family-run establishment with full central heating, tea/coffee making facilities, full English Breakfast etc. Transport available for guests. All-in-all, first class, homely accommodation with a friendly welcome for all.

LEAMINGTON SPA. Mrs R. Gibbs, Hill Farm, Lewis Road, Radford Semele, Leamington Spa CV31 1UX

(01926 337571). Working farm. Guests are welcome all year round to this comfortable, centrally heated farmhouse on a 350 acre mixed farm. Ideally situated for Warwick, Coventry, Stratford-upon-Avon, Leamington Spa, Royal Showground, Birmingham, NEC and the Cotswolds. Three pretty double bedrooms and two twin rooms with washbasins, tea and coffee facilities and TV. Some are en suite. Guests' sittingroom with colour TV; lovely conservatory for breakfast dining and excellent Breakfast Menu. Car preferable, ample parking. Spacious five van site also available. Farm Holiday Bureau member. FHG past Diploma Winner. Bed and Breakfast from £18 to £25 per person. **AA/ETC** ◆◆◆◆

SHIPSTON-ON-STOUR. Mrs Fox, Kirby Farm, Whatcote, Shipston-on-Stour CV36 5EQ (01295

680525). Kirby Farm is situated in beautiful countryside within easy reach of Cotswolds, Stratford-upon-Avon, Banbury, Warwick Castle and many other places of interest. Our spacious, stone built, fully centrally heated farmhouse is set in 450 arable acres and a long driveway gives it an "off the beaten track" feel. Visitors will receive a warm welcome. Bedrooms have tea/coffee making facilities and en suite accommodaton is available. Breakfast is served in separate dining room and guests have access to their own drawing room with TV and log fire on cold evenings. Bed and Breakfast from £16.

STRATFORD-UPON-AVON. Mrs Marion J. Walters, Church Farm, Dorsington, Stratford-upon-Avon

CV37 8AX (01789 720471; Fax: 01789 720830; Mobile: 0831 504194). Working farm. Situated on the Heart of England Way. A warm and friendly welcome awaits you all year at our 127 acre mixed farm with woodlands and stream which you may explore. Ideal for walking. Our Georgian Farmhouse is situated on the edge of an extremely pretty village. Stratford-upon-Avon, Warwick, National Exhibition Centre, Royal Showground, Cotswolds, Evesham and Worcester all within easy driving distance. Family, twin and double bedrooms, all with tea/coffee facilities; most en suite with TV, some in converted stable block. Cot and high chair available. Central heating. Gliding, fishing, boating and horse riding nearby. Full Fire Certificate held. Bed and Breakfast from £19. Write or phone for further details. **ETC** ◆◆◆
e-mail: chfarmdorsington@aol.com

> ## Please mention The Farm Holiday Guide when writing to enquire about accommodation

STRATFORD-UPON-AVON. Mrs Julia Downie, Holly Tree Cottage, Birmingham Road, Pathlow, Stratford-upon-Avon CV37 0ES (Tel & Fax: 01789 204461). Period cottage dating back to 17th century, with beams, antiques, tasteful furnishings and friendly atmosphere. Large picturesque gardens with extensive views over the countryside. Situated three miles north of Stratford towards Henley-in-Arden on A3400, convenient for overnight stops or longer stays, and ideal for theatre visits. Excellent base for touring Shakespeare country, Heart of England, Cotswolds, Warwick Castle and Blenheim Palace. Well situated for National Exhibition Centre. Double, twin and family accommodation with en suite and private facilities; colour TV and tea/coffee in all rooms. Full English Breakfast. Restaurant and pub meals nearby. Bed and Breakfast from £24. Telephone for information.

STRATFORD-UPON-AVON. Mrs R.M. Meadows, Monk's Barn Farm, Shipston Road, Stratford-upon-Avon CV37 8NA (01789 293714; Fax: 01789 205886). Working farm. Two miles south of Stratford-upon-Avon on the A3400 is Monk's Barn, a 75 acre mixed farm welcoming visitors all year. The farm dates back to the 16th century, although the pretty house is more recent. The double, single and twin rooms, most with en suite facilities, are provided in the main house and the cleverly converted milking parlour. The two ground floor rooms are suitable for some disabled guests. Visitors lounge. Beautiful riverside walk to the village. Tea/coffee making facilities and colour TV in rooms. Sorry, no pets. Non-smokers preferred. Details on request. Bed and Breakfast from £17. **AA ◆◆◆◆.**

STRATFORD-UPON-AVON. Mrs Sally Gray, Rectory Farm, Clifford Chambers, Stratford-upon-Avon CV37 8AA (01789 414355). Rectory Farm is a delightful home converted from attractive farm buildings and barn with self-contained bed and breakfast accommodation with private front door, where you will be our only guests. Double bedroom overlooking Warwickshire countryside, a twin bedded room, bathroom with shower, spacious and tastefully furnished private sitting room for guests with TV, tea/coffee making facilities. Ample car parking, children's outdoor play equipment, gardens. Countryside location but only two miles from Stratford town centre, Cotswolds close by. Pub within walking distance. Bed and Breakfast from £22.

STRATFORD-UPON-AVON. Mrs M. Turney, Cadle Pool Farm, The Ridgway, Stratford-upon-Avon CV37 9RE (01789 292494). Working farm. Situated in picturesque grounds, this charming oak-panelled and beamed family home is situated two miles from Stratford-upon-Avon. The Royal Shakespeare Theatre is only eight minutes away by car. Ideal touring centre for Warwick, Kenilworth, Oxford and the Cotswolds. Accommodation comprises one family and one double room, both with en suite bathroom and TV, and another double bedroom with private bathroom. All have tea/coffee making facilities. There is an antique oak dining room and guest lounge. The gardens and ornamental pool are particularly attractive, with peacocks and ducks roaming freely. Children over ten years welcome. Rates per person with en suite £26.00, without £24.00.

FREE or REDUCED RATE entry to Holiday Visits and Attractions — see our READERS' OFFER VOUCHERS on pages 43-60

WARWICK. Mr and Mrs D. Clapp, The Croft, Haseley Knob, Warwick CV35 7NL (Tel & Fax: 01926 484447). Join David and Pat in their country guest house and share the friendly family atmosphere, the picturesque rural surroundings, home cooking and very comfortable accommodation. Bedrooms, most en suite, have colour TV, tea/coffee making equipment. Ground floor en suite bedrooms available. Centrally located for touring Warwick (Castle), Stratford (Shakespeare), Coventry (Cathedral), and Birmingham. Also ideal for the businessman visiting the National Exhibition Centre or Birmingham Airport, both about 15 minutes. No smoking inside. Ample parking. Mobile home available, also caravan parking. Large gardens. Open all year. French spoken. Bed and Full English Breakfast from £23 per person sharing a double/twin room. **ETC** ◆◆◆◆

WARWICK. Mrs J. Stanton, Redlands Farm, Banbury Road, Lighthorne, Near Warwick CV35 0AH (01926 651241). A beautifully restored 15th century farmhouse built of local stone, the "Old Farm House" is set in two acres of garden with its own swimming pool, well away from the main road yet within easy travelling distance of Stratford and Warwick, and handy for the Cotswolds. Guest accommodation is one double (with bathroom), one single and one family bedrooms, all with tea making facilities; bathroom; beamed lounge with TV; diningroom. Rooms are centrally heated and the farmhouse also has open fires. Bed and Breakfast from £18. Children welcome – facilities available. No pets. A car is recommended to make the most of your stay. AA QQQ.

WILTSHIRE

BATH near. Mrs Dorothy Robinson, Boyds Farm, Gastard, Near Corsham SN13 9PT (Tel & Fax: 01249713146). Welcome Host. Dorothy and Andrew Robinson warmly welcome guests to Boyds Farm which is a family-run working farm with a pedigree herd of Hereford Cattle. The farmhouse is a delightful 16th century Listed building surrounded by beautiful mature gardens. Near to Bath, Lacock, Bradford-on-Avon, Castle Combe, Stonehenge, etc. Accommodation comprises one double en suite, one family or twin with private bathroom and one double with private shower room, all well furnished with tea/coffee facilities, electric blankets, etc; guest lounge with log fire for cooler nights. Featured in the "Daily Express," "The Sunday Observer," and "Sunday Mail". Rates from £20 to £25 per person. **ETC** ◆◆◆◆◆ *SILVER AWARD.* e-mail: dorothyrobinson@boydsfarm.freeserve.co.uk

CHIPPENHAM. Mrs Julie McDonough, Fairfield Farm, Upper Wraxall, Chippenham SN14 7AG (01225 891750; Fax: 01225 891050). Fairfield is a friendly farmhouse in Beaufort country, eight miles from Georgian Bath, three miles from beautiful Castle Combe en route to Bristol (12 miles). Large garden, wonderful views. One double/family room, one twin, both with private bathrooms, TV and tea/coffee making facilities. Excellent pubs nearby. A warm welcome awaits you. Closed Christmas. Non-smoking. Bed and Breakfast from £20. **ETC** ◆◆◆◆ e-mail: mcdonoug@globalnet.co.uk

DEVIZES. Marlene and Malcolm Nixon, Higher Green Farm, Poulshot, Devizes SN10 1RW (Tel & Fax: 01380 828355).

Welcome to our peaceful 17th century timbered farmhouse facing the village green and cricket pitch. Excellent traditional inn nearby. Our dairy farm is situated between Bath and Salisbury, close to many National Trust properties. Ideal for Stonehenge, Longleat, Avebury and Lacock. One double, one twin, two single rooms. Tea making facilities. Guests' lounge, colour TV. Take A361 from Devizes, after two miles left to Poulshot, farm opposite Raven Inn. Open March to November. Children and pets welcome. Non-smoking. Bed and Breakfast from £18. ETC ◆◆◆.

MALMESBURY. Mrs Edwards, Stonehill Farm, Charlton, Malmesbury SN16 9DY (01666 823310).

Superbly located on the edge of the Cotswolds in lush rolling countryside. We invite you to stay with us on our family run dairy farm and offer you Bed and Breakfast in our farmhouse, in three pretty rooms, one en suite, all with tea/coffee tray, and TV. Delicious Breakfasts using homemade preserves and local honey. Visit quiet villages, stately homes, market towns, walk in the countryside, or stay at the farm and watch the cows being milked. Spend days in Bath, Oxford, Stonehenge or the delightful Cotswold hills. Tariff from £20 per person. Pets very welcome.

MALMESBURY. Mrs Susan Barnes, Lovett Farm, Little Somerford, Near Malmesbury SN15 5BP (Tel & Fax: 01666 823268; mobile: 07808 858612).

Working farm. Enjoy traditional hospitality at our delightful farmhouse just three miles from the historic town of Malmesbury with its wonderful Norman Abbey and gardens and central for Cotswolds, Bath, Stratford, Avebury and Stonehenge. Two attractive en suite bedrooms with delightful views, each with tea/coffee making facilities, colour television and radio. Delicious full English breakfast served in our cosy diningroom/lounge. Central heating throughout. Bed and Breakfast from £23. Non-smoking accommodation. Open all year. Farm Holiday Bureau Member. ETC/AA ◆◆◆◆
e-mail: lovetts_farm@hotmail.com

MELKSHAM. Barbara Pullen, Frying Pan Farm, Broughton Gifford, Melksham SN12 8LL (01225 702343; Fax: 01225 793652).

FRYING PAN FARM

A warm welcome awaits you at our cosy farmhouse overlooking meadowland. We are situated to the east of Bath making us an ideal base for visiting the city or touring the surrounding countryside with Bradford-on-Avon, Lacock, Stonehenge and numerous National Trust Properties within easy driving distance. The accommodation consists of two en suite rooms, one double and one twin, with beverage trays and TV. Good pub food available in the village - one mile. Closed Christmas and New Year.

MELKSHAM near. Pam Hole, Church Farm, Atworth, Melksham SN12 8JA (Tel & Fax: 01225 702215)

Church Farm is a friendly family-run dairy farm in the village of Atworth just off the A365 Bath to Melksham Road. The farmhouse is a Grade 11 Listed building situated in an acre of garden with uninterrupted views of the countryside, with a fish pool and patio area for you to relax and take in the sunshine! Large lounge for sole use of guests. All bedrooms have TV, clock/radio, tea/coffee making facilities. Full English breakfast with locally grown produce when available. Within 10 minutes' walk of good local pub. Rates from £20 to £25 per person per night.
e-mail: churchfarm@tinyonline.co.uk
website: www.churchfarm-atworth.freeserve.co.uk

SALISBURY. Mrs Suzi Lanham, Newton Farmhouse, Southampton Road, Whiteparish, Salisbury

SP5 2QL (01794 884416). This Listed 16th century farmhouse on the borders of the New Forest was formerly part of the Trafalgar Estate and is situated eight miles south of Salisbury, convenient for Stonehenge, Romsey, Winchester, Portsmouth and Bournemouth. All rooms have pretty en suite facilities and are delightfully decorated, six with genuine period four-poster beds. The beamed diningroom houses a collection of Nelson memorabilia and antiques, and has flagstone floors and an inglenook fireplace with an original brick-built bread oven. The superb English breakfast is complemented by fresh fruits, home-made breads and preserves and free-range eggs. Dinner is available by arrangement using home-grown kitchen garden produce wherever possible. A swimming pool is idyllically set in the extensive well-stocked gardens and children are most welcome in this non-smoking establishment. **ETC/AA** ◆◆◆◆◆ *SILVER AWARD. 3 EGGCUPS, 1 LADLE.*
e-mail: reservations@newtonfarmhouse.co.uk
website: www.newtonfarmhouse.co.uk

TROWBRIDGE. Mrs Susan Cottle, Church Farm, Steeple Ashton, Trowbridge BA14 6EL (01380

870518). Lovely old farmhouse dating back to the 16th century in centre of beautiful village. Ideally situated for Bath, Salisbury, Longleat, Stourhead, Castle Combe, Lacock and Avebury. Spacious rooms, one double with washbasin, one family, tea/coffee facilities. Guests' bathroom. Homely atmosphere, use of lounge, TV. Log fire in winter. Tea and homemade cake on arrival. No smoking in bedrooms. Open all year except Christmas and New Year. Bed and Breakfast from £20. **ETC** ◆◆◆◆.
e-mail: church.farm@farmline.com

WARMINSTER. Mrs M. Hoskins, Spinney Farmhouse, Chapmanslade, Westbury BA13 4AQ (01373

832412). Working farm. Off A36, three miles west of Warminster; 16 miles from historic city of Bath. Close to Longleat, Cheddar and Stourhead. Reasonable driving distance to Bristol, Stonehenge, Glastonbury and the cathedral cities of Wells and Salisbury. Pony trekking and fishing available locally and an 18 hole golf course within walking distance. Washbasins, tea/coffee-making facilities and shaver points in all rooms. Family room available. Guests' lounge with colour TV. Central heating. Children and pets welcome. Ample parking. Open all year. Enjoy farm fresh food in a warm, friendly family atmosphere. Bed and Breakfast from £19 per night. Reduction after two nights. Evening Meal £11.

PLEASE MENTION THIS GUIDE WHEN YOU WRITE

OR PHONE TO ENQUIRE ABOUT ACCOMMODATION.

IF YOU ARE WRITING, A STAMPED,

ADDRESSED ENVELOPE IS ALWAYS APPRECIATED.

FREE or REDUCED RATE entry to
Holiday Visits and Attractions — see our
READERS' OFFER VOUCHERS on pages 43-60

WORCESTERSHIRE

Lower Field Farm offers genuine farmhouse comfort and hospitality in a late 17th century Cotswold stone and brick farmhouse looking out on to the Cotswold Hills. Broadway two miles. Delightful rooms have tea/coffee facilities, TV and en suite bathrooms. Ground floor room available for those who find stairs difficult. This peaceful location provides an ideal base from which to explore the Cotswolds, Stratford-upon-Avon, Warwick Castle, Cheltenham, Oxford and beyond. We can provide Evening Meals by arrangement, or there is a wealth of good eating houses nearby, Open all year. Bed with full English Breakfast from £22.50 per person. Pets and children welcome.

For enquiries, bookings or a free colour brochure contact:
Jane Hill, Lower Field Farm, Willersey, Broadway, Worcs WR11 5HF 01386 858273 or 0403 343996
Fax: 01386 854608
e-mail: lowerfield.farm@virgin.net

BROADWAY. Mrs Sarah Bent, Bowers Hill Farm, Bowers Hill, Near Willersey, Broadway WR11 5HG (01386 834585; Fax: 01386 830234). Enjoy peace and tranquillity on our 80-acre working farm with historic interest - medieval fields, old gas lamps, and lovely antiques - set alongside high quality modern comforts. View large garden and animals grazing whilst breakfasting in our new 40' conservatory. Friendly hosts. Great location for touring Worcestershire villages, Bredon Hills, the Cotswolds, and Shakespeare Country. Non-smoking bedrooms. TV lounge. Colour TV, tea and coffee, hairdryer and clock/radio in all rooms (one super-kingsize, one double and one family). Children welcome. Farm assistance always appreciated. **ETC/AA ◆◆◆◆.**
e-mail: sarah@bowershillfarm.com
website: www.bowershillfarm.com

BROMSGROVE. Mrs C. Gibbs, Lower Bentley Farm, Lower Bentley, Bromsgrove B60 4JB (01527 821286). An attractive Victorian farmhouse with modern comforts on a dairy and beef farm is an ideal base for a holiday, Short Break or business stay. Overlooking peaceful countryside, we are situated five miles away from M5 and M42 between Redditch, Bromsgrove and Droitwich. The accommodation comprises spacious double, two twin rooms with en suite or private bathroom, colour TV and tea/coffee making facilities. The comfortable lounge and separate dining room overlook the large garden. Young children are welcome. We are ideally situated for visits to Stratford-upon-Avon, Warwick, Worcester, Stourbridge, Birmingham, the Black Country, the NEC and International Convention Centre. Prices from £20 per person. *AA QQQ, RAC 3 SPARKLING DIAMONDS.* **ETC ◆◆◆.**

BROMSGROVE. Mrs J. Orford, Stoke Cross Farm, Dusthouse Lane, Finstall, Bromsgrove B60 3AE (01527 876676; Fax: 01527 874729). Modern, comfortable family farmhouse in rural location on quiet country lane yet Bromsgrove town centre is only two-and-a-half miles. Convenient for M5/M42 motorways. Stratford-upon-Avon, NEC and airport are all within easy reach. Large off road parking area. Tea/coffee making facilities and TV in all rooms. Dogs are welcome by arrangement. Bed and Breakfast from £20. **ETC ◆◆◆**

GREAT MALVERN. Mrs F. W. Coates, Mill House, 16 Clarence Road, Great Malvern WR14 3EH (01684

562345). Originally a 13th century Water Mill at the foot of the beautiful Malvern Hills. Situated in tranquil grounds with croquet lawns and hill views. A few minutes' walk from the town centre or Great Malvern Station. Malvern is ideal for touring the Cotswolds, Severn and Wye Valleys and Welsh Marches. Comfortable accommodation with full central heating, washbasin and tea/coffee making facilities in all bedrooms. One double en suite, one double with shower, one twin room. Shower room, two separate WCs. Parking within grounds. NO SMOKING! No children and no pets. Bed and English Breakfast from £22. Advance booking only.

MALVERN WELLS. Mrs J.L. Morris, Brickbarns Farm, Hanley Road, Malvern Wells WR14 4HY (016845

61775; Fax: 01886 830037). Working farm. Brickbarns, a 200-acre mixed farm, is situated two miles from Great Malvern at the foot of the Malvern Hills, 300 yards from the bus service and one-and-a half miles from the train. The house, which is 300 years old, commands excellent views of the Malvern Hills and guests are accommodated in one double, one single and one family bedrooms with washbasins; two bathrooms, shower room, two toilets; sittingroom and diningroom. Children welcome and cot and babysitting offered. Central heating. Car essential, parking. Open Easter to October for Bed and Breakfast from £16 nightly per person. Reductions for children and Senior Citizens. Birmingham 40 miles, Hereford 20, Gloucester 17, Stratford 35 and the Wye Valley is just 30 miles.

UPTON-ON-SEVERN. Mrs Sandy Barker, Tiltridge Farm & Vineyard, Upper Hook Road, Upton-on-

Severn WR8 0SA (01684 592906; Fax: 01684 594142). Come and stay with us in our comfortable, mellow farmhouse on the outskirts of the attractive riverside town of Upton-on-Severn. Set in the vineyards, the house looks towards the Malvern Hills in one direction and back over the river valley in the other. We have two doubles and one twin room, all en suite with the usual facilities, and we can offer you a bumper 'Tiltridge' breakfast with eggs from our own chickens and homemade jams and marmalades. There is plenty to do and see locally, and when you come home why not relax on the terrace with a glass of our own crisp and fruity English wine! Bed and Breakfast from £26. **ETC** ◆◆◆◆.
e-mail: elgarwine@aol.com

WORCESTER near. Sylvia and Brian Wynn, The Old Smithy, Pirton, Worcester WR8 9EJ (01905 820482). A 17th century half-timbered country house set in peaceful countryside with many interesting walks. Centrally situated, within easy reach of Stratford-upon-Avon, Cotswolds, Warwick Castle, Malvern Hills, Worcester Cathedral and Royal Worcester Porcelain. Four-and-a-half miles from junction 7 of the M5 Motorway. Private guest' facilities include lounge with inglenook log fireplace, colour TV and video, bathroom/dressing room and toilet, laundry, tea/coffee, central heating, gardens. One double bedroom and one twin bedroom. Ample parking. Bed and English Breakfast from £19.50; three-course Evening Meal optional extra £9.95. Fresh local produce and home cooking. Sorry, no pets or children under 12 years. Craft Workshop (Harris Tweed and knitwear). **ETC** ◆◆◆◆

WORCESTER near. Mrs J. Morris, Knowle Farm, Suckley, Near Worcester WR6 5DJ (01886 884347). Part timbered 17th century farmhouse with 25 acres grassland, used mainly for horses. Adjacent to a small, quiet country Inn, the house is in an elevated position with unrivalled views of the Malvern Hills and offers accommodation all year round. Large colourful garden. The quaint market towns of Bromyard, Ledbury and Hereford are nearby, and Knowle Farm is in the heart of a fruit-growing area where visitors enjoy the magnificent spring blossom. Superb walking country. One double and one single bedrooms (one with washbasin); bathroom, toilet. Sittingroom with woodburner fire, diningroom. Central heating keeps the house comfortable throughout the year. Car essential – parking. Traditional hearty English Breakfast. Fresh farm eggs. Bed and Breakfast £10 (bedtime drink). No single supplement. This is a non-smoking establishment.

YORKSHIRE

 FHG

PLEASE MENTION THIS GUIDE WHEN YOU WRITE

OR PHONE TO ENQUIRE ABOUT ACCOMMODATION

IF YOU ARE WRITING, A STAMPED, ADDRESSED

ENVELOPE IS ALWAYS APPRECIATED

EAST YORKSHIRE

GREAT DRIFFIELD. Mrs Tiffy Hopper, Kelleythorpe Farm, Great Driffield YO25 9DW (01377 252297).

Friendly atmosphere, antique furniture, pretty chintzes, new bathrooms, one en-suite. Children welcome. Large garden with swings and playcastle. Bed and Breakfast from £17; optional Evening Meal from £10 by prior arrangement. 10% discount for seven nights or more. Reductions for children under 12 years.

HORNSEA. Francis Davies, The Grainary, Skipsea Grange, Hornsea Road, Skipsea YO25 8SY (01262 468745; Fax: 01262 468840).

A converted granary and outbuildings, part of an arable farm that has been in the family for five generations. Situated on the east coast within walking distance of the sea and with views to Flamborough Head. Children very welcome. One single and three double/family bedrooms, all en suite. Special romantic breaks available with jacuzzi and sauna. Guests have membership of the local leisure complex and caravan site complete with swimming pool, bars and night club. Tearoom on site, all home cooking. Evening meals by arrangement. Prices from £15.

RUDSTON. Mrs Bowden, Eastgate Farm Cottage, Rudston YO25 4UX (Tel & Fax: 01262 420150).

Friendly 18th century cottage with superb views nestling on the edge of a medieval village with its own monolith. Ideally located for moor and coastal exploration. Freshwater and sea fishing nearby. RSPB and rural walks in beautiful countryside. Horse trekking available locally. En suite bedrooms with central heating and delightful brass and iron beds. Aga-cooked dinners available. Open all year. Bed and Breakfast from £18. **ETC** ♦♦♦

FHG

Visit the FHG website
www.holidayguides.com
for details of the wide choice of accommodation
featured in the full range of FHG titles

FREE or REDUCED RATE entry to
Holiday Visits and Attractions — see our
READERS' OFFER VOUCHERS on pages 43-60

NORTH YORKSHIRE

AMPLEFORTH. Annabel Lupton, Carr House Farm, Ampleforth, Near Helmsley YO6 4ED (01347 868526 or 07977 113197). Working farm. 'Which?' Guide;

Sunday Observer recommends "Fresh air fiends' dream – good food, good walking, warm welcome". In idyllic 16th century farmhouse, sheltered in Herriot/Heartbeat countryside, half an hour to York, ideal to enjoy Moors, Dales, National Parks, coasts, famous abbeys, castles and stately homes. Romantics will love four-poster bedrooms en suite and medieval-styled bedroom in comfortable relaxing home, with large garden. Enjoy full Yorkshire Breakfasts with homemade preserves, free-range eggs, hearty Evening Meals – own produce used whenever possible and served in oak-panelled, beamed diningroom with flagstoned floor, inglenook and original brick bread oven. No children under seven and no pets. Bed and Breakfast from £17.50. Evening meal from £10. Open all year. ETC ◆◆◆

ASKRIGG. Mrs B. Percival, Milton House, Askrigg, Leyburn DL8 3HJ (01969 650217). Askrigg is

situated in the heart of Wensleydale and is within easy reach of many interesting places – Aysgarth Falls, Hardraw Falls, Bolton Castle. Askrigg is one of the loveliest villages in the dale. This is an ideal area for touring or walking. Milton House is a lovely spacious house with all the comforts of home, beautifully furnished and decor to match. All bedrooms are en suite with colour TV and tea/coffee making facilities. Visitors lounge, diningroom. Central heating. Private parking. Milton House is open all year for Bed and Breakfast. Good pub food nearby. You are sure of a friendly welcome and a homely atmosphere. Please write or phone Mrs Beryl Percival for details and brochure. ETC ◆◆◆

BENTHAM. Mrs Shirley Metcalfe, Fowgill Park Farm, High Bentham, Near Lancaster LA2 7AH (015242 61630). Working farm. Fowgill is a 200 acre stock

rearing farm, situated in an elevated position and having magnificent views of the Dales and Fells. Only 20 minutes from M6 Junction 34. A good centre for touring the Dales, Lakes, coast, and Forest of Bowland. Visit Ingleton with its waterfalls and caves only three miles away. Golf, fishing, and horse riding nearby. Beamed bedrooms have washbasins, shaver points, and tea-making facilities, two bedrooms en-suite. Comfortable beamed visitors' lounge to relax in with colour TV. Separate diningroom. Bed and Breakfast from £20. Reductions for children. Bedtime drink included. Open Easter to October. Brochure available. ETC ◆◆◆◆

CARLTON-IN-COVERDALE. (Near Leyburn). Mrs P. Lashmar, Abbots Thorn, Carlton, Leyburn DL8 4AY (01969 640620). Relax and unwind at our non-smoking home.

Friendly faces, fabulous food, superb scenery, terrific touring, wonderful walking! Set in the Yorkshire Dales National Park, Carlton-in-Coverdale is a quiet, peaceful village - yet only a short distance from so many places of interest. To complete your day, why not sample our delicious evening meals served in the informal diningroom. The oak beamed guest lounge has an open fire for those chilly evenings. We have three attractive bedrooms, two with en suite facilities and one with private bathroom, and are open all year. Brochure available on request. ETC ◆◆◆◆
e-mail: abbots.thorn@virgin.net
website: www.abbotsthorn.co.uk

*When making enquiries or bookings,
a stamped addressed envelope is always appreciated*

DANBY. Mrs B. Tindall, Rowan Tree Farm, Danby, Whitby YO21 2LE (01287 660396).

Working farm, join in. Rowan Tree Farm is situated in the heart of the North Yorkshire Moors and has panoramic moorland views. Ideal walking area and quiet location just outside the village of Danby. Accommodation comprises one twin-bedded room and one family room all with washbasin and full oil-fired central heating. Residents' lounge with colour TV. Two residents' bathrooms. Children welcome – cot provided if required. Babysitting available. Pets accepted. Good home cooking. Bed and Breakfast from £17; Evening Meals provided on request £8 each. Ample car parking space. **ETC ◆◆◆**

HARROGATE. Mrs Judy Barker, Brimham Guest House, Silverdale Close, Darley, Harrogate HG3 2PQ (01423 780948). The family-run guest house is

situated in the centre of Darley, a quiet village in unspoilt Nidderdale. All rooms en suite and centrally heated with tea/coffee making facilities and views across the Dales. Full English breakfast served between 7am and 9am in the dining room; a TV lounge/conservatory is available for your relaxation. Off street parking. Central for visits to Harrogate, York, Skipton and Ripon, or just enjoying drives through the Dales and Moors where you will take in dramatic hillsides, green hills, picturesque villages, castles and abbeys. Children welcome. Bed and Breakfast from £17.50 per person per night (double room) to £25 (single room), reductions for three nights or more. Yorkshire in Bloom Winner 1999. **ETC ◆◆◆◆**

HARROGATE. Anne and Bob Joyner, Anro Guest House, 90 King's Road, Harrogate HG1 5JX (01423 503087; Fax: 01423 561719). "Comfortable and friendly!",

"Excellent!", "Enjoyed every visit!", "Great!", "Clean, friendly, great breakfast!"- just a few of the testimonials that visitors have written in our book on leaving. Situated in a tree lined avenue in a central position close to all amenities, Conference and Exhibition Centre two minutes' walk, Valley Gardens, town, bus and rail stations near by. Our house is fully centrally heated with thermostats on all radiators, all rooms recently refurbished. Tea/coffee making facilities, colour TV, hairdryers and complimentary items in all rooms. Some rooms en suite. Home cooking. Four-course dinner plus tea or coffee upon request. Ideal centre for touring Dales/Herriot country. Bed and Breakfast from £23, dinner £14. Well recommended. **AA/ETC ◆◆◆.**
e-mail: info@theanro.harrogate.net
website: www.theanro.harrogate.net

HARROGATE. Mrs A. Wood, Field House, Clint, Near Harrogate HG3 3DS (01423 770638). Field House with its beautiful large gardens is situated five miles from Harrogate commanding lovely views over the Nidd Valley. Ideal for exploring the Dales and Moors with ancient abbeys, castles and country houses. The market towns of Skipton, Ripon and Knaresborough and the historic city of York are all within easy reach. Accommodation is in one twin and one double room with private bathroom. Private sittingroom with TV, etc. Open all year. Car essential - private parking. Bed and Breakfast from £18; excellent food within one mile. A warm welcome guaranteed in a peaceful friendly atmosphere. Telephone or SAE, please, for further details.
e-mail: annwoodclint@lineone.net

HELMSLEY. Mrs J. Milburn, Barn Close Farm, Rievaulx, Helmsley YO6 5LN (01439 798321). Working

farm. Farm Holiday Bureau member. Farming family offer homely accommodation on mixed farm in beautiful surroundings near Rievaulx Abbey. Ideal for touring, pony trekking, walking. Home-made bread, own home-produced meat, poultry, free range eggs - in fact Mrs Milburn's excellent cooking was praised in the "Daily Telegraph". Modern home - two double bedrooms with washbasins, one family room (one room en suite); all with tea/coffee making facilities. TV lounge; diningroom. Children welcome, babysitting. Open all year round. Open log fires. Storage heaters in bedrooms. Car essential - parking. Bed and Breakfast from £20 to £25; Dinner £12. Reduced rates for children under 10 sharing parents' room.

HELMSLEY near. Brenda Johnson, Hill End Farm, Chop Gate, Bilsdale TS9 7JR (01439 798278).

Hill End Farm is recommended by "Which?" the Good Bed and Breakfast Guide. If you are looking for a comfortable peaceful break with beautiful views come and join us! Excellent walking country within the North York Moors National Park with way-marked paths from the farm. Near to Captain Cook, Herriot and Heartbeat country. Guests' lounge with TV and open fire: dining room; two pretty en suite bedrooms. Bed and Breakfast £20. Children under 14 years half price. ETC ◆◆◆.

HIGH BENTHAM. Mrs Betty Clapham, Lane House Farm, High Bentham, Lancaster LA2 7DJ (015242 61479). Enjoy a relaxing break at our 17th century

beamed farmhouse, within half a mile of the Forest of Bowland, with beautiful views of the Yorkshire Dales. One mile from the market town of High Bentham, half an hour from M6. Ideal for caves, waterfalls, touring the Lakes. Bedrooms have washbasins and tea making trays. En suite facilities. Guests' lounge with colour TV. Separate dining room. Non-smoking. Children welcome and pets by arrangement. Open March to November. Bed and Breakfast £18.50 to £20. ETC ◆◆◆◆

INGLETON. Mrs Nancy Lund, Gatehouse Farm, Far Westhouse, Ingleton LA6 3NR (015242 41458/41307). Bryan and Nancy invite you to their farm which

they run with their son who lives at Lund Holme (next door). You are welcome to wander round and look at the cows, calves and sheep or stroll in the quiet country lanes and enjoy the wild flowers. Gatehouse, situated in the Yorkshire Dales National Park, is in an elevated position with beautiful views over open countryside; it was built in 1740 and retains the original oak beams. Double or twin rooms (families welcome), all with private facilities and tea/coffee trays; guests' diningroom and lounge with colour TV. M6 turnoff 34, 15 miles, one-and-a-half miles west of Ingleton, just off A65. Bed and Breakfast from £20; Evening Meal available. ETC ◆◆◆ *FARM HOLIDAY BUREAU MEMBER.*

INGLETON. Carol Brennand, Nutstile Farm, Ingleton, Via Carnforth LA6 3DT (015242 41752).

Surrounded by the outstanding beauty of the Yorkshire Dales, Nutstile is a typical working farm providing first class accommodation. The mountains, caves and waterfalls of Ingleton are immediately accessible, the Lake District also close by. Try a leisurely ride on the scenic Settle-Carlisle railway. Three bedrooms (all with views) with washbasin and tea/coffee facilities and colour TV, en suite available. Guests' lounge with TV. Children welcome. Open all year. Bed and Breakfast from £18 to £20. website: www.nutstile.co.uk

NUTSTILE

See also Colour Display Advertisement | **INGLETON. Mrs Mollie Bell, "Langber Country Guest House", Ingleton, via Carnforth LA6 3DT (015242 41587)**. Ingleton,

"Beauty Spot of the North" in the Three Peaks/Dales National Park area. Renowned for waterfalls, glens, underground caves, magnificent scenery, and Ingleboro' Mountain (2,373 feet), an excellent centre for touring Lakes, Dales and coast. Golf, fishing, swimming, bowls, and tennis in vicinity; pony trekking a few miles away. Guests are warmly welcomed to "Langber", a detached country guest house with beautiful views and 82 acres of gardens, terrace and fields. Lambs and sheep kept. Ample parking space available. Three family, three double/twin and one single bedrooms, all with washbasin and razor points, some en-suite. Bathroom and two toilets. Sunny comfortable lounge and separate diningroom. Central heating; fire precautions. Babysitting offered. Open all year except Christmas and New Year. Fire Certificate granted. Highly recommended. Bed and Breakfast from £17.50; Bed, Breakfast and Evening Meal from £24.50. Reductions for children under 13 sharing with two parents. ETC ◆◆◆

KIRKBYMOORSIDE. Mrs M. P. Featherstone, Keysbeck Farm, Farndale, Kirkbymoorside YO6 6UZ (01751 433221).Working farm. Friendly accommodation on a 300 acre farm. There are two double, one single or twin bedrooms; diningroom with open log fire where good home cooking is served. Car essential, parking. Children and pets welcome; babysitting available. Open all year round. Bed and Breakfast £15. Reduced rates for children.

LEYBURN. Mrs H.M. Richardson, Sunnyridge, Argill Farm, Harmby, Leyburn DL8 5HQ (01969 622478).

Situated on a small sheep farm in Wensleydale, Sunnyridge is a spacious bungalow in an outstanding position. Magnificent views are enjoyed from every room. In the heart of the Yorkshire Dales and the midst of Herriot country, it is an ideal centre for exploring the wide variety of activities and attractions; or a restful stop-over for travellers to Scotland. Sample Yorkshire hospitality and relax in comfortable ground floor accommodation comprising one double or twin-bedded room, one family room with en suite shower room; both non-smoking, each with colour TV and tea/coffee facilities. Guest lounge. Children welcome. Pets by arrangement. Bed and Breakfast from £18. Optional Evening Meal.

MALHAM (Yorkshire Dales National Park). Mr C. Sharp, Miresfield Farm, Skipton BD23 4DA (01729 830414).

Miresfield is situated on the edge of the village of Malham in the Yorkshire Dales National Park. An ideal centre for exploring the Dales or for visiting the City of York, Settle and Skipton. Within walking distance is Malham Cove, Gordale Scar with its spectacular waterfalls, and Malham Moor with the famous Field Centre and home of Charles Kingsley's "Water Babies". Miresfield is set in a well-kept garden and offers accommodation in 11 bedrooms, all with private facilities. There are two well furnished lounges with TV, one has open fire; conservatory. Good, old-fashioned farmhouse cooking is served in the large, beamed diningroom. Bed and Breakfast from £24 per person per night. **ETC ◆◆◆**

MASHAM near. Peter and Irene Foster, Lime Tree Farm, Hutts Lane, Grewelthorpe, Near Ripon HG4 3DA (01765 658450). Working farm, join in.

Secluded old Dales farmhouse now a Nature Reserve. Rich in wildlife and with chickens and ducks wandering around the yard. The farmhouse has beams, oak panelling, exposed stonework and open fires. Furnished with antiques. All bedrooms have their own private facilities, colour TV, tea/coffee making facilities and central heating. Ideal location for walking and touring. Bed and Breakfast from £20 per person per night. Dinner, Bed and Breakfast from £32 per person per night. Please ring for brochure. **ETC ◆◆◆◆**

NORTHALLERTON. Mary and John Pearson, Lovesome Hill Farm, Lovesome Hill, Northallerton DL6 2PB (01609 772311).

Come and enjoy the experience of staying in our 19th century farmhouse amidst a friendly atmosphere. Tastefully converted granary adjoins house with spacious, well-furnished en suite rooms which include TV and beverage facilities. Beamed ceilings are still retained in the two upstairs bedrooms. Our newly converted downstairs accommodation includes a bedroom and dining room, both of which overlook the garden and patio. Locally produced food is used when available. Situated in open countryside overlooking Hambleton Hills, four miles north of Northallerton, this is a perfect base for exploring the Dales, Moors, York and Durham. You'll "love" It. Brochure available

OTLEY. Mrs C. Beaumont, Paddock Hill, Norwood, Otley LS21 2QU (01943 465977). Converted

farmhouse on B6451 south of Bland Hill. Open fires, lovely views, in the heart of the countryside. Within easy reach of Herriot, Bronte and Emmerdale country and with attractive market towns around – Skipton, Knaresborough, Otley and Ripon. Walking, bird- watching and fishing on the nearby reservoirs. Residents' lounge with TV. Comfortable bedrooms. Non-smoking accommodation available. Children welcome. Pets by arrangement. Bed and Breakfast £15, en suite £22. ETC ◆◆

PICKERING. Mrs Ella Bowes, Banavie, Roxby Road, Thornton-le-Dale, Pickering YO18 7SX (01751

474616). Banavie is a large stone-built semi-detached house set in Thornton-le-Dale, one of the prettiest villages in Yorkshire with the stream flowing through the centre. Situated in an attractive part of the village off the main road, it is ideal for touring coast, moors, Castle Howard, Flamingo Park, Eden Camp, North Yorkshire Moors Railways and "Heartbeat" country. A real Yorkshire Breakfast is served by Mrs Bowes herself which provides a good start to the day. One family en suite bedroom, two double en suite bedrooms, all with colour TV, shaver point and tea making facilities; diningroom, lounge with TV, central heating. Children and pets welcome, cot, high chair and babysitting available. Own door keys. Car park; cycle shed. Open all year. Bed and Breakfast including Tea and Biscuits at bedtime from £18. SAE please. Thornton-le-Dale has three pubs, two restaurants and fish and chip shop in the village for meals. Welcome Host, Hygiene Certificate held. **ETC** ◆◆◆◆
e-mail: ella@banavie.fsbusiness.co.uk
website: www.smoothHound.co.uk/hotels/banavie

REETH. Richard and Rebecca Keyse, Hackney House, Reeth, Richmond DL11 6TW (01748 884302).

Situated amid the beauty of Swaledale and conveniently astride the coast to coast route, Reeth is a haven for the weary walker, cyclist or motorist. Principal cities and cultural attractions are within easy reach, or simply enjoy the peace and quiet to be found in the Dales and villages, which offer a wealth of leisure facilities and good restaurants. Hackney House offers comfortable accommodation for both the overnight guest or those who wish to stay longer. Ideal touring base. Accommodation comprises double, twin and single rooms, all centrally heated and double glazed, with colour TV and beverage making facilities. Some rooms en suite, guests have own lounge and diningroom. Bed and Breakfast from £17. Packed Lunches available. Private off-street parking. **ETC** ◆◆◆

RICHMOND. Mrs Dorothy Wardle, Greenbank Farm, Ravensworth, Richmond DL11 7HB (01325

718334). This 170 acre farm, both arable and carrying livestock, is four miles west of Scotch Corner on the A66, midway between the historic towns of Richmond and Barnard Castle, and within easy reach of Teesdale, Swaledale and Wensleydale, only an hour from the Lake District. The farm is one mile outside the village of Ravensworth with plenty of good eating places within easy reach. Guests' own lounge; dining room; two double bedrooms, one en suite and one family room. All have washbasin, tea/coffee facilities, heating and electric blankets. Children welcome. Sorry, no pets. Car essential. Bed and Breakfast from £15.00. Reductions for children and Senior Citizens. Open all year except Christmas and New Year. Luxury mobile home also available.

Please mention ***The Farm Holiday Guide*** when making enquiries about accommodation featured in these pages.

Browson Bank Farmhouse Accommodation

A newly converted granary set in 300 acres of farmland. The accommodation consists of three very tastefully furnished double/twin rooms all en suite, tea and coffee making facilities, colour TV and central heating. A large, comfortable lounge is available to relax in. Full English breakfast served. Situated six miles West of Scotch Corner (A1). Ideal location to explore the scenic countryside of Teesdale and the Yorkshire Dales and close to the scenic towns of Barnard Castle and Richmond. Terms from £18.00 per night.

Browson Bank Farmhouse, Browson Bank, Dalton, Richmond DL11 7HE
Tel: (01325) 718504 or (01325) 718246

RIPON. Mrs Maggie Johnson, Mallard Grange, Aldfield, Near Fountains Abbey, Ripon HG4 3BE (01765 620242). Working farm. Historically linked with nearby Fountains Abbey, Mallard Grange is a rambling 16th century working farm oozing character and charm in a glorious rural setting. Offering a superb level of quality and comfort, spacious rooms furnished with care and some lovely antique pieces. Four en suite bedrooms with colour TV, hair dryers, beverages and homely extras. Delicious breakfasts complemented by home-made preserves. Yorkshire Dales, historic properties, gardens, York and Harrogate are all within easy reach, making this the perfect centre for a peaceful, relaxing stay in a designated Area of Outstanding Natural Beauty. Open most of the year. Bed and Breakfast from £25.00. Brochure available. **ETC ◆◆◆◆** *SILVER AWARD*
e-mail: mallardgrange@btinternet.com

RIPON. Mrs Dorothy Poulter, Avenue Farm, Bramley Grange, Ilton Road, Grewelthorpe, Ripon HG4 3DN (01765 658348). Small dairy farm offering quiet, homely farmhouse accommodation at the foot of the Yorkshire Dales set in lovely countryside with beautiful views. Near James Herriott country. Within easy reach of A1, Ripon, York, Fountains Abbey and just three miles from Masham with the taste of Black Sheep Ale, Golf, fishing and pony trekking nearby. Avenue Farm guarantees a warm welcome with a cup of tea on arrival and bedtime drink. TV lounge. Bed and Breakfast from £14 per night.

RIPON. Mrs Pauline Spensley, Moor End Farm, Knaresborough Road, Ripon HG4 3LU (01765 677419). Relax in a peaceful, welcoming, smoke-free farmhouse. All rooms tastefully decorated and furnished. All bedrooms with washbasin, tea/coffee making facilities, TV and hairdryer. Two rooms en suite. Lounge with TV and log fire. Set in countryside yet within easy reach of Ripon, two-and-a-half miles away. Ideal centre for the Yorkshire Dales, Harrogate and York. Good pubs nearby serving bar and restaurant meals. No children and No smoking. Bed and full English Breakfast £18.50 to £23.50 per person - double/twin room. Brochure available on request. **ETC ◆◆◆**

ROBIN HOOD'S BAY. Mrs B. Reynolds, 'South View', Sledgates, Fylingthorpe, Whitby YO22 4TZ (01947 880025). Pleasantly situated, comfortable accommodation in own garden with sea and country views. Ideal for walking and touring. Close to the moors, within easy reach of Whitby, Scarborough and many more places of interest. There are two double rooms, lounge and diningroom. Bed and Breakfast from £17, including bedtime drink. Parking Spaces. Phone for further details

---

ROSEDALE. Mrs B. Brayshaw, Low Bell End Farm, Rosedale, Pickering YO18 8RE (01751 417451). Working farm. The farm is situated in the North Yorkshire Moors National Park about 15 miles from the nearest seaside resort of Whitby. Scarborough and Bridlington are within easy reach, also York, Pickering and Helmsley, all places of historic interest. The farm, a 173-acre beef and sheep farm, is one mile from the village of Rosedale Abbey and there are many lovely walks to be taken in the area. A car is essential with ample parking space. Pets by arrangement. One double, one bunk-bedded, one family rooms; bathroom and toilet; combined sitting/diningroom with colour TV. Children welcome at reduced rates. Cot, high chair, babysitting available. Central heating and open fires. Open all year. Evening Dinner, Bed and Breakfast or Bed and Breakfast. Terms on request.

ROSEDALE EAST. Mr and Mrs Harrison, Moordale House, Dale Head, Rosedale East, Pickering YO18

8RH (01751 417219). Enjoy beautiful views across the historic valley of Rosedale in the heart of the North Yorkshire moors. We offer comfortable accommodation, en suite bedrooms - one family, two double and two twin-bedded. Tea and coffee making facilities, central heating. TV lounge with open fire. Diningroom with separate tables. Good home cooking, traditional English breakfast. Warm and friendly welcome, pets by arrangement. Licensed, good parking, evening meal by arrangement. Excellent area for walking, cycling or visiting the Yorkshire coast, York and the North East.

SCARBOROUGH. Mrs M. Edmondson, Plane Tree Cottage Farm, Staintondale, Scarborough YO13 0EY

(01723 870796). This small mixed farm is situated off the beaten track, with open views of beautiful countryside and the sea. We have sheep, hens, two ginger cats and special sheep dog "Bess". This very old beamed cottage, small but homely, has one twin with bathroom and two double en suite rooms with tea maker. Meals of very high standard served with own fresh eggs and garden produce as available. Staintondale is about half-way between Scarborough and Whitby and near the North York Moors. Pretty woodland walks nearby. Car essential. Bed and Breakfast from £20 per person per night. Also six-berth caravan available. SAE please for details, or telephone. **ETC ◆◆◆**

SCARBOROUGH. Sue and Tony Hewitt, Harmony Country Lodge, Limestone Road, Burniston,

Scarborough YO13 0DG (0800 2985840). DISTINCTIVELY DIFFERENT. Peaceful and relaxing retreat, octagonal in design and set in two acres of private grounds overlooking the National Park and sea. Two miles from Scarborough and within easy reach of Whitby, York and the beautiful North Yorkshire countryside. Comfortable en suite centrally heated rooms with colour TV and all with superb views. Attractive dining room, guest lounge and relaxing conservatory. Traditional English breakfast, optional evening meal, including vegetarian. Fragrant massage available. Bed and Breakfast from £20.50 to £30.00. Non-smoking, licensed, private parking facilities. Personal service and warm, friendly Yorkshire hospitality. Spacious eight berth caravan also available for self-catering holidays. Open all year.
Please telephone or write for brochure. Children over 7 years welcome. **ETC ◆◆◆◆**
website: www.spiderweb.co.uk/Harmony

Readers are requested to mention this guidebook
when seeking accommodation (and please enclose
a stamped addressed envelope).

𝕹𝖊𝖜 𝕴𝖓𝖓

YORKSHIRE DALES NATIONAL PARK

Tel: 015242 51203   Fax: 015242 51496

ETC ★★

Member of Inns of Tradition

Keith and Barbara Mannion invite you to their friendly 18th century residential coaching inn in the picturesque Dales village of Clapham. Ideal centre for walking the three peaks of Ingleborough, Pen-y-ghent and Whernside. Kendal and Skipton 21 miles. All 19 bedrooms have full en suite facilities, colour TV and tea/coffee making facilities. Enjoy good wholesome Yorkshire food in our restaurant, or bar meals in either of our two bars. Dogs welcome. Midweek Bed and Breakfast £25 Winter.

Ring Barbara for full details on 015242 51203

SCARBOROUGH. Simon and Val Green, Killerby Cottage Farm, Killerby Lane, Cayton, Scarborough

YO11 3TP (01723 581236; Fax: 01723 585465). Simon and Val extend a warm Yorkshire welcome and invite you to share their charming farmhouse in the pleasant countryside between Scarborough and Filey. All our bedrooms are tastefully decorated and have en suite facilities, colour TV, and well-stocked beverage trays. Hearty breakfasts that will keep you going all day are served in the conservatory overlooking the lovely garden. Our 350-acre farm has diversified and we now have the Stained Glass Centre and tearoom which are open to visitors. Cayton offers easy access to Scarborough, Filey, Whitby, the North York Moors, and York. **ETC ◆◆◆◆**
e-mail: val@green-glass.demon.co.uk

SKIPTON. Mrs Heather Simpson, Low Skibeden Farmhouse, Harrogate Road, Skipton BD23 6AB

(07050 207787 / 01756 793849; Fax: 01756 793804). Detached 16th century farmhouse in private grounds one mile east of Skipton off the A59/A65 gateway to the Dales, eg Bolton Abbey - Malham, Settle. Luxury bed and breakfast with fireside treats in the lounge. All rooms are quiet, spacious, have panoramic views, washbasins, tea facilities and electric overblankets. Central heating October to May. All guests are warmly welcomed and served tea/coffee and cakes on arrival, bedtime beverages are served from 9.30pm. Breakfast is served from 7am to 8.45am in the dining room. No smoking. No pets and no children under 12 years. Safe parking. New arrivals before 10pm. Quality and value guaranteed. Bed and Breakfast from £20 per person per night for standard room with shared hot and cold facilities, en suite from £24 per person per night; single occupancy from £25-£30, in en suite £30-£40. Two place toilet with hot and cold facilities £22 per person per night. Farm cottage sometimes available. A deposit secures a room. Open all year. Credit Cards accepted. Recommended. "Welcome Host", "Which?" **AA ◆◆◆◆ ETC ★★★**
e-mail: skibhols.yorksdales@talk21.com
website: www.yorkshirenetco.uk/accgde/lowskibeden

SUTTON-ON-THE-FOREST. Susan Rowson, Goose Farm, Eastmoor, Sutton-on-the-Forest, York YO61

1ET (Tel/Fax: 01347 810577). Sleeps six. 150 year old farmhouse situated five miles from York Minster in open countryside off the B1363 and within easy access of Herriot Country and the Yorkshire coast. Large rooms, all en suite with TV and tea/coffee making facilities. Central heating throughout and as warm as the welcome to yourselves. Open all year. Bed and Breakfast from £18 to £22. Children and Pets welcome. **ETC ◆◆◆**

THIRSK. Mrs M. Fountain, Town Pasture Farm, Boltby, Thirsk YO7 2DY (01845 537298).

COMMENDED. **Working farm, join in.** A warm welcome awaits on a 180 acre mixed farm in beautiful Boltby village, nestling in the valley below the Hambleton Hills, in the midst of Herriot country and on the edge of the North York Moors National Park. An 18th century stone-built farmhouse with full central heating, comfortable en suite bedrooms (one family, one twin) with original old oak beams, and tea/coffee facilities; spacious guests' lounge with colour TV. Children and pets welcome. Good home cooking, hearty English breakfast and evening meals by arrangement. Ideal walking country and central for touring the Dales, York and East Coast. Pony trekking in village. Bed and Breakfast from £18.50. ETC ◆◆◆

WHITBY near. Mrs Pat Beale, Ryedale House, Coach Road, Sleights, Near Whitby YO22 5EQ (Tel and

Fax: 01947 810534). Exclusive to non-smokers, welcoming Yorkshire house of character at the foot of the Moors, National Park "Heartbeat" country, three-and-a-half miles form Whitby. Magnificent scenery, moors, dales, picturesque harbours, cliffs, beaches, scenic railways, superb walking - its all here! Highly commended beautifully appointed rooms with private facilities, many extras. Guests lounge; breakfast room (separate tables) with views over Esk Valley. Enjoy the large south-facing terrace and landscaped gardens, relax and be waited on! Extensive traditional and vegetarian breakfast choice. In the evenings local inns and restaurants (two within short walk). Parking available, also public transport. Bed and Breakfast double £19 to £20, single £17 to £22. Minimum stay two nights. Regret no pets or children.

YORK. Mrs K.R. Daniel, Ivy House Farm, Kexby, York YO4 5LQ (01904 489368).Working farm. Bed

and Breakfast on a mixed dairy farm six miles from the ancient city of York on the A1079. Central for the east coast, Herriot country and dales. We offer a friendly service with comfortable accommodation consisting of double or family rooms, en suite available, all with colour TV and tea/coffee making facilities. We provide a full farmhouse English Breakfast served in separate diningroom; colour TV lounge. Ample car parking with play area for children, who are most welcome. Bed and Breakfast from £16 per person. We are within easy reach of local restaurants and public houses serving excellent evening meals. AA and RAC Listed.

YORK. Mrs Susan Viscovitch, The Manor Country House, Acaster Malbis, York YO23 2UL (Tel & Fax:

01904 706723). Atmospheric Manor in rural tranquillity with our own private lake set in five-and-a-half acres of beautiful mature grounds. Close to Racecourse and only 10 minutes' car journey from the city or take the leisurely river bus (Easter to October). Conveniently situated for trips to Dales, Moors, Wolds and splendid coastline. Find us via A64 exiting for Copmanthorpe-York, Thirsk, Harrogate or Bishopthorpe (Sim Balk Lane). Centrally heated. 10 en suite bedrooms with full facilities. Cosy lounge and lounge bar; licensed. Conservatory breakfast room. Four-poster. Bed and Breakfast from £25 to £34 per person per night inclusive of VAT. For details SAE or telephone. Also see our advertisement on the Outside Back Cover of this guide. ETC ◆◆◆◆
e-mail: manorhouse@selcom.co.uk
website: www.manorhse.co.uk

Readers are requested to mention this guidebook
when seeking accommodation (and please enclose
a stamped addressed envelope).

YORK. Mont-Clare Guest House, 32 Claremont Terrace, Gillygate, York YO31 7EJ (01904 627054; Fax: 01904 651011). Take advantage and enjoy the convenience of City Centre accommodation in a quiet location close to the magnificent York Minster. A warm and friendly welcome awaits you at the Mont-Clare. All rooms are en suite, tastefully decorated and have colour TV (Satellite), radio alarm, direct-dial telephone, hairdryer, tea/coffee tray, shoe cleaning, etc. Some four-poster rooms available. All of York's attractions are within walking distance and we are ideally situated for the Yorkshire Dales, Moors and numerous stately homes. Fire and Hygiene Certificates held. Cleanliness, good food, pleasant surroundings and friendliness are our priorities. Private car park with CCTV. Open all year. Reduced rates for weekly stays. Bed and Breakfast from £25 per person per night.
e-mail: montclareY@aol.com
website: www.mont-clare.co.uk/index.htm

YORK. Peggy Swann, South Newlands Farm, Selby Road, Riccall, York YO4 6QR (01757 248203). Friendliness, comfort and good traditional cooking are always on offer to our guests. The kettle's always on the boil in our kitchen, and the comfortable lounge is yours to relax in at any time. Easy access to York and the Dales and Moors. Our farm is a strawberry and plant nursery with a five-caravan site adjacent. No smoking please.

YORK. Mr Shipley, St Paul's Hotel, 120 Holgate Road, York YO2 4BB (01904 611514). St Paul's is situated a short walk from the centre of the historic city of York, which has something to offer everyone, with museums, shopping, tours, restaurants and nightlife ranging from olde worlde pubs to the very latest in bars. Deep in the heart of Yorkshire, it is only a short drive to breathtaking views of the Yorkshire Moors and Dales. Situated in a pleasant residential location, we have six stylish rooms with en suite facilities, colour television and tea/coffee making facilities. We can provide twin, double or family accommodation and even have a four-poster room. Our residents' lounge offers the opportunity to meet other guests, relax and unwind. We pride ourselves on friendly and reliable service to make sure your stay with us is an enjoyable one. Bed and full English Breakfast from £25. Reductions for longer stays.

YORK, near Castle Howard. Sandie and Peter Turner, High Gaterley Farm, Near Welburn, York YO60 7HT (Tel & Fax: 01653 694636). High Gaterley enjoys a unique position, located within the boundaries of Castle Howard's magnificent country estate. It is ideally situated for easy access to the City of York, East Coast and the North Yorkshire Moors renowned for ruined abbeys and castles. The tranquil ambience with panoramic views over the Howardian Hills make it a perfect location for a peaceful and relaxing stay in a comfortable well-appointed farmhouse with the option of fine cuisine. En suite facilities with tea and coffee in all rooms, log fire in the drawing room, TV, non-smoking, dogs by prior arrangement. Open all year. Bed and breakfast from £19.00. Optional evening meal and special diets by arrangement. **ETC** ◆◆◆◆
e-mail: relax@highgaterley.com
website: www.highgaterley.com

WEST YORKSHIRE

HALIFAX. Pauline Hitchen, Old Crib Farm, Luddendenfoot, Halifax HX2 6JJ (01422 883285)

Overlooking the beautiful Calder Valley in this unspoilt region of the West Yorkshire countryside, Old Crib Farm, a Grade 11 Listed building, is a working dairy farm offering a warm welcome for the holidaymaker and business person alike. En suite with TV, central heating. As featured on television and in "Staying Off the Beaten Track". Children welcome. Terms from £18 to £20.

KEIGHLEY. Mrs Sylvia Lee, Far Laithe Farm, Laycock, Keighley BD22 0PU (01535 661993)

Traditional 17th century Yorkshire farm close to Haworth, Skipton and the Dales, set in the heart of open countryside. Tea making facilities and colour TV in all bedrooms. Luxury en suite facilities. Enjoy dinner in our licensed oak-furnished dining room. We pride ourselves on the quality of our food and hospitality and look forward to welcoming you to our home. Open all year. Bed and Breakfast from £19.50, Evening Meal available from £12.50. **ETC ◆◆◆◆.**

KEIGHLEY (Bronte Country). Currer Laithe Farm, Moss Carr Road, Long Lee, Keighley BD21 4SL

(01535 604387). An extensive 180 acre Pennine hill farm rearing and pasturing 140 cattle, goats and donkeys. It and the 16th century farmhouse, beamed, mullioned and with inglenook fireplace, offer panoramic views of Airedale and are covenanted to The National Trust. Satisfied guests, still returning after 19 years, create a warm, friendly atmosphere. Food is traditional Yorkshire fare. Pets and children welcome. Ground floor accommodation is frequently used by guests in wheelchairs. Bed and Breakfast en suite from £15.50; Bed, Breakfast and Evening Meal from £19. We also have two self-catering cottage flats from £70 to £160 per week. Group accommodation can be arranged, serviced or self-catering.

Please mention The Farm Holiday Guide when writing to enquire about accommodation

ENGLAND

Country Inns

BERKSHIRE

THE DUNDAS ARMS

Station Road, Kintbury, Berkshire RG17 9UT Tel: 01488 658263/658559
• Fax: 01488 658263 • E-mail: info@dundasarms.co.uk
•Website: www.dundasarms.co.uk

The inn's lovely position between the River Kennet and the canal makes it a most pleasant spot to stop for refreshment, and indeed for an overnight stay or weekend break. The comfortably furnished bedrooms are fully equipped with private bathroom, television and tea-making facilities, and enjoy relaxing views over the river. If your visit here is purely for refreshment, you will be delighted by the excellent bar food menu, which features really interesting "specials" alongside traditional favourites such as ploughmans and steak and kidney pie, and by the range of well kept real ales. For more leisurely dining, menus in the restaurant make full use of fresh local produce, and there is also an excellent wine list.

Five bedrooms, all with private bathroom; Free House with real ale; Children welcome;
Bar meals, restaurant evenings only; Non-smoking areas; Hungerford 3 miles.

CORNWALL

CRUMPLEHORN MILL
Polperro, Cornwall PL13 2RJ

Tel: 01503 272348   Fax: 01503 272914
E-mail: AndrewCrumplehorn@msn.com
website: www.crumplehorn-inn.co.uk

A complex created out of old farm buildings in 1972, the hotel, bars, restaurant and self-catering facilities exhibit character and an enlightened appreciation of the worthwhile things of life. Crumplehorn Mill has, in part, been transformed into a most attractive free house with a notable à la carte restaurant and traditional bar snacks. Food is freshly prepared and represents excellent value for money. The hotel provides accommodation in suites and bedrooms, matched only, perhaps, by the splendid self-catering flats and penthouse apartment.

Bed & Breakfast or self-catering for 2-8 persons.

CTB Approved   *CAMRA*

CUMBRIA

THE BURNMOOR INN
Boot, Eskdale Valley, Cumbria CA19 1TG
Tel: 019467 23224 • Fax: 019467 23337
• e-mail: enquiries@burnmoor.co.uk

Those searching out the unspoiled charm of the Lakes will not be disappointed in this fine old inn in the ancient village of Boot, nestling amid the hills at the foot of Scafell. Lakeland hospitality is legendary, and the proprietors, Harry and Paddington Berger, are proud upholders of this tradition, offering excellent food (both in the restaurant and the bar), fine wines and a selection of good ales. Comfortable, cosy en suite single, twin and double bedrooms make this a perfect base for walkers, climbers and ramblers all year round. Very competitive room rates make an "Escape to Eskdale" a most appealing prospect. *ETC* ◆◆◆, *AA*.

ETC/AA ★★

Bower House Inn
Eskdale, Holmrook, Cumbria CA19 1TD
Tel: 019467 23244 • Fax: 019467 23308
Email: info@bowerhouseinn.freeserve.co.uk
Website: www.bowerhouseinn.co.uk

A 17th century inn of considerable character, the Bower House is as popular with the locals as it is with tourists, always a good recommendation for any establishment. 24 bedrooms, all with private bathroom. Decor and furnishings throughout are tasteful and designed with an eye to comfort as well as style, and all guest rooms have private facilities, colour television and telephone. Cuisine is of a consistently good standard, with fresh produce from nearby farms featuring extensively in skillfully prepared and well presented dishes, and the wine cellar should satisfy the most demanding palate. Historic interest, Children welcome, Bar meals, Restaurant eveings only, Car park (60); Gosforth 6 miles. Mature gardens make a fine setting for this gem of an inn. Free House with real ale.

See also colour advertisement

DORSET

◄ THE SCOTT ARMS ►

Kingston, Corfe Castle, Dorset BH20 5LW
Tel: 01929 480270 • Fax: 01929 481570

Situated on the Isle of Purbeck, close to the Dorset Coastal Path, the Scott Arms is a traditional 18th century inn with a character all of its own. With exposed oak beams, open fireplaces, friendly atmosphere and a truly breathtaking view of Corfe Castle from our beer garden, it is easy to see why this inn has been popular for many years. We offer a superb menu every lunchtime and evening featuring our extensive specials board. To complement the food we have a selection of well-kept traditional ales, lagers, fine wines and spirits.

Country inn accommodation is available at reasonable rates, with all the amenities you would expect, including en suite facilities, tea/coffee making, hairdryer, colour television, and, of course, our full English breakfast. For that added hint of luxury, our bedrooms have four-poster beds.

GLOUCESTERSHIRE

STROUD near. Mr D. Savage, Ragged Cot Inn, Cirencester Road, Hyde, Near Stroud GL6 8PE (01453 884643; Fax: 01453 731166). Beautiful 17th Century Cotswold Coaching Inn set in attractive gardens. The Historic Inn serves numerous real ales as well as the more well known brands and offers a choice of 75 malt whiskies from its traditional beamed bars. The ten superb double or twin en suite bedrooms make the Inn the perfect base to explore the Cotswolds and is a haven for lovers of country pursuits. Dogs and horses are welcome (but please advise beforehand). Located virtually central between Stratford and Bath with Cheltenham just 15 miles away and Cirencester ten miles, there are just too many places and things of interest to list here.
website: http://home.btclick.com/ragged.cot

LINCOLNSHIRE

CONINGSBY. Mr Dennison, Lea Gate Inn, Leas Gate Road, Coningsby LN4 4RS (01526 342370; Fax: 01526 345468).

Dating from 1542 and with its ancient timbers, open fireplaces and secret recesses exuding an atmosphere absorbed through centuries of care and comfort for the weary traveller of the fens, this fine old inn is traditionl personified. This historically fascinating hostelry extends the most cheerful of welcomes from hosts, Mark and Sharon Dennison, and the new extension is now completed. Comprising of eight luxury en suite rooms all individually designed including four poster rooms and disabled facilities. One may still enjoy honest ale from the cask and the most appetising fare, including imaginative vegetarian dishes, which are served in a comfortable restaurant transformed some time ago from an old barn. Meals are served all week at lunchtimes and in the evenings and families are catered for.
e-mail: theleagateinn@breathe.net
website: www.leagateinn.co.uk

SLEAFORD. Mr P Hodson, Finch Hatton Arms Hotel, 43 Main Street, Ewerby, Sleaford NG34 9PH (01529 460363; Fax: 01529 461703).

This is something of a surprise – a fully equipped small hotel of some distinction in a picturesque little village, if not in the middle of nowhere, then precious near to it! Its success is due, in no small part, to its attractive Tudor-style bar and restaurant where traditional ales and an imaginative menu draw custom from nearby Sleaford and even Newark, Grantham, Boston and Lincoln to prove the proposition that value for money is a sure winner. The hotel wing provides first-class overnight accommodation, each room having a bath/shower en suite, remote-control colour television, direct-dial telephone and tea and coffee-making facilities and there is the promise of a hearty English breakfast in the morning.

NORFOLK

EAST NORWICH INN

Conveniently placed for the Norfolk coast, countryside and Broads, this inn stands four-square just off the A47, midway between Great Yarmouth and Norwich. The bar, known locally as 'The Cabin', is a convivial meeting place where good ale and a large variety of reasonably-priced dishes is on offer with vegetarians and children specially catered for. The traditional Sunday roast is also a popular innovation. A welcoming and informal family venue, the inn has several guest rooms situated well away from the bar area and all are particularly well equipped with bathrooms en suite, colour television and tea/ coffee-making facilities. Prices include a self-service Continental-style breakfast.

Old Road, Acle, Norwich, Norfolk NR13 3QN
Tel: 01493 751112 • Fax: 01493 751109
e-mail: eni@acle.demon.co.uk • website: www.acle.demon.co.uk

SHROPSHIRE

LUDLOW. Mr G. W. Lloyd, The Church Inn, Buttercross, Ludlow, Shropshire SY8 1AW (01584 872174;

Fax: 01584 877146). This historic inn has undergone several changes of name over the centuries – it was originally called the "Cross Keys" – but retains the fine old-fashioned traditions of good ale and good food which have ensured its lasting popularity through the ages. Nine cosy en suite bedrooms provide first-rate overnight accommodation, and a full range of catering, from freshly cut sandwiches to succulent steaks, ensures that appetites large and small will be amply satisfied. Regularly changing guest beers supplement the already extensive range of wines, spirits and ales on offer. The ancient town of Ludlow is an ideal base for exploring the border counties and the Welsh Marches, and is conveniently located for road and rail links to the Midlands. ETC/AA/RAC ◆◆◆, CAMRA, Egon Ronay.

MUCH WENLOCK. Gaskell Arms Hotel, Much Wenlock TF13 6AQ (01952 727212; Fax: 01952

728505). A fascinating little town in the beautiful Shropshire countryside, Much Wenlock is steeped in history. The mellow Gaskell Arms did not take its place until the 17th century but it is now one of the features of the town. Warm, traditional hospitality is the order of the day at this typically English wayside inn. An interesting and varied selection of hot and cold food is always available in the cosy lounge with a full à la carte menu on offer in the oak-beamed restaurant. Overnight accommodation is provided in delightfully decorated guest rooms appointed with television, telephone and tea and coffee-making facilities. Additional superior Coach House Suite, sleeps four. **ETC/AA** ◆◆◆◆
e-mail: maxine@gaskellarms.co.uk
website: www.SmoothHound.co.uk/hotels/gaskell.html

SOMERSET

MINEHEAD. Mr Napper, The Dragon House Hotel and Restaurant, Bilbrook, Near Minehead, Somerset

TA24 6HQ (Tel: 01984 640215; Fax: 01984 641340). This charming, family-run 1700's country house is located in three acres of natural beauty between Exmoor and the Somerset coast, an ideal base to explore many renowned beauty spots. All bedrooms encompass the requirements of the modern traveller, with telephone, television and en suite facilities, each room retaining its individuality. The oak-panelled restaurant is the perfect setting to enjoy an evening of fine classical and West Country cuisine, accompanied by an impressive wine list. Simpler light meals, bar snacks, drinks and refreshments are available throughout the day In the comfortable bar, conservatory, colonnaded courtyard or underneath the largest Black Poplar in England. **ETC ★★.**
e-mail: info@dragonhouse.co.uk

SUFFOLK

PEACOCK INN

**37 The Street,
Chelsworth,
Near Lavenham,
Suffolk IP7 7HU**

Tel: 01449 740758

Amidst the colour-washed cottages of the idyllic village of Chelsworth, the welcoming 'Peacock' dates from 1870 and is full of character. Only a few miles from the picturesque wool town of Lavenham with its Tudor and timber and plaster houses, this is a recommended port of call with genuine oak beams, an impressive inglenook fireplace and a beer garden for warmer weather. Cask-conditioned ales and excellent wines make the perfect complement for the fine food served every lunchtime and evening. A most rewarding place in which to stay, the inn has three comfortable bedrooms full of beams, nooks and crannies. In fact, there is not a level floor or straight wall in the pub!

WENHASTON.The Compasses Inn, The Street, Wenhaston, Near Southwold IP19 9EF (01502 478319).

De-stress and relax in a cosy little inn near Southwold and Dunwich. No early breakfasts here – start late, eat well and linger over coffee before a leisurely stroll along the lovely footpaths and commons of the village. Explore the old resorts of Southwold and Aldeburgh, the pretty villages and the magnificent unspoilt Suffolk Heritage Coast. At night try our little bar (with real fires in winter) and bistro for generous portions of home-cooked local fare, lovingly prepared – fish is bought daily (by prior order only) fresh from the coast. En suite rooms with TV, unlimited tea and coffee, fridge with real milk! No children, but dogs most welcome – free! Bed and Breakfast from £18, £22 per person en suite, £25 single. 5 nights for 4 (October/March); 4 nights for 3 (December/February). Tinsel Breaks in November.

NORTH YORKSHIRE

ROSE & CROWN HOTEL

Bainbridge, Wensleydale, North Yorkshire DL8 3EE

One of the most attractive of the Wensleydale villages with its classic green and beautiful old stone houses, Bainbridge is a delightful setting for this most picturesque hotel, which was dispensing hospitality and cheer long before Henry VIII came to the throne. Today all of the 12 guest bedrooms have the luxury of private facilities, colour television, tea and coffee makers and hairdryers. Good local produce is used extensively in the spotless kitchens, and tempting, skilfully prepared dishes are served in the large, pleasant Dales Room Restaurant overlooking the village green, as well as less formally in the snug bars.

AA
★★

Tel: 01969 650225 • Fax: 01969 650735

e-mail: stay@roseandcrownfreeserve.co.uk   website: www.yorkshire.net/stayat/roseandcrown

Self-Catering Accommodation ENGLAND

THE FHG DIPLOMA

HELP IMPROVE BRITISH TOURIST STANDARDS

You are choosing holiday accommodation from our very popular FHG Publications.
Whether it be a hotel, guest house, farmhouse or self-catering accommodation, we think you will find it hospitable, comfortable and clean, and your host and hostess friendly and helpful.

Why not write and tell us about it?

As a recognition of the generally well-run and excellent holiday accommodation reviewed in our publications, we at FHG Publications Ltd. present a diploma to proprietors who receive the highest recommendation from their guests who are also readers of our Guides. If you care to write to us praising the holiday you have booked through FHG Publications Ltd. – whether this be board, self-catering accommodation, a sporting or a caravan holiday, what you say will be evaluated and the proprietors who reach our final list will be contacted.

The winning proprietor will receive an attractive framed diploma to display on his premises as recognition of a high standard of comfort, amenity and hospitality. FHG Publications Ltd. offer this diploma as a contribution towards the improvement of standards in tourist accommodation in Britain. Help your excellent host or hostess to win it!

FHG DIPLOMA

We nominate ....

....

Because

Name ....

Address..

....

Telephone No..

ENGLAND
Self-Catering
Accommodation

LAKE DISTRICT, EDEN VALLEY, NORTH CUMBRIA/SCOTTISH BORDERS AND NORTHUMBERLAND.

We offer a wide and varied range of self-catering accommodation from large houses to small cottages in a variety of locations. Competitive rates. Free brochure. **Clark Scott-Harden, 1 Little Dockray, Penrith, Cumbria CA11 7HL (01768 868989 24hrs; Fax: 01768 865578)**
e-mail: Shirley.Thompson@csh.co.uk
website: www.csh.co.uk

CAMBRIDGESHIRE

ELY. HIll House Farm Cottage, Coveney. Sleeps 6.

Tasteful barn conversion in farm yard. Furnished to a high quality, consisting of double bedded room, twin bedded room, and a single room with full sized bunk beds. Bathroom with shower, bath and toilet, also a separate toilet and wash basin. A comfortable lounge/dining room with colour TV and video, kitchen with full sized cooker and microwave etc. Also garden, all set In qulet vIllage location with open views of Ely Cathedral and the surrounding countryslde three miles west of Ely. Easy access to Cambridge, Huntingdon and Newmarket. You are assured a warm welcome and a friendly atmosphere, in peace and tranquillity. Non-smoking, no pets; children eight years and over. £250-£350 per week. **ETC ★★★★. Mrs Hilary Nix, Hill House Farm, Main Street, Coveney CB6 2DJ (01353 778369)**

PETERBOROUGH. Mrs J. Singlehurst, Brook Farm, Lower Benefield, Peterborough PE8 5AE (01832 205215). Sleeps two adults and two children in family room.

At the beginning of a gated road we offer peace and tranquillity with picturesque walks. Granary Cottage is warm, cosy and well equipped with linen provided. Close by are the historic market towns of Oundle and Stamford and the pretty village of Rockingham. Children welcome. Open all year. Weekly terms from £150 to £250. **ETC ♥♥♥** *COMMENDED*.

CORNWALL

©MAPS IN MINUTES™ (1999)

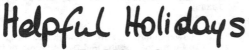

BOSCASTLE. Mrs Ann Harding, Ringford Farm, St. Juliot, Boscastle PL35 0BX (01840 250306). Working farm, join in. A two bedroomed centrally heated converted barn sleeping up to six persons comfortably. Fully equipped and has magnificent sea views. Pure spring water. Set on a 25 acre stock farm with cows, sheep, goats, pigs, ducks and chickens – you are welcome to look around and help with feeding if you so wish. Ideally situated for touring Devon and Cornwall, many footpaths to explore. Children and pets welcome. Weekly terms from £110 to £400.

BOSCASTLE. Mrs V.M. Seldon, Tregatherall Farm, Boscastle PL35 OEQ (01840 250277). Two new self-catering cottages on a warm, friendly Cornish farm, midway between Boscastle and Tintagel. Fully equipped en suite bedrooms, luxuriously furnished, sleeping four and six respectively. Oil-fired central heating and own parking. We offer out-of-season, spring and autumn short breaks. Please contact us for special offers and availablility. Brochure on request.

See also Colour Display Advertisement

BOSCASTLE (Near). Mr & Mrs J. Compton, Courtyard Farm, Lesnewth, Near Boscastle PL35 0HR (01840 261256; Fax: 01840 261794). Picturesque group of seven 17th century cottages overlooking Valency valley - area of outstanding natural beauty close to the dramatic coastline of Boscastle and Tintagel. Sleeping 2 to 8, all have individual character and are well equipped with TV/video; some with open fires and sea views. Very peaceful location, ideal for walking, beaches, Eden Project. Snooker, table tennis, swings and large playing field. Linen and towels provided. Managed by new owners Jan & Jennifer. Open year round, short breaks available, brochure on request. e-mail: courtyard.farm@virgin.net

See also Colour Display Advertisement

BUDE. Houndapitt Farm Cottages, Houndapitt Farm, Sandymouth, Bude EX23 9HW (01288 355455). Set in 100 arce estate overlooking Sandymouth Bay. We provide quality accommodation at very competitive prices. These self-catering cottages sleep from two to 9 people. They are set in the countryside surrounded by spectacular views with a choice of coastal and country walks, only one mile from the beach and ten minutes from the main town. Coarse fishing lake, large games room and adventure playground available. Terms include electricity and heating. Sorry, we do not allow pets. ETC ★★★ e-mail: info@houndapitt.co.uk website: www.houndapitt.co.uk

BUDE. Coach House and Little Coach House. Two charming cottages offering comfortable, spacious accommodation, nestled in 10 acres of ancient orchards, paddocks and ponds, yet minutes from stunning beaches and coastline of Bude and North Cornwall. 'Little Coach House' sleeps up to four people/two bedrooms and has the best views of the beautiful gardens. 'Coach House' sleeps up to eight people/four bedrooms, and has a wonderful private decking area and summerhouse, with amazing views of the ponds below. Both cottages have oak-beamed ceilings and woodburing stoves. Bed linen, electricity and logs included in the price. Ample parking. Please telephone for brochure and prices. **Mr J. M. Crocker, Cann Orchard, Howard Lane, Stratton EX23 9TD. (01288 352098).**

CAMELFORD. Ann Evelyn Ahrens, Mayrose Farm, Helstone, Camelford PL32 9RN (Tel & Fax: 01840

213509). 17th century idyllic cottages set in 20 acres in designated Area of Outstanding Natural Beauty. Spring fed lake and ponds, private gardens, exotic plants, heated swimming pool, friendly farm animals. Over 50 of our visitors are returns and recommendations from last year. Terms from £120 to £520 per week. Special breaks available. **ETC ↑↑↑↑** *COMMENDED*.

COVERACK. Polcoverack Farm Cottages, Coverack, Helston TR12 6SP (01326 281021; Fax: 01326

280683). A cluster of delightful stone built cottages approached via a private lane and set within a coastal farm providing a glorious rural setting. Coverack, one of Cornwall's most picturesque fishing villages, is within a ten minute walk. Here you will fine a sandy beach, inn, general stores and restaurants. Each cottage offers comfortable, well-equipped accommodation sleeping two to seven. They include colour television, video recorder, microwave oven, full-sized cooker, refrigerator, cafetiere, hairdryer and all bed linen. Cot and high chair if required. We also provide a laundry room, plus large games room, and ample parking. Phone for a free colour brochure. website: www.polcoverack.co.uk

CUSGARNE (near Truro). Joyce and George Clench, Saffron Meadow, Cusgarne, Truro TR4 8RW

(01872 863171). Sleeps 2. A cosy single-storey clean, detached dwelling with own enclosed garden within the grounds of Saffron Meadow, situated in a quiet hamlet. Secluded and surrounded by wooded pastureland. Bedroom with double bed and twin vanity unit. Fully tiled shower, W.C. and L.B. Comprehensively equipped kitchen/diner. Compact TV room, storage room. Hot water galore and gas included. Metered electricity. Automatic external safety lighting. Ample parking space in drive. Shop, Post Office and Inn only a short walk. Central to Truro, Falmouth and North Coast. Terms from £110 to £200 per week. Dogs welcome; £5 per week.

FALMOUTH (Near Helford River). Mrs Anne Matthews, Boskensoe Farm, Mawnan Smith,

Falmouth TR11 5JP (Tel & Fax: 01326 250257). Sleeps 6/8. BOSKENSOE FARM HOLIDAY BUNGALOW. Situated in picturesque village of Mawnan Smith, Falmouth five miles, one-and-a-half miles from lovely Helford River famous for beautiful coastal walks, gardens and scenery. Several quiet, safe beaches for bathing, also excellent sailing and fishing facilities. Bungalow has three bedrooms, colour TV, electric cooker, fridge/freezer, washing machine and microwave. Fitted with storage heaters and electric fires. Spacious garden and ample parking for cars and boats. Terms from £140 to £400. Brochure on request.

NOTE

All the information in this book is given in good faith in the belief that it is correct. However, the publishers cannot guarantee the facts given in these pages, neither are they responsible for changes in policy, ownership or terms that may take place after the date of going to press. Readers should always satisfy themselves that the facilities they require are available and that the terms, if quoted, still apply.

HELFORD RIVER. Mrs J. Jenkin, Mudgeon Farm, St Martin, Helston TR12 6BZ (01326 231202).

Mudgeon Farm runs down to the picturesque Helford River, on the Lizard Peninsula, an Area of Outstanding Natural Beauty. The cottage sleeps eight and is a tastefully restored 17th century wing of the ancient manor house, mentioned in the Domesday Book. It is equipped to a high standard with antique furniture, dishwasher and microwave. One double bedroom is en suite, the other has a four-poster. The spacious lounge has an inglenook fireplace with woodburner, and guests have their own private garden and walled patio. There are numerous safe beaches nearby. Interested visitors can watch the cows being milked, see farmyard animals and visit the ponies. Terms from £100 to £550

HELSTON. Delightful Cornish Cottage, Helston. Set in the heart of the Cornish countryside this secluded,

pretty, stone-built, beamed cottage is roughly 200 years old. Having one double and one twin bedroom, and folding bed with cot available - sleeps four to five. There is a dining area and a charming sitting room with a huge open log fire. The well-equipped kitchen has room to dine with an Aga and electric cooker. Outside are well-maintained private gardens and parking space for three or four cars. Accessing all coasts is easy from the cottage's ideal situation about two miles from Helston. For competitive prices contact: **Sue Cox, The Old Dairy, Hollington Lane, Ednaston, Ashbourne DE6 3AE (01335 361325).**
website: www.zyworld.com/suecox/information.htm

HELSTON. Mrs Julie Bray, Tregevis Farm, St. Martin, Helston TR12 6DN (01326 231265).

Sleeps 6 + cot. Come and relax at Tregevis, a working dairy farm in the picturesque Helford River area, just half a mile from the little village of St. Martin and five miles from sandy beaches. The accommodation is a self contained, spacious part of the farmhouse, very comfortable, well equipped and with a games room. The large lawn area with swings will prove popular with children, as will our farm animals. Open Easter to October. Terms from £220 to £490 per week. **ETC ★★★★.**

HELSTON. Jan Oates, Rosuick Farm, St. Martin, Helston, Cornwall TR12 6D2 (01326 231302).

Tucked away in our picturesque valley, in an area of outstanding natural beauty, Rosuick Farm offers a special holiday. Steeped in history. and each with its individual charm and character, the cottages offer quality and comfort. Four-poster beds, log fires, snooker table, private gardens, tennis court. Meet the animals on our fully organic farm, registered with the Soil Association. Produce is available from the farm shop. Discover the Helford River with its sailing and wonderful walks, and the many coves and beaches on The Lizard. Elmtree and Rosuick Cottage each sleep six and Rosuick Farmhouse sleeps ten. Open all year. £90-£700 per week.

LAUNCESTON. Mrs Kathyn Broad, Lower Dutson Farm, Launceston PL15 9SP (Tel & Fax: 01566

776456). Working farm. Sleeps 2/6. Enjoy a holiday on our traditional working farm. A warm welcome awaits you at our 17th century farmhouse. Historic Launceston with its Norman Castle (even Tescos!) is two miles away. Centrally situated for visiting National Trust houses and gardens, Dartmoor, Bodmin Moor and the beaches and harbours of Devon and Cornwall. Walk or fish along our stretch of the River Tamar for salmon and trout or try your skills at our coarse fishing lake. Well equipped cottage with three bedrooms (plus cot), two bathrooms. Enjoy the 'suntrap' just outside the front door. Children are welcome. Pet by arrangement. Terms £120 - £400. **ETC ★★★.**
e-mail: francis.broad@btclick.com

LAUNCESTON. Luxury two-bedroomed mobile home set in private site with views of a beautiful valley, with woods, three ponds with wildlife, domestic ducks and geese and sheep grazing in the fields. Fully equipped, colour TV, washing machine and all electrical appliances. Large fenced garden, safe for children, with patio and barbecue. Parking space. Central heating, gas cooker and lounge heater (gas supplied). Electricity by £1 meter. Linen supplied. Cot available. Prices from £160 per week. Apply: **Mrs A. E. Moore, Hollyvag, Lewannick, Launceston PL15 7QH (01566 782309).**

LAUNCESTON. Mrs Heather French, Higher Scarsick, Treneglos, Launceston PL15 8UH (01566 781372) Working farm. Nestled amongst the peace and tranquillity of unspoilt Cornish countryside, this well furnished and comfortable cottage is the ideal retreat for both couples and families. Very convenient for exploring the many beaches and coves on the North Cornwall Coast yet within easy driving distance of Bodmin Moor, Dartmoor and all leisure pursuits. The accommodation has three bedrooms, two double and one twin bedded, bathroom with separate shower cubicle, a fully equipped large farmhouse kitchen, lounge with open fireplace. Tariff: £120–£350 includes bed linen, night storage heaters, electricity and a very warm welcome. Short breaks from £50. No Pets.

LAUNCESTON near. Mrs A.E. Moore, Hollyvag, Lewannick, Near Launceston PL15 7QH (01566 782309). Working farm, join in. Sleeps 5. Part of 17th century farmhouse, self-contained and full of old world charm with own lawns, front and back. Set in secluded position in wooded countryside with views of the moors. Central for North and South coasts. Family farm with ducks on the pond, horses, sheep and poultry. Sleeps up to five, fully furnished with all modern conveniences, folding bed and cot available. Colour TV, fridge, electric cooker, solid fuel heater if needed. Babysitting available free. Linen not provided. Within five miles of market town; golf, fishing and riding nearby. Terms from £160 to £200. Brochure on request.

LISKEARD. Mrs Cotter, Trewalla Farm Cottages, Trewalla Farm, Minions, Liskeard PL14 6ED (Tel & Fax: 01579 342385). Sleeps 3/4 plus cot. Our small, traditionally-run farm on Bodmin Moor has rare breed pigs, sheep, hens and geese, all free-range and very friendly. The three cottages are beautifully furnished and very well equipped. Their moorland setting offers perfect peace, wonderful views, ideal walking country and a good base for exploring both coastlines – if you can tear yourself away! Linen and electricity included. Open March to December and New Year. **ETC ★★★★.**
email: cotter.trewalla@virgin.net

LISKEARD. Mrs C.Copplestone, Trethevy Farm, Darite, Liskeard PL14 5JX (01579 343186). Working farm. Sleeps eight plus cot. Relax in beautiful and peaceful surroundings in a delightful spacious 16th century Listed cottage on the edge of Bodmin Moor. An ideal location for walking, touring, visiting places of local historic interest, and the quaint fishing villages of Looe and Polperro. Within walking distance of local 17th century pub. With a Cornish cream tea to greet you, the cottage has four bedrooms (bedding provided), kitchen with cooker, fridge/freezer, washing machine and microwave. The lounge has colour TV, large granite fireplace, beamed ceilings. Private garden, ample parking. Farmhouse Bed and Breakfast also available. Details on request.

THE COTTAGES AT *Trefanny Hill*

Nr. LOOE

GORGEOUS OLD WORLD COUNTRY COTTAGES

Cornish Charm: Enchanting medieval hamlet with cottages dating back to the 15th century. Log fires, antiques and lovely country furnishings, fresh white linen, flowers and the comforts of home – for children, family, friends, or a cosy cottage for two. Nestling on a south facing hillside, with your own private garden, fabulous views, friendly farm animals including shires, fishing, lakeside and woodland walks, beautiful heated pool, tennis court and play area. Delicious home cooked cuisine in our own tiny inn (inc. fresh fish), and meals service. Open all year

O. Slaughter, Trefanny Hill, Duloe, Liskeard, Cornwall PL14 4QF
Tel: 01503 220622 • website: www.trefanny.co.uk

A COUNTRY LOVERS PARADISE – WITH AN ABUNDANCE OF COUNTRY WALKS FROM YOUR GARDEN GATE AND COASTAL WALKS ONLY FOUR MILES AWAY.

LOOE. Mrs Alison Maiklem, Katie's Cottage, Bocadden Farm, Lanreath, Looe PL13 2PG (Tel & Fax: 01503 220245). The warmest of welcomes awaits you at Katie's Cottage, a tastefully converted barn nestling peacefully in beautiful countryside. Bocadden is a 350 acre working dairy farm, six miles inland from the historic fishing villages of Looe, Polperro and Fowey. Visit the famous gardens and houses of the West Country. Very wheelchair friendly. **ETC** ○○○○ *HIGHLY COMMENDED.*

See also Colour Display Advertisement

LOOE. Tremaine Green Country Cottages, Pelynt, Near Looe PL13 2LS. Visit Tremaine Green, between Polperro and Looe, for memorable holidays. A beautiful hamlet of 11 traditional Cornish craftsmen's cottages. Clean, comfortable and well-equipped, accommodating from two to eight. Set in lovely grounds with a warm friendly atmosphere and only 12 miles from the Eden Project. Towels and linen provided. Dishwashers for four plus. Cot, highchair and occasional beds available. Putting, tennis court and games room. Pets welcome. Launderette. Pubs and restaurants within easy walking distance. Contact: **Justin and Penny Spreckley (01503 220333; Fax: 01503 220633).** e-mail: j7p@tremaine.sagehost.co.uk

---

Readers are requested to mention this guidebook when seeking accommodation (and please enclose a stamped addressed envelope).

LOOE. Mrs Angela Barrett, Tredinnick Farm, Duloe, Liskeard PL14 4PJ (01503 262997; Fax: 01503 265554). Enjoy a relaxing and tranquil holiday on our family-run farm situated in rolling countryside only three miles from Looe. The farmhouse is very comfortable and homely including en suite bedrooms. The local pub is renowned for its excellent food, only a short distance away. An ideal base for local and coastal walking. National Trust properties, golf and beaches nearby. Two units sleeping from two to ten people. Prices from £125 to £735. **ETC ★★★★.**

LOOE VALLEY. Mr & Mrs R. A. Brown, Badham Farm, St. Keyne, Liskeard PL14 4RW (Tel & Fax: 01579 343572). Once part of a Duchy of Cornwall working farm, now farmhouse and farm buildings converted to a high standard to form a six cottage complex around former farmyard. Sleeping from two to ten. All cottages are well furnished and equipped and prices include electricity, bed linen and towels. Most cottages have a garden. Five acre grounds, set in delightful wooded valley, with tennis, putting, children's play area, fishing lake, animal paddock, games room with pool and table tennis. Seperate bar. Laundry. Barbecue. Railcar from Liskeard to Looe stops at end of picnic area. Have a 'car free' day out. Children and well behaved dogs welcome. Prices from £105 per week. **ETC ♉♉♉♉ COMMENDED. GREEN TOURISM AWARD**

PADSTOW. The Brewer Family, Carnevas Farm Holiday Park, Carnevas Farm, St. Merryn, Padstow PL28 8PN (01841 520230). Bungalow/Chalets sleep 4/6. Rose Award Park 2000. Situated only half-a-mile from golden sandy beach, fishing, golf, sailing etc. Quaint harbour village of Padstow only four miles. Bungalows/chalets sleep four/six, have two bedrooms, bathroom, kitchen/diner, airing cupboard, colour TV. Caravans six-berth or eight berth, all have showers, toilets, fridge, colour TV (also separate camping and caravan facilities). Newly converted barns now available, sleep four/six persons, furnished to a high standard. AA Three Pennant site. Brochure on request. **ETC ★★★★**

PENZANCE. Mrs James Curnow, Barlowenath, St. Hilary, Penzance TR20 9DQ (01736 710409). Working farm. Cottages sleep 4/5. These two cottages are on a dairy farm, in a little hamlet right beside St. Hilary Church, with quiet surroundings and a good road approach. A good position for touring Cornish coast and most well-known places. Beaches are two miles away; Marazion two-and-a-half miles; Penzance six miles; St. Ives eight; Land's End 16. Both cottages have fitted carpets, lounge/diner with TV; modern kitchen (fridge, electric cooker, toaster, iron); bathroom with shaver point. Electricity by £1 meter, night storage heaters extra. One cottage sleeps five in three bedrooms (one double, twin divans and one single). The second cottage sleeps four in two bedrooms (twin divans in both). Linen not supplied. Cot by arrangement. Available all year. £95 to £320 weekly, VAT exempt.

PENZANCE. Mrs Catherine Wall, Trenow, Relubbus Lane, St. Hilary, Penzance TR20 9EA (01736

762308). Mini bungalow sleeps two within the grounds of an old country house. Lovely garden, surrounding rural area. Lounge/diner with cooking area, fridge, cooker, colour TV etc; shower room. Linen not provided. Beaches within easy reach, sporting activities, bird watching. No pets. Off-road Parking. Terms from £100 per week. Available all year. Please write or phone for further details.

PORT ISAAC. The Lodge, Treharrock, Port Isaac. Sleeps 6. Pleasant, south facing and convenient

bungalow, set in its own small, natural garden and surrounded by fields and woodland with streams. About two miles inland from Port Isaac, a sheltered, secluded spot at the end of driveway to Treharrock Manor. Rugged North Cornish cliffs with National Trust footpaths and lovely sandy coves in the vicinity. Excellent sandy beach at Polzeath (five miles), also pony trekking, golf etc. in the area. South-facing sun room leads on to terrace; TV. Accommodation for six plus baby. Bathroom, toilet; sittingroom; kitchen/diner. Open all year. Linen extra. Sorry, no pets. Car essential – parking. Terms from £150 to £400 per week (heating included). SAE to **Mrs E. A. Hambly, Willow Mill, St. Kew, Bodmin, Cornwall PL30 3EP (01208 841806).**

PORT ISAAC. The Dolphin, Port Isaac. Sleeps 10. This delightful house, originally an inn, is one of the most attractive in Port Isaac. Fifty yards from the sea, shops and pub. Five bedrooms, three with washbasin. Two bathrooms and WCs. Large diningroom. Cosy sittingroom. Spacious and well-equipped kitchen with electric cooker, gas-fired Aga, dishwasher, washing machine. Sun terrace. Port Isaac is a picturesque fishing village with magnificent coastal scenery all round. Nearby attractions include surfing, sailing, fishing, golf, tennis, pony trekking. Reduced rates offered for smaller families and off-peak season. Weekly terms: £360 to £650 inclusive. SAE for details to **Emily Glentworth, 30 Victoria Road, London W8 5RG (020 7937 1954)**

PORT ISAAC. Open all year. Come and enjoy being a part of a working family farm. Stay in one of our beautiful

cottages with lovely countryside views, own garden and parking. Tastefully furnished, catering for your every need, each having double glazing, microwave, fridge freezer, washer-dryer, food processor, coffee maker, colour TV and video, etc. All our animals are very friendly; meet "Barney" our Vietnamese Pot-Bellied Pig and our dogs who think visitors come to entertain them! We lamb from Christmas until March and everyone enjoys feeding the lambs. We have tennis and volleyball courts, games room and fitness room on the farm and acres of wildlife habitat to wander through. Sandy beaches, surfing, sailing, golf, riding, fishing, country pubs all within a three mile radius. We also have a large period house overlooking a wooded valley near Camelford, sleeping 12 plus cots. Moors and golf two miles, sea six miles.

Out of season Short Breaks available. **ETC ★★★** For details please send SAE to: **Henry and Shirley Symons, Trevathan, St. Endellion, Port Isaac PL29 3TT or telephone/fax (01208 880248).**
e-mail: symons@trevathanfarm.com
website: www.trevathanfarm.com

ST AUSTELL. Anita Treleaven, Trevissick Manor, Trevissick Farm, Trenarren, St Austell PL26 6BQ (Tel

& Fax: 01726 72954). Sleeps 2/4. The east wing of the manor farmhouse on our coastal mixed farm is situated between St Austell and Mevagissey Bays. Spectacular views across the gardens down the valley to the sea. Ideal for a couple or family. Meet the animals, view the milking, play tennis or take the farm trail to Hallane Cove. Close to sandy beaches, sailing, watersports, cycling, 18 hole golf. Heligan Gardens 5-10 minutes. Open all year. Terms from £140 to £390.**ETC ♛♛♛♛ COMMENDED**

ST. IVES. J. & P. Husband, Consols Farm, St. Ives TR26 2HN (01736 796151). Properties sleep 4/6/8.

A selection of four properties is available. Large cottage set in garden in quiet surroundings, sleeps eight people, sittingroom with TV; kitchen (fridge, electric cooker, etc); bathroom; five bedrooms. Also annexe flat in garden grounds; one double bed, one set bunk beds in family room; kitchen; lounge; bathroom, toilet, etc; small garden and patio. Ample parking. Situated one mile from St. Ives: Cottage flat sleeping four at end of farmhouse, on working farm. Sittingroom with TV; two bedrooms; kitchen; bathroom, toilet, etc. Flat in town of St. Ives sleeps five. One large attic room with panoramic view, one small double room, one single bedroom; kitchen, lounge; bathroom and toilet. Parking in town car park. Full details on request.

ST. KEVERNE. Mrs Rosemary Peters, Trenoweth Valley Farm Cottages, St. Keverne, Helston TR12 6QQ (01326 280910). Spacious, comfortable rural cottages, fully furnished and carpeted with well-equipped kitchen, colour TV and laundry facilities. Kitchen/diner, lounge/sittingroom, shower room/toilet. Sleeping upto six persons, each cottage has two bedrooms with duvets and covers for each bed. Surrounded by trees and fields, there is a safe play area for young children and a barbecue. Quiet, relaxing environment, midway between St. Keverne and Porthallow. Pleasant walks; beach, village shops and inns one-and-a-half miles. Open Easter to end October. Sorry, no pets. Attractive early and late prices. Terms from £70 to £345 per week. **ETC** ꭡꭡꭡ *APPROVED.*

TAMAR VALLEY. Mr and Mrs B.J. Howlett, Deer Park Farm, Luckett, Callington PL17 8NW (Tel & Fax: 01579 370292). Sleeps 4/5.

Three character cottages – traditional barn conversions – situated in the delightful rural setting of the Tamar Valley, well away from the traffic. Kit Hill Country Park, Tamar Trail both within one mile, Morwellham Quay, Cotehele House nearby. Free exclusive/private fishing on the farm – carp/roach. Nature and Heritage Trails are on the farm. St. Mellion Golf Club six miles. Also available locally, riding schools, pony trekking, swimming, sports centre, south Cornwall beaches and the quaint fishing villages of Looe and Polperro within easy reach making this an excellent base for Cornwall, Dartmoor and South Devon. Prices from £165 to £310. Regret no pets. **ETC** ꭡꭡꭡꭡ *APPROVED.*

TINTAGEL. Mrs Gillian Sanders, Fentafriddle Farm, Trewarmett, Tintagel PL34 0EX (01840 770580).

Enjoy a holiday at Fentafriddle, overlooking Trebarwith, with lovely sea views and sunsets. A spacious flat occupies the first floor of our farmhouse, with its own entrance, garden and picnic table. There are four bedrooms: one family, two double and one single. The kitchen is equipped with an electric cooker, microwave and fridge freezer. We are ideally situated for walking the coastal footpath, surfing and swimming at Trebarwith, Polzeath and Daymer Bay, cycling the Camel Trail and exploring Bodmin Moor. Bed linen supplied. Sorry no pets.

TRURO. Mrs Pamela Carbis, Chy Tyak, Trenona Farm, Ruan High Lanes, Truro TR2 5JS (01872 501339). Sleeps 6/8 plus cot.

Former farmhouse centrally situated on working beef, sheep and arable farm. Peaceful location in unspoilt countryside on Roseland Peninsula. Central for touring all parts of Cornwall. Coast path and sandy beaches three miles. Master bedroom en suite with colour TV. Handmade pine fitted kitchen and furnishings. All modern appliances including dishwasher, fridge/freezer, microwave, washer/drier, video and CD player. Central heating and gas stove. Bed linen and towels provided. Private garden/patio/parking. Wheelchair-friendly ground floor. Pets welcome. Open all year. Short breaks out of season.

e-mail: PCARBIS@compuserve.com

WADEBRIDGE. Mrs Perry, Polgrain Holiday Cottages, Higher Polgrain, St Wenn, Bodmin PL30 5PR (01637 880637; Fax: 01637 880637). Well off the beaten track, yet superbly positioned to tour the spectacular north coast, this is a holiday destination which offers the best of both worlds. Polgrain is the most perfect place to relax, unwind and enjoy the peace and tranquillity of the surrounding countryside. Once a flourishing farm and mill, the main farmhouse is now our family home, while the granite barns and mill have been converted into comfortable, well equipped holiday cottages – each with its own individual character and features. Adjoining the main farmhouse is the heated indoor swimming pool. Each cottage has a fully fitted kitchen including washing machine and microwave, and each living area is also equipped with colour TV, video recorder and compact disc hi-fi system. Alarm clock radios can be found in the bedrooms and all linen is provided free of charge. Central heating, power and lighting are all included within the price of the holiday. Each cottage also has its own patio, complete with furniture and brick built barbecue. Car parking. Tariffs and booking details on request. Open March - January. **ETC** ⟡⟡⟡⟡ *COMMENDED.*

WADEBRIDGE/BODIEVE. Sleeps 6 plus cot. 300 year old farmhouse, converted in 1990, surrounded by sunny gardens, ample parking space in front of house in quiet country crescent. Only three miles from the sandy beaches at Rock and Daymer Bay, the surfing beach at Polzeath, close to the ancient fishing harbour of Padstow. Ideal for surfing, safe bathing, walking, fishing, sailing, golf, cycling (cycle hire in Wadebridge). The excellent shops, pubs, markets at Wadebridge are half-a-mile away. Wadebridge Leisure Centre with its brand new indoor swimming pool is only a five minute walk. The house comprises lounge with wood/coal burner in fireplace, colour TV, comfortable sofa bed (double). large, cosy, well equipped kitchen/diner with fridge, electric cooker, dishwasher, microwave, double aspect windows; laundry room with automatic washing machine, tumble dryer, fridge/freezer. Three bedrooms - large master bedroom (double aspect windows) with king size bed, one twin bedroom and a bedroom with bunk beds (brand new beds, mattresses and bedding). Linen and towels on request at extra charge. Bathroom, shower, toilet. Night storage heaters. Pets by arrangement. Available all year. Terms from £120 to £490 per week (including electricity and cleaning). Saturday to Saturday bookings. Ring or write for further details. **Mrs Angela Holder, Roseley, Bodieve, Wadebridge PL27 6EG (01208 813024).**

CUMBRIA

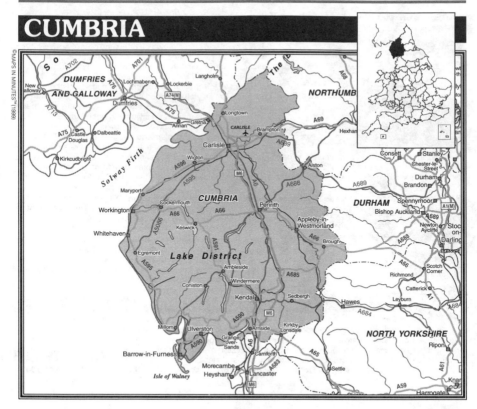

©MAPS IN MINUTES™ (1999)

AMBLESIDE. Peter and Anne Hart, Bracken Fell Cottage, Outgate, Ambleside LA22 0NH (015394 36289). Sleeps 2/4. Bracken Fell Cottage is situated in beautiful open countryside between Ambleside and Hawkshead in the picturesque hamlet of Outgate. The two/four bedroomed accommodation has central heating and is immaculately furnished. Fully equipped kitchen. Linen and electricity included. Ideally positioned for exploring the Lake District. All major outdoor activities catered for nearby. Ample parking. Patio area and two acres of gardens. Open all year. Terms from £150 per week. Sorry, no pets or children under eight years. Bed and Breakfast accommodation also available (**ETC ◆◆◆**). Non-smoking. Write or phone for brochure and tariff.
e-mail: hart.brackenfell@virgin.net
website: www.brackenfell.com

Bracken Fell

AMBLESIDE. Mrs Clare Irvine, Hole House, High Wray. HOLE HOUSE is a charming detached 17th century Lakeland cottage set in idyllic surroundings overlooking Blelham Tarn with magnificent panoramic views of the Langdale Pikes, Coniston Old Man, the Troutbeck Fells and Lake Windermere. High Wray is a quiet unspoilt hamlet set between Ambleside and Hawkshead making this an ideal base for walking or touring. This charming cottage which once belonged to Beatrix Potter has the original oak beams and feature stone staircase. It has recently been restored to provide very comfortable accommodation without losing its olde worlde charm. Accommodation consists of one double and two twin bedrooms; bathroom with shower; large spacious lounge with Sky TV and video; fitted kitchen with microwave oven, fridge/freezer, tumble dryer, automatic washing machine and electric cooker. Storage heating included in the

cost. Play area. Ample parking. Please write, or phone, for further details: **Mrs Clare Irvine, Tock How Farm, High Wray (015394 36106).**

AMBLESIDE. Mr Evans, Ramsteads Coppice, Outgate, Ambleside LA22 0NH (015394 36583). Six timber lodges of varied size and design set in 15 acres of mixed woodland with wild flowers, birds and native wild animals. There are also 11 acres of rough hill pasture. Three miles south west of Ambleside, it is an ideal centre for walkers, naturalists and country lovers. No pets. Children welcome. Open March to November.

APPLEBY-IN-WESTMORLAND. Mrs Edith Stockdale, Croft House, Bolton, Appleby-in-Westmorland CA16 6AW (Tel & Fax: 017683 61264). Sleep 2/5 and 10. Three cosy cottages recently converted from an old Westmorland style barn adjoining the owner's house. With an abundance of open stone work and oak beams and many original features. An excellent base for fell and country walking, horse-riding or as a touring base for the Lake District, beautiful Eden Valley, Scottish Borders, Hadrian's Wall and North Yorkshire Dales. Bed linen, towels, electricity and heating included in rent. Facilities include electric cooker, washing machine, fridge-freezer, microwave, colour TV, video, hi-fi and dishwasher. Stabling provided for anyone wishing to bring pony on holiday. Weekly terms from £150. Brochure.

BOWNESS-ON-WINDERMERE. 43A Quarry Rigg, Bowness-on-Windermere. Sleeps 4. Ideally situated in the centre of the village close to the lake and all amenities, the flat is in a new development, fully self-contained, and furnished and equipped to a high standard for owner's own comfort and use. Lake views, ideal relaxation and touring centre. Accommodation is for two/four people. Bedroom with twin beds, lounge with TV and video; convertible settee; separate kitchen with electric cooker, microwave and fridge; bathroom with bath/shower and WC. Electric heating. Parking for residents. Sorry, no pets. Terms from £125 to £225. Weekends and Short Breaks also available. SAE, please, for details to **Mrs E. Jones, 45 West Oakhill Park, Liverpool, Merseyside L13 4BN (Tel & Fax: 0151 228 5799).**

BOWNESS-ON-WINDERMERE. Mrs P.M. Fanstone, Deloraine, (Dept. F), Helm Road, Bowness-on-Windermere LA23 2HS (015394 45557). Deloraine spells seclusion, space, convenience and comfort for all seasons, while exploring Lakeland heritage. Parties of two/six have choice of five apartments within an Edwardian mansion, and a detached characterful cottage. Set in one-and-a-half acres of private gardens, yet only a few minutes' walk from Bowness centre and water sports. Two units command dramatic views of the Langdale Pikes and Lake at 300 foot elevation. Ground floor flat and cottage include disabled facilities. All properties have free parking, private entrances, full equipment, colour TV, electric heaters and central heating. Double glazing. Fire Prevention systems. Payphone. Washing machine. Barbecue. Sun room. Cot hire. Linen included. Four-poster beds. FREE SWIM/SAUNA TICKETS. No pets. Resident owners. Brochure on request. Terms from £130 to £430 per week. Winter Breaks available. **ETC ★★★.** *NATIONAL ACCESSIBILITY SCHEME CATEGORY 2* (FIRST IN CUMBRIA). e-mail: gordon@deloraine.demon.co.uk

BRAMPTON. Maurice and Anne Barns, Tarnside Cottages, Tarnside, Brampton CA18 1LA (01697 746675;Fax: 01697 746157). Sleeps 4. Two excellently equipped cottages, each with lounge, dining/kitchen, bathroom and twin bedroom downstairs and spiral staircase to double bedroom. Electricity, linen and logs included. Located near Eden Valley, Lake District, Hadrian's Wall and the Borders, Tarnside is an excellent base for touring the area. Open all year. From £120-£380. **ETC** ♛♛♛♛ *HIGHLY COMMMENDED*

HODYOAD COTTAGES

Hodyoad stands in its own private grounds, with extensive views of the surrounding fells in peaceful rural countryside. Mid-way between the beautiful Lakes of Loweswater and Ennerdale, six miles from Cockermouth and 17 from Keswick. Fell walking, boating, pony trekking and trout fishing can all be enjoyed within a three-and-a-half mile radius. Each cottage is fully centrally heated and has two bedrooms to sleep five plus cot. All linen provided. Lounge with colour TV. Kitchen with fitted units, cooker and fridge. Bathroom with shower, washbasin, toilet, shaver point. Laundry room with washing machine and tumble dryer. Car essential, ample parking. Sea eight miles. Open all year. From £170 to £310 per week. For further details please contact:

Mrs J. A. Cook, Hodyoad House, Lamplugh, Cumbria CA14 4TT • Tel: 01946 861338

CALDBECK near. Croft House, Brocklebank, Wigton, Near Caldbeck. This beautiful farmhouse is in a quiet country setting with large garden. Easy reach of Lake District, Scottish Borders and the Solway Firth, half-a-mile from open fells. Caldbeck is the nearest village with shops and pub. Lounge, diningroom, kitchen, three bedrooms - two double, one twin; bathroom with toilet and shower. Oil central heating, electric fire, coal, logs, cooker, fridge, colour TV, duvets all included. Bed linen and towels can be hired. Weekly terms from £160 to £250. Sorry no pets. Brochure from **Mrs Joan Todd, Wyndham Farm, Brocklebank, Wigton CA7 8DH (016974 78272).**

CONISTON. Mrs D.A. Hall (FHG), Dow Crag House, Coniston LA21 8AT (015394 41558). Two chalet bungalows to let, sleeping two/six. One mile from Coniston village on A593. Resident owner. Cleanliness assured. First bungalow has sittingroom, kitchen/diningroom, three bedrooms sleeping six; bathroom, separate toilet. Electric cooker, fridge/freezer. Night store heaters. Second bungalow comprises livingroom/kitchen, three bedrooms sleeping five, shower room. All equipped with continental quilts. Please bring own linen. Parking space. These holiday chalets are set in private garden with direct access to the Fells and Hills. Superb views overlooking Lake towards Grizedale Forest. Freedom, yet safe for children. Pets welcome by arrangement. Mountain walks, boating, fishing, tennis and bowls in village. Available March till November. Terms on application with SAE, please.

CONISTON. Townson Ground, East of Lake, Coniston LA21 8AA (015394 41272; Fax: 015394 41110). Set in an idyllic position between Grizedale Forest and the Lake, providing a spacious and relaxing scene with private access to the Lake and jetty. It is an ideal centre from which to tour and explore the beautiful Lake District National Park. The self-catering accommodation is attached to the main house, enjoying an outstanding location with views on to surrounding countryside and gardens. All units are cosy, tastefully furnished and decorated with the emphasis on quality, comfort, peace and quiet. Children welcome; one dog allowed. **ETC ★★/★★★**

Fisherground Farm Eskdale, Cumbria

Fisherground is a lovely traditional hill farm, offering accommodation in two stone cottages and three pine lodges, which share an acre of orchard. Ideal for walkers, nature lovers, dogs and children, there is space, freedom, peace and tranquillity here. Eskdale is walking country, with scores of riverside, fell or high mountain walks straight from the farm. Good pubs nearby serve excellent bar meals. ETC ★★★

Phone for a colour brochure: 01946 723319 or try our website: www.fisherground.co.uk and e-mail: holidays@fisherground.co.uk

CONISTON near. Mrs J. Halton, "Brookfield", Torver, Near Coniston LA21 8AY (015394 41328). Sleeps 2/4. This attractive, modern Bungalow property in quiet picturesque surroundings has a lovely outlook and extensive views of the Coniston mountains. It is completely detached and stands in its own half-acre of level garden and grounds. The accommodation inside is in two entirely separate self-contained units. The holiday bungalow is spacious but compact, and is suitable for two/four persons (special rate for two persons). It contains large sitting/diningroom, kitchen, utility room, two double bedrooms, bathroom and toilet. Well-equipped except for linen. Payphone. Good parking space. Village inns are handy (300 yards). Coniston three miles. Available all year. One small dog only, by arrangement. From £180 to £260 weekly. SAE for further details and terms stating number of persons and dates required. **ETC** ♉♉♉ *APPROVED/COMMENDED.*

ELTERWATER. Lane Ends Cottages, Elterwater. Three cottages are situated next to "Fellside" on the edge of Elterwater Common. Two cottages accommodate a maximum of four persons: double bedroom, twin bedded room; fully equipped kitchen/diningroom; bathroom. Third cottage sleeps five: as above plus single bedroom and separate diningroom. Electricity by meters. The cottages provide an ideal base for walking/touring holidays with Ambleside, Grasmere, Hawkshead and Coniston within a few miles. Parking for one car per cottage, additional parking opposite. Open all year; out of season long weekends available. Rates from £175 per week. Brochure on request (SAE please). **Mrs M. E. Rice, "Fellside", Elterwater, Ambleside LA22 9HN (015394 37678). ETC** ♉♉♉ *COMMENDED.*

GRIZEDALE FOREST. High Dale Park Barn, High Dale Park, Satterthwaite, Ulverston LA12 8LJ. Delightfully situated south-facing barn, newly converted, attached to owners' 17th century farmhouse, with wonderful views down secluded, quiet valley, surrounded by beautiful broadleaf woodland. Oak beams, log fires, full central heating, patio. Grizedale Visitor Centre (three miles), award-winning sculpture trails, gallery and unique sculptured playground. Grizedale Forest is one of the Lake District's richest areas of wildlife. Accommodation in two self contained units, one sleeping six, the other two plus baby; available separately or as one unit at a reduced rate. Hawkshead three miles, Beatrix Potter's home three miles. Contact: **Mr P. Brown, High Dale Park Farm, High Dale Park, Satterthwaite, Ulverston LA12 8LJ (01229 860226). ETC** ♉♉♉/♉♉♉♉ up to *HIGHLY COMMENDED.*

Readers are requested to mention this guidebook when seeking accommodation (and please enclose a stamped addressed envelope).

HAWESWATER/ULLSWATER/EDEN VALLEY. Goosemire Cottages. Over 30 traditional self-catering

holiday homes in size from one to four bedrooms, at sensible prices. Most are rustic 17th or 18th Century Lakeland cottages or lovely barn conversions, where antiquity and modern comforts have been beautifully combined. The majority of our holiday cottages are set on, or very near to Lake Ullswater (the Lake Districts second largest lake), or near Haweswater. We also have a nice selection of properties in the peaceful Eden Valley. An ideal base for walking, fishing, sailing, bird watching, touring or just relaxing in a beautiful and peaceful setting. Local pubs and post office/shop nearby. Furnished and equipped to a high standard. Log fires and central heating. Majority include heating, electric and bed linen in tariff. Pets welcome. Open all year. Short Breaks available. Details and brochure: **Goosemire Cottages, North Lodge, Longtail Hill, Bowness on Windermere LA23 3JD (015394 47477).**   website: www.goosemirecottages.co.uk

HAWKSHEAD HILL. Hatter's Cottage, Sleeps 6. 17th century detached stone cottage in secluded setting in

the southern Lake District. Located 150 yards from public roads near the hilltop between Hawkshead and Coniston. Walking and cycling from the door on footpaths, quiet lanes and forest tracks. Hatter's Cottage is beside a small stream, surrounded by gardens, fields and woodland, with mountain views. Beamed living room, fully equipped kitchen, three bedrooms. Fully renovated and heated throughout. Private garden. Rent £150-£335. ETC ★★★ **Mrs J. Gunner, Hawkshead Hill Farm, Near Hawkshead LA22 0PW (01539 436203).**
e-mail: mail@hatters-cottage.freeserve.co.uk
website: www.hatters-cottage.freeserve.co.uk

HAWKSHEAD/SAWREY. Mrs Anne Gallagher, "Hideaways", Cunsey Bridge Cottage, Cunsey Bridge,

Ambleside LA22 0LU (01539 442435; Fax: 01539 436186). Sleep 2 - 7. We offer a selection of our own family run farm cottages and individual cosy cottages and barns in this unique, picturesque area. Esthwaite Farm has been imaginatively converted into several properties, all retaining the atmosphere of the country farm and making the most of the beautiful rural position. Each property is tastefully decorated with all modern conveniences, woodburning stoves, electric central heating, comfortable seating and soft furnishings. Farm guests can enjoy free fishing on Esthwaite Water - a short stroll across the fields. In addition to the farm we have cottages in Hawkshead and Outgate village, each with its own individual charm and character. Prices include heating/logs. Dogs accepted in most properties. **ETC ★★★/★★★★.**
website: www.lakeland-hideaways.co.uk

KENDAL. Mrs E. Barnes, Brackenfold, Whinfell, Kendal LA8 9EF (01539 824238). Working farm, join in. Sleeps 5. Brackenfold is a 217 acre dairy farm set in a quiet country area. There are beautiful scenic views from the farm and also a river running through the middle of the farm which is suitable for paddling and picnicking. Brackenfold is situated centrally for touring the Lake District and the Yorkshire Dales. All children are welcome and babysitting is available. Milk can be obtained from the farm. The accommodation is part of the farmhouse and has two double bedrooms, cot; bathroom, toilet; sitting/diningroom; fully equipped kitchen with electric cooker, fridge, etc. Shops four miles, sea 20 miles. Sorry, no pets. Open March to November. SAE, please, for terms.

KENDAL. The Barns, Field End, Patton, Kendal. Two detached barns converted into five spacious architect-

designed houses. The Barns are situated on 200 acres of farmland, four miles north of Kendal. A quiet country area with River Mint passing through farmland and lovely views of Cumbrian Hills, many interesting local walks with the Dales Way Walk passing nearby. Fishing is available on the river. The Barns consist of four houses with four double bedrooms and one house with three double bedrooms. Each house fully centrally heated for early/late holidays; lounge with open fire, diningroom; kitchen with cooker, fridge, microwave and washing machine; bathroom, downstairs shower room and toilet. Many interesting features include oak beams, pine floors and patio doors. Central to Lakes and Yorkshire Dales, National Parks. Terms from £140 to £415. Electricity at cost. Pets welcome. **ETC ♀♀♀♀ COMMENDED.** For brochure of The Barns apply to **Mr and Mrs E.D. Robinson, 1 Field End, Patton, Kendal LA8 9DU (01539 824220 or 07778 596863; Fax:01539 824464.**
e-mail: fshawend@globalnet.co.uk   website: www.diva~web.co.uk.fsendhols.

KESWICK COTTAGES
Kentmere, How Lane, Keswick CA12 5RS
Superb selection of cottages and apartments in and around Keswick. All of our properties are well maintained and thoroughly clean. From a one bedroom cottage to a four bedroom house we have something for everyone. Contact us for a free colour brochure.

Tel: 01768773895   E-mail: info@keswickcottages.co.uk
Website: www.keswickcottages.co.uk

KENDAL. Mrs E. Bateman, High Underbrow Farm, Burneside, Kendal LA8 9AY (01539 721927). Working farm. Sleeps 4. The cottage adjoins the 17th century farmhouse in a sunny position with wonderful views. Ideal spot for touring the Lake District and Yorkshire Dales, with many pleasant walks around. There are two bedrooms (one with double bed, the other with two singles). Children are welcome and a cot is available. Bathroom with bath, shower, toilet and washbasin. Large livingroom/kitchen with colour TV, fitted units, fridge and cooker. Electricity by £1 coin meter. Storage heaters 50p meter. Understairs store. Fitted carpets throughout. Own entrance porch. Sorry, no pets. Shops at Burneside two miles away, Kendal four miles, Windermere eight miles. Linen provided. Car essential – parking. Terms from £150 weekly. There is also a six-berth holiday caravan to let from £140 per week.

See also Colour Display Advertisement **KESWICK. Derwentwater Manor, Portinscale, Keswick CA12 5RE (01768 772211).** This former gentleman's country residence now provides some of Lakeland's finest self-catering accommodation amid tranquil surroundings on the fringe of a picturesque village. Our tastefully converted one or two bedroomed self-catering apartments and cottages are all superbly appointed and offer a high standard of facilities. Fully fitted feature kitchens (many with dishwashers), central heating, teletext colour TVs with video, CD player and direct dial telephone. Bedrooms are complete with hair dryer, trouser press, radio alarm, welcoming tea tray, bouquet of fresh flowers and fruit basket. Beds made and towels supplied and, to be sure your holiday starts with a sparkle, a bottle of chilled Champagne. Ample free parking. Takeaway meals and grocery delivery service, and a special welcome for pets. **ETC ↑↑↑↑ HIGHLY COMMENDED.**
e-mail: info@derwentwater-hotel.co.uk
website: www.derwentwater-hotel.co.uk

KESWICK. Mr and Mrs Davis-Merry, Borrowdale Self Catering Holidays, Kiln How, Rosthwaite, Keswick CA12 5XB (017687 77356; Fax: 017687 77727). Kiln How was built in 1725 in the hamlet of Rosthwaite near the head of Borrowdale, the dale often described as the most beautiful in England. The house is ideally situated to take full advantage of many magnificent fell walks including Dalehead, Great Gable and Scafell. Choice of four self-contained, fully furnished and equipped apartments sleeping between two and six. Additional cottage for two. Private parking. Shop and pub a minute away. Outstanding scenery.
e-mail: kiln.how.@classicfm.net
website: http://users.classicfm.net/kiln.how.

KESWICK near. Mrs A.M. Trafford, Bassenthwaite Hall Farm Cottage Holidays, Bassenthwaite Village, Near Keswick CA12 4QP (Tel & Fax: 017687 76393). Working farm. By a stream with ducks! Delightful cottages charmingly restored and cared for in this attractive hamlet near Keswick. Two cosy old world farmhouses sleep 8-10 each; cottage for four/five and cute stable flat for two/three. Open all year. Storage heaters in all properties and log fires in larger properties. Special off-peak rates; weekend and mid-week breaks; farmhouse B&B. Ideally situated just two miles from Skiddaw and Bassenthwaite Lake and six miles from Keswick and Cockermouth. Mid-week and weekend breaks from £80 to £250. Available November to May except school holidays. Open all year.

KIRKBY LONSDALE near. Mrs M. Dixon, Harrison Farm, Whittington, Kirkby Lonsdale, Carnforth, Lancashire LA6 2NX (015242 71415). Properties sleep 2/8. Near Hutton Roof, three miles from Kirkby Lonsdale and central for touring Lake District and Yorkshire Dales. Coast walks on Hutton Roof Crag, famous lime stone pavings. Sleeps eight people, one room with double and single bed and one room with double and cot, while third bedroom has three single beds. Bathroom. Sittingroom, diningroom and kitchen. Everything supplied but linen. Parking space. Pets permitted. Other cottages available for two to eight people. Electric cooker, fridge, kettle, iron, immersion heater and TV. Electricity and coal extra. Terms from £160 per week. SAE brings quick reply.

See also Colour Display Advertisement

KIRKOSWALD. Crossfield Cottages with Leisure Fishing. Tranquil quality cottages overlooking fishing lakes amidst Lakeland's beautiful Eden Valley countryside. Only 30 minutes drive from Ullswater, North Pennines, Hadrian's Wall and the Scottish Borders. You will find freshly made beds for your arrival, tranquillity and freedom to roam. Good coarse and fly fishing, for residents, on your doorstep. Cottages are clean, well equipped and maintained. Laundry area. Pets very welcome. Exceptional wildlife and walking area. Escape and relax to your home in the country. ETC ★★★. SAE to **Crossfield Cottages, Kirkoswald, Penrith CA10 1EU (Tel & Fax: 01768 898711 6pm-10pm for bookings, 24hr Brochure Line).**

KIRKOSWALD. Liz Webster, Howscales, Kirkoswald, Penrith CA10 1JG (01768 898666; Fax: 01768 898710). Sleeps 2/4. COTTAGES FOR NON SMOKERS. Howscales is a former farm built in local red sandstone with the buildings grouped around a central courtyard. Located in a rural setting one-and-a-half miles from Kirkoswald. Three cottages are two storey, with the lounge, kitchen and dining areas on the first floor; the bedrooms and bathroom are on the ground floor. One is single storey at ground level, with two en suite double bedrooms. A similar cottage, for two, has been especially designed for wheel chair access. All cottages have full central heating, are equipped with colour TV and have a fully equipped kitchen/dining area with microwave, electric cooker, gas hob and fridge. Shower room and WC. Everything supplied including linen. gas and electricity paid by meter reading at end of stay. Please ring or write for our colour brochure. **ETC ♈♈♈** and **♈♈♈♈** *HIGHLY COMMENDED.*

PENRITH. Rampshowe, Orton, Penrith. Working farm, join in. Sleeps 2/8. Rampshowe is a 150 acre fell farm with sheep, lambs, beef cattle and calves. Organised pony riding nearby. Delightfully positioned in the peace and quiet of Birbeck Fells, with a river flowing through the fields, lovely waterfall and pool. Ideal area for bird-watchers. Local angling club. Shops, Post Office, pub serving snacks, Tearoom serving home-baking. Unspoilt, rural countryside, yet only five miles from M6 motorway. Accommodates eight people in three double bedrooms, cot; bathroom, toilet; colour TV, sittingroom, diningroom. All downstairs rooms and bathroom with night-store electric heaters and there is an open fire with back-boiler (wood and coal provided). Fully equipped kitchen. Fitted carpets throughout. Pets and children welcome. Car essential, ample car parking space in the farmyard. Open all year. The owner maintained house stands on its own, with garden and large farmyard. Prices from £130 to £275. SAE to **Mrs M. E. Mawson, Bow Brow, Orton, Penrith CA10 3SJ (015396 24244).**

PENRITH. Skirwith Hall Cottages. Escape to Eden! Get away from it all in one of two comfortable well-equipped cottages on dairy farm in the Eden Valley between the Lake District and the Pennine Dales. Set on the edge of the village of Skirwith in the shadow of Crossfell, the highest mountain in the Pennine range, the properties are maintained to the highest standard with every modern convenience. Accommodating two/four and five/eight people both cottages have riverside gardens and open fires. Well behaved children and pets welcome. ETC ★★★. Please contact for brochure. **Mrs L. Wilson, Skirwith Hall, Skirwith, Penrith CA10 1RH (Tel & Fax: 01768 88241).** e-mail: idawilson@aol.com website: www.eden-in-cumbria.co.uk/skirwith

STAVELY. William, Anne and Linda Batey, Brunt Knott Farm, Staveley, Kendal LA8 9QX (01539 821030; Fax: 01539 821221). Sleep 2/5.

Four cosy cottages on a small 17th century farm. Peaceful, elevated, fellside location, with superb views over Lakeland Fells. Five miles from Windemere and the historic market town of Kendal. One-and-a-half miles from Staveley village. Lovely walks from your door. Three cottages with oil central heating, one with electric storage heaters. Three cottages also have woodburner/fire. Laundry facilities. Gardens, picnic tables and parking. Ideal touring base Lakes and Yorkshire Dales. Caring resident owners. Children and pets welcome. Short breaks in low season. Tariff £145 to £310 per week. Brochure. ETC ★★★
e-mail: Linda@Bruntknott.demon.co.uk
website: www.Bruntknott.demon.co.uk

ULLSWATER. The Estate Office, Patterdale Hall Estate, Glenridding, Penrith CA11 0PJ (Tel & Fax: 017684 82308 24 hours).

Our range includes three very comfortable large coach-houses, two stone-built cottages with open fires, three-bedroomed pine lodges, six two-bedroomed cedar chalets, a unique, detached, converted dairy, and two converted bothies which make ideal, low cost accommodation for two people. All set in a private 300 acre estate between Lake Ullswater and Helvellyn and containing a working hill-farm, a Victorian waterfall wood, private lake foreshore for guests to use for boating and fishing, and 100 acres of designated ancient woodland for you to explore. Children welcome. Dogs by appointment in some of the accommodation. Colour TV, central heating, launderette, payphone. Day time electricity metered. Linen hire available. Terms from £132 to £451. Please phone for full brochure. **Coach Houses ETC** 𝓜𝓜𝓜𝓜 *COMMENDED;* **Cottages ETC** 𝓜𝓜𝓜 *COMMENDED;* **Pine Lodges ETC** 𝓜𝓜𝓜 *COMMENDED;* **Chalets ETC** 𝓜𝓜 *COMMENDED;* **The Dairy and Bothies ETC** 𝓜 *COMMENDED.*
e-mail: welcome@phel.co.uk
website: www.phel.co.uk

WHITEHAVEN. Hunting How Farmhouse, Moresby, Whitehaven. Sleeps 2/7.

17th century farmhouse on working livestock farm, one mile from the Georgian fishing port of Whitehaven with its newly built marina. A good base for exploring the Northern Lakes, Wastwater, Ennerdale, Eskdale, Keswick, Laal Ratty and Muncaster Castle, all within a short drive. The new Whitehaven Golf Course is half-a-mile away and opens in June. Farmhouse consists of four bedrooms - two double, one twin, one single. Bathroom with three-piece suite and shower over bath. Facilites include oil fired Aga cooker, microwave, dishwasher, fridge, kettle, coffee-maker, automatic washer, iron and board, hair dryer, colour TV, payphone. Oil fired central heating throughout and one bag of coal included in rent. Bed linen and towels are provided. Elevated garden with summer-house overlooking the sea and Scottish hills. Sorry, no pets or smoking in the house. Tariff from £250 - £350 per week. To book please telephone **Mrs J. Messenger (01946 693662).**

When making enquiries please mention FHG Publications

Birthwaite Edge Apartments, Windermere

Situated in extensive grounds in one of the most exclusive areas of Windermere, 10 minutes from village and Lake, this is the perfect all year round holiday base. 10 self catering apartments for two to six people. Resident proprietors personally ensure the highest standards of cleanliness and comfort. Swimming pool open May to September. Colour TV. Well equipped kitchens. Hot water included. Coin metered electricity for lighting, cooking and electric fires. Background central heating during winter. Duvets and linen provided. High chairs and cots extra. Ample car parking. Regret, no smoking and no pets. Terms from £160 to £485.

Brochure from: **Bruce and Marsha Dodsworth, Birthwaite Edge, Birthwaite Road, Windermere LA23 1BS • Tel & Fax: 015394 42861 e-mail: lakedge@lakedge.com • website: www.lakedge.com.**

WINDERMERE. Mr and Mrs F. Legge, Pinethwaite, Lickbarrow Road, Windermere LA23 2NQ (Tel & Fax: 015394 44558). Properties sleep 2/7. Pinethwaite offers more than just somewhere to stay for your Lake District holiday. Our unique cottages and apartments nestle in the heart of our private woodland, the haunt of roe deer, red squirrels and extensive bird life. A tranquil location, yet only one mile from Windermere and Bowness villages. Superb viewpoints close by. Lovely walks in our grounds and local footpaths (Cumbrian Way) through surrounding farmland and fell. Well equipped accommodation (colour TVs, microwaves, electric heating, log fires). Central washing machine/dryer. Sauna. Private parking. Children welcome but, sorry, no pets. Open all year. Short Breaks available in the Low Season. Tariffs from £170 to £500 per week. Full details in our brochure, sent on request. **ETC ★★★ and ★★★★** website: www.pinecottages.co.uk

DERBYSHIRE

AMBERGATE. Mrs Carol Oulton, Lawn Farm, Whitewells Lane (Off Holly Lane), Ambergate DE56 2DN (01773 852352). Sleeps 5. Old Pine Cottage is a conversion of an old stone barn on a working cattle and sheep farm in the Derwent Valley to the south of Matlock Bath. Its vaulted beamed ceiling, exposed stone walls, recessed windows and mellow pine doors add character to this cottage. We are ideally situated for Matlock Bath, Carsington Water, Ashbourne, Chatsworth House and Gardens, walking in the Peak District National Park and the National Tramway Museum at Crich. The cottage is comfortably furnished and well equipped with TV, video, CD radio, cooker, fridge, microwave and washing machine. Duvets, linen and towels provided. Heating by night storage heaters. Free fishing on farm. Non-smoking. Pets by arrangement. Weekly rates from £180 to £300.
e-mail: carol.oulton@farming.co.uk
website: http://members.farmline.com/jhoulton/

See also Colour Display Advertisement

ASHBOURNE. Mrs Louise Tatlow, Ashfield Farm, Calwich, Near Ashbourne DE6 2EB (01335 324279 or 324443). Working farm. Sleeps 7. Ashfield Cottage is a recently renovated oak-beamed cottage on this working farm, well situated for the Peak District and many other places of interest with beautiful views of Dove Valley and Weaver Hills. Accommodation is for seven persons in two bedrooms (one family room and one with twin beds). Well-furnished and equipped with storage heaters, colour TV, automatic washing machine, tumble dryer, fridge/freezer. Coloured bathroom suite and shower. Linen for hire. Parking space. Further details and brochure on request. **ETC ♛♛♛♛ COMMENDED.**

ASHBOURNE. Mr and Mrs Lennard, The Chop House, Windle Hill Farm, Sutton-on-the-Hill DE6 5JH (01283 732377). The Chop House has been carefully converted from the farm corn shed where animal feeds were once chopped and mixed. Providing accommodation for up to six it has three twin bedrooms, a fully equipped kitchen, large dining area and comfortable lounge. Outside there is a quiet garden and ample car parking. It features original beams and pleasant views over the farmyard, duckpond and surrounding countryside. The farm has traditional and rare breeds of livestock and poultry (some of our hens lay green eggs). Local attractions include stately homes, adventure theme parks. museums and the glorious Derbyshire countryside.

ASHBOURNE near. Throwley Moor Farm and Throwley Cottage, Ilam, Near Ashbourne. Working farm, join in. Properties sleep 7/12. Self-catering farmhouse and cottage on this beef and sheep farm near Dovedale and Manifold Valley. Approached by A52/A53 Ashbourne to Leek road, then via Calton and follow signs for Throwley and Ilam. Within easy reach of Alton Towers, cycle hire and places of historic interest. An ideal touring centre. The cottage accommodates seven people and the farmhouse 12. Sittingrooms and diningroom (kitchen/diner in cottage). Electric cookers; fridges; washing machine and dryer. Pay phone. Pets permitted. Car essential – parking. Available all year; terms according to season. Nearest shops three miles away. **ETC** ♡♡♡♡ SAE, please, for further details to **Mrs M.A. Richardson, Throwley Hall Farm, Ilam, Near Ashbourne DE6 2BB (01538 308 202/243).**

BARLOW. Mr and Mrs R. Ward, Barlow Trout, Mill Farm, Barlow, Dronfield S18 7TJ (0114 289 0543). Units sleeps 2/6. Mill Farm Holiday Cottages are situated in a conservation area with Post Office and pub/bar meals just 300 yards away; bus stop at gate. Horse riding can be arranged and coarse and fly fishing is available on site. Children and pets welcome. Central heating. Four-poster bed in three of the five units. Weekly terms from £109 to £210. Linen provided free of charge. Short break bookings accepted October – April. Please write or phone for full details. **ETC** ♡♡♡♡ *COMMENDED*

CROMFORD. Mrs Beardsley, Woodseats Farm, Willersley Lane, Cromford, Near Matlock DE4 5JG (01629 56525). Built in Derbyshire stone, Woodseats Cottages have been converted from the original cowshed. Situated on our 75 acre family-run working farm which sits on a hillside overlooking the Derwent Valley with its panoramic views. About two miles from Cromford village and Matlock Bath. Many attractions include Chatsworth House, Crich Tramway Museum, Carsington Water, Alton Towers and Bakewell. The two cottages each have two double bedrooms that sleep four plus two. They both have a shower on the first floor, and well-equipped dining kitchens with electric cooker and fridge/freezer, microwave, etc. Lounge with feature stone wall and exposed beams, TV and video. Central heating, electricity and bed linen are inclusive. Ample parking. No pets. Terms from £205 to £355 per week. Bed and Breakfast also available. Open all year.

HARTINGTON. P. Skemp, Cotterhill Farm, Biggin by Hartington, Buxton SK17 0DJ (01298 84447; Fax: 01298 84664). Two recently converted cottages, one sleeping four, the other two. Exposed beams, two-person cottage has galleried bedroom, log burner, five-piece suite in bathroom and more. High and tasteful specification. Patio, substantial garden area, wild flower meadows and barbecue. Laundry room. Phone. Glorious location in rolling countryside. Excellent views with privacy. Half-a-mile from village and pub. Tissington Trail three-quarters of a mile, two other cycle/footpath trails within three miles, nature reserve on our land leading after one-and-a-half miles to River Dove, four miles down river is Dovedale. Footpaths/bridleways surround our farm. Highly praised, personalised information pack in each cottage giving loads of advice on attractions, walks, etc. Terms from £180 to £380 per week. **ETC** ♡♡♡♡ *HIGHLY COMMENDED*.
e-mail: patrick@skemp.u-net.com
website: www.skemp.u-net.com

HARTINGTON. J. Gibbs, Wolfscote Grange Farm Cottages, Hartington, Near Buxton SK17 0AX (Tel & Fax: 01298 84342). Sleep 4/6. Charming cottages nestling beside the beautiful Dove Valley in stunning scenery. Cruck Cottage is peaceful 'with no neighbours, only sheep' and a cosy 'country living' feel. Wolfscote Cottage offers comfort for the traveller and time to relax in beautiful surroundings. It sparkles with olde worlde features, yet has all modern amenities including en suite facilities and spa bathroom. The farm trail provides walks from your doorstep to the Dales. Open all year. Weekly terms from £160 to £475. **ETC ★★★★**
e-mail: wolfscote@btinternet.com

HOPE. Crabtree Cottages, Crabtree Meadow, Aston Lane, Hope Valley, Derbyshire. Four cottages sleep 2/6. Four beautifully converted, well-equipped cottages in the grounds of a country house in Peak District National Park. Well fitted kitchens with gas rings, electric and microwave ovens. Colour TVs, videos, CD/radio/cassette players, laundry, payphone. Central heating, fuel and linen with towels included. Ample off-road parking but car not essential. Superb walking country and facilities in the area for golf, tennis, climbing, gliding, fishing, pony trekking and caving. Convenient for shops and pubs, visiting historic houses. Weekly all year £160 to £375. Short breaks in winter from £70. **Mrs P. M. Mason, Crabtree Meadow, Aston Lane, Hope Valley S33 6SA (Tel & Fax: 01433 620291). ETC ★★★★**
email: crabtree@prima.net
website: www.prima.net/crabtree

MATLOCK. Honeysuckle, Jasmine and Clematis Cottages, Middlehills Farm, Grange Mill, Matlock DE4 4HY (01629 650368). Relax, unwind, enjoy the peace and traquillity in one of our warm, welcoming cottages or static caravan. JASMINE - two bedroomed, and HONEYSUCKLE - three bedroomed, both Four Keys Commended, are full of character - stone mullions, enclosed south facing patios. CLEMATIS - two bedroomed and Four Keys Highly Commended, Accessible Category 2, is on one level and especially converted for less-able and wheelchair users. Large bathroom with support rails, wheel-in shower with shower seat. Also fully equipped static caravan for bargain breaks. Meet our friendly pot-bellied pig and Bess and Ruby are ideal playmates for children of all ages. **ETC ↟↟↟↟** *COMMENDED/HIGHLY COMMENDED.*

DEVON

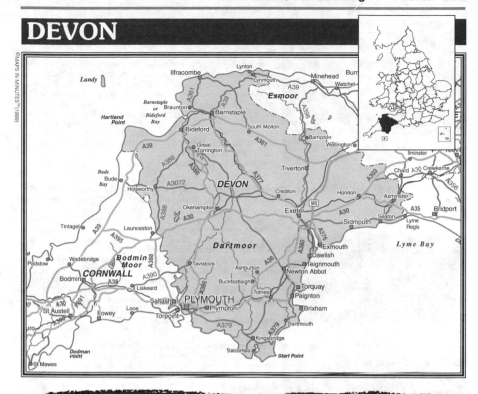

APPLEDORE. Sea Birds Cottage, Appledore. Sea edge, pretty Georgian cottage facing directly out to the

open sea. Sea Birds is a spacious cottage with large lounge, colour TV; dining room with French windows onto garden; modern fitted kitchen; three double bedrooms; bathroom, second WC downstairs; washing machine. Lawned garden at back overlooking the sea with garden furniture. Own parking. Dog welcome. Sea views from most rooms and the garden is magnificent; views of the open sea, boats entering the estuary, sunset, sea birds. Appledore is still a fishing village - fishing trips from the quay, restaurants by the water. Area has good cliff and coastal walks, stately homes, riding, swimming, golf, surfing, excellent beaches. Off peak heating. From £95. Other cottages available. Send SAE for colour brochure to **F. S. Barnes, 140 Bay View Road, Northam, Bideford EX39 1BJ (01237 473801).**
Photo shows view of sea from garden.

ASHBURTON. Mrs Angela Bell, Wooder Manor, Widecombe-in-the-Moor, Near Ashburton TQ13 7TR

(01364 621391). Modernised granite cottages and converted coach house, on 150 acre working family farm nestled in the picturesque valley of Widecombe, surrounded by unspoilt woodland, moors and granite tors. Half-a-mile from village with Post Office, general stores, inn with diningroom, church and National Trust Information Centre. Excellent centre for touring Devon, with a variety of places to visit, and exploring Dartmoor by foot or on horseback. Accommodation is clean and well equipped with colour TV, central heating, laundry room. Children welcome. Large gardens and courtyard for easy parking. Open all year, so take advantage of off-season reduced rates. Short Breaks also available. Two properties suitable for disabled visitors. Brochure available. **ETC** ♔♔♔♔ *COMMENDED.*

AXMINSTER. 2 Hillview Cottage, Dalwood, Near Axminster. A pretty semi-detached cottage set in the heart

of a delightful village surrounded by beautiful countryside. Ideal for exploring Devon, Dorset and Somerset within eight miles of the superb Lyme Bay coastline, this location offers a wealth of attractions to visit. The cottage with its low beamed ceilings upstairs comprises lounge, kitchen-diner, two bedrooms (one double, one twin), bathroom with bath and overhead shower and separate toilet. Electric cooking, microwave, fridge, automatic washing machine, colour television, video, night storage heaters, duvets. Enclosed garden with furniture. Private parking for one car, 50 yards. Bed linen and all fuel included. Children welcome. Sorry no pets and non-smokers only. Open all year (except Christmas and New Year). Short breaks available off season. Charges £190 to £320 per week. Contact: **Valerie Houghton, Homeleigh** Cottage, Tolcis Lane, Membury, Near Axminster EX13 7JF (Tel & Fax: 01404 881475).

BARNSTAPLE. Mrs Kate Price, Country Ways, Little Knowle Farm, High Bickington, Umberleigh, Near

Barnstaple EX37 9BJ (Tel & Fax: 01769 560503). Beautifully converted stone barns, all with lovely gardens and magnificent views, hidden away on a small farm. Incredibly peaceful. Walks in ancient woodland and within easy reach of Barnstaple, Exmoor and coast. The farm has rare breeds, friendly animals, play area including huge trampoline and barbecue. THE CUCKOO'S NEST has two double rooms and one bunk room, also sofa bed, THE STABLES has two bedrooms - one with king size bed and the other with two singles. THE DEN has one double bedroom and fold-out bed if required. Open all year. One unit suitable for disabled guests. Warm and well equipped. Cots on request. Short breaks available most of the year. Please telephone for further details. **ETC** ♔♔♔♔ *HIGHLY COMMENDED.*
e-mail: kate.price@virgin.net
website: www.devon-holiday.co.uk

Readers are requested to mention this guidebook
when seeking accommodation (and please enclose
a stamped addressed envelope).

Lower Hall Farm — Brayford, Barnstaple, N.Devon. EX32 7QN

● Call Mrs Shirley Barrow on 01598 710569 for brochure and more details ●

End of farm house cottage on a working mainly dairy, also with sheep and beef farm where visitors are welcome and sometimes help. Ideally situated for walking on the Tarka Trail, local beauty spots, North Devon's famous beaches and market towns of South Molton and Barnstaple. Use of tennis court, small river, walled garden with sandpit, picnic table makes it ideal for children. Accommodation which Sleeps 6, has sittingroom, dining area and kitchen, double room, twin room and bunked room. Cot and highchair available. Electricity, wood and linen included. Sorry no pets.

BARNSTAPLE. Mr and Mrs C. L. Hartnoll, Little Bray House, Brayford, Barnstaple EX32 7QG (Tel & Fax: 01598 710295). Properties sleep 2/6. Situated nine miles east of Barnstaple, Little Bray House is ideally placed for day trips to East Devon, Somerset and Cornwall, the lovely sandy surfing beaches at Saunton Sands and Woolacombe, and many places of interest both coastal and inland. Exmoor also has great charm. out of season! Come and share the pace of life and fresh air straight from the open Atlantic, and be sustained by a good healthy breakfast. Able to cater for two to ten people staying in a cottage and/or pretty twin bedded room with bathroom or en suite bedroom. Lovely gardens, walks. Prices from £18 - £20 per night person per. ETC ⸙⸙⸙

BARNSTAPLE. Mrs M. Balman, Tidicombe Farmhouse, Arlington, Near Barnstaple EX31 4SP (01271 850300). Comfortable farmhouse wing for two to eight persons. Three bedrooms - one family room, one twin-bedded room and one room with three singles. Two bathrooms, one with shower, large livingroom with log fire and galley kitchen. Linen, towels and central heating inclusive. Cot and high chair. Plenty of safe parking. Dogs allowed downstairs - £10 per week. Adjoining National Trust open countryside to explore. Ten minutes drive from coast to Exmoor or Barnstaple. Garden for children. Fishing one-and-a-half miles. Situated on Cycle Way No.56. Terms from £150 to £375 according to number of people. ETC ⸙⸙⸙⸙.

See also Colour Display Advertisement

BARNSTAPLE. North Devon Holiday Homes, 19 Cross Street, Barnstaple EX31 1BD (01271 376322 24-hour brochure service; Fax: 01271 346544). With our Free Colour Guide and unbiased recommendation and booking service, we can spoil you for choice in the beautiful unspoilt region around Exmoor and the wide sandy beaches and coves of Devon's beautiful National Trust Coast. Choose from over 400 selected properties including thatched cottages, working farms, beachside properties with swimming pools, luxury manor houses, etc. From only £89 to £890 per week. First class value assured.
e-mail: info@northdevonholidays.co.uk/
website: www.northdevonholidays.co.uk/

BIDEFORD. Mrs C. A, Thompson, Rosewood, Knotty Corner, Bideford EX39 5BT (01237 451514). Rosewood is a delightful opportunity to enjoy one of the prettiest areas in Devon. Relax on the "suntrap" patio amidst a garden full of colour! Clovelly, Rosemoor Gardens, Milky Way, Tarka Trail, coastal walks, swimming, golf, surfing, canoeing and fishing nearby. Shops and pubs one-and-a-half miles. Beaches within three miles. On the perimeter of a 45 acre stock farm Rosewood offers – attractive entrance hall leading to a large, well equipped kitchen/diningroom with electric cooker and microwave. Tastefully furnished sittingroom, TV, stereo, woodburner. Downstairs bathroom. Three bedrooms, one double, one double and single, one single. Private parking. Children welcome. Sorry, no pets. Terms from £250.

BIDEFORD near. West Titchberry Farm Cottage, Hartland, Near Bideford. Sleeps 5 adults, 1 child.

Situated on the coast near Hartland Point (follow signs to Hartland Point Lighthouse), this recently renovated farm cottage comprises (upstairs) double and family rooms (plus cot); bathroom, toilet. Downstairs is a fully fitted kitchen with dining area. Electricity for the cooker, fridge/freezer, microwave oven and washing machine is on a £1 meter. In the lounge the settee converts into a single bed; colour TV, video, wood-burning stove (logs provided free), central heating downstairs (no charge), portable heaters upstairs. The lounge door opens onto a small enclosed garden. The cottage is carpeted throughout and well appointed. Open all year. Guests have freedom of this 150-acre mixed farm. Easy access to costal footpath - quiet, unspoilt surroundings. Clovelly six miles, Hartland three miles. Sorry, no pets. Terms approximately £90 to £340 weekly according to season. SAE please **Mrs Yvonne Heard, West Titchberry Farm, Hartland, Near Bideford EX39 6AU (01237 441287).**

BIGBURY near. Miss C.M. Hodder, Bennicke Farm, Modbury, Ivybridge PL21 0SU (01548 830265). Sleeps 8. The main part of Bennicke Farmhouse is self-contained and reached from the Plymouth to Kingsbridge main road A379, by a lane quarter-of-a-mile long. Set in a quiet valley with a variety of wildlife and a large garden. Within easy reach of beaches (five miles), Dartmoor National Park (six miles) and Cornwall (15 miles). Terms from £210 to £275 per week.

BOVEY TRACEY. John and Helen Griffiths, Lookweep Farm, Liverton, Newton Abbot TQ12 6HT (01626 833277; Fax: 01626 834412). Sleeps 5. Lookweep

Farm is set within Dartmoor National Park and is perfectly placed for exploration of Dartmoor, the stunning coastline, charming villages and towns of South Devon. Shippen and Dairy cottages are two attractive, well-equipped stone cottages surrounded by open farmland and woods in this tranquil setting near Bovey Tracey and just a two mile drive from Haytor. Own gardens, ample parking, heated pool and outstanding walks right on your doorstep. Children welcome (high chairs and cots available). Pets also welcome. Short breaks available. Mastercard and Visa accepted. Please phone or write for brochure. ETC ★★★ e-mail: holidays@lookweep.co.uk

BRATTON FLEMING. Mrs A. Douglas, Friendship Farm, Bratton Fleming, Barnstaple EX31 4SQ (01598 763291 evenings). Friendship Bungalow is quietly situated down a short drive from the farmhouse, in its own garden, and surrounded by fields. There is ample parking space. The farm is situated 12 miles from Barnstaple and Ilfracombe, at the junction of roads A399 and B3358, within easy reach of the beaches of Woolacombe and Combe Martin. Exmoor is literally on the doorstep. The accommodation comprises three bedrooms (sleep six), plus cot. Linen supplied. Lounge with colour TV. Well equipped kitchen/diningroom. Bathroom, laundry room, spin dryer. Metered electricity. Weekly terms, low season from £100, high season £250.

FREE or REDUCED RATE entry to Holiday Visits and Attractions — see our READERS' OFFER VOUCHERS on pages 43-60

CHULMLEIGH near. Mrs M. E. Gay, Riddlecombe Manor Farm, Riddlecombe, Chulmleigh EX18 7NX (Tel & Fax: 01769 520335).

"An Aladdin's Cave". This is how children and their parents have described our superb games room. Which includes a play cottage, ride-on-toys (including tractors!), snooker, table tennis and much more. A friendly welcome awaits you at Manor Farmhouse, which has a very well equipped self-catering wing with lovely views and enclosed garden. A dairy and sheep farm where children can feed baby lambs, collect eggs, watch the milking and make friends with Poppy the tame sheep or Doris our adorable cow. Sleeps seven/eight plus cot, gas fired woodburner, heating throughout, cleanliness guaranteed. Woodland walks, bicycle hire nearby, handy for sea/moors. Terms from £190 per week. **ETC** ♡♡♡ *COMMENDED.*

COLYTON. Jane and Paul Galloway, Higher Watchcombe Farm. Shute, Near Colyton EX13 7QN (Tel & Fax: 01297 552424).

Range of five quality converted barns sleeping two/six. Fully equipped with microwaves, dishwashers, TV etc. Private patios and safe children's play area. Set in two-and-a-half rural acres of peaceful grounds in Area of Outstanding Natural Beauty, offering stunning views over Umborne Valley. Located two miles from the historic village of Colyton and a further two miles to the coast. Ideally situated for touring Devon, Dorset and Somerset. Many holiday activities within easy reach; also golf, swimming, riding, flying, fishing. Walking and birdwatching paradise. Open all year – short breaks available. Quality holidays at sensible prices. Call resident owners for colour brochure and further information. **ETC ★★★★**
e-mail: galloways@ukgateway.net

See also Colour Display Advertisement

COMBE MARTIN. Mr Robertson, Wheel Farm Country Cottages, Berrydown 12, Combe Martin EX34 0NT (01271 882100). COTTAGES WITH A DIFFERENCE. Near North Devon's "Blue Flag" beaches, with views of Exmoor, award winning gardens surround this high quality self-catering accommodation which has been converted from an 18th century watermill and barns. They have all the modern amenities and great rustic charm. Gas central heating, log fires, four posters, dishwashers, video, provisions and maid service, laundry room, bed linen, flowers. Inclusive indoor pool, fitness room, sauna, tennis court (tuition available). Nearby – riding, cycling, golf, walking, historic houses, gardens and family attractions. Open March to October. Spring and Autumn short breaks. **ETC ★★★★**
e-mail: holidays@wheelfarmcottages.co.uk   website:www.wheelfarmcottages.co.uk

CROYDE. Mrs Jenny Windsor, Chapel Farm, Hobbs Hill, Croyde EX33 1NE (01271 890429). Chapel Farm Self-Catering and Bed and Breakfast Holidays. The "Old Smithy Cottage" and luxury bungalow sleeping eight. Five minutes walk to the beautiful sandy beach. Surfing, horse riding, coastal paths and so much more all within easy reach of this lovely part of North Devon. Croyde village has many beautiful thatched cottages, character pubs and restaurants. Terms from £200 to £700 weekly. Colour brochure available.
website: www.chapelfarmcroyde.co.uk

CULLOMPTON. Mrs Chapman, South Farm, Blackborough, Cullompton EX15 2JE (01823 681078; Fax: 01823 680483).

Family and Fishing holidays in Devon. Comfortable and well equipped cottages. Free fishing in four well-stocked lakes - carp (double figures), roach (two to three-and-a-half pounds), chub, perch and tench. Free use of spa, sauna, tennis, outdoor heated pool (summer) and barbecue. For the children we have a games barn with table tennis, badminton, playground and trampoline. Area of Outstanding Natural Beauty with splendid views. Central to Devon tourist attractions. Open all year, wood burning stoves. Short breaks. Activity Centre ideal for residential workshops or social events. Organic box deliveries and friendly Devon milkman. Be active or relax in tranquil surroundings. Children and dogs welcome.
e-mail: chapmans@southfarm.co.uk
website: www.southfarm.co.uk

DARTMOUTH. Watermill Cottages, Hansel, Dartmouth TQ6 0LN. Delightful stone cottages set in own

secluded valley, just three miles from Slapton Sands in South Devon. Idyllic riverside setting offers perfect retreat. Wonderful walks and wildlife. Enid Blyton country for children - a whole traffic-free valley to explore, and a river to dam and paddle in. Pigs to feed, eggs to collect and lambs to bottle-feed in Spring. Five cosy well-equipped cottages sleeping three to six people. Home cooked meals available. Open all year. Winter breaks from £80. Children and dogs welcome. For brochure and further details contact: **Pam and Graham Spittle (01803 770219).**

DARTMOUTH. Mrs Stella Buckpitt, Middle Wadstray, Blackawton, Totnes TQ9 7DD (01803 712346).

Sleep 4/5. Character cottage on working farm. Pleasant rural situation. Swallow lovers' paradise. Farm walks and use of farmhouse gardens. Near Woodlands Leisure Park and Dartmouth Golf Club. Dartmouth/beaches four miles. Own parking and garden. Useful entrance room for boating gear, bicycles and wet clothes etc. Lounge/diner with woodburner and TV. Quality fitted kitchen. Two bedrooms with Dunlopillo beds for extra comfort. One 5' double (zip and link), one twin 3' bed can be used as double, extra small bed if required. Bathroom with corner bath and shower, and room for wine and candles to relax and unwind. Regret no pets or smoking indoors. Terms £140 - £400. See also entry in B & B section. Grid Ref 824513

DAWLISH. Linda Jameson, Shell Cove House, Old Teignmouth Road, Dawlish EX7 ONJ (Tel/Fax: 01626 862523). sleeps 2/10 persons. Idyllic Setting. Luxury cottage or apartment in a beautiful Georgian country house with breathtaking sea views and a virtually private beach. Nestling in four acres of grounds of outstanding natural beauty. Numerous facilities include heated pool, tennis court, badminton, croquet, bird-hide gazebo and indoor play room. Central heating, dishwashers, videos, linen and all comforts. A unique holiday. Open all year with short breaks in the Spring and Autumn.
e-mail: shellcovehouse@btclick.com

EXETER. Mrs Eileen Persey, Five Elms, Bradninch, Exeter EX5 4RD (01392 881526; Fax: 01392

881249). Sleeps 8 plus cot. Secluded luxury four-bedroomed bungalow overlooking the peaceful Colebrook Valley within easy reach of Exmoor, Dartmoor and beaches. Ideal for summer holidays or short breaks. Golf, sports centre, National Trust properties, country pubs nearby. Explore the footpaths, visit the award-winning dairy unit, fish on the 5km stretch of river, enjoy the scenery and wildlife on this 400 acre farm. Sorry no pets. Open all year. **ETC ΥΥΥΥ/ΥΥΥΥ** *COMMENDED.*
e-mail: persey.park@btinternet.com

EXMOUTH. Mrs G. Clarke, Pound House, Pound Lane, Exmouth EX8 4NP (01395 222684). Self-

catering four bedroom cottage sleeps eight. Quiet lane but very central – few minutes' walk to shops and beach. Equipped to high standard including central heating, TV and video, fridge-freezer, microwave. Integral garage. Gas, electricity and linen included in price. From £325 per week.

PEACE AND TRANQUILLITY NEAR EXETER, DEVON

The Salter family welcomes you to

HALDON LODGE FARM

Kennford, near Exeter EX6 7YG

20 minutes from Dawlish and Torbay beaches

Central for South Devon Coast and Exeter in delightful setting, Four luxury six-berth caravans in a private and friendly park. Relax and enjoy the scenery or stroll along the many forest lanes. Two private coarse fishing lakes and an attraction of farm animals, ponies and horse riding for both novice and experienced riders exploring the Teign Valley Forest. Weekly wood fire barbecue (July and August); many friendly country inns nearby. Excellent facilities including picnic tables and farm shop. Set in glorious Rural Devon, the site offers freedom and safety for all the family. Very reasonable prices. Pets accepted – exercising area. OPEN ALL YEAR.

Large six berth Caravans, two bedrooms, lounge with TV, bathroom/toilet (H/C water); Rates from £70 to £195 High Season.
Personal attention and a warm welcome assured by David and Betty Salter.

For brochure telephone (01392) 832312.

HONITON. Mrs Sue Cochrane, Droughtwell Farm, Sheldon, Honiton EX14 4QW (01404 841349). Droughtwell Farm is a small organic beef and sheep farm in open country in the Blackdown Hills, an Area of Outstanding Natural Beauty. Comfortable and self-contained, the accommodation consists of one bedroom with twin beds, sittingroom with log fire, TV and piano, kitchen and bathroom. We are six miles north of Honiton and six miles from M5. Many places are within easy reach: Sidmouth, Lyme Regis, Exeter, Dartmoor and Exmoor. Locally we have lovely walks in field and forest, there is gliding and riding nearby, or you can just relax in the garden. **ETC ★★★.**

See also Colour Display Advertisement

HOPE COVE. Mike and Judy Tromans, Hope Barton Barns, Hope Cove, Near Salcombe TQ7 3HT (01548 561393). Sleep 2/10. Nestling in its own valley, close to the sandy cove, Hope Barton Barns is an exclusive group of 17 stone barns in two courtyards and three luxury apartments in the converted farmhouse. Heated indoor pool, sauna, gym, lounge bar, tennis court, trout lake and a children's play barn. We have 35 acres of pastures and streams with sheep, goats, pigs, chickens, ducks and rabbits. Superbly furnished and fully-equipped, each cottage is unique and they vary from a studio to four bedrooms, sleeping two to ten. Ample parking. Golf, sailing and coastal walks nearby. Open all year. A perfect setting for family Summer holidays, a week's walking in Spring/Autumn or just a "get away from it all" break. Free range children and well behaved dogs welcome. For a colour brochure and rental tariff, please contact Mike or Judy. Open all year. **ETC ★★★★**

ILFRACOMBE. Mrs J. Barten, Lydford Farm, Watermouth, Ilfracombe EX34 9SJ (01271 862222). Midway between Ilfracombe and Combe Martin on the A399. Three fully equipped 28' holiday caravans individually sited on working farm with one of the most spectacular views of the Bristol Channel. Clean and comfortable, sleep four to six, colour TV, microwaves, modern kitchen and shower room, parking by vans, picnic tables. 10 minutes' walk to Harbour beach, Watermouth Castle and the South West Coastal Footpath. Regular boat trips run from Ilfracombe to Lundy Island. Regret no pets. S.A.E please.
e-mail: info@littlemeadow.co.uk
website: www.littlemeadow.co.uk

See also Colour Display Advertisement

ILFRACOMBE. Mrs E. Sansom, Widmouth Farm, Watermouth, Near Ilfracombe EX34 9RX (01271 863743; Fax: 01271 866479). Widmouth Farm has 35 acres of gardens, woodland, pastures and a private beach on National Heritage Coastline. There are 10 one, two and three bedroom cottages, some early Victorian, some conversions from farm buildings. All are comfortable and well equipped. We have sheep, goats, chickens, ducks, rabbits, guinea pigs and much wildlife (seals sometimes play off our coast). The surroundings are tranquil, the views superb and access easy (on the A399 between Ilfracombe and Combe Martin). Ideal for walking (the coastal footpath runs around the property), bird watching, painting and sea fishing. Ilfracombe Golf Club in walking distance. Pets welcome.
e-mail: sansom@intonet.co.uk

ILFRACOMBE near. Mrs M. Cowell, Lower Campscott Farm, Lee, Near Ilfracombe EX34 8LS (01271 863479). Four excellent holiday cottages on a farm with a delightful one mile walk down to the beach at Lee Bay. The cottages have been converted from the original farm buildings to a high standard. Two of the cottages will accommodate four people, one will accommodate up to six people and the large one will take eight/ten people; laundry room; linen included in the price. We also have a large, self-contained six-berth caravan to let, with Bed and Breakfast in the farmhouse. Children welcome but regret no pets. Terms from £140 to £560 weekly. Spring Mini Breaks (three nights) from £80.

INSTOW. Beach Haven Cottage. Sleeps 5. Seafront cottage overlooking the sandy beach. Instow is a quiet yachting village with soft yellow sands and a pretty promenade of shops, old houses, pubs and cafes serving drinks and meals. Beach Haven has extensive beach and sea views from the house and garden, own parking, gas fired central heating, colour TV, washing machine. Lawned garden overlooking sea with terrace and garden furniture. Coastal walks and cycle trails, boat to Lundy Island. Dog welcome. Please send SAE for colour brochure of this and other cottages to **F. I. Barnes, 140 Bay View Road, Northam, Bideford EX39 1BJ (01237 473801).**
Photo shows view from balcony of beach and sea.

KINGSBRIDGE. Allan and Marcia Green, Gara Mill, Slapton, Kingsbridge TQ7 2RE (01803 770295).

Sleeps 1-7. Set in an idyllic wooded valley, we offer two cosy flats in the 16th century mill plus seven cedar lodges along the River Gara. All are well-equipped, including microwave and colour TV. Four acre site off quiet lane, sheltered and peaceful, yet convenient for Dartmouth, Kingsbridge, Totnes. Swings, outdoor badminton court, games room, launderette. Cots available. Dogs welcome. Woodland walk on your doorstep. Two miles to beaches and spectacular coastline. From £160-£380 per week. Please ring for brochure.

KINGSBRIDGE. Sue and John Bradney, Old Cotmore Farm, Stokenham Kingsbridge TQ7 2LR (01548

580240). Sleeps 2/8. Three luxury 16th century cottages set in our grounds of nine acres in the countryside by the sea with views over farms and fields between Dartmouth and Salcombe. All very comfortably furnished and restored to a high standard. Beams, log stoves, central heating, en suite bathrooms, colour TV, microwave, fridge/freezer, washing machine, dishwasher, jacuzzi, cots and highchairs, barbecue. Beds ,made up for arrival and bathroom towels provided. Feed the ducks on the pond, pony rides, games barn, children's play area and small shop. Ring/write brochure.

See also Colour Display Advertisement

KINGSBRIDGE. Devon Connection, 87A Fore Street, Kingsbridge TQ7 1AB (01548 852572; Fax: 01548 854036). The glorious South Hams in southernmost Devon - an Area of Outstanding Natural Beauty. From sandy beaches to villages nestling in rolling hills to wooded river estuaries and the contrasting dramatic features of Dartmoor. Choose from our barns, cottages or farmhouses for your holiday retreat. Just call us for a brochure or visit our website. We will be happy to discuss your needs – walking, golf, sailing, wildlife, adventure parks and leisure centres – there is something for everyone – or just switch off and let the world go by.
website: www.devonconnection.co.uk

KINGSBRIDGE. Mr and Mrs M.B. Turner, Cross Farm, East Allington, Kingsbridge TQ9 7RW (01548

521327). Working farm, join in. Sleeps 11 plus cot. Get away from the hustle and bustle of everyday life and enjoy the peace and tranquillity of Cross Farm, surrounded by South Hams countryside of outstanding natural beauty. Children love to help feed the animals while you take a leisurely farm walk or relax in the garden. Lovely 17th century part farmhouse and delightfully converted barn; both sleep 11 in four bedrooms; equipped to very high standard including colour TV, dishwasher, microwave, washing machine, dryer, fridge freezer, showers, duvets and linen. Cleanliness guaranteed. Play area and recreation barn. Heating included for early/late holidays. Only four miles to Kingsbridge (one mile to village pub!) and close to many lovely coves and beaches. Central for Dartmoor, Salcombe, Dartmouth, Torbay; riding, fishing, golf, etc. Ideal touring area. Rough shooting on farm in season. Brochure available.

KINGSBRIDGE near. Mrs J. Tucker, Mount Folly Farm, Bigbury-on-Sea, Near Kingsbridge TQ7 4AR (01548 810267). **Working farm. Sleeps 6.** A delightful family farm, situated on the coast, overlooking the sea and sandy beaches of Bigbury Bay. Farm adjoins golf course and River Avon. Lovely coastal walks. Ideal centre for South Hams and Dartmoor. The spacious wing comprises half of the farmhouse, and is completely self-contained. All rooms attractively furnished. Large, comfortable lounge with bay windows overlooking the sea; colour TV. There are three bedrooms – one family, one double and a bunk bed; two have washbasins. The kitchen/diner has a fridge/freezer, electric cooker, microwave, washing machine and dishwasher. There is a nice garden, ideal for children. Cot and babysitting available. Sorry no smoking. Reduction for two people staying in off peak weeks. Please write or telephone for a brochure.

MORETONHAMPSTEAD. Sue Horn, Narramore Farm Cottages, Narramore Farm, Moretonhampstead TQ13 8QT (01647 440455; Fax: 01647 440031). **Sleeps 2-6.** Stressed out? Let Narramore work its magic on you! Six comfortable cottages situated on 107-acre horse stud/deer farm. A really warm pool, bubbling hot spa, satellite TV, games/laundry room, payphone, play area, fishing lake, boat, barbecue, small animals plus the opportunity to badgerwatch amidst glorious countryside - all these make us special. Colou brochure. Open all year. Terms from £85 to £525. **ETC ★★★★.**
e-mail: narramore@btinternet.com
website: www.narramorefarm.co.uk

OKEHAMPTON. East Hook Cottages, Okehampton. Sleep 2/6. In the heart of Devon on the fringe of the Dartmoor National Park, with woodland surroundings, two traditional country cottages. One mile north of the A30 at Okehampton, quiet and peaceful, 50 yards in from a country road on the Tarka Trail and Millennium cycle route (Devon Coast to Coast). The accommodation comprises of a pleasant sittingroom with log fire and TV, kitchen, bathroom and three bedrooms. Children and pets welcome. Terms from £100 to £200 per week. Open all year. Short breaks and weekends possible. The most central point for leisure in Devon. **Mrs M.E. Stevens, West Hook Farm, Okehampton EX20 1RL (01837 52305).**

SEATON. Mrs Elsie Pady, Higher Cownhayne Farm, Cownhayne Lane, Colyton, Near Seaton EX24 6HD (01297 552267). **Working farm. Properties sleep 4/8.** Higher Cownhayne is a family working farm. Accommodation consists of three self-catering farmhouse holiday apartments which are open all year round. Each apartment has all modern conveniences, with its own dining room, kitchen, bathroom and WC (no linen is provided). Tourist caravan and camping site across lane - four berth fully equipped caravan available. Animals on farm. Babysitting can be arranged. Fishing Holidays available – trout fly fishing on the River Coly on farm. Leisure facilities available to visitors one-and-a-half miles from the farm include badminton, squash, gymnasium, sauna, solarium, swimming pool and licensed restaurant . Air strip on farm for small plane enthusiasts. No pets. Terms on application, at a price families can afford to pay. Open all year.

Lower Knapp Farm

- Children's play area
- Indoor heated pool
- Sauna & Solarium
- Family run
- Open all year
- All linen provided
- Pets welcome
- Superb walking country
- ETC ★★★★

Set in 16 acres of the delightful East Devon countryside, only 5 miles from the coast, Lower Knapp Farm's 12 beautifully converted cottages (ranging from 1 to 4 bedrooms), offer an ideal location for family holidays and relaxing breaks.

LOWER KNAPP FARM, SIDBURY, SIDMOUTH, EAST DEVON EX10 0QN
Luxury self-catering country cottages
Visit our website at *www.knappfarm-holidays.co.uk*
or call Freephone **0800 915 7847** for colour brochure and tariff.
e-mail: lowknapp@aol.com • fax: 01404 871597

SIDMOUTH. Mrs B.I. Tucker, Goosemoor Farm Cottage, Newton Poppleford, Sidmouth EX10 0BL (01395 568279). Sleeps 5. Set on 25-acre mixed farm on Exeter to Lyme Regis bus route, about four miles from Sidmouth and the sea, with streams running through its meadows. Many delightful walks; carp fishing in nearby lake. Accommodation is in two bedrooms (each with washbasin), kitchen, lounge plus diner, bathroom/toilet, plus shower. Linen provided. Off road parking. Bed and breakfast available in adjoining farmhouse from £16.

SOUTH DEVON. Lower Coombe Farm and Studio. Working farm. Cottage sleeps 5. Twixt moor and sea. Cottage, split level, courtyard with small garden. TV, central heating, wood burner, microwave. From £120 to £185 per week. Mobile Home (only two on site) sleeping two adults and two children, toilet, shower, TV, small garden. From £85 to £110 per week. Working farm (sheep and horses) in secluded valley one mile from Bovey Tracey. Professional artist gives personal tuition £50 per week. Riding instruction available. Dogs by arrangement £10 per week. Quiet and peaceful. Details **Mrs S.D. Ansell, Lower Combe Farm, Lower Coombe, Bovey Tracey TQ13 9PH (Tel & Fax: 01626 832914).**

SOUTH MOLTON. Mike and Rose Courtney, West Millbrook, Twitchen, South Molton EX36 3LP

(01598 740382). Properties sleep 2/8. Adjoining Exmoor. Two fully-equipped bungalows and one farmhouse annexe in lovely surroundings bordering Exmoor National Park. Ideal for touring North Devon and West Somerset including moor and coast with beautiful walks, lovely scenery and many other attractions. North Molton village is only one mile away. All units have electric cooker, fridge/freezer, microwave and colour TV; two bungalows also have washing machine. Children's play area; cots and high chairs available free. Linen hire available. Games room. Car parking. Central heating if required. Electricity metered. Out of season short breaks. Weekly prices from £70 to £340. Colour brochure available. **ETC** ΤΪΪ up to *COMMENDED*. website: www.north-molton.co.uk

SOUTH MOLTON. Mrs Sue Hancocks, North Lee Holiday Cottages, North Lee Farm, South Molton, N. Devon EX36 3EH (Tel: 01598 740248/740675; Fax: 01598 740248). Situated on the southern edge of Exmoor on

a full working dairy farm standing in 320 acres with stunning views of Exmoor. Come and stay in one of our five tastefully decorated barn conversions set in a courtyard - sleeps two/eight. Take a ride over the moors or discover some of North Devon's scenic coastline. Hire a bicycle and head for the picturesque Tarka Trail. Short Breaks available. Pets welcome by arrangement. **ETC** ★★★★ *SELF CATERING* website: www.northleeholidaycottages.co.uk

SOUTH MOLTON. Ruth Ley, Drewstone Farm, South Molton EX36 3EF (Tel & Fax: 01769 572337).

Our 300 acre family run farm is set in the foothills of Exmoor surrounded by a wooded valley with breathtaking views and full of wildlife. We offer a superb farmhouse cottage and detached barn conversion with beams, three bedrooms, oak fitted kitchen, electric cooker, autowasher, dryer, freezer, microwave, TV and video. Each sleeps six. Heating throughout and log fires and woodburner. Furnished and equipped to the highest standards with real country cottage charm. Guests may wander amongst the farm animals, enjoy country walks, small games room, clay shooting, own trout fishing or just relax in the garden. South Molton two miles, beaches 25 minutes' drive. Children welcome. Dogs by arrangement. From £170 to £430. **ETC** ★★★.

SOUTH MOLTON near. Court Green, Bishop's Nympton, Near South Molton. Sleeps 5. A most attractive

well-equipped, south facing cottage with large garden, on edge of the village of Bishop's Nympton, three miles from South Molton. Ideal holiday centre, within easy reach of Exmoor, the coast, sporting activities and places of interest. Three bedrooms, one double, one twin-bedded with washbasin and one single. Two bathrooms with toilet. Sitting and diningrooms, large kitchen. Central heating, wood-burning stove, TV. One mile sea trout/trout fishing on River Mole. Well behaved pets welcome. Terms April to October £180 to £220. **Mrs J. Greenwell, Tregeiriog, Near Llangollen, North Wales LL20 7HU (01691 600672).**

Flear Farm Cottages

Discover nine superb cottages set in 75 acres of a beautiful South Devon valley - just five miles from the sea. As well as peace and quiet, we offer a 40ft indoor heated swimming pool, sauna, all weather tennis court, large indoor and outdoor play areas. Non-smokers only. Children and dogs welcome. Log fires and full central heating, perfect for off-season breaks. ETC ★★★★ to ★★★★★.

East Allington, Totnes, South Devon TQ9 7RF
Website: www.flearfarm.co.uk
See also colour advertisement.

'Phone (01548) 521227 or Fax (01548) 521600 For our Colour Brochure

See also Colour Display Advertisement

TORQUAY. June and Roy Lewis, Parkfield Luxury Apartments. June and Roy Lewis would like to welcome you to Parkfield Luxury Apartments which are available for 12 months of the year including short winter breaks from 1st October to 1st April. Our one, two and three bedroom accommodation comes fully appointed, each with TV and video and its own patio, most have panoramic views over rolling Devonshire countryside. Parkfield is set in an acre of landscaped grounds; children and dogs are most welcome. Parkfield offers children's play area, ample parking and kennels too. This tranquil setting nestles at the gateway to the 'English Riviera' so we're just a short drive from beaches, coastal walks, traditional pubs, steam railways and other family attractions aplenty. For more information please phone/fax or write To: **Roy and June at Parkfield Luxury Apartments, Claddon Lane, Maidencombe, Torquay TQ1 4TB (01803 328952).**

WELLINGTON. Mr and Mrs L. J. Tristram, West End, Holcombe Rogus, Wellington, Somerset TA21 0QD (01823 672384). Working farm, join in. Sleeps six. This 16th century olde worlde farm cottage in Devon has an inglenook fireplace and bread oven. It is approached by a private tarmac road and surrounded by a large garden. Situated on 180-acre family farm, over which guests are free to wander. Half-a-mile from the small village of Holcombe Rogus which has general store with Post Office, garage, public house, church. Within easy reach of Exmoor, Taunton, Exeter and the coast. Excellent walks in unspoilt countryside; extensive views. Six people accommodated in three double rooms, cot; bathroom, toilet; sitting/diningroom. Kitchen with electric cooker, fridge, microwave, washing machine, kettle, iron, etc.; glass conservatory at front of house. Linen by arrangement. Pets allowed. Car an advantage, ample parking.

Open all year. TV provided. SAE, please, for terms. Charges are from £120 per week.

See also Colour Display Advertisement

WESTWARD HO! West Pusehill Farm, Westward Ho! EX39 5AH (01237 475638). Nestling within the Kenwith Valley, our cottages are set along the beautiful North Devon coast. 11 cottages converted from farm buildings built from traditional local stone in 1854. 40ft heated outdoor pool set amongst secluded sheltered lawns. Perfectly situated to explore coast and countryside. Pets and children welcome in all areas. Resident Proprietors John and Gill have welcomed visitors for 20 years and will ensure everyone enjoys their stay. Pig on the Hill Country Inn is on site and is open seven days a week. Bar menu available lunch/evenings, excellent pint; some brewed on the premises. Skittles alley and games room; petanque boule pitch. Outdoor children's play area.
website: www.wpfcottages.co.uk

WOOLACOMBE. Mrs B.A. Watts, Resthaven Holiday Flats, The Esplanade, Woolacombe EX34 7DJ (01271 870248). Situated on the sea front opposite the beautiful Combesgate Beach, with uninterrupted views of the coastline. Two self-contained flats – ground floor sleeps five, first floor sleeps nine. Family, double and single bedrooms, all with washbasins. Comfortable lounges with sea views, colour TV and videos. Fully equipped electric kitchens. Bathrooms have bath and shower. Electricity by £1 meter. Payphone. Free lighting, parking, hot water and laundry facility. Terms from £140 to £650 per week. Please write, or phone, for brochure.

DORSET

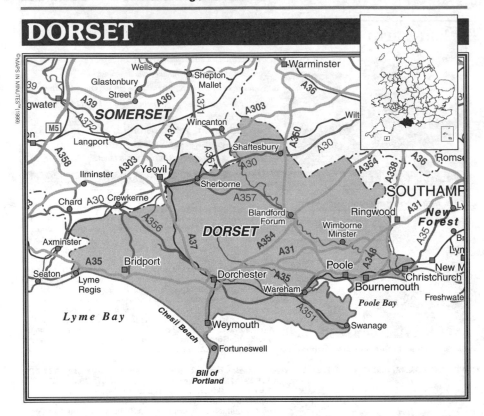

ABBOTSBURY. Mrs Mary Pengelly, Gorwell Farm, Abbotsbury, Weymouth DT3 4JX (01305 871401; Fax: 01305 871441). Sleep 2/8. You can relax, unwind and enjoy peaceful surroundings at Gorwell, a family farm situated in its own secret wooded valley. We are only one-and-a-half miles north of the historical thatched village of Abbotsbury, famous for its Swannery, Subtropical Gardens and World Heritage coastline. Central for Weymouth, Dorchester and Bridport. Very well equipped cottages are comfortable for any time of the year, with open fireplaces, central heating and double glazing. Spindle Cottage has wheelchair access and is suitable for the disabled. Enjoy Gorwell's abundance of wildlife, birdlife and flora, explore the pretty villages or wonderful footpath network, or actively enjoy watersports and golf locally. Something for all in this Area of Outstanding Natural Beauty. **ETC up to ★★★★★.**
e-mail: mary@gorwellfarm.co.uk
website: gorwellfarm.co.uk

ABBOTSBURY near. Character Farm Cottages, Langton Herring, Near Abbotsbury. Sleep 2-8. Working

farm. Four character farm cottages situated in the villages of Langton Herring and Rodden, nestling on the coastline between picturesque Abbotsbury and Weymouth. This unique part of Dorset's Heritage Coast is ideal for walking, touring, bird-watching and fishing with the added attractions of Abbotsbury's world famous Swannery, The Fleet and Weymouth's safe sandy beaches. The four cottages are all comfortably furnished with features such as open fires, beams, inglenooks, walled gardens and ample parking. Pets and children welcome. Logs and linen available. Prices from £140. **ETC ♀♀♀♀ HIGHLY COMMENDED.** Enquiries: **Mrs J. Elwood, Lower Farmhouse, Langton Herring, Weymouth DT3 4JB (01305 871187; Fax: 01305 871347).**
e-mail: jane@mayo.fsbusiness.co.uk

BEXINGTON. Mrs Josephine Pearse, Tamarisk Farm, West Bexington, Dorchester DT2 9DF (01308 897784). Sleeps 4/6. On slope overlooking Chesil Beach between Abbotsbury and Burton Bradstock. Three large (one suitable for Disabled Category 1) and two smaller cottages and two secluded chalets (ETC Graded) properties sleep fours/six. Terms from £105 to £495. Each one stands in own garden. Glorious views along West Dorset and Devon coasts. Lovely walks by sea and inland. Mixed organic farm with arable, sheep, cattle, horses and market garden – vegetables available. Sea fishing, riding in Abbotsbury, lots of tourist attractions and good markets in Bridport (six miles), Dorchester, Weymouth and Portland, all 13 miles. Good centre for touring Thomas Hardy's Wessex. Safe for children, and pets can be quite free. **ETC ★★★/★★★★.**

BLANDFORD. Mrs M. J. Waldie, The Old Rectory, Lower Blandford St. Mary, Near Blandford Forum DT11 9ND (01258 453220). Sleeps 6. Completely self-contained wing of Georgian Old Rectory, one mile from the market town of Blandford Forum, within easy reach of the south coast, Poole, Bournemouth, Salisbury and Thomas Hardy country around Dorchester. Local fishing and many places of historical interest. Accommodation for six in three rooms, one double bedded, one twin bedded and smaller room with bunk beds, cot. Large well equipped kitchen, spacious sitting/diningroom with colour TV; cloakroom downstairs; bathroom and separate toilet upstairs. Pets allowed by prior arrangement. Children welcome. Parking spaces. Use of secluded garden. Everything provided except bed linen and towels. Terms from £175 to £230 per week. May to September. SAE, please, for further details.

BLANDFORD. Orchard Cottage, Deverel Farm, Milborne St Andrew, Blandford. In the midst of Hardy

Country, one mile from Milborne St. Andrew and just two miles from the picturesque village of Milton Abbas, the cottage is within easy reach of the coast. Situated at the edge of the farmyard, 150 yards from the A354, this modern three bedroom semi-detached cottage has a large, well fenced garden and views of rolling countryside. Children welcome. Open all year. Weekly terms from £150 to £400. **ETC** ♛♛♛ *COMMENDED.* Contact: **Charlotte Martin, Deverel Farm, Milborne St. Andrew, Blandford DT11 0HX (01258 837195; Fax: 01258 837227)**

BLANDFORD near. The Lodge and the Stable. Recently converted from an old cart shed, the accommodation

has oak beams, natural stone, and wood cladding on the front. Fully fitted kitchen; carpeted throughout. Electric night storage heating, cosy in winter. The Lodge has large doorways and has been designed for easy access by the disabled. Cots and high chairs supplied; linen available. Open all year round and personally supervised to a high standard. Coarse fishing nearby, many pleasant woodland walks in the area. Ideal for touring and day trips to the coast. Also available on farm Jasmine Cottage, sleeps six, and Plumtree Cottage, sleeps four. Terms from £130 to £460. Excellent value low season. **ETC** ★★★ Contact: **Mrs Penny Cooper, Dairy House Farm, Woolland, Blandford Forum DT11 0EY (01258 817501; Fax: 01258 818060).** e-mail: penny.cooper@farming.co.uk website: http://members.farmline.com/penny_cooper

BOURNEMOUTH & DORSET. Bournemouth and Dorset Holiday Homes, Henbury View, Dullar Lane, Sturminster Marshall, Wimbourne BH21 4AD. For more than 35 years Bournemouth's oldest self catering holiday accommodation agency has provided a booking service for a broad selection of high quality houses, bungalows, cottages, flats and caravans in the Bournemouth, Poole, Dorset, Christchurch, Mudeford and New Forest areas. Some properties are near or beside the sea, others enjoy the setting of the beautiful Dorset or Hampshire countryside. All have colour TV, are fully equipped and are personally inspected for quality. Almost all units welcome children and have off-road parking, some allow pets. Prices vary widely. FOR FREE COLOUR BROCHURE AND MORE INFORMATION PLEASE TELEPHONE **01258 858580.**

BRIDPORT. Flax Cottage. Sleeps 6/8 plus cot. Bridport is an historic, small market town lying in the beautiful

rolling countryside of West Dorset, one-and-a-half miles from the coast. Flax Cottage is a charming, recently refurbished terrace cottage situated in a quiet, but central, location in Bridport. Restaurants, inns and shops are a short walk from the cottage. The cottage is well-equipped with colour TV, music centre, automatic washing machine, fridge/freezer and central heating. Prices from £250 per week. Children and pets welcome. For a brochure please phone or write to: **Mrs Margaret Barrett, 49 Newtown, Beaminster, Dorset DT8 3ER (01308 863565)**

BRIDPORT (Near). Mrs S. Norman, Frogmore Farm, Chideock, Bridport DT6 6HT (01308 456159).

Working farm. Sleeps 6. Delightful farm cottage on ninety acre grazing farm set in the rolling hills of West Dorset. Superb views over Lyme Bay, ideal base for touring Dorset and Devon or rambling the many coastal and country footpaths of the area. This fully equipped self-catering cottage sleeps six. Three bedrooms. Bed linen supplied. Cosy lounge with woodburner and colour TV, French doors to a splendid columned sun verandah. Children and well behaved dogs welcome. Car essential. Open all year. Short breaks available, also Bed and Breakfast in the 17th century farmhouse. Brochure and terms free on request.

MANOR FARM HOLIDAY CENTRE
Charmouth, Bridport, Dorset DT6 6QL
Situated in a rural valley, ten minutes' level walk from the beach.

★★★
HOLIDAY PARK

1983 Built Two-Bedroom Houses: *Sleep 4-6 *Lounge with colour TV *Fully fitted kitchen/diner *Fitted carpets *Double glazing *Central heating *Parking space.

Three-Bedroom House and Bungalow: *Sleep 4-6 each *Lounge with colour TV *Central heating available *Parking within grounds *Enclosed garden.

Luxury Six-Berth Caravans: *One or two bedrooms *Toilet *Shower *Refrigerator *Full cooker *Television *Gas fire.

FULL CENTRE FACILITIES AVAILABLE INCLUDING SWIMMING POOL, SHOP, BAR (BAR FOOD AVAILABLE), LAUNDERETTE ETC.

Send SAE for colour brochure to Mr R. E. Loosmore or Tel: 01297 560226
website: www.manorfarmholidaycentre.co.uk   See also Colour Display Advertisement in this Guide.

LANCOMBES HOUSE HOLIDAY COTTAGES

Carol & Karl Mansfield
West Milton
Bridport. DT6 3TN

Tel: 01308 485375

★★★
SELF CATERING

Lancombes House is a 200-year-old stone barn built 300 feet above sea level set in 10 acres; there are tame animals for children to play and help with including horses, ponies, goats and ducks. Farm has panoramic views to the sea only four miles away. There are four superbly converted cottages, each with its own sitting-out area, barbecue and garden furniture. They have spacious open plan living areas, most with wood burning stoves. Modern fitted kitchens, double and twin-bedded rooms. Electric central heating, shared laundry. Deep in the heart of Hardy country, this is a delightful area to explore whether on foot or horseback. There are many things to do and pets and children are very welcome. Prices start at £140 for mini-breaks; open all the year round.

See also colour advertisement

BRIDPORT near. Court Farm Cottages, Askerswell, Dorchester DT2 9EJ (01308 485668). A Grade II Listed barn has been converted into delightful holiday cottages, fully equipped with all modern conveniences to make your holiday as relaxing as possible. Wheatsheaf and Haywain sleep four and feature king-sized four-poster beds. Threshers has three bedrooms and sleeps five. South Barn has four bedrooms and two bathrooms and sleeps seven. A games room and large garden are provided for guests. Askerswell is an idyllic village in an Area of Outstanding Natural Beauty just four miles from the coast. Perfect for walking and touring holidays. Open all year. Low season short breaks available. From £195 to £650 per week. **ETC ★★★★/★★★★★.**
e-mail: courtfarmcottages@eclipse.co.uk
website: www.eclipse.co.uk/CourtFarmCottages/WEBPG2.

See also Colour Display Advertisement

DORCHESTER. Greenwood Grange Farm Cottages, Higher Bockhampton, Dorchester DT2 8QH (Tel & Fax: 01305 268874). Set in glorious rolling countryside Greenwood Grange Cottages, converted from barns built by Thomas Hardy's father in 1849. Superb leisure facilities: magnificent Roman-style indoor swimming pool, sauna, separate purpose-built fitness/games building with solarium, table tennis, table football, pool table and bar billiards, indoor and outdoor play area with swings for infants. Grounds for strolling and relaxing, two all weather tennis courts, lawns for croquet and badminton. Cottages accommodating between two and seven people. Family cottages sleeping two-six plus two luxury houses and a single storey cottage suitable for disabled. Country setting, two miles Dorchester, six miles coast.
e-mail: enquiries@greenwoodgrange.co.uk
website: www.greenwoodgrange.co.uk

DORCHESTER near. Pitt Cottage, Ringstead Bay, Near Dorchester. Sleeps 6. An attractive thatched stone

cottage, surrounded by farmland and situated on the edge of a small wood about a quarter mile from the sea, commanding outstanding views of Ringstead Bay on the Dorset Heritage Coast. The cottage is equipped to sleep six; three bedrooms (two beds in each), two bathrooms, sitting room with open fire and large kitchen/dining area. Cot/high chair; washing machine; TV; night storage heaters/electric radiators in all rooms. Car essential. Available from £150 per week. For details please send SAE (reference FHG) to: **Mrs S.H. Russell, 49 Limerston Street, London SW10 0BL or telephone 0207 351 9919.**

PITT COTTAGE

HOLDITCH. Old Forge Cottage, Holditch, Chard. Sleeps 4. Ideal for peace and seclusion in glorious

unspoilt countryside within easy reach of the sea. This delightful old world cottage with oak beams stands just outside Holditch on the Devon/Dorset/Somerset borders, affording splendid views over beautiful countryside. Charmouth and its sandy beaches seven miles distant. Lyme Regis, with safe bathing and recreational facilities eight miles. The cottage is completely modernised and tastefully furnished with fitted carpets throughout. For up to four people. One twin-bedded room and two single rooms; sittingroom with colour TV; kitchen with dining area; modern bathroom; second toilet; electric cooker, fridge, vacuum cleaner, modern sink unit, immersion heater, night storage heaters throughout (included in terms). Everything supplied except linen. Electricity charged by meter reading. Phone; walled garden; garage. Chard four-and-a-half miles. Terms £130 to £200 weekly. Open all year. Regret no children under 10 years. No pets. All enquiries to **Mrs P. A. Spice, Orchard Cottage, Duke Street, Micheldever, Near Winchester, Hants SO21 3DF (01962 774563).**

See also Colour Display Advertisement

LYME REGIS. Mr Stenson, Lyme Bay Holidays (FHG), 44 Church Street, Lyme Regis DT7 3DA (01297 443363; Fax: 01297 445576). Country and coastal cottages in and around Lyme Regis, Charmouth and West Dorset. Over 100 properties, all Tourist Board inspected. Phone for our free catalogue or help in selecting the right property for you. Terms on request. **ETC** ♦♦♦/♦♦♦♦♦.

website: www.lymebayholidays.co.uk.

LYME REGIS near. Mrs Debby Snook, Westover Farm Cottages, Wootton Fitzpaine, Bridport DT6 6NE

(01297 560451). Working farm. Sleeps 6/7. Immerse yourself in rural tranquillity. Set in an area of outstanding natural beauty, Wootton Fitzpaine nestles amidst rolling Dorset farmland. Within walking distance of the beaches and shops of Charmouth, world famous for its fossils, and three miles from the renowned Cobb at Lyme Regis. Golf, water sports and riding close by. We have two spacious, comfortable, well-furnished three-bedroomed cottages with open fires, inglenooks, heating and all amenities. Also large secluded, secure gardens with furniture, barbecues, parking. Open all year. Pets and children welcome. Logs and linen available. Guests are welcome to walk our dairy farm. Terms from £175 to £520 per week, winter breaks available. **ETC** ♦♦♦♦ COMMENDED.

e-mail: wfcottages@aol.com

Please mention *The Farm Holiday Guide* when making enquiries about accommodation featured in these pages.

PIDDLEHINTON. Mrs Pole-Carew, Higher Waterston Farm, Piddlehinton DT2 7SW (01305 848208).

When you come to Higher Waterston you will relax, unwind and enjoy the beauty of the Piddle Valley, one of Dorset's best kept secrets. The pretty villages and thatched pubs, grazing sheep, horses and their foals, hovering buzzards are all around us. We are only four miles from the historic county town of Dorchester and nine miles from the sea. The exceptionally well equipped, comfortable cottages are open all year round. Exposed beams and log fires, videos and dishwashers are in each of the four cottages. Arranged around a central grass courtyard with a large games barn, Higher Waterston Farm also caters for the energetic with its hard tennis court, badminton, table tennis and basketball. **ETC ÏÏÏÏÏ** *COMMENDED.*

SHERBORNE. Mrs J. Warr, Trill Cottages, Trill House, Thornford, Sherborne DT9 6HF (01935 872305).

Two cottages situated in the Blackmore Vale only five miles from both Sherborne and Yeovil, and one mile from the villages of Yetminster and Thornford. Ideally placed for exploring the wonderful counties of Dorset and Somerset, where there is so much to see and do. The cottages are comfortably furnished, accommodation in each comprising of three bedrooms (one double bed and four singles), lounge with colur TV and an open fire, diningroom, well equipped kitchen with fridge and microwave, bathroom and toilet. A cot and high chair are available on request. Electricity by £1 slot meter. Storage heating. Quiet, peaceful and safe for children. We regret that we do not allow pets. **ETC ÏÏÏ** *COMMENDED.*
e-mail: trill.cottages@ic24.net

SHERBORNE. White Horse Farm, Middlemarsh, Sherborne DT9 5QN (01963 210222). Toad Hall sleeps 4; Badger's sleeps 2; Ratty's sleeps 2/4, Moley's sleeps 2. Set in beautiful Hardy countryside, we have four chalet/bungalows furnished to high standards and surrounded by three acres of paddock and garden with a duck pond. We lie between

the historic towns of Sherborne, Dorchester and Cerne Abbas. Delightful coastal attractions are some 30-40 minutes' drive away. Situated next door to an inn serving good food, we welcome children, partially disabled guests and pets. All cottages have central heating, colour TV and video recorders with unlimited free video-film rental. Electricity, bed linen, towels inclusive. Ample parking. Good value at £140 to £340 per week. Discounted two weeks or more. B&B holidays available in our attractive farmhouse. **David, Hazel, Mary and Gerry Wilding (01963 210222). ETC ★★★**
e-mail: enquiries@whitehorsefarm.co.uk
website: www.whitehorsefarm.co.uk

STURMINSTER NEWTON. Mrs Sheila Martin, Moorcourt Farm, Moorside, Marnhull, Sturminster Newton DT10 1HH (Tel & Fax: 01258 820271). Working farm. Sleeps four. Ground floor flat with own entrance and front

door key. It is part of the farmhouse, kept immaculately clean and furnished to the highest order. We are a 117 acre dairy farm in the middle of the Blackmore Vale. Guests are welcome to wander round, watch the farm activities and laze in the large garden - we have some garden loungers for your use. We are very central for touring with easy access to New Forest, Longleat Wildlife Park, Cheddar, Stonehenge and the lovely Dorset coast. Accommodation for four people in two double bedrooms, one with a double bed, the other with twin beds. Bathroom, separate toilet. Sittingroom with colour TV and door leading straight onto the back garden. Well equipped kitchen/diner, with fridge/freezer, microwave and washing machine; all utensils colour co-ordinated, matching crockery, etc. Beds made up with fresh linen on arrival. Towels, tea towels, etc provided. Electric heaters in all rooms. Electricity payable by meter, units to be read at the start and finish of your holiday. Sheila creates a friendly atmosphere here "down on the farm" and does her best to make your holiday an enjoyable one. Open April to November. Car essential. Sorry, no pets. Weekly terms from £180 to £280. SAE please.

STURMINSTER NEWTON. Mrs J. Miller, Lower Fifehead Farm, Fifehead St. Quinton, Sturminster Newton DT10 2AP (01258 817335). Come and stay with us

on our 400 acre dairy farm. Our lovely Listed 17th century farmhouse with interesting mullion windows is pictured and mentioned in Dorset Books. We have three bedrooms - one double en suite, one double and one twin, each with private bathroom, own sitting room, TV and large garden. Tea and coffee making. No evening meals but we can recommend the local places. We also have a self-contained one bedroom flat with en suite bathroom, private sitting room as well as a self-catering annexe sleeping four/five. Bed and Breakfast from £20 per person. Three-day breaks from £55 per person (B&B **ETC** ◆◆◆). Right in the heart of the Blackmore Vale and "Hardy" country; lovely walks, fishing and riding can be arranged.

See also Colour Display Advertisement

WAREHAM. Lulworth Country Cottages. Five family owned properties on historic 1200 acre estate. Coastguard Cottage, 400 yards from Lulworth Cove, sleeps seven; Home Farm, sleeps seven; St. Mary's sleeps 10, 48 East Lodge sleeps four and 49 East Lodge sleeps three. All cottages are well equipped with washing machines, tumble dryers, fridge/freezers, microwaves, dishwashers and colour TV. Central heating, duvets with linen, and electricity all inclusive. Secure gardens and parking. Situated in an area of exceptional natural beauty. Open throughout the year. Short breaks by arrangement. For brochure contact: **Mrs E.S. Weld, Lulworth Castle House, Wareham BH20 5QS (Tel & Fax: 01929 400100).**

WAREHAM (Near). Mrs M. J. M. Constantinides, "Woodlands", Hyde, Near Wareham BH20 7NT (01929 471239). Secluded house, formerly Dower House of Hyde Estate, stands alone on a meadow of the River Piddle in four-and-a-half acres in the midst of "Hardy Country". The Maisonette comprises upstairs lounge with colour TV; one bedroom (two single beds); downstairs large kitchen/diner, small entrance hall, bathroom; electric cooker (in addition to Aga cooker), refrigerator. Independent side entrance. Extra bedroom (two single beds) on request at £30 per week. Visitors are welcome to use house grounds; children can fish or play in the boundary stream. Pleasant walks in woods and heath nearby. Golf course half-a-mile, pony trekking/riding nearby. All linen included, beds ready made and basic shopping arranged on arrival day. Aga will be lit and maintained on request. Ideal for a quiet holiday far from the madding crowd. Cot and high chair available and children welcome to bring their pets. SAE, please, for terms and further particulars.

FREE or REDUCED RATE entry to Holiday Visits and Attractions — see our READERS' OFFER VOUCHERS on pages 43-60

DURHAM

CONSETT. The Cottage and Dairy Cottage. Two adjoining self-contained units each comprising one double and one twin bedroom, kitchen, bathroom and comfortable living area. Colour TV, private garden and patio furniture, heating and linen are all included in the price. We are a working sheep farm just north of the village of Castleside on the A68 heading towards Corbridge and offer easy access to the Roman Wall, Durham City, the Metro Centre, Beamish Museum and lots more. Pass the Fleece Inn Pub on the north side of the village, take a left turn after a short distance, left again down a very steep hill, the road is signposted 'Derwent Grange', follow this and we are the farm on the right. Terms from £150 to £175 Low Season, £175 to £200 High Season. Please contact for further information: **Kay Elliot, Derwent Grange Farm, Castleside, Consett DH8 9BN (01207 508358).**
e-mail: ekelliot@aol.com

HARWOOD-IN-TEESDALE. Upper Teesdale Estate, Raby Estate Office, Middleton-in-Teesdale, Barnard Castle DL12 0QH (01833 640209; Fax: 01833 640963). HONEY POT AND FROG HALL sleeping four and six respectively, are two former farmhouses remotely situated in completely unspoilt countryside in the heart of the North Pennines area of outstanding natural beauty, with the National Nature Reserve, Cauldron Snout and High Force Waterfalls close by, a haven for walkers, naturalists and fishermen. Ideally situated for touring Durham, Cumbria, the Yorkshire Dales and Lake District. Both cottages have background heating are simply furnished yet fully equipped; fuel for open fires is included in price. Cot and high chair available. Please write for a brochure. **ETC** 🍴 *APPROVED.*

LANCHESTER. Mrs Pat Gibson, Hall Hill Farm, Lanchester, Durham DH7 0TA (Tel & Fax: 01388 730300). Two country cottages. Well equipped and comfortable. Both cottages have one double and one twin room - sleeps up to four people. Downstairs is a livingroom and large kitchen/dinningroom, upstairs two bedrooms and bathroom. Kitchen contains washing machine/tumble dryer, microwave and fridge/freezer. Linen and towels are provided. Both cottages are heated. The cottages are in an ideal location for Durham City and Beamish Museum. You will have a free pass for the week to visit our own open farm. Prices from £160 per week. Children welcome. Sorry no pets. Please write or telephone for brochure. **ETC** 🍴🍴🍴🍴 *COMMENDED.*
e-mail: hhf@freenetname.co.uk
website: www.hallhillfarm.co.uk

MIDDLETON-IN-TEESDALE. North Wythes Hill Cottage, Lunedale, Middleton-in-Teesdale. Working farm. Sleeps 6/7. Cosy secluded cottage on the Pennine Way route with large enclosed garden, situated on working hill farm with sheep, cattle and duck pond. Sleeps six to seven in three bedrooms. Open fire and beamed ceilings. All fuel and linen included in rent. An Area of Outstanding Natural Beauty. Weekly terms from £175 to £360; three-day winter breaks fully inclusive £125. Brochure on request. Please contact: **Mrs J. Dent, Laneside, Middleton-in-Teesdale DL12 0RY (01833 640573).**

MIDDLETON-IN-TEESDALE. Mrs Scott, Westfield Cottage, Laithkirk, Middleton-in-Teesdale. Barnard Castle DL12 0PN (01833 640942). Sleeps 6. Westfield Cottage is a Grade II Listed building very recently renovated and furnished to a high standard. Situated on a working farm in beautiful Teesdale which is excellent touring, cycling and walking country with the Pennine and Teesdale Ways close by. The Cumbrian border is about six miles away. Ample parking area; free fishing. About half a mile from the local village. Open all year. From £185-£380. **ETC ★★★**

GLOUCESTERSHIRE

HEREFORDSHIRE

WILTSHIRE

©MAPS IN MINUTES™ (1999)

CHELTENHAM. Mr & Mrs J. Close, Coxhorne Farm, London Road, Charlton Kings, Cheltenham, Gloucestershire GL52 6UY (01242 236599). Cosy, well-equipped. Non-smoking. Self-contained appartment with open aspects, attached to the farmhouse of a 100 acre livestock farm. Situated on the eastern outskirts of Cheltenham, on the edge of the Cotswold Escarpment. Comfortably furnished, with full central heating, payphone and plenty of parking space. Electricity and bed linen included in rental. Ideal position for visiting the lovely Regency town of Cheltenham and the mellow villages of the Cotswolds. Sorry, no pets allowed. Terms £140 to £185 per week. ETC ★★★

CIRENCESTER. Mrs Randall, Warrens Gorse Cottages, Home Farm, Warrens Gorse, Cirencester GL7 7JD (01285 831261). Sleep 3/4/5. Two-and-a-half miles from the Roman town of Cirencester, these attractive cottages, personally attended by the owners, are ideally situated for touring the Cotswolds, Lying near the farmhouse in a hamlet surrounded by fields on the 100 acre farm of cattle and sheep, the cottages, each with its own garden, are well equipped and comfortably furnished. Easy parking, golf club and water sports nearby. From £160 - £220. Open April - October. **ETC** ★★

DURSLEY. Two Springbank, 37 Hopton Road, Upper Cam, Dursley. A recently renovated Victorian mid-terraced cottage, situated in a pleasant rural location one mile from the market town of Dursley where the amenities include a swimming pool and sports centre. Ideal location for keen walkers with the Cotswold Way only a short distance away. On the ground floor, accommodation comprises a comfortable sittingroom with colour TV and electric fire. A large archway leads into a dining area with freestanding multi-fuel stove, set in a tiled alcove with oak surround. Through a half-door to the rear is a fitted kitchen with fridge/freezer, electric cooker and microwave. A conservatory with washing machine gives access to the rear of the property. Two bedrooms are situated on the first floor, one double and one twin, with a cot and high chair available on request. Terms from £126 to £207 per week. **ETC** ♙♙♙ *COMMENDED*. **Mrs F.A. Jones, Little Gables, 32 Everlands, Cam, Dursley, Gloucestershire GL11 5NL (01453 543047).**

DURSLEY near. Gerald and Norma Kent, Hill House, Crawley Hill, Uley, Dursley GL11 5BH (01453 860267). Sleeps 2. The flat is a separate part of this Cotswold stone house which stands in four-and-a-half acres and is situated on top of a hill with beautiful views of the surrounding countryside. The accommodation consists of double bedroom, kitchen with cooker, microwave, fridge, etc., lounge with TV and video, toilet and shower. Car port and garden area. We supply a comprehensive set of maps and tourist information as well as routes to the many places of interest in the area. Bed linen and towels not supplied. Electricity by meter. Open all year. Sorry, no pets. Non-smoking. Terms from £120 per week. Please telephone, or write, for brochure.

HAMPSHIRE

LYNDHURST. Penny Farthing Hotel, Romsey Road, Lyndhurst SO43 7AA (02380 284422; Fax: 02380 284488). The Penny Farthing is a cheerful small Hotel ideally situated in Lyndhurst village centre, the capital of the "New Forest". The hotel offers en suite single, double, twin and family rooms with direct dial telephones, tea/coffee tray, colour TV and clock radios. We also have some neighbouring cottages available as hotel annexe rooms or on a self-catering basis. These have been totally refitted, much with "Laura Ashley" and offer a quieter, more exclusive accommodation. The hotel has a licensed bar, private car park and bicycle store. Lyndhurst has a charming variety of shops, restaurants, pubs and bistros and the "New Forest Information Centre and Museum. **AA/RAC/ETC** ◆◆◆◆. website: www.pennyfarthinghotel.co.uk

SWAY. Mrs H.J. Beale, Hackney Park, Mount Pleasant Lane, Sway, Lymington SO41 8LS (01590 682049). Properties sleep 4/6. Situated in commanding and tranquil setting two miles from Lymington and Sway village. Delightful residence in own extensive grounds adjoining New Forest heath with superb walks, rides and drives. Apartments to sleep six (further bedrooms available). Coach House cottage to sleep five. Comfortable and modern, colour TV, bed linen and electricity included. Pets by prior arrangement. First class stables for those wishing to bring own horse and excellent riding facilities in the area. Many famous places of interest nearby. Close to Isle of Wight ferry and within six miles of sandy beaches, 15 miles Bournemouth and Southampton. Open all year.

HEREFORDSHIRE

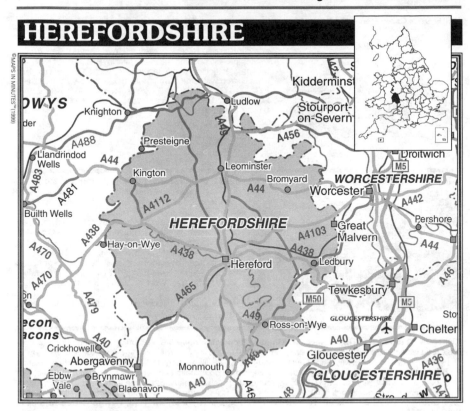

©MAPS IN MINUTES™ (1999)

FELTON. Marjorie and Brian Roby, Felton House, Felton, Herefordshire HR1 3PH (Tel & Fax: 01432 820366). The Lodge is a spotlessly clean, cosy, restful cottage in the beautiful grounds of Felton House, the former rectory, just off A417 between Hereford, Leominster and Bromyard. The Lodge has been restored to its Victorian character but with the convenience of electric heating, a modern kitchen, two shower rooms, a diningroom and a sittingroom with TV. Guests are accommodated in one double, one twin and one single bedroom and a cot is available. Linen may be hired. Children, and pets with responsible owners are most welcome. Private parking, patio and garden. Weekly terms £150 to £250 exclusive of electricity. Brochure available.
website: www.SmoothHound.co.uk/hotels/felton.html
www.herefordshirebandb.co.uk

GOODRICH. Mainoaks Farm Cottages, Goodrich, Ross-on-Wye. Six units sleeping 2,4,6 & 7. Mainoaks is a 15th century listed farm which has been converted to form six cottages of different size and individual character. It is set in 80 acres of pasture and woodland beside the River Wye in an area of outstanding natural beauty and an SSSI where there is an abundance of wildlife. All cottages have exposed beams, pine furniture, heating throughout, fully equipped kitchens with microwaves, washer/dryer etc., colour TV. Private gardens, barbecue area and ample parking. Linen and towels provided. An ideal base for touring the local area with beautiful walks, fishing, canoeing, pony trekking, golf, bird-watching or just relaxing in this beautiful tranquil spot. Open throughout the year. Short breaks available. Pets by arrangement. brochure on request. ETC ★★★

to ★★★★ *HIGHLY COMMENDED* **Mrs P. Unwin, Hill House, Chase End, Bromsberrow, Ledbury, Herefordshire HR8 1SE (Tel: 01531 650448).**

HEREFORD. Carey Dene and Rock House, Hereford. Sleeps 4/8 + cot. Working farm. Two oak-beamed

cottages on traditional farm overlooking River Wye. Beautiful area between Hereford and Ross-on-Wye, for a peaceful holiday or a short break. Access to the river, two minutes' walk to pub serving meals. Washing machine. microwave, colour TV, central heating. Electricity and linen included in charge. Open all year. Pets and children welcome. Non-smoking. Prices from £170 to £390. **ETC** ♙♙/♙♙♙♙ *COMMENDED*. Please contact: **Mrs Rita Price, Folly Farm, Holme Lacy, Hereford HR2 6LS (Tel & Fax: 01432 870259)**

HEREFORD. Mrs S. Dixon, Swayns Diggins, Harewood End, Hereford HR2 8JU (01989 730358). This

highly recommended small first floor flat is completely self-contained at one end of the main house. The bedroom, sitting room and private balcony all face south with panoramic views over farmland towards Ross and Symonds Yat. The well-equipped kitchen overlooks the garden with grand views towards Orcop Hill and the Black Mountains. Open all year, rental from £130 to £140 per week includes electricity, linen, heating, colour TV. Ideal base for exploring the beautiful Wye Valley, Herefordshire, Gloucestershire and the historic Welsh Marches. There is much to see and do in the area. Write or phone for further particulars.

KINGTON. The Harbour, Upper Hergest, Kington. Properties sleep 5/9. This bungalow is on a good second-class road facing south with beautiful views from its elevated position, across the Hergest Ridge and Offa's Dyke. The Welsh border is a mile away. Shops are two-and-a-half miles away. Kington Golf Club nearby. Accommodation for five/nine in two double rooms (one with extra single bed) downstairs and two double dormer bedrooms; two cots; bathroom, toilet; sittingroom (TV); diningroom; sun porch for relaxing; kitchen with electric cooker, fridge, food store and usual equipment. No linen. Children and pets welcome. Car essential - parking. Available all year. SAE, please, to **Mr A. J. Welson, New House Farm, Upper Hergest, Kington, Herefordshire HR5 3EW (01544 230533).**

LEOMINSTER. Mrs E. Thomas, Woonton Court Farm, Leysters, Leominster HR6 0HL (Tel & Fax: 01568

750232) Enjoy traditional hospitality and experience authentic country life at our working family farm. The Mill House Flat, a comfortably converted former cider house, provides the freedom of self catering for up to five guests. (We also offer bed and breakfast in our Tudor farmhouse). The flat's master bedroom has one large double bed and one single, with washbasin, and the second bedroom has twin beds (suitable for one adult or two children) with adjacent bathroom. The characterful sittingroom has a television and a kitchen area with all facilities. Central heating, linen and electricity included. Laundry, cot, highchair, baby sitting and groceries available. Patio garden and ample parking. We welcome you walking the farm (strong footwear advised); observe the animals; enjoy free-range eggs and local produce; and appreciate the peace and tranquillity of the local scenery. Terms from £180 to £260 per week. Brochure on request. **ETC** ♙♙♙♙ *COMMENDED*.

DOCKLOW MANOR

HOLIDAY COTTAGES IN RURAL HEREFORDSHIRE FOR 2–6 PEOPLE

Quietly secluded in ten acres of garden/ woodland, the delightfully renovated stone cottages are grouped around an attractive stone-walled pond amidst shrubs, roses and honeysuckle. The cottages are homely, cosy and spotlessly clean. Fitted carpets, well equipped kitchens, colour TV, electric blankets. Laundry facilities. Bed linen is provided and beds are made up for your arrival. Cottages for 5/6 people have two bathrooms. Wander round our rambling gardens and meet our friendly peacock and ducks. The more energetic can play croquet, lawn tennis, table tennis or take a dip in our outdoor **SWIMMING POOL**. Docklow is an ideal base for Ludlow, the Welsh border castles and market towns, Wye Valley, Brecon and Malvern Hills.

OPEN ALL YEAR INCLUDING CHRISTMAS AND NEW YEAR. SHORT BREAKS LOW SEASON.

For brochure and tourist information: Tel: 01568 760643 Fax: 01568 760565 Website: www.docklow-manor.co.uk E-mail: enquiries@docklow-manor.co.uk

Carole and Malcolm Ormerod, Docklow Manor, Leominster, Herefordshire.

PRESTEIGNE. Mrs F. Johnstone, Brick House Farm, Byton, Presteigne LD8 2HY (01544 267306; Fax: 01544 260601). "Something for everyone" on our smallholding in peaceful North Herefordshire. With three bedrooms and one-and-a-half bathrooms downstairs, our cottage sleeps six. Upstairs is a wonderful open-plan living area, with views across the gardens and valley. Extra accommodation in the farmhouse Bed and Breakfast from £17.50 per person. Children are encouraged to join in with daily animal care-they really feel like farmers and many vote it their best holiday ever. Made-up beds, fresh flowers, heating, lighting, laundry and logs included in the price. Free range eggs and seasonal produce available. Dogs welcome. £200 - £400. Couples 20% discount outside the high season. **WTB ★★★★★.**
e-mail: dmfj@johnstone.kc3.co.uk
website: www.kc3.co.uk/chamber/brickhouse/index.html

See also Colour Display Advertisement

ROSS-ON-WYE. Langstone Court Farmhouse. 14th century farmhouse. Lounge and diningroom each measure 15 x 18 feet. Farmhouse wing sleeps 18 plus cots, Cidermill flat sleeps six to eight plus cot or can be let as one unit sleeping up to 26 plus cots. Very popular for hen parties, birthdays and family get-togethers. Two ground floor bedrooms, one double, one single. Central heating, log fires, laundry, payphone, bike storage, dishwashers. Set in beautiful Herefordshire countryside. Large groups please book early. Short Breaks available all year except August. Colour brochure: **Lesley Saunders, Dales Barn, Langstone, Llangarron, Ross-on-Wye HR9 6NR (01989 770747).**

ISLE OF WIGHT

ISLE OF WIGHT. Island Cottage Holidays. Charming cottages in lovely rural surroundings and close to the sea

- situated throughout the Isle of Wight. Beautiful views, attractive gardens, delightful country walks. Dogs and horses welcome at many properties. Some cottages on farms, some with swimming pools, and some only a short walk from lovely sandy beaches. All equipped to a high standard and graded for quality by the Tourist Board. Open all year. Terms from £100 to £950 per week. Short breaks available in low season (3 nights) £85 to £179. For a brochure please contact: **Mrs Honor Vass, The Old Vicarage, Kingston, Wareham, Dorset BH20 5LH (01929 480080; Fax: 01929 481070). ETC ★★★/★★★★★**
e-mail:enq@islandcottageholidays.com
website: www.islandcottageholidays.com

TOTLAND BAY. 3 Seaview Cottages, Broadway, Totland Bay. Sleeps 5. This well-modernised cosy old coastguard cottage holds the Farm Holiday Guide Diploma for the highest standard of accommodation. It is warm and popular throughout the year. Four day winter break £39; a week in summer £242. Located close to two beaches in beautiful walking country near mainland links. It comprises lounge/dinette/ kitchenette; two bedrooms (sleeping five); bathroom/toilet. Well furnished, fully heated, TV, selection of books and other considerations. Another cottage is also available at Cowes, Isle of Wight. Non-smokers only. **ETC ⛺. Mrs C. Pitts, 11 York Avenue, New Milton, Hampshire BH25 6BT (01425 615215).**

KENT

GOUDHURST. Three Chimneys Farm Holiday Cottages, Bedgebury Road, Goudhurst TN17 2RA (Tel

& Fax: 01580 212175) Set on top of a hill at the end of a one mile track, on the edge of Bedgebury Forest, Three Chimneys is a haven of tranquillity, yet only an hour from London. The five cottages (and two B&B rooms) are individually and tastefully furnished. The cottages are well equipped and all bed linen is included. Central heating; telephone. There is a tennis court and the forest is perfect for visitors who like to walk or cycle. Goudhurst is centrally placed for visiting the castles and gardens of the South East.
e-mail: fullerthreechimneys@btinternet.com
website: www.holiday-rentals.com/index.cfm/property/2691.htm

KENT/SUSSEX BORDER. Alex Hillier, Risebridge Farm Holiday Cottages, Goudhurst, Cranbrook TN17 1HN (01580 212097). Sleep 2/8. 100 acre mixed farm. Group of seven cottages converted from an oast house and traditional farm buildings with extensive leisure facilities including indoor pool, squash, tennis, badminton and gymnasium. Children welcome. Terms: Low Season £180 to £490; High Season £385 to £785 per week. **ETC ★★★.**

Please mention **The Farm Holiday Guide** when making enquiries
about accommodation featured in these pages.

LANCASHIRE

©MAPS IN MINUTES™ (1999)

CLITHEROE. Mrs P. M. Gifford, Rakefoot Farm, Chaigley, Clitheroe BB7 3LY (01995 61332/07889 279063). Cottage sleeps seven adults and one child in three en suite bedrooms, one ground floor. Byre: sleeps four adults and two children in two en suite bedrooms all groundfloor. Freezer and dishwasher in fully fitted kitchens, woodburners in lounge. Little Barn: sleeps two adults in one en suite bedroom all ground floor. Granary: sleeps five adults in two bedrooms. Three properties internally interconnected. Babysitting, maid, meals service available. Indoor and outdoor play areas. Gardens, patios, laundry. Bed and Breakfast also available. Winner Of NWTB Silver Award For Self Catering Holiday Of The Year 2000. **ETC ★★★** to ★★★★.

LUNE VALLEY. Barbara Mason, Oxenforth Green, Tatham, Lancaster LA2 8P (015242 61784).

Working farm, join in. Sleeps 4 plus cot. Cottage and static caravan on working farm with panoramic views of Ingleborough and surrounding hills. Central for Lakes, dales and coast. Good walking, fishing and horse-riding nearby. Guests are welcome to watch the day-to-day workings of the farm. Our cottage sleeps four in one double and one twin room with lounge, fitted kitchen, ground and first floor shower rooms. The caravan sleeps four in one double and two bunkbeds, with washbasin, shower, flushing toilet, colour TV. Garden and garden chairs available. Children welcome. One dog welcome. Three-quarters-of-a-mile to nearest pub. Prices from £200 to £270 per week. Caravan from £110 per week.

SOUTHPORT. Mr W.H. Core, Sandybrook Farm, 52 Wyke Cop Road, Scarisbrick, Southport PR8

5LR (01704 880337). Welcome to our small arable farm and 18th century Barn, which has been converted into five superbly equipped holiday apartments. Many of the Barn's original features have been retained and it is furnished in traditional style but also offers all modern amenities. The Barn is situated three-and-a-half miles from the seaside town of Southport and five miles from the historic town of Ormskirk with lots of places to visit in the surrounding area. Families are welcome and cot and high chairs are available. One apartment equipped for wheelchair/disabled guests. Central heating, bed linen and towels are provided free of charge.

LINCOLNSHIRE

ALFORD near. Manor Farm Cottage, Near Alford. Comfortable cottage in rural countryside, midway between the coast and Lincolnshire Wolds. Well equipped including colour TV, washing machine, microwave and freezer. Rose garden including picnic table. Suitable area for pets to exercise. Pets and children welcome. Ample parking space. For futher details please contact: **Mrs E.M. Farrow, Manor Farm, Strubby, Alford LN13 0LW (01507 450228). ETC** *APPROVED*.

See also Colour Display Advertisement

ALFORD near. Mrs Stubbs, Woodthorpe Hall Country Cottages, Near Alford LN13 0DD (01507 450294). Very well appointed luxury one and three bedroomed cottages, overlooking the golf course, all with central heating, colour TV, microwave, washer, dryer, dishwasher and fridge freezer. Woodthorpe is situated approximately six miles from the coastal resort of Mablethorpe and offers easy access to the picturesque Lincolnshire Wolds. Adjacent facilities include golf, fishing, garden centre, aquatic centre, snooker, pool and restaurant with bar and family room. **ETC** ★★★★.

SKEGNESS. Mr and Mrs K. Bennett, Field Farm, Station Road, Burgh-Le-Marsh PE24 5ES (Tel & Fax: 01754 810372). Sleeps 2-4. Working farm. Self-contained one bedroom farmhouse flat on working farm. Sleeps two to four with sofabed in living area. Fully equipped, fridge freezer, electric cooker, shower room, storage heaters for winter. Features include attractive beams, electric fire, patio doors into large porch entrance. Static caravan sleeps four to six available March to October, fully equipped with fridge, gas cooker, shower, etc. The farm is 250 yards from the A158, with plenty of ample safe parking. Conveniently situated between the coast/Fantasy Island (six miles) and attractive Wolds with its many interesting small towns. Abundant fishing lakes. Good migratory bird-watching nine miles. Bed and Breakfast available next door. Terms from £140 per week. Non-smokers only please. No pets.

NORFOLK

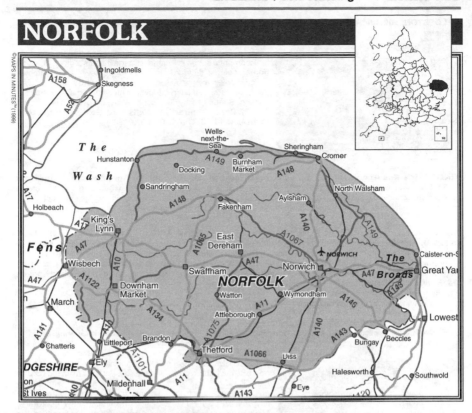

See also Colour Display Advertisement **CLIPPESBY. Clippesby Holidays, Clippesby Hall, Clippesby, Near Great Yarmouth NR29 3BL (01493 367800; Fax: 01493 367809).** IN NORFOLK BROADS NATIONAL PARK between Norwich and Great Yarmouth. Luxury lodges and woodland cottages in a peaceful country setting. Touring, walking, cycling, boating, bird-watching, fishing, exploring local nature reserves and tourist attractions. Short breaks and longer stays all year round. From May to September we have: swimming, lawn tennis, crazy golf, family pub. Summertime apartments, award-winning touring park and more. Send for colour brochure. **ETC ⚑⚑ to ⚑⚑⚑⚑ up to** COMMENDED. ✓✓✓✓✓ EXCELLENT. David Bellamy Gold Conservation Award.
e-mail: holidays@clippesby.com
website: clippesby.com

See also Colour Display Advertisement **DEREHAM. Mrs G.V. Howes, Church Farm Cottages, Brisley, Dereham NR20 5LL (Tel and Fax: 01362 668332).** Peace and tranquillity in owner supervised cottage between Dereham and Fakenham. Kept to a very high standard of cleanliness and comfort, it has full oil fired central heating, log fires, colour TV, video, washing machine, dishwasher, fridge freezer, microwave, tumble dryer, outside drying etc. It has a lawned garden and plenty of parking space. Open all year. Linen, logs and heating are included in price. Sorry no pets. Weekly price £100 to £200 for two, £188 to £348 for four. Short breaks available from October to April from £60 to £256. **ETC ★★★/★★★★.**

GELDESTON. Hillside, 15 Kells Way, Geldeston, Beccles. Sleeps 4/6. This bungalow situated in small

country village, very quiet and near River Waveney, is within easy reach of Great Yarmouth, Norwich, Lowestoft, Southwold and seaside. Accommodates four/six people; one double, one twin bedroom; bed settee in lounge, storage heaters, colour TV, wood burner, beams; diningroom; bathroom/shower, toilet; kitchen, electric cooker, microwave, etc. Carpets throughout. Cot available. Sorry, no pets. Bed linen supplied. Open all year. Car essential - parking. Shops nearby. Terms on request. Special winter rates. **Mrs M. Rolt, "Conifer", 17 Kells Way, Geldeston, Beccles, Suffolk NR34 0LU (01508 518689).**

KINGS LYNN. Mrs Angela Ringer, Sid's Cottage, Goslings, c/o The Grange, West Rudham, Kings Lynn PE31 8SY (Tel & Fax: 01485 528229). Sleeps 4 in 2 bedrooms. Semi-detached single storey stable conversion - wheelchair friendly. Use of indoor heated pool - linen provided, central heating, gas fire, colour TV, microwave, dishwaher, washer/dryer, Carp fishing. Open views. Sorry no children or pets.

NORWICH. Haveringland Hall Park, Cawston, Norwich NR10 4PN (01603 871302; Fax: 01603 879223). Peaceful and secluded site in the grounds of the former Haveringland Hall Estate. The spacious and low density park is noted for its 12 acre coarse fishing lake, its woodland walks and beautiful specimen trees in the arboretum. A few self-catering holiday static caravans are for hire from £190 per week. Also touring and camping fields with hook-ups and amenity block. Ideally situated to tour Norfolk: the Broads, the varied coastline and Norwich are minutes away. Fishermen, walkers, nature lovers and cyclists welcome.
e-mail: haveringland@claranet.com
website: www.haveringlandhall.co.uk

SHERINGHAM. Beeston Hills Lodge. Non-smoking seaside holiday accommodation in Sheringham. Our

house which is marvellously located next to the Norfolk Coastal Path, cliffs and ocean, obtains good views of the sea and green. Beeston Hills Lodge is one of the highest dwellings here, located opposite the putting green and the sea. Set back from the road so there is no passing traffic, the house is equipped with a four-poster king-sized bed, an old piano, satellite system, video player and several colour TVs with boosted feeds to the bedrooms. Mini/Bargain breaks available. Garden with garden furniture. Car parking for two cars. 10 to 20 minutes' drive from the golf course and cinema. The Lodge can accommodate up to eight people in four bedrooms (cot available if required), all with sea views, including one bedroom with a shower and washbasin. There is also a bathroom with WC and two further WC's. Fitted carpets, central heating and storage heaters. Well behaved children and pets welcome. Pillows and duvets provided. Terms from £302 per week, early booking discounts available. Please contact for further details. **(01603 766716 or 0771 3751156; Fax: 001 775 5422519)**
e-mail: enquiries@bhlodge.co.uk
website: www.bhlodge.co.uk/lodge.htm

SPIXWORTH. Mrs Sheelah Cook, Grange Farm, Buxton Road, Spixworth, Norwich NR10 3PR (01603

898190; Fax: 01603 897176). Delightful 18th century coachman's cottage and award-winning stables conversion and Lodge cottage in seclusion on our farm. Ideal for exploring Norwich, the Broads and the coast. Very well furnished and equipped. Central heating and log fires. Families welcome. Secure garden and space to relax. Barn games room and outdoor play area. Swimming and tennis, walks and fishing available. Short breaks from £120 or weekly from £190 to £550. We offer a warm welcome, please ring or write for further details. **ETC** ⚬⚬⚬⚬ 🏠🏠🏠🏠 *HIGHLY COMMENDED.*

WINTERTON-ON-SEA. Timbers, The Lane, Winterton-on-Sea. Sleeps 5. Comfortable, well-furnished ground floor flat in attractive timber cottage situated in quiet seaside village just eight miles north of Great Yarmouth. Broad sandy beach and sand dunes (nature reserve) for pleasant walks. Three miles from Norfolk Broads (boating and fishing). Flat is carpeted throughout and is fully equipped for self-catering family holidays. Ideal for children, and pets are welcome. One double, one twin-bedded and one single bedroom. Sleeps five plus cot. Bed linen provided and maid service every other day for general cleaning. Beamed sittingroom with colour TV. Secluded garden. Car parking. Available May to September. Terms from £200 to £320 per week. For full details write to **Miss E. Isherwood, 11 Birnbeck Court, 98 Bells Hill, Barnet EN5 2TD (0208 441 3493).**

WINTERTON-ON-SEA. Church Farm Cottages. Sleep 4/5 plus cot. Five minutes' walk from Winterton's famous sand dunes, Church Farm is a cluster of traditional farm buildings, set in four acres of fields and gardens. Excellent centre fro Broads and beach. The main single-storey range of outbuildings recently converted into three very comfortable holiday cottages, each with separate enclosed garden. original features - flint walls inside and out, Norfolk pantiles, low ceilings - carefully preserved, cosy and atmospheric, as well as clean and well equipped - continental showers, microwaves, washing machines, etc. Secure car par. Use of more than an acre of play field. Secure bicycle storage. Rates from £175 to £350 per week. Short breaks available. Children and pets welcome. **June and Patrick Carpmael, Church Farm, Black Street, Winterton-on-Sea, Norfolk NR29 4AP (01493 393224).**

On the River Bure at Horning, a popular resort on the Broads

NORTHUMBERLAND

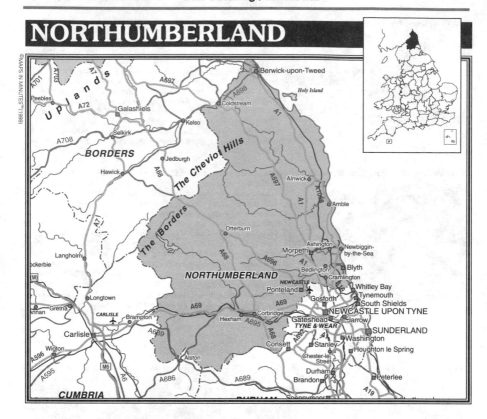

©MAPS IN MINUTES™ (1999)

ALNWICK. **Jackie Stothard, Northfield Farm, Glanton, Alnwick NE66 4AG (01665 578203).** Traditional farmhouse in south facing garden, with panoramic views of the Cheviot hills, minutes from the A697. Access down a long private driveway, with safe play areas for children in the extensive grounds. A separate wing of the owners home, it is extremely spacious and very comfortably furnished and equipped. An ideal base, the Scottish Borders and splendid coastline are easily reached. National Park five minutes. Double and twin bedrooms. Wood burning stove. Colour TV and video. Dishwasher, microwave, automatic washing machine, fridge. Electricity, full night storage heating and linen included. Basket of logs on arrival thereafter at cost. SORRY NO PETS.

ALNWICK. **Mrs J.M. Gilroy, White House Folly Farm NE66 2LW (01665 579265).** Stone-built semi-detached cottage situated in an elevated position with beautiful views, on a working farm just four miles north of the attractive, historic town of Alnwick - famous for its castle. The cottage is well decorated and carpeted throughout and provides a comfortable base for sightseeing, or simply relax in this fascinating area of Northumberland. The cottage has a sittingroom, diningroom, kitchen with washer, dryer, dishwasher, freezer, microwave and payphone, cloakroom, two bedrooms, bathroom. Shops and pubs four miles away in Alnwick and just one mile from bus route. Children welcome, cot and high chair available. Sorry no pets. Enclosed garden, ample parking. Electricity by meter reading. Weekly terms from £130 to £270. Brochure available. **ETC ★★★** *SELF CATERING.*

BAMBURGH. East Burton Farm Holiday Cottages, Bamburgh NE69 7AR (01668 214213; Fax: 01668 214538).

The Bungalow: stands in its own grounds at the top of the farm road. Sleeps five people in a double, a twin and a single bedroom; separate bathroom and toilet; lounge, kitchen/dining lounge with wonderful views of the Farne Islands and Bamburgh Castle. Washing machine, dryer, microwave, two colour TVs, video. Open fire and night storage heaters. Sheets, towels and fuel included. No1 East Burton Cottage: a low bungalow type cottage joining onto a group of terraced cottages.Very private with a large garden and superb views. Sleeps five in a double, a twin and a single bedroom. Lounge, new kitchen, bathroom with shower. Night storage heaters, open fire. Sheets, towels and fuel included. Terms for each property £250-£500 per week. Bed and Breakfast also available at Burton Hall. Contact **Eve Humphreys.**
e-mail: evehumphreys@aol.com

BELFORD. Mrs K. Burn, Fenham-Le-Moor Farmhouse, Belford NE70 7PN (Tel & Fax: 01668 213247).

A comfortably furnished farm cottage situated in peaceful surroundings on a quiet road half-a-mile from the shore and Lindisfarne Nature Reserve, an Area of Outstanding Natural Beauty, close to Holy Island, Bamburgh and within easy reach of Cheviot Hills. An ideal area for golf, beaches and walking. Electricity, linen and fuel for open fire included in rent. Terms from £190 to £380 per week. Please telephone for further details. **ETC** ☆☆☆ *COMMENDED.*

BERWICK-UPON-TWEED. Mrs S. Wight, Gainslawhill Farm, Berwick-upon-Tweed TD15 1SZ (01289 386210).

Well-equipped cottage with own walled garden on mixed farm, three miles from Berwick-upon-Tweed, situated between the rivers Tweed and Whiteadder (last farm in England). Ideal position for touring north Northumberland and the border country. Good beaches, golf, riding nearby. Lovely walks along both rivers. Trout fishing. Sleeps six, cot available. Pets welcome. Livingroom with open fire, colour TV, telephone. Three bedrooms (linen provided), kitchen with dining area, fridge/freezer, automatic washing machine, microwave oven. Bathroom. Night store heaters. Terms from £250.

CORNHILL-ON-TWEED near. Hawthorn Cottage.

In a quiet, rural location on a family farm, this traditional stone-built cottage (formerly two) has a panoramic view and a lovely enclosed garden. It is only 20 minutes' drive to Lindisfarne and the beautiful Northumberland Coast. The cottage is attractively furnished and looked after by the owner. It consists of a spacious living room with dining area, log/coal fire, colour TV and French window looking into the garden. Two double and one single bedrooms; bathroom; kitchen with electric cooker, fridge/freezer, spin dryer and microwave. There are five night storage heaters and three electric heaters. Conveniently situated for touring the Border's many castles, abbeys and stately homes, excellent golf courses and good eating places. Logs and coal are free. One pet only. Available March to November. Brochure on request. Contact: **Mrs D.C.S. Tweedie, Buchtrig, Hownam, Jedburgh TD8 6NJ (01835 840230).**

HALTWHISTLE near. Mr and Mrs Knox, Close-A-Burn, Cawburn, Haltwhistle NE49 9PN (01434 320764). Sleeps 4/5. In whatever season you visit, for however long you stay, a warm welcome is assured at Close-a-Burn. Set in its own seven acres of quiet countryside, the cottage, which was converted from an old cow byre, now has all you could need for a relaxing holiday in the beautiful Northumberland National Park, including your own uninterrupted views of Hadrian's Wall at Cawfields, and the North Pennine Moors beyond. The Cottage itself is comfortable and well equipped with a private garden, sheltered patio and barbecue area. There are two bedrooms. We also provide our guests with a 'Taste of Northumberland' welcome pack. Terms £150 to £275 per week. **ETC** ♙♙♙ *COMMENDED.*

HEXHAM. Isaac's Cottage. Situated in the hills between Northumberland and Durham, Isaac's Cottage overlooks the River Allen. Surrounded by open fields and with the benefit of fishing in the little river only a field away, this cottage is a paradise for families wanting a 'get away from it all' holiday in lovely countryside. The cottage consists of three bedrooms - one double and one twin, family bathroom. Facilites include - electric cooker, microwave, fridge, kettle, toaster, coffee maker, slow cooker. Automatic washing machine. Colour TV. Oil-fired central heating, logs for the open fire, electricity included in the rent. Bed-linen and a selection of hand towels. Cot and high chair. Ample parking. Prices from £180 - £350 per week. **ETC** ♙♙♙♙ *HIGHLY COMMENDED.* **Mrs Heather Robson, Allenheads Farm, Allenheads, Hexam NE47 9HJ (01434 685312).**

MORPETH. Mr & Mrs A.P. Coatsworth, Gallowhill Farm, Whalton, Morpeth NE61 3TX (01661 881241). Working farm. Sleeps 4-6. Relax in our two spacious stone-built cottages. Recently converted and modernised to give you every facility you require. Electric cooker, fridge, freezer, dishwasher, washer/dryer, microwave, colour TV. Located in the heart of Northumberland on a very tidy farm with private gardens. Bolam Lake two miles, Belsay Castle four miles, coast 20 minutes, Hadrian's Wall 30 minutes, to name only a few attractions. All linen, heating, electricity included in price. Sorry, no pets. All children welcome. Brochure on request. Terms £210 to £400. **ETC** ♙♙♙♙♙ *HIGHLY COMMENDED.*

ROTHBURY. Mrs H. Farr, Lorbottle, West Steads, Thropton, Morpeth NE65 7JT (01665 574672). Working farm. Sleeps 2/5. Semi-detached newly modernised cottages on 320 acre mixed farm, lying in the beautiful Whittingham Vale, surrounded by peaceful rolling hills and unspoilt countryside, four-and-a-half miles from Rothbury. Double glazed, full gas central heating and fire. Well-equipped modern kitchen. Cooking by electricity (included in price), own parking and back garden. Panoramic views from all windows. Colour TV. Very central and ideal for visiting all parts of Northumbria. Gas by meter reading. Children allowed to look around the farm. Alnwick 15 miles, Border region 25 miles, Kielder Water and Hadrian's Wall 30 miles. All bed linen supplied. Single, twin and double beds. No dogs please (sheep nearby). Details on request. Some cottages **ETC** ★★★

SEAHOUSES. Mrs Julie Gregory, Springhill Farm, Seahouses NE68 7UR (Tel & Fax01665 720351/720399). Springhill Cottages are peacefully positioned at the side of a winding country lane, which leads three-quarters-of-a-mile to sandy beaches, stretching between the fishing village of Seahouses, gateway to the Farne Island Nature Reserve, and Bamburgh village, which nestles beneath its magnificent castle. We offer a perfect base for exploring Northumberland and the Scottish Borders. Cosy log fires and deserted beaches make our Short Winter Breaks very popular. SPRINGHILL COTTAGE sleeps five, COPYWELL COTTAGE sleeps four. Both have well equipped kitchens with washing machines, electric showers/heating. Bed linen is inclusive in rent. Both cottages are non-smoking. More information available on request. **ETC ★★★★.**
e-mail: www.springhillfarm.ntb.org.uk

WOOLER. Mrs Logan, Fenton Hill Farm Cottages, Fenton Hill NE71 6JJ (01668 216228; Fax: 01668 216228). Sleep 4/6. Come and relax and enjoy the peace and beauty of Fenton Hill. We have four delightful cottages, furnished and equipped to a high standard. Cosy, home from home comfort with open fires and lovely views of the Cheviot Hills, surrounded by countryside. Ideal for family holiday, walking, bird watching, cycling or just to retreat from the pressures and busyness of life. Centrally situated for beaches, Scottish Borders, hills, castles and picturesque valleys. Many have discovered Fenton Hill and returned year after year. Open all year, each season having its particular attraction. Out of season breaks from £30 per night. **ETC ★★★★.**
e-mail: hlogan3437@aol.com

OXFORDSHIRE

BANBURY. Mrs Jeffries, Anita's Holiday Cottages, The Yews, Mollington, Banbury OX17 1AZ (01295 750731). 'The Shippon' and 'The Byre' are a tastefully converted cow-barn with quality as the byword. Beautifully fitted kitchen, a lovely en suite bedroom with fully fitted shower room. A comfortable sitting room, colour TV, fully heated, and a patio area. Central for Cotswolds, Oxford, Stratford or just enjoy the surrounding countryside. Cottages sleep two plus two and two can be joined to make larger cottage. Ideal for family and friends. Close to M40, Junction 12. Short breaks available. Linen included. Sorry no pets. Non-smoking. Ample parking.

PANGBOURNE near. "Brambly Thatch" Holiday Cottage, Coombe End Farm, Whitchurch Hill, Near Pangbourne, Reading. Brambly Thatch is an attractive, thatched, 17th century farm cottage, located on a working mixed (dairy and arable) farm, at the southern end of the Chiltern Hills. The cottage is about two miles north of Pangbourne, seven miles north-west of Reading, and about 20 miles south of Oxford. London is within easy reach. With the River Thames, Chiltern beech woods and countryside nearby, there is the chance to go walking, boating, driving or picknicking. One double bedroom, one single bedroom, and bathroom/W.C. upstairs; while downstairs there are the kitchen, main living room, dining room, and third bedroom. Fully equipped kitchen, VCR, colour TV, and telephone. Small garden. No pets, except by special arrangement. Smoking discouraged. **ETC ŤŤŤ COMMENDED.** Contact: **Mr J. N. Hatt, Merricroft Farming, Goring Heath, Reading, Berkshire RG8 7TA (01189 843121).**
e-mail:hatts@merricroft.demon.co.uk

SHROPSHIRE

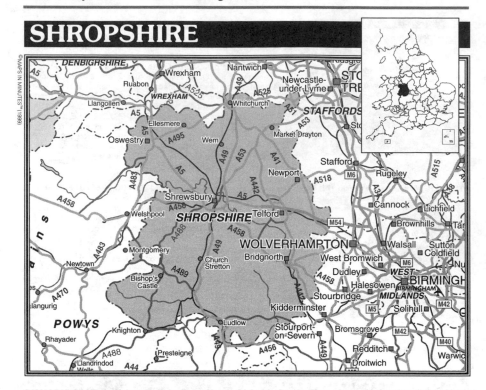

BISHOP'S CASTLE. Walcot Hall, Lydbury North, Bishop's Castle. Flats sleep 4/9. Spacious flats in Stately Home. Secluded location in own grounds; splendid scenery and ideal area for peaceful holiday for young and old. All flats fully furnished and recently decorated and sleep four/nine. Larger parties by arrangement. Village shop half a mile; local market towns, castles, villages and hill country of the Border Counties provide opportunities for exploration and walking. Coarse fishing in pools and lake. Boats and bicycles available, and riding locally. Terms from £182 to £295 weekly. **Mrs M. Smith, 41 Cheval Place, London SW7 1EW (020 7581 2782)**

CRAVEN ARMS. Mrs B. Freeman, Upper House, Clunbury, Craven Arms SY7 0HG (01588 660629).

Welcome to Horseshoe Cottage which is situated in the beautiful gardens of Upper House (17th century Listed) in Clunbury, a village of archaeological interest in a designated area of outstanding natural beauty – A. E. Housman countryside. This private self-catering cottage is completely furnished and equipped; being on one level the accommodation is suitable for elderly and disabled persons. Colour TV. Sleeps four; cot available. Children and pets welcome. Ample parking. This Welsh Border countryside is rich in medieval history, unspoilt villages and natural beauty. Enjoy walking on the Long Mynd and Offa's Dyke, or explore Ludlow and Ironbridge. £135 to £170 per week. Please write or phone for further details.

CRAVEN ARMS. Mrs Davies, Hesterworth Holidays, Hesterworth, Hopesay, Craven Arms SY7 8EX

(Tel & Fax: 01588 660487). A selection of comfortable country cottages and apartments, surrounded by 12 acres of beautiful gardens and grounds. Large dining room ideal for families or groups, residential licence. Meal service and short breaks available. We truly believe that there is no better centre in Britain for the bird watcher, walker, historian, motorist or for people who love the countryside. Groups welcome. Open all year. Half a mile from Aston-on-Clun off B4368. Ludlow 10 miles. Also Bed and Breakfast. Self-catering £103 - £367 per week. **ETC ★★/★★★.** website: www.go2.co.uk/hesterworth

CRAVEN ARMS. Mrs C.A. Morgan, Strefford Hall, Strefford, Craven Arms SY7 8DE (Tel & Fax: 01588 672383). Set in the lovely South Shropshire countryside surrounded by fields and close to Wenlock Edge. The Coachhouse provides two luxury self-catering units. Swallows Nest on the ground floor is ideal for frail or disabled guests. Wrens Nest is on the first floor. Each consists of double en suite bedroom, fitted kitchen, large sitting/diningroom with colour TV; central heating and linen included. Fitted carpets. Patio area with seating. Ample parking to the side of the Coachhouse. Terms £185 to £250 per week. Also Bed and Breakfast available in the farmhouse.

LUDLOW. Hazel Cottage, Duxmoor, Onibury, Craven Arms. Sleeps 4. Beautifully restored, semi-detached, yet private, period cottage, set in its own extensive cottage-style garden with its own drive and ample parking space. Amidst peaceful surroundings and panoramic views of the countryside, it is situated five miles north of historic Ludlow and one-and-a-half miles from the A49. The cottage retains all its original features and fittings with traditional decorations and is fully furnished as a home, with antiques throughout. It comprises a comfortable living room with a victorian range for coal and log fire; TV, wireless and telephone; diningroom with bread oven; fully equipped kitchen, hall, Victorian bathroom; two bedrooms (one double and one twin-bedded) with period washbasin. Electric central heating throughout. All linen included. Tourist information. Open all year. Short Breaks from £120. No pets. Terms from £180 to £360 per week. **ETC ♥♥♥♥** *HIGHLY COMMENDED*. **Mrs Rachel Sanders, Duxmoor Farm, Onibury, Craven Arms SY7 9BQ (01584 856342).**

LUDLOW. Sally and Tim Loft, Goosefoot Barn, Pinstones, Diddlebury, Craven Arms, Shropshire SY7 9LB (01584 861326). Converted in 2000 from stone and timbered barns, the three cottages are individually decorated and equipped to the highest standards. Fresh linen and towels are also provided for your comfort. Each cottage has en suite facilities and private garden or seating area. Situated in a secluded valley with walks from the doorstep through beautiful Corvedale. Ideally located for exploring South Shropshire, only eight miles from Ludlow. Cottages sleep up to six people. There is a games room with a full sized snooker table. Short Breaks available. A real break from the ordinary. Prices from £190 per week. Children and pets welcome. Non-smoking accommodation available. Awaiting ETC inspection.
e-mail: sally@goosefoot.freeserve.co.uk

LYDBURY NORTH. The Powis Arms, Lydbury North SY7 8PR (01588 680232). Caravan site available at our country pub. Good food from snacks to full à la carte with friendly and professional service available. Parking. Fishing and walking. Ideally situated for exploring Shropshire and the Welsh Borders and mediaeval towns of Ludlow and Shrewsbury. Nearby are the world famous Ironbridge and walking or bicycling country of Offa's Dyke, the Long Mynd, Stiperstones and Wenlock Edge. Self-catering flats and Bed & Breakfast accommodation also available.

OSWESTRY near. Mr and Mrs Breeze, Lloran Isaf, Llansilin, Near Oswestry SY10 7QX (01691 791376 or 01691 780318). Working farm. Beautiful bungalow set on a working farm in its own valley which has wonderful scenery and walks. Kitchen with microwave, washer/dryer, fridge, cooker; lounge/dining area with colour TV and woodburning stove, small charge for logs; three bedrooms – one twin with double and single bed, one double, one single (duvets supplied but no linen); separate toilet and bathroom. Fitted carpets and electric heating in bedrooms and lounge; barbecue, garden furniture in enclosed garden. One-and-a-half miles from village, wonderful touring area with lots of attractions. Open all year. Pets welcome. Sorry no children. Prices from £80. Electricity by meter reading. **WTB ❀❀❀.**

SOMERSET

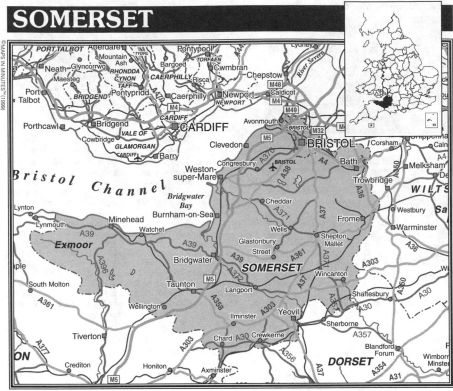

©MAPS IN MINUTES™ (1999)

FREE or REDUCED RATE entry to
Holiday Visits and Attractions — see our
READERS' OFFER VOUCHERS on pages 43-60

Leigh Farm Pensford, Near Bristol BS39 4BA
TELEPHONE OR FAX: 01761 490281

Leigh Farm is situated in the old mining village of Pensford. 7 miles to Bristol and 8 miles to Bath. Overlooking the floodlit pool; a 3-bedroomed cottage sleeping 6 plus baby. Terraced bungalow conversion built tastefully in natural stone with original oak beams. One or two bedroomed, with shower room, WC and basin. TV. Night storage heating. Bed linen is not supplied but can be hired. Cot and high chair available. Private Carp and Tench fishing. Wander round the ponds where Duck and Moorhen nest. Park and ride for both cities near, and plenty of Tourist Information for your use. Safe floodlit car park. Open all year. No pets. £150-£400 weekly. *For brochure contact Josephine Smart.*

Withy Grove Farm ★★

Come and enjoy a relaxing and friendly holiday "Down on the Farm" set in beautiful Somerset countryside. Peaceful rural setting adjoining River Huntspill, famed for its coarse fishing. The farm is ideally situated for visiting the many local attractions including Cheddar Gorge, Glastonbury, Weston-super-Mare and the lovely sandy beach of Burnham-on-Sea. Self-catering cottages are tastefully converted, sleeping 4-5. Fully equipped with colour TV.

★ Heated Swimming Pool
★ Licensed Bar and Entertainment *(in high season)*
★ Games Room   ★ Skittle Alley   ★ Laundry

For more information please contact: **Mrs Wendy Baker, Withy Grove Farm, East Huntspill, Near Burnham-on-Sea, Somerset TA9 3NP. Telephone: 01278 784471.**

See also colour advertisement

BATH near. Mrs Audrey Rich, Whitnell Farm, Binegar, Emborough, Near Bath BA3 4UF (01749 840277). Whitnell Farm is a family working farm with holiday homes for two to eight on the edge of a pretty Mendip village in the most beautiful area of Somerset, between Wells and Bath and very central for touring. Ideal for a family holiday. Wildlife parks, caves, castles, stately homes, golf, riding and fishing; 20 miles to the beach. Open all year. Caravans welcome. Please telephone for further details.

See also Colour Display Advertisement

BATH near. Mrs S. Bowles, Church Farm, Winsley, Bradford-on-Avon, Wiltshire BA15 2JH (Tel & Fax: 01225 722246). Delightful single storey cottages, formerly an old cow byre, tastefully converted with exposed beams and vaulted ceilings. Working farm with sheep and horses. Countryside location in an Area of Outstanding Natural Beauty. Bath five miles. Kennet and Avon Canal three-quarters of a mile for boating, cycling and walking. Village shop and pub 500 metres. Fully equipped. Video. Ample parking. Enclosed garden with patio furniture. Welcome pack. Short breaks when available. Colour brochure. ETC ★★★★
e-mail: churchfarmcottages@compuserve.com
website: www.bath.co.uk/churchfarmcottages

EXMOOR. Mrs Jones, Higher Town, Dulverton TA22 9RX (01398 341272). Our property is set in 80 acres of National Park, half-a-mile from open moorland and visitors are welcome to walk over our beef and sheep farm. The bungalow is situated on its own with lovely views, lawn and parking space. It sleeps six with one bunk-bedded room, double bedroom and one bedroom with two single beds. Bedding, linen and electricity are provided. The bathroom and toilet are separate and the bath also has a shower over. The lounge has an open fire and colour TV, the kitchen has electric cooker, fridge freezer and washer dryer. Centrally heated and double glazed. SAE please for further information.

EXMOOR. Penny & Roger Webber, Hindon Farm, Near Minehead TA24 8SH (Tel & Fax: 01643 705244). "For a real taste of country life". Charming cottage and 18th century farmhouse on our 500-acre organic stock farm adjoining heather moors, South West coast path, and thatched village of Selworthy for 'scrummy' cream teas. All within National Trust Estate – wonderful walks and riding, bring dogs and horses. Waymarked farm trail with picnic wood – organic picnic basket available. Organic lamb, Aberdeen Angus beef, free-range pork, bacon, ham, sausages, all available direct from our farm shop or S-O-D-S will deliver. Free organic produce basket for self-catering accommodation guests. Escape to where buzzards soar and the red deer roam. Minehead three miles, Dunster Castle six miles. Real farm, real food, relax. Award winners from Exmoor National Park for conservation and commitment to 'green' principles.
website: www.hindonfarm.co.uk

PLEASE SEND A STAMPED ADDRESSED ENVELOPE WITH ENQUIRIES

GLASTONBURY. Mrs M. Moon, West Town Farm, Baltonsborough, Glastonbury BA6 8QX (01458

850217). Spacious, fully furnished flat in wing of 17th century farmhouse, situated in lovely Somerset countryside. Ideal for touring – Glastonbury, Wells, Cheddar, Wookey, Longleat – and midway between south and north coast seaside resorts. Self-contained with own bathroom/toilet/shower. Lounge/diner with TV and electric fire; fitted kitchen with electric cooker, fridge and microwave. One bedroom with double and single beds, washbasin; second bedroom with two single beds, washbasin; cot. Central heating. Large walled garden with lawns. Visitors must supply own linen. Children most welcome. Sorry, no pets. Holder of FHG Diploma. SAE for full details, terms and dates available.

GLASTONBURY. Mrs A. Coles, Middlewick Farm Holiday Cottages, Wick Lane, Glastonbury BA6 8JW

(Tel & Fax: 01458 832351). Working farm. Sleeps 2/6. Eight delightful cottages with luxury indoor heated swimming pool set in 20 acres of cottage gardens, meadows and apple orchards. The cottages have country style decor with olde worlde charm. The smallest cottage sleeps two, the largest six plus cot. In total, the eight cottages sleep 30 people. The accommodation is set around a courtyard and gardens. They have a wealth of inglenooks and beamed ceilings. Each has its own character and all are cosy and comfortable. Some ground floor accommodation available. Central for many places of interest. Terms from £180 to £598. **ETC up to** ♀♀♀♀ *COMMENDED*.

PORLOCK. Lucott Farm, Porlock, Minehead. Sleeps 2/10. Isolated farmhouse on Exmoor, with wood burning fireplaces and all modern conveniences. It lies at the head of Horner Valley and guests will delight in the wonderful scenery. Plenty of pony trekking in the area. Ten people accommodated in four double and two single bedrooms, cot; bathroom, two toilets; sittingroom; diningroom. Kitchen has oil-fired Aga and water heater. No linen supplied. Shops three miles; sea four miles. Car essential - parking. Open all year. Terms (including fuel) on application with SAE please to **Mrs E.A. Tucker, West Luccombe Cottage, Porlock, Minehead TA24 8MT (01643 862810).**

SHEPTON MALLET. Mrs J.A. Boyce, Knowle Farm, West Compton, Shepton Mallet BA4 4PD (01749

890482; Fax: 01749 890405). Working farm. Cottages sleep 2/5/8. Four charming cottages superbly converted from old barns and furnished to a high standard. Pretty gardens to relax in and separate play area for children. Two cottages have kitchen/diner, separate lounge, colour TV, the other two have kitchen, lounge/diner, colour TV. Cot, high chair by prior arrangement. Bed linen supplied; towels by request. Situated in quiet secluded countryside yet close to Wells, Glastonbury, Bath, etc, and approximately five miles from Wells and Mendip Golf Clubs. Area also has a wide selection of family attractions. Sorry no pets. Terms: £180 to £450. Car essential, ample parking. Payphone for guests. Open all year. **ETC** ♀♀♀♀ *COMMENDED*.

SIMONSBATH. Jane Styles, Wintershead Farm, Simonsbath, Exmoor TA24 7LF (01643 831222;

Fax: 01643 831628). Hidden away in that place on Exmoor which you normally only find once you're already on holiday, and can never remember where you saw it! Wintershead offers you the peace and tranquillity you need to recharge the batteries after the stresses of everyday life. Five self-catering cottages to suit all your needs. Short breaks available from November to March. Please telephone, fax or write for a colour brochure. **ETC** ♀♀♀♀ *HIGHLY COMMENDED*.
website: www.wintershead.co.uk

Wintershead

TAUNTON. Mrs Joan Greenway, Woodlands Farm, Bathealton, Taunton TA4 2AH (01984 623271).

You can be assured of a warm and friendly welcome on our family-run dairy farm, with a small carp pond. Children are welcome and will enjoy feeding the animals. We are in the heart of beautiful unspoilt countryside within easy reach of the north and south coasts and Exmoor. The cottage sleeps five people and is furnished to a high standard to enjoy a relaxing holiday. The kitchen has washing machine, microwave, etc. Bathroom with bath and shower. Electricity, central heating and bed linen included in the tariff. Terms from £135 to £295 per week. Please write or phone for colour brochure.

YEOVIL. Mrs P. Trott, Richmond House and Barrow Farm Holiday Cottages, North Barrow, Yeovil BA22 7LZ (Tel & Fax: 01963 240543). Richmond House sleeps 16, Wisteria, Saddlery, Stable and Byre sleep 4/8. Richmond

House is a beautifully restored former rectory. Large elegant rooms, perfect for large groups. Saddlery, Stable and Byre are tastefully converted stone barns with original beams, very comfortably equipped. Wisteria is a pretty stone cottage, attractive and welcoming. Heated outdoor pool in sheltered garden during main summer season. From £112 per week. Open all year. **ETC** ♛♛♛♛ *COMMENDED.*

STAFFORDSHIRE

LEEK. Edith and Alwyn Mycock, 'Rosewood Cottage and Rosewood Flat', Lower Berkhamsytch Farm, Bottom House, Near Leek ST13 7QP (Tel and Fax: 01538 308213). Each sleeps 6. Situated in Staffordshire Moorlands,

one cottage and one flat overlooking picturesque countryside. Fully equipped, comfortably furnished and carpeted throughout. Cottage, all on ground floor, is suitable for the less able. An ideal base for visits to Alton Towers, the Potteries and Peak District. Patio, play area. Cot and high chair available. Laundry room with auto washer and dryer. Electricity and fresh linen inclusive. **ETC** ★★★.

SUFFOLK

HITCHAM. Old Wetherden Hall Cottage. Sleeps 6 plus cot. 15th century Listed oak-beamed house, with

large open inglenook fireplace (logs supplied). Full central heating. Surrounded by large moat stocked with carp and various other fish. Private fishing available. Abundance of wildlife with picturesque secluded setting. Large spacious garden. Close to Lavenham and Bury St. Edmunds, well positioned to explore Suffolk. £175-£350 per week. Open all year. **ETC ŤŤŤ** *COMMENDED.* **Mrs J. C. Elsden, Old Wetherden Hall, Hitcham, Ipswich IP7 7PZ (Tel & Fax: 01449 740574)** e-mail: farm@wetherdenhall.force9.co.uk

KESSINGLAND. Kessingland Cottages, Rider Haggard Lane, Kessingland. Sleeps 6. An exciting three-

bedroom recently built semi-detached cottage situated on the beach, three miles south of sandy beach at Lowestoft. Fully and attractively furnished with colour TV and delightful sea and lawn views from floor-to-ceiling windows of lounge. Accommodation for up to eight people. Well-equipped kitchen with electric cooker, fridge, electric immersion heater. Electricity by £1 coin meter. Luxurious bathroom with coloured suite. No linen or towels provided. Only a few yards to beach and sea fishing. One mile to wildlife country park with mini-train. Buses quarter-of-a-mile and shopping centre half-a-mile. Parking, but car not essential. Children and disabled persons welcome. Available 1st March to 7th January. Weekly terms from £50 In early March and late December to £225 in peak season. SAE to **Mr S. Mahmood, 156 Bromley Road, Beckenham, Kent BR3 6PG (Tel & Fax: 020-8650 0539).**

SAXMUNDHAM. Mrs Mary Kitson, White House Farm, Sibton, Saxmundham IP17 2NE (01728 660260). Working farm. Sleeps 4/6 adults; 2/4 children. The flat is a self-contained part of late Georgian farmhouse standing in 130 acres of quiet farmland with a variety of livestock. Fishing on farm. Accommodation in three double bedrooms (two double/two single beds) plus cot; livingroom with TV; shower/toilet on first floor. Entrance hall, kitchen/diner on ground floor. Full central heating. Situated one-and-a-half miles from village shops, etc. Ten miles from coast at Dunwich, Minsmere Bird Sanctuary, Snape Maltings. Linen optional. Pets permitted. Car essential - parking. Available all year. Terms from £130 to £190 per week. SAE, please, for further details.

WALSHAM-LE-WILLOWS. Bridge Cottage, Walsham-le-Willows, Near Bury St. Edmunds. . Sleeps 5.

Bridge Cottage is illustrated in the book "English Cottages", with introduction by John Betjeman. Built in the 17th century it has been attractively modernised. There are fitted carpets and comfortable beds; centrally heated and well furnished. The kitchen is well equipped with electric cooker and fridge/deep-freeze. Plenty of hot water. Children and well-behaved pets are welcome. Electricity and heating included in rent. Colour TV. Tennis court and swimming pool available in summer by arrangement. Walsham-le-Willows is in the centre of East Anglia (11 miles from Bury St. Edmunds) and has shops and Post Office. Available all year. Terms from £190 to £300. **ETC ŤŤŤ** *APPROVED.* **Mrs H. M. Russell, The Beeches, Walsham-le-Willows, Near Bury St. Edmunds IP31 3AD (01359 259227; Fax: 01359 258206)..**

EAST SUSSEX

LEWES near. Mrs Elizabeth Hollington, Duck Barn, Telscombe Village, Near Lewes BN7 3HY (01273

301844; Fax: 01273 300935). The Coach House, a skilfully converted, flint cottage in this exquisite, sheltered South Downs hamlet has generous accommodation: large open-plan living space, wide oak spiral stair , one twin, one double bedroom. The sunny, walled garden is set within mature trees. The village boasts a Norman church, an ancient manor and instant access to walks with spectacular Downs and sea views. Classy Lewes 10 minutes by car, cultural, stylish Brighton and the coast 15 minutes more. Day trips to London and France very possible. Central heating, wood stove, TV, video, washing machine, dryer. Sleeps four/five plus small child. Dogs by arrangement. £230 to £550 per week, mini breaks available. ETC ♌♌♌♌ *HIGHLY COMMENDED.*

WEST SUSSEX

HENFIELD. The Holiday Flat and Cottage, New Hall, Small Dole, Henfield BN5 9YJ (01273 492546). New Hall is the manor house of Henfield, it stands in three-and-a-half acres of mature gardens, surrounded by farmland with abundant footpaths. The holiday cottage is the original 1600 AD farmhouse. It has one en suite bedroom with large livingroom with a folding bed, diningroom and kitchen. A door opens into the walled garden. Holiday flat is the upper-part of the dairy wing. Its front door opens from a Georgian courtyard. It has three bedrooms sleeping five, lounge/diner, kitchen and bathroom. Both units are fully equipped and comfortably furnished. Children welcome. Open all year. Terms from £150 to £305 per week. Send SAE for details, or phone **Mrs M. W. Carreck. ETC** ♌♌♌ *COMMENDED.*

WILTSHIRE

CHIPPENHAM. Mr D. Humphrey, Roward Farm, Draycot Cerne, Chippenham SN15 4SG (01249

758147). Sleep 2/4. Roward Farm offers three holiday cottages, converted from traditional farm buildings. Overlooking open fields, they provide the perfect base for visiting the Cotswolds and Bath, with Castle Combe, Lacock Abbey and Bowood House all close by. All cottages are fully-equipped and furnished to a high standard. Laundry facilities are available and bed linen, towel and tea towels are provided. Barbecue facilities also available. One cottage has one double bedroom plus sofa bed in the living room, the other has one double and one twin. Welcome pack on arrival. Non-smoking throughout. Well behaved pets are welcome. Please call or write for brochure and terms. **ETC** ♌♌♌♌ *HIGHLY COMMENDED.*

DEVIZES. Colin and Cynthia Fletcher, Lower Foxhangers Farm, Rowde, Devizes SN10 1SS (Tel & Fax: 01380 828795). Sleep 4/6. Enjoy your holiday with us on our small farm/marina with its many diverse attractions. Hear the near musical clatter of the windlass heralding the lock gate opening and the arrival of yet another narrowboat. Relax on the patios of our rural retreats – four holiday mobile homes sleeping four/six in a setting close to the canal locks. Bed and Breakfast accommodation in 18th century spacious farmhouse from £19.50 per person. Also available weekly hire with our narrowboat holidays or small camp site with electricity and facilities. Self-catering rates from £180 per week.

MALMESBURY. John and Edna Edwards, Stonehill Farm, Charlton, Malmesbury SN16 9DY (01666 823310). Sleeps 2/3. Superbly located on the edge of the Cotswolds in lush rolling countryside. We invite you to stay with us on our family-run dairy farm in two comfortable, well equipped cottages, converted from farm buildings. Each comprises lounge, kitchen/diner, bathroom, bedroom. Visit quiet villages, stately homes, market towns, walk in the countryside or stay at the farm and watch the cows being milked. Spend days in Bath, Oxford, Stonehenge or the Cotswold hills. Tariff from £180 to £230 per week including power, heat and linen. Pets very welcome.

SALISBURY. Mr G. Gould, The Old Stables, Bridge Farm, Lower Road, Britford, Salisbury SP5 4DY (01722 349002; Fax: 01722 349003). Sleeps 5/6. Newly converted 19th century stable block. Peacefully situated in village close to Salisbury. Three units, traditionally and individually decorated, spiral staircases and exposed beams. Downstairs one en suite double/twin room, upstairs one double, one single and shower room. Ground floor is wheelchair accessible/disabled friendly. Washing machine, microwave, TV, central heating. Bedding provided, payphone available. Own patios, shared garden within chalk thatched wall. Ideal touring base. Stonehenge, Avebury, New Forest, Longleat, Wilton House all within easy reach. Town and Cathedral five minutes' drive. Non-smoking. Open all year.
e-mail: mail@old-stables.co.uk
website: www.old-stables.co.uk

WORCESTERSHIRE

EVESHAM. Mrs Daphne Stow, Hall Farm Country Holidays, Sedgeberrow, Evesham WR11 6UB (Tel & Fax: 01386 881298). Six cottages of character converted from 19th century barns in peaceful village setting in Vale of Evesham. Ranging from three bedrooms/two bathrooms to one and two bedrooms (all en suite) they all have many original features and a wealth of old timbers. Furnished and equipped to a very high standard they have a welcoming atmosphere. Set amidst large lawned gardens. Ample parking, heated outdoor pool (summer months), grass tennis court. Only a short drive to many Cotswold beauty spots, interesting towns (Worcester, Cheltenham, Stratford-on-Avon), farm parks and pick-your-own. **ETC ★★★/★★★★.**
e-mail: daphnestow@aol.com

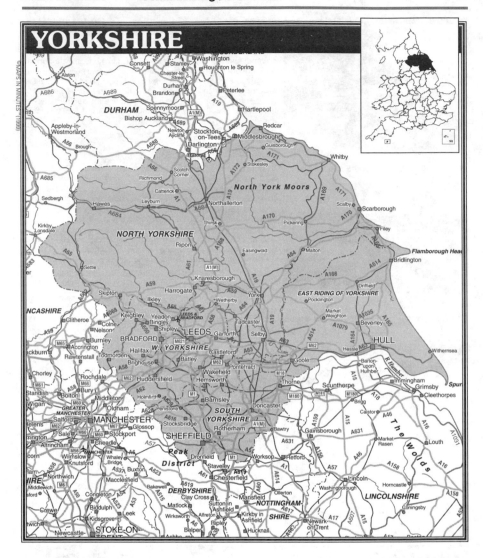

NORTH YORKSHIRE

ASKRIGG. Fern Croft, 2 Mill Lane, Askrigg. Sleeps four. A modern cottage enjoying quiet location on edge of village with open fields rising immediately behind. Attractive and compact, this Wensleydale village is an ideal centre for Dales, with facilities for everyday needs, including two shops, Post office, restaurant and a couple of pubs. Furnished to a high standard for four, ground floor accommodation comprises large comfortable lounge/diner with colour TV and well-equipped kitchen. Upstairs there are two double bedrooms with a double and twin beds respectively, and modern bathroom. Storage heating included, other electricity by meter. Regret no pets. Terms from £125 to £250 weekly. Brochure: **Mr and Mrs K. Dobson (01689 838450**

ASKRIGG/WENSLEYDALE. Mrs E. Scarr, Coleby Hall, Askrigg, Leyburn DL8 3DX (01969 650216). Working farm. Sleeps 5 plus cot. Situated in Wensleydale, half-a-mile from Bainbridge and one mile from Askrigg, Coleby Hall is a 17th century gabled farmhouse with stone mullioned windows, the west end being to let. A stone spiral staircase leads to two bedrooms; linen provided. The kitchen is equipped with electric cooker, fridge, crockery, etc., and coal fire. The lounge has an inglenook coal fire and TV. Oil fired central heating throughout. Coleby has lovely views and is an ideal situation for walking, fishing and driving round the Yorkshire Dales. Children and pets welcome. Terms from £170 per week.

CROPTON/PICKERING. Mrs R. Feaster, High Farm, Cropton, Pickering YO18 8AL (01751 417461).Sleeps 2/6. Three luxury holiday cottages, ideally situated on the edge of quiet, unspoilt village with fine views over the North Yorkshire Moors National Park. No longer a working farm, the buildings have been thoughtfully and sympathetically converted into single storey cottages, individually designed and furnished to offer every comfort in this peaceful rural location. Being in the heart of Ryedale, there is easy access to the Moors, coast and York. Stroll to the New Inn, which offers both bar and restaurant meals and has its own brewery. The beautiful one acre garden is planted with trees, shrubs and roses and has a barbecue. Private parking. Children welcome. Regret, no pets. Terms from £140 to £475 per week. **ETC** ♕♕♕♕♕ *HIGHLY COMMENDED.*

GRASSINGTON near. Mrs Judith M. Joy, Jerry and Ben's, Hebden, Skipton BD23 5DL (01756 752369; Fax: 01756 753370). Properties sleep 3/6/8/9. Jerry and Ben's stands in two acres of grounds in one of the most attractive parts of the Yorkshire Dales National Park. Seven properties; Ghyll Cottage (sleeps eight); Mamie's Cottage (sleeps eight); Paradise End (sleeps six); Robin Middle (sleeps six); High Close (sleeps nine); Cruck Rise (sleeps six); Raikes Side (sleeps two/three). All have parking, electric cooker, microwave, toaster, fridge, colour TV, electric heating and immersion heater; lounge, dining area, bathroom with shower; cots if required. Fully equipped, including linen if requested. Washing machine and telephone available. Ghyll and Mamie's Cottages now have dishwashers. Well behaved pets accepted. Open all year. Fishing and bathing close by. Terms from £90 to £350. SAE, please for detailed brochure. Suitable for some disabled guests.

When making enquiries or bookings, a stamped addressed envelope is always appreciated

HAWES. Pru Phillips, Gaudy House Farm, Gayle, near Hawes DL8 3NA (Tel 01969 667231). Sleeps

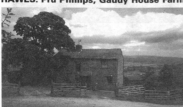

two/six. Traditional stone barns converted into three spacious self-contained dwellings with log fires. Sleeping two/five people. Set in 25 acres of farmland. Peaceful, comfortable, unique setting on the Pennine Way with magnificent views over Wensleydale, ideal for exploring the Dales. One mile from the market town of Hawes. Reasonable rentals all year round from £140 to £320 per week. **ETC** ♉♉ *APPROVED*.

HELMSLEY near. Mrs Rickatson, Summerfield Farm, Harome, Near Helmsley, York YO6 5JJ (01439

748238). Working farm, join in. Sleeps 6. Enjoy walking or touring in North Yorkshire Moors National Park. Lovely area 20 miles north of historic city of York. Modernised, comfortable and well-equipped farmhouse wing; sleeps four/six plus cot. Kitchen equipped with electric cooker, fridge, microwave and automatic washing machine. Sit beside a log fire in the evenings. Linen supplied. Weekly terms from £90 to £210. Mid-week and weekend bookings are possible in winter. Trout stream on farm. For further information send SAE, or phone.

PICKERING. Mrs Sue Cavill, Badger Cottage, Stape, Pickering YO18 8HR (01751 476108). Comfortable

self-catering on small, remote, moorland farm. Seven miles from Pickering on edge of Cropton Forest. Wonderful area for touring, walking, cycling or riding. Accommodation available for guests' horses. Cottage is converted from original stone milking parlours, so all on ground floor. Open-plan well-equipped kitchen, dining and sittingroom with sofa bed and cosy woodburning stove. Spacious bedroom with double and single beds, en suite shower room. Parking space and a garden to sit in. Linen and power included. Terms £140 to £200 per week.

RATHMELL, (near Settle). Rosemary Hyslop, Field House, Rathmell, Settle (01729 840234; Fax:

01729 840775). Sleeps two-ten. Situated on a working sheep farm, Layhead Farm Cottages are a group of three, with lovely views of rolling countryside and Penyghent in the background. Four miles from busy little market town of Settle we are the ideal base from which to explore the Yorkshire Dales. LAYHEAD FARMHOUSE, recently renovated to a high standard, has oil-fired central heating from Rayburn in kitchen/dining room, open fire in lounge. Attractive garden with furniture and barbecue. CRAGGS and COBBLESTONES are the result of a conversion of an original stone barn into two superb cottages with all modern amenities. Cobbled courtyard with garden furniture and colourful tubs. Pets welcome. Colour brochure available. Prices from £190 to £570. **ETC** ♉♉♉♉ *HIGHLY COMMENDED*.
e-mail: rosehyslop@easynet.co.uk

ROBIN HOOD'S BAY. Ken and Nealia Pattinson, South House Farm, Fylingthorpe, Whitby YO22 4UQ

(01947 880243). Two super detached stone cottages on this 180 acre farm only a short distance walk from the beach at Boggle Hole. Situated in a National Park this is wonderful walking country with the North York Moors all around. The cottages have two and three bedrooms and are fully equipped and centrally heated. Llama and pony trekking nearby. Sorry no pets. Terms from £80 to £350.

SCARBOROUGH. Peter and Maggie Martin, Gowland Farm, Gowland Lane, Cloughton, Scarborough

YO13 0DU (01723 870924). Sleeps 2/7. Four charming converted stone barns situated within the beautiful North Yorkshire Moors National Park enjoying wonderful views of Harwood Dale and only two miles from the coast. The cottages have been sympathetically converted from traditional farm buildings, furnished and fitted to a very high standard, retaining the old features as well as having modern comforts. They are fully carpeted, warm and cosy with central heating and double glazing. Electric fires and colour TVs in all lounges. Well equipped kitchens. All linen and bedding provided (duvets). Large garden with plenty of car parking space. Garden furniture and laundry facilities. Sorry, no pets. Open all year. From £105 to £435 per week. Bed, Breakfast and Evening Meal also available from April to October. White Rose Award Self-Catering Holiday of the Year runner-up 1993. **ETC ⅋⅋⅋/⅋⅋⅋⅋** *HIGHLY COMMENDED.*

SKIPTON. Mrs Brenda Jones, New Close Farm, Kirkby Malham, Skipton BD23 4DP (Tel & Fax 01729

830240). Sleeps 5. A supa dupa cottage on New Close Farm in the heart of Craven Dales with panoramic views over the Aire Valley. Excellent area for walking, cycling, fishing, golf and touring. Two double and one single bedrooms; bathroom. Colour TV and video. Full central heating and double glazing. Bed linen and all amenities included in the price. Low Season £225, High Season £275; deposit required. Sorry, no young children, no pets. Non-smokers preferred. The weather can't be guaranteed but your comfort can. FHG Diploma Award Winner.

WHITBY. Nick Eddleston, Greenhouses Farm Cottages, Greenhouses Farm, Lealholm, Near Whitby

YO21 2AD (01947 897486). The three cottages have been converted from the traditional farm buildings. The old world character has been retained with the thick stone walls, exposed beams and red pantile roofs typical of North Yorkshire. Set in the tiny hamlet of Greenhouses and enjoying splendid views over open countryside, the cottages offer a very quiet and peaceful setting for a holiday. All the cottages are equipped with colour TV, electric cooker, fridge/freezer, microwave and automatic washing machine. Linen, fuel and lighting are all included in the price. There are ample safe areas for children to play. Sorry, no pets. Prices from £173 to £488 per week. Winter Breaks from £131.

WHITBY near. Mr and Mrs Geoffrey Hepworth, Land of Nod Farm, Near Whitby YO21 2BL (01947 840325). Sleeps 6 plus cot. Attached sandstone bungalow, situated in the clean air, carefree part of North Yorkshire Moors National Park. All five windows face south across pastures, the sittingroom window also faces east across six miles of widening valley to Whitby Abbey headland. Runswick Bay is three miles northward. The holiday property is separated from the farm house by a dividing passage. There are three compact bedrooms, one of which has two single beds and cot. Modern toilet facilities and shower. Kitchen/diner fully equipped with electric cooker, microwave, fridge; spin dryer, colour TV. Bed linen, electricity included in hire. Small charge for pets. No telephone bookings. Non-smoking. Owner attended. For availability, enquiries and brochure phone: 01947 840325. Rates from £87 Low Season to £162 High Season per week.

YORK. Orillia Cottages, Stockton-on-the-Forest, York. Four converted farmworkers' cottages in a courtyard setting at the rear of the 300-year-old farmhouse in Stockton-on-the-Forest; three miles from York. Golf course nearby, pub 200 yards away serves food. Post Office, newsagents and general stores within easy reach. Convenient half-hourly bus service to York and the coast. Fully furnished and equipped for two to eight, the cottages comprise lounge with colour TV, etc; kitchen area with microwave oven, grill and hob. Bedrooms have double bed or twin beds. Gas central heating. Non-smokers preferred. Children and pets welcome. Available Easter to October. Short Breaks may be available. Terms from £150 to £360 weekly includes heating, linen, etc. Contact: **Mike Cundall, Orillia House, 89 The Village, Stockton-on-the-Forest, York YO3 9UP (01904 400600).**

YORK. Sunset Cottages, Grimston Manor Farm, Gilling East, York YO62 4HR. Working farm.

Six beautiful cottages lovingly converted from the granaries of our family farm. Superbly situated in the heart of the Howardian Hills, on the outskirts of the National Park and only 17 miles north of the historic city of York, Herriot country. With panoramic views, these warm and comfortable cottages retain their original mellow beams and interesting stonework while still providing all the modern comforts you rightfully expect in a well-designed self-catering cottage. Full central heating. Personally supervised by the resident owners, Heather and Richard Kelsey. Sorry, no pets (sheep country). Prices from £150 to £350. **ETC** ♔♔♔♔ *COMMENDED*. Please write, or phone for brochure to **Mr and Mrs R. J. Kelsey, Grimston Manor Farm, Gilling East, York YO62 4HR (01347 888654; Fax: 01347 888347).**
website: www.sunsetcottages.co.uk

YORK. Mrs M.S.A. Woodliffe, Mill Farm, Yapham, Pocklington, York YO4 2PH (01759 302172). Three attractive self-catering choices on the farm. 12 miles from York with fine views of the Yorkshire Wolds. WOODLEA, detached house, sleeping five/six people, with fully equipped kitchen, dining area, large lounge with colour TV, bathroom, downstairs cloakroom and three bedrooms. BUNGALOW adjacent to farmhouse sleeps two/four with kitchen, bathroom, lounge/diningroom with colour TV and double bed settee, twin room with cot. Children and pets welcome. STUDIO adjacent to farmhouse, sleeps two. Modern kitchen, lounge/diningroom with colour TV, twin bedroom, bathroom/toilet. Parking for all. Open all year. Shopping and other amenities at Pocklington (two miles). Eating out, stately homes, a variety of activities available locally; coast 28 miles. SAE for details.

Caravan &
Camping Holidays
ENGLAND

THE FHG DIPLOMA

HELP IMPROVE
BRITISH TOURIST STANDARDS

You are choosing holiday accommodation from our very popular FHG Publications.
Whether it be a hotel, guest house, farmhouse or self-catering accommodation, we think you will find it hospitable, comfortable and clean, and your host and hostess friendly and helpful.

Why not write and tell us about it?

As a recognition of the generally well-run and excellent holiday accommodation reviewed in our publications, we at FHG Publications Ltd. present a diploma to proprietors who receive the highest recommendation from their guests who are also readers of our Guides. If you care to write to us praising the holiday you have booked through FHG Publications Ltd. – whether this be board, self-catering accommodation, a sporting or a caravan holiday, what you say will be evaluated and the proprietors who reach our final list will be contacted.

The winning proprietor will receive an attractive framed diploma to display on his premises as recognition of a high standard of comfort, amenity and hospitality. FHG Publications Ltd. offer this diploma as a contribution towards the improvement of standards in tourist accommodation in Britain. Help your excellent host or hostess to win it!

FHG DIPLOMA

We nominate ....

....

Because

Name ....

Address..

....

Telephone No..

ENGLAND
Caravan & Camping Holidays

BUDE. Mrs E. Haworth, Newlands Farm, Youlstone, Morwenstowe, Bude EX23 9PT (01288 331474). CARAVAN AND TENTS. One luxury six-berth caravan. Two separate bedrooms; shower and WC. Fridge, cooker, hot and cold water, gas fire, continental quilts and pillows, no linen. Electric light, 3-point plug sockets, TV. Disabled persons welcome. Well behaved pets accepted. Three touring van or tent spaces. Sited in enclosed south-facing area, picnic table and barbecue. The site offers a quiet farm holiday with coastal walks and beaches nearby. The farm is a 220 acre working dairy farm on North Devon/Cornwall border, one mile from A39. Rates from £150. Write or phone for further details.

BUDE. Willow Valley Holiday Park, Bush, Bude EX23 9LB (01288 353104). Our camp site, which is only two miles from Bude and the sandy surfing beaches, is set in a beautiful valley. There is a small river meandering through the site which adds to its beauty. We are only a small site, with 2 pitches on four acres of land and, as these are not arranged in rows but around the edges of the site, there are always plenty of open spaces. We have toilets, showers, dishwashing area and a laundry. We also have a children's adventure playground which is in full view of most pitches, but not set amongst them. Dogs on leads are very welcome and we have seven acres of land in which they can run free. We also have a wide variety of pets on site including chickens, ducks, rabbits and peacocks. Open 31st March to 31st October, but enquiries are welcome anytime. For further details please write or telephone for a brochure and price list.

LOOE. Mr and Mrs G. Veale, Trelay Farmpark, Pelynt, Looe PL13 2JX (01503 220900). Trelay Farmpark is a small, peaceful, friendly, family-run site. It is quiet, uncommercialised and surrounded by farmland. The park lies on a gentle south facing slope offering wide views of open countryside. Excellent new facilities include hot showers/launderette and disabled suite with wheelchair access. The three acre camping field is licensed for 55 tourers/tents etc. Good access, generous pitches, hook-ups. In adjoining area (1.5 acres) are 20 holiday caravans in a garden-like setting. Two new luxury caravans and two available for dog owners. The village of Pelynt which is half-a-mile away has shops, Post Office, restaurants, pub. Looe and Polperro are both just three miles away. Controlled dogs welcome. **ETC** ✓✓✓✓✓

CUMBRIA

BRAMPTON. Mrs O.R. Campbell, Irthing Vale Caravan Park, Old Church Lane, Brampton, Near Carlisle CA8 2AA (016977 3600). Popular with tourists whose prime concern is cleanliness, peace and quietness with the personal attention of the owner, this four-and-a-half acre park has pitches for 20 touring caravans, motorised caravans plus space for camping. There is a small site shop, laundry room, mains water and drainage and electric hook-ups. In fact all the amenities one would expect on a quiet, modern caravan park. We are very close to Hadrian's (Roman) Wall and convenient for having days out discovering romantic Scottish Border country. The ideal site for walking, sailing, fishing and golf. Open 1st March until 31st October. Terms from £8.50 per car/caravan plus two persons. Special reductions for hikers and cyclists. Caravan and Camping Club Listed site, AA ★★★
website: www.ukparks.com

CONISTON. Mrs E. Johnson, Spoon Hall, Coniston LA21 8AW (015394 41391). Caravans sleep 6. Three 33ft caravans situated on a 50 acre working hill farm one mile from Coniston, overlooking Coniston Lake. All have flush-toilet, shower, gas cookers, fires and water heaters, electric lighting and fridge plus colour TV. Children are welcome. Pets are allowed free. Available March to October. Pony trekking arranged from farm. Weekly terms on request.

NEWBY BRIDGE. Oak Head Caravan Park, Ayside, Grange-over-Sands LA11 6JA (015395 31475). Family owned and operated. Select, quiet, clean wooded site in the picturesque fells of the Lake District. Easy access from M6 Junction 36, 14 miles A590. On-site facilities include flush toilets, hot showers, hot and cold water, deep sinks for washing clothes, washing machine, tumble dryers and spin dryers, iron and deep freeze; hair dryers. Milk and gas on sale. Tourers (30 pitches) £10 per night (including electricity and VAT); Tents (30 pitches) £8 per night up to four persons. Open March 31st to October 31st.

POOLEY BRIDGE/LAKE ULLSWATER. Parkfoot Caravan and Camping Park, Howtown Road, Pooley Bridge, Penrith CA10 2NA (017684 86309; Fax: 017684 86041). Family-run park set in magnificent Lakeland scenery. Country Club, licensed bar, restaurant, take-away, games room. Free lake access with boat launching. Car parking. Ideal for watersports, sailing, boating, canoeing, windsurfing and fishing. Tennis court, mountain biking (hire available) and pony trekking from the Park. Private access to Barton Fell for walking. Modern toilets, hot showers, hair dryers, shaver points; fully equipped laundry room. Public telephones. Shop. Adventure playground and children's playgrounds. Camping fields have level and hill sites with views of Lake Ullswater. Grass and hardstanding pitches for touring caravans. Electric hook-ups. Self-catering log cabins and houses for hire. SAE, or telephone, for brochure.

FHG PUBLICATIONS LIMITED
publish a large range of well-known accommodation guides. We will be happy to send you details or you can use the order form at the back of this book.

ETC ★★★

Waterside House Campsite

Waterside House, Howtown Road, Pooley Bridge, Penrith CA10 2NA   Tel & Fax: 017684 86332

Farm and campsite situated about one mile from Pooley Bridge. Genuine Lakeside location with beautiful views of Lake Ullswater and Fells. Ideal for windsurfing, canoeing, boating, fell walking and fishing, table tennis, volleyball. Boat, canoe and mountain bike hire on site. Play area, shop and gas exchange also. SAE or telephone for brochure. Open March to October. Directions: M6 Junction 40, A66 follow signs for Ullswater, A592 to Pooley Bridge, one mile along Howtown Road on right - signposted.

WASDALE. Mrs Ruth Knight, Church Stile Farm, Wasdale, Seascale CA20 1ET (019467 26252). A quiet, secluded farm park on a working family farm welcoming tents, motor caravans and dormobiles, no touring caravans. It is approximately one-and-a-half miles to Wastwater Lake and the nearest fells, Scafell is five miles. This is an excellent walking and climbing area with glorious scenery. Nine miles to Muncaster Castle and the Ravenglass and Eskdale Railway. Ideal for touring the rest of the Lake District. Children and pets welcome. Children's play area. Facilities include showers, toilets, washbasins, laundry room, hot and cold water and electricity throughout the toilet block. Electric hook-ups. Two country hotels in the village for either food or drink. Price list supplied on request. Open March to November.

DERBYSHIRE

BUXTON near. Mr and Mrs J. Melland, The Pomeroy Caravan Park, Street House Farm, Flagg, Near Buxton SK17 9QG (01298 83259). Working farm. This site for 30 caravans is situated five miles from Buxton, in the heart of the Peak District National Park. Ideal base for touring by car or walking. Site adjoins northern-end of now famous Tissington and High Peak Trail. Only nine miles from Haddon Hall and ten from Chatsworth House. Landscaped to the latest model standards for caravan sites; tourers and campers will find high standards here. Toilet block with showers, washing facilities and laundry; mains electric hook-up points. Back-packers welcome. Large rally field available. Children welcome; dogs on lead. Touring rates £6 to £6.50 for two people per night. Open Easter to end of October. SAE for brochure please. **ETC ✓✓✓**

BUXTON near. R.J. Macara, Newhaven Caravan and Camping Park, Newhaven, Near Buxton SK17 0DT (01298 84300). Delightful site in the heart of the Peak District providing an ideal centre for touring the Derbyshire Dales, walking, climbing, potholing, etc. Convenient for visiting Chatsworth, Haddon House, Hardwick House, Alton Towers, Matlock and the Dams. Two first class toilet blocks providing FREE hot water; electric hook-ups. Children's playground, playroom, fully stocked shop supplying Calor and Camping gas, fresh groceries, etc. Laundry. Ice pack freezing facilities. Restaurant adjacent. Tents, motor vans, caravans. Pets and children welcome. AA Three Pennant site. Terms from £7.25 per night, discount for seven nights or more. SAE for brochure. **ETC ★★★**

DEVON

ASHBURTON. Parkers Farm Holiday Park, Ashburton TQ13 7LJ (01364 652598; Fax: 01364 654004).

A friendly, family-run farm site, set in 400 acres and surrounded by beautiful countryside. 12 miles to the sea and close to Dartmoor National Park. Ideal for touring Devon/Cornwall. Perfect for children and pets with all farm animals, play area and plenty of space to roam, also large area for dogs. Holiday cottages and caravans fully equipped except for linen. Level touring site with some hard standings. Electric hook-up. Free showers in fully tiled block, laundry room and games room. Small family bar, restaurant, shop and phone. Prices start from £90 Low Season to £380 High Season. Good discounts for couples. To find us: From Exeter take A38 to Plymouth till you see "26 miles Plymouth" sign; take second left at Alston Cross signposted to Woodland and Denbury. British Farm Toursit Award. 1999 Gold Award for Quality and Service. Silver David Bellamy Conservation Award. Practical Caravan Top 100 Parks 1998. **ETC** ★★★, **AA** *FOUR PENNANTS*, **RAC** *RECOMMENDED*.
e-mail: parkersfarm@btconnect.com
website: www.parkersfarm.co.uk

BIDEFORD. Mrs J.A. Fox, Highstead Farm, Bucks Cross, Bideford EX39 5DX (01237 431201). Large

and attractive modern caravan on a private farm site with fine sea views nearby. Just off the A39 Bideford/Bude road close to the coast of North Devon and convenient for Clovelly, Bideford and Westward Ho! Luxury accommodation for six adults (sleeping accommodation for up to 11 at extra charge) with bath/shower, separate toilet, fully equipped kitchen including microwave, gas fire and colour TV. Babysitting also available. Pets welcome by arrangement. Linen supplied as extra. Shopping, beaches, local attractions within easy reach. Car essential but good walking country. Open March to October from £95 weekly low season.

BIDEFORD. Mrs Sarah Hunt, Greencliff Farm, Abbotsham, Bideford EX39 1JL (01237 424674). Only

one caravan, peaceful situation, panoramic sea views, beautiful North Devon coastline. Mixed farm, Tudor farmhouse, easy access cliffs (coastal footpath) and rocky shore (prawning and surfing - for the experienced). Sleeps six in one double plus bunks. Gas cooker, fridge, hot and cold water, flush toilet, colour TV and fan heater. Separate building with toilet plus shower. Village amenities one mile, sandy beach at Westward Ho! three miles; water sports on Taw/Torridge estuary. Historic market town of Bideford two miles and convenient for Clovelly, Exmoor, Lundy. Price from £85 to £130 per week.

BRANSCOMBE. Mrs A.E. White, Berry Barton, Branscombe, Near Seaton EX12 3BD (01297 680208).
Our park stands above the picturesque old village of Branscombe with thatched cottages, bakery museum and smithy. There are two freehouses in the village, the nearest within easy walking distance. We offer a quiet, peaceful holiday for both retired people and families; there is a large area for children to play. The site is on our 300 acre dairy and mixed farm, with one mile of coastline. Riding available on site on Shetland ponies and larger horses. There are many lovely walks with golf and fishing within easy reach, as are Seaton and Sidmouth (5 miles), the fishing village of Beer (3 miles), and the motorway (17 miles). Six berth caravans available from March to November. Mains water; flush toilets; mains electricity; colour TV; fridge. All caravans have toilets; showers and hot water. Laundry room; showers; supermarket within easy reach. One dog per van permitted. Terms on application.

PLEASE SEND A STAMPED ADDRESSED ENVELOPE WITH ENQUIRIES

CHITTLEHAMHOLT (North Devon). Snapdown Farm Caravans, Chittlehamholt. 12 only, six-berth caravans with all facilities in beautiful unspoilt country setting down our quiet lane. Very peaceful, quiet and secluded, and well away from busy roads. Each with hard standing for car and each with outside seats and picnic table. Table tennis. Children's play area in small wood adjoining. Laundry room. PLENTY OF SPACE - field and woodland walks on farm. Lots of wildlife. Help feed and milk the goats. Within easy reach of sea and moors. Well behaved pets welcome. Terms: £90 to £240 including gas and electricity. Reductions for couples early and late season. Illustrated brochure from **Mrs M. Bowen, Snapdown Cottage, Chittlehamholt, Umberleigh EX37 9PF (01769 540708).**

See also Colour Display Advertisement **COLYTON. Bonehayne Farm, Colyton EX24 6SG. Working farm.** Enjoy a relaxing holiday, deep in the tranquil Devon countryside, on a 250-acre working farm. Situated on the banks of the River Coly, ideal for trout fishing, or spot a kingfisher in a beautiful sheltered valley. Two miles from Colyton and four-and-a-half miles from coast, is situated our spacious self-catering cottage. It is part of the farmhouse (south-facing), with many olde worlde features, and is fully equipped, including a four-poster. There are also two luxury caravans, each on its own site (south-facing), situated in the farmhouse's spacious garden. They are well-equipped; laundry room, barbecue, picnic tables and chairs. Bed and Breakfast also available. Details from **Mrs S. Gould (01404 871416) or Mrs R. Gould (01404 871396).**
e-mail: thisfarm33@netscapeonline.co.uk
website: www.members.netscapeonline.co.uk/thisfarm33

See also Colour Display Advertisement **COMBE MARTIN. Stowford Farm Meadows Touring Park, Combe Martin EX34 0PW (01271 882476; Fax: 01271 883053).** Situated at the heart of North Devon's glorious countryside, and on the western edge of Exmoor National Park, this site has a superb rural setting. Site renowned for superb range of facilities and excellent value for money. Facilities include four modern luxury amenity blocks, laundry facilities, the old stable bars and indoor heated swimming pool. Shop, snooker, games room, horse riding, golf, sports field, undercover mini-zoo, petorama, crazy golf, kiddies kars and cycle hire. Recently developed 70 acres of woodland nature trails and woodland walks. Prices from £4.00 per unit per night, electric hook-up from £1. Pets welcome. AA 5 Pennants. "Premier Park". "Practical Caravan Regional Choice 1998," "Caravan Life UK Best Sites" sixth place out of 185. "Most Popular Feature: Summer Parking- Easter to November, only £60". "Why Tow?". **ETC** ✓✓✓

CULLOMPTON. Mr A. R. Davey, Pound Farm, Butterleigh, Cullompton EX15 1PH (01884 855 208). Working farm. Sleeps 6. A Pound Farm holiday combines finest English scenery with traditional beauty of village of Butterleigh, half-a-mile away. Enjoy family break from April to November on this 80-acre sheep and beef farm. Spacious comfortable caravan accommodation for six, in grass paddock with paths and parking for two cars. Enter by road. Well-equipped. Hot and cold water, shower. Electric power points (8) £1 coin metre. All cutlery, utensils, blankets and pillows. Washroom/utility room. Adjoining caravan has flush toilet, double drainer, stainless steel sink unit in utility room with shaving point, hot/cold water, electric light and two-bar heater. Farmstead within sight of caravans. Visitors free to walk over the farm. South and North coast 45 to 60 minutes' drive. Four miles from M5, Cullompton, North Devon link road (A361), Tiverton, Silverton, Bickleigh thatched olde worlde village in heart of beautiful Exe Valley. Pets allowed. Free coarse fishing, no closed season - carp, tench, perch, roach, rudd. Terms from £140 to £160. FHG Diploma Winner.

HONITON. Francis Wigram, Riggles Farm, Upottery, Honiton EX14 4SP (01404 891229). Working farm. Caravans sleeps 6. Two beautifully situated caravans on 300 acre beef, sheep, arable farm six miles from Honiton, with easy access to many lovely beaches, moors and local attractions. Visitors welcome on farm, well behaved pets accepted. Children's play area, table tennis, darts. Linen hire, washing machine and dryer. Caravans set in two peaceful acres near farmhouse. Each is fully equipped for two/six people. Two separate bedrooms and spacious living areas. Own bathroom with shower, flush toilet, washbasin. Gas cooker, heater, colour TV, fridge. Terms from £95 to £225 per week (10% reduction for couples, not school holidays). For brochure please write or telephone.
e-mail: rigglesfarm@farming.co.uk
website: www.braggscottage.co.uk

Edge of Teign Valley Forest

HALDON LODGE FARM
KENNFORD, NEAR EXETER
Tel: (01392) 832312

Delightful modern caravans only five miles Exeter and short distance Dawlish, Teignmouth and Torbay, from £70 to £195 (high season). Lounge (TV), two bedrooms, kitchen, bathroom, (washbasin and toilet). Attractive private grounds in peaceful surroundings, forest walks, famous village inns, three well stocked fishing lakes, farm food and shop nearby. Small private camping site, pony trekking or riding holiday available; special welcome to inexperienced riders also the personal service of a small family-run private site.

RIDING & TREKKING • PETS WELCOME • OPEN ALL YEAR • ENQUIRIES D. L. SALTER

KINGSBRIDGE. Mrs Meacher, Mounts Farm Touring Park, The Mounts, Near East Allington, Kingsbridge TQ9 7QJ (01548 521591). Mounts Farm is a family-run site in the heart of South Devon. On site facilities include FREE hot showers, flush toilets, FREE hot water in washing-up room, razor points, laundry, information room, electric hook-ups and site shop. We welcome tents, touring caravans and motor caravans. Large pitches in level, sheltered fields. No charges for awnings. Children and pets welcome. Situated three miles north of Kingsbridge, Mounts Farm is an ideal base for exploring Dartmouth, Salcombe, Totnes, Dartmoor and the many safe sandy beaches nearby. Please telephone or write for a free brochure. Self-catering cottage also available.

TOTNES. J. and E. Ball, Higher Well Farm and Holiday Park, Stoke Gabriel, Totnes TQ9 6RN (01803 782289). A quiet secluded farm park welcoming tents, motor caravans and touring caravans. It is less than one mile from the riverside village of Stoke Gabriel and within four miles of Torbay beaches. Central for touring South Devon. Facilities include new toilet/shower block for 2001 with dishwashing and family rooms. Electric hook-ups and hard standings. Launderette, shop and payphone. Also static caravans to let from £120 per week or £17 per night. **ETC ★★**.

WOOLACOMBE. Mrs Gilbert, North Morte Farm Caravan and Camping, Dept. FHG, Mortehoe, Woolacombe EX34 7EG (01271 870381). The nearest camping and caravan park to the sea, in perfectly secluded beautiful coastal country. Our family-run park, adjoining National Trust land, is only 500 yards from Rockham Beach, yet only five minutes' walk from the village of Mortehoe with a Post Office, petrol station/garage, shops, cafes and pubs – one of which has a children's room. Four to six berth holiday caravans for hire and pitches for tents, dormobiles and touring caravans, electric hook-ups available. We have hot showers and flush toilets, laundry room, shop and off-licence; Calor gas and Camping Gaz available; children's play area. Dogs accepted but must be kept on lead. Open Easter to end September. Brochure available.

NORTH MORTE FARM CARAVAN & CAMPING PARK

FHG

Visit the website

www.holidayguides.com

for details of the wide choice of accommodation featured in the full range of FHG titles

DORSET

MANOR FARM HOLIDAY CENTRE
Charmouth, Bridport, Dorset DT6 6QL
Situated in a rural valley. Charmouth beach a level ten minutes' walk away.

Luxury 6-berth Caravans for Hire with toilet/shower, refrigerator, full cooker, colour TV, gas fire.

30-acre Tourist Park for touring caravans, dormobiles and tents

Centre facilities include • Toilets • Hotel showers • Licensed bar with family room • Bar food available • Amusement room • Launderette • Shop and Off-licence • Swimming pool • Electric hook-up points • Calor Gas and Camping Gaz • Ice pack service • Chemical disposal unit • Disabled facilities

Send SAE for colour brochure to Mr R. B. Loosmore or Tel. 01297 560226

website: www.manorfarmholidaycentre.co.uk   *See also Colour Display Advertisement*

LYME REGIS. Mrs J. Tedbury, Little Paddocks, Yawl Hill Lane, Lyme Regis DT7 3RW (01297 443085).

Sleeps 6. A six-berth caravan on Devon/Dorset border in a well-kept paddock overlooking Lyme Bay and surrounding countryside. Situated on a smallholding with animals, for perfect peace and quiet. Lyme Regis two-and-a-half miles, Charmouth three-and-a-half miles. Both have safe beaches for children. Easy driving distance to resorts of Seaton, Beer and Sidmouth. The caravan is fully equipped except linen. It has shower room with handbasin and toilet inside as well as flush toilet just outside. Electric light, fridge and TV. Calor gas cooker and fire. Car can be parked alongside. Dogs welcome. Terms from £90. Also fully equipped chalet for two from £75. SAE, please.

See also Colour Display Advertisement

WIMBORNE. Woolsbridge Manor Farm Caravan Park, Three Legged Cross, Wimborne, Dorset BH21 6RA (01202 826369). Situated approximately three-and-a-half-miles from the New Forest market town of Ringwood – easy access to the south coast. Seven acres level, semi-sheltered, well-drained spacious pitches. Quiet country location on a working farm, ideal and safe for families. Showers, mother/baby area, laundry room, washing up area, chemical disposal, payphone, electric hook-ups, battery charging. Children's play area on site. Site shop. Dogs welcome on leads. Fishing adjacent. Moors Valley Country Park golf course one mile. Pub and restaurant 10 minutes' walk. **AA** *THREE PENNANTS*. **ETC** ✓✓✓

FHG

PLEASE MENTION THIS GUIDE WHEN YOU WRITE

OR PHONE TO ENQUIRE ABOUT ACCOMMODATION

IF YOU ARE WRITING, A STAMPED, ADDRESSED

ENVELOPE IS ALWAYS APPRECIATED

LINCOLNSHIRE

GRANTHAM. Mrs D. Coradine, Woodland Waters, Willoughby Road, Ancaster, Grantham NG32 3RT

(Tel & Fax:01400 230888). 72 acres of beautiful wooded walks. Four fishing lakes. Touring, camping, statics, luxury lodges. Rallies welcome, bar/restaurant (also available for private hire). Four golf courses nearby. Hook-ups with adjoining water taps. Open all year.
e-mail: info@woodlandwaters.co.uk
website: www.woodlandwaters.co.uk

MARKET RASEN. Mr Robert Cox, Manor Farm Caravan Site, Manor Farm, East Frisby, Market Rasen

LN8 2DB (01673 878258). A small 15 touring caravan and six tent site ideal for visiting Lincoln and the Lincolnshire Wolds. Set in three acres over two level fields - one for families, the other for solitude. New toilet block for the year 2000. Ideal cycling country neighbouring a Saxon settlement reconstruction. Tents, caravans, caravanettes, trailer tents welcome. Electric hook-ups, toilets, hot showers, gas exchange and small animals area. Cycles/tandems for hire. We also have a gypsy-style caravan for hire. Ten miles from Lincoln.

FHG PUBLICATIONS

publish a large range of well-known accommodation guides. We will be happy to send you details or you can use the order form at the back of this book.

NORFOLK

NORTHUMBERLAND

ALNWICK. Mrs J.W. Bowden, "Anvil-Kirk", 8 South Charlton Village, Alnwick NE66 2NA (01665

579324). One six-berth caravan on single private site. Hard standing and lovely spacious surroundings. Three-quarters of a mile from the A1; six miles north of Alnwick and six miles also from the lovely clean beaches of Beadnell, Seahouses, Craster Village; nine miles from the Cheviot Hills. Many castles nearby – Bamburgh and Alnwick being the largest; wild cattle and bird sanctuaries; Ingram Valley for the hill walker, Berwick and Morpeth markets. Holy Island is a must with its tiny castle and harbour with fishing boats. Many places to eat out within a radius of 10 miles. The caravan has mains water and electricity; electric cooker, fridge, microwave, TV. End bedroom (bunk beds); flush toilet in bathroom. Open Easter to October. Children and pets welcome. Milk and papers delivered daily. Terms from £165 to £195 per week. One Rose Award. SAE, please. Also Bed and Breakfast available in house from £18 to £20 per night.

NORTH NORTHUMBERLAND. Mrs Ann Gold, Barmoor South Moor, Lowick, Berwick-upon-Tweed TD15

2QF (01289 388205). If you enjoy the tranquillity of the countryside, but would like to be within easy reach of the beautiful Northumbrian coastline, Cheviot Hills and Scottish Borders you will find we are the perfect location. Our working farm is two miles from Lowick village and half way between Wooler and Berwick-upon-Tweed, just off the B6525. We have two six-berth caravans to let situated on a peaceful site of five caravans, adjacent to the farmyard. Both have mains services, including shower, toilet, TV and fridge. Dogs welcome. £115 - £210 per week. Open Easter to end of October. **ETC ★★★★**
HOLIDAY PARK
e-mail: BARRGOLD@farming.co.uk

SHROPSHIRE

CRAVEN ARMS. Mrs S. Thomas, Llanhowell Farm, Hopton Castle, Craven Arms SY7 0QG (01588 660307). Comfortable and well equipped mobile home (30'x10'). Single site with own lawn, located on an upland working family farm. Sleeps four to five in two separate bedrooms, kitchen includes full cooker, fridge and microwave. Lounge area includes colour TV and gas fire. Shower room with all services. Linen included. Local village pubs provide good food. Historic town of Ludlow approximately 14 miles. Booking concessions for two people or less and long lets. 10% deposit required on booking. Prices on application.

SOMERSET

DULVERTON. Mrs M.M. Jones, Higher Town, Dulverton TA22 9RX (01398 341272). Working farm.

Caravans sleep 8. Our farm is situated half-a-mile from open moorland, one mile from the Devon/Somerset border and four miles from Dulverton. 80 acres of the farm is in the Exmoor National Park. We let two caravans which are quarter-of-a-mile apart and do not overlook each other, and have lovely views, situated in lawns with parking space. Both are eight berth, with a double end bedroom, bunk bedroom, shower, flush toilet, hot/cold water and colour TV. The caravans are modern and fully equipped except linen. Cot and high chair available. One caravan new for season 1999 with three bedrooms. Visitors are welcome to watch the milking or walk over our beef and sheep farm. Riding and fishing nearby. Open May to October. Price from £85, includes gas and electricity.

TAUNTON. Mr and Mrs D.A. Small, Ashe Farm Caravan and Camping Site, Thornfalcon, Taunton TA3 5NW (01823 442567; Fax: 01823 443372).

In the vale of Taunton Deane, quiet farm site, with 30 touring pitches and two holiday caravans. Sheltered mowed meadow with easy access quarter-mile off A358, four miles south east of Taunton. Showers, toilet, hot water, deep sinks, shaver points, electric hook-ups, telephone, shop, games room and tennis court, laundry. AA Three Pennants. Pets welcome. Ideal touring site within easy reach of North and South coasts and Quantock and Blackdown Hills, Exmoor and the Somerset Levels. The fully equipped holiday caravans sleep six. Open April to October, from £3.25 per person. From M5 Junction 25, take A358 for two-and-a-half miles, then turn right at "Nags Head". **ETC ★★**

WIVELSCOMBE. Mrs A. Taylor, Waterrow Touring Park, Near Wivelscombe, Taunton TA4 2AZ (01984 623464; Fax: 01984 624280).

One only three-bedroom holiday home with uninterrupted views across the Tone Valley. The luxury specification includes accommodation for up to six (maximum four adults), shower room, fitted galley kitchen, colour TV, linen included. Well behaved dogs welcome. We also have separate facilities for caravans, motor-homes and tents on our touring park bordered by woods and the River Tone. Attractive landscaping with spacious pitches in a peaceful setting where you can relax and watch the buzzards soaring overhead. Excellent touring area close to the Somerset/Devon border and Exmoor, with fishing, walking, golf, etc., available locally. Good pubs three minutes walk. Park open all year. Please ring for brochure. **ETC ★★, AA** *TWO PENNANTS*
e-mail: taylor@waterrowpark.u-net.com
website: www.waterrowpark.u-net.com

When making enquiries or bookings, a stamped addressed envelope is always appreciated

STAFFORDSHIRE

COTTON. Star Caravan Park, Cotton, Near Alton Towers, Stoke-on-Trent ST10 3DW (01538 702256/702219/702564). Situated off the B5417 road, between Leek and Cheadle, within ten miles of the market towns of Ashbourne and Uttoxeter, with Alton Towers just three-quarters-of-a-mile away. A family-run site where your enjoyment is our main concern. Site amenities include large children's play area, shop, toilet block with free showers, etc. laundry room with drying and ironing facilities, electric hook-ups, etc. Dogs welcome but must be kept on a leash. Open 1st March to 31st October. £5 per night for two persons. Special rates for groups and parties of campers (Scouts, schools, etc.). Static caravans for hire. Brochure and further details available. **ETC ★★★, AA** *THREE PENNANTS.* website: www.starcaravanpark.co.uk

NORTH YORKSHIRE

WHITBY (Near). Partridge Nest Farm, Eskdaleside, Sleights, Whitby YO22 5ES (01947 810450). Set in beautiful Esk Valley, six caravans on secluded site in 45 acres of interesting land reaching up to the moors. Beautiful views. Just five minutes from the sea and the ancient fishing town of Whitby. The North Yorkshire Moors Steam Railway starts two miles away at Grosmont. Ideal for children, bird-watchers and all country lovers. Each caravan has mains electricity, gas cooker, fire, colour TV, fridge and shower/WC. Ideal touring centre. Riding lessons available on our own horses/ponies. Terms from £140 to £255. Two double Bed and Breakfast rooms also available from £16 per person.

PLEASE MENTION THIS GUIDE WHEN YOU WRITE OR PHONE TO ENQUIRE ABOUT ACCOMMODATION

IF YOU ARE WRITING, A STAMPED, ADDRESSED ENVELOPE IS ALWAYS APPRECIATED

FREE or REDUCED RATE entry to Holiday Visits and Attractions — see our READERS' OFFER VOUCHERS on pages 43-60

ENGLAND

Activity Holidays

DEVON

Edge of Teign Valley Forest

HALDON LODGE FARM
KENNFORD, NEAR EXETER
Tel: (01392) 823312

Delightful modern caravans only five miles Exeter and short distance Dawlish, Teignmouth and Torbay, from £70 to £195 (high season). Lounge (TV), two bedrooms, kitchen, bathroom (washbasin and toilet). Attractive private grounds in peaceful surroundings, forest walks, famous village inns, three well stocked fishing lakes, farm food and shop nearby. Small private camping site, pony trekking or riding holiday available; special welcome to inexperienced riders also the personal service of a small family-run private site.

RIDING & TREKKING • PETS WELCOME • OPEN ALL YEAR • ENQUIRIES D. L. SALTER

ASHBURTON. Parkers Farm Holiday Park, Ashburton TQ13 7LJ (01364 652598; Fax: 01364 654004).

A friendly, family-run farm site, set in 400 acres and surrounded by beautiful countryside. 12 miles to the sea and close to Dartmoor National Park. Ideal for touring Devon/Cornwall. Perfect for children and pets with all farm animals, play area and plenty of space to roam, also large area for dogs. Holiday cottages and caravans fully equipped except for linen. Level touring site with some hard standings. Electric hook-up. Free showers in fully tiled block, laundry room and games room. Small family bar, restaurant, shop and phone. Prices start from £90 Low Season to £380 High Season. Good discounts for couples. To find us: From Exeter take A38 to Plymouth till you see "26 miles Plymouth" sign; take second left at Alston Cross signposted to Woodland and Denbury. British Farm Tourist Award. 1999 Gold Award for Quality and Service. Silver David Bellamy Conservation Award. Practical Caravan Top 100 Parks 1998. **ETC ★★★, AA** *FOUR PENNANTS,* **RAC** *RECOMMENDED.*
e-mail: parkersfarm@btconnect.com
website: www.parkersfarm.co.uk

DEVON, AXMINSTER. Mrs C. M. Putt, Highridge Guest House, Lyme Road, Axminster EX13 5BQ

(01297 34037). BOARD: FISHING. River, fly and coarse fishing – 18 different venues available. We have detailed information on each venue including maps and photos of fish. Ideal for a good day's fishing. All facilities including bait, fridge, drying room. Large lounge, good food, packed lunches available. Pretty gardens with wildfowl and ponds. Terms from £16.50 per night Bed and Breakfast, Evening Meal from £8.50.

SOMERSET

SOMERSET, CHEDDAR. Broadway House Holiday Touring Caravan and Camping Park, Cheddar BS27 3DB (01934 742610; Fax: 01934 744950). SELF-CATERING: GENERAL. Cheddar Gorge - "England's Grand Canyon." A totally unique five star caravan and camping family experience. One of the most interesting inland parks in the West Country. A family business specialising in family holidays. A free cuddle with the llamas a speciality. Prices include the use of the heated outdoor swimming pool and entrance to the Bar/Family room. Activities on the park include archery, shooting; mountain bike/tandem hire; table tennis, crazy golf, boules, croquet, skate-board ramps. **ETC ★★★★** AA 5 Pennants, RAC Appointed, David Bellamy Gold Award.
e-mail: enquiries@broadwayhouse.uk.com
website: www.broadwayhouse.uk.com

Board Accommodation
SCOTLAND

Ratings You Can Trust

ENGLAND

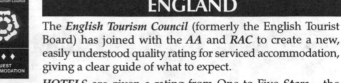

The *English Tourism Council* (formerly the English Tourist Board) has joined with the *AA* and *RAC* to create a new, easily understood quality rating for serviced accommodation, giving a clear guide of what to expect.

HOTELS are given a rating from One to Five *Stars* – the more Stars, the higher the quality and the greater the range of facilities and level of services provided.

GUEST ACCOMMODATION, which includes guest houses, bed and breakfasts, inns and farmhouses, is rated from One to Five *Diamonds*. Progressively higher levels of quality and customer care must be provided for each one of the One to Five Diamond ratings.

HOLIDAY PARKS, TOURING PARKS and CAMPING PARKS are now also assessed using *Stars*. Standards of quality range from a One Star (acceptable) to a Five Star (exceptional) park.

Look out also for the new *SELF-CATERING* Star ratings. The more *Stars* (from One to Five) awarded to an establishment, the higher the levels of quality you can expect. Establishments at higher rating levels also have to meet some additional requirements for facilities.

NB Some self-catering properties had not been assessed at the time of going to press and in these cases the old-style KEY symbols will still be shown.

SCOTLAND

Star Quality Grades will reflect the most important aspects of a visit, such as the warmth of welcome, efficiency and friendliness of service, the quality of the food and the cleanliness and condition of the furnishings, fittings and decor.

THE MORE STARS,
THE HIGHER THE STANDARDS.

The description, such as Hotel, Guest House, Bed and Breakfast, Lodge, Holiday Park, Self-catering etc tells you the type of property and style of operation.

In England, Scotland and Wales, all graded properties are inspected annually by Tourist Authority trained Assessors.

WALES

Places which score highly will have an especially welcoming atmosphere and pleasing ambience, high levels of comfort and guest care, and attractive surroundings enhanced by thoughtful design and attention to detail

STAR QUALITY GUIDE FOR SERVICED ACCOMMODATION AND HOLIDAY PARKS

★★★★★ *Exceptional quality*
★★★★ *Excellent quality*
★★★ *Very good quality*
★★ *Good quality*
★ *Fair to good quality*

SELF-CATERING ACCOMMODATION

The *DRAGON GRADES* spell out the quality. They range from Grade 1 (simple and reasonable) to Grade 5 (excellent quality). The grades reflect the overall quality, not the range of facilities.

SCOTLAND

Board Accommodation

The Black Watch Museum
Balhousie Castle, Perth PH1 5HR
Tel: 0131 310 8530

Two-and-a-half centuries of treasures of the 42nd/73rd Highland regiments.
The Museum displays by means of pictures, weapons, uniforms and medals
the 250 year history of Scotland's Senior Highland Regiment.

Admission is FREE — donations to Museum Fund.

Opening Times: *May to September* (*Monday to Saturday incl. Public Holidays*):
10am to 4.30pm. *NB Closed last Saturday of June.*
October to April: (*Monday to Friday*) 10am to 3.30pm.
Closed 23rd December to 6th January.

See also Colour Display Advertisement BRECHIN. **Brechin Castle Centre, Haughmuir, by Brechin, Angus** (**01356 626813**). One of the largest tourist attractions in Angus and a great day out for all the family. High quality Garden Centre and Coffee Shop. Country Park with ornamental lake. Picnic and enjoy the tranquillity, walk around the park to the farm, touch the animals. Summer Events. Brochure on request.

PLEASE MENTION THIS GUIDE WHEN YOU WRITE

OR PHONE TO ENQUIRE ABOUT ACCOMMODATION

IF YOU ARE WRITING, A STAMPED, ADDRESSED

ENVELOPE IS ALWAYS APPRECIATED

FREE or REDUCED RATE entry to
Holiday Visits and Attractions — see our
READERS' OFFER VOUCHERS on pages 43-60

ABERDEENSHIRE, BANFF & MORAY

FOCHABERS. Mrs Alexia Shand, Castlehill Farm, Blackdam, Fochabers IV32 7LJ (Tel & Fax: 01343 820351).

Comfortable accommodation on working farm at edge of forest with panoramic views to Ben Aigen. Lovely trails to walk or cycle. Deer and badgers are some of the woodland's inhabitants in addition to the birdlife. Ideal base for touring, golf, fishing, sandy beaches and old fishing villages locally. The famous Speyside Way, Whisky and Castle Trails are nearby. Accommodation comprises one double room and one family/twin room both with washbasin and tea/coffee making facilities, full central heating and electric blankets. Guest lounge with coal fire. After an active day enjoy this peaceful overnight stop. A warm welcome awaits you from your welcome host. STB ★★★ *B&B.*

METHLICK. Mrs Christine Staff, Sunnybrae Farm, Gight, Methlick, Ellon AB41 7JA (01651 806456).

Working farm. Comfortable accommodation on a working farm situated in a quiet, peaceful location with superb views. Close to Castle, Whisky and Stone Circle Trails. Centrally located for many places of interest. One twin and one double bedrooms, both en suite and one single room. All rooms have tea/coffee making facilities. Guest lounge with colour TV. Full central heating. Full farmhouse breakfast. Ample parking space. Open all year. Pets welcome. Bed and Breakfast from £18; reduced rates for children. A warm welcome awaits all guests. STB ★★ *B&B.*

PETERHEAD. Carrick Guest House, 16 Merchant Street, Peterhead AB42 1DU (Tel & Fax: 01779 470610). Comfortable accommodation centrally situated for all amenities. Two minutes' walk from main shopping centre, harbour and beach. All rooms en suite, colour television, hospitality tray, trouser press, hairdryer. Full central heating. Good car parking. Bed and Breakfast from £20 to £25 per person. STB ★★ *GUEST HOUSE.*

ARGYLL & BUTE

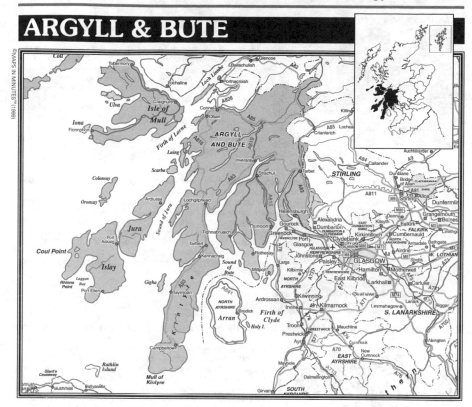

©MAPS IN MINUTES™ (1999)

ARDMADDY, (Near Oban). Mrs D. Gilbert, Ardshellach Farm, Ardmaddy, near Oban PA34 4QY

(01852 300218). Working beef-cattle and sheep farm situated on the Ardmaddy road 12 miles from Oban on the B844 to Easdale and approximately one mile before the Bridge over the Atlantic and Ardmaddy Castle Gardens. This quiet accommodation is 400 yards from the sea overlooking Luing and Scarba and comprises one room sleeping two/four. Bathroom with bath and shower adjacent. TV lounge. Children welcome. Bed and Breakfast from £15 includes evening cup of tea. Bar meals available by Atlantic Bridge.

ARROCHAR. Mrs C. Bowen, The Roadman's Cottage, Rest and Be Thankful, By Arrochar G83 7AS

(01301 702 557). By itself in breathtakingly beautiful Glen Croe, seven miles from Loch Lomond on the A83 with Inveraray 15 miles. Scenic routes to Campbeltown or Oban, the west coast and islands. Access to easy walks in Argyll Forest Park which is rich in flora and fauna. Hillwalking and climbing on Munros. Adjacent to farmland, good fishing on Loch Long. I bake my own bread and enjoy cooking local produce. Traditional and vegetarian menus are offered. Bed and Breakfast £15 to £16. Dinner £10. One double or family room, one twin room. **STB ★★** *B&B*

CARRADALE. Mrs D. MacCormick, Mains Farm, Carradale, Campbeltown PA28 6QG (01583 431216).

Working farm. From April to October farmhouse accommodation is offered at Mains Farm, five minutes' walk from safe beach, forestry walks with views of Carradale Bay and Arran. Near main bus route and 15 miles from airport. Golf, sea/river fishing, pony trekking, canoeing locally. Comfortable accommodation in one double, one single, one family bedrooms; guests' sitting/diningroom with coal/log fire; bathroom, toilet. Heating in rooms according to season. Children welcome at reduced rates, cot and high chair available. Pets by prior arrangement. The house is not suitable for disabled visitors. Good home cooking and special diets catered for. Bed and Breakfast from £17. Tea making facilities in rooms. STB ★★ B&B.

DALMALLY. Eredine House, South-East Lochaweside, Eredine PA33 1BP (Tel & Fax: 01866 844207).

This magnificent Georgian house is beautifully positioned on an elevated site commanding spectacular views over Loch Awe and the surrounding hills. The secluded grounds consist mainly of attractive mature trees; a mile of private shoreline on the loch provides a private beach. Bed and Breakfast accommodation is available in the main house, and there are two fully equipped cottages for self-catering. Situated on the B840, eight miles north-east of Ford and 10 miles south-west of Portsonachan. Details on request.

HELENSBURGH. Mrs Elizabeth Howie, Drumfork Farm, Helensburgh G84 7JY (01436 672329).

Traditional sandstone farmhouse, extensively refurbished, all rooms en suite, some with sea view. Organic food served and we offer packed lunches, afternoon teas and high teas. The Victorian seaside town of Helensburgh, with its wide streets and stylish architecture, is port of call for paddle steamer 'Waverley' and home to Hill House by Charles Rennie MacKintosh. Open all year. Non-smoking. Babysitting available. Bed and Breakfast from £18 per person per night. STB ★★★ B & B.
e-mail: drumforkfarm@aol.com.uk.

INVERARAY. Mrs M Semple, Killean Farmhouse, Inveraray PA32 8XT (01499 302474).

Killean Farmhouse is located just a few miles outside Inveraray. Ideally situated for walking, climbing, pony trekking or just touring. There's fishing for trout, pike or salmon and opportunities to enjoy boating, water skiing or windsurfing. The whole area is steeped in history and the town of Inveraray itself is a classic example of 18th century Scottish town planning. With all this in mind the cottages provide high quality accommodation for family holidays.

LOCHGOILHEAD. Mrs Rosemary Dolan, The Shorehouse Inn, Lochgoilhead PA24 8AJ (01301 703340). Friendly informal Inn, fully licensed, has seven letting rooms, central heating and double glazing. There are two family, three twin, one single and one double bedrooms. Residents' lounge, a bar of unusual character and licensed restaurant. Home cooking, bar meals. Formerly the old manse on a historic site with lochside and panoramic views looking southward down Loch Goil, situated in the village on the shore. Local amenities include water sports, fishing, pony trekking, tennis, bowls, golf, swimming pool, curling in winter and a good area for hill walking. Some rooms with private facilities. Fully licensed. One hour travel time from Glasgow. Open all year round. Ideal for winter or summer breaks. Rates from £16 per person Bed and Breakfast, en suite £20 per person.

OBAN. Mrs K. Lambie, Thistle-Doo, Kilchrenan, By Taynuilt, Oban PA35 1HF (01866 833339). Awe-inspiring view of Loch Awe from our friendly family-run establishment. Ideal for all outdoor activities, fishing, hill walking, forest trails, Winter Ski (Glencoe 30 miles). Our peaceful, relaxing situation gives you easy access to visit castles, gardens, Highland Games and local shows. 20 miles east of Oban, taking the B845 off the A85 at Taynuilt to the shore of Loch Awe. Oban gives you ferry crossings to the Western Isles. All rooms en suite with TV, radio and tea/coffee making facilities. Open all year. Bed and Breakfast from £20. **STB** ★★★ *B & B.*

Oban, from Ardentraive Bay, Kerrera

AYRSHIRE & The Island of Arran

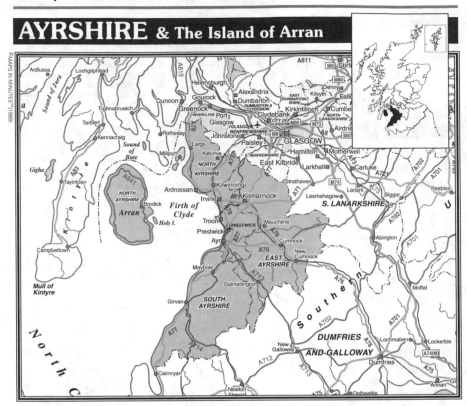

©MAPS IN MINUTES™ (1999)

AYR. Mrs Agnes Gemmell, Dunduff Farm, Dunure, Ayr KA7 4LH (01292 500225).

DUNDUFF FARM

Tel: 01292 500225 Fax: 01292

Welcome to Dunduff Farm where a warm, friendly atmosphere awaits you. Situated just south of Ayr at the coastal village of Dunure, this family-run beef and sheep unit of 600 acres is only 15 minutes from the shore providing good walks and sea fishing and enjoying close proximity to Dunure Castle and Park. Accommodation is of a high standard yet homely and comfortable. Bedrooms have washbasins, radio alarm, tea/coffee making facilities, central heating, TV, hair dryer and en suite facilities (the twin room has private bathroom). There is also a small farm cottage available sleeping two/four people. Bed and Breakfast from £23 per person; weekly rate £130. Cottage £250 per week. Colour brochure available. **STB** ★★★★ *B&B*, **AA/RAC** ◆◆◆◆◆

BEITH. Mrs Jane Gillan, Shotts Farm, Beith KA15 1LB (01505 502273). Comfortable friendly accommodation is offered on this 160 acre dairy farm situated one-and-a-half miles from the A736 Glasgow to Irvine road; well placed to visit golf courses, country parks, or leisure centre, also ideal for the ferry to Arran or Millport and for many good shopping centres all around. A high standard of cleanliness is assured by Mrs Gillan who is a first class cook holding many awards, food being served in the diningroom with its beautiful picture windows. Three comfortable bedrooms (double, family and twin), all with tea-making facilities, central heating and electric blankets. Two bathrooms with shower; sittingroom with colour TV. Children welcome. Bed and Breakfast from £14. Dinner can be arranged. **STB** ★★★ *B&B*, **AA** ★★★

DUNLOP. Mrs W. Burns, East Langton Farm, Dunlop KA3 4DS (01560 482978). A warm welcome in peaceful surroundings, close to all amenities. Twentry minutes to Glasgow or Prestwick Airport, also 20 minutes from the coast with spectacular views overlooking the Isle of Arran, Dalry and the Kilbirnie hills, and Ben Lomond in the distance. Very quiet, peaceful countryside. One double and two twin rooms, all with private bathroom/shower, TV with Teletext, radio alarm, tea/coffee making facilities and hair-dryer. Terms from £18.50 to £22.50 per person.

KILMARNOCK. Mrs M. Howie, Hill House Farm, Grassyards Road, Kilmarnock KA3 6HG (01563 523370). Enjoy a peaceful holiday on a working dairy farm two miles east of Kilmarnock. We offer a warm welcome with home baking for supper, choice of farmhouse breakfasts with own preserves. Three large comfortable bedrooms with lovely views over Ayrshire countryside, en suite facilities, tea/coffee making facilities, electric blankets, central heating; TV lounge, sun porch, diningroom and garden. Excellent touring base with trips to coast, Arran, Burns country and Glasgow nearby. Easy access to A77 and numerous golf courses. Children very welcome. Bed and Breakfast from £18 to £20 (including supper). Self-catering cottages also available. **STB ★★★★ B&B.**

LARGS. Mrs M. Watson, South Whittlieburn Farm, Brisbane Glen, Largs KA30 8SN (01475 675881; Fax: 01475 675080). Why not try our superb farmhouse accommodation? With lovely peaceful panoramic views on our working sheep farm. Ample parking. Only 5 minutes' drive from popular tourist resort of Largs. (near ferries to islands, and 45 minutes from Glasgow/Prestwick airports). Hillwalking, golf, riding, fishing, diving available. All rooms en suite, TV's, radio alarms, tea/coffee facilities, hairdryers, lounge, payphone. Central heating. Packed lunches and special diets catered for. Bed and Breakfast from £20. Reduced rates for children under 11 years. Open all year. Certified caravan and camping site on farm with electric hook-ups. toilet, shower, hot/cold washbasins from £6 per night. Please enquire about holiday caravans to hire. Warm friendly hospitality, delicious breakfasts, highly recommended. A warm welcome from Mary Watson. Enjoy a great holiday at South Whittlieburn Farm! **STB ★★★★ B&B. AA QQQQ SELECTED, RAC LISTED. CHOSEN BY "WHICH?" 'BEST BED & BREAKFAST'. WELCOME HOST.**

MAUCHLINE. Mrs J. Clark, Auchenlongford, Sorn, Mauchline KA5 6JF (01290 550761). The farm is situated in the hills above the picturesque village of Sorn, with its Castle set on a promontory above the River Ayr, and nearby its 17th century church. It is only 19 miles east from the A74 and 20 miles inland from the town of Ayr. Accommodation can be from a choice of three attractive, furnished bedrooms and there is also a large well appointed residents' lounge. Full Scottish breakfast is served with home made jams and marmalade; traditional High Tea and/or Dinners are also available on request. Bed and Breakfast £18; Bed, Breakfast and Evening Meal £28. Brochure available.

BORDERS

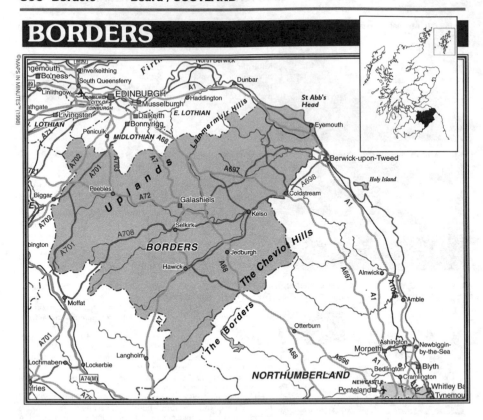

BIGGAR. Mrs Rosemary Harper, South Mains Farm, Biggar ML12 6HF (01899 860226). Working farm.

South Mains Farm is a working family farm, situated in an elevated position with good views, on the B7016 between Biggar and Broughton. An ideal place to take a break on a North/South journey. Edinburgh 29 miles, Peebles 11 miles. Well situated for touring the Border regions in general. A comfortable bed and excellent breakfast provided in this centrally heated and well-furnished farmhouse, which has two double and one single bedrooms. Open all year. Car essential, parking. Terms £16 per night which includes light supper of home-made scones, etc. If you are interested just ring, write or call in. Warm welcome assured.

DUNS. Mrs Rosemary Gaston, Ravelaw, Duns TD11 3NQ (01890 870207)

Ravelaw is a working arable farm, situated between the Lammermuir and Cheviot Hills, in a lovely rural setting. You are assured of an excellent breakfast and comfortable rooms. One en suite bathroom with shower, one en suite family room with shower and one double room with private bathroom. There is ample parking and real log fires on chilly evenings. We are placed mid-way between Edinburgh (45 miles) to north and Newcastle (60 miles) to south. The historic towns of Duns, Kelso and Berwick-upon-Tweed are all nearby with a wealth of castles and large houses to visit e.g. Floors Castle, Kelso; Manderston House, Duns; and Paxton House near Berwick-upon-Tweed. Open all year. Terms from £20 per night. Ideally placed for walking, shooting, fishing or golf.

GREENLAW. Mrs Carruthers, Bridgend House, 36 West High Street, Greenlaw TD10 6XA (01361

810270). Bridgend is on the scenic A697 road between Newcastle (68 miles south) and Edinburgh (38 miles north). Built in 1816, it retains many original features besides having three en suite bedrooms and one bedroom with private bathroom; lounge with colour TV, books, games and a real fire in winter. Traditional and wholefood breakfasts, home-baking and cooking with local produce in season. Parking available in courtyard. Trout fishing in River Blackadder from the pretty garden. Book one of our Special Weekend Breaks and come and unwind in the beautiful Scottish Borders. Bed and Breakfast from £18 to £20 per night depending on two people sharing.

TRAQUAIR. Mrs J. Caird, The Old School House, Traquair, Innerleithen EH44 6PL (Tel & Fax: 01896

830425). The Old School House has been recently modernised with wheelchair access. Stands above picturesque Traquair village, with spectacular views of the River Tweed valley. The Southern Upland Way passes close by; perfect walking and riding country. Nearby is Innerleithen Golf Course, historic Traquair House and Kailzie Garden with fishing lake. Salmon and trout fishing on Tweed; horses can be hired. Peebles is an attractive Border town with splendid woollen shops and a swimming pool .Edinburgh 35 minutes by car. Children and dogs welcome; stabling available; resident cats, dogs, ponies, hens and sometimes puppies. Log fire, home-cooked evening meals on request.

DUMFRIES & GALLOWAY

ANNAN. Mrs Mary Forrest, Hurkledale Farm, Cummertrees, Annan DG12 5QA (01461 700228). A warm

welcome awaits you at Hurkledale. Have a relaxing comfortable break here at our mixed farm. Our farmhouse is spacious and comfortable with panoramic views over the Solway Firth. All rooms are en suite or with private facilities and have hair dryers, television, radio and tea/coffee trolley. Enjoy walking, bird watching at Caerlaverock, and golf at Powfoot. Our quiet roads are suitable for cycling. Personal attention and quality guaranteed. Bed and Breakfast from £22 per person, Evening Meal from £10 per person.
e-mail: marykforrest@hotmail.com

CANONBIE. Mrs Steele, North Lodge, Canonbie DG14 0TF (013873 71409). A warm welcome awaits

you at this small family-run guest house situated approximately one mile south of the village of Canonbie, on the tourist route A7 to Edinburgh. Canonbie village is renowned for its fishing - private fishing on the "Willow Pool" can be arranged. NORTH LODGE is a 19th century cottage set in beautiful gardens and was recently extended to include five double/twin bedrooms, four en suite, the other has private facilities. The ground floor en suite room is suitable for the disabled traveller (Grade 1 classification). Within easy reach of Hadrian's Wall, the Lake District, Carlisle, Dumfries, Moffat, Kielder Dam, Hawick, Gretna and many more interesting places. An ideal touring base. Breaks available. Please telephone for further details.

CANONBIE. Miss G. Matthews, Four Oaks, Canonbie DG14 OTF (013873 71329).

Bed and Breakfast accommodation in comfortable, peaceful family home, with open views of lovely rolling countryside and farmland. Near the village of Canonbie, off the A7 just north of Carlisle, providing an excellent base for touring the Borderlands. Near River Esk. Accommodation provided in one twin room en suite, one double room with en suite bathroom with bath and shower. Cot available. Visitors' lounge with TV, tea/coffee making facilities, Garden and good parking.

CASTLE DOUGLAS. Mrs C. Pickup, Craigadam, Castle Douglas DG7 3HU (Tel & Fax: 01556 650233).

Working farm. A family-run 18th century farmhouse situated in the hills looking across Galloway. All bedrooms are en suite and there is a lovely oak-panelled dining room which offers Cordon Bleu cooking using local produce such as venison, pheasant, salmon. Oak-panelled billiards room. Come home in the evening to comfort, warmth and good Scottish hospitality. Fish on our own trout loch. The area offers much to the traveller with its lovely beaches, hill and forest walks, sailing, fishing, bird watching, pony trekking, golfing, as well as many places of historic and local interest. Please telephone **Richard or Celia** for further details. **STB ★★★★**B&B
website: www.craigadam.com

CASTLE DOUGLAS. Mrs P. Keith, Airds Farm, Crossmichael, Castle Douglas DG7 3BG (01556 670418). Airds Farm overlooks Loch Ken and the picturesque

church and village of Crossmichael. Guests can enjoy rambling in the nearby Airds Glen or relaxing in our terraced garden or conservatory. Airds is totally non-smoking, for the benefit of our guests. Rooms, mostly with scenic view, have washbasins, TV and tea/coffee making facilities. Airds is ideally situated for all holiday activities, including golf, fishing, walking, birdwatching and visiting the many gardens, castles and places of interest to be found within the Dumfries and Galloway area. **STB ★★★** GUEST HOUSE.
e-mail: alan@airds.com
website: www.airds.com

CASTLE DOUGLAS. Mrs Jessie Shaw, High Park Farm, Balmaclellan, Castle Douglas DG7 3PT (Tel

& Fax: 01644 420298). Enjoy a holiday amidst beautiful scenery while staying at our comfortable farmhouse situated by Loch Ken. High Park is a family-run dairy, beef and sheep farm offering accommodation in one family room, one twin bedroom (upstairs), one double bedroom (ground floor); all have washbasins, shaver points, tea/coffee making facilities, colour TV. Central heating, comfort, cleanliness and good food guaranteed. Open Easter to October. Bed and Breakfast from £16. Brochure on request. **STB ★★** B&B
e-mail: high.park@farming.co.uk
website: www.dalbeattie.com/farmholidays/qhpbm.htm

CROSSMICHAEL (Galloway). Mr James C. Grayson, Culgruff House Hotel, Crossmichael DG7 3BB

(01556 670230). Culgruff is a former Baronial Mansion standing in its own grounds of over 35 acres, overlooking the beautiful Ken Valley and the loch beyond. The hotel is comfortable, ideal for those seeking a quiet, restful holiday. An excellent position for touring Galloway and Burns country. The hotel is half-a-mile from A713 Castle Douglas to Ayr road, four miles from Castle Douglas and A75 to Stranraer. Many places of interest in the region - picturesque Solway coast villages, gardens, castles (including Culzean), the Ayrshire coast. For holiday activities - tennis, riding, pony trekking, bowls, golf, fishing (salmon, fly, coarse and sea), boating, water ski-ing, windsurfing, swimming etc. Lovely walks. All rooms have washbasins (some en suite), electric blankets, tea/coffee facilities; ample bathroom/toilet facilities. All bedrooms have TVs. Large family rooms available. One of the lounges has colour TV; diningroom. Central heating. Children under 10 years at reduced rates. Cot. Non-smoking accommodation if required. Car advisable, parking. Bed and Breakfast from £12 per person in large family rooms, doubles from £18 per person. Open from Easter to October. Restricted October to Easter. Home of author James Crawford.

MOFFAT. Mr and Mrs W. Gray, Barnhill Springs Country Guest House, Moffat DG10 9QS (01683

220580). Barnhill Springs is an early Victorian country mansion standing in its own grounds overlooking Upper Annandale. Situated half-a-mile from the A74/M, the house and its surroundings retain an air of remote peacefulness. Internally it has been decorated and furnished to an exceptionally high standard of comfort. Open fire in lounge. Accommodation includes family, double, twin and single rooms, some en suite. Open all year. Children welcome; pets welcome FREE of charge. Bed and Breakfast from £20; Evening Meal (optional) £14. **STB ★★** *GUEST HOUSE.* **AA ◆◆◆**

DUNDEE & ANGUS

BRECHIN. Rosemary Beatty, Brathinch Farm, By Brechin DD9 7QX (01356 648292; Fax: 01356 648003). Working farm. Brathinch is an 18th century farmhouse on a family-run working arable farm, with a large garden, situated off the B966 between Brechin and Edzell. Rooms have private or en suite bathroom, TV and tea/coffee making facilities. Shooting, fishing, golf, castles, stately homes, wildlife, swimming and other attractions are all located nearby. Easy access to Angus Glens and other country walks. Open all year. We look forward to welcoming you. **STB ★★★** *B&B*.

CARNOUSTIE. Mrs E. Watson, Balhousie Farm, Carnoustie, Dundee DD7 6LG (01241 853533). Balhousie Farm House Bed and Breakfast is on a family-run farm two-and-a-half miles from Carnoustie. Tastefully furnished bedrooms overlooking mature gardens and rural scenes. Three-quarters-of-a-mile off main A92 Dundee to Arbroath road and within easy reach of many historic sites, tourist attractions and numerous golf courses. Self-catering also available.
e-mail: balhousie@msn.com

KIRRIEMUIR by. Mr and Mrs D. Clark, Purgavie Farm, Lintrathen, By Kirriemuir (Tel & Fax: 01575 560213; mobile: 07850 392794). Purgavie has been farmed by the same family since 1902 and is situated at the foot of Glen Isla, the most westerly of the lovely Glens of Angus. An ideal base for touring, hillwalking, fishing, downhill and cross country skiing and pony trekking, etc. All bedrooms have colour TV, clock radio, hair dryer, tea making facilities, electric blankets and central heating. Full Scottish Breakfast. Two self-catering properties also available, Brankam - STB ★★★ *SELF-CATERING*, and Tipperwhig - STB ★★★★ *SELF-CATERING*. Please send for our colour brochure giving full details. **STB ★★★★** *B&B*.
website: www.purgavie@aol.com

EDINBURGH & LOTHIANS

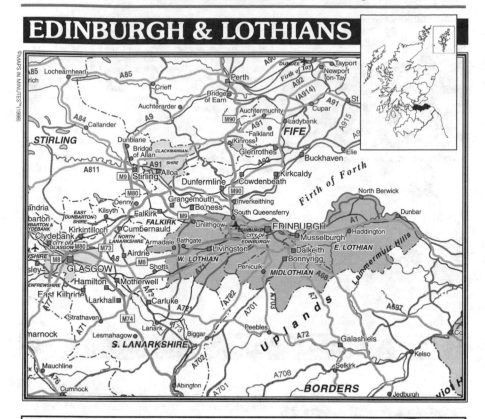

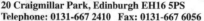

MUSSELBURGH. Inveresk House, Inveresk Village, Musselburgh EH21 7UA (0131-665 5855; Fax:

0131-665 0578). Historic Mansion house and award- winning Bed & Breakfast. Family-run "home from home". Situated in three acres of garden and woodland. Built on the site of a Roman settlement from 150 AD, the remains of a bathhouse can be found hidden in the garden. Three comfortable en suite rooms. Original art and antiques adorn the house. Edinburgh's Princes Street seven miles from Inveresk House. Good bus routes. Families welcome. Off street parking. Telephone first. Price from £35pp. Family room £100 to £120.
e-mail: chute.inveresk@btinternet.com

PATHHEAD. Mrs Anne Gordon, "Fairshiels", Blackshiels, Pathhead EH7 5SX (01875 833665)

We are situated on the A68, three miles south of Pathhead at the picturesque village of Fala. The house is an 18th century coaching inn (Listed building). All bedrooms have washbasins and tea/coffee making facilities; one is en suite. All the rooms are comfortably furnished. We are within easy reach of Edinburgh and the Scottish Borders. A warm welcome is extended to all our guests - our aim is to make your stay a pleasant one. Cost is from £16 per person; children two years to 12 years £9.00, under two years FREE.

FIFE

ST ANDREWS. Cambo House, Kingsbarns, St Andrews KY16 8QD (01333 450313; Fax: 01333

450987). Tucked away in the ancient Kingdom of Fife only 15 minutes from medieval St Andrews is the enchanting wooded coastal estate of Cambo – our family home since 1688. Enjoy traditional hospitality in a style not found elsewhere. 18 holes of championship links golf, romantic walled garden (Good Garden Guide selected), spectacular snowdrops, four-poster beds in wonderful historic mansion. Bed and Breakfast or Self Catering in one of our apartments (East and West Wing interconnect to sleep 16) or traditional farm cottages. Games room, sauna, play area, trampoline, tennis and safe cycling. Breakfasts and dinners can also be arranged for self catering guests. Bed and Breakfast from £38 to £42 per person per night, Self Catering from £190 to £695 per week. **STB ★★★★** *B&B*; **★★/★★★** *S/C*.
e-mail:cambohouse@compuserve.com
website: www.camboestate.com

ST. ANDREWS. Mrs Anne Duncan, Spinkstown Farmhouse, St. Andrews KY6 8PN. (Tel & Fax:

01334 473475). Working farm. Only two miles from St. Andrews on the picturesque A917 road to Crail, Spinkstown is a uniquely designed farmhouse with views of the sea and surrounding countryside. Bright and spacious, it is furnished to a high standard. Accommodation consists of double and twin rooms, all en suite and with tea/coffee making facilities; diningroom and lounge with colour TV. Substantial farmhouse breakfast to set you up for the day; evening meals are by arrangement only. The famous Old Course, historic St. Andrews and several National Trust properties are all within easy reach, as well as swimming, tennis, putting, bowls, horse riding, country parks, nature reserves, beaches and coastal walks. Plenty of parking available. Bed and Breakfast from £20; Evening Meal £12. **STB ★★★★** *B&B*. **AA ◆◆◆◆.**
e-mail: anne-duncan@lineone.net

Newton of Nydie Farmhouse Bed & Breakfast

A working Scottish farm situated in the Kingdom of Fife. Three miles from St Andrews, ideally situated for Perth, Edinburgh and Dundee, not forgetting the picturesque fishing villages of East Fife. St Andrews boasts several golf courses including the famous Old & Royal Ancient clubhouses. Beautiful sandy beaches with Blue Flag awards and historic castles. This area also boasts one of the driest and sunniest climates in the UK. A warm welcome awaits all who stay.

Self-catering bungalow sleeps 6, in rural position on the farm, see brochure for details.

Sam and Doreen Wood, Newton of Nydie, Strathkinness, St Andrews, Fife KY16 9SL

STB ★★★   Tel: 01334 850204   e-mail: nydiefarmhouse@talk21.com

---

TAYPORT. Mrs M. Forgan, B&B, 23 Castle Street, Tayport DD6 9AE (01382 552682; Fax: 01382 552692). A warm, friendly welcome awaits you at this family run B&B. Five minutes' drive from Dundee, 15 minutes' drive from St Andrews. Good bus service. Near many local attractions and surrounded by golf courses. An ideal touring base - one hour's drive from Edinburgh, two hours to Inverness. Cyclists and walkers welcome. Situated on the River Tay only one minute's walk from the picturesque harbour and a short walk to Tentsmuir Forest and the four miles sandy beach - ideal for birdwatchers and walkers. Five minute drive to Kinshaldy Riding Stables. Good traditional home cooked Scottish breakfast. Special diets catered for. Evening Meals on request. Children free when sharing with adults. Discounts available for longer stays. Smoking outside only please. Accommodation consists of two twin, one double, all with wash hand basin, tea making facilities, colour TV and video. Bed and Breakfast from £15 to £19 per person. Welcome Host/Scotland's Best. **STB ★★** *B&B.* website: www.forgan.ukf.net/

PLEASE MENTION THIS GUIDE WHEN YOU WRITE

OR PHONE TO ENQUIRE ABOUT ACCOMMODATION

IF YOU ARE WRITING, A STAMPED, ADDRESSED

ENVELOPE IS ALWAYS APPRECIATED

FREE or REDUCED RATE entry to Holiday Visits and Attractions — see our READERS' OFFER VOUCHERS on pages 43-60

HIGHLANDS

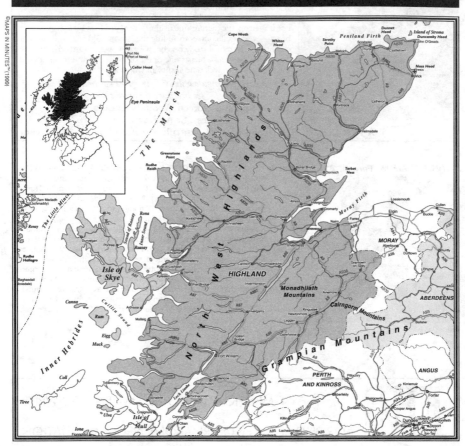

HIGHLANDS (Mid)

AULTBEA. Mrs H. MacLeod, The Croft, Aultbea IV22 2JA (01445 731352). Guests are assured of a warm welcome at The Croft, which stands on its own just yards away from the sea and the village of Aultbea, overlooking Loch Ewe and the Torridon Hills. Lots of hill walking and climbing within easy reach and Inverewe sub-tropical gardens are only five miles away. Unrestricted access to house and guests are provided with their own keys. One twin, two double rooms, all with washbasins and tea making facilities; bathroom with shower, toilet; sitting/diningroom. All modern conveniences. Car essential – parking. Open from March to October. Bed and Breakfast from £18.

HIGHLANDS SOUTH

FORT WILLIAM. Mrs A. Grant, Glen Shiel Guest House, Achintore Road, Fort William PH33 6RW

(01397 702271; Fax: 01397 202271). Modern purpose-built guest house situated near the shore of Loch Linnhe with panoramic views of the surrounding mountains. Accommodation comprises three en suite double bedrooms, one twin-bedded room and one family room, all with colour TV and tea making facilities. Non-smoking accommodation available. Large car park. Garden. Bed and Breakfast from £16 to £20. Directions: on the A82 one-and-a-half miles south of Fort William. **STB** ★★ *GUEST HOUSE.*

FORT WILLIAM. Norma and Jim McCallum, "The Neuk", Corpach, Fort William PH33 7LR (01397 772244). The Neuk is fully centrally heated and double glazed throughout to ensure maximum comfort of guests. Two family, one twin and one double bedrooms, all en suite and have colour TV and refreshment facilities. Guests' dining room and smoking lounge. Payphone. Situated north-west of Fort William in the village of Corpach offering panoramic views over Mamore Mountains, Ben Nevis and Loch Linnhe. An ideal base for exploring the surrounding area either walking, cycling or motoring. Open all year. Whatever the weather you can always be sure of a warm welcome. Bed and Breakfast from £18 - £40. Evening meal £11. Brochure available.

See also Colour Display Advertisement

FORT WILLIAM. Mrs Cameron, Strone Farm, By Banavie, Fort William PH33 7PB (Tel & Fax: 01397 712773). A friendly welcome awaits you in our beautiful farmhouse which sits in a rural setting with magnificent panoramic views of Ben Nevis and Caledonian Canal. All double bedrooms tastefully decorated with en suite facilities and hostess tray. Large lounge with woodburning stove. Fresh food well presented. Open February to September. Bed and Breakfast from £18-£25, Evening Meal from £11. Self-catering also available - see advertisement in Colour Section of this guide for details. **STB** ★★★ *B&B*

INVERNESS. Mrs E. MacKenzie, The Whins, 114 Kenneth Street, Inverness IV3 5QG (01463 236215). Comfortable, homely accommodation awaits you here 10 minutes' walking distance from town centre, bus and railway stations, Inverness being an excellent touring base for North, West and East bus and railway journeys. Bedrooms have TV and tea making facilities, washbasin and heating off-season. Bathroom has a shared shower and toilet. Two double/twin rooms from £15 per person per night. Write or phone for full details. Non-smoking.

INVERNESS. Mrs A. McLean, Waternish, 15 Clachnaharry Road, Inverness IV3 8QH (01463 230520). Delightful bungalow in beautiful setting overlooking Moray Firth and Black Isle. On main A862 road to Beauly, just five minutes to Inverness town centre. Ideal touring centre for north and west. Canal cruises and golf course nearby and lovely walks by banks of Caledonian Canal. Loch Ness is just 15 minutes drive. Accommodation comprises three double/twin rooms, one en suite, all with tea/coffee making facilities and colour TV. Comfortable lounge. Full Scottish Breakfast. Private car parking. Open March to October. Bed and Breakfast from £14.

LANARKSHIRE

HARTHILL. Mrs H. Stephens, Blair Mains Farm, Harthill ML7 5TJ (01501 751278). Attractive farmhouse on small farm – 72 acres. Immediately adjacent to Junction 5 of M8 motorway. Ideal centre for touring, with Edinburgh, Glasgow, Stirling 30 minutes' drive. Fishing (trout and coarse) and golf nearby. One double, three twin and two single (three with en suite); bathroom; sittingroom, diningroom; sun porch. Central heating. Children welcome – babysitting offered. Pets welcome. Car essential – parking. Bed and Breakfast from £16; weekly rates available. Reduced rates for children. Open all year.

PERTH & KINROSS

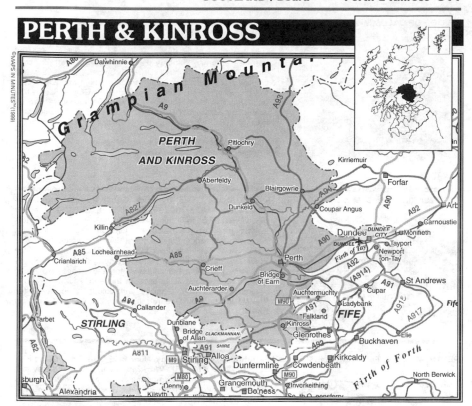

©MAPS IN MINUTES™ (1999)

ABERNETHY. Mrs M. Mackenzie, Gattaway Farm, Abernethy PH2 9LQ (01738 850746; Fax: 01738 850925). Join us in our Georgian/Victorian farmhouse set in 600 acres of farmland with lovely views over Strathearn. Ideal as a base for touring or taking part in a variety of activities - Gleneagles and St Andrews are just two of the nearby golf courses. Fishing, hill walking and skiing within easy reach. The house is centrally heated and all rooms are en suite with electric blankets and tea/coffee facilities. TV lounge for residents. Downstairs bedroom is suitable for disabled guests. Enjoy home cooking with some home-grown produce, dinner is recommended and available on request. Brochure available. **STB** ★★★ *B&B, CATEGORY 1 UNASSISTED WHEELCHAIR ACCESS.*
e-mail: tarduff@aol.com
website: www.SmoothHound.co.uk/hotels/gattaway.html

BLAIRGOWRIE. Mrs Alison Constable, Tomlea Farm, Ballintuim, Blairgowrie PH10 7NL (Tel & Fax: 01250 881383). Tomlea is a traditional family-run hill farm in quiet and peaceful surroundings in the picturesque glen of Strathardle. We are located in the heart of Perthshire, gateway to the Scottish Highlands, ideally situated for outings to Balmoral, Glamis and Blair Castles. Guests can enjoy scenic walks around the farm, golf on many local courses, fishing and skiing at nearby Glenshee. All bedrooms have central heating, tea/coffee making facilities and superb views of the surrounding hills. There is a guest TV lounge with an open log fire, clothes drying facilities for hillwalkers and skiers, large garden and ample private parking. Evening meal can be provided by arrangement or a bar meal can be enjoyed at a nearby hotel. **STB** ★★★ *B&B.*
e-mail: aliconstable@tomlea-farm.demon.co.uk

BRIDGE OF CALLY. Mrs Josephine MacLaren, Blackcraig Castle, Bridge of Cally PH10 7PX (01250 886251 or 0131-551 1863). A beautiful castle of architectural interest situated in spacious grounds. Free trout fishing on own stretch of River Ardle. Excellent centre for hill walking, golf and touring - Braemar, Pitlochry (Festival Theatre), Crieff, Dunkeld, etc. Glamis Castle within easy reach by car. Four double, two twin, two family and two single bedrooms, eight with washbasin; two bathrooms, three toilets. Cot, high chair. Dogs welcome free of charge. Car essential - free parking. Open for guests from 1st July to 7th September. £24.00 per person per night includes full Breakfast plus night tea/coffee and home baking at 10pm in the beautiful drawing room which has a log fire. Reduced rates for children under 14 years. Enquiries November to end June to **1 Inverleith Place, Edinburgh EH3 5QE.**

CRIANLARICH. Mr & Mrs A. Chisholm, Tigh Na Struith, The Riverside Guest House, Crianlarich FK20 8RU (01838 300235; Fax: 01838 300268). Voted the Best Guest House in Britain by the British Guild of Travel Writers in 1984, this superbly sited Guest House comprises six bedrooms, each with unrestricted views of the Crianlarich mountains. The three-acre garden leads down to the River Fillan, a tributary of the River Tay. Personally run by the owners, Janice and Sandy Chisholm, Tigh Na Struith allows visitors the chance to relax and enjoy rural Scotland at its best. To this end, each bedroom is centrally heated, double glazed, with colour TV and tea/coffee making facilities. Open March to November. Bed and Breakfast from £16 per person.

PERTH. Mrs Mary Fotheringham, Craighall Farmhouse, Forgandenny, Near Bridge of Earn, Perth PH2 9DF (01738 812415). Working farm. Come and stay in a modern and warm farmhouse with a cheerful, friendly atmosphere situated in lovely Earn Valley, half-a-mile west of village of Forgandenny on B935 and only six miles south of Perth. True Highland hospitality and large choice for breakfast served in diningroom overlooking fields where a variety of cattle, sheep and lambs graze. Farm produce used. Open all year, the 1000 acre arable and stock farm is within easy reach of Stirling, Edinburgh, St. Andrews, Glasgow and Pitlochry. Fishing, golf, tennis, swimming locally. Hill walking amid lovely scenery. All rooms en suite. Tea making facilities. Sitting room. Cot and reduced rates for children. Sorry, no pets. Central heating. Car not essential. Parking. Bed and Breakfast from £19.50. Mid-week bookings taken. **AA/RAC** *ACCLAIMED.*

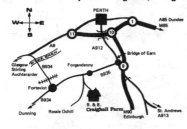

See also Colour Display Advertisement **PITLOCHRY. Blair Castle, Blair Atholl, Pitlochry, Perthshire (01796 481207).** "A great day inside and out". Blair Castle, Scotland's most visited private Historic House, is where you can experience 700 years of history in one day. Browse through 32 rooms of fascinating treasures. Explore the beautiful grounds. Marvel at our 'Hercules Walled Garden' project. New licensed restaurant. New gift shop. New children's playground. Open daily 10am to 6pm (last entry 5pm) from 1st April to 27th October 2000. Telephone for information, leaflets or party booking information.

PITLOCHRY. Mrs Ruth MacPherson-MacDougall, Dalnasgadh House, Killiecrankie, By Pitlochry PH16 5LN (01796 473237).. Attractive country house in grounds of two acres amidst magnificent Highland scenery. Close to National Trust Centre in Pass of Killiecrankie, historic Blair Castle nearby. Only seven minutes from Pitlochry with its famous Festival Theatre. Easy touring distance to Queen's View, Loch Tummel, Balmoral, Braemar, Glamis Castle, Scone Palace and Aviemore. Only six guests accommodated at one time. All bedrooms have washbasins, shaver points, electric blankets and tea/coffee making facilities. Lounge with colour TV. Shower room with toilet and washbasin; bathroom with bath, shower, toilet and washbasin. Centrally heated throughout. Sorry no pets. No smoking. Open Easter to October. Fire Certificate Awarded. Write, telephone or please call in to enquire about terms. **AA/RAC** ◆◆

SCONE. Mrs Irene Millar, Blackcraigs Farm, Scone PH2 7PJ (01821 640254) 18th century farmhouse set in well maintained garden. A warm welcome awaits you; relax and enjoy the quiet, peaceful surroundings. Comfortable bedrooms all with colour TV and tea/coffee making facilities. Elegant residents' lounge with an open fire. The Fair City of Perth has lots of charm and amenities and is an ideal touring area. From Perth take the A94 and travel four miles to find your perfect holiday. Open all year. Bed and Breakfast £18 to £20. **STB ★★★** B&B.

See also Colour Display Advertisement

STANLEY. Mrs Ann Guthrie, Newmill Farm, Stanley PH1 4QD (01738 828281. This 330 acre farm is situated on the A9, six miles north of Perth. Accommodation comprises twin and double en suite rooms and a family room with private bathroom; lounge, sittingroom, diningroom; bathroom, shower room and toilet. Bed and Breakfast from £18; Evening Meal on request. The warm welcome and supper of excellent home baking is inclusive. Reductions and facilities for children. Pets accepted. The numerous castles and historic ruins around Perth are testimony to Scotland's turbulent past. Situated in the area known as "The Gateway to the Highlands", the farm is ideally placed for those seeking some of the best unspoilt scenery in Western Europe. Many famous golf courses and trout rivers in the Perth area. **STB ★★★** B&B.
e-mail: guthrienewmill@sol.co.uk
website: www.newmillfarm.com

RENFREWSHIRE

JOHNSTONE. Mrs Capper, Auchans Farm, Johnstone PA6 7EE (01505 320131). Family-run working farm with large farmhouse offering Bed and Breakfast accommodation. All bedrooms are centrally heated and have colour TV and tea/coffee making facilities. Only five minutes from Glasgow Airport, convenient for City Centre and for touring Burns Country, Loch Lomond, Trossachs, etc. Excellent salmon and trout fishing on River Gryffe close by, permits available. Children welcome. Parking. Open all year. Bed and Breakfast £18 to £20 per person per night.

KILBARCHAN. Mrs Diana Douglas, Gladstone Farmhouse, Burntshields Road, By Johnstone PA10 2PB (01505 702579). The 300-year-old white stone-built farmhouse of Gladstone is situated in beautiful, quiet countryside on the outskirts of the old weaving village of Kilbarchan. We are just 10 minutes away from Glasgow Airport on a direct route and 20 minutes from Glasgow City Centre. We are a very convenient 'stepping stone' for many places of interest, and also have many local amenities. All the comfortable bedrooms have washbasins, colour TV and tea/coffee facilities. **STB ★★** B&B

STIRLING & DISTRICT

BLAIRLOGIE. Mrs Margaret Logan, Blairmains Farm, Manor Loan, Blairlogie, Stirling FK9 5QA

(01259 761338). Working farm. Charming, traditional stone farmhouse set in attractive gardens on a working dairy farm with a herd of pedigree Holstein cattle. Adjacent to a picturesque conservation village and close to the Wallace Monument and Stirling University. Three-and-a-half miles from Stirling. Edinburgh airport is 30 minutes' drive and Glasgow airport 45 minutes. Ideal base for touring and walking. Accommodation is in one double and two twin rooms with shared bathroom. Very comfortable TV lounge. Ample private parking at this non-smoking establishment. Children welcome. Sorry no pets. Bed and Breakfast terms – double or twin £18 to £20; single £20 to £22. Room only £16. A warm Scottish welcome awaits you.

DENNY. Mrs Jennifer Steel, The Topps Farm, Fintry Road, Denny FK6 5JF (01324 822471; Fax: 01324

823099) A modern farmhouse guesthouse in a beautiful hillside location with stunning, panoramic views. Family, double or twin-bedded rooms available, all en suite with tea/coffee, shortbread, TV, radio, telephone. Food a speciality ("Taste of Scotland " listed). Restaurant open to all non-residents. A la carte menu only. Easy access to all major tourist attractions. Your enjoyment is our aim and pleasure! Children welcome, pets by arrangement. Open all year. Bed and Breakfast from £20; Evening Meal from £12. **STB ★★** *GUEST HOUSE*

DRYMEN. Mrs Julia Cross, Easter Drumquhassle Farm, Gartness Road, Drymen G63 0DN (01360

660893). Join us in this quiet rural setting, with spectacular views. Ideal base for touring Loch Lomond and Central Scotland. Situated on the West Highland Way. Accommodation consists of one double, one twin and one family room, all en suite. Children and pets welcome. Bed and Breakfast from £16.50 to £25. Evening Meal from £10. **STB ★★★** *B&B*. **AA ◆◆◆.**
e-mail: julia.macx@aol.com

ORKNEY ISLANDS

BURRAY. Mrs Woodward, Vestlaybanks, Burray KW17 2SX (Tel: 01856 731305; Fax: 01856 731401).

"What a wonderful situation", is what most guests say when they arrive at Vestlaybanks. Overlooking the whole of Scapa Flow, Vestlaybanks is an ideal base for seeing all that Orkney has to offer. Our spacious comfortable rooms have en suite facilities, TV, tea/coffee making facilities and many other extras which make our guests feel at home. We provide three-course evening meals, highly recommended by previous guests, using local produce and organic vegetables when in season. Relax and recharge your batteries here. Ideal for birdwatchers and nature-lovers. None of our guests has regretted coming to Vestlaybanks. Escape the rat race and live life in the slow lane at Vestlaybanks. Self-catering caravan also available. Pets allowed in caravan only. *GREEN AWARD. WELCOME HOST.* STB ★★★★ *B&B*.
e-mail: vestlaybanks@btinternet.com
website: www.orkneyislands.com/vestlaybanks

KIRKWALL. Mrs D. Flett, The Albert Hotel, Mounthoolie Lane, Kirkwall KW15 1JZ (Tel: 01856 876000; Fax: 01856 875397) Situated in Kirkwall town centre

close to all local attractions the Albert Hotel makes an ideal base for your stay in Orkney. The Bothy Bar is a must for the tourist, sit by the cosy fire, enjoy the authentic surroundings whilst sampling our local ales or whiskies, delicious bar menu and snacks served daily. Most Sunday evening local musicians play traditional music, come along and join in. Enjoy that special occasion and dine in the Stables Restaurant where we serve the best Orkney Beef, Lamb and Seafood. Matchmakers Lounge Bar serves family lunches and bar suppers seven days-a-week. Lunches 12-2pm, suppers 5-9.30pm, Dinners 6-9.30pm. All major credit cards accepted. Call us for information on Special Break Offers. STB★★★ *HOTEL*
e-mail: enquiries@alberthotel.co.uk

KIRKWALL. John D. Webster, Lav'rockha Guest House, Inganess Road, Kirkwall KW15 1SP (Tel & Fax: 01856 876103). Situated a short walk from the Highland Park

Distillery and Visitor Centre, and within reach of all local amenities. Lav'rockha is the perfect base for exploring and discovering Orkney. We offer high quality accommodation at affordable rates. All our rooms have en suite WC and power shower, tea/coffee tray, hairdryer, radio alarm clock and remote-control colour TV. Those with young children will appreciate our family room with reduced children's rates, children's meals and child minding service. We also have facilities for the disabled, with full unassisted wheelchair access from our private car park. All our meals are prepared to a high standard using fresh produce as much as possible. Bed and Breakfast from £22 per person. Special winter break prices available. **STB ★★★★** *GUEST HOUSE, WINNER OF BEST B&B ORKNEY; FOOD AWARDS.*
e-mail: lavrockha@orkney.com
website: www.orkneyislands.co.uk/lavrockha/

ORPHIR. Mrs Ann Hewison, The Noust, Orphir KW17 2RB (01856 811348). Come and soak up the peace

and quiet of the unspoilt Orkney Islands. Visit the many well preserved archeological remains, explore the smaller islands, and enjoy the beautiful land and seascapes. The Noust is a modern centrally heated family home in the country. The guest lounge, overlooking Scapa Flow, is equipped with fridge, TV, kettle, iron, etc., and the bedrooms have TV, hairdryer and clock radio. Meals at The Noust are thoughtfully prepared and give opportunity to enjoy local homemade food.

WESTRAY. Beltane House. Papa Westray is one of the most northerly islands in Orkney, with sandy beaches,

inquisitive seals, maritime heath, bird reserve, Arctic Tern colonies and excellent views of cliff-nesting birds, rare flowers and a wealth of important archaeological sites. All this within easy walking of the Papay Co-op - the local shop, hostel and guest house. The guest house has four en suite rooms and a restaurant open to non-residents (booking only). Bed and Breakfast from £23.50 per person, hostel £8, dinner £16.50. Bookings and more information please contact **The Papay Community Co-operative, Beltane House, Papa Westray, Orkney KW17 2BU (01857 644267) STB ★★** *GUEST HOUSE.*
e-mail: papaycoop@orkney.com

Readers are requested to mention this guidebook
when seeking accommodation (and please enclose
a stamped addressed envelope).

THE FHG DIPLOMA

HELP IMPROVE BRITISH TOURIST STANDARDS

You are choosing holiday accommodation from our very popular FHG Publications.
Whether it be a hotel, guest house, farmhouse or self-catering accommodation, we think you will find it hospitable, comfortable and clean, and your host and hostess friendly and helpful.

Why not write and tell us about it?

As a recognition of the generally well-run and excellent holiday accommodation reviewed in our publications, we at FHG Publications Ltd. present a diploma to proprietors who receive the highest recommendation from their guests who are also readers of our Guides. If you care to write to us praising the holiday you have booked through FHG Publications Ltd. – whether this be board, self-catering accommodation, a sporting or a caravan holiday, what you say will be evaluated and the proprietors who reach our final list will be contacted.

The winning proprietor will receive an attractive framed diploma to display on his premises as recognition of a high standard of comfort, amenity and hospitality. FHG Publications Ltd. offer this diploma as a contribution towards the improvement of standards in tourist accommodation in Britain. Help your excellent host or hostess to win it!

FHG DIPLOMA

We nominate ....

....

Because

Name ....

Address...

....

Telephone No...

Self-Catering Accommodation SCOTLAND

ABERDEENSHIRE, BANFF & MORAY

Bremners of Foggie

Old School, Aberchirder AB54 7XS
Tel & Fax: 01466 780260
or 01466 780510
website: www.bremnersoffoggie.co.uk

Two and three bedroomed houses to let in quiet country village. Only 20 minutes' drive from coast at Banff and Portsoy. Weekly terms from £150 to £250; electricity extra. Sleeps 6/8. STB ★★★ SELF-CATERING

See also Colour Display Advertisement | **ABERDEEN. The Robert Gordon University, Business and Vacation Accommodation, Customer Services Dept, Schoolhill, Aberdeen AB10 1FR (01224 262134; Fax: 01224 262144).** Situated in the heart of Aberdeen and offering a wide variety of accommodation to visitors from June through to August. Aberdeen is ideal for visiting Royal Deeside, castles and historic buildings, playing golf or visiting the Malt Whisky Trail. The city itself is a place to discover and Aberdonians are a friendly and welcoming people. Self-catering accommodation available for individuals or groups of people at superb rates. Each flat is self-contained, centrally heated, fully furnished and suitable for children or disabled guests. All have colour TV and some have microwave facilities. Bed linen and cooking utensils are provided, as is a 'welcome pack' of basic groceries. Each residence has laundry facilities and a telephone as well as car parking. ASSC MEMBER. **STB ★ & ★★** *SELF-CATERING*.
e-mail: accommodation@rgu.ac.uk   website: www.scotland2000.com/rgu

ALFORD. Mrs A. MacAdam, West Balnakelly, Cushnie, Alford AB33 8LD (019755 81312). Sleeps 2.

Well equipped modern timber chalet situated at 1000ft on working hill farm. Twin-bedded room; open-plan living room/kitchen with mini kitchen, fridge; shower room and WC. Double glazing, colour TV, electric blankets, central heating; garden. Ideal centre for walking, golf, touring Royal Deeside, Castle and Whisky Trails. £100 to £110 per week including linen and electricity. Regret no pets.

See also Colour Display Advertisement | **ELGIN. Mrs J.M. Shaw, North East Farm Chalet, Sheriffston, Elgin IV30 8LA (01343 842695).** An "A" frame chalet and Elgin situated on a working farm, fully equipped for two to six people, colour TV, bed linen, duvets. Beautiful rural location in Moray - famous for flowers - district of lowlands, highlands, rivers, forests, lovely beaches, historic towns, welcoming people. Excellent local facilities. Moray golf tickets available. From £170 to £300. January to December. ASSC MEMBER. **STB ★★** *SELF-CATERING*.
e-mail: jennifer.shaw@moray.gov.uk

See also Colour Display Advertisement | **HUNTLY. Mrs Cruickshank, Logie Newton Farm, By Huntly AB54 6BB (01464 841229; Fax: 01464 841277). Sleeps 4/6.** A warm welcome awaits you at Logie Newton Farm, a delightful holiday retreat eight miles east of Huntly. Set in the heart of Grampian, Dykeside and Tanaree are charming single storey cottages where comfort and Scottish hospitality are priorities. The farm has its own walks, children's lead rein pony rides, stone circles and even the site of a Roman Camp! Both cottages have lounge with open fire, colour TV, video, payphone, hi-fi, books, games and toys. A fully-fitted kitchen, bathroom, electric blankets and duvets are also provided. Laundry room on site. Cots and high chairs available. Well behaved pets welcome. Large garden with safe children's play area. Locally available eating facilities range from small pubs to country hotels and private castles. Please call or write for our brochure. ASSC MEMBER. **STB ★★★★** *SELF-CATERING*.
www.logienewton.co.uk

See also Colour Display Advertisement INVERURIE. Mr and Mrs P. A. Lumsden, Kingsfield House, Kingsfield Road, Kintore, Inverurie AB51 0UD (01467 632366; Fax: 01467 632399). 'The Greenknowe' is a comfortable detached and renovated cottage in a quiet location at the southern edge of the village of Kintore. It is in an ideal situation for touring castles, historic sites and distilleries, or for walking, fishing and even golf. The cottage is all on one level with a large south-facing sittingroom overlooking the garden. It sleeps four people in one double and one twin room. a cot is available. Parking adjacent. Open from March to November. Prices from £225 to £350 per week, inclusive of electricity (the cottage is all-electric) and linen. Walkers Welcome Scheme. ASSC MEMBER. **STB** ★★★ *SELF-CATERING*.
e-mail: kfield@clara.net

TOMINTOUL. Mrs Shearer, Croughly Farm, Tomintoul AB37 9EN (01807 580476). Sleeps 4 to

6. Croughly Farm lies in a peaceful valley, two miles from Tomintoul, with views of the Cairngorm Mountains and surrounding scenery. Whisky and castle trails are nearby, the Lecht Ski Centre is only a 15 minute drive away, and fishing can be arranged on the River Avon. The 16th century wing has been renovated and converted into this comfortable self-catering cottage. One double and one twin bedrooms plus extra sofa-bed allows for four to six people. With colour TV, fully equipped kitchen, bathroom, utility room and lounge with open fire providing all the necessary comforts. There is ample parking, a private water supply and it is only two miles away from shops and Post Office. Advance ordering of provisions available. Terms from £200 to £280 per week. **STB** ★★ *SELF-CATERING*.

See also Colour Display Advertisement TURRIFF. Mrs O.E. Bates, Forglen Holiday Cottages, Forglen Estate, Turriff AB53 4JP (01888 562918/562518; Fax: 01888 562252). The Estate lies along the beautiful Deveron River and our traditional stone cottages (modernised and well equipped) nestle in individual seclusion. Visitors are free to wander and explore one of the ancient baronies of Scotland. The sea is only nine miles away, and the market town of Turriff only two miles, with its golf course, swimming pool etc. Many places of interest including the Cairngorms, Aviemore, picturesque fishing villages and castles, all within easy reach on uncrowded roads. Wildlife haven. See our Highland cattle. Terms from £145 weekly, including VAT and heating. Special winter lets. Ten cottages sleeping six to nine. Children and reasonable dogs welcome. Please telephone for brochure. **STB** ★/★★ *SELF-CATERING*.

FREE or REDUCED RATE entry to Holiday Visits and Attractions — see our READERS' OFFER VOUCHERS on pages 43-60

ARGYLL & BUTE

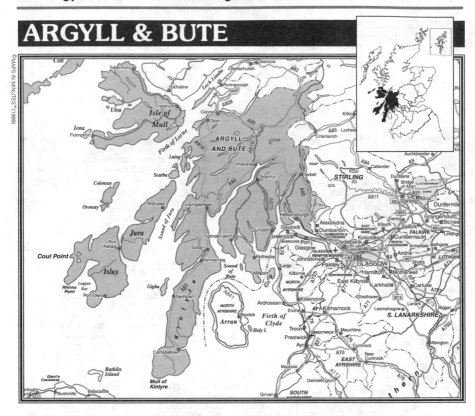

©MAPS IN MINUTES™ (1999)

APPIN. Ardtur Cottages, Appin. Two adjacent cottages in secluded surroundings on promontory between Port Appin and Castle Stalker, opposite north end of Isle of Lismore. Ideal centre for hill walking, climbing etc.(Glencoe and Ben Nevis half hour drive). Direct access across the field to sea (Loch Linnhe). Tennis court available by arrangement. Boat hire, pony trekking, fly fishing all available locally. Accommodation in first cottage for eight people in four double bedrooms, large dining/sittingroom/kitchenette and two bathrooms. Second cottage accommodates six people in three twin-bedded rooms, dining/sittingroom/kitchenette and bathroom. Everything is provided except linen. Shops one mile; sea 200 yards. Pets allowed. Car essential, parking. Open March/October. Terms from £165 to £375 weekly. SAE, please for full details to **Mrs J. Pery, Ardtur, Appin PA38 4DD (01631 730223 or 0162 834172)** e-mail: pery@eurobell.co.uk

APPIN. Appin Holiday Homes. Midway between Oban and Fort William in the Scottish Highlands. Fine hill and shoreline walks amid natural beauty. Warm welcoming lodges and lochside caravan, set apart within landscaped park. Fishing (free), boating, cycling, pony-trekking, Sealife Centre, Castle Stalker, licensed inn nearby. Lots do do and see. Price guide £155 to £375 per unit weekly. Sleep two/five. Free colour brochure. **Mr and Mrs I.F. Weir, Appin Holiday Homes, Appin PA38 4BQ (01631 730287).** ASSC MEMBER. STB ★★★★ *SELF-CATERING*
e-mail: info@appinholidayhomes.co.uk
website: www.appinholidayhomes.co.uk

Mr & Mrs E. Crawford, Blarghour Farm, Lochaweside, By Dalmally, Argyll PA33 1BW
Tel: (01866) 833246; Fax: (01866) 833338
E-mail: blarghour@aol.com Website: www.blarghour.com

At Blarghour, a working hill farm on the shores of lovely Loch Awe, the holiday guest has a choice of high quality, well appointed, centrally heated, double glazed accommodation of individual character, each enjoying its own splendid view over loch and mountains in this highly scenic area.

Barn House sleeps two in one ground floor bedroom with twin or zip-linked beds, has a bathroom adjacent to bedroom and open lounge/dining/kitchen on the first floor which is well lit and has a pleasing view.

Stable House accommodates four in two first floor bedrooms with twin or zip-linked bed arangements, has one bathroom and large lounge/dining room with an elegant spiral staircase and full length windows with an oustanding view.

Barr-beithe Bungalow sleeps five in three bedrooms, one twin or zip-linked, one double and one single. There is a bathroom and shower room. The lounge/dining/sun lounge enjoys an outstanding loch view.

Upper Blarghour House sleeps eight in three bedrooms, two with twin or zip-linked beds and one with twin beds and bunk beds. There is a bathroom and shower room on the first floor and a cloakroom on the ground floor. The large lounge/dining/sun lounge overlooks a spectacular view as does the balcony leading from the master bedroom.

All have modern kitchens with fridge/freezer, washer/dryer, microwave and electric cooker and the two larger houses have dishwashers. Cots and high chairs arc available in the two larger houses. All have telephones and televisions. Linen and towels are supplied.

Cars may be parked beside each house. Barn and Stable Houses are unsuitable for children under five years. No pets are allowed. Open all year. The area, centrally situated for touring, offers opportunities for walking, bird-watching, boating and fishing. Golf is available at Dalmally and Inveraray.

Colour brochure sent on request.   *See also colour advertisement*

See also Colour Display Advertisement **ARDFERN. Lerigoligan, Ardfern, By Oban.** This 19th century cottage has been enlarged to sleep up to eight, but is cosy for two, four or six. The elevated position, 300 feet above Loch Craignish, and the privacy of two acres, with the new lounge commanding panoramic views, creates an ideal location for a refreshing holiday. Riding, fishing, sailing, bird-watching, archeological sites. Separate games room with Table Tennis. Barbeque. No TV or telephone. Shop, Inn, Post Office nearby. Graduated rates £150 - £450 p.w. Open all year. Booking address. **Mrs Jean Reid, Creag-na-Mara, Tarbert Road, Ardrishaig, Argyll PA30 8ER (01546 602852).**

See also Colour Display Advertisement **CONNEL. West Coast Character Cottages.** Interesting selection of five individual privately owned holiday homes beautifully located (some with loch views) in rural areas within easy driving distance of Oban. All equipped/presented to a high standard and personally supervised by the local owners. Walking, fishing and many other pursuits to be enjoyed amongst wonderful scenery. Sleep two to seven. Call for a brochure. **Tigh Beag, Connel, By Oban PA37 1PJ (Tel & Fax: 01631 710504; Mobile: 07808 109005).** ASSC MEMBER.
e-mail: Ejtricker@aol.com

CRINAN FERRY. The Ferryman's Cottage, Crinan Ferry, Lochgilphead. Sleeps 6. The Ferryman's Cottage is situated on the end of a peninsula overlooking Crinan Moss and is surrounded by sandy beaches and spectacular views. It is a paradise for children and bird-watchers. The traditional stone cottage sleeps six in three bedrooms. There is an all-electric kitchen, wood panelled sittingroom with open fire, diningroom and a bathroom. The cottage is comfortable and charming. Duvets with covers are provided, linen on request. **STB ★★** *SELF-CATERING.* SAE for details to **Mrs Rachel Walker, The Change House, Crinan Ferry, Lochgilphead PA31 8QH (01546 510232).**

Self-catering Holidays in Unspoilt Argyll at
THE HIGHLAND ESTATE OF ELLARY AND CASTLE SWEEN

One of the most beautiful areas of Scotland with a wealth of historical associations such as St Columba's Cave, probably one of the first places of Christian worship in Britain, also Castle Sween, the oldest ruined castle in Scotland, and Kilmory Chapel where there is a fascinating collection of Celtic slabs.

PEACE, SECLUSION, OUTSTANDING SCENERY AND COMPLETE FREEDOM TO PURSUE INDIVIDUAL HOLIDAY PASTIMES.

Loch, sea and burn fishing, swimming, sailing and observing a wide variety of wildlife can all be enjoyed on the estate and there are many attractive paths and tracks for the walker. Various small groups of cottages, traditional stone-built as well as modern, are strategically scattered throughout the estate. All have wonderful views and are near to attractive stretches of shore; in many cases there is safe anchorage for boats close by. Most of the cottages accommodate 6, but one will take 8. All units are fully equipped except linen. TV reception is included.

For further details, brochure and booking forms please apply to: **ELLARY ESTATE OFFICE**

By Lochgilphead, Argyll PA31 8PA
01880 770209/770232
or 01546 850223; Fax: 01880 770386
e-mail: info@ellary.com   website: www.ellary.com

DALMALLY by. Mrs E. Fellowes, Inistrynich, By Dalmally PA33 1BQ (01838 200256; Fax: 01838 200253).

Three cottages situated on a private estate surrounded by beautiful scenery. Garden Cottage (four bedrooms), Millside Cottage (two bedrooms) and Inistrynich Cottage (two bedrooms). Situated five miles from Dalmally, 11 miles from Inveraray, 28 miles from Oban and each has a garden area. They all have convector heaters in all rooms and an open fire in the livingroom. All have electric cooker, microwave, fridge, immersion heater, electric kettle, iron, hoover, washing machine and colour TV; cot and high chair available on request. Dogs allowed by arrangement. Car essential – ample parking space. Ideal centre for touring mainland and Western Isles. Hill-walking, forest walks, fishing, boat trips, pony trekking and golf all within easy reach. Colour brochure available on request. **STB ★★★** SELF-CATERING

LOCH AWE. Innis Chonain, Loch Awe, Dalmally (01838 200220).

Attractive three bedroom cottage on private 20 acre island (vehicle access by bridge from main A85 road). Superb situation on this beautiful loch with complete privacy, but only half-a-mile to shops. Ideal touring centre, Inveraray 17 miles, Oban 20 miles. Cottage has three bedrooms sleeping five/six persons. Modern furnishings, colour TV/video, electric heating, gas cooking, washing machine/dryer. Linen not provided. Boat with free fishing on loch. Children welcome, pets with permission. Ample parking. Rates from £195 to £395 per week. Full details from **J. C. D. Somerville, Ashton House, Pattingham Road, Perton, Wolverhampton WV6 7HD (01902 700644).**

When making enquiries or bookings, a stamped addressed envelope is always appreciated

LOCH CRINAN. Poltalloch Estate. A selection of charming self catering cottages, each unique in its history and

character, and enhanced by the natural beauty of Loch Crinan. All have been attractively modernised and furnished, with care taken in the retention of many traditional and historically interesting features. The cottages offer varying accommodation for two to five persons in comfort. Eating out is no problem with many good restaurants in the area. Salmon fishing, hill walking and safe sandy beaches can all be enjoyed on the estate. Terms and further details on application. **STB ★★★★** *SELF-CATERING*. SAE please. **Susan Malcolm, Duntrune Castle, Kilmartin PA31 8QQ (01546 510283).**
e-mail: info@ellary.com
website: www.ellary.com

Mother Brown's

See also Colour Display Advertisement   **LOCHGILPHEAD (By). Ellary Estate Office, By Lochgilphead (01880 770232/770209 or 01546 850223). Properties sleep 6/8.** Ellary affords peace and seclusion amidst outstanding scenery, plus complete freedom to pursue holiday pastimes for young and old alike. The range of accommodation is wide - small groups of cottages and chalets on Ellary, and super luxury and luxury caravans at Castle Sween. Cottages accommodate six to eight. All units fully equipped except for linen. The estate, beautiful at all times of the year, is suitable for windsurfing, fishing, swimming, wildlife observation and numerous walks. Further details and brochure on request.

LOCHGOIL. Darroch Mhor, Carrick Castle, Loch Goil, Argyll PA24 8AF (01301 703249/703432).

Sleep 4. Five self-catering chalets on the shores of Loch Goil in the heart of Argyll Forest Park with superb lochside views. Chalets are fully equipped except linen. Colour TV, fitted kitchen, carpeted. Pets very welcome. Open all year. Weekly rates £120-£295; reductions for two people. Short breaks available.

See also Colour Display Advertisement   **OBAN. Highland Hideaways.** Several high quality self-catering properties of individual character in outstanding coastal, town and country locations in Argyll including the Oban area and around Loch Awe. Sleeping two to 12 from £130 to £950 per week. **Up to STB ★★★★**. For further details please contact: **Highland Hideaways, 5/7 Stafford Street, Oban PA34 5NJ (01631 562056; Fax: 01631 566778).** ASSC MEMBER.
e-mail: info@highlandhideaways.co.uk

See also Colour Display Advertisement   **OBAN. Cologin Farm Holiday Chalets.** All Scottish Glens have

their secrets: let us share ours with you – and your pets ! Our cosy holiday chalets, set on an old farm in a peaceful private glen, can sleep from two to six people in comfort. They all have private parking, central heating, colour TV and bed linen. Tranquil country glen, just three miles from Oban. Free fishing and dinghy use on our hill loch. Excellent walks for you and your dogs. Home-cooked food and licensed bar in our converted farm-house byre. A safe haven for pets and children. A friendly, family run complex with a good range of facilities. Call now for our colour brochure and find out more. Open all year round. Rates from £120 to £420 per week. Autumn Gold breaks and mid-week deals also available. Oban. **STB ★★ to ★★★★** *SELF CATERING*. ASSC MEMBER. **Mrs Linda Battison, Cologin Farmhouse, Lerags, By Oban PA34 4SE**
e-mail: cologin@oban.org.uk

OBAN. Lagnakeil Highland Lodges, Lerags, Oban PA34 4SE. Our timber lodges are nestled in seven acres of scenic wooded glen overlooking Loch Feochan, only three-and-a-half miles from Oban - "Gateway to the Highlands". Lodges are fully equipped to a high standard, including linen and towels. Country pub only a short walk away. Senior Citizen discount. Free loch fishing. Special Breaks from £38 per lodge per night, weekly from £170. Our colour brochure will tell lots more. Please phone or write to: **Colin and Jo Mossman (01631 562746; Fax: 01631 570225).** ASSC MEMBER.
e-mail: lagnakeil@aol.com
website: www.lagnakeil.co.uk

OBAN by. Mrs H.M. McCorkindale, Scammadale Farm, Kilninver, By Oban PA34 4UU (01852 316282; Fax: 01852 316223). Working farm. Sleeps 7. Wing of old Scottish farmhouse of character with own entrance, it stands in a beautiful position overlooking Loch Scammadale, 13 miles from Oban which has a lively night life and is the starting point for boat trips to the islands. Fishing in loch and river free to residents – includes boat. Furnishings simple and comfortable. Sleeps seven in one family bedroom, one twin-bedded room and a small single bedroom; bathroom/toilet; sitting/diningroom; colour TV. Kitchen has gas cooker and fridge etc. Guests must supply own linen. Sorry, no pets. Shops 13 miles away; sea five miles. Car essential – parking. Garage available. Terms from £130 to £200 weekly, including gas, lights and hot water. Electric fire and TV metered. SAE, please.

OBAN (By). Eleraig Highland Chalets, Kilninver, By Oban PA34 4UX (Tel & Fax: 01852 200225). Sleep 4/7. These seven well-equipped, widely spaced chalets are set in breathtaking scenery in a private glen 12 miles south of Oban, close to Loch Tralaig, with free brown trout fishing and boating - or bring your own boat. Peace and tranquillity are features of the site, located within an 1800 acre working sheep farm. Walkers' and bird-watchers' paradise. Children and pets are especially welcome (dogs free). Cots and high chairs are available, also free. Gliding, water skiing and other sports pastimes and evening entertainment are available locally. Car parking by each chalet. Open March to January. From £205 per week per chalet including electricity and bed linen. Colour brochure from resident owners **Anne and Robin Grey. STB ★★** *SELF-CATERING.*
website: www.scotland2000.com/eleraig

PORT APPIN. The Cottage, Port Appin. Sleeps 7. Situated on small bay 50 yards from beach. Sheltered position, completely on its own, five minutes from the village. Area offers hill-walking, pony trekking, boating, windsurfing, sea fishing. Ideal for children. Oban and Fort William are within easy reach. Accommodation: four bedrooms (one en suite); diningroom; sittingroom, kitchen and bathroom. Sleeps seven. Fully equipped. Electric cooker, fridge/freezer, washing machine, colour TV. No linen. Heating by electricity and coal fires. Available March-September £275 to £350 weekly. For details send SAE to **Mrs A. V. Livingstone, Bachuil, Isle of Lismore, By Oban PA34 5UL or telephone 01631 760256.**

Terms quoted in this publication may be subject to increase if rises in costs necessitate

FARM HOLIDAY GUIDE DIPLOMA

STB ★ SELF-CATERING

SKIPNESS ESTATE

This unspoilt, peaceful, West Highland estate with its own historic castle, medieval chapel and way-marked walks has traditional cottages to let all year round. Each cottage has an open fire and television; some cottages have a rowing dinghy in summer. Laundry facilities are available alongside the Seafood Cabin at Skipness Castle. Properties sleep 4 – 10.

All cottages have magnificent views and beautiful surrounding countryside and coastline. Safe, sandy beaches can be enjoyed on the estate, with fishing, pony trekking and golf nearby. Local ferries to Arran, Gigha, Islay, Jura and Northern Ireland. PETS WELCOME. Apply for rates and further details:

Sophie James, Skipness Castle, By Tarbert, Argyll PA29 6XU

Tel: 01880 760207; Fax: 01880 760208 Email: sophie@skipness.freeserve.co.uk

---

See also Colour Display Advertisement | **TARBERT. Dunmore Court, West Loch Tarbert. Sleep 5/7.** Four cottages in architect design conversion of home farm on the estate of Dunmore House. Spacious accommodation furnished to the highest standards, all have stone fireplaces for log fires. Bird-watching, sailing, sea fishing and unrestricted walking. Easy access to island ferries. Pets welcome. Open all year. Colour brochure. From £165-£425. **STB ★★★ to ★★★★** *SELF-CATERING*. Conact: **Amanda Minshall, Dunmore Court, Near Tarbert, Argyll PA29 6XZ (01880 820654)** *ASSC MEMBER*

TAYNUILT. Mrs R. Campbell-Preston, Inverawe House, Taynuilt PA35 1HU (01866 822446; Fax: 01800 822274). Cottages sleep 2/6. Inverawe House, set amid some of the most beautiful scenery in Scotland, overlooks the River Awe. It is ideally situated for a family holiday with fishing, tennis and walking. The estate has four well stocked lochs and salmon and sea trout fishing is available on the river. Only five minutes from the small village of Taynuilt or 20 minutes from Oban, this charming Victorian sea port has much to offer the visitor. Inverawe has two delightful cottages adjoining the house sleeping five to six people, and charming secluded cottage, sleeping two, on the banks of Loch Etive. Dogs welcome. Fantastic prices from £125 to £325 per week.

Please mention The Farm Holiday Guide when writing to enquire about accommodation

TAYNUILT. Mrs I. Olsen, Airdeny Chalets, Airdeny, Taynuilt PA35 1HY (01866 822648; Fax: 01866

822665). Our chalets are in a field on our private land, well away from any main road. Glorious views of Ben Cruachan (3,650 ft) and Glen Etive, the area offers wonderful opportunities for lovely walks, climbs and peaceful secluded privacy. Ideal location for children, plenty of parking space alongside each chalet. Oban is just 12 miles away and from there one can take steamer tours to the inner and outer islands. Chalets are equipped to a very high standard and comprise two bedrooms - one twin-bedded and one double, bathroom and shower, livingroom and fully fitted kitchen (all electric). ASSC member. **STB ★★★** *SELF CATERING.*

TAYVALLICH. Cariel and Ternait, Tayvallich, By Lochgilphead. Sleeps 7 & 4/8. Two charming, well

equipped, modern bungalows with superb view of Tayvallich Bay. CARIEL sleeps seven and TERNAIT sleeps four or eight with annexe. Both have two bathrooms plus showers, games room and open fire. Walk in the woods and hills, picnic on the beach, explore the headlands. Ideally situated to visit the Western Isles. Sample the local seafood at the Tayvallich Inn (two minutes' walk). Terms from £150 to £450 per week. For details telephone **01793 782361 or 0270 5838667** or SAE **Jeanie Wright, Watchfield House, Watchfield, Swindon, Wiltshire SN6 8TD.**

AYRSHIRE & The Island of Arran

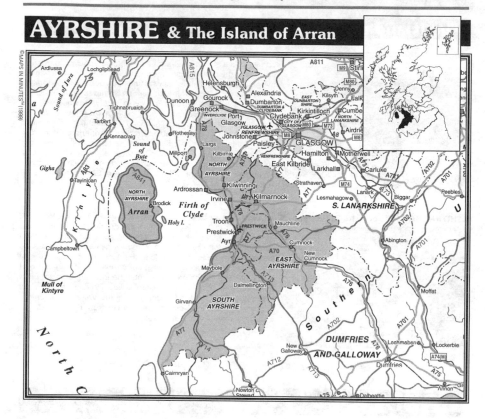

BALLANTRAE. Mrs M. Drummond, Balnowlart Farm, Ballantrae KA26 0LA (01465 831343).
Working farm. Sleeps six. Luxury country-lodge situated in lovely Stinchar Valley near old fishing village of Ballantrae, with shopping facilities, sea-fishing, tennis court, putting green, bowling, golf courses within easy reach. Beautiful scenery, places of historic interest, many unspoilt beaches, with rock formation said to be oldest in the world. Ideal spot for touring the "Burns' Country, Alloway", also panoramic views at Glen Trool in "Bonnie Galloway". Daily sailings from Stranraer and Cairnryan to Northern Ireland. Accommodation for six comprises sitting/diningroom with open fires (fuel included), three bedrooms (two double, one twin), bathroom with electric shower, fully equipped electric kitchen, immerser. Heating. Metered electricity. Telephone. Tastefully furnished throughout. Linen included. Ample parking - car essential. Pets by arrangement. Available all year. Terms from £130 per week. STB ★★★ SELF-CATERING

See also Colour Display Advertisement NEWMILNS. Mr and Mrs Reynolds, Loudoun Mains Country Cottages, Newmilns, Ayrshire KA16 9LG (Tel: 01560 321246; Fax: 01560 320657).** All bed linen and towels are provided. Heating is by electricity (meter) and the cottages are double-glazed and insulated for your comfort. Convenient parking and laundry room. Cots available on request. Pets welcome by special arrangement. Leisure Club with heated indoor pool. Varied wild life and country walks in the surrounding area. Fishing, horse riding, squash nearby. Loudoun 'Gowf' Club and Loudoun Castle Theme Park a few minutes away. Ayrshire coast and Glasgow less than thirty minutes away. Edinburgh, Stirling and Loch Lomond within sixty miles. Post Office and shops less than two miles.
e-mail: salesandinfo@loudounmains.co.uk
website: www.loudounmains.co.uk

The Island of Arran

PIRNMILL. Mrs Dale, The Wee Rig, Pirnmill, By Brodick, Isle of Arran KA27 8HP (01770 850228).

Situated on a slightly elevated site, within a spacious garden to the side of the main house, in a unique secluded position flanked by sheltering woodlands but with fine open outlook to panoramic views and sunsets over the Kilbrannan Sound to Kintyre. Across the road the low tide reveals a clean sandy expanse which is habitat to various seabirds. Wider exploration of our unspoiled picturesque island, termed "Scotland in miniature" offers much variety with rugged mountains, rolling farmlands, interesting bird/wildlife, castles, distillery, golf (seven courses), walking, cycling, ponies plus various visitor centres, swimming facilities, etc. An overall sense of peace and relaxation which we warmly welcome you to share with us. Terms from £200 per week. **STB ★★★** *SELF-CATERING.*

WHITING BAY. Mr and Mrs S. Pairman, 'Seabank', Largiebeg, Whiting Bay, Isle of Arran KA27 8RL (01770 700301). Sleeps 4.

Self-contained red sandstone house two miles south of Whiting Bay, set in peaceful surroundings with own garden overlooking beach and panoramic views across the Firth of Clyde to the Ayrshire coastline. Ideally situated for hill walking, golfing, pony trekking, fishing and bird watching. The house has two double bedrooms; linen supplied but not towels. Sitting/dining room, colour TV/video. Kitchen has electric cooker, fridge/freezer, automatic washing machine. Parking for two cars. Sorry no pets. Prices from £170 to £250. e-mail: seabank@freezone.co.uk

BORDERS

See also Colour Display Advertisement

JEDBURGH. Mill House, Letterbox and Stockman's Cottages. Three recently renovated, quality Cottages, each sleeping four, on a working farm three miles from Jedburgh. Ideal centres for exploring, sporting holidays or getting away from it all. Each cottage has two public rooms (ground floor available). Minimum let two days. Terms £190–£310. Open all year. Bus three miles, airport 54 miles. Green Tourism Business Award – SILVER. **STB ★★★★** *SELF-CATERING.* **Mrs A. Fraser, Overwells, Jedburgh TD8 6LT (01835 863020; Fax: 01835 864334).** ASSC MEMBER. website: www.overwells.co.uk

NEWCASTLETON. Pamela Copeland, Bailey Mill Courtyard Apartments and Trekking Centre, Bailey Mill, Newcastleton TD9 0TR (Tel & Fax: 016977 48617).

A warm welcome awaits you from Pam and Ian on this small farm holiday complex, nestling on the Roxburghshire/Cumbrian border. The rural self-contained apartments create a courtyard setting or enjoy Bed and Breakfast or Full Board riding holidays in the farmhouse. Colour TV and Sky link; heating (oil), electricity and linen included in the rent. On site sauna, solarium, toning table, games room, laundry, babysitting, fully licensed bar and meal service. Enjoy walking or trekking through surrounding forests. Central touring area for Lake District, Hadrian's Wall and Scotland. Colour brochure available. Self-catering £78-£498; Bed and Breakfast from £20 per person. **STB ★★/★★★** *SELF CATERING.*

Greenhope Cottage

Mrs Alison Landale, Green Hope, Ellem Ford, Duns, Berwickshire TD11 3SG

Situated in beautiful surroundings in Lammermuir Hills. Perfect for relaxing, walking and visiting all Scottish Borders attractions. Next door to East Lothian and only one hour from Scotland's capital Edinburgh. Accommodation comprises: Garden flat sleeps 2 to 4 persons, Green Hope cottage sleeps 6 to 8 persons. Fully equipped, no TV. The perfect riverside hideaway - totally secluded. Golf course, fishing, wonderful walks and beautiful beaches within easy reach. Terms from £200 Self-catering depending on season. Bed and Breakfast accommodation also available nearby. Video available. Facilities for disabled.

Tel: 01361 890242 • Fax: 01361 890295

DUMFRIES & GALLOWAY

CASTLE DOUGLAS. Cala-Sona, Auchencairn, Castle Douglas. Sleeps 6. A stone-built house in centre of Auchencairn village, near shops, Post Office and garage. To let, furnished. Equipped for six persons. Linen supplied. Two bedrooms (one double bed; two single beds); cot available. Bathroom, bedroom with double bed, livingroom and kitchenette with electric cooker, fridge and geyser. Auchencairn is a friendly seaside village and you can enjoy a peaceful holiday here on the Solway Firth where the Galloway Hills slope down to the sea. Many places of historic interest to visit, also cliffs, caves and sandy beaches. A haven for ornithologists. SAE brings prompt reply. Car essential – parking. **Mrs Mary Gordon, 7 Church Road, Auchencairn, Castle Douglas DG7 1QS (01556 640345).**

CASTLE DOUGLAS. Mrs R. Agnew, Glenlee Holiday Houses, New Galloway, Castle Douglas DG7 3SF (01644 430212; Fax: 01644 430340). Sleeps 2/7. Five charming cottages around a central courtyard, superbly converted from the former home farm of Glenlee Estate. Two miles (3km) from New Galloway and Dalry in a peaceful woodland setting. Each spacious cottage has its own individual character. Magnificent walks round a wooded glen. Free trout fishing. Children welcome, cot available. Eating out facilities within two miles. Shops nearby. Open March to November. Terms from £200 per week per unit. Electricity extra. Pets welcome. **STB ★★★** *SELF-CATERING.*

See also Colour Display Advertisement

DALBEATTIE. Mrs Colquhoun, Barend Holiday Village, Sandyhills, Dalbeattie DG5 4NU (01387 780663; Fax: 01387 780283). Barend Holiday Village, near Sandyhills, on the beautiful south west coast of Scotland, with sixteen golf courses within a twenty mile drive; yet only one hour's drive from England. Our Scandinavian style log chalets are centrally heated for all year round use, with TV and video. All chalets have decks or verandahs, some overlooking the loch, or the adjacent Colvend 18 hole golf course. On-site launderette, bar, restaurant, sauna and indoor heated pool. The two and three bedroomed chalets, accommodate up to eight people, are £240 - £640 p.w., including linen, heating and swimming. Short breaks all year round from £145 for four. Pets welcome. **STB ★★★** *SELF-CATERING.* ASSC MEMBER.
website: www.barendholidayvillage.co.uk

See also Colour Display Advertisement DUMFRIES. **David and Gill Stewart, Gubhill Farm, Ae, Dumfries DG1 1RL (01387 860648).** Listed farm steading flats in peaceful, pastoral valley surrounded by wooded hills and forest lanes. Two bedrooms each plus sofa bed and cot. TV, linen and central heating provided. Electricity metered. Outside facilities include drying room, bicycle shed, stable, dog run, barbecue and picnic area. Management is eco-sound and nature friendly. Lower flat (Category One Disability) and forest walks are wheelchair compatible. Village shop: one-and-a-half miles, Thornhill one mile, Dumfries 11 miles, riding four miles, fishing and mountain bike course two miles. Queensberry (697 metres) five miles. Upstairs flat - STB ★★★ *SELF-CATERING*. ASSC MEMBER.
e-mail: stewart@creaturefeature.freeserve.co.uk

KIRKCUDBRIGHT. Mrs Dunlop, High Kirkland Holiday Cottages, Cannee, Kirkcudbright DG6 4XD (01557 330684). Sleep 6 and 10. Two traditional stone-built Galloway cottages, recently reconstructed and attractively situated in an elevated position on a farm. Beautiful country walks with abundant animal and bird life, wildlife park nearby, golf, tennis, bowling, fishing and attractive beaches in close proximity. Kirkcudbright is an attractive old town, famed for its many artists, and is only one mile from the cottages. Cottages have metered electricity and are fully equipped, with payphone and shared garden. Blankets and duvets are provided, linen and towels available for an extra fee. Children and pets welcome. Private parking. Open all year. From £180 to £350 per week for the smaller cottage and £200 to £500 for the larger. STB ★★★ *SELF-CATERING*.

PORTPATRICK. Mr A. D. Bryce, Commercial Inn, Portpatrick DG9 8JW (01776 810277). Sea front situation with unrestricted views of harbour and boats, overlooking small sandy beach with safe bathing. Golf, bowling, tennis and sea angling, scenic cliff walks and ideal country roads for touring. Shops and restaurants nearby. Area is of great historical and archaeological interest and enjoys a mild climate. Self-catering flats, three bedrooms; cottage, two bedrooms. Electric heating,cooking etc. Prepayment coin meter. Terms from £150 to £200 per week. Parking at door. Please write or telephone for further details.

DUNDEE & ANGUS

BROUGHTY FERRY. Kingennie Fishings and Holiday Lodges, Kingennie, Broughty Ferry DD5 3RD (01382 350777; Fax: 01382 350400). The four modern Lodges provide luxury self-catering holiday accommodation; all have colour TV and are well insulated and centrally heated. Set in secluded woodland, they enjoy views over the fishing ponds below, where experts and beginners alike can try their skills. GLENCLOVA, sleeping up to seven has been specially designed for disabled visitors, GLENISLA and GLENESK, sleeping four to six, both enjoy lovely views. THE BARD'S NEUK is situated in a quiet secluded corner site. The nearby towns, villages, beaches and countryside around the area provide many fascinating and enjoyable trips all of which can be covered within a day. Pets welcome. Terms from £205 to £465 for Esk, Clova and Isla Cottages; from £363 to £747 for The Bard's Neuk. STB ★★★★ *SELF-CATERING*.
e-mail: kingennie@easynet.co.uk
website: www.kingennie-fishings.com

See also Colour Display Advertisement KIRRIEMUIR. **Glenprosen Cottages.** Glenprosen is one of the lovely, secret, Glens of Angus, foothills of the Cairngorms, and one of the most accessible, yet least spoilt parts of the Scottish Highlands. Only 40 minutes from Dundee, and one-and-a-half hours from Edinburgh, the hills reach to over 3000 ft and the glen is exceptionally rich in wildlife. Peter Pan was conceived in these hills, James Barrie, spent his best holidays here.A wide range of completely individual self-catering cottages, and houses. All traditionally stone built, but fully modernised and comfortable. Wide range of size (two-eight) from shepherd's cottage, to Georgian mansion. Visit our website or ring for brochure **01575 540302.** ASSC MEMBER.
website: www.glenprosen.co.uk

KIRRIEMUIR, Mrs M. Marchant, Welton Farm, The Welton of Kingoldrum, By Kirriemuir, Angus DD8 5HY (Tel & Fax: 01575 574743). Three luxurious self-catering properties (two with en suite facilities) on a secluded 275 acre working farm, situated in a spectacular setting with superb panoramic views at the gateway to the glorious Angus Glens. Peaceful and relaxing with abundance of birds and wildlife. Ideal for hillwalking and birdwatching. An excellent base for outdoor pursuits including fishing, riding, skiing, shooting, golf, and touring the glens, coast and castles (including Glamis). Many visitor attractions in the area. A wide variety of comfortable, high standard accommodation, sleeping two/four. Central heating, hot water, linen and towels included in rental. Facilities include payphone, laundry and ironing facilities, microwave, electric cooker, fridge freezer, dishwasher, colour TV, cot, bed settee, electric blankets, radio alarm, hairdryer, garden furniture, parking. Open all year. Short breaks available. Welcome Host. ASSC Member. Prices £160 to £330. **STB ★★★/★★★★** *SELF-CATERING*.
e-mail: weltonholidays@btinternet.com
website: http://homepages.go.com/~thewelton/index.htm

EDINBURGH & LOTHIANS

WEST CALDER by. Mrs Geraldine Hamilton, Crosswoodhill Farm, By West Calder EH55 8LP (01501 785205 Fax: 01501 785308). **3 Properties Sleep 4/6.** Imagine the best of both worlds. . . two stunning cities, Edinburgh and Glasgow, within an hour's drive and. . . midway. . . Crosswoodhill, a haven of rural tranquillity. Situated on the A70, just 18 miles from the heart of historic Edinburgh, our 1700 acre livestock farm is perfectly placed for exploring Fife, the Borders, Rob Roy and Braveheart country. Visit castles, stately homes, museums, galleries, fine shops; enjoy leisure pursuits close by. Or simply relax; it's a perfect place to unwind. Choose between Midcrosswood, a gem of a cottage on the scenic Pentland Hills, Steading Cottage or a self-contained wing of our handsome 200 year-old farmhouse with its own garden. Comfort, charm, warmth, tradition and a friendly welcome await you. All properties are superbly equipped, including colour TV, video, electric cooker, microwave, washing machine, tumble dryer, dishwasher, fridge, freezer, pay-phone, all bed linen and towels. Bath and power shower. Central heating. Extras: home-grown peat/coal for multi-fuel stoves, oil, electricity by meter reading. Dogs by arrangement (sheep country). Own transport essential. From £260 to £570 weekly. Two cottages wheelchair friendly. **STB ★★★ to ★★★★** *SELF-CATERING*. ASSC MEMBER.
e-mail: crosswd@globalnet.co.uk
website: www.crosswoodhill.co.uk

FIFE

CUPAR (near St Andrews). Mrs Morna Chrisp, Scotstarvit Farm, Cupar KY15 5PA (Tel & Fax 01334 653591). Working Farm. Scotstarvit is ideally situated just off the A916 by 16th century ancient monument of Scotstarvit Tower in an Area of Outstanding Natural Beauty with breathtaking views. The stone built cottage with spacious rooms is well appointed with all mod cons: colour TV/teletext, microwave, washer/dryer, central heating. A log fire is optional if desired. All rooms ground level with south-facing enclosed sheltered garden on little lane by the farm. Private parking. Scotstarvit is enviably placed for accessing all areas along with many golf courses and leisure activities surrounding us: less than five minutes' drive to Cupar our market town and to the historic village of Ceres. 10 minutes to St. Andrews and Fife's quaint little fishing villages. The cities of Edinburgh, Dundee, Perth and Aberdeen are all within easy reach for a day trip. Personal attention. From £140 to £300 per week. Two person discounts. Short breaks. Open all year. Quality farmhouse Bed and Breakfast also from £16 per night. **STB ★★★** *SELF CATERING.*
e-mail: chrisp.scotstarvit@ukgateway.net

See also Colour Display Advertisement   **NEWPORT-ON-TAY. Mr and Mrs Ramsay, Balmore, 3 West Road, Newport-on-Tay DD6 8HH (01382 542274; Fax: 01382 542927). Sleeps 5/6.** Situated on the southern shore of the Tay Estuary, Thorndene is the secluded and self-contained west wing of a large Listed house situated in a three acre walled garden. On the ground floor, it has entry through a paved courtyard, and has its own garden. It is bright and sunny, equipped to a high standard, carpeted throughout, with central heating. There are two double bedrooms – one with a shower en suite, a single bedroom, large sittingroom, diningroom, sun lounge, tiled bathroom with bath and shower, fitted kitchen with washing machine, dishwasher, microwave and breakfast bar. Terms from £185 to £390. Brochure available. **STB ★★★** *SELF-CATERING.* ASSC MEMBER.
e-mail: allan.ramsay@ukgateway.net

HIGHLANDS

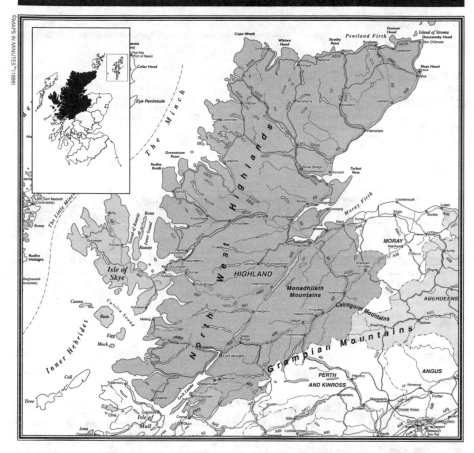

HIGHLANDS (North)

DORNOCH. Highland Glen Lodges. Superb luxury lodges set on a hillside in the Northern Highlands. Panoramic mountain views from your armchair or private balcony. Centrally located for touring the north. Glorious walks from the lodges. Each lodge is beautifully furnished and cosy at any time of the year. Dogs welcome. Open all year. Sleeps 4. Bed linen and towels included. Free electricity. Digital Satellite TV, video, fully fitted kitchen, bathroom with power shower. Ground floor accommodation with parking by the door. Credit card and secure online bookings available. Short and weekend breaks available. **Highland Glen Lodges, Southlins, High Street, Dornoch, Sutherland IV25 3SH (01862 811579; Fax: 01862 811479). STB ★★★★**
SELF-CATERING. ASSC MEMBER
website: www.highlandlodges.co.uk

LOCHCARRON. The Cottage, Stromecarronach, Lochcarron West, Strathcarron. Working farm, join in. Sleeps 2. The small, stone-built Highland cottage is fully equipped and has a double bedroom, shower room and open plan kitchen/livingroom (with open fire). It is secluded with panoramic views over Loch Carron and the mountains. River, sea and loch fishing are available. Hill walking is popular in the area, and there is a small local golf course. Nearby attractions include the Isle of Skye, Inverewe Gardens, the Torridon and Applecross Hills and the historic Kyle Railway Line. Visitors' dogs are welcome provided they are kept under control at all times. For full particulars, write or telephone **Mrs A.G. Mackenzie, Stromecarronach, Lochcarron West, Strathcarron IV54 8YH (01520 722284).**

See also Colour Display Advertisement **LOCHINVER. Clashmore Holiday Cottages, Lochinver. Sleeps 2-5.** Our three croft cottages at Clashmore are the ideal base for a holiday in the Highlands. They are cosy and fully equipped, with linen provided. Nearby there are sandy beaches, mountains and lochs for wild brown trout fishing. Children welcome, but sorry – no pets. Open all year. Terms from £160 to £330. **STB ★★★** *SELF-CATERING*. Contact: **Mr and Mrs Mackenzie, Lochview, 216 Clashmore, Stoer, Lochinver, Sutherland IV27 4JQ (Tel & Fax: 01571 855226).** ASSC MEMBER.
e-mail: clashcotts@aol.com

HIGHLANDS (Mid)

See also Colour Display Advertisement **POOLEWE. Innes Maree Bungalows, Poolewe IV22 2JU (Tel & Fax 01445 781454).** Only a few minutes' walk from the world-famous Inverewe Gardens in magnificent Wester Ross. A purpose built complex of six superb modern bungalows, all equipped to the highest standards of luxury and comfort. Each bungalow sleeps six with main bedroom en suite. Children and pets welcome. Terms from £175 to £425 inclusive of bed linen and electricity. Brochure available. **STB ★★★★** *SELF-CATERING*. ASSC MEMBER
e-mail: innes-maree@lineone.net
website: www.assc.co.uk/innesmaree

TORRIDON. 11 Diabaig, Torridon. Holiday cottage in quiet location overlooking Diabaig Bay with glorious views

out to Skye. The cottage is well-equipped and sleeps six in two double and one twin-bedded rooms. Kitchen with electric cooker, automatic washing machine and fridge, etc; livingroom with electric fire and colour TV. All linen supplied. Pets welcome. Car parking beside house. Open January to December. Prices from £160 to £220 per week. The area around Loch Torridon offers a wide range of outdoor activities, from low-level walks to spectacular hill climbing. Fishing and sailing are also well catered for, with local boat hire available. Permit-free brown trout fishing on the hill lochs and permits for salmon fishing are also available. Contact: **.Mrs Christine Duncan, Hazelbank, Diabaig IV2 2HE (01445 790259).**

HIGHLANDS SOUTH

AVIEMORE. Aviemore – Heart of the Scottish Highlands. For that special vacation enjoy the stunning beauty of the Highlands and the Cairngorm Mountains from our choice of cosy lodges and superbly appointed villas. Great locations; peaceful and relaxing setting. Sky TV, video, payphone, barbecue. Pets welcome. Mini breaks. Many activities available; leisure pool and restaurants nearby. Open all year. Free brochure from: **Premier Vacations – telephone 0870 7019966 ; Fax: 0870 7019955**. ASSC MEMBER.
e-mail: reservations@premiervacations.net
website: www.premiervacations.net

CROY. Mrs Strachan, Balblair Cottages, Balblair, Croy IV2 5PH (01667 493 407). Three cottages, imaginatively created from a stone farm steading, on a small livestock holding, 10 miles east of Inverness. Each cottage has its own south facing garden with patio furniture, double glazing, electric central heating and wood burning stove, making Balblair an ideal all year round base for a Highland holiday. Cawdor Castle, Fort George, Clava Cairns, Inverness and Nairn are all within ten miles, while Loch Ness, the Cairngorms, the Isle of Skye and even John O' Groats can be visited in a day by car. Golf courses are in abundance. Bed linen and towels are provided; telephone. Children and pets welcome. ASSC MEMBER.

CULLODEN (By Inverness). Blackpark Farm, Westhill, Inverness IV2 5BP (01463 790620; Fax: 01463 794262). This newly built holiday home is located one mile from Culloden Battlefield with panoramic views over Inverness and beyond. Fully equipped with many extras to make your holiday special, including oil fired central heating to ensure warmth on the coldest of winter days. Ideally based for touring the Highlands including Loch Ness, Skye etc. Extensive information is available on our website. A Highland welcome awaits you. ASSC MEMBER
e-mail: i.alexander@blackpark.co.uk
website: www.blackpark.co.uk

DALCROSS. Easter Dalziel Farm Holiday Cottages, Dalcross IV1 2JL (Tel & Fax: 01667 462213). Three cosy, traditional stone-built cottages in a superb central location, ideal for touring, sporting activities and observing wildlife. Woodland and coastal walks. The cottages are fully equipped including linen and towels. Pets by arrangement. Terms from £130 low season to £415 high season per cottage per week. Recommended in 'The Good Holiday Cottage Guide'. Open all year for long or short breaks. Brochure on request. **STB ★★★** and **★★★★** *SELF CATERING*. ASSC MEMBER.

DRUMNADROCHIT. H. Brook, Lochletter Lodges, Balnain, Glenurquhart, Inverness IV63 6TJ (01456 476313; Fax: 01456 476301). Situated in beautiful Glenurquhart. Plodda, Divach and Guisachan Lodges all have double bed, one twin bedded room and two adult sized bunk bedded rooms. Bathrooms have shower, toilet etc. Glomach is a two bedded Lodge with one double and one twin bedded room with extra stowaway beds. Full bathroom facilities. Access for disabled. Electricity inclusive. Badminton and games room on site; washing machine and tumble dryer; space for two cars. Linen provided, delicious home made bread available. Walking, cycling, golf and fishing. ASSC MEMBER.
e-mail: mary@lochletter.freeserve.co.uk
website: www.lochletter.freeserve.co.uk

FORT WILLIAM. Great Glen Holidays, Torlundy, Fort William PH33 6SW (01397 703015: Fax 01397 703304) Sleeps 4/6. Eight timber chalets situated in woodland with spectacular mountain scenery. These spacious two bedroom lodges are attractively furnished with linen provided. On working Highland farm. Riding, fishing and walking on farm. Ideal for family holidays and an excellent base for touring; four miles from town. Prices from £250 to £420 per week. **STB ★★** *SELF-CATERING*.

INVERGARRY. High Garry Lodges, Invergarry. Four Scandinavian lodges set in an elevated position with superb views. Double glazed, electric central heating. One twin, two double bedrooms, lounge with breakfast bar and well equipped kitchen and bathroom. Terms from £160 to £440. Also one newly converted cottage nestling at a lower level within the confines of this small working farm. One double and one twin bedroom, tastefully renovated to a high standard. Terms from £190 to £470. Visitors may participate at feeding times on the farm. Ideal for touring the West Highlands. Fishing, walking, golf and bird-watching nearby. Brochure available. **STB ★★★** *SELF-CATERING.* Contact: **Mr and Mrs Wilson (01809 501226; Fax: 01809 501307).** ASSC MEMBER.

KINCRAIG. Loch Insh Chalets, Kincraig, PH21 1NU (01540 651272 Fax: 01540 651208). Just six miles south of Aviemore these superb log chalets are set in 14 acres of woodland in the magnificent Spey Valley, surrounded on three sides by forest and rolling fields with the fourth side being half a mile of beach frontage. Free watersports hire for guests, 8.30-10am/4-5.30pm daily. Watersports, salmon fishing, archery, dry ski slope skiing. Hire/instruction available by the hour, day or week mid April to end October. Boathouse Restaurant on the shore of Loch Insh offers coffees, bar meals, children's meals and evening à la carte. Large gift shop and bar. Children's adventure area, interpretation trail, ski slope, mountain bike hire and stocked trout lochan are open all year round. Ski hire and instruction available December-April. ASSC MEMBER.
e-mail: office@lochinsh.com
website: www.lochinsh.com

KINGUSSIE. Alvie Holiday Cottages. A secluded and beautiful Highland Estate with breathtaking views over the Spey Valley and the Cairngorm Mountains beyond. Woodland walks, fishing on the River Spey plus many other family activities available nearby. Three traditional farm cottages or two flats in the Estate's Edwardian shooting lodge. All furnished to the most comfortable standards. For further details visit our website or contact: **Alvie Estate Office, Kincraig, Kingussie PH21 1NE (01540 651255/651249; Fax: 01540 651380).** ASSC MEMBER.
website: www.alvie-estate.co.uk

KIRKHILL (near Inverness). Mr M. R. Fraser, Reelig House, Reelig Glen, Kirkhill, Near Inverness IV5 7PP (01463 831208; Fax: 01463 831413). Properties sleep 4/5. Holiday cottages and chalets in secluded woodland positions only eight miles from Inverness, capital of the Highlands. People staying here have enjoyed the freedom and the solitude; the tall trees and water of the Fairy Glen; the countryside with all the untrammelled joys of nature is at the door, butterflies find what butterflies need. Yet they have been glad of the nearness to shops, the pleasures of Inverness and of Beauly only 10 minutes' drive away. Pony trekking, sandy beaches and organised pastimes not far off. Central for touring West Coast to North, Central Highlands, Glen Affric, Culloden, Aviemore, Speyside and Moray Firth coast. The holiday homes are fully equipped except for linen and towels (unless these are specially asked for), with electric fires, night storage heater, fridge, four-ring cooker, microwave, shaving socket and colour TV. Reduced rates spring and autumn. Please ask for brochure and booking details. **STB ★/★★** *SELF-CATERING.*
e-mail: reelig@aol.com
website: www.reelig.com

LOCH NESS (SOUTH). 'Giusaichean', Ault-na-Goire, Errogie. Sleeps 4/6 plus cot. Secluded but not isolated. Giusaichean is a converted croft at Loch Ness, centrally placed for touring the Highlands. Two double bedrooms upstairs, also bathroom with bidet, shower and bath. Downstairs second WC and kitchen with electric hob and oven, microwave, washing machine, tumble dryer, dishwasher, fridge and freezer. Spacious lounge with wood-burning stove, colour TV. Oil central heating and electricity free. Payphone. Fenced garden, safe for pets and children. Open all year. Other self catering also in Loch Ness area. **STB ★★★★** *SELF CATERING.* For brochure, contact **Rosemary and Andy Holt, Wilderness Cottages, Island Cottage, Inverfarigaig, Inverness IV2 6XR. Tel/Fax: 01456 486631** ASSC MEMBER.
e-mail: andy@wildernesscottages.com
website: www.wildernesscottages.com

SPEAN BRIDGE. Riverside Lodges, Invergloy, Spean Bridge PH34 4DY (Tel & Fax 01397 712684). Peace and quiet are synonymous with Riverside, where our three identical lodges each sleep up to six people. Accessible from the A82 but totally hidden from it, our 12 acres of woodland garden front on Loch Lochy. Cots, linen, boat, fishing tackle, barbecue, all for hire. Pets welcome. There is a nominal charge for fishing on our stocked lochan or you can fish free from our shingle beach on Loch Lochy. Brochure gladly provided. **STB** ★★★ *SELF-CATERING*. ASSC MEMBER.
e-mail: riverside.lodges@dial.pipex.com
web: www.ykm09.dial.pipex.com

TOMICH. Tomich Holidays. Sleep 4-6. Our magnificent farm steading houses three courtyard cottages and a heated indoor pool. Two storey wooden chalets are also available and have been designed to blend into the natural birch woodland. The Victorian Dairy, a listed building of classic architectural quality, sleeps four. All have central heating, hot water and electricity included in the price. Whatever the weather, summer or winter, your comfort is assured. Tomich is in the depths of the Highlands, near Glen Affric and close to Loch Ness, an ideal base for walking, touring or relaxing. Open all year. Pets welcome. Terms from £165 to £505. Bookings/colour brochure: **Donald and Sue Fraser, Tomich Holidays, Guisachan Farm, Tomich IV4 7LY (01456 415332; Fax: 01456 415499). STB** ★★★/★★★★ *SELF-CATERING*. ASSC MEMBER.
e-mail: tomicholidays@zetnet.co.uk
website: www.tomicholidays.zetnet.co.uk

LANARKSHIRE

BIGGAR (Clyde Valley). Carmichael Country Cottages, Carmichael Estate Office, Westmains, Carmichael. Biggar ML12 6PG (01899 308336; Fax: 01899 308481). Working farm, join in. Sleep 2/7. These 200-year-old stone cottages nestle among the woods and fields of our 700-year-old family estate. Still managed by the descendants of the original Chief of Carmichael. We guarantee comfort, warmth and a friendly welcome in an accessible, unique, rural and historic time capsule. We farm deer, cattle and sheep and sell meats and tartan - Carmichael of course! Children and pets welcome. Open all year. Terms from £180 to £480. 15 cottages with a total of 32 bedrooms. We have the ideal cottage for you. Private tennis court and fishing loch; cafe, farm shop and visitor centre. Pony trekking. Off-road driving course. **STB** ★★/★★★★ *SELF-CATERING*. FHB Member. ASSC MEMBER.
e-mail: chiefcarm@aol.com
website: www.carmichael.co.uk/cottages

PERTH & KINROSS

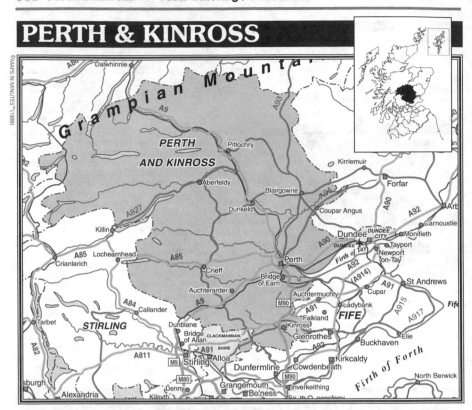

©MAPS IN MINUTES™ (1999)

ABERFELDY. Mrs Pamela McDiarmid, Mains of Murthly, Aberfeldy PH15 2EA (01887 820427). Sleeps three/five. Two beautifully situated stone-built holiday cottages overlooking Aberfeldy on a working farm, one-and-a-quarter miles from town. Fully equipped for three to five persons. Dining/sittingroom, kitchen, bathroom with shower and bath. Everything supplied except linen. Log fires. Children welcome. Pets accepted. Ample parking. Fishing available on private stretch of River Tay. Golf courses nearby and new recreation centre with swimming pool in Aberfeldy. Available all year, with terms from £150. SAE please for further details. ASSC MEMBER. **STB** ★★★ *SELF-CATERING.*

ABERFELDY. Mr Robin Menzies, Mains of Taymouth Cottages. Kenmore, Aberfeldy PH15 2HN (01887 830226; Fax: 01887 830211). Mains of Taymouth cottages are set in magnificent Highland Perthshire by the village of Kenmore amidst the finest scenery Scotland has to offer. We are surrounded by lovely walks, good fishing, Kenmore Golf Course is on our doorstep and activities abound from water sports and mountain biking to Highland Adventure safaris. Our five cottages are based around an 18th century courtyard and vary from a cosy two bedroomed cottage to an extensive luxury four bedroom with en-suite facilities, large garden and sauna. All cottages are traditional stone built and tastefully modernised with full central heating, open fires, dishwashers and all other mod cons you would possibly need. The cottages are in a quiet private setting with easy access to the golf course and restaurant and everything the area has to offer.
e-mail: info@taymouth.co.uk
website: www.taymouth.co.uk

BLAIRGOWRIE. Mrs K.A.L. Saddler, Inverquiech, Alyth, Blairgowrie PH11 8JR (01828 632463). Working farm. Cottage sleeps 4. Recently refurbished farm cottage with oil-fired central heating. Everything essential for self-catering including colour television, microwave, electric cooker, fridge and vacuum, bath and shower. Farm is bordered by River Isla and Alyth Burn. Free fishing allowed. There are two bedrooms, one double with twin beds and one smaller with bunk beds. Electric blankets, duvets, linen and towels provided. Small garden and double garage with washing machine and tumble dryer. Pets welcome. Golfing, riding, walking, fishing and skiing nearby. Terms £175-£240 includes electricity, oil, coal and logs for open fire. Brochure available. **STB ★★★** *SELF-CATERING.*

See also Colour Display Advertisement

DUNKELD by. Laighwood Holidays, Butterstone, By Dunkeld PH8 0HB (01350 724241). Properties sleep 2-8. A de luxe detached house, comfortably accommodating eight, created from the west wing of a 19th century shooting lodge with panoramic views. Two popular cottages sleeping four, situated on our hill farm with beautiful views. Two well-equipped apartments adjoining Butterglen House near Butterstone Loch. Butterstone lies in magnificent countryside (especially Spring/Autumn), adjacent to Nature Reserve (ospreys). Central for walking, touring, historic houses, golf and fishing. Private squash court and hill loch (wild brown trout) on the farm. Sorry no pets. Terms: House £385 to £580; Cottages and Apartments £130 to £300. ASSC MEMBER. **STB ★★★/★★★★** *SELF-CATERING.*
e-mail: holidays@laighwood.co.uk
website: www.laighwood.co.uk

KILLIN. Springwood. Springwood is a modern bungalow set on a private road overlooking the River Lochay. It is in a secluded position on the edge of the village yet within walking distance of shops and local facilities. Furnished to a high standard throughout, extras include dishwasher, microwave, automatic washer. There are well laid out gardens to the front and rear, with patio and garden furniture. Prices, which include bedding, towels and electricity, range from £210 per week. Offering a truly relaxing holiday. **STB ★★★** *SELF-CATERING.* Details from **Mrs C.A. Campbell, Ledcharrie, Luib, Crianlarich FK20 8QT (Tel & Fax: 01567 820532).**

See also Colour Display Advertisement

LOCH EARN. Riverside Log Cabins. Sitting on the bank of the River Earn, in an Area of Outstanding Natural Beauty, these three bedroom cabins are ideally situated to explore most of Scotland. Oban and the West Coast (via Glencoe), St Andrews, Stirling and the shopping and cultural Meccas of Glasgow and Edinburgh are all within a 90 minute drive. Many local golf courses, beautiful walks, fishing, sailing, water skiing, riding and country sports nearby. Inverness and Loch Ness (including the monster?) provide an excellent day trip. Colour brochure available on request. **STB ★★★★** *SELF-CATERING.* For details contact **Office:- Willoughby, Gordon Road, Crieff PH7 4BL (Tel & Fax: 01764 654048)**
e-mail: riverside@logcabins.demon.co.uk

RANNOCH. Mrs N. Robertson, Camusericht Farm, Bridge of Gaur, Rannoch, By Pitlochry PH17 2QD (01882 633219 or 01882 633277). Sleeps 5. Situated in the rugged and romantic hills of Scotland where River Gaur runs into Loch Rannoch: Bothy Cottage. Contains livingroom with multi-fuel stove; kitchenette; shower and toilet; two bedrooms with one single and two double beds. Fully furnished except linen. Children welcome. Tariff £120 per week, excluding electricity. Plenty of swimming and fishing. SAE for futher details.

STRATHTAY. Carnish, Strathtay. Sleeps 4. Modern semi-detached bungalow, comfortably furnished, on edge of small village. Aberfeldy five miles, Pitlochry nine miles; near golf course. Sleeps four in two double bedrooms; electric blankets; duvets; fully equipped except linen; fridge; all-electric; parking. Utility room with washing machine and freezer. No children, no pets. Weekly terms plus electricity. **Mrs Kidd, Eiriostadh, Strathtay, Pitlochry PH9 0PG (01887 840322)**

SCOTTISH ISLANDS

Islay

BRIDGEND. Blackpark Croft House. Situated in a stunning location with breathtaking views, near to safe sandy beaches, ideal for family holidays. The house is exceptionally well-appointed and has a wonderfully presented interior. It sleeps eight people, and consists of one family, and two double bedrooms; two bathrooms with shower facility; large kitchen with all mod cons and a large sittingroom with open fire, which heats the entire house. Bed linen and towels are provided. Price £400 per week. Also, two self-catering apartments situated in the idyllic village of Port Charlotte, with all mod cons. All enquiries to **Mrs M. Shaw, 10 An-Creagan Place, Port Charlotte (01496 850355).**

Mull

GRULINE. Mrs McFarlane, Torlochan, Gruline, Isle of Mull PA71 6HR (01680 300380: Fax: 01680

300664). Torlochan is situated in the centre of the Isle of Mull, with panoramic views over Loch Na Keal. We are a small working croft with 26 acres in which you can enjoy the antics of our animals, which include llamas, sheep, goats, pigs and varieties of poultry. Pets free of charge. A friendly welcome awaits you, your children and pets at our "Oasis in the desert". More information and colour brochure available from Diane McFarlane.

Orkney Islands

HOLM. Ms M.A. Fox, Craebreck House, Holm KW17 2RX (01856 781220). Self-catering farmhouse

with four bedrooms, sleeping seven. Situated five miles from Hoy, accommodation comprises of a modernised two storey house, double glazed and centrally heated, with conservatory, lounge, shower room and fully equipped kitchen/diner. Most rooms provide wonderful views to the Southern Isles, Scapa Flow and Hoy. Orkney is a must for those who like scenery, space, safety and peace. Added interests include birdwatching, geology, archaeology, fishing, sailing, diving, many crafts, good eating, malt whisky distillery, museums, exhibitions and really friendly people. Easy to reach several other islands for day trips. Prices from £160 to £335 per week, heating included. Open all year. Brochure available. **STB** ★★★★ SELF-CATERING.

HOY. Rackwick Hostel, Hoy KW16 3NJ. Sleeps eight. The hostel accommodates up to eight people in two

ORKNEY ISLANDS COUNCIL

dormitories, each sleeping four. It lies in the Rackwick valley with magnificent cliff scenery, only two miles from the Old Man of Hoy. The area is of special interest to climbers, botanists, ornithologists and geologists. No linen. Cooking is by gas, with cooking utensils, cutlery and crockery provided; one toilet/ shower room. Limited camping is available with use of hostel amenities. Terms from £6.25 (jumiors) £7.00 (adults) per night for hostel, from £2.00 (juniors) £2.75 (adults) per night camping. Sorry, no dogs (except Guide Dogs). Open March to September (special out of season opening for groups can be arranged). **The Department of Education and Recreation Services, Orkney Islands Council, School Place, Kirkwall KW15 1NY (01856 873535 ext.2404; Fax: 01856 870302).**

SCOTLAND
Caravan & Camping Holidays

ARGYLL & BUTE

caolasnacon
Caravan & Camping Park, Kinlochleven PA40 4RS

There are 20 static six-berth caravans for holiday hire on this lovely site with breathtaking mountain scenery on the edge of Loch Leven — an ideal touring centre. Caravans have electric lighting, Calor gas cookers and heaters, toilet, shower, fridge and colour TV. There are two toilet blocks with hot water and showers and laundry facilities. Children are welcome and pets allowed. Open from April to October. Milk, gas, soft drinks available on site; shops three miles. Sea loch fishing, hill walking and boating; boats and rods for hire, fishing tackle for sale.

Weekly rates for vans from £180; 10% reductions on two week bookings.
Tourers from £7.50 nightly. 7½ acres for campers — Rates from £5.25 nightly.

For details contact Mrs Patsy Cameron — 01855 831279

BORDERS

COLDINGHAM. Scoutscroft Holiday Centre, Coldingham TD14 5NB (01890 771338; Bookings Hotline: 0800 169 3786; Fax: 01890 771746). Scoutscroft enjoys a superb position within a few minutes' walk from a safe, sandy beach. Holiday homes available for let (none over five years old), varying from six-berth de luxe to super de luxe models All are fully equipped with mains services, flush toilets etc. There is also a touring and camping park for all types of tourers, motor homes, and tents – excellent facilities. Amenities at the Centre include a bar/lounge with entertainment during the summer months, a family bar, restaurant, and fast food takeaway.
e-mail: jhamilton@scoutscroftholidaycentre.fsnet.co.uk
website: www.scoutscroftholidaycentre.fsnet.co.uk

HIGHLANDS (North)

JOHN O'GROATS. John O'Groats Caravan and Camping Site, John O'Groats KW1 4YS (01955 611329). At end of A99 on seafront beside "last house in Scotland", caravan and camping site with showers, launderette, electric hook-ups and disabled toilet. Caravans, caravanettes and tents welcome. Booking office for day trips to Orkney Islands on site. Hotel, restaurant, cafe, harbour 150 metres. Magnificent cliff scenery with sea birds galore including puffins, guillemots, skuas within one-and-a-half-miles. Seals are often seen swimming to and fro and there is a seal colony only four miles away. From the site you can see the wide panorama of the Orkney Islands, the nearest of which is only seven miles away. Prices from £7 per night. Public telephone on site. **STB ★★★**

HIGHLANDS (Mid)

ACHNASHEEN. Mr A.J. Davis, Gruinard Bay Caravan Park, Laide, By Achnasheen, Wester Ross IV22 2ND (Tel & Fax: 01445 731225).  An invitation to the most beautiful part of North West Scotland. Situated just a stone's throw from the beach, Gruinard Bay Caravan Park offers the perfect setting for a holiday or a stopover on the West Coast of Scotland. Family owned and operated, the park boasts magnificent views across the Bay, and from the beach you can take in the breathtaking views of the mountains of Coigach, the Summer Isles and Gruinard Island. Limited number of static vans available for hire, all fully serviced and equipped (including duvets and linen) with no additional charge for gas and electricity. For up-to-the-minute availability and tariff information please telephone and we will be pleased to advise you. **STB ✓✓✓✓.**

PERTH & KINROSS

COMRIE. West Lodge Caravan Park, Comrie PH6 2LS (01764 670354).  Two to six berth static caravans with gas cooker, running water, toilet, electric fridge, lighting, colour TV and gas fire. Crockery, cutlery, cooking utensils, blankets and pillows are provided. Sheets and towels can be hired. All caravans also have showers. One modern shower block on site, complete with washing machine, tumble dryer, showers and hot and cold running water; shop. Fishing, golf, tennis, bowling, hill-walking and canoeing all within easy reach. Watersports available on nearby Loch Earn. Ideal for touring, 23 miles north of Stirling and 23 miles west of Perth. Terms from £20 to £32 nightly, £100 to £220 weekly; VAT, electricity and gas included. Open 1st April to 31st October. **STB ★★★** SELF-CATERING.

DUNKELD. Kilvrecht Caravan Park, Inverpark, Dunkeld PH8 0JR (01350 727284; Fax: 01350 728635).  Secluded campsite on a level open area in quiet and secluded woodland setting. Close by is the Black Wood of Rannoch, a remnant of the Ancient Caledonian Forest which once blanketed Scotland. There is fishing available for brown trout on Loch Rannoch and there is nothing to beat a sunny day on the shores of the loch for those who wish to relax. There is a Forest Park centre and shop at the Queen's View where you will find full details of walks and activities. Several trails begin from the campsite. Please write, fax or telephone for further information.

Board
Accommodation
WALES

Ratings You Can Trust

ENGLAND

The *English Tourism Council* (formerly the English Tourist Board) has joined with the *AA* and *RAC* to create a new, easily understood quality rating for serviced accommodation, giving a clear guide of what to expect.

HOTELS are given a rating from One to Five *Stars* – the more Stars, the higher the quality and the greater the range of facilities and level of services provided.

GUEST ACCOMMODATION, which includes guest houses, bed and breakfasts, inns and farmhouses, is rated from One to Five *Diamonds*. Progressively higher levels of quality and customer care must be provided for each one of the One to Five Diamond ratings.

HOLIDAY PARKS, TOURING PARKS and CAMPING PARKS are now also assessed using *Stars*. Standards of quality range from a One Star (acceptable) to a Five Star (exceptional) park.

Look out also for the new *SELF-CATERING* Star ratings. The more *Stars* (from One to Five) awarded to an establishment, the higher the levels of quality you can expect. Establishments at higher rating levels also have to meet some additional requirements for facilities.

NB Some self-catering properties had not been assessed at the time of going to press and in these cases the old-style *KEY* symbols will still be shown.

SCOTLAND

Star Quality Grades will reflect the most important aspects of a visit, such as the warmth of welcome, efficiency and friendliness of service, the quality of the food and the cleanliness and condition of the furnishings, fittings and decor.

THE MORE STARS,
THE HIGHER THE STANDARDS.

The description, such as Hotel, Guest House, Bed and Breakfast, Lodge, Holiday Park, Self-catering etc tells you the type of property and style of operation.

In England, Scotland and Wales, all graded properties are inspected annually by Tourist Authority trained Assessors.

WALES

Places which score highly will have an especially welcoming atmosphere and pleasing ambience, high levels of comfort and guest care, and attractive surroundings enhanced by thoughtful design and attention to detail

STAR QUALITY GUIDE FOR SERVICED ACCOMMODATION AND HOLIDAY PARKS

★★★★★	*Exceptional quality*
★★★★	*Excellent quality*
★★★	*Very good quality*
★★	*Good quality*
★	*Fair to good quality*

SELF-CATERING ACCOMMODATION

The *DRAGON GRADES* spell out the quality. They range from Grade 1 (simple and reasonable) to Grade 5 (excellent quality). The grades reflect the overall quality, not the range of facilities.

ANGLESEY & GWYNEDD

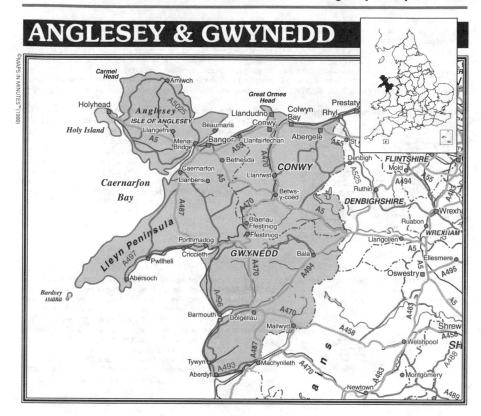

ANGLESEY. Mrs J Bown, Drws-y-Coed, Llannerch-y-medd, Anglesey LL71 8AD (01248 470473).

Welcome to Drws-y-Coed. Enjoy excellent hospitality, food and tranquil surroundings with panoramic views of Snowdonia. Centrally situated to explore Anglesey's coastline and attractions. 25 minutes to the Port of Holyhead. Beautifully decorated and furnished en suite bedrooms with all facilities, to make your stay most enjoyable. Inviting spacious lounge with a log fire. The freshly cooked breakfasts are served in the cosy diningroom with separate tables. Games room. Interesting historic farmstead and walks on a 550 acre beef, sheep and arable farm. Attractive garden with a gazebo to relax in. Non-smoking establishment. Open all year. Bed and Breakfast from £22.50 – £24.50. **WTB** ★★★★ FARM, Farm Holiday Guide Diploma, WTB Rural Tourism Award.

BALA. Mrs C. A. Morris, Tai'r Felin Farm, Frongoch, Bala LL23 7NS (01678 520763). Working farm.

Tai'r Felin Farm is a working farm, situated three miles north of Bala (A4212 and B4501). Double and twin bedrooms available with beverage tray and clock radio. Beamed lounge with colour TV and log fire when the weather is cooler. Excellent base for touring Snowdonia National Park, watersports, walking, fishing, etc. National White Water Centre is nearby. Hearty breakfast, with packed lunches and snacks available on request. Recommended for excellent cooking and friendly atmosphere. Relax and enjoy a homely welcome. Bed and Breakfast from £16. Walkers and cyclists welcome. Reductions for longer stays. **WTB** ★★ FARM

BALA. Mrs S.E. Edwards, Bryn Melyn, Rhyduchaf, Bala LL23 7PG (01678 520376). Working farm. Bryn Melyn, Rhyduchaf is situated in the beautiful countryside of Bala, and offers accommodation all year. The house is stone-built and stands on 56 acres of mixed farmland. Home cooking and home produced food makes this a real home from home. Two double and one twin bedrooms, all with washbasins; two bathrooms, toilet; sittingroom; diningroom; central heating. With tea and coffee facilities. Children welcome at reduced rates. Sorry, no pets. A car is necessary to ensure that visitors derive all the pleasure that this region offers. Parking space. Sea 28 miles. Good recreation facilities in the area. Evening Dinner, Bed and Breakfast from £175 weekly or Bed and Breakfast £16 per person, with Dinner £25. No smoking. Mrs Edwards is a Farm Holiday Guide Diploma winner. **WTB** ★★

CAERNARFON. Gwyndaf and Jane Lloyd Rowlands, Pengwern, Saron, Llanwnda, Caernarfon LL54

5UH (Tel & Fax: 01286 831500; mobile: 07778 411780), Charming, spacious farmhouse of character, situated between mountains and sea. Unobstructed views of Snowdonia. Well-appointed bedrooms, all en suite. Set in 130 acres of land which runs down to Foryd Bay. Jane has a cookery diploma and provides excellent meals with farmhouse fresh food, including home-produced beef and lamb. Excellent access. Children welcome. Open February to November. Bed and Breakfast from £22 to £28; Evening Meal from £13. **WTB** ★★★★ *FARM,* AA QQQQQ.

CAERNARFON near. Paula and David Foster, Tan y Gaer, Rhosgadfan, Near Caernarfon LL54 7LE

(01286 830943). Set in spectacular scenery with views to the top of Snowdon and over the Irish Sea, this farmhouse with beams and open fires offers a restful atmosphere from which to enjoy beautiful North Wales. Riding, climbing, walking and beaches are all close by. The home-made bread and farmhouse cooking are done on the 'Aga' and much of the food is home produced. Guests have their own diningroom and lounge with TV, books, etc. and the en suite bedrooms are spacious. Bed and Breakfast from £20, evening meal optional. Reductions for weekly stays. Telephone for details, brochure on request.

DOLGELLAU. Mrs Griffiths, Llwyn Tal Cen, Brithdir, Dolgellau LL40 2RY (01341 450276).

Situated in an acre of rhododendron and azalea gardens, Llwyn Tal Cen offers a warm welcome and outstanding views, together with peace and quiet. Our location, about four miles east of Dolgellau, makes an ideal centre for hill-walkers and nature lovers. We offer good fresh food, organic whenever possible. Traditional and vegetarian fare are both available. Bed and Breakfast from £17 to £21; Evening Meal £11. En suite rooms available. Reduced rates are available for children. Ample parking. To find us take narrow lane from the centre of the village of Brithdir (telephone box) past the village hall and wooden houses for about half-a-mile until you reach a crossroads, turn right, Llwyn Tal Cen is on the right in the trees after about 200 yards. **WTB** ★ *GUEST HOUSE*

DOLGELLAU. Mrs W. Smith, Maesneuadd Farm, Llanfachreth, Dolgellau LL40 2DH (01341 450256).

Maesneuadd Farm is situated in a peaceful area of outstanding natural beauty. Our 200-year-old farmhouse with log fires and oak beams offers excellent accommodation in a friendly, relaxing atmosphere. All bedrooms are en suite. We offer fresh eggs and home-grown vegetables. Walks can be taken over the farm, through gardens and bluebell woodland, by streams and hillsides with breathtaking mountain views. We are four-and-a-half miles from Dolgellau and 20 minutes from the beach. Ideal for touring, walking, fishing, cycling. Colour TV in lounge. No smoking or pets. Bed and Breakfast from £18 to £22 per person. **WTB** ★★★ *FARM.* Self-catering cottage also available (WTB Five Stars).

HARLECH. Mrs G.M. Evans, Glanygors, Llandanwg, Harlech LL46 2SD (01341 241410).

This detached house with two acres of land is situated 400 yards from sandy beach, and has beautiful views of the mountains. It is one-and-a-half miles from Harlech Castle, golf club and swimming pool, and within a quarter-mile of train station. Ideal place for bird-watching. Private access to beach. Presenting good home-cooking in a homely and relaxed atmosphere and run by a Welsh-speaking family. Open all year. Central heating and electric blankets for winter months. Accommodation comprises two double, one twin and one family bedrooms, all with washbasin, TV and tea-making facilities; bathroom, toilet; TV lounge and diningroom. Reduced rates for children and senior citizens. Bed and Breakfast from £16 per night; Evening Meal optional. Caravan to let.

LLANERCHRYMEDD. Margaret and Richard Hughes, Llwydiarth Fawr, Llanerchymedd, Isle of Anglesey LL71 8DF (01248 470321/470540).

Llwydiarth Fawr is a stylish, secluded and special place to stay. Guests invariably appreciate its air of spaciousness, its quiet luxury, its superior standards, its antiques, its warmth of welcome, its delicious food and its unbeatable value for money. The bedrooms are furnished to the highest standards, all en suite with colour TV, tea/coffee making facilities and central heating. Llwydiarth Fawr's central location makes it the perfect base from which to explore all of Anglesey, or just enjoy the relaxing setting. Nature walks, a lake for private fishing and bird watching are all available within the grounds, while children can play in complete security in the farmland surroundings. Open all year except Christmas. Non-smoking.

LLANRUG. Mrs C. MacKinnon, Plas Tirion Farm, Llanrug, Caernarfon LL55 4PY (Tel & Fax: 01286673190).

Peacefully located in 300 acres of lowland pastures, commanding panoramic views of Snowdonia and historic Caernarfon. Ideally situated for touring North Wales. Traditional stone farmhouse, offering guests warm and comfortable accommodation. All en suite bedrooms with beverage facilities and TV. Children welcome. Mid week breaks April to May and September to October. Open April to October. Bed and Breakfast from £20 per person per night; Evening Meal available. WTB ★★★★ FARM.

TRAWSFYNYDD. Penny Osborne and Margaret Roberts, Old Mill Farmhouse, Fron Oleu Farm, Trawsfynydd LL41 4UN (Tel & Fax: 01766 540397).

In the heart of Snowdonia National Park midway between Porthmadog and Dolgellau, Fron Oleu Farm offers plenty of wide open space to roam amongst a variety of safe, friendly animals, with beautiful views over the lake to the mountains beyond. Bedrooms are situated adjacent to the farmhouse, each with individual front door, private bathroom, TV, tea making facilities and heating. A two bedroomed family suite is available, as well as double, twin and family rooms. Ideal base for visiting mountains, lakes, rivers, castles, slate and copper mines and National Park properties; plenty of nearby sporting activities. Please telephone for further information.

NORTH WALES

BETWS-Y-COED. Mrs E. Jones, Maes-y-Garnedd Farm, Capel Garmon, Llanrwst, Betws-y-Coed

(01690 710428). Working farm. This 140-acre mixed farm is superbly situated on the Rooftop of Wales as Capel Garmon has been called, and the Snowdonia Range, known to the Welsh as the "Eyri", visible from the land. Two miles from A5. Surrounding area provides beautiful country scenery and walks. Safe, sandy beaches at Llandudno and Colwyn Bay. Salmon and trout fishing (permit required). Mrs Jones serves excellent home-produced meals with generous portions including Welsh lamb and roast beef. Gluten-free and coeliacs' wheat-free diets can be arranged. Packed lunches, with flask of coffee or tea. One double and one family bedrooms with washbasins; bathroom, toilet; sittingroom, dining room. Children welcome; cot, high chair and babysitting available. Regret, no pets. Car essential, ample parking. Open all year. Bed and Breakfast; Evening Meal optional. SAE brings prompt reply with details of terms. Reductions for children. Bala Lakes, Bodnant Gardens, Ffestiniog Railway, slate quarries, Trefriw Woollen Mills nearby. Member of AA. **WTB ★** *FARM*

BETWS-Y-COED. Mrs Florence Jones, Maes Gwyn Farm, Pentrefoelas, Betws-y-Coed LL24 0LR

(01690 770668). Maes Gwyn is a mixed farm of 90-97 hectares, situated in lovely quiet countryside, about one mile from the A5, six miles from the famous Betws-y-Coed. The sea and Snowdonia Mountains about 20 miles. Very good centre for touring North Wales, many well-known places of interest. House dates back to 1665. It has one double and one family bedrooms with washbasins and tea/coffee making facilities; bathroom with shower, toilet; lounge with colour TV and diningroom. Children and Senior Citizens are welcome at reduced rates and pets are permitted. Car essential, ample parking provided. Good home cooking. Six miles to bus/railway terminal. Open May/November for Bed and Breakfast from £15. SAE, please, for details. **WTB ★★★** *FARM*

BETWS-Y-COED. Jim and Lilian Boughton, Bron Celyn Guest House, Lon Muriau, Llanrwst Road, Betws-y-Coed LL24 0HD (01690 710333; Fax: 01690

710111). A warm welcome awaits you at this delightful guest house overlooking the Gwydyr Forest and Llugwy/Conwy Valleys and village of Betws-y-Coed in Snowdonia National Park. Ideal centre for touring, walking, climbing, fishing and golf. Also excellent overnight stop en-route for Holyhead ferries. Easy walk into village and close to Conwy/Swallow Falls and Fairy Glen. Most rooms en suite, all with colour TV and beverage makers. Lounge. Full central heating. Garden. Car park. Open all year. Full hearty breakfast, packed meals, snacks, evening meals - special diets catered for. Bed and Breakfast from £19 to £26, reduced rates for children under 12 years. Special out of season breaks. **WTB ★★★** *GUEST HOUSE.*
e-mail: broncelyn@betws-y-coed.co.uk
website: www.betws-y-coed.co.uk/broncelyn

BETWS-Y-COED near. Mrs Eleanore Roberts, Awelon, Plas Isa, Llanrwst LL26 0EE (01492 640047).

Awelon once formed part of the estate of William Salisbury, translator of the New Testament into Welsh in the 16th century. With three-foot thick outer walls, it has now been modernised and is an attractive small guest house. Three bedrooms with en suite available; colour TV and teamakers; cosy lounge; central heating ensures a comfy stay. Private parking. Llanrwst, a busy market town at the centre of the beautiful Conway Valley, is close to Snowdonia, Bodnant Gardens and North Wales coast. A warm Welsh welcome awaits all guests. Bed and Breakfast from £16, en suite from £18.50 per person. A good choice of hotels, pubs and cafes in Llanrwst for evening meals. All home cooking. Children and pets welcome. Recommended by "Which?" Magazine.

LLANWRST. Mrs Menna Williams, Tyddyn Du, Nant-y-Rhiw, Llanwrst, Conwy LL26 0TG (Tel & Fax: 01492 640189). Tyddyn Du is a traditional farmhouse offering a homely Welsh welcome. Oak doors and deep windowsills evoke a sense of the past, and the rooms have been recently redecorated. There is a substantial garden where guests can sit and enjoy spectacular views of the Snowdonia Range. The farm itself is a busy one, with Welsh Black Cattle and Welsh Mountain Sheep. It is situated within five miles of Betws-y-Coed and attractions, and 20 minutes from the coast. Open April to November. Bed and Breakfast from £17. **WTB** ★★ *FARM*.

MACHYNLLETH. Mrs Lynwen Edwards, Bryn Sion Farm, Cwm Cywarch, Dinas Mawddwy, Machynlleth SY20 9JG (01650 531251). A very warm welcome awaits you when you visit Bryn Sion Farm, situated in the quiet, unspoilt valley of Cywarch at the foot of Arran Fawddwy (3000 ft). We are within reach of the beach and fishing and shooting are available on the farm. Bryn Sion is a mixed farm of 708 acres offering a variety of good farmhouse breakfasts and bedtime tea/coffee. Log fire in sittingroom in the evenings. Central heating throughout. One twin en suite and one double en suite with TV, tea making facilities and shaving points. Car essential - parking. Open April to November for Bed and Breakfast from £18 per person. SAE, please with enquiries.

RUTHIN. Mrs Ella Williams, Tyddyn Chambers, Pwllglas, Ruthin LL15 2LS (01824 750683). A traditional sheep and dairy working farm set in scenic countryside with close proximity to Snowdonia and many other North Wales attractions. Your hosts are a typical Welsh-speaking musical family. Your stay will be enhanced by tasting our home-cooking and enjoyment of the peaceful surroundings. One double room, one twin room and one family room, all en suite. Open all year except Christmas and New Year Bed and Breakfast from £18 to £22; Evening Meal available from £10. **WTB** ★★ *FARM*.

Please mention *The Farm Holiday Guide* when making enquiries about accommodation featured in these pages.

CARDIGANSHIRE

ABERAERON. Mrs Christine Jones, Frondolau Farm Guest House, Heol Llain Prysg, Llanon SY23 5HZ (01974 202354). Frondolau is a period house in a quiet location and is part of a working dairy farm. Situated five miles north of Aberaeron and ten miles south of Aberystwyth we are ideally placed for visiting Ceredigion's many beautiful beaches and mountains. Bedrooms have tea/coffee facilities, clock radio, double glazing and central heating. A large sitting room with wood fire is available for your use. Relax and enjoy being a welcome guest with home-produced food from the farm and garden. B&B from £16 per person with special rates available for short breaks (five days plus). Open all year. Brochure available. **WTB ★★** *B&B, WELCOME HOST AWARD, TASTE OF WALES.*

See also Colour Display Advertisement   **ABERYSTWYTH. Mrs Lisa Bumford, Brynglas Farm, Chancery, Aberystwyth SY23 4DF (Tel & Fax: 01970 612799).** Bed and Breakfast with a difference - a unique experience. Your own self-contained cottage with the breakfast being served therein. Set in the heart of Cardigan Bay - ideal base for exploring mid-Wales. Situated on a small family-run working farm, only four miles south of Aberystwyth, surrounded by lovely panoramic views. Ideal for families. Dogs welcomed. Come and discover this lovely location and enjoy the tranquillity. Short breaks available. Brochure available on request. **WTB ★★★** *B&B, WELCOME HOST AWARD.*
e-mail: blue.grass@lineone.net

WHITLAND. Mrs A. Windsor, Forest Farm, Whitland SA43 0LS (01994 240066). Forest Farm is a mixed livestock farm, situated on the A40 in the rolling hillside of the Taf Valley, with beautiful walks around the farm and woodlands and fishing on the River Taf, which runs through the farm (salmon and trout). Within easy reach of the coastal areas (Tenby and Saundersfoot) and shopping areas of Carmarthen and Swansea. A homely atmosphere, fully centrally heated. TV lounge for guests, diningroom with separate tables – good home-cooked breakfast. Plenty of good restaurants and pubs nearby. En suite bedrooms. Ample parking space.

CARMARTHENSHIRE

CARMARTHEN. Mrs Margaret Thomas, Plas Farm, Llangynog, Carmarthen SA33 5DB (Tel & Fax: 01267 211492). Working farm. Welcome Host. Situated six miles west of Carmarthen town along the A40 towards St. Clears. Quiet location, ideal touring base. Working farm run by the Thomas family for the past 100 years. Very spacious, comfortable farmhouse. En suite rooms available, all with tea/coffee making facilities, colour TV and full central heating. TV lounge. Evening meals available at local country inn nearby. Good golf course minutes away. Plas Farm is en route to Fishguard and Pembroke Ferries. Bed and Breakfast from £18 per person. Children under 16 years sharing family room half price. Special mid-week breaks available. A warm welcome assured. **WTB ★★★** *FARM.*

WHITLAND. Mrs O. Ebsworth, Brunant Farm, Whitland SA34 0LX (Tel/Fax: 01994 240421). 'Never enough time to enjoy this to the full, never enough words to say how splendid it was.' – John Carter (Wish You Were Here). Welcome to our 200 year old farmhouse, centrally situated for touring, beaches, walking or just relaxing. Comfortable spacious bedrooms, all en suite, tea/coffee facilities, TV, hairdryers. Good home cooking, comfortable lounge, separate tables in dining room. No smoking. Open April to September. Bed & Breakfast £20 – £22. Evening meal £12.

FREE or REDUCED RATE entry to Holiday Visits and Attractions – see our READERS' OFFER VOUCHERS on pages 43-60

PEMBROKESHIRE

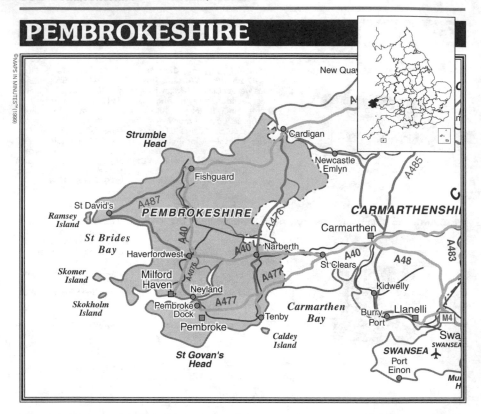

©MAPS IN MINUTES™ (1999)

FISHGUARD near. Heathfield Mansion, Letterston, Near Fishguard SA62 5EG (01348 840263).

A Grade II Listed Georgian country house in 16 acres of pasture and woodland, Heathfield is the home of former Welsh rugby international, Clive Rees and his wife Angelica. This is an ideal location for the appreciation of Pembrokeshire's many natural attractions. There is excellent golf, riding and trout fishing in the vicinity and the coast is only a few minutes' drive away. The accommodation is very comfortable and two of the three bedrooms have en suite bathrooms. The cuisine and wines are well above average. This is a most refreshing venue for a tranquil and wholesome holiday. Bed and Breakfast from £20 to £24 per person per night; Dinner by prior arrangement. **WTB** ★★★ *GUEST HOUSE.*

GOODWICK. Mrs M.P. Miller, Siriole Guest House, 2 Siriole, Quay Road, Goodwick SA64 0BS (01348

872375). Beautifully run Bed and Breakfast with spacious accommodation overlooking Fishguard Bay and the Preseli hills. In a quiet location with ample parking and close to Goodwick village and a short walk to the main ferry terminal to Rosslare - ideal for day trips to Ireland. We are centrally located for walks along the splendid Pembrokeshire National Coastal Path and numerous attractions. All rooms are en suite with shower/toilet, tea/coffee facilities and colour TV; some have sea views. Children and pets welcome. Bed and Breakfast £19per person for sea-view rooms £17 per person for back rooms. Reductions for longer stays. Open all year.

HAVERFORDWEST Mrs M. E. Davies, Cuckoo Mill Farm, Pelcomb Bridge, St. David's Road,

Haverfordwest SA62 6EA (01437 762139). Working farm. There is a genuine welcome to our mixed working family farm. Quietly set in beautiful countryside surrounded by animals and wild life. Comfortable well appointed accommodation. Bedrooms with tea/coffee tray, radio, TV and en suite. Excellent quality food using home and local produce. Families welcome. Deductions for children and Senior Citizens. Open January to December. Pretty flowers, lawns in relaxed surroundings. Personal attention. Unrestricted access. Ideally situated central Pembrokeshire for coastline walks. Sandy beaches. Bird islands, castles, City of St. David's, Tenby. Bed and Breakfast; Bed, Breakfast and Evening Dinner. Terms on application. **WTB ★★★**, *GOLD WELCOME HOST AWARD, TASTE OF WALES.* .

HAVERFORDWEST. Mr and Mrs Patrick, East Hook Farm, Portfield Gate, Haverfordwest, Pembroke

SA62 3LN (01437 762211). Howard and Jen welcome you to their Georgian Farmhouse surrounded by beautiful countryside, four miles from the coastline and three miles from Haverfordwest. Double, twin and family suite available, all en suite. Pembrokeshire produce used for dinner and breakfast. Dinner £14 per person. Bed and Breakfast from £20 to £22 per person. **WTB ★★★** *FARMHOUSE.*

HAVERFORDWEST. Joyce Canton, Nolton Haven Farm, Nolton Haven, Haverfordwest SA62 1NH

(01437 710263). The farmhouse is beside the beach on a 200 acre mixed farm, with cattle, calves and lots of show ponies. It has a large lounge which is open to guests all day as are all the bedrooms. Single, double and family rooms; two family rooms en suite, four other bathrooms. Pets and children most welcome, babysitting free of charge. 50 yards to the beach, 75 yards to the local inn/restaurant. Pony trekking, surfing, fishing, excellent cliff walks, boating and canoeing are all available nearby. Riding holidays and short breaks all year a speciality. Colour brochure on request.

See also Colour Display Advertisement

HAVERFORDWEST. Mrs Margaret Williams, Skerryback, Sandy Haven, St Ishmaels, Haverfordwest SA62 3DN (Tel: 01646 636598; Fax: 01646 636595). Our 18th century farmhouse is a working farm set in a sheltered garden adjoining the Pembrokeshire coast footpath. It is an ideal situation for walkers and bird lovers to explore the secluded coves and sandy beaches of the area, or take a boat trip to see the puffins on Skomer Island. The two attractive double rooms, both en suite, look out across horses grazing in the meadow; the guests' lounge has a colour TV and central heating backed up by log fires on chilly evenings. A welcoming cup of tea/coffee on arrival plus hospitality trays in the bedrooms. Skerryback breakfasts are a real treat, the perfect way to start a day of strenuous walking or just relaxing on the nearest beach. **WTB ★★★** *FARMHOUSE* .

FREE or REDUCED RATE entry to Holiday Visits and Attractions — see our READERS' OFFER VOUCHERS on pages 43-60

MARTINS HAVEN/MARLOES. Mrs Christina Chetwynd, East Hook Farm, Marloes, Haverfordwest SA62 3BJ (01646 636291). Farm on Pembrokeshire Coast Path offering Bed and Breakfast, camping, caravans, horse and pony riding, cycle hire, sea fishing, bird-watching and walking. Convenient for boat trips to Skomer and Skokholm Islands and next to Marloes Mere Nature Reserve. 110 acres of natural unspoilt beauty. Bedrooms with washbasin, TV and tea/coffee making facilities available. Reception room on site. Transport to Martins Haven for boat trips, diving and Marine Nature Reserve. Bed and Breakfast £16 per person per night. Children welcome.

MOYLEGROVE. Alan and Joy Bloss, Trewidwal, Moylegrove, Near Cardiganshire SA43 3BY (01239

881651). Trewidwal is a former farmhouse situated in beautiful, peaceful surroundings in the Pembrokeshire National Park, with wonderful hill and coastal views. Abundant wildlife. Easy (largely footpath) access to coastal path (one mile). Lifts provided if required. Sandy beaches nearby. Accommodation in one en suite family room, one double (with private access) and one single room. TV, tea/coffee facilities and provision for guests to make their own simple picnic food. Evening meals/lighter snacks (including special diets) by arrangement. Home produce. Pets welcome by arrangement. Drying facilities for walkers. Bed and Breakfast £15 to £18 per night.
e-mail: alan.bloss@btinternet.com

PRESELI HILLS. Mrs Vivienne Lockton,

Dolau Isaf Farm, Mynachlog-Ddu, Clunderwen SA66 7SB (Tel & Fax: 01994 419327). Working farm, join in. Our peaceful farm with superb views, nestles below the Bluestones in the Preseli hills and offers you every comfort. En-suite rooms with king-size beds, courtesy trays and guests sitting room with colour TV, lots of books and a log fire for the cooler evenings. See our baby lambs and delightful mohair kids. Enjoy freshly cooked meals made with our own local quality produce. Excellent walking and many beaches a short drive away. Something for every season or if you prefer just relax in this tranquil atmosphere and unwind. In sympathy with our surroundings we have a Non-smoking policy. **WTB** ★★★ *FARM, WELCOME HOST GOLD.*
e-mail: vivlockton@tinyworld.co.uk

SAUNDERSFOOT. Mrs Joy Holgate, Carne Mountain Farm, Reynalton, Kilgetty SA68 0PD (01834

860546). Working farm. We warmly welcome you to our lovely 200-year-old farmhouse set amidst the peace and tranquillity of the beautiful Pembrokeshire countryside. Distant views of Preseli Mountains, yet only three-and-a-half miles from Saundersfoot. Pretty, picturesque bedrooms with colour TV, washbasins, tea/coffee tray, central heating. Dining room with interesting plate collection, and attractive beamed sitting room with books and maps. Delicious traditional farmhouse breakfast; vegetarians very welcome. Let the strain and stress slip away as you enjoy the peaceful atmosphere and friendly farmyard animals. Bed and Breakfast from £17.00. Welcome Host and Farmhouse Award. Quality six-berth caravan in pretty, peaceful setting with lawn and patio. From £120 per week including linen.

POWYS

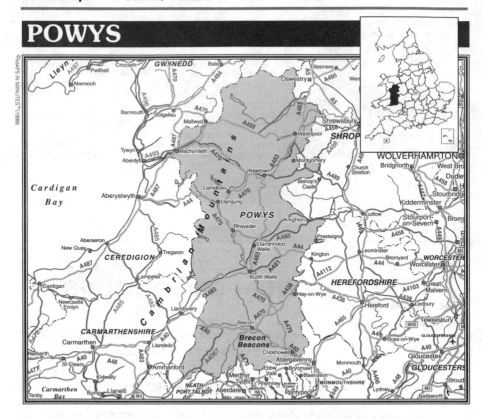

BRECON. Mrs M. J. Mayo, Maeswalter, Heol Senni, Near Brecon LD3 8SU (01874 636629). Maeswalter

is a 300-year-old farmhouse in the mountainous Brecon Beacons National Park. There are three tastefully decorated bedrooms: one double en suite, one standard double and a family room sleeping three. The comfortable lounge/dining room features exposed timbers. Visitors can roam freely through the grounds where there are seats to sit and admire the scenery and wildlife. Also private apartment (en suite double bedroom and private sittingroom) with basic cooking facilities. The apartment and all bedrooms have colour TV and beverage tray with tea/coffee making facilities, chocolate and biscuits. Rates per room: en suite double £39 per night, standard double £36, family room £50; reductions for longer stays.

MAESWALTER

BRECON. Mrs Pamela Boxhall, The Old Mill, Felinfach, Brecon LD3 0UB (01874 625385). A 16th century

converted corn mill peacefully situated in its own grounds. Inglenook fireplace, exposed beams, en suite rooms, beverage trays, TV lounge. Ideal for country pursuits or just relaxing. Within easy reach of Brecon Beacons, Black Mountains, Hay-on-Wye and local pubs within walking distance. Packed lunches by arrangement. Children welcome. Terms: double room with private bathroom from £18.50 per person; twin en suite room from £20.00 per person, single from £20.00 per person per night. Reductions for weekly stays. Welcome Host. **WTB ★★★** *B&B*.

BRECON. Mrs Carol Morgan, Blaencar Farm, Sennybridge, Brecon LD3 8HA (01874 636610). Enjoy the warmth and quality of a true Welsh welcome on a working family farm in the heart of the Brecon Beacons National Park.

Eight miles west of Brecon, this lovingly refurbished farmhouse with a wealth of charm and character offers superior accommodation and comfort for discerning guests looking for something special. Three luxurious en suite bedrooms have all facilities. The peace and tranquillity of this quiet, accessible location provides an ideal base for relaxation, touring and exploring in unspoilt countryside. Friendly country pub a pleasant 15-minute walk. **WTB ★★★★★,** *TASTE OF WALES MEMBER, WELCOME HOST GOLD.*
e-mail: carol@blaencar.co.uk
website: www.blaencar.co.uk

BRECON. Mrs A. Harpur, Llanbrynean Farm, Llanfrynach, Brecon LD3 7BQ (01874 665222).

Llanbrynean is a fine, traditional, Victorian farmhouse peacefully situated on the edge of the picturesque village of Llanfrynach, three miles south-east of Brecon. We are in an ideal spot for exploring the area - the Brecon Beacons rise behind the farm and the Brecon/Monmouth canal flows through the fields below. We are a working family sheep farm with wonderful pastoral views and a large garden. The house is spacious and comfortable with a friendly, relaxed atmosphere. We have two double en suite bedrooms and one twin with private bathroom. All have tea/coffee facilities. There is a sitting room with log fire. Bed and Breakfast from £18 per person. Excellent pub food within easy walking distance.

BRECON. Mrs Eileen Williams, Upper Farm, Llechfaen, Brecon LD3 7SP (01874 665269). Working farm. A modernised farmhouse offering Bed and Breakfast only, situated just off the A40 Brecon to Abergavenny road, two miles from Brecon town. A 64-acre dairy farm in the heart of the National Park directly facing Brecon Beacons. Ideal for touring, with golf, trekking and fishing nearby and many Welsh craft shops to visit. Two double and one family bedrooms with washbasin and tea/coffee making facilities; bathroom, toilet; sittingroom; diningroom. Cot, babysitting, reduced rates for children. Open all year. Car essential - parking. No pets.

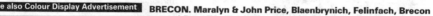
See also Colour Display Advertisement

BRECON. Maralyn & John Price, Blaenbrynich, Felinfach, Brecon LD3 0TS (Tel & Fax: 01874 623433). Blaenbrynich is an early 18th century farmhouse which provides quality en suite accommodation. All rooms have colour television and tea/coffee making facilities. Breakfast in the warm diningroom with inglenook fireplace or in the sunny garden room with magnificent views. Guests are guaranteed a warm family welcome. Conveniently situated on the A470 at the gateway to the Brecon Beacons National Park in some of Wales' most outstanding scenery, it is an ideal base for walking, cycling, riding and exploring Wales. No smoking and regretfully no pets. Self-catering apartment also available. Bed and Breakfast from £38 double room, £25 single room, £50 family room. Self-catering from £150 per week.
e-mail: jprice2044@aol.com

BRECON near. Gwyn and Hazel Davies, Caebetran Farm, Felinfach, Brecon LD3 0UL (Tel & Fax: 01874 754460). Working farm, join in. A warm welcome, a cup of

tea and home-made cakes await you when you arrive at Caebetran. Visitors are welcome to see the cattle and sheep on the farm. There are breathtaking views of the Brecon Beacons and the Black Mountains and just across a field is a 400 acre common, ideal for walking, bird-watching or just relaxing. Ponies and sheep graze undisturbed, while buzzards soar above you. The farmhouse dates back to the 17th century and has been recently modernised to give the quality and comfort visitors expect today. There are many extras in the rooms to give that special feel to your holiday. The rooms are all en suite and have colour TV and tea making facilities. The diningroom has separate tables, there is also a comfortable lounge with colour TV and video. Caebetran is an ideal base for exploring this beautiful, unspoilt part of the country with pony trekking, walking, birdwatching, wildlife, hang-gliding and so much more. For a brochure and terms please write, telephone or fax. "Arrive as visitors and leave as our friends". Winners of the 'FHG Diploma' for Wales 1998 and 1999. *WELCOME HOST.*

BUILTH WELLS. C. Davies, Gwern-y-Mynach, Llanafan Fawr, Builth Wells LD2 3PN (01597 860256).

Working farm. Gwern-y-Mynach Farm is a working sheep farm near Builth Wells in mid-Powys where golf, rugby, bowls, cricket and a new sports hall are all available. Our house is centrally heated throughout. Guest accommodation comprises one single room and one double room with bathroom en suite. Situated in a lovely area, ideal for walking, enjoying the open mountains and watching the Red Kites in flight. Close to the farm in the forest we have Greenwood chair making, steam bending and coracle making, which attract people from overseas to the classes. Also nearby the oldest pub in Powys – The Red Lion, voted best pub in Powys for food. Please write or telephone for further information and tariff.

BUILTH WELLS. Mrs N. Jones, Ty-Isaf Farm, Erwood, Builth Wells LD2 3SZ (01982 560607).

Ty-Isaf is a mixed working farm in the Wye Valley, with cattle, sheep, ponies and plenty of dogs. All bedrooms have washbasin, tea/coffee making facilities and full central heating. It is situated just off the A470 near Erwood village, and is an ideal spot from which to tour Mid-Wales, being within easy reach of Elan Valley, the Black Mountains and Brecon Beacons, Llangorse Lake and Hay-on-Wye, famous for its bookshops, including what is claimed to be the largest second-hand bookshop in the world. Bed and Breakfast or Bed and Breakfast and Evening Meal with good home cooking. Bed and Breakfast £15 per person.

GLADESTRY. Mrs M.E. Hughes, Stonehouse Farm, Gladestry, Kington, Herefordshire HR5 3NU (01544 370651). Working farm. Large Georgian farmhouse,

modernised whilst retaining its character, situated on Welsh border with Offa's Dyke Footpath going through its 380 acres of mixed farming. Beautiful unspoiled area for walking. Many places of interest within driving distance such as Elan Valley Dams, Devil's Bridge, Llangorse Lake, Kington golf course. Guests are accommodated in one double and one twin-bedded rooms, with washbasins; bathroom, two toilets; sitting and diningroom. TV. Homely informal atmosphere with home produced food and home cooking. Vegetarian meals on request. Good food available nearby at village inn. Children welcome. Babysitting available. Bed and Breakfast from £15; Evening Meals by arrangement.

HAY-ON-WYE. Annie and John McKay, Hafod-y-Garreg, Erwood, Builth Wells LD2 3TQ (01982 560400). A medieval farmhouse, nestling on a wooded hillside

in an Area of Special Scientific Interest, well off the beaten track, above, reputedly, the most picturesque part of the River Wye. A short drive from Hay-on-Wye 'Town of Books', and Brecon and the Beacons National Park. Alternatively, leave your car and step through our gate into a walkers' paradise, steeped in ancient Celtic history. Drink spring water from the tap, and have an enormous breakfast with our free-range eggs. Enjoy a delicious candlelit supper with log fires in the massive inglenook. Bed and Breakfast from £17.50.

LLANDRINDOD WELLS. Mrs Diane Evans, Dolberthog Farm, Off Howey Road, Llandrindod Wells LD1 5PH (01597 822255). A warm, friendly welcome awaits you at

Dolberthog Farm, situated in quiet countryside one mile south of Llandrindod Wells. Enjoy a relaxing holiday with a breath of fresh air, scenic walks, river fishing and birdwatching. It is an ideal spot from which to tour Mid-Wales, being within easy reach of Elan Valley, Powys Castle, Brecon Beacons and many more places of interest. En suite private bathroom facilities. Beverage trays. Traditional cooking using farm produce. Children welcome. Safe parking. Gas central heating. Bed and Breakfast from £18 to £21, Bed, Breakfast and Evening Meal from £28 to £31, weekly £180 to £200. Brochure available. *WELCOME HOST. FARM AND GUEST HOUSE AWARD.*

LLANDRINDOD WELLS. Mrs Ruth Jones, Holly Farm, Howey, Llandrindod Wells LD1 5PP (Tel & Fax:

01597 822402). Tastefully restored Tudor farmhouse on working farm in peaceful location. En suite bedrooms with breathtaking views over fields and woods, colour TV, beverage trays. Two lounges with log fires. Renowned for excellent food. Wonderful area for wildlife, walking, cycling, near Red Kite feeding station. Safe parking. Bed , breakfast and evening meals available. Bed and Breakfast from £20. Brochure on request. **WTB ★★★** *FARM,* **AA ◆◆◆◆,** *TASTE OF WALES TOURISM AWARD, FARM HOLIDAY BUREAU MEMBER.*

LLANIDLOES. Mrs L. Rees, Esgairmaen, Y Fan, Llanidloes SY18 6NT (01686 430272). "Croeso Cynnes"

a warm welcome awaits you at Esgairmaen, a working farm one mile from Clywedog reservoir where fishing and sailing can be enjoyed, an ideal base for walking, bird watching and exploring nearby forests. The house commands magnificent views of unspoilt countryside, only 29 miles from the coast. One double and one family room, both en suite with tea/coffee making facilities. Central heating. Open April to October. Children and pets welcome. Camping also available. We offer peace and tranquillity.

LLANWRTHWL. Gaynor Tyler, Dyffryn Farm, Llanwrthwl, Llandrindod Wells LD1 6NU (01597 811017;

Fax: 01597 810609). Idyllically situated amidst the magnificent scenery of the Upper Wye Valley, Dyffryn, dating from the 17th century, is an ideal base from which to explore this unspoilt area of 'Wild Wales' with its wonderful walking, cycling, pony-trekking, bird-watching and fishing. The beautiful Elan Valley is close by. Slate floors, beams, stone walls and woodburning stoves all add their charm to this serene old house. We have two double and one twin bedrooms, en suite facilities and a lovely relaxing hayloft lounge. A cosy self-catering cottage is also available. Enjoy our wholesome food and a warm welcome. No smoking. Bed and Breakfast from £20. Self catering from £130 to £275. Brochure available. **WTB ★★** *FARM.*
e-mail: dyffrynfm@cs.com
website: www.rhayader.co.uk/dyffryn

MONTGOMERY. Ceinwen Richards, The Drewin Farm, Churchstoke, Montgomery SY15 6TW (Tel &

Fax: 01588 620325). A family-run mixed farm set on hillside overlooking panoramic views of the most beautiful countryside. The Drewin is a charming 17th century farmhouse retaining much of its original character with oak beams and large inglenook fireplace, separate lounge; twin and family rooms, both en suite and all modern amenities with colour TV. Full central heating. Offa's Dyke footpath runs through the farm - a wonderful area for wildlife. Ideal base for touring the many beauty spots around. Good home cooking and a very warm welcome await our visitors. Bed and Breakfast from £20; Bed, Breakfast and Evening Meal from £30. Featured in The Travel Show. Holder of Essential Food Hygiene Certificate and Farmhouse Award from Wales Tourist Board, 1999/2000 winner of AA Best Breakfast in Wales Award. Open April to October. **AA ◆◆◆◆**

PENYBONT-FAWR. Mrs Anne Evans, Glanhafon, Penybont-Fawr SY10 0EW (01691 860377). Working farm, join in. Secluded farmhouse in the Upper Tanat Valley, ideal for a peaceful break. Glanhafon is a working sheep farm with hill walks on the farm. Bordering the Berwyn Mountains, it is a wonderful area for walking, bird-watching, or touring, with Lake Vyrnwy, RSPB Centre, and Pistyll Falls - one of the seven wonders of Wales- just seven miles away. Many other places of interest within easy reach, including Powys and Chirk Castle, Snowdonia, Erddig and the market towns of Shrewsbury and Oswestry. There are three attractive bedrooms, all en suite, with tea making facilities. Guests' own sittingroom. Ample parking. Children and pets welcome. Open Easter till October. Bed and Breakfast from £16. **WTB** ★★ *FARM*

RHAYADER. Carl and Ann Edwards, Beili Neuadd, Rhayder LD6 5NS (Tel & Fax: 01597 810211). Beautifully situated in quiet, secluded countryside with delightful views and its own stream, trout pools and woodland, Beili Neuadd is only two miles away from the smalll market town of Rhayder. The stone-built farmhouse, parts of which date back to the 16th century, has been sensitively restored to retain its original charm and character with exposed beams, polished oak floors, log fires and pretty furnishings. Single, double and twin bedded rooms with private shower and bathrooms, central heating, tea and coffee making facilities. Self-catering bunk house accommodation available in our recently converted stone barn. Special facilities for wheelchair users and families as well as for the outdoor enthusiast. Bed and Breakfast rates from £22 to £24. **WTB** ★★★★
e-mail: ann-carl@thebeili.freeserve.co.uk

See also Colour Display Advertisement   **TALGARTH. Mrs Bronwen Prosser, Upper Genffordd Farm Guest House, Talgarth LD3 0EN (01874 711360).** Set amongst the most spectacular scenery of the Brecon Beacons National Park, Upper Genfford Farm is an ideal base for exploring the Black Mountains, Wye Valley and the Brecon Beacons, an area of outstanding beauty, rich in historical and archaeological interest, with Roman camps and Norman castles. Picturesque mountain roads will lead you to reservoirs, the Gower coast with its lovely sandy beaches and Llangorse Lake - well known for all kinds of water sports. The charming Guest House accommodation includes one double and one twin-bedded room, both with en suite facilities. they are beautifully decorated and furnished, including tea/coffee making facilities, central heating, colour TV and hairdryer. the cosy lounge has a wealth of personal bric-a-brac, maps and paintings. Very much a home from home, with colour TV and books. Guests are made welcome with home-made cakes and tea on arrival. The local pub and restaurant is nearby and Hay-on-Wye, 'The Town of Books', is a short distance away. bed and Breakfast from £18 to £20 per person. Also fully equipped self-catering cottage with microwave. Bathroom with shower. Ample parking on attractive patio adjacent to cottage. Play area for children, also a friendly pony. terms from £150 to £180 weekly. Awarded Plaque of Recommendation from the Welsh Tourist Board. Nominated "Landlady of the Year" 1999. Winner of FHG Diploma. **AA** ◆◆◆ AA QQQQ

WELSHPOOL. Mrs Joyce Cornes, Cwmllwynog, Llanfair, Caereinion, Welshpool SY21 0HF (Tel & Fax: 01938 810791). Built in the early 17th century Cwmllwynog is a traditional long farmhouse of character on a working dairy farm. We have a spacious garden with a stream at the bottom and a lot of unusual plants. All bedrooms have colour TV and drink making facilities. Double room en suite, twin with washbasins and private bathroom. Delicious home-cooked meals cooked. We can help you with routes. Open January-November. **WTB** ★★★ *FARMHOUSE,* **AA** ◆◆◆◆

Readers are requested to mention this guidebook
when seeking accommodation (and please enclose
a stamped addressed envelope).

SOUTH WALES

COWBRIDGE near. Mrs Sue Beer, Plas Llanmihangel, Llanmihangel, Near Cowbridge CF71 7LQ

(01446 774610). Plas Llanmihangel is the finest medieval Grade I Listed manor house in the beautiful Vale of Glamorgan. We offer a genuine warmth of welcome, delightful accommodation, first class food and service in our wonderful home. The baronial hall, great log fires, the ancient tower and acres of beautiful historic gardens intrigue all who stay in this fascinating house. Its long history and continuous occupation have created a spectacular building in romantic surroundings unchanged since the sixteenth century. A great opportunity to experience the ambience and charm of a past age, featured in "Distinctly Different." Guests are accommodated in three double rooms. Bed and Breakfast from £28. High quality home-cooked Evening Meal available on request. **WTB ★★** *GUEST HOUSE.*

MONMOUTH. Rosemary and Derek Ringer, Church Farm Guest House, Mitchel Troy, Monmouth

NP25 4HZ (01600 712176). A spacious and homely 16th century former farmhouse with oak beams and inglenook fireplaces, set in large attractive garden with stream. An excellent base for visiting the Wye Valley, Forest of Dean and Black Mountains. All bedrooms have washbasins, tea/coffee making facilities and central heating; most are en suite. Own car park. Colour TV. Non-smoking. Terrace and barbecue area. Bed and Breakfast from £20 to £23.50 per person. Evening Meal by arrangement. We also offer self-guided Walking Holidays and Short Breaks. Separate "Wysk Walks" brochure on request. **WTB ★★** *GUEST HOUSE,* **AA ◆◆◆**

NEATH. Mrs S. Brown, Green Lantern Guest House, Hawdref Ganol Farm, Cimla, Neath SA12 9SL

(01639 631884). Family-run 18th century luxury centrally heated farmhouse, set in its own 45 acres with beautiful scenic views over open countryside. Close to Afan Argoed and Margam Parks; 10 minutes from M4; one mile from birthplace of Richard Burton. Ideal for walking, cycling, horse riding from farm. Colour TV. Tea/coffee making facilities in all rooms, en suite availability. Pets welcome by arrangement. We offer luxury accommodation at an affordable price. Safe off-road parking. Central for Swansea, Neath and Port Talbot. Want to be impressed, try us. Terms from £23, reductions for children. West Glamorgan's only AA QQQQQ Premier selected Guest House. **WTB ★★★★** *B&B*
e-mail: stuart.brown7@virgin.net
website: http://freespace.virgin.net/stuart.brown7/

THE FHG DIPLOMA

HELP IMPROVE
BRITISH TOURIST STANDARDS

You are choosing holiday accommodation from our very popular FHG Publications.
Whether it be a hotel, guest house, farmhouse or self-catering accommodation, we think you will find it hospitable, comfortable and clean, and your host and hostess friendly and helpful.

Why not write and tell us about it?

As a recognition of the generally well-run and excellent holiday accommodation reviewed in our publications, we at FHG Publications Ltd. present a diploma to proprietors who receive the highest recommendation from their guests who are also readers of our Guides. If you care to write to us praising the holiday you have booked through FHG Publications Ltd. – whether this be board, self-catering accommodation, a sporting or a caravan holiday, what you say will be evaluated and the proprietors who reach our final list will be contacted.

The winning proprietor will receive an attractive framed diploma to display on his premises as recognition of a high standard of comfort, amenity and hospitality. FHG Publications Ltd. offer this diploma as a contribution towards the improvement of standards in tourist accommodation in Britain. Help your excellent host or hostess to win it!

FHG DIPLOMA

We nominate ....

....

Because

Name ....

Address..

....

Telephone No..

WALES

Self-catering

ANGLESEY & GWYNEDD

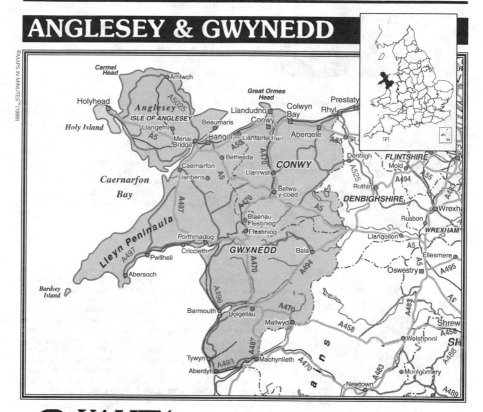

©"MAPS IN MINUTES" (1999)

QUALITY COTTAGES

ABERSOCH. Quality Cottages. Around the magnificent Welsh coast. Away from the madding crowd. Near safe sandy beaches. A small specialist agency offering privacy, peace and unashamed luxury. Wales Tourist Board 1989 Award Winner. Residential standards - dishwashers, microwaves, washing machines, central heating, log fires, no slot meters. Linen provided. Pets welcome free. All in coastal areas famed for scenery, walks, wild flowers, birds, badgers and foxes. Free colour brochure. **S.C. Rees, Quality Cottages, Cerbid, Solva, Haverfordwest, Pembrokeshire SA62 6YE (01348 837871).**
website: www.qualitycottages.co.uk

BALA near. Rhyd Fudr, Llanuwchllyn, Near Bala. Sleeps 6. Stone farm cottage set in an isolated position

with views of five mountain peaks and Bala Lake. Accommodation comprises three bedrooms, plus cot; two sittingrooms; sun room; kitchen; bathroom. Garage. Multi-fuel burning stove and most modern conviences but no TV. Fully-equipped including washing machine and telephone. Linen not supplied. Mountain stream and lovely walks on the doorstep. Sea, 45 minutes by car; Snowdon, one hour. Children welcome. Terms from £180. Apply: **Mrs J. H. Gervis, Nazeing Bury, Nazeing, Essex EN9 2JN (0199 289 2331) or Mrs G. E. Evans, Pant-y-Ceubren, Llanuwchllyn, Bala (01678 540252).**

BEDDGELERT. Bron Eifion, Rhyd Ddu, Beddgelert. Sleeps 6. Attractive semi-detached house on edge of

small village in National Park at foot of Snowdon. Splendid mountain and valley walks from village including path up Snowdon. Lakes nearby. Excellent centre for seaside, historic castles and houses, golf, riding, fishing and touring. Three bedrooms; two livingrooms; bathroom; modern kitchen, fridge, airing cupboard, heaters. Well equipped. Mountain view, terrace, rough garden. Inn (serving meals) nearby. Sorry, no pets. High season £150 to £285 per week; low season £65 to £140 per week. Short Breaks by arrangement. Open all year. Apply: **Davies, 218 Clive Road, London SE21 8BS (020 8670 2756).**

BEDDGELERT. Beudy Coed, Oerddwr, Beddgelert. Sleeps 4. Beautifully renovated shepherd's cottage one

mile from Aberglaslyn Pass, situated in a secluded, elevated position overlooking the River Glaslyn. The views towards the mountain ranges are breathtaking. Ideal central location for exploring Snowdonia, walking, fishing, horse riding, yet only four miles away from Porthmadog's sandy beaches. Perfect setting for relaxing amongst the scenery. Accommodation to sleep four persons in double and twin-bedded rooms. Linen supplied. Lounge/diner with stone fireplace, colour TV, fitted carpets. Fully equipped kitchen; shower room. Patio area in enclosed garden with table and benches. Ample car parking. Pets welcome. Contact: **Mrs Madge Williams, Berllan, Borth-y-Gest, Porthmadog, Gwynedd LL49 9UE (01766 513784).**

CRICCIETH. Betws-Bach & Rhos-Dhu, Ynys, Criccieth LL52 0PB (Tel & Fax: 01758 720047; 01766

810295). A truly romantic, memorable and special place to stay and relax in comfort. Old world farmhouse and period country cottage. Situated just off the B4411 road in tranquil surroundings. Equipped with washing/ drying machines, dishwashers, microwaves, freezers, colour TV, old oak beams, inglenook with log fires, full central heating. Snooker table, pitch 'n' putt; romantic four-poster bed;sauna and jacuzzi. Open all year – Winter Weekends welcomed. Ideal for couples. Sleep two–six plus cot. Own fishing and shooting rights, wonderful walks, peace and quiet with Snowdonia and unspoilt beaches on our doorstep. For friendly personal service please phone, fax or write to **Mrs Anwen Jones. Wales Tourist Board Grade 5.**
e-mail: cottages@rhos.freeserve.co.uk
website: www.rhos-cottages.co.uk

BRYN BRAS CASTLE

Welcome to beautiful Bryn Bras Castle – enchanting castle Apartments, elegant Tower-House within unique romantic turreted Regency Castle (Listed Building) in the gentle foothills of Snowdonia. Centrally situated amidst breathtaking scenery, ideal for exploring North Wales' magnificent mountains, beaches, resorts, heritage and history. Near local country inns/restaurants, shops. Each spacious apartment is fully self-contained, gracious, peaceful, clean, with distinctive individual character, comfortable furnishings, generously and conveniently appointed from dishwasher to fresh flowers, etc. Inclusive of VAT. Central heating, hot water, linen. All highest WTB grade. 32 acres of tranquil landscaped gardens, sweeping lawns, woodland walks of natural beauty, panoramic hill walks overlooking the sea, Anglesey and Mount Snowdon. Mild climate. Enjoy the comfort, warmth, privacy and relaxation of this castle of timeless charm in truly serene surroundings. Open all year, including for Short Breaks. Sleep 2-4 persons. **Regret no young children.** Brochure sent with pleasure

Llanrug, Near Caernarfon, North wales LL554RE

Tel & Fax: Llanberis (01286) 870210

E-mail: holidays@brynbrascastle.co.uk   Website: www.brynbrascastle.co.uk

---

CRICCIETH. Mrs L. Hughes Jones, Tyddyn Heilyn, Chwilog LL53 6SW (01766 810441). Freshly renovated but keeping its antique features, charming, very cosy stonebuilt farm cottage in tranquil, unspoilt countryside with sea on either side, sheltered by Snowdonia Mountains in distant background. Comfortably sized kitchen full of electrical gadgets, microwave, washing machine; spacious lounge with colour TV. Capricorn bathroom suite has full size Twingrip bath and shower. Victorian furnished bedrooms have new mattresses with choice of duvets and blankets. As well as flower and shrub beds, there is an olde worlde character to the front and back courtyards - ample parking space here. Also, but not in cottage vicinity, furnished home sleeping up to six persons. Passing through this farmland, the renowned Lon Goed walk has six mile roadway of oak and ash trees and In the flowered hedgerows too there are species of rare birds.

Llanystumdwy, the home village of Earl Lloyd George with its commemorative museum, two fishing rivers, riding school, pets and rabbit farm, the church, cafes and a pub, is one mile away. Write or phone for the moderate terms of the two holiday accommodation properties. No pets. Let anytime of the year. Highly Commended.

CRICCIETH. Quality Cottages. Around the magnificent Welsh coast. Away from the madding crowd. Near safe sandy beaches. A small specialist agency offering privacy, peace and unashamed luxury. Wales Tourist Board 1989 Award Winner. Residential standards - dishwashers, microwaves, washing machines, central heating, log fires, no slot meters. Linen provided. Pets welcome free. All in coastal areas famed for scenery, walks, wild flowers, birds, badgers and foxes. Free colour brochure. **S.C. Rees, Quality Cottages, Cerbid, Solva, Haverfordwest, Pembrokeshire SA62 6YE (01348 837871).**
website: www.qualitycottages.co.uk

CRICCIETH. Mrs M. Williams, Gaerwen Farm, Ynys, Criccieth LL52 0NU (01766 810324). Sleeps 7. This 200 acre dairy/mixed farm is situated four-and-a-half miles inland from Criccieth and beaches. An ideal centre for enjoying climbing, fishing, pony trekking and quiet country walks with extensive views of Snowdonia and Cardigan Bay. Within easy reach of various historic places nearby. Accommodation is self-contained in furnished farmhouse, comprising TV/video lounge with inglenook fireplace and oak beams, electric fire; fitted kitchen with electric cooker, automatic washing machine, fridge/freezer and microwave; diningroom; two double bedrooms, one twin-bedded room and one single bedroom, with duvets and bed linen; bathroom/shower with washbasin and toilet. Children most welcome, cot and babysitting available. Pets welcome. Car essential. Electricity provided. Weekly terms from £125 to £320. Short Breaks offered. Phone: 01766 810324.

HARLECH near. Mrs A.M. Wells, Yr-Ogof, Ynys, Talsarnau LL47 6TL (01766 780058). Sleeps 4/5. This comfortable, old-fashioned cottage is three miles from Harlech and just five minutes' walk to Ynys Beach. Convenient for shops. Lovely mountain views from cottage windows. Swimming pool at Harlech. Very attractive area with lovely walks. Also fishing nearby. All modern conveniences. Accommodation to sleep four/five persons in double and twin bedded rooms; bathroom, toilet, also downstairs toilet; lounge with oak beams and colour TV; kitchen/diner with electric cooker, microwave, fridge, etc. Everything supplied except linen. Extra charge for electricity used. Economy 7 central heating. Parking. Guaranteed clean home-from-home. Vacant May to September. Lower charges May to June. SAE, please for terms and further details or phone.

**LLANBEDR. Mrs Beti Wyn Jones, Pensarn Farm, Llanbedr, Gwynedd LL45 2HS (01341 241285).
Working farm. Sleeps 4 adults, 2 children.** Self-catering, semi-detached cottage in beautiful surroundings, ideal for a peaceful and relaxing holiday. The accommodation consists of modern kitchen, lounge/diner, two bedrooms, bathroom and toilet on ground floor; one bedroom, shower/toilet upstairs. Night storage heaters. Ample parking space and garden. Children and pets welcome. It is situated one mile from the picturesque village of Llanbedr, quarter-of-a-mile off the main Barmouth to Harlech road. Convenient for beach, mountains, golf course, fishing and pleasant walks up the River Artro to the Nantcol and Cwm Bychan Valleys. Terms from £170 to £250 per week.

LLANBEDROG. Mrs L. O. Williams, Bodwrog, Llanbedrog, Pwllheli LL53 7RE (01758 740341).
Modernised all-electric farmhouse accommodation to let without attendance although occasional free babysitting may be arranged. The 80 acre mixed farm offers stupendous views over the bays and headlands towards Snowdonia. Lleyn Peninsula is exceptionally mild - ideal for out of season holidays. Shooting is available on farm. Double glazing. Three double bedrooms accommodating six (cot provided); lounge, colour TV; kitchen/diningroom with mahogany units, microwave, Parker Knoll suite. Bathroom and toilet. Linen supplied. Cleanliness assured. One house-trained pet welcome. Car preferable, ample concreted parking area. Shopping less than one mile away. Also available, six-berth private 32ft Galaxy Kingsley caravan (shower, flush toilet, fridge, colour TV, microwave, etc). Glorious sandy beach one- and-a-half miles away by car but only one mile across fields. Village pub with Les Routiers listed restaurant three-quarters -of-a-mile, leisure centre five miles. Farmhouse terms from £150 weekly inclusive of electricity and bed linen. Mid-week or weekend bookings accepted during winter period and possibly March to May and in October. Caravan from £120 per week inclusive of electricity, gas and pillowcases. SAE for prompt reply. **WTB** *FOUR DRAGONS STANDARD*

PORTHMADOG (Snowdonia). Felin Parc Cottages. Discover this idyllic 17th century riverside millhouse and  charming wool manager's cottage in superb waterfall valley between Porthmadog and Beddgelert. Mill (WTB 4 Dragons) with large character beamed livingroom, period furnishings, wood stove, central heating, colour TV. Luxury kitchen, modernised bathroom/cloakroom. Sleeps eight/ten in four bedrooms and self-contained annexe. Secluded terraces (barbecue/floodlighting) adjoin Mill pool and falls. Cottage (WTB 3 Dragons) sleeping four/six in two bedrooms, and self-contained gable annexe with similar facilities, is delightfully situated overlooking ancient fording bridge. Superb local scenery with Snowdon, Portmeirion, Ffestiniog Railway all nearby. Cottage Terms £175 to £390 and Mill £200 to £700 weekly. Brochure, photographs:- **Mr and Mrs O. Williams-Ellis, San Giovanni, 4 Sylvan Road, London SE19 2RX (020 8653 3118).**

PWLLHELI. Mrs C.A. Jones, Rhedyn, Mynytho, Pwllheli LL53 7PS (01758 740669) Sleeps 4. Rhedyn  is a small farm overlooking the beautiful Nanhoran Valley, and the farm cottage, accommodating four people, is offered for hire between April and November. It is two miles from Llanbedrog and Abersoch, both noted for their safe bathing. Children are made especially welcome. The house has two double bedrooms; bathroom and toilet; combined sitting/diningroom with TV; kitchen with immersion heater, washing machine, microwave oven. Calor gas stove and fridge. Linen supplied. Pets permitted. One mile from shops and two from the sea. Car essential, ample parking. SAE, for further details and terms.

PWLLHELI. Mrs M. Adams, Cae'r Ferch Uchaf, Pencaenewydd LL53 6DJ (01766 810660). Cedarwood  chalet on a secluded smallholding consisting of three bedrooms, all with fitted wardrobes; large lounge with colour TV; luxury shower room with WC, additional WC in boiler room; kitchen/diner. The chalet is double glazed, centrally heated and open all year. The area is superb for walking and cycling, with quiet country roads throughout. The area is good for photography also. We are very central for all beaches and just a few miles from Snowdon. Charges are from £180 to £240 according to season. 50p power meter. Dogs by arrangement only. Please write or ring for details.

Superb stone cottages lovingly converted from the traditional Welsh barns near our Grade II listed farmhouse. We have four cottages, two for couples only and two sleeping up to four (so we are never over-crowded), each one furnished and equipped to the highest of standards but all retaining their own individual character. The cottages are set in 20 acres of beautiful mountainside grounds and each has panoramic sea or valley views and excellent walking from the doorstep. Guests are welcome to use our outdoor swimming pool and to help us with our varied collection of animals, most of whom are either rare breeds, rescued or both.

Please telephone Wendy Jervis on 01654 711404 for a brochure or visit our website at: www.geufron.com

Geufron Farm Cottages, Bryncrug, Gwynedd

See also Colour Display Advertisement

PWLLHELI. Mrs S. Ellis, W. M. Gwynfryn Farm Holidays, Gwynfryn Farm, Pwllheli LL53 5UF (Tel & Fax: 01758 612536). Take a relaxed care-free holiday on this organic dairy farm. Quality self-catering cottages sleep two-eight. Comfort and cleanliness assured. Explore the Lleyn Peninsula where the Welsh language flourishes. Varied activities to suit your needs. Indoor heated swimming pool, sauna and jacuzzi. Cooked dishes available. Colour brochure. Weekly terms and short break rates available. **WTB** *FOUR/FIVE DRAGONS*
e-mail: fhg@gwynfryn.freeserve.co.uk.

TYWYN. Coastal House, Tywyn, Gwynedd. Two minutes' walk to sandy beach. Two minutes' walk to pub/bar meals. Fully equipped as own home. Garden front and rear. Garage. Eight doors from the home bakery. Tal-y-Llyn Steam Railway walking distance. Pets welcome FREE OF CHARGE. Three bedrooms. Sleeps five Terms £164-£214 per week. Enquiries: **Mr Ian Weston, 18 Elizabeth Road, Basingstoke, Hampshire RG22 6AX (01256 352364; Evenings: 01256 412233).**
e-mail: ianweston@iname.com

NORTH WALES

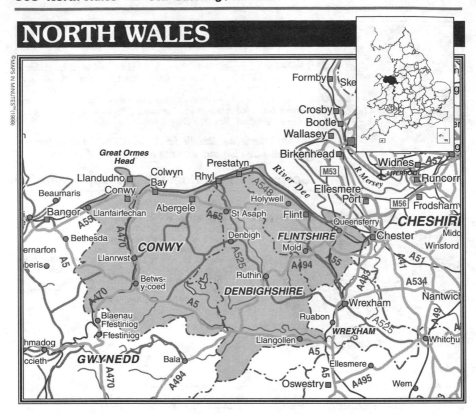

©MAPS IN MINUTES™ (1999)

BETWS-Y-COED. Jim and Lilian Boughton, Bron Celyn, Lôn Muriau, Llanrwst Road, Betws-y-Coed LL24 0HD (01690 710333; Fax: 01690 710111). Our cosy 200-year-old converted coach house has been tastefully refurbished and offers accommodation for up to four persons. Upstairs: one double room with space for a cot, and one bunk-bedded room with full length/width bunk beds. All bed linen is provided but not towels. Downstairs: lounge with colour TV and wood-burning stove (ample supply of chopped timber available). Kitchen with fridge, electric cooker, microwave, toaster and water heater. Shower room and toilet. Electric storage heaters fitted throughout. Metered electricity (read arrival/departure). Open all year. Ideal centre for walking, climbing, fishing or simply just relaxing! Terms £150 to £325per week. Short Breaks available.
e-mail: broncelyn@betws-y-coed.co.uk
website: www.betws-y-coed.co.uk/broncelyn/

BETWS-Y-COED. Dol-llech, Capel Curig, Near Betws-y-Coed. Sleeps 7. Detached farmhouse in beautiful Welsh countryside within easy reach of popular climbs and for rambling through magnficent Snowdonia scenery. Its location gives good access for touring Snowdonia and North Wales coast. Lounge with open fire, diningroom with woodburner, kitchen, bathroom and toilet. Four bedrooms, two double, one twin and one single. Microwave, washing machine, tumble dryer, fridge/freezer, cooker; open fire in lounge. Economy 7 heaters. Private parking for three cars. Small sitting-out area with picnic table and barbecue. Electricity on card meter. Bed linen and first £5 of electricity included in rent. Shops and pub one-and-a-quarter miles. Terms from £150 to £300 per week. Details from: **Gwen Williams Tyn Twll, Eglwys Bach, Colwyn Bay, Conwy LL28 5SB (01492 580391).**

BETWS-Y-COED. Mr W. R. Sudbury, Glan-y-Borth Holiday Village, Betws Road, Llanrwst, Betws-y-Coed

LL26 0HE (01492 641543; Fax: 01492 641369). Glan-y-Borth nestles peacefully on the banks of the River Conwy. Fully equipped bungalows with home from home comfort – sleep two to eight persons. Six bungalows designed for wheelchairs. Magnificent scenery with an abundance of attractions and activities, mountain railways, walking, canoeing, castles and sandy beaches. Please contact Bill between 8am and 9pm daily. Short breaks available. Open all year. Pets by arrangement. **WTB** *GRADE THREE.*

LLANDUDNO. Mrs A. I. Roberts, Oaklands Holiday Flats and Flatlets, 19 Caroline Road, Llandudno

LL30 2TY (01492 583820 or 875450). Situated in a quiet, tree-lined, residential area in central Llandudno – an ideal base for touring beautiful Snowdonia. You are within minutes of all that Llandudno has to offer; main shopping centre, both beaches and promenades, pier, the Oval with cricket, bowling, tennis, theatres, cinemas, gardens, yachting, children's boating and swimming pools. Convenient for Railway Station and coach park. Self-contained flatlets for one, two, three and four persons; two/four room flats for two/six persons (some on ground floor with toilet and shower). Cooking and heating by gas. Well-furnished with fitted carpets throughout. Private key. No restrictions. Children welcome, and small house-trained pet welcome. Linen, cutlery and crockery provided. Colour TV available for all flats and flatlets

Under personal supervision. Guests' payphone. Reduced terms for early/late season and winter breaks. Member of Wales Tourist Board and annually inspected. New fire prevention system. Open all year round from £100 to £330 weekly. SAE for brochure stating number of persons and dates required. **WTB** *GRADE THREE*

CARDIGANSHIRE

©MAPS IN MINUTES™ (1999)

Cardigan Bay

Tywyn
A493
Aberdyfi
Machyn
A4

Aberystwyth

A487

A44

Llangurig
A470
A470

PO

Rhayad

A485

Aberaeron
New Quay
A487

CEREDIGION

Tregaron

Lampeter

Cardigan

Newcastle Emlyn

A485
A482

A483

Llandovery

B

ABERPORTH. Quality Cottages. Around the magnificent Welsh coast. Away from the madding crowd. Near safe, sandy beaches. A small specialist agency offering privacy, peace and unashamed luxury. Wales Tourist Board 1989 Award Winner. Residential standards - dishwashers, microwaves, washing machines, central heating, log fires, no slot meters. Linen provided. Pets welcome free. All in coastal areas famed for scenery, walks, wild flowers, birds, badgers and foxes. Free colour brochure. **S.C. Rees, Quality Cottages, Cerbid, Solva, Haverfordwest, Pembrokeshire SA62 6YE (01348 837871).**
website: www.qualitycottages.co.uk

See also Colour Display Advertisement

ABERYSTWYTH. Mrs Lisa Bumford, Blue Grass Cottages, Brynglas Farm, Chancery, Aberystwyth SY23 4DF (Tel: 01970 612799). Set in the heart of Cardigan Bay - ideal base for exploring mid-Wales. Situated on a small family-run working farm, only four miles south of Aberystwyth, surrounded by lovely panoramic views. The cottages are of a very high standard and fully equipped. All on one level with one step outside the front door. Linen and towels are supplied with the beds made up and ready for use. Ample off-road parking and a warm welcome for dogs. Come and discover this lovely location and enjoy the tranquillity. Short breaks available. Brochure available on request.
WTB ★★★★
e-mail: blue.grass@lineOne.net

Please mention *The Farm Holiday Guide* when making enquiries about accommodation featured in these pages.

CARDIGAN. Jennie Donaldson, Gorslwyd Farm, Tanygroes, Cardigan SA43 2HZ (01239

810593; Fax: 01239 811569). In the country by the sea, close to sandy beaches and holiday activities. Country style cottages in beautiful, peaceful setting that includes Prince of Wales award winning gardens, nature trail, barbecue, adventure play area, countryside museum, farm animals, games room and laundry facilities. Comfortable, well-equipped and maintained two or three bedroom cottages. Gorslwyd is secluded but not remote, an ideal base from which to explore and enjoy west and mid Wales. Weekly terms from £150 to £350 per cottage. Designed and equipped to be ACCESSIBLE TO WHEELCHAIR USERS throughout. **WTB** *FOUR DRAGONS AWARD.*

CARDIGAN near. Quality Cottages. Around the magnificent Welsh coast. Away from the madding crowd. Near safe sandy beaches. A small specialist agency offering privacy, peace and unashamed luxury. Wales Tourist Board 1989 Award Winner. Residential standards - dishwashers, microwaves, washing machines, central heating, log fires, no slot meters. Linen provided. Pets welcome free. All in coastal areas famed for scenery, walks, wild flowers, birds, badgers and foxes. Free colour brochure. **S.C. Rees, Quality Cottages, Cerbid, Solva, Haverfordwest, Pembrokeshire SA62 6YE (01348 837871).**
website: www.qualitycottages.co.uk

LLANGRANNOG. Quality Cottages. Around the magnificent Welsh coast. Away from the madding crowd. Near safe, sandy beaches. A small specialist agency offering privacy, peace and unashamed luxury. Wales Tourist Board 1989 Award Winner. Residential standards - dishwashers, microwaves, washing machines, central heating, log fires, no slot meters. Linen provided. Pets welcome free. All in coastal areas famed for scenery, walks, wild flowers, birds, badgers and foxes. Free colour brochure. **S.C. Rees, Quality Cottages, Cerbid, Solva, Haverfordwest, Pembrokeshire SA62 6YE (01348 837871).**
website: www.qualitycottages.co.uk

See also Colour Display Advertisement   **MYDROILYN. Hillside Cottages, Blaenllanarth, Mydroilyn, Lampeter SA48 7RJ (01570 470374).** Stone farm buildings, recently converted Into four cottages, providing a modern standard of comfort in a traditional setting. Sleep two to three (terms £115 to £215), or sleep four to eight (terms £180 to £340). Gas, electricity and linen included in price. All have shower-room and fully-equipped kitchen. Colour TV; shared laundry-room; facilities for children. Special terms for Short Breaks. Open Easter to October. Situated in a secluded rural area abundant with wildlife. Only five miles from sandy beaches and picturesque harbours of Cardigan Bay. Within easy reach of National Trust coastal footpaths, sites of historic and cultural interest, steam railways, castles and breathtaking mountain scenery. Bird watching, fishing and pony trekking nearby. AA Approved. Open all year. Full details from. **Chris and Jeff Strudgeon**

PEMBROKESHIRE

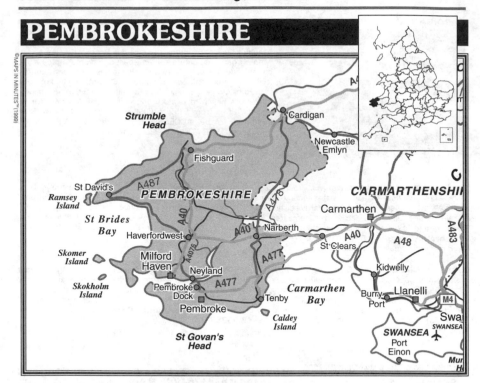

©MAPS IN MINUTES™ (1999)

BOSHERTON. **Quality Cottages.** Around the magnificent Welsh coast. Away from the madding crowd. Near safe sandy beaches. A small specialist agency offering privacy, peace and unashamed luxury. Wales Tourist Board 1989 Award Winner. Residential standards - dishwashers, microwaves, washing machines, central heating, log fires, no slot meters. Linen provided. Pets welcome free. All in coastal areas famed for scenery, walks, wild flowers, birds, badgers and foxes. Free colour brochure. **S.C. Rees, Quality Cottages, Cerbid, Solva, Haverfordwest, Pembrokeshire SA62 6YE (01348 837871).**
website: www.qualitycottages.co.uk

BROAD HAVEN / LITTLE HAVEN. Haven Cottages, Whitegates Farm, Little Haven, Haverfordwest SA62 3LA (01437 781552; Fax 01437 781386). Sleep 2/12. Situated 200 yards' level walk from beautiful sandy beach in the old village of Broad Haven, close to shops and pubs. On Coastal Path, ideal for walkers, bird watchers, windsurfers and family beach holidays. Linen provided. TV. Laundry room. Pets welcome. Available all year. Organic poultry and ostriches reared. Special rates for breaks available. Bed and Breakfast also available in farmhouse. Details on request. **WTB ★★★** *SELF-CATERING.* e-mail:welshhaven@aol.com

GOODWICK. Mrs Rosemary Johns, Carne Farm, Goodwick SA64 0LB (01348 891665). Working farm, join in. Sleeps 6. Stone cottage adjoining farmhouse sleeps six in three bedrooms, also a spacious residential caravan for six with two bedrooms, each with its own garden where children can play safely. In peaceful countryside on 350 acre dairy and sheep farm between Fishguard and Strumble Head, three miles from the sea. Within easy reach of many beaches by car, ideal for walking and bird-watching. No linen supplied. Children welcome. Washing machine in cottage. TV, microwave, cots, high chairs. Baby sitting available. You can be sure of a warm welcome and visitors can feed calves and watch the milking.

QUALITY COTTAGES

AROUND THE MAGNIFICENT WELSH COAST

Away from the Madding Crowd • Near safe sandy beaches

A small specialist agency with over 38 years experience of providing quality self-catering, offers privacy, peace and unashamed luxury. The first Wales Tourist Board Self-Catering Award Winner. Highest residential standards.

Dishwashers, Microwaves, Washing Machines, Central Heating. No Slot meters.

LOG FIRES • LINEN PROVIDED • PETS WELCOME FREE!

All in coastal areas famed for scenery, walks, wild-flowers, birds, badgers and foxes.

Away from the madding crowd

Free colour brochure from F.G. Rees "Quality Cottages", Cerbid, Solva, Haverfordwest, Pembrokeshire SA62 6YE
Telephone: (01348) 837871 • Website: www.qualitycottages.co.uk

---

CROFT FARM & CELTIC COTTAGES
PEMBROKESHIRE *(Featured in Daily Mail)*

Unique smallholding offering luxury indoor leisure facilities to complement superbly equipped and maintained traditional stone cottages. Open all year.
Indoor heated pool, sauna, spa pool, gym and recreation room. Near the stunning Pembrokeshire coastal cliff path, sandy beaches, ancient forest and National Park.
Friendly farm animals to help feed. Well-maintained colourful gardens, orchard and barbecue.

WTB
★★★★★

For a brochure please contact Andrew and Sylvie Gow, Croft Farm & Celtic Cottages, Croft, Near Cardigan, Pembrokeshire SA43 3NT Tel/Fax: 01239 615179 e-mail: croftfarm@bigfoot.com website: www.croft-holiday-cottages.co.uk

---

WEST LAMBSTON

Near. Portfield Gate, Haverfordwest, Pembrokeshire, SA62 3LG
Charles & Joy Spiers • Tel & Fax: 01437 710038

Non-working farm centrally positioned for beautiful coastal walks and many sandy beaches. Sleeps four in two bedrooms and cot. Autowasher, electric and microwave cookers. Fridge/Freezer, and ironing equipment. Cosy window seat and charming oak beamed inglenook. TV and video. Pets by arrangement. Linen inclusive. Open all year. Special rates for short breaks. October to March.

Terms from £150 to £390

FHG

FHG PUBLICATIONS

publish a large range of well-known accommodation guides. We will be happy to send you details or you can use the order form at the back of this book.

NARBERTH. Susan Lloyd, East Llanteg Farm, Llanteg, Narberth SA67 8QA (01834 831336). Two charming and spacious self-catering cottages (Crunwere and Hayloft), sleeping four and five respectively; each has cot and highchair. Both are comfortably furnished with all modern facilities, including fitted kitchens with dishwasher, washing machine, fridge, oven and hob etc. The spacious lounges and bedrooms are provided with colour TV and there is a video in each lounge. Both cottages have central heating and full double glazing, making them ideal for out-of-season breaks. **WTB** ★★★★★

e-mail: www.pfh.co.uk/east.llanteg/index.html

NEWGALE. Quality Cottages. Around the magnificent Welsh coast. Away from the madding crowd. Near safe, sandy beaches. A small specialist agency offering privacy, peace and unashamed luxury. Wales Tourist Board 1989 Award Winner. Residential standards - dishwashers, microwaves, washing machines, central heating, log fires, no slot meters. Linen provided. Pets welcome free. All in coastal areas famed for scenery, walks, wild flowers, birds, badgers and foxes. Free colour brochure. **S.C. Rees, Quality Cottages, Cerbid, Solva, Haverfordwest, Pembrokeshire SA62 6YE (01348 837871).**
website: www.qualitycottages.co.uk

ST. DAVID'S. Quality Cottages. Around the magnificent Welsh coast. Away from the madding crowd. Near safe sandy beaches. A small specialist agency offering privacy, peace and unashamed luxury. Wales Tourist Board 1989 Award Winner. Residential standards - dishwashers, microwaves, washing machines, central heating, log fires, no slot meters. Linen provided. Pets welcome free. All in coastal areas famed for scenery, walks, wild flowers, birds, badgers and foxes. Free colour brochure. **S.C. Rees, Quality Cottages, Cerbid, Solva, Haverfordwest, Pembrokeshire SA62 6YE (01348 837871).**
website: www.qualitycottages.co.uk

SOLVA. Quality Cottages. Around the magnificent Welsh coast. Away from the madding crowd. Near safe sandy beaches. A small specialist agency offering privacy, peace and unashamed luxury. Wales Tourist Board 1989 Award Winner. Residential standards - dishwashers, microwaves, washing machines, central heating, log fires, no slot meters. Linen provided. Pets welcome free. All in coastal areas famed for scenery, walks, wild flowers, birds, badgers and foxes. Free colour brochure. **S.C. Rees, Quality Cottages, Cerbid, Solva, Haverfordwest, Pembrokeshire SA62 6YE (01348 837871).**
website: www.qualitycottages.co.uk

TENBY. Quality Cottages. Around the magnificent Welsh coast. Away from the madding crowd. Near safe, sandy beaches. A small specialist agency offering privacy, peace and unashamed luxury. Wales Tourist Board 1989 Award Winner. Residential standards - dishwashers, microwaves, washing machines, central heating, log fires, no slot meters. Linen provided. Pets welcome free. All in coastal areas famed for scenery, walks, wild flowers, birds, badgers and foxes. Free colour brochure. **S.C. Rees, Quality Cottages, Cerbid, Solva, Haverfordwest, Pembrokeshire SA62 6YE (01348 837871).**
website: www.qualitycottages.co.uk

See also Colour Display Advertisement

WHITLAND. Mrs Angela Colledge, Gwarmacwydd, Llanfallteg, Whitland SA34 0XH (01437 563260; Fax: 01437 563839). Gwarmacwydd is a country estate of over 450 acres, including two miles of riverbank. Come and see a real farm in action, the hustle and bustle of harvest, newborn calves and lambs. Children are welcomed. On the estate are five character stone cottages, Tourist Board Grade Four. Each cottage has been lovingly converted from traditional farm buildings, parts of which are over 200 years old. Each cottage is fully furnished and equipped with all modern conveniences. All electricity and linen included. All cottages are heated for year-round use. Colour brochure available. **WTB** *GRADE FOUR SELF-CATERING.*
e-mail: info@a-farm-holiday.org
website: www.a-farm-holiday.org

POWYS

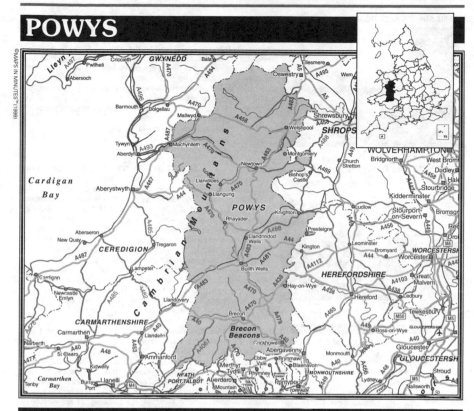

©MAPS IN MINUTES™ (1999)

LLANDRINDOD WELLS. Phillip and Patricia Harley, Gaer Cottage, Hundred House, Llandrindod Wells

LD1 5RU (Tel & Fax: 01982 570208). Gaer Cottage is a comfortable, well equipped, recently restored Welsh cottage. It has oil-fired central heating throughout. There are large south-facing windows and a conservatory. The kitchen and utility are well stocked with pots and pans for up to eight people. There is a fan oven, microwave, fridge/freezer, dishwasher and automatic washing machine. The lounge is very spacious providing a dining table with seating for eight, comfortable chairs and a bed-settee. There is a TV and video. Upstairs there are two en suite bedrooms; one has a double bed and the other has three single beds, two of which can join together to form a double
e-mail: unwind@gaercottage.co.uk
website: www.gaercottage.co.uk

LLANFAIR CAEREINION. Mr A. L. Annal, Bryn Erica, Llangyniew, Llanfair Caereinion SY21 0JT (01938 500149). Holiday caravan, single sited, four/six berth, modern, heated and fully equipped with microwave, freezer, refrigerator and TV. Situated in the Vale of Meiford it enjoys beautiful views and is ideal for relaxing, walking, fishing, local golf club and access to the Welsh coastline. Pets are welcome in the caravan and a cattery/kennel is provided with heated chalet and secure outside run built to FAB specification should you wish to have that day out on your own. We also provide a pet sitting service whilst you are out. Book now for 2001. Seasonal prices are inclusive. Please telephone for details.
e-mail: erica@micro-plus-web.net

NEWTOWN. Mrs D. Pryce, Aberbechan Farm, Newtown SY16 3BJ (01686 630675). Working farm, join in. Sleeps 10. This part of quaint Tudor farmhouse with its lovely oak beams is situated in picturesque countryside on a mixed farm with trout fishing and shooting in season. Newtown three miles, Welshpool, Powis Castle and Llanfair Light Railway, 14 miles; 45 miles to coast. The accommodation sleeps ten persons in four double and two single bedrooms, also cot. Two bathrooms, two toilets. Sitting/diningroom with colour TV. Fully fitted kitchen with fridge, electric cooker, washing machine and dishwasher. Log fires and off-peak heaters. Electricity on meter. Large lawn with swing. Everything supplied for visitors' comfort. Linen available for overseas guests at extra cost. Car essential to obtain the best from the holiday. Farm produce available in season. Village shop one-and-a-half miles away. Open all year. SAE please.

See also Colour Display Advertisement   TALGARTH. Mrs Bronwen Prosser, Upper Genfford Farm Guest House, Talgarth LD3 0EN (01874 711360). Set amongst the most spectacular scenery of the Brecon Beacons National Park, Upper Genfford Farm is an ideal base for exploring the Black Mountains, Wye Valley and the Brecon Beacons, an area of outstanding beauty, rich in historical and archaeological interest, with Roman camps and Norman castles. Picturesque mountain roads will lead you to reservoirs, the Gower coast with its lovely sandy beaches and Llangorse Lake - well known for all kinds of water sports. The local pub and restaurant is quarter-of-a-mile away and Hay-on-Wye, "The Town of Books" is a short distance away. Our self-catering cottage is fully equipped with fridge freezer, electric cooker, microwave and oil-fired Rayburn for cooking. There is a cosy, comfortable lounge with colour TV, open log fire (logs provided), pretty bathroom and two attractive bedrooms (one with two single beds, the second with one double and one single). Bathroom with shower. Ample parking in attractive patio adjacent to the cottage. Play area for children, also a friendly pony. terms from £150 to £180 weekly. Also charming Guest House accommodation, beautifully decorated and furnished. Home-made cakes and tea on arrival. Bed and Breakfast £18 to £20 per person. Awarded Plaque of Recommendation from the Welsh Tourist Board. Nominated "Landlady of the Year" 1999. Winner of FHG Diploma. **AA ◆◆◆. AA** QQQQ.

SOUTH WALES

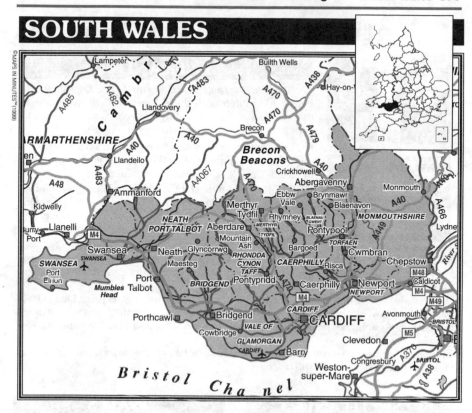

LLANELLEN (Abergavenny near). Mrs M. R. Bevan, Llanellen-Court Farm, Llanellen, Abergavenny NP7 9HT (Tel & Fax: 01873 853332). Situated two miles from Abergavenny, 'Gateway to Wales', which has a busy market three times a week. Llanellen Court Farm is within an Area of Outstanding Natural Beauty and offers four beautifully furnished 'cottage type' bungalows, each with large patio and own garden. Fully equipped with microwave, washing machine, and brand new sofa beds (fully sprung) for extra comfort. Bed linen and towels provided. Cot available (no linen). Excellent walking country, golf, fishing, pony trekking and beautiful castles nearby. Llanellen-Court is a working poultry farm, sheep and cattle also. Regretfully no pets or smoking. **WTB ★★★★★** *SELF-CATERING..*

Ratings You Can Trust

ENGLAND

The **English Tourism Council** (formerly the English Tourist Board) has joined with the **AA** and **RAC** to create a new, easily understood quality rating for serviced accommodation, giving a clear guide of what to expect.

HOTELS are given a rating from One to Five **Stars** – the more Stars, the higher the quality and the greater the range of facilities and level of services provided.

GUEST ACCOMMODATION, which includes guest houses, bed and breakfasts, inns and farmhouses, is rated from One to Five **Diamonds**. Progressively higher levels of quality and customer care must be provided for each one of the One to Five Diamond ratings.

HOLIDAY PARKS, TOURING PARKS and CAMPING PARKS are now also assessed using **Stars**. Standards of quality range from a One Star (acceptable) to a Five Star (exceptional) park.

Look out also for the new **SELF-CATERING** Star ratings. The more **Stars** (from One to Five) awarded to an establishment, the higher the levels of quality you can expect. Establishments at higher rating levels also have to meet some additional requirements for facilities.

NB Some self-catering properties had not been assessed at the time of going to press and in these cases the old-style **KEY** symbols will still be shown.

SCOTLAND

Star Quality Grades will reflect the most important aspects of a visit, such as the warmth of welcome, efficiency and friendliness of service, the quality of the food and the cleanliness and condition of the furnishings, fittings and decor.

THE MORE STARS, THE HIGHER THE STANDARDS.

The description, such as Hotel, Guest House, Bed and Breakfast, Lodge, Holiday Park, Self-catering etc tells you the type of property and style of operation.

In England, Scotland and Wales, all graded properties are inspected annually by Tourist Authority trained Assessors.

WALES

Places which score highly will have an especially welcoming atmosphere and pleasing ambience, high levels of comfort and guest care, and attractive surroundings enhanced by thoughtful design and attention to detail

STAR QUALITY GUIDE FOR SERVICED ACCOMMODATION AND HOLIDAY PARKS

★★★★★ *Exceptional quality*
★★★★ *Excellent quality*
★★★ *Very good quality*
★★ *Good quality*
★ *Fair to good quality*

SELF-CATERING ACCOMMODATION

The **DRAGON GRADES** spell out the quality. They range from Grade 1 (simple and reasonable) to Grade 5 (excellent quality). The grades reflect the overall quality, not the range of facilities.

WALES
Caravan & Camping Holidays

ANGLESEY & GWYNEDD

BALA. Mrs S.E. Edwards, Bryn Melyn, Rhyduchaf, Bala LL23 7PG (01678 520376). Sleeps 6. One six-berth caravan available on Bryn Melyn, a 56 acre mixed farm in the village of Rhyduchaf, two miles from Bala situated in beautiful countryside. The caravan has a bathroom, inside flush toilet, hot and cold water, electric light, gas cooker, gas heater, fridge, colour TV. Fully equipped with blankets, microwave, etc. Children welcome. Sorry, no pets allowed. Open from April to September. Electricity on slot motor (£1). Weekly terms £85. Bed and Breakfast and Evening Meals available. SAE please for further details.

NORTH WALES

ABERGELE. Mr and Mrs T.P. Williams, Pen Isaf Caravan Park, Llangernyw, Abergele LL22 8RN (01745 860276). This small caravan site in beautiful unspoilt countryside is ideal for touring North Wales and is situated 10 miles from the coast and 12 miles from Betws-y-Coed. The eight-berth caravans are fully equipped except for linen and towels and have shower, flush toilet, hot and cold water, Calor gas cooker, electric light and fridge. Fresh eggs and milk can be obtained from the farm on which this 20 caravan site is situated. Children especially will enjoy a holiday here, there being ample space and facilities for fishing and pony riding. Pets are allowed but must be kept under control. Open March to October. Terms on application with SAE, please.

RHYL. Mrs Phasey, Palins Holiday Park, Morfa Avenue, Kinmel Bay, Rhyl LL18 5LE (01745 342672; Fax: 01745 344110).

Palins Holiday Park is situated between Rhyl and Abergele on the A548 Towyn Coast Road. You are assured of the warmest welcome, all our staff are totally committed to ensuring that your holiday will be one you remember and hopefully you will decide to visit again and again. Heated indoor pool with waterchute and toddlers' area, children's play area, cabaret club, bingo and disco. Tudor Lounge with full size snooker table, pool, darts and colour TV. Mexican Theme Wine Bar and Restaurant, supermarket, fish and chip shop, cafe and launderette. All holiday homes have two or three bedrooms all equipped to the highest standard; bed linen and towels not provided. Dogs by arrangement only. Families only. Palins Holiday Park is a superb place from which to explore North Wales and its many attractions. **WTB** ✓✓✓✓.

CARDIGANSHIRE

ABERPORTH. Mrs S. Jones, Manorafon Caravan Park, Sarnau, Llandyssul SA44 6QH (01239 810564).
Sleeps 6. Quiet, peaceful site of 11 caravans, fully equipped except linen, all six-berth with end bedrooms. All essential facilities provided. Bathroom facilities with hot water on tap in each van; Calor gas cooker, electric lighting and heating. Toilets and washbasins, showers, shaving points. Calor and Camping Gaz sold. Available Easter to October. Children welcome. No dogs. Only half-a-mile from the pleasant Penbryn beach and nine miles from the market towns of Cardigan and Newcastle Emlyn. One-and-a-half-acres for campers and tourers.

ABERYSTWYTH. Mrs Anne Bunton, Cwmergyr Farm, Ponterwyd, Aberystwyth SY23 3LB (01970

890301). This spacious six-berth caravan is sited in its own enclosure on a 250 acre sheep farm in the beautiful Cambrian Mountains, 16 miles east of Aberystwyth off the A44. Accommodation consists of two bedrooms, bathroom (flush toilet, vanity unit and shower); kitchen (fridge and gas cooker); spacious lounge with colour TV and spectacular views; gas fire and hot and cold water throughout. Linen not supplied. No pets allowed. Car essential with ample parking. Within 15 mile radius there are sandy beaches, fishing, golf, pony trekking, steam railway, scenic drives and walks. An ideal location to explore mid-Wales. A stream runs through the property and the farm animals always fascinate the children. Open 1st April to 31st October. Terms from £100 to £150 per week (all gas and electricity included).

PEMBROKESHIRE

LITTLE HAVEN. David and Kaye James, Hasguard Cross Caravan Park, Little Haven, Haverfordwest SA62 3SL (Tel & Fax: 01437 781443). The

Park is situated in the centre of Pembrokeshire National Park on the Dale peninsula within easy reach of the many beaches, coastal walks and water sports. The Park covers three-and-a-quarter acres of level grassland tastefully screened with trees, with beautiful views of the countryside overlooking the Milford Haven and St Brides Bay. The Park caters for the hire of modern holiday homes with colour TV; touring and motor caravans have electric hook up available and the usual facilities. A warm welcome in the Hasguard Inn awaits you where good food and beer is available every evening. **WTB ✓✓✓✓**

SOUTH WALES

MERTHYR TYDFIL. Grawen Caravan and Camping Park, Grawen Farm, Cwm-Taff, Cefn Coed, Merthyr Tydfil CF48 2HS (01685 723740). Clean modern

facilities. Picturesque surroundings with forest, mountain, reservoir walks from site. Reservoir trout fishing. Ideally located for touring, visiting places of historic interest and enjoying scenic views. Available April to October. Easy access A470 Brecon Beacons road, one-and-a-half miles Cefn Coed, three-and-a-half miles Merthyr Tydfil, two miles from A456 known as the Heads of the Valleys. Pets welcome. Terms from £8 per night for tent, two adults +50p per child; caravans from £9 per night for 2 adults +50p per child (price includes car). 16 electric hook-ups. **WTB ✓✓✓**

Isle of Man

Self-Catering

ST MARKS. P. M. Hine, Ballagarey Farm Cottages, St. Marks, IM9 3AH (01624 822174; Fax: 01624 825118). Manx stone barn converted into three superb units - two units each sleeping four and the third sleeping six. Bedrooms on the ground floor with open plan spacious living and kitchen on the first floor thus enjoying the beauty of the Manx countryside. All units equipped to the highest standard. Large shared lawn with children's play area. Additional cottage with one double bedroom. Hall, kitchen and lounge on the ground floor. All have payphones. Close to Millennium Way footpath. Convenient for all golf courses south of Island. Three miles from local village of Ballasalla providing for all your holiday requirements. ooooo *HIGHLY COMMENDED.*
e-mail: info@farmcottagesisleofman.com
website: www.farmcottagesisleofman.com

White Rocks, near Portrush, Antrim, Northern Ireland

NORTHERN IRELAND

Board Accommodation

FERMANAGH

ENNISKILLEN. Mrs M. Love, View Point, 5 Mullnaskea Road, Garvary, Enniskillen BT74 4JQ (Tel & Fax:

028 6632 7321). Just off the B80, about three miles from Enniskillen, View Point is ideally situated to allow easy access to a wide range of Fermanagh tourist attractions. Within minutes of Enniskillen, tourists can relax in the quiet rural setting, amid beautiful countryside while enjoying an extensive breakfast and dinner menu. Two rooms en suite; one twin standard and one double with handbasin and shower. Three rooms have TV, all have central heating, hairdryer, and tea/coffee making facilities. Places of Interest within easy reach include Ardhowen Theatre, Belleek Pottery, Castle Coole, Devenish Island and Enniskillen Castle. Castle Archdale Country Park and Carrybridge; boating, water skiing, etc nearby. Children welcome. Bed and Breakfast from £16.50 to £18; single supplement £3. **NITB** *APPROVED.*

NORTHERN IRELAND

Caravan & Camping Holidays

TYRONE

See also Colour Display Advertisement

DUNGANNON. Dungannon Park Caravan and Camping, Dungannon. Set in 70 acres of beautiful parkland surrounding an idyllic stillwater lake, the caravan park is situated in the heartland of Ulster, less than one mile away from the motorway to Belfast, and is within easy walking distance of the town of Dungannon. Relax and enjoy the many facilities available - up to three miles of scenic park walks, barbecue site and picnic area and children's play area. We have twelve fully serviced caravan sites and access for up to eight tents. Stillwater Rainbow Trout fly fishery. Terms: Caravans £8 per night, Tents £6. ✓✓✓✓, **AA** *THREE PENNANTS*. For more informations contact: **Dungannon and South Tyrone Borough Council (028 8772 7327; Fax: 028 8772 9169).**

REPUBLIC OF IRELAND

Board Accommodation

Co. CORK

BANTRY. Mrs Agnes Hegarty, Hillcrest Farm, Ahakista, Durrus, Bantry (00 353 27 67045). Seaside farm. Charming old-style farmhouse, newly renovated, retaining traditional character. Situated in picturesque peaceful setting overlooking harbour and Dunmanus Bay, quarter-of-a-mile from Ahakista village on the Sheep's Head Peninsula. Magnificent sea and mountain scenery; swimming, fishing, boating and five minutes' walk to the sea. Irish pubs and restaurants close by. Bantry 12 miles, Durrus six miles. Ideal centre for touring the Peninsulas of West Cork and Kerry. Signposted in Durrus. Four guest bedrooms, three with bath/shower en suite, one with washbasin; two are family rooms. Ground floor room available. Tea/coffee making facilities and electric blankets in all bedrooms. Bathroom. Spacious dining room with stone walls; sittingroom with old world fireplace and log fire. Play/games room, antiques, swing, lovely garden with mature trees. Warm hospitality. Fresh farm vegetables and home baking. Babysitting. On new Sheeps Head Way walking route. Bed and Breakfast from (Ir)£18 to £20; Dinner (Ir)£14, High Tea (Ir) £12. 25% reductions for children sharing with parents. Extensive breakfast menu. Award Winner of Farmhouse of the Year 1991/2. Also to let, modern seaside bungalow for self catering. Fully equipped and in superb location, from (Ir)£130 to (Ir)£360 per week. Available all year. e-mail: agneshegarty@oceanfree.net

Co. KILDARE

CASTLEDERMOT. Mr G. D. Greene, Kilkea Lodge Farm, Castledermot (00 353 50345112). Kilkea

Lodge has belonged to the Greene family since 1740. Set in 260 acres of prime tillage and rolling parklands this tranquil setting offers guests the opportunity to relax in the comfort of log fires and traditional Irish hospitality. Accommodation comprises two double and one twin-bedded rooms en suite, and one single room and one family suite. First class traditional home cooking. Riding Centre on site run by Marion Greene and offering a variety of instructional and fun holidays under qualified supervision. Children welcome. French spoken. Open all year round except Christmas. Bed and Breakfast from £30 to £35 per person; single supplement £5. Dinner from £15 to £20. Advance booking essential. Brochure available.

REPUBLIC OF IRELAND

Self-Catering

Co. KERRY

ANNASCAUL. Mrs M. Sayers, Kilmurry Farm, Minard Castle, Annascaul (066 91 57173; from UK 00 353 66 9157173). Self-catering accommodation apartment. Two bedrooms. Sleeps four. All modern conveniences overlooking Dingle Bay and sandy beach. Dingle renowned for Dingle Dolphin. Terms on request.

LAURAGH. Creveen Lodge Caravan and Camping Park, Healy Pass Road, Lauragh (00 353 64 83131; from Ireland 064 83131). Attractive two-storey dormer-style farmhouse attached to proprietors' residence, 200 yards from roadside, with magnificent views of sea and countryside. The 80-acre mixed farm is conveniently situated for fishing, mountain climbing, Derreen Gardens, shops and old Irish pub: 16 miles south of Kenmare. Accommodation for six/eight persons in three double and one single room, all with washbasin; cot. Sittingroom with large stone fireplace, TV; separate diningroom. Kitchen has gas cooker; full oil-fired central heating and storage heating; washing machine and dryer. Everything supplied including linen. Children and pets welcome; high chair, and babysitting arranged. Car essential parking Available all year. April and October £120; June and September £170 per week; July and August £270 per week; rest of the year by arrangement. Gas and electricity extra.

REPUBLIC OF IRELAND
Caravan & Camping Holidays

Co. KERRY

See also Colour Display Advertisement

KILLORGLIN. West's Caravan Park, Killarney Road, Killorglin, Co. Kerry (00 353 66 9761240; FREEPHONE 0800 374424 from Britain). A perfect holiday location, in an area of outstanding natural beauty. Static caravans with showers for hire. Tennis, fishing, play area, laundry on park. Killarney National Park, Gap of Dunloe, caves, Dingle Peninsula (dolphin), Tralee (Aquadome), horse riding all nearby. Wonderful central location. Outdoor pursuits centre, pubs, restaurants and sandy beaches within easy reach. IR£109-£359. Recommended by: BH&HPA, ITB, AA, ADAC, RAC, MCCI and our customers.

FOR THE MUTUAL GUIDANCEOF GUEST AND HOST

Every year literally thousands of holidays, short breaks and overnight stops are arranged through our guides, the vast majority without any problems at all. In a handful of cases, however, difficulties do arise about bookings, which often could have been prevented from the outset.

It is important to remember that when accommodation has been booked, both parties – guests and hosts – have entered into a form of contract. We hope that the following points will provide helpful guidance.

GUESTS: When enquiring about accommodation, be as precise as possible. Give exact dates, numbers in your party and the ages of any children. State the number and type of rooms wanted and also what catering you require – bed and breakfast, full board etc. Make sure that the position about evening meals is clear – and about pets, reductions for children or any other special points.

Read our reviews carefully to ensure that the proprietors you are going to contact can supply what you want. Ask for a letter confirming all arrangements, if possible.

If you have to cancel, do so as soon as possible. Proprietors do have the right to retain deposits and under certain circumstances to charge for cancelled holidays if adequate notice is not given and they cannot re-let the accommodation.

HOSTS: Give details about your facilities and about any special conditions. Explain your deposit system clearly and arrangements for cancellations, charges etc. and whether or not your terms include VAT.

If for any reason you are unable to fulfil an agreed booking without adequate notice, you may be under an obligation to arrange suitable alternative accommodation or to make some form of compensation.

While every effort is made to ensure accuracy, we regret that FHG Publications cannot accept responsibility for errors, omissions or misrepresentations in our entries or any consequences thereof.
Prices in particular should be checked because we go to press early. We will follow up complaints but cannot act as arbiters or agents for either party.

Website Directory

A quick-reference guide to holiday accommodation with e-mail addresses and websites, conveniently arranged by country and county, with full contact details

•LONDON

Hotel
Stanley House Hotel, 19 – 21 Belgrave Road, VICTORIA, London SW1V 1RB
020 7834 5042
• e-mail: cmahotel@aol.com
• website: www.affordablehotelsonline.com

Hotel
St Georges Hotel, 23 Belgrave Road, LONDON SW1V 1RB
020 7828 2061
• e-mail: cmahotel@aol.com
• website: www.affordablehotelsonline.com

Hotel
Colliers Hotel, 97 Warwick Way, LONDON SW1V 1QL
020 7834 6931
• e-mail: cmahotel@aol.com
• website: www.affordablehotelsonline.com

•CORNWALL

Guest House
Mrs C. Carruthers, The Clearwater, 50 Melvill Road, FALMOUTH, Cornwall TR11 4DF
01326 311344
• e-mail: clearwater@lineone.net
• website: www.clearwaterhotel.co.uk

County House Hotel
Parc-An-Ithan House Hotel, Sithney, NEAR HELSTON, Cornwall
TR13 0RN
01326 572565
• e-mail: parc-hotel@btinternet.com
• website: www.visitweb.com/parc

Self-Catering
Mr & Mrs Cotter, Trewalla Farm, Minions, LISKEARD, Cornwall PL14 6ED
01579 342385
• e-mail: cotter.trewalla@virgin.net
• website: www.selfcateringcornwall.net

Guest House
Jan & Jeff Loveridge, Harescombe Lodge, Watergate, NEAR LOOE, Cornwall PL13 2NE
01503 263158
• e-mail: harescombe@dial.pipex.com
• website: www.harescombe.dial.pipex.com

Hotel
Lostwithiel Hotel, Golf & Country Club, Lower Polscoe, LOSTWITHIEL, Cornwall PL22 0HQ
01208 873550
• e-mail: reception@golf-hotel.co.uk
• website:www.golf-hotel.co.uk

Hotel
Seavista Hotel, Mawgan Porth, NEAR NEWQUAY, Cornwall TR8 4AL
01637 860276
• e-mail: crossd@supanet.com
• website: www.seavistahotel.co.uk

Self-Catering
Cornish Horizons Holiday Cottages, Higher Trehemborne, St Merryn, PADSTOW Cornwall PL28 8JU
01841 520889
• e-mail: cottages@cornishhorizons.co.uk
• website: www.cornishhorizons.co.uk

Self-Catering
Angela Clark, Darrynane Cottages, Darrynane,ST BREWARD, Bodmin Moor, Cornwall PL30 4LZ
01208 850885
• e-mail: darrynane@eclipse.co.uk
• website: www.darrynane.co.uk

Guest House
Mr & Mrs Clark, Trewerry Mill, Trerice, ST NEWLYN EAST, Cornwall TR8 5GS
01872 510345
• e-mail: trewerry.mill@which.net
• website: www.connexions.co.uk\trewerry.mill

Self-catering
Mrs Lynda Spring, Trethevy Manor, Trethevy, TINTAGEL, Cornwall PL34 0BG
01840 770636
• e-mail: manor1151@talk21.com
• website: www.cornwall-online.co.uk/trethevy-manor

CORNWALL (Contd)

Hotel
Rosevine Hotel, Porthcurnick Beach ,St
Mawes, TRURO, Cornwall TR2 5EW
01872 580206
• e-mail: info@rosevine.co.uk
• website: www.rosevine.co.uk

B&B/Self-Catering
Mrs Pamela Carbis, Trenona Farm, Ruan
High Lanes, TRURO, Cornwall TR2 5JS
01872 501339
• e-mail: pcarbis@compuserve.com
• website: www.connexions.co.uk/trenona

•CUMBRIA

B&B/Self-Catering
Mr and Mrs P. Hart,Bracken Fell, Outgate,
AMBLESIDE, Cumbria LA22 0NH
015394 36289
• e-mail: hart.brackenfell@virgin.net
• website: www.brackenfell.com

Self-Catering
Lakelovers, The New Toffee Loft, Kendal
Road, BOWNESS, Cumbria LA23 3RA
01539 488855
• e-mail: bookings@lakelovers.co.uk
• website: www.lakelovers.co.uk

Self-Catering
The Coppermines at Coniston, The Estate
Office, The Bridge, CONISTON, Cumbria
LA21 8HJ
01539 441765
• e-mail: bookings@coppermines.co.uk
• website: www.coppermines.co.uk

Self-Catering
Mr and Mrs E.D. Robinson, 1 Field End,
Patton, KENDAL, Cumbria LA8 9DU
01539 824220
• e-mail: fshawend@globalnet.co.uk
• website: www.diva~web.co.uk.fsendhols

B & B
Mr & Mrs M. Rooney, Villa Lodge, Cross
Street, WINDERMERE, Cumbria LA23 1AE
01539 443318
• e-mail: rooneym@btconnect.com
• website: www.villa-lodge.co.uk

Self-Catering
Mr and Mrs F. Legge, Pinethwaite Holiday
Cottages, Luckbarrow Road, WINDERMERE
Cumbria LA23 2NQ
01539 444558
• e-mail: legge@pinethwaite.freeserve.co.uk
• website: www.pinecottages.co.uk

Guest House
Mr Brian Fear, Cambridge House, 9 Oak
Street, WINDERMERE, Cumbria LA23 1EN
01539 443846
• e-mail: reservations@cambridge-
house.fsbusiness.co.uk
• website: www.cambridge-
house.fsbusiness.co.uk

•DEVON

B & B
Mr C.D. Moore, Gages Mill, Buckfastleigh
Road, ASHBURTON, Devon TQ13 7JW
01364 652391
• e-mail: moore@gagesmill.co.uk
• website: www.gagesmill.co.uk

Farmhouse B&B
Jaye Jones & Helen Asher, Twitchen Farm,
Challacombe, BARNSTAPLE,
Devon EX31 4TT
01598 763568
• e-mail: holidays@twitchen.co.uk
• website: www.twitchen.co.uk

Self-Catering
Mrs L. Nash, Swincombe Farm,
Challacombe, NEAR BARNSTAPLE, Devon
EX31 4TU
01598 763506
• e-mail: nash@lineone.com
• website: www.jcjdatacomm.co.uk\nash

Hotel
Fingals at Old Coombe Manor, Dittisham,
NEAR DARTMOUTH, Devon TQ6 0JA
01803 722398
• e-mail: richard@fingals.co.uk
• website: www.fingals.co.uk

Self-Catering
Mrs Sue Horn, Narramore Farm Cottages,
Narramore Farm, MORETONHAMPSTEAD,
Devon TQ13 8QT
01647 440455
• e-mail: narramore@btinternet.com
• website: www.narramorefarm.co.uk

Hotel
Lodge Hill Farm Hotel, TIVERTON,
Devon EX16 5PA
01884 251200
• e-mail: lodgehill@dial.pipex.com
• website: www.lodgehill.co.uk

Visit the FHG website
www.holidayguides.com
for a wide choice of holiday accommodation

•DORSET

Country House B&B

Mrs Martine Tree, The Old Rectory,
Winterbourne Steepleton, DORCHESTER,
Dorset DT2 9LG
01305 889468
• e-mail: trees@eurobell.co.uk
• website: www.trees.eurobell.co.uk

Guest House

Lydwell Guest House, Lyme Road, Uplyme,
LYME REGIS, Dorset DT7 3TJ
01297 443522
• e-mail: lydwell@britane16.fsbusiness.co.uk
• website: www.SmoothHound.co.uk

•GLOUCESTERSHIRE

B & B

Mr S. D. Gwilliam, Dryslade Farm, English
Bicknor, COLEFORD, Gloucestershire GL16
7PA
01594 860259
• e-mail: gwilliam@dryslade.freeserve.co.uk
• website: www.fweb.org.uk/dryslade

Lodge

Mr Paul Korn, Symonds Yat Rock Lodge,
Hillersland, NEAR COLEFORD,
Gloucestershire GL16 7NY
01594 836191
• e-mail: enquiries@rocklodge.co.uk
• website: www.rocklodge.co.uk

Hotel

Speech House Hotel, COLEFORD, Forest of
Dean, Gloucestershire GL16 7EL
01594 822607
• e-mail: relax@thespecchhouse.co.uk
• website: www.thespeechhouse.co.uk

•HAMPSHIRE

Guest House

Mrs Lewis, Our Bench, Lodge Road,
Pennington, LYMINGTON, Hampshire SO41
8HH
01590 673141
• e-mail: enquiries@ourbench.co.uk
• website: www.ourbench.co.uk

B & B

Graham & Sandra Tubb, Hamilton House,
95 Victoria Road North, Southsea,
PORTSMOUTH, Hampshire PO5 1PS
02392 823502
• e-mail: sandra@hamiltonhouse.co.uk
• website: www.hamiltonhouse.co.uk

•LANCASHIRE

B & B

Mr & Mrs M. Smith, The Old Coach House,
50 Dean St, BLACKPOOL, Lancashire FY4
1BP
01253 349195
• e-mail:
blackpool@theoldcoachhouse.freeserve.co.uk
• website:
www.theoldcoachhouse.freeserve.co.uk

B & B

Mrs Melanie Smith ,Capernwray House,
Capernwray, CARNFORTH, Lancashire LA6
1AE
01524 732363
• e-mail: thesmiths@capernwrayhouse.com
• website: www.capernwrayhouse.com

Hotel

Rosedale Hotel, 11 Talbot Street,
SOUTHPORT, Lancashire PR8 1HP
0800 0738133
• e-mail: info@rosedalehotelsouthport.co.uk
• website: www.rosedalehotelsouthport.co.uk

•LEICESTERSHIRE

B & B

Mrs A.T. Hutchinson and Mrs A.M. Knight
The Greenway and Knaptoft House Farm,
Bruntingthorpe Road, Near Shearsby,
LUTTERWORTH, Leicestershire LE17 6PR
011624 78388
• e-mail: info@knaptoft.com
• website: www.knaptoft.com

•LINCOLNSHIRE

Guest House

Edward King House, The Old Palace,
LINCOLN, Lincolnshire LN2 1PU
01522 528778
• e-mail: ekh@oden-org.uk
• website: www.lincoln.anglican.org/ekh

B&B

Mrs B. Moss, Keddington House Host
Home, 5 Keddington Road, LOUTH,
Lincolnshire LN11 0AA
01507 603973
• e-mail: beverly@keddingtonhouse.co.uk
• website: www.keddingtonhouse.co.uk

•NORFOLK

Hotel

Ffolkes Arms Hotel, Lynn Road, Hillington, KING'S LYNN, Norfolk PE31 6BJ
01485 600210
• e-mail: ffolkespub@aol.com
• website: www.ffolkes-arms-hotel.co.uk

B&B

Mrs M.A. Hemmant, Poplar Farm, Sisland, Loddon, NORWICH, Norfolk NR14 6EF
01508 520706
• e-mail: milly@hemmant.myhome.org.uk
• website: www.farm-holidays.co.uk

•NORTHUMBERLAND

Self-Catering

Mrs Vicki Taylor, Quality Self Catering, Letton Lodge, ALNMOUTH, Northumberland NE66 2RJ
01665 830633
• e-mail: lettonlodge@aol.com
• website: www.alnmouth.co.uk

Self-catering

Northumbria Coast and Country Cottages, Riverbank Road, ALNMOUTH, Northumberland NE66 2RH
01665 830783
• e-mail: cottages@nccc.demon.co.uk
• website: www.northumbriacottages.com

Self-catering/B&B

Mrs Vicki Taylor, Quality Self Catering, Letton Lodge, ALNMOUTH, Northumberland NE66 2RJ
01665 830633
• e-mail: alnmouth@aol.com
• website: www.alnmouth.co.uk

•OXFORDSHIRE

Self-Catering

Mrs W. Church, Cottage in the Country, Forest Gate, Forge Lane, MILTON-UNDER-WYCHWOOD, Oxfordshire OX7 6JZ
01993 831495
• e-mail: cottage@cottageinthecountry.co.uk
• website: www.cottageinthecountry.co.uk

Visit the FHG website
www.holidayguides.com
for a wide choice of holiday accommodation

•SOMERSET

Farm

Mr & Mrs Rowe, Ash-Wembdon Farm, Wembdon, BRIDGWATER, Somerset TA5 2BD
01278 453097
• e-mail: mary.rowe@btinternet.com
• website: www.farmaccommodation.co.uk

Hotel

Braeside Hotel, 2 Victoria Park, WESTON-SUPER-MARE, Somerset BS23 2HZ
01934 626642
• e-mail: info@thebraesidehotel.co.uk
• website: www.braesidehotel.co.uk

•STAFFORDSHIRE

Guest House

Mrs Griffiths, Prospect House Guest House, 334 Cheadle Road, Cheddleton, LEEK, Staffordshire ST13 7BW
01782 550639
• e-mail: prospect@talk21.com
• website:
www.touristnetuk.com/wm/prospect/index.htm

•SUFFOLK

Guest House

Kay Dewsbury, Manor House Guest House, The Green, Beyton, BURY ST EDMUNDS, Near Suffolk IP30 9AF
01359 270960
• e-mail: manorhouse@thegreenbeyton.com
• website: www.beyton.com

Guest House/Tearoom

Mr & Mrs Bowles, Ship Stores, 22 Callis St, CLARE, Sudbury, Suffolk CO10 8DX
01787 277834
• e-mail: shipclare@aol.com
• website: www.ship-stores.co.uk

Self-Catering

Melanie Reiger, Mill House, Water Run, Hitcham, IPSWICH, Suffolk IP7 7LN
01449 740315
• e-mail: hitcham@aol.com
• website: www.millhouse-hitcham.co.uk

Pet Hotel

Pakefield Pet Hotel, London Road, Pakefield, LOWESTOFT, Suffolk NR33 7PG
01502 563399
• e-mail: marion@pakefieldpethotel.fsnet.co.uk
• website: www.pakefieldpethotel.co.uk

•SURREY

Guest House

Mr. A. Grinsted, The Lawn Guest House, 30 Massetts Road, HORLEY, Surrey RH5 7DE
01293 775751
• e-mail: info@lawnguesthouse.co.uk
• website: www.lawnguesthouse.co.uk

Hotel

Chase Lodge Hotel, 10 Park Road, Hampton, Wick, KINGSTON UPON THAMES, Surrey KT1 4AS
02089 431862
• e-mail: chaselodgehotel@aol.com
• website: www.chaselodgehotel.com

•EAST SUSSEX

B & B

Mr Mundy, The Homestead, Homestead Lane, Valebridge Road, BURGESS HILL, East Sussex RH15 0RQ
01444 246899
• e-mail: homestead@burgess-hill.co.uk
• website: www.burgess-hill.co.uk

Guest House

Mrs J. P. Hadfield, Jeake's House, Mermaid Street, RYE, East Sussex TN31 7ET
01797 222828
• e-mail: Jeakeshouse@btInternet.com
• website: www.jeakeshouse.com

•WEST SUSSEX

B & B

Deborah S. Collinson, The Old Priory, 80 North Bersted Street, BOGNOR REGIS, West Sussex PO22 9AQ
01243 863580
• e-mail: old.priory@mcmail.com
• website: www.old.priory.mcmail.com

•WARWICKSHIRE

Guest House

Mr & Mrs K Wheat, Hollyhurst Guest House, 47 Priory Road, KENILWORTH, Warwickshire CV8 1LL
01926 853882
• e-mail: admin@hollyhurstguesthouse.co.uk
• website: www.hollyhurstguesthouse.co.uk

•NORTH YORKSHIRE

Guest House

Mr & Mrs R. Joyner, Anro Guest House, 90 Kings Road, HARROGATE, North Yorkshire HG1 5JX
01423 503087
• e-mail: info@theanro.harrogate.net
• website: www.theanro.harrogate.net

Guest House

Mr & Mrs C. Richardson, The Coppice, 9 Studley Road, HARROGATE, North Yorkshire HG1 5JU
01423 569626
• e-mail: coppice@harrogate.com
• website: www.harrogate.com/coppice

B&B/Self-catering

Mrs S. Robinson, Valley View Farm, Old Byland, HELMSLEY, North Yorkshire YO6 5LG
01439 798221
• e-mail: sally@valleyviewfarm.com
• website: www.valleyviewfarm.com

Guest House

Mrs Ella Bowes, Banavie, Roxby Road, Thornton-Le-Dale, PICKERING, North Yorkshire YO18 7SX
01751 474616
• e-mail: ella@banavie.fsbusiness.co.uk
• website: www.SmoothHound.co.uk/hotels

Hotel / Inn

The Queens Arms, Litton, NEAR SKIPTON, North Yorkshire BD23 5QJ
01756 770208
• e-mail: queensarms.litton@amserve.net
• website:
www.yorkshiredales.net/stayat/queens

Caravans

Mr & Mrs Tyerman, Partridge Nest Farm, Eskdaleside, Sleights, WHITBY, North Yorkshire YO22 5ES
01947 810450
• e-mail: pnfarm@aol.com
• website: www.tmis.uk.com/partridge-nest/

SCOTLAND

•ARGYLL & BUTE

Hotel

Willowburn Hotel, Clachan Seil, BY OBAN,
Argyll PA34 4TJ
01852 300276
• e-mail: willowburnhotel@virgin.net
• website: www.willowburn.co.uk

•DUNDEE & ANGUS

Self-Catering

Mrs M. Marchant, The Welton of
Kingoldrum, Welton Farm, KIRRIEMUIR,
Angus DD8 5HY
01575 574743
• e-mail: weltonholidays@btinternet.com
• website:
http://homepages.go.com/~thewelton/index.htm

•EDINBURGH & LOTHIANS

Guest House

Irene Cheape, Crion Guest House, 33 Minto
Street, EDINBURGH, Lothians EH9 2BT
0131 667 2708
• e-mail:
wcheape@gilmourhouse.freeserve.co.uk
• website: www.edinburghbedbreakfast.com

Guest House

John and Muriel Hamilton, Southdown
Guest House, 20 Craigmillar Park,
EDINBURGH, Lothians EH16 5PS
0131 667 2410
• e-mail: haml20@aol.com
• website:
www.SmoothHound.co.uk/hotels/southdow.html

Self-Catering

Premier Vacations, 5 St Peters Buildings,
EDINBURGH, Lothians EH3 9PG
0131 221 9001
• e-mail: reservations@premiervacations.net
• website: www.premiervacations.net

Guest House

Mr David Martin, Spylaw Bank House, 2
Spylaw Ave, Colinton, EDINBURGH,
Lothians EH13 0LR
0131 441 5022
• e-mail: angelaatspylawbank.freeserve.co.uk
• website: www.spylawbank.freeserve.co.uk

B & B

The Stuarts, 17 Glengyle Terrace,
EDINBURGH, Lothians EH3 9LN
0131 229 9559
• e-mail: fhg@the-stuarts.com
• website: www.the-stuarts.com

Guest House

Ben Doran Guest House, 11 Mayfield
Gardens, EDINBURGH, Lothians EH9 2AX
0131 667 8488
• e-mail: info@bendoran.com
• website: www.bendoran.com

Guest House

Mrs Lamb, Priory Lodge, 8 The Loan,
SOUTH QUEENSFERRY, West Lothian EH30
9NS
0131 331 4345
• e-mail: calmyn@aol.com
• website: www.queensferry.com

•FIFE

Self-Catering

Mr Potter, Carvenom Farm Cottage,
Carvenom House, BY ANSTRUTHER, Fife
KY10 3JU
01333 311823
• e-mail: gtpotter@aol.com
• website: www.carvenom.btinternet.co.uk

Hotel

The Golf Hotel, ELIE, Fife KY9 1EF
01333 330209
• e-mail: golf@standrews.co.uk
• website: www.golfhotel.co.uk

•HIGHLANDS

Guest House

Mrs Sandra Silke, Westwood, Lower
Balmacaan, DRUMNADROCHIT, Inverness-
shire IV63 6WU
01456 450826
• e-mail: sandra@westwoodbb.freeserve.co.uk
• website: www.westwoodbb.freeserve.co.uk

B&B/Self-Catering

Mr A. Allan, Torguish House & Holiday
Homes, DAVIOT, Inverness-shire IV1 2XQ
01463 772308
• e-mail: torguish@torguish.com
• website: www.torguish.com

Visit the FHG website **www.holidayguides.com** for a wide choice of holiday accommodation

Farm/Croft

Ian & Pamela Grant, Greenfield Croft, Insh,
By KINGUSSIE, Inverness-shire PH21 1NT
01540 661010
• e-mail: farmhouse@kincraig.com
• website: www.kincraig.com/greenfield

Self-Catering

Mr J. Fleming, Dell of Abernethy Cottages,
NETHYBRIDGE, Inverness-shire PH25 3DL
01463 224358
• website:
www.nethybridge.comdellofabernethy.htm

Self-Catering

Mrs Dean, Fhuarain Forest Cottages & Lazy
Duck Hostel, Badanfhuarain,
NETHYBRIDGE, Inverness-shire PH25 3ED
01479 821642
• e-mail: lazy.duck@virgin.net
• website: www.forestcottages.com

Guest House

Dreamweavers, Earendil, Mulomir, BY
SPEAN BRIDGE, Inverness-shire PH34 4EQ
01397 712548
• e-mail: helen@dreamweavers.co.uk
• website: www.dreamweavers.co.uk

Self-Catering

Mr & Mrs Allen, Wildside Highland Lodges.
WHITEBRIDGE, Inverness-shire IV1 2UN
01456 486373
• e-mail: info@wildside lodges.com
• website: www.wildsidelodges.com

•PERTH & KINROSS

Self-Catering

Mr Alastair Steeple, Altamount Chalets,
Coupar Angus Road, BLAIRGOWRIE,
Perthshire PH10 6JN
01250 873324
• e-mail: alastair@altamountchalets.co.uk
• website: www.altamountchalets.co.uk

Hotel

The Highland House Hotel, South Church
Street, CALLANDER, Perth FK17 8BN
01877 330269
• e-mall: highland.house.hotel@lineone.net
• website: www.highlandhousehotel.co.uk

Hotel

The Birnam House Hotel, Birnam,
DUNKELD, Perthshire PH8 0BQ
01350 727462
• e-mail: email@birnamhousehotel.co.uk
• website: www.birnamhousehotel.co.uk

Self-Catering

Mrs F. Bruges, Laighwood Holidays,
Butterstone, BY DUNKELD, Perthshire PH8
0HB
01350 724241
• e-mail: holidays@laighwood.co.uk
• website: www.laighwood.co.uk

Self-Catering

Mrs W. Marshall, Duncrub Holidays,
Dalreoch, DUNNING, Perthshire PH12 0DJ
01764 684368
• e-mail: info@duncrub-holidays.com
• website: www.duncrub-holidays.com

Hotel

Killiecrankie Hotel, Pass of Killiecrankie, BY
PITLOCHRY, Perthshire PH16 5LG
01796 473220
• e-mail: enquiries@killiecrankiehotel.co.uk
• website: www.killiecrankiehotel.co.uk

Guest House

Mrs Hilary Pratt, Bonskeid House,
PITLOCHRY, Perthshire PH16 5NP
01796 473208
• e-mail: bonskeid@aol.com
• website: www.bonskeid-house.co.uk

•ORKNEY ISLANDS

Hotel

Cleaton House Hotel, Cleaton, WESTRAY,
Orkney KW17 2DB
01857 677508
• e-mail: cleaton@orkney.com
• website: www.orkneyhotel.com

WALES

• ANGLESEY & GWYNEDD

Guest House

Mr & Mrs D. Pender, Bryn Bella Guest House, Llanrwst Road, BETWS-Y-COED, Gwynedd LL24 0HD
01690 710627
• e-mail: brynbella@clara.net
• website: www.brynbella.co.uk

• NORTH WALES

B & B

Mrs Janet Shaw, Bryn, Sychnant Pass Road, CONWY, North Wales LL32 8NS
01492 592449
• e-mail: b&b@bryn.org.uk
• website: www.bryn.org.uk

Hotel

Caerlyr Hall Hotel, Conwy Old Road, Penmaenmawr, CONWY, North Wales LL34 6SW
01492 623518
• website:
www.nwi.co.uk/snowdonia/caerlyrhall

• POWYS

Guest House

Mr & Mrs Jackson, The Beacons, 16 Bridge Street, BRECON, Powys LD3 8AH
01874 623339
• e-mail: beacons@brecon.co.uk
• website: www.beacons.brecon.co.uk

B&B

Cambrian Cruisers, Ty Newydd, Pencelli, BRECON, Powys LD3 7LJ
01874 665315
• e-mail: cambrian@talk21.com
• website: www.cambriancruisers.co.uk

Guest House

Mr & Mrs P. Roberts, York House, Cusop, HAY-ON-WYE, Powys HR3 5QX
01497 820705
• e-mail: roberts@yorkhouse59.fsnet.co.uk
• website: www.hay-on-wye.co.uk/yorkhouse

IRELAND

Caravan & Camping/Self-catering

Belleek Caravan & Camping Park, BALLINA, Co. Mayo, Republic of Ireland
00353 9671533
• e-mail: lenahan@indigo.ie
• website: http://indigo.ie/~lenahan

Index of towns and counties.
Please also refer to Contents pages 38-39

PLEASE NOTE

All the information in this book is given in good faith in the belief that it is correct. However, the publishers cannot guarantee the facts given in these pages, neither are they responsible for changes in policy, ownership or terms that may take place after the date of going to press. Readers should always satisfy themselves that the facilities they require are available and that the terms, if quoted, still apply.

BOOKING

FOR THE MUTUAL GUIDANCE OF GUEST AND HOST

Every year literally thousands of holidays, short breaks and overnight stops are arranged through our guides, the vast majority without any problems at all. In a handful of cases, however, difficulties do arise about bookings, which often could have been prevented from the outset.

It is important to remember that when accommodation has been booked, both parties – guests and hosts – have entered into a form of contract. We hope that the following points will provide helpful guidance.

GUESTS: When enquiring about accommodation, be as precise as possible. Give exact dates, numbers in your party and the ages of any children. State the number and type of rooms wanted and also what catering you require – bed and breakfast, full board etc. Make sure that the position about evening meals is clear – and about pets, reductions for children or any other special points.

Read our reviews carefully to ensure that the proprietors you are going to contact can supply what you want. Ask for a letter confirming all arrangements, if possible.

If you have to cancel, do so as soon as possible. Proprietors do have the right to retain deposits and under certain circumstances to charge for cancelled holidays if adequate notice is not given and they cannot re-let the accommodation.

HOSTS: Give details about your facilities and about any special conditions. Explain your deposit system clearly and arrangements for cancellations, charges etc. and whether or not your terms include VAT.

If for any reason you are unable to fulfil an agreed booking without adequate notice, you may be under an obligation to arrange suitable alternative accommodation or to make some form of compensation.

While every effort is made to ensure accuracy, we regret that FHG Publications cannot accept responsibility for errors, omissions or misrepresentations in our entries or any consequences thereof. Prices in particular should be checked because we go to press early. We will follow up complaints but cannot act as arbiters or agents for either party.

FHG Diploma Winners 2000

Each year we award a small number of diplomas to holiday proprietors whose services have been specially commended by our readers. The following were our FHG Diploma Winners for 2000.

England

CUMBRIA

- Mr & Mrs Haskell, Borwick Lodge, Outgate, Hawkshead, Cumbria LA22 0PU (015394 36332).

- Mrs Val Sunter, Higher House Farm, Oxenholme Lane, Natland, Kendal, Cumbria LA9 7QH (015395 61177).

DEVON

- Jenny Fox, Highstead Farm, Bucks Cross, Bideford, Devon EX39 5DX (01237 431201).

DORSET

- Mr & Mrs Reynolds, The Vine Hotel, 22 Southern Rd, Southbourne, Bournemouth, Dorset BH6 3SR (01202 428309).

HAMPSHIRE

- Mrs Ellis, Efford Cottage Guest House, Milford Road, Everton, Lymington, Hampshire SO41 0JD (015906 42315).

KENT

- Pam & Arthur Mills, Cloverlea, Bethersden, Ashford, Kent TN26 3DU (01233 820353)

Wales

ANGLESEY & GWYNEDD

- Jim & Marion Billingham, Preswylfa, Aberdovey, Gwynedd LL35 0LE (01654 767239)

NORTH WALES

- Bob & Nesta Wivell, Pen-Y-Bont Fawr, Cynwyd, Near Corwen, North Wales LL21 0ET (01490 412663)

Scotland

ABERDEENSHIRE, BANFF & MORAY

- Garth Hotel, Grantown on Spey, Morayshire PH26 3HN (01479 872836)

PERTH & KINROSS

- The Windlestrae Hotel, The Muirs, Kinross, Tayside KY13 7AS (01577 863217)

HELP IMPROVE BRITISH TOURIST STANDARDS

Why not write and tell us about the holiday accommodation you have chosen from one of our popular publications?

Complete a nomination form giving details of why you think YOUR host or hostess should win one of our attractive framed diplomas.

ONE FOR YOUR FRIEND 2001

FHG Publications have a large range of attractive holiday accommodation guides for all kinds of holiday opportunities throughout Britain. They also make useful gifts at any time of year. Our guides are available in most bookshops and larger newsagents but we will be happy to post you a copy direct if you have any difficulty. We will also post abroad but have to charge separately for post or freight. *The inclusive cost of posting and packing the guides to you or your friends in the UK is as follows:*

Recommended
SHORT BREAK HOLIDAYS
in Britain.
'Approved' accommodation for
quality bargain breaks
£5.50 inc p&p

BED AND BREAKFAST STOPS.
Over 1000 friendly and
comfortable overnight stops.
Non-smoking, Disabled and
Special Diets Supplements.
£6.00 inc p&p

BRITAIN'S BEST HOLIDAYS
A quick-reference general guide
for all kinds of holidays.
£4.50 inc p&p.

SELF-CATERING HOLIDAYS
in Britain
Over 1000 addresses throughout
for Self-catering and caravans
in Britain.
£5.50 inc p&p.

Recommended
WAYSIDE AND COUNTRY INNS
of Britain
Pubs, Inns and small hotels.
£5.50 inc p&p.

Recommended
COUNTRY HOTELS OF BRITAIN
Including Country Houses, for
the discriminating
£5.50 inc p&p

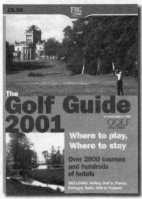